# THE BODLEY HEAD
# Bernard Shaw

VOLUME

# V

THE BODLEY HEAD

# Bernard Shaw

COLLECTED PLAYS WITH

THEIR PREFACES

[VOLUME V]

Heartbreak House

Augustus Does His Bit, Annajanska

Back to Methuselah

Jitta's Atonement

*MAX REINHARDT*

THE BODLEY HEAD

LONDON SYDNEY

TORONTO

EDITORIAL SUPERVISOR

# Dan H. Laurence

ISBN 0 370 01394 8
Printed and bound in Great Britain for
Max Reinhardt, The Bodley Head Ltd
9 Bow Street, London, WC2E 7AL
by William Clowes & Sons Ltd, Beccles
Set in Monotype Plantin Light
*First published 1919, 1921, 1926, 1930*
*Revised and reprinted in the Collected Edition 1930*
*Reprinted in the Standard Edition 1931*
(Back to Methuselah *further revised for*
*World's Classics edition 1945*)
*This edition first published 1972*

# Publisher's Note

Bernard Shaw was, throughout his publishing career, an inveterate reviser. His most extensive revision of his plays was undertaken in 1930–32 for the Collected Edition. This text was subsequently reset and issued in 1931–32 as the Standard Edition: it contained corrections but no further textual revision. Shaw, however, did make further alterations in some of the plays and prefaces in the Standard Edition in later years. Accordingly, to ensure a definitive text, we have set type for the Bodley Head edition from the last printing of each volume of plays in the Standard Edition which was authorized for press by Shaw in his lifetime.

Shaw had strong personal opinions about style in printing, many of them highly idiosyncratic, and as he was his own publisher he had no difficulty implementing them. His spellings and contractions were often bizarre (*enterprize* and *wernt*), and sometimes archaic (*shew* for *show*, as in the title of his play *The Shewing-up of Blanco Posnet*). He had equally strong convictions about the superfluous use of punctuation, noting in *The Author* in April 1902:

"The apostrophes in ain't, don't, haven't, etc., look so ugly that the most careful printing cannot make a page of colloquial dialogue as handsome as a page of classical dialogue. Besides, shan't should be sha''n't, if the wretched pedantry of indicating the elision is to be carried out. I have written aint, dont, havnt, shant, shouldnt and wont for twenty years with perfect impunity, using the apostrophe only where its omission would suggest another word: for example, hell for he'll. There is not the faintest reason for persisting in the ugly and silly trick of peppering pages with these uncouth bacilli. I also write thats, whats, lets, for the colloquial forms of that is, what is, let us; and I have not yet been prosecuted."

Throughout this definitive edition we have undertaken to follow Shaw's dictates in all matters of spelling and punctuation. Except for a small number of corrections of obvious misprints, the texts are faithfully reproduced.

One additional technical matter must be noted here. Shaw's aesthetics of typography required that italics be reserved for stage directions. In all editions of Shaw's plays up to and including the Collected Edition emphasis within dialogue passages was obtained by letter-spacing. For technical reasons, however, Shaw's printer (William Maxwell, director of R. & R. Clark, Edinburgh) prevailed upon him to permit the setting of emphasised words in the Standard Edition in a slightly larger type. In the present edition the original spaced lettering has been restored. This move, we like to think, would have pleased Shaw.

# CONTENTS

[ 7 ]

Jitta's Atonement
by Siegfried Trebitsch
translated by Bernard Shaw

# Heartbreak House:
# A Fantasia in the Russian Manner on English Themes

### WITH

*Preface: Heartbreak House and Horseback Hall*

*"G.B.S." Explains*

*Bernard Shaw on Heartbreak House*

*Letter to the Editor of the* Daily News, *24 October 1921*

*Mr Shaw's Characteristic Speech at Matinee*

*Shaw on the Play's Reception*

Composition begun 4 March 1916; completed May 1917. (Shaw stated on several occasions that the play was begun before the war, but all surviving evidence contradicts this.) Published in *Heartbreak House, Great Catherine, & Playlets of the War*, 1919. First presented by the Theatre Guild at the Garrick Theatre, New York, on 10 November 1920.

Ellie Dunn    *Elizabeth Risdon*
Nurse Guinness    *Helen Westley*
Captain Shotover    *Albert Perry*
Lady Utterword    *Lucile Watson*
Hesione Hushabye    *Effie Shannon*
Mazzini Dunn    *Erskine Sanford*
Hector Hushabye ("Marcus Darnley")
                                    *Fred Eric*
Alfred "Boss" Mangan    *Dudley Digges*
Randall Utterword    *Ralph Roeder*
The Burglar (Billy Dunn)    *Henry Travers*

Period—Late September

ACT I *Captain Shotover's Villa in Sussex—the Poop. Evening*

ACT II *The Same. After Dinner*

ACT III *The Garden, astern of the Poop. Night*

# Heartbreak House
# and Horseback Hall

---

*Contents*

[ 11 ]

---

## WHERE HEARTBREAK HOUSE STANDS

Heartbreak House is not merely the name of the play which follows this preface. It is cultured, leisured Europe before the war. When the play was begun not a shot had been fired; and only the professional diplomatists and the very few amateurs whose hobby is foreign policy even knew that the guns were loaded. A Russian playwright, Tchekov, had produced four fascinating dramatic studies of Heartbreak House, of which three, The Cherry Orchard, Uncle Vanya, and The Seagull, had been performed in England. Tolstoy, in his Fruits of Enlightenment, had shewn us through it in his most ferociously contemptuous manner. Tolstoy did not waste any sympathy on it: it was to him the house in which Europe was stifling its soul; and he knew that our utter enervation and futilization in that overheated drawingroom atmosphere was delivering the world over to the control of ignorant and soulless cunning and energy, with the frightful consequences which have now overtaken it. Tolstoy was no pessimist: he was not disposed to leave the house standing if he could bring it down about the ears of its pretty and amiable voluptuaries; and he wielded the pickaxe with a will. He treated the case of the inmates as one of opium poisoning, to be dealt with by seizing the patients roughly and exercising them violently until they were broad awake. Tchekov, more of a fatalist, had no faith in these charming people extricating themselves. They would, he thought, be sold up and sent adrift by the bailiffs; therefore he had no scruple in exploiting and even flattering their charm.

## THE INHABITANTS

Tchekov's plays, being less lucrative than swings and roundabouts, got no further in England, where theatres are only ordinary commercial affairs, than a couple of performances by the Stage Society. We stared and said, "How Russian!" They did not strike me in that way. Just as Ibsen's intensely Norwegian plays exactly fitted every middle and professional class suburb in Europe, these intensely Russian plays fitted all the country houses in Europe in which the pleasures of music, art, literature, and the theatre had supplanted hunting, shooting, fishing, flirting, eating, and drinking. The same nice people, the same utter futility. The nice people could read; some of them could write; and they were the only repositories of culture who had social opportunities of contact with our politicians, administrators, and newspaper proprietors, or any chance of sharing or influencing their activities. But they shrank from that contact. They hated politics. They did not wish to realize Utopia for the common people: they wished to realize their favourite fictions and poems in their own lives; and, when they could, they lived without scruple on incomes which they did nothing to earn. The women in their girlhood made themselves look like variety theatre stars, and settled down later into the types of beauty imagined by the previous generation of painters. They took the only part of our society in which there was leisure for high culture, and made it an economic, political, and, as far as practicable, a moral vacuum; and as Nature, abhorring the vacuum, immediately filled it up with sex and with all sorts of refined pleasures, it was a very delightful place at its best for moments of relaxation. In other moments it was disastrous. For prime ministers and their like, it was a veritable Capua.

## HORSEBACK HALL

But where were our front benchers to nest if not here? The alternative to Heartbreak House was Horseback Hall, consisting of a prison for horses with an annex for the ladies and gentlemen who rode them, hunted them, talked about them, bought them and sold them, and gave nine-tenths of their lives to them, dividing the other tenth between charity, church-going (as a substitute for religion), and conservative electioneering (as a substitute for politics). It is true that the two establishments got mixed at the edges. Exiles from the library, the music room, and the picture gallery would be found languishing among the stables, miserably discontented; and hardy horse-women who slept at the first chord of Schumann were born, horribly misplaced, into the garden of Klingsor; but sometimes one came upon horsebreakers and heartbreakers who could make the best of both worlds. As a rule, however, the two were apart and knew little of one another; so the prime minister folk had to choose between barbarism and Capua. And of the two atmospheres it is hard to say which was the more fatal to statesmanship.

## REVOLUTION ON THE SHELF

Heartbreak House was quite familiar with revolutionary ideas on paper. It aimed at being advanced and
freethinking, and hardly ever went to church or kept
the Sabbath except by a little extra fun at week-ends.
When you spent a Friday to Tuesday in it you found
on the shelf in your bedroom not only the books of
poets and novelists, but of revolutionary biologists and
even economists. Without at least a few plays by
myself and Mr Granville Barker, and a few stories by
Mr H. G. Wells, Mr Arnold Bennett, and Mr John
Galsworthy, the house would have been out of the
movement. You would find Blake among the poets,
and beside him Bergson, Butler, Scott Haldane, the
poems of Meredith and Thomas Hardy, and, generally speaking, all the literary implements for forming
the mind of the perfect modern Socialist and Creative
Evolutionist. It was a curious experience to spend
Sunday in dipping into these books, and on Monday
morning to read in the daily paper that the country
had just been brought to the verge of anarchy because a new Home Secretary or chief of police, without an idea in his head that his great-grandmother
might not have had to apologize for, had refused to
"recognize" some powerful Trade Union, just as a
gondola might refuse to recognize a 20,000-ton liner.

In short, power and culture were in separate com-
partments. The barbarians were not only literally in
the saddle, but on the front bench in the House of
Commons, with nobody to correct their incredible
ignorance of modern thought and political science but
upstarts from the counting-house, who had spent
their lives furnishing their pockets instead of their
minds. Both, however, were practised in dealing with

money and with men, as far as acquiring the one and exploiting the other went; and although this is as undesirable an expertness as that of the medieval robber baron, it qualifies men to keep an estate or a business going in its old routine without necessarily understanding it, just as Bond Street tradesmen and domestic servants keep fashionable society going without any instruction in sociology.

## THE CHERRY ORCHARD

The Heartbreak people neither could nor would do anything of the sort. With their heads as full of the Anticipations of Mr H. G. Wells as the heads of our actual rulers were empty even of the anticipations of Erasmus or Sir Thomas More, they refused the drudgery of politics, and would have made a very poor job of it if they had changed their minds. Not that they would have been allowed to meddle anyhow, as only through the accident of being a hereditary peer can anyone in these days of Votes for Everybody get into parliament if handicapped by a serious modern cultural equipment; but if they had, their habit of living in a vacuum would have left them helpless and ineffective in public affairs. Even in private life they were often helpless wasters of their inheritance, like the people in Tchekov's Cherry Orchard. Even those who lived within their incomes were really kept going by their solicitors and agents, being unable to manage an estate or run a business without continual prompting from those who have to learn how to do such things or starve.

From what is called Democracy no corrective to this state of things could be hoped. It is said that every people has the Government it deserves. It is more to the point that every Government has the electorate it deserves; for the orators of the front bench can edify or debauch an ignorant electorate at will. Thus our democracy moves in a vicious circle of reciprocal worthiness and unworthiness.

## NATURE'S LONG CREDITS

Nature's way of dealing with unhealthy conditions is unfortunately not one that compels us to conduct a solvent hygiene on a cash basis. She demoralizes us with long credits and reckless overdrafts, and then pulls us up cruelly with catastrophic bankruptcies. Take, for example, common domestic sanitation. A whole city generation may neglect it utterly and scandalously, if not with absolute impunity, yet without any evil consequences that anyone thinks of tracing to it. In a hospital two generations of medical students may tolerate dirt and carelessness, and then go out into general practice to spread the doctrine that fresh air is a fad, and sanitation an imposture set up to make profits for plumbers. Then suddenly Nature takes her revenge. She strikes at the city with a pestilence and at the hospital with an epidemic of hospital gangrene, slaughtering right and left until the innocent young have paid for the guilty old, and the account is balanced. And then she goes to sleep again and gives another period of credit, with the same result.

This is what has just happened in our political hygiene. Political science has been as recklessly neglected by Governments and electorates during my lifetime as sanitary science was in the days of Charles the Second. In international relations diplomacy has been a boyishly lawless affair of family intrigues, commercial and territorial brigandage, torpors of pseudo-goodnature produced by laziness, and spasms of ferocious activity produced by terror. But in these islands we muddled through. Nature gave us a longer credit than she gave to France or Germany or Russia. To British centenarians who died in their beds in 1914, any dread of having to hide underground in London from the shells of an enemy seemed more remote and fantastic than a dread of the appearance of a colony of cobras and rattlesnakes in Kensington Gardens. In the prophetic works of Charles Dickens we were warned against many evils which have since come to pass; but of the evil of being slaughtered by a foreign foe on our own doorsteps there was no shadow. Nature gave us a very long credit; and we abused it to the utmost. But when she struck at last she struck with a vengeance. For four years she smote our firstborn and heaped on us plagues of which Egypt never dreamed. They were all as preventible as the great Plague of London, and came solely because they had not been prevented. They were not undone by winning the war. The earth is still bursting with the dead bodies of the victors.

## THE WICKED HALF CENTURY

It is difficult to say whether indifference and neglect are worse than false doctrine; but Heartbreak House and Horseback Hall unfortunately suffered from both. For half a century before the war civilization had been going to the devil very precipitately under the influence of a pseudo-science as disastrous as the blackest Calvinism. Calvinism taught that as we are predestinately saved or damned, nothing that we do can alter our destiny. Still, as Calvinism gave the individual no clue as to whether he had drawn a lucky number or an unlucky one, it left him a fairly strong interest in encouraging his hopes of salvation and allaying his fear of damnation by behaving as one of the elect might be expected to behave rather than as one of the reprobate. But in the middle of the XIX century naturalists and physicists assured the world, in the name of Science, that salvation and damnation are all nonsense, and that predestination is the central truth of religion, inasmuch as human beings are produced by their environment, their sins and good deeds being only a series of chemical and mechanical reactions over which they have no control. Such figments as mind, choice, purpose, conscience, will, and so forth, are, they taught, mere illusions, produced because they are useful in the continual struggle of the human machine to maintain its environment in a favourable condition, a process incidentally involving the ruthless destruction or subjection of its competitors for the supply (assumed to be limited) of subsistence available. We taught Prussia this religion; and Prussia bettered our instruction so effectively that we presently found ourselves confronted with the necessity of destroying Prussia to prevent Prussia destroying us. And that has just ended in each destroying the other to an extent doubtfully reparable in our time.

It may be asked how so imbecile and dangerous a creed ever came to be accepted by intelligent beings. I will answer that question more fully in my next volume of plays, which will be entirely devoted to the subject. For the present I will only say that there were better reasons than the obvious one that such sham science as this opened a scientific career to very stupid men, and all the other careers to shameless rascals, provided they were industrious enough. It is true that this motive operated very powerfully; but when the new departure in scientific doctrine which is associated with the name of the great naturalist Charles Darwin began, it was not only a reaction against a barbarous pseudo-evangelical teleology intolerably obstructive to all scientific progress, but was accompanied, as it happened, by discoveries of extraordinary interest in physics, chemistry, and that lifeless method of evolution which its investigators called Natural Selection. Howbeit, there was only one result possible in the ethical sphere, and that was the banishment of conscience from human affairs, or, as Samuel Butler vehemently put it, "of mind from the universe."

## HYPOCHONDRIA

Now Heartbreak House, with Butler and Bergson and Scott Haldane alongside Blake and the other major poets on its shelves (to say nothing of Wagner and the tone poets), was not so completely blinded by the doltish materialism of the laboratories as the uncultured world outside. But being an idle house it was a hypochondriacal house, always running after cures. It would stop eating meat, not on valid Shelleyan grounds, but in order to get rid of a bogey called Uric Acid; and it would actually let you pull all its teeth out to exorcize another demon named Pyorrhea. It was superstitious, and addicted to table-rapping, materialization séances, clairvoyance, palmistry, crystal-gazing and the like to such an extent that it may be doubted whether ever before in the history of the world did soothsayers, astrologers, and unregistered therapeutic specialists of all sorts flourish as they did during this half century of the drift to the abyss. The registered doctors and surgeons were hard put to it to compete with the unregistered. They were not clever enough to appeal to the imagination and sociability of the Heartbreakers by the arts of the actor, the orator, the poet, the winning conversationalist. They had to fall back coarsely on the terror of infection and death. They prescribed inoculations and operations. Whatever part of a human being could be cut out without necessarily killing him they cut out; and he often died (unnecessarily of course) in consequence. From such trifles as uvulas and tonsils they went on to ovaries and appendices until at last no one's inside was safe. They explained that the human intestine was too long, and that nothing could make a child of Adam healthy except short circuiting the pylorus by cutting a length out of the lower intestine and fastening it directly to the stomach. As their mechanist theory taught them that medicine was the business of the chemist's laboratory, and surgery of the carpenter's shop, and also that Science (by which they meant their practices) was so important that no consideration for the interests of any individual creature, whether frog or philosopher, much less the vulgar commonplaces of sentimental ethics, could weigh for a moment against the remotest off-chance of an addition to the body of scientific knowledge, they operated and vivisected and inoculated and lied on a stupendous scale, clamoring for and actually acquiring such legal powers over the bodies of their fellow-citizens as neither king, pope, nor parliament dare ever have claimed. The Inquisition itself was a Liberal institution compared to the General Medical Council.

## THOSE WHO DO NOT KNOW HOW TO LIVE
## MUST MAKE A MERIT OF DYING

Heartbreak House was far too lazy and shallow to extricate itself from this palace of evil enchantment. It rhapsodized about love; but it believed in cruelty. It was afraid of the cruel people; and it saw that cruelty was at least effective. Cruelty did things that made money, whereas Love did nothing but prove the soundness of Larochefoucauld's saying that very few people would fall in love if they had never read about it. Heartbreak House, in short, did not know how to live, at which point all that was left to it was the boast that at least it knew how to die: a melancholy accomplishment which the outbreak of war presently gave it practically unlimited opportunities of displaying. Thus were the firstborn of Heartbreak House smitten; and the young, the innocent, the hopeful expiated the folly and worthlessness of their elders.

## WAR DELIRIUM

Only those who have lived through a first-rate war, not in the field, but at home, and kept their heads, can possibly understand the bitterness of Shakespear and Swift, who both went through this experience. The horror of Peer Gynt in the madhouse, when the lunatics, exalted by illusions of splendid talent and visions of a dawning millennium, crowned him as their emperor, was tame in comparison. I do not know whether anyone really kept his head completely except those who had to keep it because they had to conduct the war at first hand. I should not have kept my own (as far as I did keep it) if I had not at once understood that as a scribe and speaker I too was under the most serious public obligation to keep my grip on realities; but this did not save me from a considerable degree of hyperaesthesia. There were of course some happy people to whom the war meant nothing: all political and general matters lying outside their little circle of interest. But the ordinary war-conscious civilian went mad, the main symptom being a conviction that the whole order of nature had been reversed. All foods, he felt, must now be adulterated. All schools must be closed. No advertisements must be sent to the newspapers, of which new editions must appear and be bought up every ten minutes. Travelling must be stopped, or, that being impossible, greatly hindered. All pretences about fine art and culture and the like must be flung off as an intolerable affectation; and the picture galleries and museums and schools at once occupied by war workers. The British Museum itself was saved only by a hairsbreadth. The sincerity of all this, and of much more which would not be believed if I chronicled it, may be established by one conclusive instance of the general craziness. Men were seized with the illusion that they could win the war by giving away money. And they not only subscribed millions to Funds of all sorts with no discoverable object, and to ridiculous voluntary organizations for doing what was plainly the business of the civil and military authorities, but actually handed out money to any thief in the street who had the presence of mind to pretend that he (or she) was "collecting" it for the annihilation of the enemy. Swindlers were emboldened to take offices; label themselves Anti-Enemy Leagues; and simply pocket the money that was heaped on them. Attractively dressed young women found that they had nothing to do but parade the streets, collecting-box in hand, and live gloriously on the profits. Many months elapsed before, as a first sign of returning sanity, the police swept an Anti-Enemy secretary into prison *pour encourager les autres*, and the passionate penny collecting of the Flag Days was brought under some sort of regulation.

## MADNESS IN COURT

The demoralization did not spare the Law Courts. Soldiers were acquitted, even on fully proved indictments for wilful murder, until at last the judges and magistrates had to announce that what was called the Unwritten Law, which meant simply that a soldier could do what he liked with impunity in civil life, was not the law of the land, and that a Victoria Cross did not carry with it a perpetual plenary indulgence. Unfortunately the insanity of the juries and magistrates did not always manifest itself in indulgence. No person unlucky enough to be charged with any sort of conduct, however reasonable and salutary, that did not smack of war delirium had the slightest chance of acquittal. There were in the country, too, a certain number of people who had conscientious objections to war as criminal or unchristian. The Act of Parliament introducing Compulsory Military Service thoughtlessly exempted these persons, merely requiring them to prove the genuineness of their convictions. Those who did so were very ill-advised from the point of view of their own personal interest; for they were persecuted with savage logicality in spite of the law; whilst those who made no pretence of having any objection to war at all, and had not only had military training in Officers'

Training Corps, but had proclaimed on public occasions that they were perfectly ready to engage in civil war on behalf of their political opinions, were allowed the benefit of the Act on the ground that they did not approve of this particular war. For the Christians there was no mercy. In cases where the evidence as to their being killed by ill treatment was so unequivocal that the verdict would certainly have been one of wilful murder had the prejudice of the coroner's jury been on the other side, their tormentors were gratuitously declared to be blameless. There was only one virtue, pugnacity: only one vice, pacifism. That is an essential condition of war; but the Government had not the courage to legislate accordingly; and its law was set aside for Lynch law.

The climax of legal lawlessness was reached in France. The greatest Socialist statesman in Europe, Jaurès, was shot and killed by a gentleman who resented his efforts to avert the war. M. Clemenceau was shot by another gentleman of less popular opinions, and happily came off no worse than having to spend a precautionary couple of days in bed. The slayer of Jaurès was recklessly acquitted: the would-be slayer of M. Clemenceau was carefully found guilty. There is no reason to doubt that the same thing would have happened in England if the war had begun with a successful attempt to assassinate Keir Hardie, and ended with an unsuccessful one to assassinate Mr Lloyd George.

## THE LONG ARM OF WAR

The pestilence which is the usual accompaniment of war was called influenza. Whether it was really a war pestilence or not was made doubtful by the fact that it did its worst in places remote from the battle-fields, notably on the west coast of North America and in India. But the moral pestilence, which was un-questionably a war pestilence, reproduced this pheno-menon. One would have supposed that the war fever would have raged most furiously in the countries actually under fire, and that the others would be more reasonable. Belgium and Flanders, where over large districts literally not one stone was left upon another as the opposed armies drove each other back and forward over it after terrific preliminary bombard-ments, might have been pardoned for relieving their feelings more emphatically than by shrugging their shoulders and saying "C'est la guerre." England, inviolate for so many centuries that the swoop of war on her homesteads had long ceased to be more credible than a return of the Flood, could hardly be expected to keep her temper sweet when she knew at last what it was to hide in cellars and underground railway stations, or lie quaking in bed, whilst bombs crashed, houses crumbled, and aircraft guns distributed shrap-nel on friend and foe alike until certain shop windows in London, formerly full of fashionable hats, were filled with steel helmets. Slain and mutilated women and children, and burnt and wrecked dwellings, excuse a good deal of violent language, and produce a wrath on which many suns go down before it is appeased. Yet it was in the United States of America, where nobody slept the worse for the war, that the war fever went beyond all sense and reason. In European Courts there was vindictive illegality: in American Courts there was raving lunacy. It is not for me to chronicle the extravagances of an Ally: let some candid American do that. I can only say that to us sitting in our gardens in England, with the guns in France making themselves felt by a throb in the air as unmistakeable as an audible sound, or with tightening hearts studying the phases of the moon in London in their bearing on the chances whether our houses would be standing or ourselves alive next morning, the newspaper accounts of the sentences American Courts were passing on young girls and old men alike for the expression of opinions which were being uttered amid thundering applause before huge audiences in England, and the more private records of the methods by which the American War Loans were raised, were so amazing that they would put the guns and the possibilities of a raid clean out of our heads for the moment.

## THE RABID WATCHDOGS OF LIBERTY

Not content with these rancorous abuses of the existing law, the war maniacs made a frantic rush to abolish all constitutional guarantees of liberty and well-being. The ordinary law was superseded by Acts under which newspapers were seized and their printing machinery destroyed by simple police raids *à la Russe*, and persons arrested and shot without any pretence of trial by jury or publicity of procedure or evidence. Though it was urgently necessary that production should be increased by the most scientific organization and economy of labor, and though no fact was better established than that excessive duration and intensity of toil reduces production heavily instead of increasing it, the factory laws were suspended, and men and women recklessly overworked until the loss of their efficiency became too glaring to be ignored. Remonstrances and warnings were met either with an accusation of pro-Germanism or the

[ 27 ]

formula, "Remember that we are at war now." I have said that men assumed that war had reversed the order of nature, and that all was lost unless we did the exact opposite of everything we had found necessary and beneficial in peace. But the truth was worse than that. The war did not change men's minds in any such impossible way. What really happened was that the impact of physical death and destruction, the one reality that every fool can understand, tore off the masks of education, art, science, and religion from our ignorance and barbarism, and left us glorying grotesquely in the licence suddenly accorded to our vilest passions and most abject terrors. Ever since Thucydides wrote his history, it has been on record that when the angel of death sounds his trumpet the pretences of civilization are blown from men's heads into the mud like hats in a gust of wind. But when this scripture was fulfilled among us, the shock was not the less appalling because a few students of Greek history were not surprised by it. Indeed these students threw themselves into the orgy as shamelessly as the illiterate. The Christian priest joining in the war dance without even throwing off his cassock first, and the respectable school governor expelling the German professor with insult and bodily violence, and declaring that no English child should ever again be taught the language of Luther and Goethe, were kept in countenance by the most impudent repudiations of every decency of civilization and every lesson of political experience on the part of the very persons who, as university professors, historians, philosophers, and men of science, were the accredited custodians of culture. It was crudely natural, and perhaps necessary for recruiting purposes, that German militarism and German dynastic ambition should be painted by journalists and recruiters in black and red as European dangers (as in fact they are), leaving it to be inferred that our own militarism and our own political constitution are millennially democratic (which they certainly are not); but when it came to frantic denunciations of German chemistry, German biology, German poetry, German music, German literature, German philosophy, and even German engineering, as malignant abominations standing towards British and French chemistry and so forth in the relation of heaven to hell, it was clear that the utterers of such barbarous ravings had never really understood or cared for the arts and sciences they professed and were profaning, and were only the appallingly degenerate descendants of the men of the seventeenth and eighteenth centuries who, recognizing no national frontiers in the great realm of the human mind, kept the European comity of that realm loftily and even ostentatiously above the rancors of the battle-field. Tearing the Garter from the Kaiser's leg, striking the German dukes from the roll of our peerage, changing the King's illustrious and historically appropriate surname for that of a traditionless locality, was not a very dignified business; but the erasure of German names from the British rolls of science and learning was a confession that in England the little respect paid to science and learning is only an affectation which hides a savage contempt for both. One felt that the figure of St George and the Dragon on our coinage should be replaced by that of the soldier driving his spear through Archimedes. But by that time there was no coinage: only paper money in which ten shillings called itself a pound as confidently as the people who were disgracing their country called themselves patriots.

## THE SUFFERINGS OF THE SANE

The mental distress of living amid the obscene din of all these carmagnoles and corobberies was not the only burden that lay on sane people during the war. There was also the emotional strain, complicated by the offended economic sense, produced by the casualty lists. The stupid, the selfish, the narrow-minded, the callous and unimaginative were spared a great deal. "Blood and destruction shall be so in use that mothers shall but smile when they behold their infants quartered by the hands of war," was a Shakespearean prophecy that very nearly came true; for when nearly every house had a slaughtered son to mourn, we should all have gone quite out of our senses if we had taken our own and our friends' bereavements at their peace value. It became necessary to give them a false value; to proclaim the young life worthily and gloriously sacrificed to redeem the liberty of mankind, instead of to expiate the heedlessness and folly of their fathers, and expiate it in vain. We had even to assume that the parents and not the children had made the sacrifice, until at last the comic papers were driven to satirize fat old men, sitting comfortably in club chairs, and boasting of the sons they had "given" to their country.

No one grudged these anodynes to acute personal grief; but they only embittered those who knew that the young men were having their teeth set on edge because their parents had eaten sour political grapes. Then think of the young men themselves! Many of them had no illusions about the policy that led to the war: they went clear-sighted to a horribly repugnant duty. Men essentially gentle and essentially wise, with really valuable work in hand, laid it down voluntarily and spent months forming fours in the barrack yard, and stabbing sacks of straw in the public eye, so that they might go out to kill and maim men as gentle as themselves. These men, who were perhaps, as a class, our most efficient soldiers (Frederick Keeling, for example), were not duped for a moment by the hypocritical melodrama that consoled and stimulated the others. They left their creative work to drudge at destruction, exactly as they would have left it to take their turn at the pumps in a sinking ship. They did not, like some of the conscientious objectors, hold back because the ship had been neglected by its officers and scuttled by its wreckers. The ship had to be saved, even if Newton had to leave his fluxions and Michael Angelo his marbles to save it; so they threw away the tools of their beneficent and ennobling trades, and took up the bloodstained bayonet and the murderous bomb, forcing themselves to pervert their divine instinct for perfect artistic execution to the effective handling of these diabolical things, and their economic faculty for organization to the contriving of ruin and slaughter. For it gave an ironic edge to their tragedy that the very talents they were forced to prostitute made the prostitution not only effective, but even interesting; so that some of them were rapidly promoted, and found themselves actually becoming artists in war, with a growing relish for it, like Napoleon and all the other scourges of mankind, in spite of themselves. For many of them there was not even this consolation. They "stuck it," and hated it, to the end.

### EVIL IN THE THRONE OF GOOD

This distress of the gentle was so acute that those who shared it in civil life, without having to shed blood with their own hands, or witness destruction with their own eyes, hardly care to obtrude their own woes. Nevertheless, even when sitting at home in safety, it was not easy for those who had to write and speak about the war to throw away their highest conscience, and deliberately work to a standard of inevitable evil instead of to the ideal of life more abundant. I can answer for at least one person who found the change from the wisdom of Jesus and St Francis to the morals of Richard III and the madness of Don Quixote extremely irksome. But that change had to be made; and we are all the worse for it, except those for whom it was not really a change at all, but only a relief from hypocrisy.

Think, too, of those who, though they had neither to write nor to fight, and had no children of their own to lose, yet knew the inestimable loss to the world of four years of the life of a generation wasted on destruction. Hardly one of the epoch-making works of the human mind might not have been aborted or destroyed by taking their authors away from their natural work for four critical years. Not only were Shakespears and Platos being killed outright; but many of the best harvests of the survivors had to be sown in the barren soil of the trenches. And this was no mere British consideration. To the truly civilized man, to the good European, the slaughter of the German youth was as disastrous as the slaughter of the English. Fools exulted in "German losses." They were our losses as well. Imagine exulting in the death of Beethoven because Bill Sikes dealt him his death blow!

## STRAINING AT THE GNAT
### AND SWALLOWING THE CAMEL

But most people could not comprehend these

sorrows. There was a frivolous exultation in death for its own sake, which was at bottom an inability to realize that the deaths were real deaths and not stage ones. Again and again, when an air raider dropped a bomb which tore a child and its mother limb from limb, the people who saw it, though they had been reading with great cheerfulness of thousands of such happenings day after day in their newspapers, suddenly burst into furious imprecations on "the Huns" as murderers, and shrieked for savage and satisfying vengeance. At such moments it became clear that the deaths they had not seen meant no more to them than the mimic deaths of the cinema screen. Sometimes it was not necessary that death should be actually witnessed: it had only to take place under circumstances of sufficient novelty and proximity to bring it home almost as sensationally and effectively as if it had been actually visible.

For example, in the spring of 1915 there was an appalling slaughter of our young soldiers at Neuve Chapelle and at the Gallipoli landing. I will not go so far as to say that our civilians were delighted to have such exciting news to read at breakfast. But I cannot pretend that I noticed either in the papers, or in general intercourse, any feeling beyond the usual one that the cinema show at the front was going splendidly, and that our boys were the bravest of the brave. Suddenly there came the news that an Atlantic liner, the Lusitania, had been torpedoed, and that several well-known first class passengers, including a famous theatrical manager and the author of a popular farce, had been drowned, among others. The others included Sir Hugh Lane; but as he had only laid the country under great obligations in the sphere of the fine arts, no great stress was laid on that loss.

Immediately an amazing frenzy swept through the country. Men who up to that time had kept their heads now lost them utterly. "Killing saloon passengers! What next?" was the essence of the whole agitation; but it is far too trivial a phrase to convey the faintest notion of the rage which possessed us. To me, with my mind full of the hideous cost of Neuve Chapelle, Ypres, and the Gallipoli landing, the fuss about the Lusitania seemed almost a heartless impertinence, though I was well acquainted personally with the three best-known victims, and understood, better perhaps than most people, the misfortune of the death of Lane. I even found a grim satisfaction, very intelligible to all soldiers, in the fact that the civilians who found the war such splendid British sport should get a sharp taste of what it was to the actual combatants. I expressed my impatience very freely, and found that my very straightforward and natural feeling in the matter was received as a monstrous and heartless paradox. When I asked those who gaped at me whether they had anything to say about the holocaust of Festubert, they gaped wider than before, having totally forgotten it, or rather, having never realized it. They were not heartless any more than I was; but the big catastrophe was too big for them to grasp, and the little one had been just the right size for them. I was not surprised. Have I not seen a public body for just the same reason pass a vote for £30,000 without a word, and then spend three special meetings, prolonged into the night, over an item of seven shillings for refreshments?

## LITTLE MINDS AND BIG BATTLES

Nobody will be able to understand the vagaries of public feeling during the war unless they bear constantly in mind that the war in its entire magnitude did not exist for the average civilian. He could not conceive even a battle, much less a campaign. To the suburbs the war was nothing but a suburban squabble. To the miner and navvy it was only a series of bayonet fights between German champions and English ones. The enormity of it was quite beyond most of us. Its episodes had to be reduced to the dimensions of a railway accident or a shipwreck before it could produce any effect on our minds at all. To us the ridiculous bombardments of Scarborough and Ramsgate were colossal tragedies, and the battle of Jutland a mere ballad. The words "after thorough artillery preparation" in the news from the front meant nothing to us; but when our seaside trippers learned that an elderly gentleman at breakfast in a week-end marine hotel had been interrupted by a bomb dropping into his egg-cup, their wrath and horror knew no bounds. They declared that this would put a new spirit into the army, and had no suspicion that the soldiers in the trenches roared with laughter over it for days, and told each other that it would do the blighters at home good to have a taste of what the army was up against. Sometimes the smallness of view was pathetic. A man would work at home regardless of the call "to make the world safe for democracy." His brother would be killed at the front. Immediately he would throw up his work and take up the war as a family blood feud against the Germans. Sometimes it was comic. A wounded man, entitled to his discharge, would return to the trenches with a grim determination to find the Hun who had wounded him and pay him out for it.

It is impossible to estimate what proportion of us, in khaki or out of it, grasped the war and its political antecedents as a whole in the light of any philosophy of history or knowledge of what war is. I doubt whether it was as high as our proportion of higher mathematicians. But there can be no doubt that it was prodigiously outnumbered by the comparatively ignorant and childish. Remember that these people had to be stimulated to make the sacrifices demanded by the war, and that this could not be done by appeals to a knowledge which they did not possess, and a comprehension of which they were incapable. When the armistice at last set me free to tell the truth about the war at the following general election, a soldier said to a candidate whom I was supporting "If I had known all that in 1914, they would never have got me into khaki." And that, of course, was precisely why it had been necessary to stuff him with a romance that any diplomatist would have laughed at. Thus the natural confusion of ignorance was increased by a deliberately propagated confusion of nursery bogey stories and melodramatic nonsense, which at last overreached itself and made it impossible to stop the war before we had not only achieved the triumph of vanquishing the German army and thereby overthrowing its militarist monarchy, but made the very serious mistake of ruining the centre of Europe, a thing that no sane European State could afford to do.

### THE DUMB CAPABLES AND THE NOISY INCAPABLES

Confronted with this picture of insensate delusion and folly, the critical reader will immediately counterplead that England all this time was conducting a war which involved the organization of several millions of fighting men and of the workers who were supplying them with provisions, munitions, and transport, and that this could not have been done by a mob of hysterical ranters. This is fortunately true. To pass from the newspaper offices and political platforms and club fenders and suburban drawing-rooms to the Army and the munition factories was to pass from Bedlam to the busiest and sanest of workaday worlds. It was to rediscover England, and find solid ground for the faith of those who still believed in her. But a necessary condition of this efficiency was that those who were efficient should give all their time to their business and leave the rabble raving to its hearts' content. Indeed the raving was useful to the efficient, because, as it was always wide of the mark, it often distracted attention very conveniently from operations that would have been defeated or hindered by publicity. A precept which I endeavored vainly to popularize early in the war, "If you have anything to do go and do it: if not, for heaven's sake get out of the way," was only half carried out. Certainly the capable people went and did it; but the incapables would by no means get out of the way: they fussed and bawled and were only prevented from getting very seriously into the way by the blessed fact that they never knew where the way was. Thus whilst all the efficiency of England was silent and invisible, all its imbecility was deafening the heavens with its clamor and blotting out the sun with its dust. It was also unfortunately intimidating the Government by its blusterings into using the irresistible powers of the State to intimidate the sensible people, thus enabling a despicable minority of would-be lynchers to set up a reign of terror which could at any time have been broken by a single stern word from a responsible minister. But our ministers had not that sort of courage: neither Heartbreak House nor Horseback Hall had bred it, much less the suburbs. When matters at last came to the looting of shops by criminals under patriotic pretexts, it was the police force and not the Government that put its foot down. There was even one deplorable moment, during the submarine scare, in which the Government yielded to a childish cry for the maltreatment of naval prisoners of war, and, to our great disgrace, was forced by the enemy to behave itself. And yet behind all this public blundering and misconduct and futile mischief, the effective England was carrying on with the most formidable capacity and activity. The ostensible England was making the empire sick with its incontinences, its ignorances, its ferocities, its panics, and its endless and intolerable blarings of Allied national anthems in season and out. The esoteric England was proceeding irresistibly to the conquest of Europe.

## THE PRACTICAL BUSINESS MEN

From the beginning the useless people set up a shriek for "practical business men." By this they meant men who had become rich by placing their personal interests before those of the country, and measuring the success of every activity by the pecuniary profit it brought to them and to those on whom they depended for their supplies of capital. The pitiable failure of some conspicuous samples from the first batch we tried of these poor devils helped to give the whole public side of the war an air of monstrous and hopeless farce. They proved not only that they were useless for public work, but that in a well-ordered nation they would never have been allowed to control private enterprise.

## HOW THE FOOLS SHOUTED THE WISE
## MEN DOWN

Thus, like a fertile country flooded with mud, England shewed no sign of her greatness in the days when she was putting forth all her strength to save herself from the worst consequences of her littleness. Most of the men of action, occupied to the last hour of their time with urgent practical work, had to leave to idler people, or to professional rhetoricians, the presentation of the war to the reason and imagination of the country and the world in speeches, poems, manifestos, picture posters, and newspaper articles. I have had the privilege of hearing some of our ablest commanders talking about their work; and I have shared the common lot of reading the accounts of that work given to the world by the newspapers. No two experiences could be more different. But in the end the talkers obtained a dangerous ascendancy over the rank and file of the men of action; for though the great men of action are always inveterate talkers and often very clever writers, and therefore cannot have their minds formed for them by others, the average man of action, like the average fighter with the bayonet, can give no account of himself in words even to himself, and is apt to pick up and accept what he reads about himself and other people in the papers, except when the writer is rash enough to commit himself on technical points. It was not uncommon during the war to hear a soldier, or a civilian engaged on war work, describing events within his own experience that reduced to utter absurdity the ravings and maunderings of his daily paper, and yet echo the opinions of that paper like a parrot. Thus, to escape from the prevailing confusion and folly, it was not enough to seek the company of the ordinary man of action: one had to get into contact with the master spirits. This was a privilege which only a handful of people could enjoy. For the unprivileged citizen there was no escape. To him the whole country seemed mad, futile, silly, incompetent, with no hope of victory except the hope that the enemy might be just as mad. Only by very resolute reflection and reasoning could he reassure himself that if there was nothing more solid beneath these appalling appearances the war could not possibly have gone on for a single day without a total breakdown of its organization.

## THE MAD ELECTION

Happy were the fools and the thoughtless men of action in those days. The worst of it was that the fools were very strongly represented in parliament, as fools not only elect fools, but can persuade men of action to elect them too. The election that immediately followed the armistice was perhaps the maddest that has ever taken place. Soldiers who had done voluntary and heroic service in the field were defeated by persons who had apparently never run a risk or spent a farthing that they could avoid, and who even had in the course of the election to apologize publicly for bawling Pacifist or Pro-German at their opponent. Party leaders seek such followers, who can always be depended on to walk tamely into the lobby at the party whip's orders, provided the leader will make their seats safe for them by the process which was called, in derisive reference to the war rationing system, "giving them the coupon." Other incidents were so grotesque that I cannot mention them without enabling the reader to identify the parties, which would not be fair, as they were no more to blame than thousands of others who must necessarily be nameless. The general result was patently absurd; and the electorate, disgusted at its own work, instantly recoiled to the opposite extreme, and cast out all the coupon candidates at the earliest bye-elections by equally silly majorities. But the mischief of the general election could not be undone; and the Government had not only to pretend to abuse its European victory as it had promised, but actually to do it by starving the enemies who had thrown down their arms. It had, in short, won the election by pledging itself to be thriftlessly wicked, cruel, and vindictive; and it did not find it as easy to escape from this pledge as it had from nobler ones. The end, as I write, is not yet; but it is clear that this thoughtless savagery will recoil on the heads of the Allies so severely that we shall be forced by the sternest necessity to take up our share of healing the Europe we have wounded almost to death instead of attempting to complete her destruction.

## THE YAHOO AND THE ANGRY APE

Contemplating this picture of a state of mankind so recent that no denial of its truth is possible, one understands Shakespear comparing Man to an angry ape, Swift describing him as a Yahoo rebuked by the superior virtue of the horse, and Wellington declaring that the British can behave themselves neither in victory nor defeat. Yet none of the three had seen war as we have seen it. Shakespear blamed great men, saying that "Could great men thunder as Jove himself does Jove would ne'er be quiet; for every pelting petty officer would use his heaven for thunder:

nothing but thunder." What would Shakespear have said if he had seen something far more destructive than thunder in the hand of every village laborer, and found on the Messines Ridge the craters of the nineteen volcanoes that were let loose there at the touch of a finger that might have been a child's finger without the result being a whit less ruinous? Shakespear may have seen a Stratford cottage struck by one of Jove's thunderbolts, and have helped to extinguish the lighted thatch and clear away the bits of the broken chimney. What would he have said if he had seen Ypres as it is now, or returned to Stratford, as French peasants are returning to their homes today, to find the old familiar signpost inscribed "To Stratford, 1 mile," and at the end of the mile nothing but some holes in the ground and a fragment of a broken churn here and there? Would not the spectacle of the angry ape endowed with powers of destruction that Jove never pretended to, have beggared even his command of words?

And yet, what is there to say except that war puts a strain on human nature that breaks down the better half of it, and makes the worse half a diabolical virtue? Better for us if it broke it down altogether; for then the warlike way out of our difficulties would be barred to us, and we should take greater care not to get into them. In truth, it is, as Byron said, "not difficult to die," and enormously difficult to live: that explains why, at bottom, peace is not only better than war, but infinitely more arduous. Did any hero of the war face the glorious risk of death more bravely than the traitor Bolo faced the ignominious certainty of it? Bolo taught us all how to die: can we say that he taught us all how to live? Hardly a week passes now without some soldier who braved death in the field so recklessly that he was decorated or specially commended for it, being haled before our magistrates for having failed to resist the paltriest temptations of peace, with no better excuse than the old one that "a man must live." Strange that one who, sooner than do honest work, will sell his honor for a bottle of wine, a visit to the theatre, and an hour with a strange woman, all obtained by passing a worthless cheque, could yet stake his life on the most desperate chances of the battle-field! Does it not seem as if, after all, the glory of death were cheaper than the glory of life? If it is not easier to attain, why do so many more men attain it? At all events it is clear that the kingdom of the Prince of Peace has not yet become the kingdom of this world. His attempts at invasion have been resisted far more fiercely than the Kaiser's. Successful as that resistance has been, it has piled up a sort of National Debt that is not the less oppressive because we have no figures for it and do not intend to pay it. A blockade that cuts off "the grace of our Lord" is in the long run less bearable than the blockades which merely cut off raw materials; and against that blockade our Armada is impotent. In the blockader's house, he has assured us, there are many mansions; but I am afraid they do not include either Heartbreak House or Horseback Hall.

### PLAGUE ON BOTH YOUR HOUSES!

Meanwhile the Bolshevist picks and petards are at work on the foundations of both buildings; and though the Bolshevists may be buried in the ruins, their deaths will not save the edifices. Unfortunately they can be built again. Like Doubting Castle, they have been demolished many times by successive Greathearts, and rebuilt by Simple, Sloth, and Presumption, by Feeble Mind and Much Afraid, and by all the jurymen of Vanity Fair. Another generation of "secondary education" at our ancient public schools and the cheaper institutions that ape them will be quite sufficient to keep the two going until the next war.

For the instruction of that generation I leave these pages as a record of what civilian life was during the war: a matter on which history is usually silent. Fortunately it was a very short war. It is true that the people who thought it could not last more than six months were very signally refuted by the event. As Sir Douglas Haig has pointed out, its Waterloos lasted months instead of hours. But there would have been nothing surprising in its lasting thirty years. If it had not been for the fact that the blockade achieved the amazing feat of starving out Europe, which it could not possibly have done had Europe been properly organized for war, or even for peace, the war would have lasted until the belligerents were so tired of it that they could no longer be compelled to compel themselves to go on with it. Considering its magnitude, the war of 1914–18 will certainly be classed as the shortest in history. The end came so suddenly that the combatants literally stumbled over it; and yet it came a full year later than it should have come if the belligerents had not been far too afraid of one another to face the situation sensibly. Germany, having failed to provide for the war she began, failed again to surrender before she was dangerously exhausted. Her opponents, equally improvident, went as much too close to bankruptcy as Germany to starvation. It was a bluff at which both were bluffed. And, with the usual irony of war, it remains doubtful whether Germany and Russia, the defeated, will not be the gainers; for the victors are already busy fastening on themselves the chains they have struck from the limbs of the vanquished.

## HOW THE THEATRE FARED

Let us now contract our view rather violently from the European theatre of war to the theatre in which the fights are sham fights, and the slain, rising the moment the curtain has fallen, go comfortably home to supper after washing off their rosepink wounds. It is nearly twenty years since I was last obliged to introduce a play in the form of a book for lack of an opportunity of presenting it in its proper mode by a performance in a theatre. The war has thrown me back on this expedient. Heartbreak House has not yet reached the stage. I have withheld it because the war has completely upset the economic conditions which formerly enabled serious drama to pay its way in London. The change is not in the theatres nor in the management of them, nor in the authors and actors, but in the audiences. For four years the London theatres were crowded every night with thousands of soldiers on leave from the front. These soldiers were not seasoned London playgoers. A childish experience of my own gave me a clue to their condition. When I was a small boy I was taken to the opera. I did not then know what an opera was, though I could whistle a good deal of opera music. I had seen in my mother's album photographs of all the great opera singers, mostly in evening dress. In the theatre I found myself before a gilded balcony filled with persons in evening dress whom I took to be the opera singers. I picked out one massive dark lady as Alboni, and wondered how soon she would

[ 45 ]

stand up and sing. I was puzzled by the fact that I was made to sit with my back to the singers instead of facing them. When the curtain went up, my astonishment and delight were unbounded.

### THE SOLDIER AT THE THEATRE FRONT

In 1915 I saw in the theatres men in khaki in just the same predicament. To everyone who had my clue to their state of mind it was evident that they had never been in a theatre before and did not know what it was. At one of our great variety theatres I sat beside a young officer, not at all a rough specimen, who, even when the curtain rose and enlightened him as to the place where he had to look for his entertainment, found the dramatic part of it utterly incomprehensible. He did not know how to play his part of the game. He could understand the people on the stage singing and dancing and performing gymnastic feats. He not only understood but intensely enjoyed an artist who imitated cocks crowing and pigs squeaking. But the people who pretended that they were somebody else, and that the painted picture behind them was real, bewildered him. In his presence I realized how very sophisticated the natural man has to become before the conventions of the theatre can be easily acceptable, or the purpose of the drama obvious to him.

Well, from the moment when the routine of leave for our soldiers was established, such novices, accompanied by damsels (called flappers) often as innocent as themselves, crowded the theatres to the doors. It was hardly possible at first to find stuff crude enough to nurse them on. The best music-hall comedians ransacked their memories for the oldest quips and the most childish antics to avoid carrying the military

spectators out of their depth. I believe that this was a
mistake as far as the novices were concerned. Shakespear, or the dramatized histories of George Barnwell,
Maria Martin, or the Demon Barber of Fleet Street,
would probably have been quite popular with them.
But the novices were only a minority after all. The
cultivated soldier, who in time of peace would look
at nothing theatrical except the most advanced post-
Ibsen plays in the most artistic settings, found himself, to his own astonishment, thirsting for silly jokes,
dances, and brainlessly sensuous exhibitions of pretty
girls. The author of some of the most grimly serious
plays of our time told me that after enduring the
trenches for months without a glimpse of the female
of his species, it gave him an entirely innocent but
delightful pleasure merely to see a flapper. The reaction from the battle-field produced a condition of
hyperaesthesia in which all the theatrical values were
altered. Trivial things gained intensity and stale
things novelty. The actor, instead of having to coax
his audiences out of the boredom which had driven
them to the theatre in an ill humor to seek some sort
of distraction, had only to exploit the bliss of smiling
men who were no longer under fire and under military
discipline, but actually clean and comfortable and in
a mood to be pleased with anything and everything
that a bevy of pretty girls and a funny man, or even a
bevy of girls pretending to be pretty and a man pretending to be funny, could do for them.

Then could be seen every night in the theatres old-
fashioned farcical comedies, in which a bedroom,
with four doors on each side and a practicable window
in the middle, was understood to resemble exactly the
bedroom in the flats beneath and above, all three
inhabited by couples consumed with jealousy. When

these people came home drunk at night; mistook their neighbor's flats for their own; and in due course got into the wrong beds, it was not only the novices who found the resulting complications and scandals exquisitely ingenious and amusing, nor their equally verdant flappers who could not help squealing in a manner that astonished the oldest performers when the gentleman who had just come in drunk through the window pretended to undress, and allowed glimpses of his naked person to be descried from time to time. Men who had just read the news that Charles Wyndham was dying, and were thereby sadly reminded of Pink Dominos and the torrent of farcical comedies that followed it in his heyday until every trick of that trade had become so stale that the laughter they provoked turned to loathing: these veterans also, when they returned from the field, were as much pleased by what they knew to be stale and foolish as the novices by what they thought fresh and clever.

## COMMERCE IN THE THEATRE

Wellington said that an army moves on its belly. So does a London theatre. Before a man acts he must eat. Before he performs plays he must pay rent. In London we have no theatres for the welfare of the people: they are all for the sole purpose of producing the utmost obtainable rent for the proprietor. If the twin flats and twin beds produce a guinea more than Shakespear, out goes Shakespear, and in come the twin flats and the twin beds. If the brainless bevy of pretty girls and the funny man outbid Mozart, out goes Mozart.

## UNSER SHAKESPEAR

Before the war an effort was made to remedy this by establishing a national theatre in celebration of the tercentenary of the death of Shakespear. A committee was formed; and all sorts of illustrious and influential persons lent their names to a grand appeal to our national culture. My play, The Dark Lady of The Sonnets, was one of the incidents of that appeal. After some years of effort the result was a single handsome subscription from a German gentleman. Like the celebrated swearer in the anecdote when the cart containing all his household goods lost its tailboard at the top of the hill and let its contents roll in ruin to the bottom, I can only say, "I cannot do justice to this situation," and let it pass without another word.

## THE HIGHER DRAMA PUT OUT OF ACTION

The effect of the war on the London theatres may now be imagined. The beds and the bevies drove every higher form of art out of it. Rents went up to an unprecedented figure. At the same time prices doubled everywhere except at the theatre pay-boxes, and raised the expenses of management to such a degree that unless the houses were quite full every night, profit was impossible. Even bare solvency could not be attained without a very wide popularity. Now what had made serious drama possible to a limited extent before the war was that a play could pay its way even if the theatre were only half full until Saturday and three-quarters full then. A manager who was an enthusiast and a desperately hard worker, with an occasional grant-in-aid from an artistically disposed millionaire, and a due proportion of those rare and happy accidents by which plays of the higher sort turn out to be potboilers as well, could hold out for some years, by which time a relay might arrive in the person of another enthusiast. Thus and not otherwise occurred that remarkable revival of the British drama at the beginning of the century which made my own career as a playwright possible in England. In America I had already established myself, not as part of the ordinary theatre system, but in association with the exceptional genius of Richard Mansfield. In Germany and Austria I had no difficulty: the system of publicly aided theatres there, Court and Municipal, kept drama of the kind I dealt in alive; so that I was indebted to the Emperor of Austria for magnificent productions of my works at a time when the sole official attention paid me by the British Court was the announcement to the English-speaking world that certain plays of mine were unfit for public performance, a substantial set-off against this being that the British Court, in the course of its private playgoing, paid no regard to the bad character given me by the chief officer of its household.

Howbeit, the fact that my plays effected a lodgment on the London stage, and were presently followed by the plays of Granville Barker, Gilbert Murray, John Masefield, St John Hankin, Laurence Housman, Arnold Bennett, John Galsworthy, John Drinkwater, and others which would in the XIX century have stood rather less chance of production at a London theatre than the Dialogues of Plato, not to mention revivals of the ancient Athenian drama, and a restoration to the stage of Shakespear's plays as he wrote them, was made economically possible solely by a supply of theatres which could hold nearly twice as much money as it cost to rent and maintain them. In such theatres work appealing to a relatively small class of cultivated persons, and therefore attracting only from half to three-quarters as many spectators as the more popular pastimes, could nevertheless keep going in the hands of young adventurers who were doing it for its own sake, and had not yet been forced by advancing age and responsibilities to consider the commercial value of their time and energy too closely. The war struck this foundation away in the manner I have just described. The expenses of running the cheapest westend theatres rose to a sum which exceeded by twenty-five per cent the utmost that the higher drama can, as an ascertained matter of fact, be depended on to draw. Thus the higher drama, which has never really been a commercially sound speculation, now became an impossible one. Accordingly, attempts are being made to provide a refuge for it in suburban theatres in London and repertory theatres in the provinces. But at the moment when the army has at last disgorged the survivors of the gallant band of dramatic pioneers whom it swallowed, they find that the economic conditions which formerly made their work no worse than precarious now put it out of the question altogether, as far as the west end of London is concerned.

## CHURCH AND THEATRE

I do not suppose many people care particularly. We are not brought up to care; and a sense of the national importance of the theatre is not born in mankind: the natural man, like so many of the soldiers at the beginning of the war, does not know what a theatre is. But please note that all these soldiers who did not know what a theatre was, knew what a church was. And they had been taught to respect churches. Nobody had ever warned them against a church as a place where frivolous women paraded in their best clothes; where stories of improper females like Potiphar's wife, and erotic poetry like the Song of Songs, were read aloud; where the sensuous and sentimental music of Schubert, Mendelssohn, Gounod, and Brahms was more popular than severe music by greater composers; where the prettiest sort of pretty pictures of pretty saints assailed the imagination and senses through stained-glass windows; and where sculpture and architecture came to the help of painting. Nobody ever reminded them that these things had sometimes produced such developments of erotic idolatry that men who were not only enthusiastic amateurs of literature, painting, and music, but famous practitioners of them, had actually exulted when mobs and even regular troops under express command had mutilated church statues, smashed church windows, wrecked church organs, and torn up the sheets from which the church music was read and sung. When they saw broken statues in churches, they were told that this was the work of wicked godless rioters, instead of, as it was, the work partly of zealots bent on driving the world, the flesh, and the devil out of the temple, and partly of insurgent men who had become intolerably poor because the temple had become a den of thieves. But all the sins and perversions that were so carefully hidden from them in the history of the Church were laid on the shoulders of the Theatre: that stuffy, uncomfortable place of penance in which we suffer so much inconvenience on the slenderest chance of gaining a scrap of food for our starving souls. When the Germans bombed the Cathedral of Rheims the world rang with the

horror of the sacrilege. When they bombed the Little
Theatre in the Adelphi, and narrowly missed bomb-
ing two writers of plays who lived within a few yards
of it, the fact was not even mentioned in the papers.
In point of appeal to the senses no theatre ever built
could touch the fane at Rheims: no actress could rival
its Virgin in beauty, nor any operatic tenor look otherwise than a fool beside its David. Its picture glass was
glorious even to those who had seen the glass of
Chartres. It was wonderful in its very grotesques:
who would look at the Blondin Donkey after seeing
its leviathans? In spite of the Adam-Adelphian
decoration on which Miss Kingston had lavished so
much taste and care, the Little Theatre was in comparison with Rheims the gloomiest of little conven-
ticles: indeed the cathedral must, from the Puritan
point of view, have debauched a million voluptuaries
for every one whom the Little Theatre had sent home
thoughtful to a chaste bed after Mr Chesterton's
Magic or Brieux's *Les Avariés*. Perhaps that is the
real reason why the Church is lauded and the Theatre
reviled. Whether or no, the fact remains that the lady
to whose public spirit and sense of the national value
of the theatre I owed the first regular public performance of a play of mine had to conceal her action
as if it had been a crime, whereas if she had given the
money to the Church she would have worn a halo for
it. And I admit, as I have always done, that this state
of things may have been a very sensible one. I have
asked Londoners again and again why they pay half
a guinea to go to a theatre when they can go to St
Paul's or Westminster Abbey for nothing. Their only
possible reply is that they want to see something new
and possibly something wicked; but the theatres
mostly disappoint both hopes. If ever a revolution

makes me Dictator, I shall establish a heavy charge for admission to our churches. But everyone who pays at the church door shall receive a ticket entitling him or her to free admission to one performance at any theatre he or she prefers. Thus shall the sensuous charms of the church service be made to subsidize the sterner virtue of the drama.

## THE NEXT PHASE

The present situation will not last. Although the newspaper I read at breakfast this morning before writing these words contains a calculation that no less than twenty-three wars are at present being waged to confirm the peace, England is no longer in khaki; and a violent reaction is setting in against the crude theatrical fare of the four terrible years. Soon the rents of theatres will once more be fixed on the assumption that they cannot always be full, nor even on the average half full week in and week out. Prices will change. The higher drama will be at no greater disadvantage than it was before the war; and it may benefit, first, by the fact that many of us have been torn from the fools' paradise in which the theatre formerly traded, and thrust upon the sternest realities and necessities until we have lost both faith in and patience with the theatrical pretences that had no root either in reality or necessity; second, by the startling change made by the war in the distribution of income. It seems only the other day that a millionaire was a man with £50,000 a year. Today, when he has paid his income tax and super tax, and insured his life for the amount of his death duties, he is lucky if his net income is £10,000, though his nominal property remains the same. And this is the result of a Budget which is called "a respite for the rich." At the other end of the scale millions of persons have had regular incomes for the first time in their lives; and their men have been regularly clothed, fed, lodged, and taught to make up their minds that certain things have to be done, also for the first time in their lives. Hundreds of thousands of women have been taken out of their domestic cages and tasted both discipline and independence. The thoughtless and snobbish middle classes have been pulled up short by the very unpleasant experience of being ruined to an unprecedented extent. We have all had a tremendous jolt; and although the widespread notion that the shock of the war would automatically make a new heaven and a new earth, and that the dog would never go back to his vomit nor the sow to her wallowing in the mire, is already seen to be a delusion, yet we are far more conscious of our condition than we were, and far less disposed to submit to it. Revolution, lately only a sensational chapter in history or a demagogic claptrap, is now a possibility so imminent that hardly by trying to suppress it in other countries by arms and defamation, and calling the process anti-Bolshevism, can our Government stave it off at home.

Perhaps the most tragic figure of the day is the American President who was once a historian. In those days it became his task to tell us how, after that great war in America which was more clearly than any other war of our time a war for an idea, the conquerors, confronted with a heroic task of reconstruction, turned recreant, and spent fifteen years in abusing their victory under cover of pretending to accomplish the task they were doing what they could to make impossible. Alas! Hegel was right when he said that we learn from history that men never learn anything from history. With what anguish of mind the President sees that we, the new conquerors, for-getting everything we professed to fight for, are sitting down with watering mouths to a good square meal of ten years revenge upon and humiliation of our prostrate foe, can only be guessed by those who know, as he does, how hopeless is remonstrance, and how happy Lincoln was in perishing from the earth before his inspired messages became scraps of paper. He knows well that from the Peace Conference will come, in spite of his utmost, no edict on which he will be able, like Lincoln, to invoke "the considerate judg-ment of mankind, and the gracious favor of Almighty God." He led his people to destroy the militarism of Zabern; and the army they rescued is busy in Cologne imprisoning every German who does not salute a British officer; whilst the Government at home, asked whether it approves, replies that it does not propose even to discontinue this Zabernism when the Peace is concluded, but in effect looks forward to making Germans salute British officers until the end of the world. That is what war makes of men and women. It will wear off; and the worst it threatens is already proving impracticable; but before the humble and contrite heart ceases to be despised, the President and I, being of the same age, will be dotards. In the mean-time there is, for him, another history to write; for me, another comedy to stage. Perhaps, after all, that is what wars are for, and what historians and play-wrights are for. If men will not learn until their lessons are written in blood, why, blood they must have, their own for preference.

## THE EPHEMERAL THRONES AND THE ETERNAL THEATRE

To the theatre it will not matter. Whatever Bastilles

fall, the theatre will stand. Apostolic Hapsburg has collapsed; All Highest Hohenzollern languishes in Holland, threatened with trial on a capital charge of fighting for his country against England; Imperial Romanoff, said to have perished miserably by a more summary method of murder, is perhaps alive or perhaps dead: nobody cares more than if he had been a peasant; the lord of Hellas is level with his lackeys in republican Switzerland; Prime Ministers and Commanders-in-Chief have passed from a brief glory as Solons and Caesars into failure and obscurity as closely on one another's heels as the descendants of Banquo; but Euripides and Aristophanes, Shakespear and Molière, Goethe and Ibsen remain fixed in their everlasting seats.

## HOW WAR MUZZLES THE DRAMATIC POET

As for myself, why, it may be asked, did I not write two plays about the war instead of two pamphlets on it? The answer is significant. You cannot make war on war and on your neighbor at the same time. War cannot bear the terrible castigation of comedy, the ruthless light of laughter that glares on the stage. When men are heroically dying for their country, it is not the time to shew their lovers and wives and fathers and mothers how they are being sacrificed to the blunders of boobies, the cupidity of capitalists, the ambition of conquerors, the electioneering of demagogues, the Pharisaism of patriots, the lusts and lies and rancors and bloodthirsts that love war because it opens their prison doors, and sets them in the thrones of power and popularity. For unless these things are mercilessly exposed they will hide under the mantle of the ideals on the stage just as they do in real life.

And though there may be better things to reveal, it may not, and indeed cannot, be militarily expedient to reveal them whilst the issue is still in the balance. Truth telling is not compatible with the defence of the realm. We are just now reading the revelations of our generals and admirals, unmuzzled at last by the armistice. During the war, General A, in his moving despatches from the field, told how General B had covered himself with deathless glory in such and such a battle. He now tells us that General B came within an ace of losing us the war by disobeying his orders on that occasion, and fighting instead of running away as he ought to have done. An excellent subject for comedy now that the war is over, no doubt; but if General A had let this out at the time, what would have been the effect on General B's soldiers? And had the stage made known what the Prime Minister and the Secretary of State for War who overruled General A thought of him, and what he thought of them, as now revealed in raging controversy, what would have been the effect on the nation? That is why comedy, though sorely tempted, had to be loyally silent; for the art of the dramatic poet knows no patriotism; recognizes no obligation but truth to natural history; cares not whether Germany or England perish; is ready to cry with Brynhild, "Lass' uns verderben, lachend zu grunde geh'n" sooner than deceive or be deceived; and thus becomes in time of war a greater military danger than poison, steel, or trinitrotoluene. That is why I had to withhold Heartbreak House from the footlights during the war; for the Germans might on any night have turned the last act from play into earnest, and even then might not have waited for their cues.

*June 1919.*

# [ACT I]

---

*The hilly country in the middle of the north edge of
Sussex, looking very pleasant on a fine evening at the
end of September, is seen through the windows of a room
which has been built so as to resemble the after part of an
old-fashioned high-pooped ship with a stern gallery; for
the windows are ship built with heavy timbering, and
run right across the room as continuously as the stability
of the wall allows. A row of lockers under the windows
provides an unupholstered window-seat interrupted by
twin glass doors, respectively halfway between the stern
post and the sides. Another door strains the illusion a
little by being apparently in the ship's port side, and yet
leading, not to the open sea, but to the entrance hall of
the house. Between this door and the stern gallery are
bookshelves. There are electric light switches beside the
door leading to the hall and the glass doors in the stern
gallery. Against the starboard wall is a carpenter's
bench. The vice has a board in its jaws; and the floor is
littered with shavings, overflowing from a waste-paper
basket. A couple of planes and a centrebit are on the
bench. In the same wall, between the bench and the
windows, is a narrow doorway with a half door, above
which a glimpse of the room beyond shews that it is a
shelved pantry with bottles and kitchen crockery.*

*On the starboard side, but close to the middle, is a
plain oak drawing-table with drawing-board, T-square,
straightedges, set squares, mathematical instruments,
saucers of water color, a tumbler of discolored water,
Indian ink, pencils, and brushes on it. The drawing-
board is set so that the draughtsman's chair has the*

*window on its left hand. On the floor at the end of the table, on his right, is a ship's fire bucket. On the port side of the room, near the bookshelves, is a sofa with its back to the windows. It is a sturdy mahogany article, oddly upholstered in sailcloth, including the bolster, with a couple of blankets hanging over the back. Between the sofa and the drawing-table is a big wicker chair, with broad arms and a low sloping back, with its back to the light. A small but stout table of teak, with a round top and gate legs, stands against the port wall between the door and the bookcase. It is the only article in the room that suggests (not at all convincingly) a woman's hand in the furnishing. The uncarpeted floor of narrow boards is caulked and holystoned like a deck.*

*The garden to which the glass doors lead dips to the south before the landscape rises again to the hills. Emerging from the hollow is the cupola of an observatory. Between the observatory and the house is a flagstaff on a little esplanade, with a hammock on the east side and a long garden seat on the west.*

*A young lady, gloved and hatted, with a dust coat on, is sitting in the window-seat with her body twisted to enable her to look out at the view. One hand props her chin: the other hangs down with a volume of the Temple Shakespear in it, and her finger stuck in the page she has been reading.*

*A clock strikes six.*

*The young lady turns and looks at her watch. She rises with an air of one who waits and is almost at the end of her patience. She is a pretty girl, slender, fair, and intelligent looking, nicely but not expensively dressed, evidently not a smart idler.*

*With a sigh of weary resignation she comes to the draughtsman's chair; sits down; and begins to read*

*Shakespear. Presently the book sinks to her lap; her eyes close; and she dozes into a slumber.*

*An elderly womanservant comes in from the hall with three unopened bottles of rum on a tray. She passes through and disappears in the pantry without noticing the young lady. She places the bottles on the shelf and fills her tray with empty bottles. As she returns with these, the young lady lets her book drop, awakening herself, and startling the womanservant so that she all but lets the tray fall.*

---

THE WOMANSERVANT. God bless us! [*The young lady picks up the book and places it on the table*]. Sorry to wake you, miss, I'm sure; but you are a stranger to me. What might you be waiting here for now?

THE YOUNG LADY. Waiting for somebody to shew some signs of knowing that I have been invited here.

THE WOMANSERVANT. Oh, youre invited, are you? And has nobody come? Dear! dear!

THE YOUNG LADY. A wild-looking old gentleman came and looked in at the window; and I heard him calling out "Nurse: there is a young and attractive female waiting in the poop. Go and see what she wants." Are you the nurse?

THE WOMANSERVANT. Yes, miss: I'm Nurse Guinness. That was old Captain Shotover, Mrs Hushabye's father. I heard him roaring; but I thought it was for something else. I suppose it was Mrs Hushabye that invited you, ducky?

THE YOUNG LADY. I understood her to do so. But really I think I'd better go.

NURSE GUINNESS. Oh, dont think of such a thing, miss. If Mrs Hushabye has forgotten all about it, it will be a pleasant surprise for her to see you, wont it?

THE YOUNG LADY. It has been a very unpleasant surprise to me to find that nobody expects me.

NURSE GUINNESS. Youll get used to it, miss: this house is full of surprises for them that dont know our ways.

CAPTAIN SHOTOVER [*looking in from the hall suddenly: an ancient but still hardy man with an immense white beard, in a reefer jacket with a whistle hanging from his neck*] Nurse: there is a hold-all and a handbag on the front steps for everybody to fall over. Also a tennis racquet. Who the devil left them there?

THE YOUNG LADY. They are mine, I'm afraid.

THE CAPTAIN [*advancing to the drawing-table*] Nurse: who is this misguided and unfortunate young lady?

NURSE GUINNESS. She says Miss Hessy invited her, sir.

THE CAPTAIN. And had she no friend, no parents, to warn her against my daughter's invitations? This is a pretty sort of house, by heavens! A young and attractive lady is invited here. Her luggage is left on the steps for hours; and she herself is deposited in the poop and abandoned, tired and starving. This is our hospitality. These are our manners. No room ready. No hot water. No welcoming hostess. Our visitor is to sleep in the toolshed, and to wash in the duckpond.

NURSE GUINNESS. Now it's all right, Captain: I'll get the lady some tea; and her room shall be ready before she has finished it. [*To the young lady*] Take off your hat, ducky; and make yourself at home [*she goes to the door leading to the hall*].

THE CAPTAIN [*as she passes him*] Ducky! Do you suppose, woman, that because this young lady has been insulted and neglected, you have the right to address her as you address my wretched children, whom you have brought up in ignorance of the commonest decencies of social intercourse?

NURSE GUINNESS. Never mind him, doty. [*Quite unconcerned, she goes out into the hall on her way to the kitchen*].

THE CAPTAIN. Madam: will you favor me with your name? [*He sits down in the big wicker chair*].

THE YOUNG LADY. My name is Ellie Dunn.

THE CAPTAIN. Dunn! I had a boatswain whose name was Dunn. He was originally a pirate in China. He set up as a ship's chandler with stores which I have every reason to believe he stole from me. No doubt he became rich. Are you his daughter?

ELLIE [*indignant*] No: certainly not. I am proud to be able to say that though my father has not been a successful man, nobody has ever had one word to say against him. I think my father is the best man I have ever known.

THE CAPTAIN. He must be greatly changed. Has he attained the seventh degree of concentration?

ELLIE. I dont understand.

THE CAPTAIN. But how could he, with a daughter? I, madam, have two daughters. One of them is Hesione Hushabye, who invited you here. I keep this house: she upsets it. I desire to attain the seventh degree of concentration: she invites visitors and leaves me to entertain them. [*Nurse Guinness returns with the tea-tray, which she places on the teak table*]. I have a second daughter who is, thank God, in a remote part of the Empire with her numskull of a husband. As a child she thought the figure-head of my ship, the Dauntless, the most beautiful thing on earth. He resembled it. He had the same expression: wooden yet enterprising. She married him, and will never set foot in this house again.

NURSE GUINNESS [*carrying the table, with the tea-things on it, to Ellie's side*] Indeed you never were more mistaken. She is in England this very moment. You have been told three times this week that she is coming home for a year for her health. And very glad you should be to see your own daughter again after all these years.

THE CAPTAIN. I am not glad. The natural term of the affection of the human animal for its offspring is six years. My daughter Ariadne was born when I was forty-six. I am now eighty-eight. If she comes, I am not at home. If she wants anything, let her take it. If she asks for me, let her be informed that I am extremely old, and have totally forgotten her.

NURSE GUINNESS. Thats no talk to offer to a young lady. Here, ducky, have some tea; and dont listen to him [*she pours out a cup of tea*].

THE CAPTAIN [*rising wrathfully*] Now before high heaven they have given this innocent child Indian tea: the stuff they tan their own leather insides with. [*He seizes the cup and the tea-pot and empties both into the leathern bucket*].

ELLIE [*almost in tears*] Oh, please! I am so tired. I should have been glad of anything.

NURSE GUINNESS. Oh, what a thing to do! The poor lamb is ready to drop.

THE CAPTAIN. You shall have some of my tea. Do not touch that fly-blown cake: nobody eats it here except the dogs. [*He disappears into the pantry*].

NURSE GUINNESS. Theres a man for you! They say he sold himself to the devil in Zanzibar before he was captain; and the older he grows the more I believe them.

A WOMAN'S VOICE [*in the hall*] Is anyone at home? Hesione! Nurse! Papa! Do come, somebody; and take in my luggage.

*Thumping heard, as of an umbrella, on the wainscot.*

[ 64 ]

NURSE GUINNESS. My gracious! It's Miss Addie, Lady Utterword, Mrs Hushabye's sister: the one I told the Captain about. [*Calling*] Coming, Miss, coming.

*She carries the table back to its place by the door, and is hurrying out when she is intercepted by Lady Utterword, who bursts in much flustered. Lady Utterword, a blonde, is very handsome, very well dressed, and so precipitate in speech and action that the first impression (erroneous) is one of comic silliness.*

LADY UTTERWORD. Oh, is that you, Nurse? How are you? You dont look a day older. Is nobody at home? Where is Hesione? Doesnt she expect me? Where are the servants? Whose luggage is that on the steps? Where's Papa? Is everybody asleep? [*Seeing Ellie*] Oh! I beg your pardon. I suppose you are one of my nieces. [*Approaching her with outstretched arms*] Come and kiss your aunt, darling.

ELLIE. I'm only a visitor. It is my luggage on the steps.

NURSE GUINNESS. I'll go get you some fresh tea, ducky. [*She takes up the tray*].

ELLIE. But the old gentleman said he would make some himself.

NURSE GUINNESS. Bless you! he's forgotten what he went for already. His mind wanders from one thing to another.

LADY UTTERWORD. Papa, I suppose?

NURSE GUINNESS. Yes, Miss.

LADY UTTERWORD [*vehemently*] Dont be silly, nurse. Dont call me Miss.

NURSE GUINNESS [*placidly*] No, lovey [*she goes out with the tea-tray*].

LADY UTTERWORD [*sitting down with a flounce on the sofa*] I know what you must feel. Oh, this house, this house! I come back to it after twenty-three years;

and it is just the same: the luggage lying on the steps, the servants spoilt and impossible, nobody at home to receive anybody, no regular meals, nobody ever hungry because they are always gnawing bread and butter or munching apples, and, what is worse, the same disorder in ideas, in talk, in feeling. When I was a child I was used to it: I had never known anything better, though I was unhappy, and longed all the time —oh, how I longed!—to be respectable, to be a lady, to live as others did, not to have to think of everything for myself. I married at nineteen to escape from it. My husband is Sir Hastings Utterword, who has been governor of all the crown colonies in succession. I have always been the mistress of Government House. I have been so happy: I had forgotten that people could live like this. I wanted to see my father, my sister, my nephews and nieces (one ought to, you know), and I was looking forward to it. And now the state of the house! the way I'm received! the casual impudence of that woman Guinness, our old nurse! really Hesione might at least have been here: some preparation might have been made for me. You must excuse my going on in this way; but I am really very much hurt and annoyed and disillusioned: and if I had realized it was to be like this, I wouldnt have come. I have a great mind to go away without another word [*she is on the point of weeping*].

ELLIE [*also very miserable*] Nobody has been here to receive me either. I thought I ought to go away too. But how can I, Lady Utterword? My luggage is on the steps; and the station fly has gone.

*The Captain emerges from the pantry with a tray of Chinese lacquer and a very fine tea-set on it. He rests it provisionally on the end of the table; snatches away the drawing-board, which he stands on the floor against the table legs; and puts the tray in the space thus cleared. Ellie pours out a cup greedily.*

THE CAPTAIN. Your tea, young lady. What! another lady! I must fetch another cup [*he makes for the pantry*].

LADY UTTERWORD [*rising from the sofa, suffused with emotion*] Papa! Dont you know me? I'm your daughter.

THE CAPTAIN. Nonsense! my daughter's upstairs asleep. [*He vanishes through the half door*].

*Lady Utterword retires to the window to conceal her tears.*

ELLIE [*going to her with the cup*] Dont be so distressed. Have this cup of tea. He is very old and very strange: he has been just like that to me. I know how dreadful it must be: my own father is all the world to me. Oh, I'm sure he didnt mean it.

*The Captain returns with another cup.*

THE CAPTAIN. Now we are complete. [*He places it on the tray*].

LADY UTTERWORD [*hysterically*] Papa: you cant have forgotten me. I am Ariadne. I'm little Paddy Patkins. Wont you kiss me?

[*She goes to him and throws her arms round his neck*].

THE CAPTAIN [*woodenly enduring her embrace*] How can you be Ariadne? You are a middle-aged woman: well preserved, madam, but no longer young.

LADY UTTERWORD. But think of all the years and years I have been away, Papa. I have had to grow old, like other people.

THE CAPTAIN [*disengaging himself*] You should grow out of kissing strange men: they may be striving to attain the seventh degree of concentration.

LADY UTTERWORD. But I'm your daughter. You havnt seen me for years.

THE CAPTAIN. So much the worse! When our relatives are at home, we have to think of all their good points or it would be impossible to endure them. But when they are away, we console ourselves for their absence by dwelling on their vices. That is how I have come to think my absent daughter Ariadne a perfect fiend; so do not try to ingratiate yourself here by impersonating her [*he walks firmly away to the other side of the room*].

LADY UTTERWORD. Ingratiating myself indeed! [*With dignity*] Very well, papa. [*She sits down at the drawing-table and pours out tea for herself*].

THE CAPTAIN. I am neglecting my social duties. You remember Dunn? Billy Dunn?

LADY UTTERWORD. Do you mean that villainous sailor who robbed you?

THE CAPTAIN [*introducing Ellie*] His daughter. [*He sits down on the sofa*].

ELLIE [*protesting*] No—

*Nurse Guinness returns with fresh tea.*

THE CAPTAIN. Take that hogwash away. Do you hear?

NURSE. Youve actually remembered about the tea! [*To Ellie*] O, miss, he didnt forget you after all! You have made an impression.

THE CAPTAIN [*gloomily*] Youth! beauty! novelty! They are badly wanted in this house. I am excessively old. Hesione is only moderately young. Her children are not youthful.

LADY UTTERWORD. How can children be expected to be youthful in this house? Almost before we could speak we were filled with notions that might have been all very well for pagan philosophers of fifty, but were certainly quite unfit for respectable people of any age.

NURSE. You were always for respectability, Miss Addy.

LADY UTTERWORD. Nurse: will you please remember that I am Lady Utterword, and not Miss Addy, nor lovey, nor darling, nor doty? Do you hear?

NURSE. Yes, ducky: all right. I'll tell them all they must call you my lady. [*She takes her tray out with undisturbed placidity*].

LADY UTTERWORD. What comfort? what sense is there in having servants with no manners?

ELLIE [*rising and coming to the table to put down her empty cup*] Lady Utterword: do you think Mrs Hushabye really expects me?

LADY UTTERWORD. Oh, dont ask me. You can see for yourself that Ive just arrived; her only sister, after twenty-three years absence! and it seems that *I* am not expected.

THE CAPTAIN. What does it matter whether the young lady is expected or not? She is welcome. There are beds: there is food. I'll find a room for her myself [*he makes for the door*].

ELLIE [*following him to stop him*] Oh please— [*he goes out*]. Lady Utterword: I dont know what to do. Your father persists in believing that my father is some sailor who robbed him.

LADY UTTERWORD. You had better pretend not to notice it. My father is a very clever man; but he always forgot things; and now that he is old, of course he is worse. And I must warn you that it is sometimes very hard to feel quite sure that he really forgets.

*Mrs Hushabye bursts into the room tempestuously, and embraces Ellie. She is a couple of years older than Lady Utterword, and even better looking. She has magnificent black hair, eyes like the fishpools of Heshbon, and a nobly modelled neck, short at the back and low between her shoulders in front. Unlike her sister she is*

[ 69 ]

*uncorseted and dressed anyhow in a rich robe of black pile that shews off her white skin and statuesque contour.*

MRS HUSHABYE. Ellie, my darling, my pettikins [*kissing her*]: how long have you been here? Ive been at home all the time: I was putting flowers and things in your room; and when I just sat down for a moment to try how comfortable the armchair was I went off to sleep. Papa woke me and told me you were here. Fancy your finding no one, and being neglected and abandoned. [*Kissing her again*], My poor love! [*She deposits Ellie on the sofa. Meanwhile Ariadne has left the table and come over to claim her share of attention*]. Oh! youve brought someone with you. Introduce me.

LADY UTTERWORD. Hesione: is it possible that you dont know me?

MRS HUSHABYE [*conventionally*] Of course I remember your face quite well. Where have we met?

LADY UTTERWORD. Didnt Papa tell you I was here? Oh! this is really too much. [*She throws herself sulkily into the big chair*].

MRS HUSHABYE. Papa!

LADY UTTERWORD. Yes: Papa. Our papa, you unfeeling wretch. [*Rising angrily*] I'll go straight to a hotel.

MRS HUSHABYE [*seizing her by the shoulders*] My goodness gracious goodness, you dont mean to say that youre Addy!

LADY UTTERWORD. I certainly am Addy; and I dont think I can be so changed that you would not have recognized me if you had any real affection for me. And papa didnt think me even worth mentioning!

MRS HUSHABYE. What a lark! Sit down [*she pushes her back into the chair instead of kissing her, and posts herself behind it*]. You do look a swell. Youre much handsomer than you used to be. Youve made the acquaintance of Ellie, of course. She is going to marry a perfect hog of a millionaire for the sake of her father, who is as poor as a church mouse; and you must help me to stop her.

ELLIE. Oh please, Hesione.

MRS HUSHABYE. My pettikins, the man's coming here today with your father to begin persecuting you; and everybody will see the state of the case in ten minutes; so whats the use of making a secret of it?

ELLIE. He is not a hog, Hesione. You dont know how wonderfully good he was to my father, and how deeply grateful I am to him.

MRS HUSHABYE [to Lady Utterword] Her father is a very remarkable man, Addy. His name is Mazzini Dunn. Mazzini was a celebrity of some kind who knew Ellie's grandparents. They were both poets, like the Brownings; and when her father came into the world Mazzini said "Another soldier born for freedom!" So they christened him Mazzini; and he has been fighting for freedom in his quiet way ever since. Thats why he is so poor.

ELLIE. I am proud of his poverty.

MRS HUSHABYE. Of course you are, pettikins. Why not leave him in it, and marry someone you love?

LADY UTTERWORD [rising suddenly and explosively] Hesione: are you going to kiss me or are you not?

MRS HUSHABYE. What do you want to be kissed for?

LADY UTTERWORD. I dont want to be kissed; but I do want you to behave properly and decently. We are sisters. We have been separated for twenty-three years. You ought to kiss me.

MRS HUSHABYE. Tomorrow morning, dear, before you make up. I hate the smell of powder.

LADY UTTERWORD. Oh! you unfeeling—[she is interrupted by the return of the captain].

[ 71 ]

THE CAPTAIN [*to Ellie*] Your room is ready. [*Ellie rises*]. The sheets were damp; but I have changed them [*he makes for the garden door on the port side*].

LADY UTTERWORD. Oh! What about my sheets?

THE CAPTAIN [*halting at the door*] Take my advice: air them; or take them off and sleep in blankets. You shall sleep in Ariadne's old room.

LADY UTTERWORD. Indeed I shall do nothing of the sort. That little hole! I am entitled to the best spare room.

THE CAPTAIN [*continuing unmoved*] She married a numskull. She told me she would marry anyone to get away from home.

LADY UTTERWORD. You are pretending not to know me on purpose. I will leave the house.

*Mazzini Dunn enters from the hall. He is a little elderly man with bulging credulous eyes and earnest manners. He is dressed in a blue serge jacket suit with an unbuttoned mackintosh over it, and carries a soft black hat of clerical cut.*

ELLIE. At last! Captain Shotover: here is my father.

THE CAPTAIN. This! Nonsense! not a bit like him [*he goes away through the garden, shutting the door sharply behind him*].

LADY UTTERWORD. I will not be ignored and pretended to be somebody else. I will have it out with papa now, this instant. [*To Mazzini*] Excuse me. [*She follows the Captain out, making a hasty bow to Mazzini, who returns it*].

MRS HUSHABYE [*hospitably, shaking hands*] How good of you to come, Mr Dunn! You dont mind papa, do you? He is as mad as a hatter, you know, but quite harmless, and extremely clever. You will have some delightful talks with him.

MAZZINI. I hope so. [*To Ellie*] So here you are, Ellie,

dear. [*He draws her arm affectionately through his*]. I must thank you, Mrs Hushabye, for your kindness to my daughter. I'm afraid she would have had no holiday if you had not invited her.

MRS HUSHABYE. Not at all. Very nice of her to come and attract young people to the house for us.

MAZZINI [*smiling*] I'm afraid Ellie is not interested in young men, Mrs Hushabye. Her taste is on the graver, solider side.

MRS HUSHABYE [*with a sudden rather hard brightness in her manner*] Wont you take off your overcoat, Mr Dunn? You will find a cupboard for coats and hats and things in the corner of the hall.

MAZZINI [*hastily releasing Ellie*] Yes—thank you—I had better— [*he goes out*].

MRS HUSHABYE [*emphatically*] The old brute!

ELLIE. Who?

MRS HUSHABYE. Who! Him. He. It [*pointing after Mazzini*]. "Graver, solider tastes," indeed!

ELLIE [*aghast*] You dont mean that you were speaking like that of my father!

MRS HUSHABYE. I was. You know I was.

ELLIE [*with dignity*] I will leave your house at once. [*She turns to the door*].

MRS HUSHABYE. If you attempt it, I'll tell your father why.

ELLIE [*turning again*] Oh! How can you treat a visitor like this, Mrs Hushabye?

MRS HUSHABYE. I thought you were going to call me Hesione.

ELLIE. Certainly not now?

MRS HUSHABYE. Very well: I'll tell your father.

ELLIE [*distressed*] Oh!

MRS HUSHABYE. If you turn a hair—if you take his part against me and against your own heart for a moment, I'll give that born soldier of freedom a piece of my mind that will stand him on his selfish old head for a week.

ELLIE. Hesione! My father selfish! How little you know—

*She is interrupted by Mazzini, who returns, excited and perspiring.*

MAZZINI. Ellie: Mangan has come: I thought youd like to know. Excuse me, Mrs Hushabye: the strange old gentleman—

MRS HUSHABYE. Papa. Quite so.

MAZZINI. Oh, I beg your pardon: of course: I was a little confused by his manner. He is making Mangan help him with something in the garden; and he wants me too—

*A powerful whistle is heard.*

THE CAPTAIN'S VOICE. Bosun ahoy! [*the whistle is repeated*].

MAZZINI [*flustered*] Oh dear! I believe he is whistling for me [*He hurries out*].

MRS HUSHABYE. Now my father is a wonderful man if you like.

ELLIE. Hesione: listen to me. You dont understand. My father and Mr Mangan were boys together. Mr Ma—

MRS HUSHABYE. I dont care what they were: we must sit down if you are going to begin as far back as that [*She snatches at Ellie's waist, and makes her sit down on the sofa beside her*]. Now, pettikins: tell me all about Mr Mangan. They call him Boss Mangan, dont they? He is a Napoleon of industry and disgustingly rich, isnt he? Why isnt your father rich?

ELLIE. My poor father should never have been in business. His parents were poets; and they gave him

[ 74 ]

the noblest ideas; but they could not afford to give
him a profession.

MRS HUSHABYE. Fancy your grandparents, with their
eyes in fine frenzy rolling! And so your poor father
had to go into business. Hasnt he succeeded in it?

ELLIE. He always used to say he could succeed if he
only had some capital. He fought his way along, to
keep a roof over our heads and bring us up well; but
it was always a struggle: always the same difficulty of
not having capital enough. I dont know how to
describe it to you.

MRS HUSHABYE. Poor Ellie! I know. Pulling the devil
by the tail.

ELLIE [hurt] Oh no. Not like that. It was at least
dignified.

MRS HUSHABYE. That made it all the harder, didnt
it? *I* shouldnt have pulled the devil by the tail with
dignity. I should have pulled hard—[between her
teeth] hard. Well? Go on.

ELLIE. At last it seemed that all our troubles were at
an end. Mr Mangan did an extraordinarily noble thing
out of pure friendship for my father and respect for
his character. He asked him how much capital he
wanted, and gave it to him. I dont mean that he lent
it to him, or that he invested it in his business. He
just simply made him a present of it. Wasnt that
splendid of him?

MRS HUSHABYE. On condition that you married him?

ELLIE. Oh no, no, no. This was when I was a child.
He had never even seen me: he never came to our
house. It was absolutely disinterested. Pure generosity.

MRS HUSHABYE. Oh! I beg the gentleman's pardon.
Well, what became of the money?

ELLIE. We all got new clothes and moved into another
house. And I went to another school for two years.

MRS HUSHABYE. Only two years?

ELLIE. That was all; for at the end of two years my father was utterly ruined.

MRS HUSHABYE. How?

ELLIE. I dont know. I never could understand. But it was dreadful. When we were poor my father had never been in debt. But when he launched out into business on a large scale, he had to incur liabilities. When the business went into liquidation he owed more money than Mr Mangan had given him.

MRS HUSHABYE. Bit off more than he could chew, I suppose.

ELLIE. I think you are a little unfeeling about it.

MRS HUSHABYE. My pettikins: you mustnt mind my way of talking. I was quite as sensitive and particular as you once; but I have picked up so much slang from the children that I am really hardly presentable. I suppose your father had no head for business, and made a mess of it.

ELLIE. Oh, that just shews how entirely you are mistaken about him. The business turned out a great success. It now pays forty-four per cent after deducting the excess profits tax.

MRS HUSHABYE. Then why arnt you rolling in money?

ELLIE. I dont know. It seems very unfair to me. You see, my father was made bankrupt. It nearly broke his heart, because he had persuaded several of his friends to put money into the business. He was sure it would succeed; and events proved that he was quite right. But they all lost their money. It was dreadful. I dont know what we should have done but for Mr Mangan.

MRS HUSHABYE. What! Did the Boss come to the rescue again, after all his money being thrown away?

ELLIE. He did indeed, and never uttered a reproach to my father. He bought what was left of the business—the buildings and the machinery and things—from the official trustee for enough money to enable my father to pay six and eightpence in the pound and get his discharge. Everyone pitied papa so much, and saw so plainly that he was an honorable man, that they let him off at six-and-eightpence instead of ten shillings. Then Mr Mangan started a company to take up the business, and made my father a manager in it to save us from starvation; for I wasnt earning anything then.

MRS HUSHABYE. Quite a romance. And when did the Boss develop the tender passion?

ELLIE. Oh, that was years after, quite lately. He took the chair one night at a sort of people's concert. I was singing there. As an amateur, you know: half a guinea for expenses and three songs with three encores. He was so pleased with my singing that he asked might he walk home with me. I never saw anyone so taken aback as he was when I took him home and introduced him to my father: his own manager. It was then that my father told me how nobly he had behaved. Of course it was considered a great chance for me, as he is so rich. And—and—we drifted into a sort of understanding—I suppose I should call it an engagement—[*she is distressed and cannot go on*].

MRS HUSHABYE [*rising and marching about*] You may have drifted into it; but you will bounce out of it, my pettikins, if I am to have anything to do with it.

ELLIE [*hopelessly*] No: it's no use. I am bound in honor and gratitude. I will go through with it.

MRS HUSHABYE [*behind the sofa, scolding down at her*] You know, of course, that it's not honorable or grateful to marry a man you dont love. Do you love this Mangan man?

ELLIE. Yes. At least—

MRS HUSHABYE. I dont want to know about "the least": I want to know the worst. Girls of your age fall in love with all sorts of impossible people, especially old people.

ELLIE. I like Mr Mangan very much; and I shall always be—

MRS HUSHABYE [*impatiently completing the sentence and prancing away intolerantly to starboard*]— grateful to him for his kindness to dear father. I know. Anybody else?

ELLIE. What do you mean?

MRS HUSHABYE. Anybody else? Are you in love with anybody else?

ELLIE. Of course not.

MRS HUSHABYE. Humph! [*The book on the drawing-table catches her eye. She picks it up, and evidently finds the title very unexpected. She looks at Ellie, and asks, quaintly*] Quite sure youre not in love with an actor?

ELLIE. No, no. Why? What put such a thing into your head?

MRS HUSHABYE. This is yours, isnt it? Why else should you be reading Othello?

ELLIE. My father taught me to love Shakespear.

MRS HUSHABYE [*flinging the book down on the table*] Really! your father does seem to be about the limit.

ELLIE [*naïvely*] Do you never read Shakespear, Hesione? That seems to me so extraordinary. I like Othello.

MRS HUSHABYE. Do you indeed? He was jealous, wasnt he?

ELLIE. Oh, not that. I think all the part about jealousy is horrible. But dont you think it must have been a wonderful experience for Desdemona, brought up so quietly at home, to meet a man who had been out in the world doing all sorts of brave things and having terrible adventures, and yet finding something in her that made him love to sit and talk with her and tell her about them?

MRS HUSHABYE. Thats your idea of romance, is it?

ELLIE. Not romance, exactly. It might really happen.

*Ellie's eyes shew that she is not arguing, but in a day-dream. Mrs Hushabye, watching her inquisitively, goes deliberately back to the sofa and resumes her seat beside her.*

MRS HUSHABYE. Ellie darling: have you noticed that some of those stories that Othello told Desdemona couldnt have happened?

ELLIE. Oh no. Shakespear thought they could have happened.

MRS HUSHABYE. Hm! Desdemona thought they could have happened. But they didnt.

ELLIE. Why do you look so enigmatic about it? You are such a sphinx: I never know what you mean.

MRS HUSHABYE. Desdemona would have found him out if she had lived, you know. I wonder was that why he strangled her!

ELLIE. Othello was not telling lies.

MRS HUSHABYE. How do you know?

ELLIE. Shakespear would have said if he was. Hesione: there are men who have done wonderful things: men like Othello, only, of course, white, and very hand-some, and—

MRS HUSHABYE. Ah! Now we're coming to it. Tell me all about him. I knew there must be somebody, or youd never have been so miserable about Mangan: youd have thought it quite a lark to marry him.

ELLIE [*blushing vividly*] Hesione: you are dreadful.

[ 79 ]

But I dont want to make a secret of it, though of course I dont tell everybody. Besides, I dont know him.

MRS HUSHABYE. Dont know him! What does that mean?

ELLIE. Well, of course I know him to speak to.

MRS HUSHABYE. But you want to know him ever so much more intimately, eh?

ELLIE. No no: I know him quite—almost intimately.

MRS HUSHABYE. You dont know him; and you know him almost intimately. How lucid!

ELLIE. I mean that he does not call on us. I—I got into conversation with him by chance at a concert.

MRS HUSHABYE. You seem to have rather a gay time at your concerts, Ellie.

ELLIE. Not at all: we talk to everyone in the green-room waiting for our turns. I thought he was one of the artists: he looked so splendid. But he was only one of the committee. I happened to tell him that I was copying a picture at the National Gallery. I make a little money that way. I cant paint much; but as it's always the same picture I can do it pretty quickly and get two or three pounds for it. It happened that he came to the National Gallery one day.

MRS HUSHABYE. One student's day. Paid sixpence to stumble about through a crowd of easels, when he might have come in next day for nothing and found the floor clear! Quite by accident?

ELLIE [*triumphantly*] No. On purpose. He liked talking to me. He knows lots of the most splendid people. Fashionable women who are all in love with him. But he ran away from them to see me at the National Gallery and persuade me to come with him for a drive round Richmond Park in a taxi.

MRS HUSHABYE. My pettikins, you have been going

it. It's wonderful what you good girls can do without anyone saying a word.

ELLIE. I am not in society, Hesione. If I didnt make acquaintances in that way I shouldnt have any at all.

MRS HUSHABYE. Well, no harm if you know how to take care of yourself. May I ask his name?

ELLIE [*slowly and musically*] Marcus Darnley.

MRS HUSHABYE [*echoing the music*] Marcus Darnley! What a splendid name!

ELLIE. Oh, I'm so glad you think so. I think so too; but I was afraid it was only a silly fancy of my own.

MRS HUSHABYE. Hm! Is he one of the Aberdeen Darnleys?

ELLIE. Nobody knows. Just fancy! He was found in an antique chest—

MRS HUSHABYE. A what?

ELLIE. An antique chest, one summer morning in a rose garden, after a night of the most terrible thunderstorm.

MRS HUSHABYE. What on earth was he doing in the chest? Did he get into it because he was afraid of the lightning?

ELLIE. Oh no, no: he was a baby. The name Marcus Darnley was embroidered on his babyclothes. And five hundred pounds in gold.

MRS HUSHABYE [*looking hard at her*] Ellie!

ELLIE. The garden of the Viscount—

MRS HUSHABYE. —de Rougemont?

ELLIE [*innocently*] No: de Larochejaquelin. A French family. A vicomte. His life has been one long romance. A tiger—

MRS HUSHABYE. Slain by his own hand?

ELLIE. Oh no: nothing vulgar like that. He saved the life of the tiger from a hunting party: one of King Edward's hunting parties in India. The King was furious: that was why he never had his military services properly recognized. But he doesnt care. He is a Socialist and despises rank, and has been in three revolutions fighting on the barricades.

MRS HUSHABYE. How can you sit there telling me such lies? You, Ellie, of all people! And I thought you were a perfectly simple, straightforward, good girl.

ELLIE [rising, dignified but very angry] Do you mean to say you dont believe me?

MRS HUSHABYE. Of course I dont believe you. Youre inventing every word of it. Do you take me for a fool?

*Ellie stares at her. Her candor is so obvious that Mrs Hushabye is puzzled.*

ELLIE. Goodbye, Hesione. I'm very sorry. I see now that it sounds very improbable as I tell it. But I cant stay if you think that way about me.

MRS HUSHABYE [catching her dress] You shant go. I couldnt be so mistaken: I know too well what liars are like. Somebody has really told you all this.

ELLIE [flushing] Hesione: dont say that you dont believe him. I couldnt bear that.

MRS HUSHABYE [soothing her] Of course I believe him, dearest. But you should have broken it to me by degrees. [Drawing her back to her seat] Now tell me all about him. Are you in love with him?

ELLIE. Oh no. I'm not so foolish. I dont fall in love with people. I'm not so silly as you think.

MRS HUSHABYE. I see. Only something to think about—to give some interest and pleasure to life.

ELLIE. Just so. Thats all, really.

MRS HUSHABYE. It makes the hours go fast, doesnt it? No tedious waiting to go to sleep at nights and wondering whether you will have a bad night. How delightful it makes waking up in the morning! How much better than the happiest dream! All life transfigured! No more wishing one had an interesting book to read, because life is so much happier than any book! No desire but to be alone and not to have to talk to anyone: to be alone and just think about it.

ELLIE [*embracing her*] Hesione: you are a witch. How do you know? Oh, you are the most sympathetic woman in the world.

MRS HUSHABYE [*caressing her*] Pettikins, my pettikins: how I envy you! and how I pity you!

ELLIE. Pity me! Oh, why?

*A very handsome man of fifty, with mousquetaire moustaches, wearing a rather dandified curly brimmed hat, and carrying an elaborate walking-stick, comes into the room from the hall, and stops short at sight of the women on the sofa.*

ELLIE [*seeing him and rising in glad surprise*] Oh! Hesione: this is Mr Marcus Darnley.

MRS HUSHABYE [*rising*] What a lark! He is my husband.

ELLIE. But how—[*she stops suddenly; then turns pale and sways*].

MRS HUSHABYE [*catching her and sitting down with her on the sofa*] Steady, my pettikins.

THE MAN [*with a mixture of confusion and effrontery, depositing his hat and stick on the teak table*] My real name, Miss Dunn, is Hector Hushabye. I leave you to judge whether that is a name any sensitive man would care to confess to. I never use it when I can possibly help it. I have been away for nearly a month; and I had no idea you knew my wife, or that you were coming here. I am none the less delighted to find you in our little house.

ELLIE [*in great distress*] I dont know what to do.

[ 83 ]

Please, may I speak to papa? Do leave me. I cant bear it.

MRS HUSHABYE. Be off, Hector.

HECTOR. I—

MRS HUSHABYE. Quick, quick. Get out.

HECTOR. If you think it better—[*he goes out, taking his hat with him but leaving the stick on the table*].

MRS HUSHABYE [*laying Ellie down at the end of the sofa*] Now, pettikins, he is gone. Theres nobody but me. You can let yourself go. Dont try to control yourself. Have a good cry.

ELLIE [*raising her head*] Damn!

MRS HUSHABYE. Splendid! Oh, what a relief! I thought you were going to be broken-hearted. Never mind me. Damn him again.

ELLIE. I am not damning him: I am damning myself for being such a fool. [*Rising*] How could I let myself be taken in so? [*She begins prowling to and fro, her bloom gone, looking curiously older and harder*].

MRS HUSHABYE [*cheerfully*] Why not, pettikins? Very few young women can resist Hector. I couldnt when I was your age. He is really rather splendid, you know.

ELLIE [*turning on her*] Splendid! Yes: splendid looking, of course. But how can you love a liar?

MRS HUSHABYE. I dont know. But you can, fortunately. Otherwise there wouldnt be much love in the world.

ELLIE. But to lie like that! To be a boaster! a coward!

MRS HUSHABYE [*rising in alarm*] Pettikins: none of that, if you please. If you hint the slightest doubt of Hector's courage, he will go straight off and do the most horribly dangerous things to convince himself that he isnt a coward. He has a dreadful trick of getting out of one third-floor window and coming in at another, just to test his nerve. He has a whole drawerful of Albert Medals for saving people's lives.

ELLIE. He never told me that.

MRS HUSHABYE. He never boasts of anything he really did: he cant bear it; and it makes him shy if anyone else does. All his stories are made-up stories.

ELLIE [*coming to her*] Do you mean that he is really brave, and really has adventures, and yet tells lies about things that he never did and that never happened?

MRS HUSHABYE. Yes, pettikins, I do. People dont have their virtues and vices in sets: they have them anyhow: all mixed.

ELLIE [*staring at her thoughtfully*] Theres something odd about this house, Hesione, and even about you. I dont know why I'm talking to you so calmly. I have a horrible fear that my heart is broken, but that heartbreak is not like what I thought it must be.

MRS HUSHABYE [*fondling her*] It's only life educating you, pettikins. How do you feel about Boss Mangan now?

ELLIE [*disengaging herself with an expression of distaste*] Oh, how can you remind me of him, Hesione?

MRS HUSHABYE. Sorry, dear. I think I hear Hector coming back. You dont mind now, do you, dear?

ELLIE. Not in the least. I am quite cured.

*Mazzini Dunn and Hector come in from the hall.*

HECTOR [*as he opens the door and allows Mazzini to pass in*] One second more, and she would have been a dead woman!

MAZZINI. Dear! dear! what an escape! Ellie, my love: Mr Hushabye has just been telling me the most extraordinary—

ELLIE. Yes: Ive heard it [*She crosses to the other side of the room*].

HECTOR [*following her*] Not this one: I'll tell it to you after dinner. I think youll like it. The truth is, I made it up for you, and was looking forward to the pleasure of telling it to you. But in a moment of impatience at being turned out of the room, I threw it away on your father.

ELLIE [*turning at bay with her back to the carpenter's bench, scornfully self-possessed*] It was not thrown away. He believes it. I should not have believed it.

MAZZINI [*benevolently*] Ellie is very naughty, Mr Hushabye. Of course she does not really think that. [*He goes to the bookshelves, and inspects the titles of the volumes*].

*Boss Mangan comes in from the hall, followed by the Captain. Mangan, carefully frock-coated as for church or for a director's meeting, is about fiftyfive, with a careworn, mistrustful expression, standing a little on an entirely imaginary dignity, with a dull complexion, straight, lustreless hair, and features so entirely commonplace that it is impossible to describe them.*

CAPTAIN SHOTOVER [*to Mrs Hushabye, introducing the newcomer*] Says his name is Mangan. Not able-bodied.

MRS HUSHABYE [*graciously*] How do you do, Mr Mangan ?

MANGAN [*shaking hands*] Very pleased.

CAPTAIN SHOTOVER. Dunn's lost his muscle, but recovered his nerve. Men seldom do after three attacks of delirium tremens [*he goes into the pantry*].

MRS HUSHABYE. I congratulate you, Mr Dunn.

MAZZINI [*dazed*] I am a lifelong teetotaler.

MRS HUSHABYE. You will find it far less trouble to let papa have his own way than try to explain.

MAZZINI. But three attacks of delirium tremens, really!

MRS HUSHABYE [*to Mangan*] Do you know my husband, Mr Mangan [*she indicates Hector*].

MANGAN [*going to Hector, who meets him with outstretched hand*] Very pleased. [*Turning to Ellie*] I hope, Miss Ellie, you have not found the journey down too fatiguing. [*They shake hands*].

MRS HUSHABYE. Hector: shew Mr Dunn his room.

HECTOR. Certainly. Come along, Mr Dunn. [*He takes Mazzini out*].

ELLIE. You havnt shewn me my room yet, Hesione.

MRS HUSHABYE. How stupid of me! Come along. Make yourself quite at home, Mr Mangan. Papa will entertain you [*She calls to the Captain in the pantry*] Papa: come and explain the house to Mr Mangan.

*She goes out with Ellie. The Captain comes from the pantry.*

CAPTAIN SHOTOVER. Youre going to marry Dunn's daughter. Dont. Youre too old.

MANGAN [*staggered*] Well! Thats fairly blunt, Captain.

CAPTAIN SHOTOVER. It's true.

MANGAN. She doesnt think so.

CAPTAIN SHOTOVER. She does.

MANGAN. Older men than I have—

CAPTAIN SHOTOVER [*finishing the sentence for him*]— made fools of themselves. That, also, is true.

MANGAN [*asserting himself*] I dont see that this is any business of yours.

CAPTAIN SHOTOVER. It is everybody's business. The stars in their courses are shaken when such things happen.

MANGAN. I'm going to marry her all the same.

CAPTAIN SHOTOVER. How do you know?

MANGAN [*playing the strong man*] I intend to. I mean to. See? I never made up my mind to do a thing yet that I didnt bring it off. Thats the sort of man I am;

and there will be a better understanding between us when you make up your mind to that, Captain.

CAPTAIN SHOTOVER. You frequent picture palaces.

MANGAN. Perhaps I do. Who told you?

CAPTAIN SHOTOVER. Talk like a man, not like a movy. You mean that you make a hundred thousand a year.

MANGAN. I dont boast. But when I meet a man that makes a hundred thousand a year, I take off my hat to that man, and stretch out my hand to him and call him brother.

CAPTAIN SHOTOVER. Then you also make a hundred thousand a year, hey?

MANGAN. No. I cant say that. Fifty thousand, perhaps.

CAPTAIN SHOTOVER. His half brother only [*he turns away from Mangan with his usual abruptness, and collects the empty tea-cups on the Chinese tray*].

MANGAN [*irritated*] See here, Captain Shotover. I dont quite understand my position here. I came here on your daughter's invitation. Am I in her house or in yours?

CAPTAIN SHOTOVER. You are beneath the dome of heaven, in the house of God. What is true within these walls is true outside them. Go out on the seas; climb the mountains; wander through the valleys. She is still too young.

MANGAN [*weakening*] But I'm very little over fifty.

CAPTAIN SHOTOVER. You are still less under sixty. Boss Mangan: you will not marry the pirate's child [*he carries the tray away into the pantry*].

MANGAN [*following him to the half door*] What pirate's child? What are you talking about?

CAPTAIN SHOTOVER [*in the pantry*] Ellie Dunn. You will not marry her.

[ 88 ]

MANGAN. Who will stop me?

CAPTAIN SHOTOVER [*emerging*] My daughter [*he makes for the door leading to the hall*].

MANGAN [*following him*] Mrs Hushabye! Do you mean to say she brought me down here to break it off?

CAPTAIN SHOTOVER [*stopping and turning on him*] I know nothing more than I have seen in her eye. She will break it off. Take my advice: marry a West Indian negress: they make excellent wives. I was married to one myself for two years.

MANGAN. Well, I am damned!

CAPTAIN SHOTOVER. I thought so. I was, too, for many years. The negress redeemed me.

MANGAN [*feebly*] This is queer. I ought to walk out of this house.

CAPTAIN SHOTOVER. Why?

MANGAN. Well, many men would be offended by your style of talking.

CAPTAIN SHOTOVER. Nonsense! It's the other sort of talking that makes quarrels. Nobody ever quarrels with me.

*A gentleman, whose firstrate tailoring and frictionless manners proclaim the wellbred West Ender, comes in from the hall. He has an engaging air of being young and unmarried, but on close inspection is found to be at least over forty.*

THE GENTLEMAN. Excuse my intruding in this fashion; but there is no knocker on the door; and the bell does not seem to ring.

CAPTAIN SHOTOVER. Why should there be a knocker? Why should the bell ring? The door is open.

THE GENTLEMAN. Precisely. So I ventured to come in.

CAPTAIN SHOTOVER. Quite right. I will see about a room for you [*he makes for the door*].

[ 89 ]

THE GENTLEMAN [*stopping him*] But I'm afraid you dont know who I am.

CAPTAIN SHOTOVER. Do you suppose that at my age I make distinctions between one fellowcreature and another? [*He goes out. Mangan and the newcomer stare at one another*].

MANGAN. Strange character, Captain Shotover, sir.

THE GENTLEMAN. Very.

CAPTAIN SHOTOVER [*shouting outside*] Hesione: another person has arrived and wants a room. Man about town, well dressed, fifty.

THE GENTLEMAN. Fancy Hesione's feelings! May I ask are you a member of the family?

MANGAN. No.

THE GENTLEMAN. I am. At least a connexion.

*Mrs Hushabye comes back.*

MRS HUSHABYE. How do you do? How good of you to come!

THE GENTLEMAN. I am very glad indeed to make your acquaintance, Hesione. [*Instead of taking her hand he kisses her. At the same moment the Captain appears in the doorway*]. You will excuse my kissing your daughter, Captain, when I tell you that—

CAPTAIN SHOTOVER. Stuff! Everyone kisses my daughter. Kiss her as much as you like [*he makes for the pantry*].

THE GENTLEMAN. Thank you. One moment, Captain, [*The Captain halts and turns. The gentleman goes to him affably*]. Do you happen to remember—but probably you dont, as it occurred many years ago—that your younger daughter married a numskull.

CAPTAIN SHOTOVER. Yes. She said she'd marry anybody to get away from this house. I should not have recognized you: your head is no longer like a walnut. Your aspect is softened. You have been boiled in bread and milk for years and years, like other married men. Poor devil! [*He disappears into the pantry*].

MRS HUSHABYE [*going past Mangan to the gentleman and scrutinizing him*] I dont believe you are Hastings Utterword.

THE GENTLEMAN. I am not.

MRS HUSHABYE. Then what business had you to kiss me?

THE GENTLEMAN. I thought I would like to. The fact is, I am Randall Utterword, the unworthy younger brother of Hastings. I was abroad diplomatizing when he was married.

LADY UTTERWORD [*dashing in*] Hesione: where is the key of the wardrobe in my room? My diamonds are in my dressing-bag: I must lock it up—[*recognizing the stranger with a shock*] Randall: how dare you? [*She marches at him past Mrs Hushabye, who retreats and joins Mangan near the sofa*].

RANDALL. How dare I what? I am not doing anything.

LADY UTTERWORD. Who told you I was here?

RANDALL. Hastings. You had just left when I called on you at Claridge's; so I followed you down here. You are looking extremely well.

LADY UTTERWORD. Dont presume to tell me so.

MRS HUSHABYE. What is wrong with Mr Randall, Addy?

LADY UTTERWORD [*recollecting herself*] Oh, nothing. But he has no right to come bothering you and papa without being invited [*she goes to the window-seat and sits down, turning away from them ill-humoredly and looking into the garden, where Hector and Ellie are now seen strolling together*].

MRS HUSHABYE. I think you have not met Mr Mangan, Addy.

LADY UTTERWORD [*turning her head and nodding coldly to Mangan*] I beg your pardon. Randall: you have flustered me so: I made a perfect fool of myself.

MRS HUSHABYE. Lady Utterword. My sister. My younger sister.

MANGAN [*bowing*] Pleased to meet you, Lady Utterword.

LADY UTTERWORD [*with marked interest*] Who is that gentleman walking in the garden with Miss Dunn?

MRS HUSHABYE. I dont know. She quarrelled mortally with my husband only ten minutes ago; and I didn't know anyone else had come. It must be a visitor. [*She goes to the window to look*]. Oh, it is Hector. Theyve made it up.

LADY UTTERWORD. Your husband! That handsome man?

MRS HUSHABYE. Well, why shouldnt my husband be a handsome man?

RANDALL [*joining them at the window*] One's husband never is, Ariadne [*he sits by Lady Utterword, on her right*].

MRS HUSHABYE. One's sister's husband always is, Mr Randall.

LADY UTTERWORD. Dont be vulgar, Randall. And you, Hesione, are just as bad.

*Ellie and Hector come in from the garden by the starboard door. Randall rises. Ellie retires into the corner near the pantry. Hector comes forward; and Lady Utterword rises looking her very best.*

MRS HUSHABYE. Hector: this is Addy.

HECTOR [*apparently surprised*] Not this lady.

LADY UTTERWORD [*smiling*] Why not?

HECTOR [*looking at her with a piercing glance of deep but respectful admiration, his moustache bristling*] I thought—[*pulling himself together*] I beg your pardon,

Lady Utterword. I am extremely glad to welcome you at last under our roof [*he offers his hand with grave courtesy*].

MRS HUSHABYE. She wants to be kissed, Hector.

LADY UTTERWORD. Hesione! [*but she still smiles*].

MRS HUSHABYE. Call her Addy; and kiss her like a good brother-in-law; and have done with it. [*She leaves them to themselves*].

HECTOR. Behave yourself, Hesione. Lady Utterword is entitled not only to hospitality but to civilization.

LADY UTTERWORD [*gratefully*] Thank you, Hector. [*They shake hands cordially*].

*Mazzini Dunn is seen crossing the garden from starboard to port.*

CAPTAIN SHOTOVER [*coming from the pantry and addressing Ellie*] Your father has washed himself.

ELLIE [*quite self-possessed*] He often does, Captain Shotover.

CAPTAIN SHOTOVER. A strange conversion! I saw him through the pantry window.

*Mazzini Dunn enters through the port window door, newly washed and brushed, and stops, smiling benevolently, between Mangan and Mrs Hushabye.*

MRS HUSHABYE [*introducing*] Mr Mazzini Dunn, Lady Ut—oh, I forgot: youve met. [*Indicating Ellie*] Miss Dunn.

MAZZINI [*walking across the room to take Ellie's hand, and beaming at his own naughty irony*] I have met Miss Dunn also. She is my daughter. [*He draws her arm through his caressingly*].

MRS HUSHABYE. Of course: how stupid! Mr Utter word, my sister's-er-

RANDALL [*shaking hands agreeably*] Her brother-in-law, Mr Dunn. How do you do?

MRS HUSHABYE. This is my husband.

HECTOR. We have met, dear. Dont introduce us any more. [*He moves away to the big chair, and adds*] Wont you sit down, Lady Utterword? [*She does so very graciously*].

MRS HUSHABYE. Sorry. I hate it: it's like making people shew their tickets.

MAZZINI [*sententiously*] How little it tells us, after all! The great question is, not who we are, but what we are.

CAPTAIN SHOTOVER. Ha! What are you?

MAZZINI [*taken aback*] What am I?

CAPTAIN SHOTOVER. A thief, a pirate, and a murderer.

MAZZINI. I assure you you are mistaken.

CAPTAIN SHOTOVER. An adventurous life; but what does it end in? Respectability. A ladylike daughter. The language and appearance of a city missionary. Let it be a warning to all of you [*he goes out through the garden*].

DUNN. I hope nobody here believes that I am a thief, a pirate, or a murderer. Mrs Hushabye: will you excuse me a moment? I must really go and explain. [*He follows the Captain*].

MRS HUSHABYE [*as he goes*] It's no use. Youd really better—[*but Dunn has vanished*] We had better all go out and look for some tea. We never have regular tea; but you can always get some when you want: the servants keep it stewing all day. The kitchen veranda is the best place to ask. May I shew you? [*She goes to the starboard door*].

RANDALL [*going with her*] Thank you, I dont think I'll take any tea this afternoon. But if you will shew me the garden—?

MRS HUSHABYE. Theres nothing to see in the garden except papa's observatory, and a gravel pit with a cave where he keeps dynamite and things of that sort. However, it's pleasanter out of doors: so come along.

RANDALL. Dynamite! Isnt that rather risky?

MRS HUSHABYE. Well, we dont sit in the gravel pit when theres a thunderstorm.

LADY UTTERWORD. Thats something new. What is the dynamite for?

HECTOR. To blow up the human race if it goes too far. He is trying to discover a psychic ray that will explode all the explosives at the will of a Mahatma.

ELLIE. The Captain's tea is delicious, Mr Utterword.

MRS HUSHABYE [*stopping in the doorway*] Do you mean to say that youve had some of my father's tea? that you got round him before you were ten minutes in the house?

ELLIE. I did.

MRS HUSHABYE. You little devil! [*She goes out with Randall*].

MANGAN. Wont you come, Miss Ellie?

ELLIE. I'm too tired. I'll take a book up to my room and rest a little. [*She goes to the bookshelf*].

MANGAN. Right. You cant do better. But I'm disappointed. [*He follows Randall and Mrs Hushabye*].

*Ellie, Hector, and Lady Utterword are left. Hector is close to Lady Utterword. They look at Ellie, waiting for her to go.*

ELLIE [*looking at the title of a book*] Do you like stories of adventure, Lady Utterword?

LADY UTTERWORD [*patronizingly*] Of course, dear.

ELLIE. Then I'll leave you to Mr Hushabye. [*She goes out through the hall*].

HECTOR. That girl is mad about tales of adventure. The lies I have to tell her!

LADY UTTERWORD [*not interested in Ellie*] When you

saw me what did you mean by saying that you thought, and then stopping short? What did you think?

HECTOR [*folding his arms and looking down at her magnetically*] May I tell you?

LADY UTTERWORD. Of course.

HECTOR. It will not sound very civil. I was on the point of saying "I thought you were a plain woman."

LADY UTTERWORD. Oh for shame, Hector! What right had you to notice whether I am plain or not?

HECTOR. Listen to me Ariadne. Until today I have seen only photographs of you; and no photograph can give the strange fascination of the daughters of that supernatural old man. There is some damnable quality in them that destroys men's moral sense, and carries them beyond honor and dishonor. You know that, dont you?

LADY UTTERWORD. Perhaps I do, Hector. But let me warn you once for all that I am a rigidly conventional woman. You may think because I'm a Shotover that I'm a Bohemian, because we are all so horribly Bohemian. But I'm not. I hate and loathe Bohemianism. No child brought up in a strict Puritan household ever suffered from Puritanism as I suffered from our Bohemianism.

HECTOR. Our children are like that. They spend their holidays in the houses of their respectable schoolfellows.

LADY UTTERWORD. I shall invite them for Christmas.

HECTOR. Their absence leaves us both without our natural chaperons.

LADY UTTERWORD. Children are certainly very inconvenient sometimes. But intelligent people can always manage, unless they are Bohemians.

HECTOR. You are no Bohemian; but you are no Puritan either: your attraction is alive and powerful. What sort of woman do you count yourself?

LADY UTTERWORD. I am a woman of the world, Hector; and I can assure you that if you will only take the trouble always to do the perfectly correct thing, and to say the perfectly correct thing, you can do just what you like. An ill-conducted, careless woman gets simply no chance. An ill-conducted, careless man is never allowed within arms length of any woman worth knowing.

HECTOR. I see. You are neither a Bohemian woman nor a Puritan woman. You are a dangerous woman.

LADY UTTERWORD. On the contrary, I am a safe woman.

HECTOR. You are a most accursedly attractive woman. Mind: I am not making love to you. I do not like being attracted. But you had better know how I feel if you are going to stay here.

LADY UTTERWORD. You are an exceedingly clever lady-killer, Hector. And terribly handsome. I am quite a good player, myself, at that game. Is it quite understood that we are only playing?

HECTOR. Quite. I am deliberately playing the fool, out of sheer worthlessness.

LADY UTTERWORD [*rising brightly*] Well, you are my brother-in-law. Hesione asked you to kiss me. [*He seizes her in his arms, and kisses her strenuously*]. Oh! that was a little more than play brother-in-law. [*She pushes him suddenly away*]. You shall not do that again.

HECTOR. In effect, you got your claws deeper into me than I intended.

MRS HUSHABYE [*coming in from the garden*] Dont let me disturb you: I only want a cap to put on daddiest. The sun is setting; and he'll catch cold [*she makes for the door leading to the hall*].

LADY UTTERWORD. Your husband is quite charming,

darling. He has actually condescended to kiss me at last. I shall go into the garden: it's cooler now [*she goes out by the port door*].

MRS HUSHABYE. Take care, dear child. I dont believe any man can kiss Addy without falling in love with her. [*She goes into the hall*].

HECTOR [*striking himself on the chest*] Fool! Goat!

*Mrs Hushabye comes back with the Captain's cap.*

HECTOR. Your sister is an extremely enterprising old girl. Wheres Miss Dunn?

MRS HUSHABYE. Mangan says she has gone up to her room for a nap. Addy wont let you talk to Ellie: she has marked you for her own.

HECTOR. She has the diabolical family fascination. I began making love to her automatically. What am I to do? I cant fall in love; I cant hurt a woman's feelings by telling her so when she falls in love with me. And as women are always falling in love with my moustache I get landed in all sorts of tedious and terrifying flirtations in which I'm not a bit in earnest.

MRS HUSHABYE. Oh, neither is Addy. She has never been in love in her life, though she has always been trying to fall in head over ears. She is worse than you, because you had one real go at least, with me.

HECTOR. That was a confounded madness. I cant believe that such an amazing experience is common. It has left its mark on me. I believe that is why I have never been able to repeat it.

MRS HUSHABYE [*laughing and caressing his arm*] We were frightfully in love with one another, Hector. It was such an enchanting dream that I have never been able to grudge it to you or anyone else since. I have invited all sorts of pretty women to the house on the chance of giving you another turn. But it has never come off.

HECTOR. I dont know that I want it to come off. It was damned dangerous. You fascinated me; but I loved you; so it was heaven. This sister of yours fascinates me; but I hate her; so it is hell. I shall kill her if she persists.

MRS HUSHABYE. Nothing will kill Addy: she is as strong as a horse. [*Releasing him*] Now *I* am going off to fascinate somebody.

HECTOR. The Foreign Office toff? Randall?

MRS HUSHABYE. Goodness gracious, no! Why should I fascinate him?

HECTOR. I presume you dont mean the bloated capitalist, Mangan?

MRS HUSHABYE. Hm! I think he had better be fascinated by me than by Ellie. [*She is going into the garden when the Captain comes in from it with some sticks in his hand*]. What have you got there, daddiest?

CAPTAIN SHOTOVER. Dynamite.

MRS HUSHABYE. Youve been to the gravel pit. Dont drop it about the house: theres a dear. [*She goes into the garden, where the evening light is now very red*].

HECTOR. Listen, O sage. How long dare you concentrate on a feeling without risking having it fixed in your consciousness all the rest of your life?

CAPTAIN SHOTOVER. Ninety minutes. An hour and a half. [*He goes into the pantry*].

*Hector, left alone, contracts his brows, and falls into a daydream. He does not move for some time. Then he folds his arms. Then, throwing his hands behind him, and gripping one with the other, he strides tragically once to and fro. Suddenly he snatches his walking-stick from the teak table, and draws it; for it is a sword-stick. He fights a desperate duel with an imaginary antagonist, and after many vicissitudes runs him through the body up to the hilt. He sheathes his sword and throws it on the sofa, falling into another reverie as he does so. He looks straight into the eyes of an imaginary woman; seizes her by the arms; and says in a deep and thrilling tone "Do you love me!" The Captain comes out of the pantry at this moment; and Hector, caught with his arms stretched out and his fists clenched, has to account for his attitude by going through a series of gymnastic exercises.*

CAPTAIN SHOTOVER. That sort of strength is no good. You will never be as strong as a gorilla.

HECTOR. What is the dynamite for?

CAPTAIN SHOTOVER. To kill fellows like Mangan.

HECTOR. No use. They will always be able to buy more dynamite than you.

CAPTAIN SHOTOVER. I will make a dynamite that he cannot explode.

HECTOR. And that you can, eh?

CAPTAIN SHOTOVER. Yes: when I have attained the seventh degree of concentration.

HECTOR. Whats the use of that? You never do attain it.

CAPTAIN SHOTOVER. What then is to be done? Are we to be kept for ever in the mud by these hogs to whom the universe is nothing but a machine for greasing their bristles and filling their snouts?

HECTOR. Are Mangan's bristles worse than Randall's lovelocks?

CAPTAIN SHOTOVER. We must win powers of life and death over them both. I refuse to die until I have invented the means.

HECTOR. Who are we that we should judge them?

CAPTAIN SHOTOVER. What are they that they should judge us? Yet they do, unhesitatingly. There is enmity between our seed and their seed. They know it and act on it, strangling our souls. They believe in themselves. When we believe in ourselves, we shall kill them.

HECTOR. It is the same seed. You forget that your pirate has a very nice daughter. Mangan's son may be a Plato: Randall's a Shelley. What was my father?

CAPTAIN SHOTOVER. The damndest scoundrel I ever met. [*He replaces the drawing-board; sits down at the table; and begins to mix a wash of color*].

HECTOR. Precisely. Well, dare you kill his innocent grandchildren?

CAPTAIN SHOTOVER. They are mine also.

HECTOR. Just so. We are members one of another. [*He throws himself carelessly on the sofa*]. I tell you I have often thought of this killing of human vermin. Many men have thought of it. Decent men are like Daniel in the lion's den: their survival is a miracle; and they do not always survive. We live among the Mangans and Randalls and Billie Dunns as they, poor devils, live among the disease germs and the doctors and the lawyers and the parsons and the restaurant chefs and the tradesmen and the servants and all the rest of the parasites and blackmailers. What are our terrors to theirs? Give me the power to kill them; and I'll spare them in sheer—

CAPTAIN SHOTOVER [*cutting in sharply*] Fellow feeling?

HECTOR. No. I should kill myself if I believed that. I must believe that my spark, small as it is, is divine, and that the red light over their door is hell fire. I should spare them in simple magnanimous pity.

CAPTAIN SHOTOVER. You cant spare them until you have the power to kill them. At present they have the power to kill you. There are millions of blacks over the water for them to train and let loose on us.

Theyre going to do it. Theyre doing it already.

HECTOR. They are too stupid to use their power.

CAPTAIN SHOTOVER [*throwing down his brush and coming to the end of the sofa*] Do not deceive yourself: they do use it. We kill the better half of ourselves every day to propitiate them. The knowledge that these people are there to render all our aspirations barren prevents us having the aspirations. And when we are tempted to seek their destruction they bring forth demons to delude us, disguised as pretty daughters, and singers and poets and the like, for whose sake we spare them.

HECTOR [*sitting up and leaning towards him*] May not Hesione be such a demon, brought forth by you lest I should slay you?

CAPTAIN SHOTOVER. That is possible. She has used you up, and left you nothing but dreams, as some women do.

HECTOR. Vampire women, demon women.

CAPTAIN SHOTOVER. Men think the world well lost for them, and lose it accordingly. Who are the men that do things? The husbands of the shrew and of the drunkard, the men with the thorn in the flesh. [*Walking distractedly away towards the pantry*] I must think these things out. [*Turning suddenly*] But I go on with the dynamite none the less. I will discover a ray mightier than any X-ray: a mind ray that will explode the ammunition in the belt of my adversary before he can point his gun at me. And I must hurry. I am old: I have no time to waste in talk [*he is about to go into the pantry, and Hector is making for the hall, when Hesione comes back*].

MRS HUSHABYE. Daddiest: you and Hector must come and help me to entertain all these people. What on earth were you shouting about?

HECTOR [*stopping in the act of turning the doorhandle*] He is madder than usual.

MRS HUSHABYE. We all are.

HECTOR. I must change [*he resumes his door opening*].

MRS HUSHABYE. Stop, stop. Come back, both of you. Come back [*They return, reluctantly*]. Money is running short.

HECTOR. Money! Where are my April dividends?

MRS HUSHABYE. Where is the snow that fell last year?

CAPTAIN SHOTOVER. Where is all the money you had for that patent lifeboat I invented?

MRS HUSHABYE. Five hundred pounds; and I have made it last since Easter!

CAPTAIN SHOTOVER. Since Easter! Barely four months! Monstrous extravagance! I could live for seven years on £500.

MRS HUSHABYE. Not keeping open house as we do here, daddiest.

CAPTAIN SHOTOVER. Only £500 for that lifeboat! I got twelve thousand for the invention before that.

MRS HUSHABYE. Yes, dear; but that was for the ship with the magnetic keel that sucked up submarines. Living at the rate we do, you cannot afford life-saving inventions. Cant you think of something that will murder half Europe at one bang?

CAPTAIN SHOTOVER. No. I am ageing fast. My mind does not dwell on slaughter as it did when I was a boy. Why doesnt your husband invent something? He does nothing but tell lies to women.

HECTOR. Well, that is a form of invention, is it not? However, you are right: I ought to support my wife.

MRS HUSHABYE. Indeed you shall do nothing of the sort: I should never see you from breakfast to dinner. I want my husband.

HECTOR [*bitterly*] I might as well be your lapdog.

MRS HUSHABYE. Do you want to be my breadwinner, like the other poor husbands?

HECTOR. No, by thunder! What a damned creature a husband is anyhow!

MRS HUSHABYE [*to the Captain*] What about that harpoon cannon?

CAPTAIN SHOTOVER. No use. It kills whales, not men.

MRS HUSHABYE. Why not? You fire the harpoon out of a cannon. It sticks in the enemy's general; you wind him in; and there you are.

HECTOR. You are your father's daughter, Hesione.

CAPTAIN SHOTOVER. There is something in it. Not to wind in generals: they are not dangerous. But one could fire a grapnel and wind in a machine gun or even a tank. I will think it out.

MRS HUSHABYE [*squeezing the Captain's arm affectionately*] Saved! You are a darling, daddiest. Now we must go back to these dreadful people and entertain them.

CAPTAIN SHOTOVER. They have had no dinner. Dont forget that.

HECTOR. Neither have I. And it is dark: it must be all hours.

MRS HUSHABYE. Oh, Guinness will produce some sort of dinner for them. The servants always take jolly good care that there is food in the house.

CAPTAIN SHOTOVER [*raising a strange wail in the darkness*] What a house! What a daughter!

MRS HUSHABYE [*raving*] What a father!

HECTOR [*following suit*] What a husband!

CAPTAIN SHOTOVER. Is there no thunder in heaven?

HECTOR. Is there no beauty, no bravery, on earth?

MRS HUSHABYE. What do men want? They have their food, their firesides, their clothes mended, and our love at the end of the day. Why are they not satisfied? Why do they envy us the pain with which we bring them into the world, and make strange dangers and torments for themselves to be even with us?

CAPTAIN SHOTOVER [*weirdly chanting*]

I built a house for my daughters, and opened the
doors thereof,

That men might come for their choosing, and their
betters spring from their love;

But one of them married a numskull;

HECTOR [*taking up the rhythm*]

The other a liar wed;

MRS HUSHABYE [*completing the stanza*]

And now must she lie beside him, even as she made
her bed.

LADY UTTERWORD [*calling from the garden*] Hesione! Hesione! Where are you?

HECTOR. The cat is on the tiles.

MRS HUSHABYE. Coming, darling, coming [*she goes quickly into the garden*].

*The Captain goes back to his place at the table.*

HECTOR [*going into the hall*] Shall I turn up the lights for you?

CAPTAIN SHOTOVER. No. Give me deeper darkness. Money is not made in the light.

# [ACT II]

*The same room, with the lights turned up and the curtains drawn. Ellie comes in, followed by Mangan. Both are dressed for dinner. She strolls to the drawing-table. He comes between the table and the wicker chair.*

MANGAN. What a dinner! I dont call it a dinner: I call it a meal.

ELLIE. I am accustomed to meals, Mr Mangan, and very lucky to get them. Besides, the captain cooked some macaroni for me.

MANGAN [*shuddering liverishly*] Too rich: I cant eat such things. I suppose it's because I have to work so much with my brain. Thats the worst of being a man of business: you are always thinking, thinking, thinking. By the way, now that we are alone, may I take the opportunity to come to a little understanding with you?

ELLIE [*settling into the draughtsman's seat*] Certainly. I should like to.

MANGAN [*taken aback*] Should you? That surprises me; for I thought I noticed this afternoon that you avoided me all you could. Not for the first time either.

ELLIE. I was very tired and upset. I wasn't used to the ways of this extraordinary house. Please forgive me.

MANGAN. Oh, thats all right: I dont mind. But Captain Shotover has been talking to me about you. You and me, you know.

ELLIE [*interested*] The Captain! What did he say?

MANGAN. Well, he noticed the difference between our ages.

ELLIE. He notices everything.

MANGAN. You dont mind, then?

ELLIE. Of course I know quite well that our engagement—

MANGAN. Oh! you call it an engagement.

ELLIE. Well, isnt it?

MANGAN. Oh, yes, yes: no doubt it is if you hold to it. This is the first time youve used the word; and I didnt quite know where we stood: thats all. [*He sits down in the wicker chair; and resigns himself to allow her to lead the conversation*]. You were saying—?

ELLIE. Was I? I forget. Tell me. Do you like this part of the country? I heard you ask Mr Hushabye at dinner whether there are any nice houses to let down here.

MANGAN. I like the place. The air suits me. I shouldnt be surprised if I settled down here.

ELLIE. Nothing would please me better. The air suits me too. And I want to be near Hesione.

MANGAN [*with growing uneasiness*] The air may suit us; but the question is, should we suit one another? Have you thought about that?

ELLIE. Mr Mangan: we must be sensible, mustnt we? It's no use pretending that we are Romeo and Juliet. But we can get on very well together if we choose to make the best of it. Your kindness of heart will make it easy for me.

MANGAN [*leaning forward, with the beginning of something like deliberate unpleasantness in his voice*] Kindness of heart, eh? I ruined your father, didnt I?

ELLIE. Oh, not intentionally.

MANGAN. Yes I did. Ruined him on purpose.

ELLIE. On purpose!

MANGAN. Not out of ill-nature, you know. And youll admit that I kept a job for him when I had finished with him. But business is business; and I ruined him as a matter of business.

ELLIE. I dont understand how that can be. Are you trying to make me feel that I need not be grateful to you, so that I may choose freely?

MANGAN [*rising aggressively*] No. I mean what I say.

ELLIE. But how could it possibly do you any good to ruin my father? The money he lost was yours.

MANGAN [*with a sour laugh*] Was mine! It is mine, Miss Ellie, and all the money the other fellows lost too. [*He shoves his hands into his pockets and shews his teeth*]. I just smoked them out like a hive of bees. What do you say to that? A bit of a shock, eh?

ELLIE. It would have been, this morning. Now! you cant think how little it matters. But it's quite interesting. Only, you must explain it to me. I dont understand it. [*Propping her elbows on the drawing-board and her chin on her hands, she composes herself to listen with a combination of conscious curiosity with unconscious contempt which provokes him to more and more unpleasantness, and an attempt at patronage of her ignorance*].

MANGAN. Of course you dont understand: what do you know about business? You just listen and learn. Your father's business was a new business; and I dont start new businesses: I let other fellows start them. They put all their money and their friends' money into starting them. They wear out their souls and bodies trying to make a success of them. Theyre what you call enthusiasts. But the first dead lift of the thing is too much for them; and they havnt enough financial experience. In a year or so they have either to let the whole show go bust, or sell out to a new lot of fellows for a few deferred ordinary shares: that is, if theyre lucky enough to get anything at all. As likely as not the very same thing happens to the new lot. They put in more money and a couple of years more work; and then perhaps they have to sell out to a third lot. If it's really a big thing the third lot will have to sell out too, and leave their work and their money behind them. And thats where the real business man comes in: where I come in. But I'm cleverer than some: I dont mind dropping a little money to start the process. I took your father's measure. I saw that he had a sound idea, and that he would work himself silly for it if he got the chance. I saw that he was a child in business, and was dead certain to outrun his expenses and be in too great a hurry to wait for his market. I knew that the surest way to ruin a man who doesnt know how to handle money is to give him some. I explained my idea to some friends in the city, and they found the money; for I take no risks in ideas, even when theyre my own. Your father and the friends that ventured their money with him were no more to me than a heap of squeezed lemons. Youve been wasting your gratitude: my kind heart is all rot. I'm sick of it. When I see your father beaming at me with his moist, grateful eyes, regularly wallowing in gratitude, I sometimes feel I must tell him the truth or burst. What stops me is that I know he wouldnt believe me. He'd think it was my modesty, as you did just now. He'd think anything rather than the truth, which is that he's a blamed fool, and I am a man that knows how to take care of himself. [*He throws himself back into the big chair with large self-approval*]. Now what do you think of me, Miss Ellie?

ELLIE [*dropping her hands*] How strange! that my mother, who knew nothing at all about business, should have been quite right about you! She always said—not before papa, of course, but to us children—that you were just that sort of man.

MANGAN [*sitting up, much hurt*] Oh! did she? And yet she'd have let you marry me.

ELLIE. Well, you see, Mr Mangan, my mother married a very good man—for whatever you may think of my father as a man of business, he is the soul of goodness—and she is not at all keen on my doing the same.

MANGAN. Anyhow, you dont want to marry me now, do you?

ELLIE [*very calmly*] Oh, I think so. Why not?

MANGAN [*rising aghast*] Why not!

ELLIE. I dont see why we shouldnt get on very well together.

MANGAN. Well, but look here, you know—[*he stops, quite at a loss*].

ELLIE [*patiently*] Well?

MANGAN. Well, I thought you were rather particular about people's characters.

ELLIE. If we women were particular about men's characters, we should never get married at all, Mr Mangan.

MANGAN. A child like you talking of "we women"! What next! Youre not in earnest?

ELLIE. Yes I am. Arnt you?

MANGAN. You mean to hold me to it?

ELLIE. Do you wish to back out of it?

MANGAN. Oh no. Not exactly back out of it.

ELLIE. Well?

*He has nothing to say. With a long whispered whistle, he drops into the wicker chair and stares before him like a beggared gambler. But a cunning look soon comes into his face. He leans over towards her on his right elbow, and speaks in a low steady voice.*

MANGAN. Suppose I told you I was in love with another woman!

ELLIE [*echoing him*] Suppose I told you I was in love with another man!

MANGAN [*bouncing angrily out of his chair*] I'm not joking.

ELLIE. Who told you *I* was?

MANGAN. I tell you I'm serious. Youre too young to be serious; but youll have to believe me. I want to be near your friend Mrs Hushabye. I'm in love with her. Now the murder's out.

ELLIE. I want to be near your friend Mr Hushabye. I'm in love with him. [*She rises and adds with a frank air*] Now we are in one another's confidence, we shall be real friends. Thank you for telling me.

MANGAN [*almost beside himself*] Do you think I'll be made a convenience of like this?

ELLIE. Come, Mr Mangan! you made a business convenience of my father. Well, a woman's business is marriage. Why shouldnt I make a domestic convenience of you?

MANGAN. Because I dont choose, see? Because I'm not a silly gull like your father. That why.

ELLIE [*with serene contempt*] You are not good enough to clean my father's boots, Mr Mangan; and I am paying you a great compliment in condescending to make a convenience of you, as you call it. Of course you are free to throw over our engagement if you like; but, if you do, youll never enter Hesione's house again: I will take care of that.

MANGAN [*gasping*] You little devil, youve done me [*On the point of collapsing into the big chair again he recovers himself*] Wait a bit, though: youre not so cute as you think. You cant beat Boss Mangan as easy as that. Suppose I go straight to Mrs Hushabye and tell her that youre in love with her husband.

ELLIE. She knows it.

MANGAN. You told her!!!

ELLIE. She told me.

MANGAN [*clutching at his bursting temples*] Oh, this is a crazy house. Or else I'm going clean off my chump. Is she making a swop with you—she to have your husband and you to have hers?

ELLIE. Well, you dont want us both, do you?

MANGAN [*throwing himself into the chair distractedly*] My brain wont stand it. My head's going to split. Help! Help me to hold it. Quick: hold it: squeeze it: Save me. [*Ellie comes behind his chair; clasps his head hard for a moment; then begins to draw her hands from his forehead back to his ears*]. Thank you. [*Drowsily*] Thats very refreshing. [*Waking a little*] Dont you hypnotize me, though. Ive seen men made fools of by hypnotism.

ELLIE. [*steadily*] Be quiet. Ive seen men made fools of without hypnotism.

MANGAN [*humbly*] You dont dislike touching me, I hope. You never touched me before, I noticed.

ELLIE. Not since you fell in love naturally with a grown-up nice woman, who will never expect you to make love to her. And I will never expect him to make love to me.

MANGAN. He may, though.

ELLIE [*making her passes rhythmically*] Hush. Go to sleep. Do you hear? You are to go to sleep, go to sleep, go to sleep; be quiet, deeply deeply quiet; sleep, sleep, sleep, sleep, sleep, sleep.

*He falls asleep. Ellie steals away; turns the light out; and goes into the garden.*

*Nurse Guinness opens the door and is seen in the light which comes in from the hall.*

GUINNESS [*speaking to someone outside*] Mr Mangan's

not here, ducky: theres no one here. It's all dark.

MRS HUSHABYE [*without*] Try the garden. Mr Dunn and I will be in my boudoir. Shew him the way.

GUINNESS. Yes, ducky. [*She makes for the garden door in the dark; stumbles over the sleeping Mangan; and screams*] Ahoo! Oh Lord, sir! I beg your pardon, I'm sure: I didnt see you in the dark. Who is it? [*She goes back to the door and turns on the light*]. Oh, Mr Mangan, sir, I hope I havnt hurt you plumping into your lap like that. [*Coming to him*] I was looking for you, sir. Mrs Hushabye says will you please— [*noticing that he remains quite insensible*] Oh, my good Lord, I hope I havnt killed him. Sir! Mr Mangan! Sir! [*She shakes him; and he is rolling inertly off the chair on the floor when she holds him up and props him against the cushion*]. Miss Hessy! Miss Hessy! Quick, doty darling. Miss Hessy! [*Mrs Hushabye comes in from the hall, followed by Mazzini Dunn*]. Oh, Miss Hessy, Ive been and killed him.

*Mazzini runs round the back of the chair to Mangan's right hand, and sees that the nurse's words are apparently only too true.*

MAZZINI. What tempted you to commit such a crime, woman?

MRS HUSHABYE [*trying not to laugh*] Do you mean you did it on purpose?

GUINNESS. Now is it likely I'd kill any man on purpose. I fell over him in the dark; and I'm a pretty tidy weight. He never spoke nor moved until I shook him; and then he would have dropped dead on the floor. Isnt it tiresome?

MRS HUSHABYE [*going past the nurse to Mangan's side, and inspecting him less credulously than Mazzini*] Nonsense! he is not dead: he is only asleep. I can see him breathing.

[ 113 ]

GUINNESS. But why wont he wake?

MAZZINI [*speaking very politely into Mangan's ear*] Mangan! My dear Mangan! [*he blows into Mangan's ear*].

MRS HUSHABYE. Thats no good [*she shakes him vigorously*]. Mr Mangan: wake up. Do you hear? [*He begins to roll over*]. Oh! Nurse, nurse: he's falling: help me.

*Nurse Guinness rushes to the rescue. With Mazzini's assistance, Mangan is propped safely up again.*

GUINNESS [*behind the chair; bending over to test the case with her nose*] Would he be drunk, do you think, pet?

MRS HUSHABYE. Had he any of papa's rum?

MAZZINI. It cant be that: he is most abstemious. I am afraid he drank too much formerly, and has to drink too little now. You know, Mrs Hushabye, I really think he has been hypnotized.

GUINNESS. Hip no what, sir?

MAZZINI. One evening at home, after we had seen a hypnotizing performance, the children began playing at it; and Ellie stroked my head. I assure you I went off dead asleep; and they had to send for a professional to wake me up after I had slept eighteen hours. They had to carry me upstairs; and as the poor children were not very strong, they let me slip; and I rolled right down the whole flight and never woke up. [*Mrs Hushabye splutters*]. Oh, you may laugh, Mrs Hushabye; but I might have been killed.

MRS HUSHABYE. I couldnt have helped laughing even if you had been, Mr Dunn. So Ellie has hypnotized him. What fun!

MAZZINI. Oh no, no, no. It was such a terrible lesson to her: nothing would induce her to try such a thing again.

MRS HUSHABYE. Then who did it? *I* didnt.

MAZZINI. I thought perhaps the Captain might have done it unintentionally. He is so fearfully magnetic: I feel vibrations whenever he comes close to me.

GUINNESS. The Captain will get him out of it anyhow, sir: I'll back him for that. I'll go fetch him [*she makes for the pantry*].

MRS HUSHABYE. Wait a bit. [*To Mazzini*] You say he is all right for eighteen hours?

MAZZINI. Well, *I* was asleep for eighteen hours.

MRS HUSHABYE. Were you any the worse for it?

MAZZINI. I dont quite remember. They had poured brandy down my throat, you see; and—

MRS HUSHABYE. Quite. Anyhow, you survived. Nurse, darling: go and ask Miss Dunn to come to us here. Say I want to speak to her particularly. You will find her with Mr Hushabye probably.

GUINNESS. I think not ducky: Miss Addy is with him. But I'll find her and send her to you. [*She goes out into the garden*].

MRS HUSHABYE [*calling Mazzini's attention to the figure on the chair*] Now, Mr Dunn, look. Just look. Look hard. Do you still intend to sacrifice your daughter to that thing?

MAZZINI [*troubled*] You have completely upset me, Mrs Hushabye, by all you have said to me. That anyone could imagine that I—I, a consecrated soldier of freedom, if I may say so—could sacrifice Ellie to anybody or anyone, or that I should ever have dreamed of forcing her inclinations in any way, is a most painful blow to my—well, I suppose you would say to my good opinion of myself.

MRS HUSHABYE [*rather stolidly*] Sorry.

MAZZINI [*looking forlornly at the body*] What is your objection to poor Mangan, Mrs Hushabye? He looks all right to me. But then I am so accustomed to him.

MRS HUSHABYE. Have you no heart? Have you no sense? Look at the brute! Think of poor weak innocent Ellie in the clutches of this slavedriver, who spends his life making thousands of rough violent workmen bend to his will and sweat for him: a man accustomed to have great masses of iron beaten into shape for him by steam-hammers! to fight with women and girls over a halfpenny an hour ruthlessly! a captain of industry, I think you call him, dont you? Are you going to fling your delicate, sweet, helpless child into such a beast's claws just because he will keep her in an expensive house and make her wear diamonds to shew how rich he is?

MAZZINI [*staring at her in wide-eyed amazement*] Bless you, dear Mrs Hushabye, what romantic ideas of business you have! Poor dear Mangan isnt a bit like that.

MRS HUSHABYE [*scornfully*] Poor dear Mangan indeed!

MAZZINI. But he doesnt know anything about machinery. He never goes near the men: he couldnt manage them: he is afraid of them. I never can get him to take the least interest in the works: he hardly knows more about them than you do. People are cruelly unjust to Mangan: they think he is all rugged strength just because his manners are bad.

MRS HUSHABYE. Do you mean to tell me he isnt strong enough to crush poor little Ellie?

MAZZINI. Of course it's very hard to say how any marriage will turn out; but speaking for myself, I should say that he wont have a dog's chance against Ellie. You know, Ellie has remarkable strength of character. I think it is because I taught her to like Shakespear when she was very young.

MRS HUSHABYE [*contemptuously*] Shakespear! The next thing you will tell me is that you could have made a great deal more money than Mangan. [*She retires to the sofa, and sits down at the port end of it in the worst of humors*].

MAZZINI [*following her and taking the other end*] No: I'm no good at making money. I dont care enough for it, somehow. I'm not ambitious! that must be it. Mangan is wonderful about money: he thinks of nothing else. He is so dreadfully afraid of being poor. I am always thinking of other things: even at the works I think of the things we are doing and not of what they cost. And the worst of it is, poor Mangan doesnt know what to do with his money when he gets it. He is such a baby that he doesnt know even what to eat and drink: he has ruined his liver eating and drinking the wrong things; and now he can hardly eat at all. Ellie will diet him splendidly. You will be surprised when you come to know him better: he is really the most helpless of mortals. You get quite a protective feeling towards him.

MRS HUSHABYE. Then who manages his business, pray?

MAZZINI. I do. And of course other people like me.

MRS HUSHABYE. Footling people, you mean.

MAZZINI. I suppose youd think us so.

MRS HUSHABYE. And pray why dont you do without him if youre all so much cleverer?

MAZZINI. Oh, we couldnt: we should ruin the business in a year. I've tried; and I know. We should spend too much on everything. We should improve the quality of the goods and make them too dear. We should be sentimental about the hard cases among the workpeople. But Mangan keeps us in order. He is down on us about every extra halfpenny. We could never do without him. You see, he will sit up all night thinking of how to save sixpence. Wont Ellie make him jump, though, when she takes his house in hand!

MRS HUSHABYE. Then the creature is a fraud even as a captain of industry!

MAZZINI. I am afraid all the captains of industry are what you call frauds, Mrs Hushabye. Of course there are some manufacturers who really do understand their own works; but they dont make as high a rate of profit as Mangan does. I assure you Mangan is quite a good fellow in his way. He means well.

MRS HUSHABYE. He doesnt look well. He is not in his first youth, is he?

MAZZINI. After all, no husband is in his first youth for very long, Mrs Hushabye. And men cant afford to marry in their first youth nowadays.

MRS HUSHABYE. Now if *I* said that, it would sound witty. Why cant you say it wittily? What on earth is the matter with you? Why dont you inspire everybody with confidence? with respect?

MAZZINI [*humbly*] I think that what is the matter with me is that I am poor. You dont know what that means at home. Mind: I dont say they have ever complained. Theyve all been wonderful: theyve been proud of my poverty. Theyve even joked about it quite often. But my wife has had a very poor time of it. She has been quite resigned—

MRS HUSHABYE [*shuddering involuntarily*]!!

MAZZINI. There! You see, Mrs Hushabye. I dont want Ellie to live on resignation.

MRS HUSHABYE. Do you want her to have to resign herself to living with a man she doesnt love?

MAZZINI [*wistfully*] Are you sure that would be worse than living with a man she did love, if he was a footling person?

MRS HUSHABYE [*relaxing her contemptuous attitude, quite interested in Mazzini now*] You know, I really think you must love Ellie very much; for you become quite clever when you talk about her.

MAZZINI. I didnt know I was so very stupid on other subjects.

MRS HUSHABYE. You are, sometimes.

MAZZINI [*turning his head away; for his eyes are wet*] I have learnt a good deal about myself from you, Mrs Hushabye; and I'm afraid I shall not be the happier for your plain speaking. But if you thought I needed it to make me think of Ellie's happiness you were very much mistaken.

MRS HUSHABYE [*leaning towards him kindly*] Have I been a beast?

MAZZINI [*pulling himself together*] It doesnt matter about me, Mrs Hushabye. I think you like Ellie; and that is enough for me.

MRS HUSHABYE. I'm beginning to like you a little. I perfectly loathed you at first. I thought you the most odious, self-satisfied, boresome elderly prig I ever met.

MAZZINI [*resigned, and now quite cheerful*] I daresay I am all that. I never have been a favorite with gorgeous women like you. They always frighten me.

MRS HUSHABYE [*pleased*] Am I a gorgeous woman, Mazzini? I shall fall in love with you presently.

MAZZINI [*with placid gallantry*] No you wont, Hesione. But you would be quite safe. Would you believe it that quite a lot of women have flirted with me because I quite safe? But they get tired of me for the same reason.

MRS HUSHABYE [*mischievously*] Take care. You may not be so safe as you think.

MAZZINI. Oh yes, quite safe. You see, I have been in

love really: the sort of love that only happens once. [*softly*] Thats why Ellie is such a lovely girl.

MRS HUSHABYE. Well, really, you are coming out. Are you quite sure you wont let me tempt you into a second grand passion?

MAZZINI. Quite. It wouldnt be natural. The fact is, you dont strike on my box, Mrs Hushabye; and I certainly dont strike on yours.

MRS HUSHABYE. I see. Your marriage was a safety match.

MAZZINI. What a very witty application of the expression I used! I should never have thought of it.

*Ellie comes in from the garden, looking anything but happy.*

MRS HUSHABYE [*rising*] Oh! here is Ellie at last. [*She goes behind the sofa*].

ELLIE [*on the threshold of the starboard door*] Guinness said you wanted me: you and papa.

MRS HUSHABYE. You have kept us waiting so long that it almost came to—well, never mind. Your father is a very wonderful man [*she ruffles his hair affectionately*]: the only one I ever met who could resist me when I made myself really agreeable. [*She comes to the big chair, on Mangan's left*]. Come here. I have something to shew you. [*Ellie strolls listlessly to the other side of the chair*]. Look.

ELLIE [*contemplating Mangan without interest*] I know. He is only asleep. We had a talk after dinner; and he fell asleep in the middle of it.

MRS HUSHABYE. You did it, Ellie. You put him asleep.

MAZZINI [*rising quickly and coming to the back of the chair*] Oh, I hope not. Did you, Ellie?

ELLIE [*wearily*] He asked me to.

MAZZINI. But it's dangerous. You know what happened to me.

ELLIE [*utterly indifferent*] Oh, I daresay I can wake him. If not, somebody else can.

MRS HUSHABYE. It doesnt matter, anyhow, because I have at last persuaded your father that you dont want to marry him.

ELLIE [*suddenly coming out of her listlessness, much vexed*] But why did you do that, Hesione? I do want to marry him. I fully intend to marry him.

MAZZINI. Are you quite sure, Ellie? Mrs Hushabye has made me feel that I may have been thoughtless and selfish about it.

ELLIE [*very clearly and steadily*] Papa. When Mrs Hushabye takes it on herself to explain to you what I think or dont think, shut your ears tight; and shut your eyes too. Hesione knows nothing about me: she hasnt the least notion of the sort of person I am, and never will. I promise you I wont do anything I dont want to do and mean to do for my own sake.

MAZZINI. You are quite, quite sure?

ELLIE. Quite, quite sure. Now you must go away and leave me to talk to Mrs Hushabye.

MAZZINI. But I should like to hear. Shall I be in the way?

ELLIE [*inexorable*] I had rather talk to her alone.

MAZZINI [*affectionately*] Oh, well, I know what a nuisance parents are, dear. I will be good and go. [*He goes to the garden door*]. By the way, do you remember the address of that professional who woke me up? Dont you think I had better telegraph to him.

MRS HUSHABYE [*moving towards the sofa*] It's too late to telegraph tonight.

MAZZINI. I suppose so. I do hope he'll wake up in the course of the night. [*He goes out into the garden*].

ELLIE [*turning vigorously on Hesione the moment her father is out of the room*] Hesione: what the devil do you mean by making mischief with my father about Mangan?

MRS HUSHABYE [*promptly losing her temper*] Dont you dare speak to me like that, you little minx. Remember that you are in my house.

ELLIE. Stuff! Why dont you mind your own business? What is it to you whether I choose to marry Mangan or not?

MRS HUSHABYE. Do you suppose you can bully me, you miserable little matrimonial adventurer?

ELLIE. Every woman who hasnt any money is a matrimonial adventurer. It's easy for you to talk: you have never known what it is to want money; and you can pick up men as if they were daisies. I am poor and respectable—

MRS HUSHABYE [*interrupting*] Ho! respectable! How did you pick up Mangan? How did you pick up my husband? You have the audacity to tell me that I am a—a—a—

ELLIE. A siren. So you are. You were born to lead men by the nose: if you werent, Marcus would have waited for me, perhaps.

MRS HUSHABYE [*suddenly melting and half laughing*] Oh, my poor Ellie, my pettikins, my unhappy darling! I am so sorry about Hector. But what can I do? It's not my fault: I'd give him to you if I could.

ELLIE. I dont blame you for that.

MRS HUSHABYE. What a brute I was to quarrel with you and call you names! Do kiss me and say youre not angry with me.

ELLIE [*fiercely*] Oh, dont slop and gush and be sentimental. Dont you see that unless I can be hard—as hard as nails—I shall go mad. I dont care a damn about your calling me names: do you think a woman in my situation can feel a few hard words?

MRS HUSHABYE. Poor little woman! Poor little situation!

ELLIE. I suppose you think youre being sympathetic. You are just foolish and stupid and selfish. You see me getting a smasher right in the face that kills a whole part of my life: the best part that can never come again; and you think you can help me over it by a little coaxing and kissing. When I want all the strength I can get to lean on: something iron, something stony, I dont care how cruel it is, you go all mushy and want to slobber over me. I'm not angry; I'm not unfriendly; but for God's sake do pull yourself together; and dont think that because youre on velvet and always have been, women who are in hell can take it as easily as you.

MRS HUSHABYE [*shrugging her shoulders*] Very well. [*She sits down on the sofa in her old place*]. But I warn you that when I am neither coaxing and kissing nor laughing, I am just wondering how much longer I can stand living in this cruel, damnable world. You object to the siren: well, I drop the siren. You want to rest your wounded bosom against a grindstone. Well [*folding her arms*], here is the grindstone.

ELLIE [*sitting down beside her, appeased*] Thats better: you really have the trick of falling in with everyone's mood; but you dont understand, because you are not the sort of woman for whom there is only one man and only one chance.

MRS HUSHABYE. I certainly dont understand how your marrying that object [*indicating Mangan*] will console you for not being able to marry Hector.

ELLIE. Perhaps you dont understand why I was quite a nice girl this morning, and am now neither a girl nor particularly nice.

MRS HUSHABYE. Oh yes I do. It's because you have

made up your mind to do something despicable and wicked.

ELLIE. I dont think so, Hesione. I must make the best of my ruined house.

MRS HUSHABYE. Pooh! Youll get over it. Your house isnt ruined.

ELLIE. Of course I shall get over it. You dont suppose I'm going to sit down and die of a broken heart, I hope, or be an old maid living on a pittance from the Sick and Indigent Roomkeeper's Association. But my heart is broken, all the same. What I mean by that is that I know that what has happened to me with Marcus will not happen to me ever again. In the world for me there is Marcus and a lot of other men of whom one is just the same as another. Well, if I cant have love, that no reason why I should have poverty. If Mangan has nothing else, he has money.

MRS HUSHABYE. And are there no young men with money?

ELLIE. Not within my reach. Besides, a young man would have the right to expect love from me, and would perhaps leave me when he found I could not give it to him. Rich young men can get rid of their wives, you know, pretty cheaply. But this object, as you call him, can expect nothing more from me than I am prepared to give him.

MRS HUSHABYE. He will be your owner, remember. If he buys you, he will make the bargain pay him and not you. Ask your father.

ELLIE [*rising and strolling to the chair to contemplate their subject*] You need not trouble on that score, Hesione. I have more to give Boss Mangan than he has to give me: it is I who am buying him, and at a pretty good price too, I think. Women are better at that sort of bargain than men. I have taken the Boss's measure;

and ten Boss Mangans shall not prevent me doing far more as I please as his wife than I have ever been able to do as a poor girl. [*Stooping to the recumbent figure*] Shall they, Boss? I think not. [*She passes on to the drawing-table, and leans against the end of it, facing the windows*]. I shall not have to spend most of my time wondering how long my gloves will last, anyhow.

MRS HUSHABYE [*rising superbly*] Ellie: you are a wicked sordid little beast. And to think that I actually condescended to fascinate that creature there to save you from him! Well, let me tell you this: if you make this disgusting match, you will never see Hector again if I can help it.

ELLIE [*unmoved*] I nailed Mangan by telling him that if he did not marry me he should never see you again [*she lifts herself on her wrists and seats herself on the end of the table*].

MRS HUSHABYE [*recoiling*] Oh!

ELLIE. So you see I am not unprepared for your playing that trump against me. Well, you just try it: thats all. I should have made a man of Marcus, not a

MRS HUSHABYE [*flaming*] You dare! [household pet.

ELLIE [*looking almost dangerous*] Set him thinking about me if you dare.

MRS HUSHABYE. Well, of all the impudent little fiends I ever met! Hector says there is a certain point at which the only answer you can give to a man who breaks all the rules is to knock him down. What would you say if I were to box your ears?

ELLIE [*calmly*] I should pull your hair.

MRS HUSHABYE [*mischievously*] That wouldnt hurt me. Perhaps it comes off at night.

ELLIE [*so taken aback that she drops off the table and runs to her*] Oh, you dont mean to say, Hesione, that your beautiful black hair is false?

MRS HUSHABYE [*patting it*] Dont tell Hector. He believes in it.

ELLIE [*groaning*] Oh! Even the hair that ensnared him false! Everything false!

MRS HUSHABYE. Pull it and try. Other women can snare men in their hair; but I can swing a baby on mine. Aha! you cant do that, Goldylocks.

ELLIE [*heartbroken*] No. You have stolen my babies.

MRS HUSHABYE. Pettikins: dont make me cry. You know, what you said about my making a household pet of him is a little true. Perhaps he ought to have waited for you. Would any other woman on earth forgive you?

ELLIE. Oh, what right had you to take him all for yourself! [*Pulling herself together*] There! You couldnt help it: neither of us could help it. He couldnt help it. No: dont say anything more: I cant bear it. Let us wake the object. [*She begins stroking Mangan's head, reversing the movement with which she put him to sleep*]. Wake up, do you hear? You are to wake up at once. Wake up, wake up, wake—

MANGAN [*bouncing out of the chair in a fury and turning on them*] Wake up! So you think Ive been asleep, do you? [*He kicks the chair violently back out of his way, and gets between them*]. You throw me into a trance so that I cant move hand or foot—I might have been buried alive! it's a mercy I wasnt—and then you think I was only asleep. If youd let me drop the two times you rolled me about, my nose would have been flattened for life against the floor. But Ive found you all out, anyhow. I know the sort of people I'm among now. Ive heard every word youve said, you and your precious father, and [*to Mrs Hushabye*] you too. So I'm an object, am I? I'm a thing, am I? I'm a fool that hasnt sense enough to feed myself properly, am

I? I'm afraid of the men that would starve if it werent for the wages I give them, am I? I'm nothing but a disgusting old skinflint to be made a convenience of by designing women and fool managers of my works, am I? I'm—

MRS HUSHABYE [*with the most elegant aplomb*] Sh-sh-sh-sh-sh! Mr Mangan: you are bound in honor to obliterate from your mind all you heard while you were pretending to be asleep. It was not meant for you to hear.

MANGAN. Pretending to be asleep! Do you think if I was only pretending that I'd have sprawled there helpless, and listened to such unfairness, such lies, such injustice and plotting and backbiting and slandering of me, if I could have up and told you what I thought of you! I wonder I didnt burst.

MRS HUSHABYE [*sweetly*] You dreamt it all, Mr Mangan. We were only saying how beautifully peaceful you looked in your sleep. That was all, wasnt it, Ellie? Believe me, Mr Mangan, all those unpleasant things came into your mind in the last half second before you woke. Ellie rubbed your hair the wrong way; and the disagreeable sensation suggested a disagreeable dream.

MANGAN [*doggedly*] I believe in dreams.

MRS HUSHABYE. So do I. But they go by contraries, dont they?

MANGAN [*depths of emotion suddenly welling up in him*] I shant forget, to my dying day, that when you gave me the glad eye that time in the garden, you were making a fool of me. That was a dirty low mean thing to do. You had no right to let me come near you if I disgusted you. It isnt my fault if I'm old and havnt a moustache like a bronze candlestick as your husband has. There are things no decent woman would do to a man—like a man hitting a woman in the breast.

*Hesione, utterly shamed, sits down on the sofa and covers her face with her hands. Mangan sits down also on his chair and begins to cry like a child. Ellie stares at them. Mrs Hushabye, at the distressing sound he makes, takes down her hands and looks at him. She rises and runs to him.*

MRS HUSHABYE. Dont cry: I cant bear it. Have I broken your heart? I didnt know you had one. How could I?

MANGAN. I'm a man aint I?

MRS HUSHABYE [*half coaxing, half rallying, altogether tenderly*] Oh no: not what I call a man. Only a Boss: just that and nothing else. What business has a Boss with a heart?

MANGAN. Then youre not a bit sorry for what you did, nor ashamed?

MRS HUSHABYE. I was ashamed for the first time in my life when you said that about hitting a woman in the breast, and I found out what I'd done. My very bones blushed red. Youve had your revenge, Boss. Arnt you satisfied?

MANGAN. Serve you right! Do you hear? Serve you right! Youre just cruel. Cruel.

MRS HUSHABYE. Yes: cruelty would be delicious if one could only find some sort of cruelty that didnt really hurt. By the way [*sitting down beside him on the arm of the chair*], whats your name? It's not really Boss, is it?

MANGAN [*shortly*] If you want to know, my name's Alfred.

MRS HUSHABYE [*springing up*] Alfred!! Ellie: he was christened after Tennyson!!!

MANGAN [*rising*] I was christened after my uncle, and

never had a penny from him, damn him! What of it?

MRS HUSHABYE. It comes to me suddenly that you are a real person: that you had a mother, like anyone else. [*Putting her hands on his shoulders and surveying him*] Little Alf!

MANGAN. Well, you have a nerve.

MRS HUSHABYE. And you have a heart, Alfy, a whimpering little heart, but a real one. [*Releasing him suddenly*] Now run and make it up with Ellie. She has had time to think what to say to you, which is more than I had [*she goes out quickly into the garden by the port door*].

MANGAN. That woman has a pair of hands that go right through you.

ELLIE. Still in love with her, in spite of all we said about you?

MANGAN. Are all women like you two? Do they never think of anything about a man except what they can get out of him? You werent even thinking that about me. You were only thinking whether your gloves would last.

ELLIE. I shall not have to think about that when we are married.

MANGAN. And you think I am going to marry you after what I heard there!

ELLIE. You heard nothing from me that I did not tell you before.

MANGAN. Perhaps you think I cant do without you.

ELLIE. I think you would feel lonely without us all now, after coming to know us so well.

MANGAN [*with something like a yell of despair*] Am I never to have the last word?

CAPTAIN SHOTOVER [*appearing at the starboard garden door*] There is a soul in torment here. What is the matter?

[ 129 ]

MANGAN. This girl doesnt want to spend her life wondering how long her gloves will last.

CAPTAIN SHOTOVER [*passing through*] Dont wear any. I never do [*he goes into the pantry*].

LADY UTTERWORD [*appearing at the port garden door, in a handsome dinner dress*] Is anything the matter?

ELLIE. This gentleman wants to know is he never to have the last word?

LADY UTTERWORD [*coming forward to the sofa*] I should let him have it, my dear. The important thing is not to have the last word, but to have your own way.

MANGAN. She wants both.

LADY UTTERWORD. She wont get them, Mr Mangan. Providence always has the last word.

MANGAN [*desperately*] Now you are going to come religion over me. In this house a man's mind might as well be a football. I'm going. [*He makes for the hall, but is stopped by a hail from the Captain, who has just emerged from his pantry*].

CAPTAIN SHOTOVER. Whither away, Boss Mangan?

MANGAN. To hell out of this house: let that be enough for you and all here.

CAPTAIN SHOTOVER. You were welcome to come: you are free to go. The wide earth, the high seas, the spacious skies are waiting for you outside.

LADY UTTERWORD. But your things, Mr Mangan. Your bags, your comb and brushes, your pyjamas—

HECTOR [*who has just appeared in the port doorway in a handsome Arab costume*] Why should the escaping slave take his chains with him?

MANGAN. Thats right, Hushabye. Keep the pyjamas, my lady; and much good may they do you.

HECTOR [*advancing to Lady Utterword's left hand*] Let

us all go out into the night and leave everything behind us.

MANGAN. You stay where you are, the lot of you. I want no company, especially female company.

ELLIE. Let him go. He is unhappy here. He is angry with us.

CAPTAIN SHOTOVER. Go, Boss Mangan; and when you have found the land where there is happiness and where there are no women, send me its latitude and longitude; and I will join you there.

LADY UTTERWORD. You will certainly not be comfortable without your luggage, Mr Mangan.

ELLIE [*impatient*] Go, go: why dont you go? It is a heavenly night: you can sleep on the heath. Take my waterproof to lie on: it is hanging up in the hall.

HECTOR. Breakfast at nine, unless you prefer to breakfast with the Captain at six.

ELLIE. Good night, Alfred.

HECTOR. Alfred! [*He runs back to the door and calls into the garden*] Randall: Mangan's Christian name is Alfred.

RANDALL [*appearing in the starboard doorway in evening dress*] Then Hesione wins her bet.

*Mrs Hushabye appears in the port doorway. She throws her left arm round Hector's neck; draws him with her to the back of the sofa; and throws her right arm round Lady Utterword's neck.*

MRS HUSHABYE. They wouldnt believe me, Alf.

*They contemplate him.*

MANGAN. Is there any more of you coming in to look at me, as if I was the latest thing in a menagerie.

MRS HUSHABYE. You are the latest thing in this menagerie.

*Before Mangan can retort, a fall of furniture is*

*heard from upstairs; then a pistol shot, and a yell of pain. The staring group breaks up in consternation.*

MAZZINI'S VOICE [*from above*] Help! A burglar! Help!

HECTOR [*his eyes blazing*] A burglar!!!

MRS HUSHABYE. No, Hector: youll be shot [*but it is too late: he has dashed out past Mangan, who hastily moves towards the bookshelves out of his way*].

CAPTAIN SHOTOVER [*blowing his whistle*] All hands aloft! [*He strides out after Hector*].

LADY UTTERWORD. My diamonds! [*She follows the Captain*].

RANDALL [*rushing after her*] No, Ariadne. Let me.

ELLIE. Oh, is papa shot? [*she runs out*].

MRS HUSHABYE. Are you frightened, Alf?

MANGAN. No. It aint my house, thank God.

MRS HUSHABYE. If they catch a burglar, shall we have to go into court as witnesses, and be asked all sorts of questions about our private lives?

MANGAN. You wont be believed if you tell the truth.

*Mazzini, terribly upset, with a duelling pistol in his hand, comes from the hall, and makes his way to the drawing-table.*

MAZZINI. Oh, my dear Mrs Hushabye, I might have killed him [*He throws the pistol on the table and staggers round to the chair*]. I hope you wont believe I really intended to.

*Hector comes in, marching an old and villainous looking man before him by the collar. He plants him in the middle of the room and releases him.*

*Ellie follows, and immediately runs across to the back of her father's chair, and pats his shoulders.*

RANDALL [*entering with a poker*] Keep your eye on this door, Mangan. I'll look after the other [*he goes to the starboard door and stands on guard there*].

*Lady Utterword comes in after Randall, and goes between Mrs Hushabye and Mangan.*

*Nurse Guinness brings up the rear, and waits near the door, on Mangan's left.*

MRS HUSHABYE. What has happened?

MAZZINI. Your housekeeper told me there was somebody upstairs, and gave me a pistol that Mr Hushabye had been practising with. I thought it would frighten him; but it went off at a touch.

THE BURGLAR. Yes, and took the skin off my ear. Precious near took the top off my head. Why dont you have a proper revolver instead of a thing like that, that goes off if you as much as blow on it?

HECTOR. One of my duelling pistols. Sorry.

MAZZINI. He put his hands up and said it was a fair cop.

THE BURGLAR. So it was. Send for the police.

HECTOR. No, by thunder! It was not a fair cop. We were four to one.

MRS HUSHABYE. What will they do to him?

THE BURGLAR. Ten years. Beginning with solitary. Ten years off my life. I shant serve it all: I'm too old. It will see me out.

LADY UTTERWORD. You should have thought of that before you stole my diamonds.

THE BURGLAR. Well, youve got them back, lady: havnt you? Can you give me back the years of my life you are going to take from me?

MRS HUSHABYE. Oh, we cant bury a man alive for ten years for a few diamonds.

THE BURGLAR. Ten little shining diamonds! Ten long black years!

LADY UTTERWORD. Think of what it is for us to be dragged through the horrors of a criminal court, and have all our family affairs in the papers! If you were a native, and Hastings could order you a good beating and send you away, I shouldnt mind; but here in England there is no real protection for any respectable person.

THE BURGLAR. I'm too old to be giv a hiding, lady. Send for the police and have done with it. It's only just and right you should.

RANDALL [*who has relaxed his vigilance on seeing the burglar so pacifically disposed, and comes forward swinging the poker between his fingers like a well-folded umbrella*] It is neither just nor right that we should be put to a lot of inconvenience to gratify your moral enthusiasm, my friend. You had better get out, while you have the chance.

THE BURGLAR [*inexorably*] No. I must work my sin off my conscience. This has come as a sort of call to me. Let me spend the rest of my life repenting in a cell. I shall have my reward above.

MANGAN [*exasperated*] The very burglars cant behave naturally in this house.

HECTOR. My good sir: you must work out your salvation at somebody else's expense. Nobody here is going to charge you.

THE BURGLAR. Oh, you wont charge me, wont you?

HECTOR. No. I'm sorry to be inhospitable; but will you kindly leave the house?

THE BURGLAR. Right. I'll go to the police station and give myself up. [*He turns resolutely to the door; but Hector stops him*].

HECTOR. }Oh no. You mustnt do that.

RANDALL. } No, no. Clear out, man, cant you; and dont be a fool.

MRS HUSHABYE. } Dont be so silly. Cant you repent at home?

LADY UTTERWORD. You will have to do as you are told.

THE BURGLAR. It's compounding a felony, you know.

MRS HUSHABYE. This is utterly ridiculous. Are we to be forced to prosecute this man when we dont want to?

THE BURGLAR. Am I to be robbed of my salvation to save you the trouble of spending a day at the sessions? Is that justice? Is it right? Is it fair to me?

MAZZINI [*rising and leaning across the table persuasively as if it were a pulpit desk or a shop counter*] Come, come! let me shew you how you can turn your very crimes to account. Why not set up as a locksmith? You must know more about locks than most honest men?

THE BURGLAR. Thats true, sir. But I couldnt set up as a locksmith under twenty pounds.

RANDALL. Well, you can easily steal twenty pounds. You will find it in the nearest bank.

THE BURGLAR [*horrified*] Oh what a thing for a gentleman to put into the head of a poor criminal scrambling out of the bottomless pit as it were! Oh, shame on you, sir! Oh, God forgive you! [*He throws himself into the big chair and covers his face as if in prayer*].

LADY UTTERWORD. Really, Randall!

HECTOR. It seems to me that we shall have to take up a collection for this inopportunely contrite sinner.

LADY UTTERWORD. But twenty pounds is ridiculous.

THE BURGLAR [*looking up quickly*] I shall have to buy a lot of tools, lady.

LADY UTTERWORD. Nonsense: you have your burgling kit.

THE BURGLAR. Whats a jemmy and a centrebit and an acetylene welding plant and a bunch of skeleton keys? I shall want a forge, and a smithy, and a shop, and fittings. I cant hardly do it for twenty.

HECTOR. My worthy friend, we havnt got twenty pounds.

THE BURGLAR [*now master of the situation*] You can raise it among you, cant you?

MRS HUSHABYE. Give him a sovereign, Hector; and get rid of him.

HECTOR [*giving him a pound*] There! Off with you.

THE BURGLAR [*rising and taking the money very ungratefully*] I wont promise nothing. You have more on you than a quid: all the lot of you, I mean.

LADY UTTERWORD [*vigorously*] Oh, let us prosecute him and have done with it. I have a conscience too, I hope; and I do not feel at all sure that we have any right to let him go, especially if he is going to be greedy and impertinent.

THE BURGLAR [*quickly*] All right, lady, all right. Ive no wish to be anything but agreeable. Good evening, ladies and gentlemen; and thank you kindly.

*He is hurrying out when he is confronted in the doorway by Captain Shotover.*

CAPTAIN SHOTOVER [*fixing the burglar with a piercing regard*] Whats this? Are there two of you?

THE BURGLAR [*falling on his knees before the Captain in abject terror*] Oh my Good Lord, what have I done? Dont tell me it's your house Ive broken into, Captain Shotover.

*The Captain seizes him by the collar; drags him to his feet; and leads him to the middle of the group, Hector falling back beside his wife to make way for them.*

CAPTAIN SHOTOVER [*turning him towards Ellie*] Is that your daughter? [*He releases him*].

THE BURGLAR. Well, how do I know, Captain? You know the sort of life you and me has led. Any young lady of that age might be my daughter anywhere in the wide world, as you might say.

CAPTAIN SHOTOVER [*to Mazzini*] You are not Billy Dunn. This is Billy Dunn. Why have you imposed on me?

THE BURGLAR [*indignantly to Mazzini*] Have you been giving yourself out to be me? You, that nigh blew my head off! Shooting yourself, in a manner of speaking!

MAZZINI. My dear Captain Shotover, ever since I came into this house I have done hardly anything else but assure you that I am not Mr William Dunn, but Mazzini Dunn, a very different person.

THE BURGLAR. He dont belong to my branch, Captain. Theres two sets in the family: the thinking Dunns and the drinking Dunns, each going their own ways. I'm a drinking Dunn: he's a thinking Dunn. But that didnt give him any right to shoot me.

CAPTAIN SHOTOVER. So youve turned burglar, have you?

THE BURGLAR. No, Captain: I wouldnt disgrace our old sea calling by such a thing. I am no burglar.

LADY UTTERWORD. What were you doing with my diamonds?

GUINNESS. What did you break into the house for if youre no burglar?

RANDALL. Mistook the house for your own and came in by the wrong window, eh?

THE BURGLAR. Well, it's no use my telling you a lie: I can take in most captains, but not Captain Shotover, because he sold himself to the devil in Zanzibar, and can divine water, spot gold, explode a cartridge in your pocket with a glance of his eye, and see the truth hidden in the heart of man. But I'm no burglar.

CAPTAIN SHOTOVER. Are you an honest man?

THE BURGLAR. I dont set up to be better than my fellow-creatures, and never did, as you well know,

Captain. But what I do is innocent and pious. I enquire about for houses where the right sort of people live. I work it on them same as I worked it here. I break into the house; put a few spoons or diamonds in my pocket; make a noise; get caught; and take up a collection. And you wouldnt believe how hard it is to get caught when youre actually trying to. I have knocked over all the chairs in a room without a soul paying any attention to me. In the end I have had to walk out and leave the job.

RANDALL. When that happens, do you put back the spoons and diamonds?

THE BURGLAR. Well, I dont fly in the face of Providence, if thats what you want to know.

CAPTAIN SHOTOVER. Guinness: you remember this man?

GUINNESS. I should think I do, seeing I was married to him, the blackguard!

HESIONE            ⎱exclaiming ⎰Married to him!
LADY UTTERWORD ⎰together     ⎱Guinness!!

THE BURGLAR. It wasnt legal. Ive been married to no end of women. No use coming that over me.

CAPTAIN SHOTOVER. Take him to the forecastle [*he flings him to the door with a strength beyond his years*].

GUINNESS. I suppose you mean the kitchen. They wont have him there. Do you expect servants to keep company with thieves and all sorts?

CAPTAIN SHOTOVER. Land-thieves and water-thieves are the same flesh and blood. I'll have no boatswain on my quarter-deck. Off with you both.

THE BURGLAR. Yes, Captain. [*He goes out humbly*].

MAZZINI. Will it be safe to have him in the house like that?

GUINNESS. Why didnt you shoot him, sir? If I'd

known who he was, I'd have shot him myself. [*She goes out*].

MRS HUSHABYE. Do sit down, everybody. [*She sits down on the sofa*]

*They all move except Ellie. Mazzini resumes his seat. Randall sits down in the window seat near the starboard door, again making a pendulum of his poker, and studying it as Galileo might have done. Hector sits on his left, in the middle. Mangan, forgotten, sits in the port corner. Lady Utterword takes the big chair. Captain Shotover goes into the pantry in deep abstraction. They all look after him; and Lady Utterword coughs consciously.*

MRS HUSHABYE. So Billy Dunn was poor nurse's little romance. I knew there had been somebody.

RANDALL. They will fight their battles over again and enjoy themselves immensely.

LADY UTTERWORD [*irritably*] You are not married; and you know nothing about it, Randall. Hold your tongue.

RANDALL. Tyrant!

MRS HUSHABYE. Well, we have had a very exciting evening. Everything will be an anticlimax after it. We'd better all go to bed.

RANDALL. Another burglar may turn up.

MAZZINI. Oh, impossible! I hope not.

RANDALL. Why not? there is more than one burglar in England.

MRS HUSHABYE. What do you say, Alf?

MANGAN [*huffily*] Oh, I dont matter. I'm forgotten. The burglar has put my nose out of joint. Shove me into a corner and have done with me.

MRS HUSHABYE [*jumping up mischievously, and going to him*] Would you like a walk on the heath, Alfred? With me?

ELLIE. Go, Mr Mangan. It will do you good. Hesione will soothe you.

MRS HUSHABYE [*slipping her arm under his and pulling him upright*] Come, Alfred. There is a moon: it's like the night in Tristan and Isolde. [*She caresses his arm and draws him to the port garden door*].

MANGAN [*writhing but yielding*] How you can have the face—the heart—[*he breaks down and is heard sobbing as she takes him out.*]

LADY UTTERWORD. What an extraordinary way to behave! What is the matter with the man?

ELLIE [*in a strangely calm voice, staring into an imaginary distance*] His heart is breaking: that is all. [*The Captain appears at the pantry door, listening*]. It is a curious sensation: the sort of pain that goes mercifully beyond our powers of feeling. When your heart is broken, your boats are burned: nothing matters any more. It is the end of happiness and the beginning of peace.

LADY UTTERWORD [*suddenly rising in a rage, to the astonishment of the rest*] How dare you?

HECTOR. Good heavens! Whats the matter?

RANDALL [*in a warning whisper*] Tch—tch—tch! Steady.

ELLIE [*surprised and haughty*] I was not addressing you particularly, Lady Utterword. And I am not accustomed to be asked how dare I.

LADY UTTERWORD. Of course not. Anyone can see how badly you have been brought up.

MAZZINI. Oh, I hope not, Lady Utterword. Really!

LADY UTTERWORD. I know very well what you meant. The impudence!

ELLIE. What on earth do you mean?

CAPTAIN SHOTOVER [*advancing to the table*] She means that her heart will not break. She has been longing all her life for someone to break it. At last she has become afraid she has none to break.

LADY UTTERWORD [*flinging herself on her knees and throwing her arms round him*] Papa: dont say you think Ive no heart.

CAPTAIN SHOTOVER [*raising her with grim tenderness*] If you had no heart how could you want to have it broken, child?

HECTOR [*rising with a bound*] Lady Utterword: you are not to be trusted. You have made a scene [*he runs out into the garden through the starboard door*].

LADY UTTERWORD. Oh! Hector, Hector! [*she runs out after him*].

RANDALL. Only nerves, I assure you [*He rises and follows her, waving the poker in his agitation*] Ariadne! Ariadne! For God's sake be careful. You will— [*he is gone*].

MAZZINI [*rising*] How distressing! Can I do anything, I wonder?

CAPTAIN SHOTOVER [*promptly taking his chair and setting to work at the drawing-board*] No. Go to bed. Goodnight.

MAZZINI [*bewildered*] Oh! Perhaps you are right.

ELLIE. Goodnight, dearest. [*She kisses him*].

MAZZINI. Goodnight, love. [*He makes for the door, but turns aside to the bookshelves*]. I'll just take a book [*he takes one*]. Goodnight. [*He goes out, leaving Ellie alone with the Captain*].

*The Captain is intent on his drawing. Ellie, standing sentry over his chair, contemplates him for a moment.*

ELLIE. Does nothing ever disturb you, Captain Shotover?

CAPTAIN SHOTOVER. Ive stood on the bridge for eighteen hours in a typhoon. Life here is stormier; but I can stand it.

ELLIE. Do you think I ought to marry Mr Mangan?

CAPTAIN SHOTOVER [*never looking up*] One rock is as good as another to be wrecked on.

ELLIE. I am not in love with him.

CAPTAIN SHOTOVER. Who said you were?

ELLIE. You are not surprised?

CAPTAIN SHOTOVER. Surprised! At my age!

ELLIE. It seems to me quite fair. He wants me for one thing: I want him for another.

CAPTAIN SHOTOVER. Money?

ELLIE. Yes.

CAPTAIN SHOTOVER. Well, one turns the cheek: the other kisses it. One provides the cash: the other spends it.

ELLIE. Who will have the best of the bargain, I wonder?

CAPTAIN SHOTOVER. You. These fellows live in an office all day. You will have to put up with him from dinner to breakfast; but you will both be asleep most of that time. All day you will be quit of him; and you will be shopping with his money. If that is too much for you, marry a seafaring man: you will be bothered with him only three weeks in the year, perhaps.

ELLIE. That would be best of all, I suppose.

CAPTAIN SHOTOVER. It's a dangerous thing to be married right up to the hilt, like my daughter's husband. The man is at home all day, like a damned soul in hell.

ELLIE. I never thought of that before.

CAPTAIN SHOTOVER. If youre marrying for business, you cant be too businesslike.

ELLIE. Why do women always want other women's husbands?

CAPTAIN SHOTOVER. Why do horse-thieves prefer a horse that is broken-in to one that is wild?

ELLIE [*with a short laugh*] I suppose so. What a vile world it is!

CAPTAIN SHOTOVER. It doesnt concern me. I'm nearly out of it.

ELLIE. And I'm only just beginning.

CAPTAIN SHOTOVER. Yes; so look ahead.

ELLIE. Well, I think I am being very prudent.

CAPTAIN SHOTOVER. I didnt say prudent. I said look ahead.

ELLIE. Whats the difference?

CAPTAIN SHOTOVER. It's prudent to gain the whole world and lose your own soul. But dont forget that your soul sticks to you if you stick to it; but the world has a way of slipping through your fingers.

ELLIE [*wearily, leaving him and beginning to wander restlessly about the room*] I'm sorry, Captain Shotover; but it's no use talking like that to me. Old-fashioned people are no use to me. Old-fashioned people think you can have a soul without money. They think the less money you have, the more soul you have. Young people nowadays know better. A soul is a very expensive thing to keep: much more so than a motor car.

CAPTAIN SHOTOVER. Is it? How much does your soul eat?

ELLIE. Oh, a lot. It eats music and pictures and books and mountains and lakes and beautiful things to wear and nice people to be with. In this country you cant have them without lots of money: that is why our souls are so horribly starved.

CAPTAIN SHOTOVER. Mangan's soul lives on pigs' food.

ELLIE. Yes: money is thrown away on him. I suppose his soul was starved when he was young. But it will not be thrown away on me. It is just because I want to save my soul that I am marrying for money. All the women who are not fools do.

CAPTAIN SHOTOVER. There are other ways of getting money. Why dont you steal it?

ELLIE. Because I dont want to go to prison.

CAPTAIN SHOTOVER. Is that the only reason? Are you quite sure honesty has nothing to do with it?

ELLIE. Oh, you are very very old-fashioned, Captain. Does any modern girl believe that the legal and illegal ways of getting money are the honest and dishonest ways? Mangan robbed my father and my father's friends. I should rob all the money back from Mangan if the police would let me. As they wont, I must get it back by marrying him.

CAPTAIN SHOTOVER. I cant argue: I'm too old: my mind is made up and finished. All I can tell you is that, old-fashioned or new-fashioned, if you sell yourself, you deal your soul a blow that all the books and pictures and concerts and scenery in the world wont heal [*he gets up suddenly and makes for the pantry*].

ELLIE [*running after him and seizing him by the sleeve*] Then why did you sell yourself to the devil in Zanzibar?

CAPTAIN SHOTOVER [*stopping, startled*] What?

ELLIE. You shall not run away before you answer. I have found out that trick of yours. If you sold yourself, why shouldnt I?

CAPTAIN SHOTOVER. I had to deal with men so degraded that they wouldnt obey me unless I swore at them and kicked them and beat them with my fists. Foolish people took young thieves off the streets; flung them into a training ship where they were taught to fear the cane instead of fearing God; and thought theyd made men and sailors of them by private subscription. I tricked these thieves into believing I'd sold myself to the devil. It saved my soul from the kicking and swearing that was damning me by inches.

ELLIE [*releasing him*] I shall pretend to sell myself to Boss Mangan to save my soul from the poverty that is damning me by inches.

CAPTAIN SHOTOVER. Riches will damn you ten times deeper. Riches wont save even your body.

ELLIE. Old-fashioned again. We know now that the soul is the body, and the body the soul. They tell us they are different because they want to persuade us that we can keep our souls if we let them make slaves of our bodies. I am afraid you are no use to me, Captain.

CAPTAIN SHOTOVER. What did you expect? A Savior, eh? Are you old-fashioned enough to believe in that?

ELLIE. No. But I thought you were very wise, and might help me. Now I have found you out. You pretend to be busy, and think of fine things to say, and run in and out to surprise people by saying them, and get away before they can answer you.

CAPTAIN SHOTOVER. It confuses me to be answered. It discourages me. I cannot bear men and women. I have to run away. I must run away now [*he tries to*].

ELLIE [*again seizing his arm*] You shall not run away from me. I can hypnotize you. You are the only person in the house I can say what I like to. I know you are fond of me. Sit down. [*She draws him to the sofa*].

CAPTAIN SHOTOVER [*yielding*] Take care: I am in my dotage. Old men are dangerous: it doesnt matter to them what is going to happen to the world.

*They sit side by side on the sofa. She leans affectionately against him with her head on his shoulder and her eyes half closed.*

[ 145 ]

ELLIE [*dreamily*] I should have thought nothing else mattered to old men. They cant be very interested in what is going to happen to themselves.

CAPTAIN SHOTOVER. A man's interest in the world is only the overflow from his interest in himself. When you are a child your vessel is not yet full; so you care for nothing but your own affairs. When you grow up, your vessel overflows; and you are a politician, a philosopher, or an explorer and adventurer. In old age the vessel dries up: there is no overflow: you are a child again. I can give you the memories of my ancient wisdom: mere scraps and leavings; but I no longer really care for anything but my own little wants and hobbies. I sit here working out my old ideas as a means of destroying my fellow-creatures. I see my daughters and their men living foolish lives of romance and sentiment and snobbery. I see you, the younger generation, turning from their romance and sentiment and snobbery to money and comfort and hard common sense. I was ten times happier on the bridge in the typhoon, or frozen into Arctic ice for months in darkness, than you or they have ever been. You are looking for a rich husband. At your age I looked for hardship, danger, horror, and death, that I might feel the life in me more intensely. I did not let the fear of death govern my life; and my reward was, I had my life. You are going to let the fear of poverty govern your life; and your reward will be that you will eat, but you will not live.

ELLIE [*sitting up impatiently*] But what can I do? I am not a sea captain: I cant stand on bridges in typhoons, or go slaughtering seals and whales in Greenland's icy mountains. They wont let women be captains. Do you want me to be a stewardess?

CAPTAIN SHOTOVER. There are worse lives. The

stewardesses could come ashore if they liked; but they sail and sail and sail.

ELLIE. What could they do ashore but marry for money? I dont want to be a stewardess: I am too bad a sailor. Think of something else for me.

CAPTAIN SHOTOVER. I cant think so long and continuously. I am too old. I must go in and out. [*He tries to rise*].

ELLIE [*pulling him back*] You shall not. You are happy here, arnt you?

CAPTAIN SHOTOVER. I tell you it's dangerous to keep me. I cant keep awake and alert.

ELLIE. What do you run away for? To sleep?

CAPTAIN SHOTOVER. No. To get a glass of rum.

ELLIE [*frightfully disillusioned*] Is that it? How disgusting! Do you like being drunk?

CAPTAIN SHOTOVER. No: I dread being drunk more than anything in the world. To be drunk means to have dreams; to go soft; to be easily pleased and deceived; to fall into the clutches of women. Drink does that for you when you are young. But when you are old: very very old, like me, the dreams come by themselves. You dont know how terrible that is: you are young: you sleep at night only, and sleep soundly. But later on you will sleep in the afternoon. Later still you will sleep even in the mornings; and you will awake tired, tired of life. You will never be free from dozing and dreams: the dreams will steal upon your work every ten minutes unless you can awaken yourself with rum. I drink now to keep sober; but the dreams are conquering: rum is not what it was: I have had ten glasses since you came; and it might be so much water. Go get me another: Guinness knows where it is. You had better see for yourself the horror of an old man drinking.

[ 147 ]

ELLIE. You shall not drink. Dream. I like you to dream. You must never be in the real world when we talk together.

CAPTAIN SHOTOVER. I am too weary to resist or too weak. I am in my second childhood. I do not see you as you really are. I cant remember what I really am. I feel nothing but the accursed happiness I have dreaded all my life long: the happiness that comes as life goes, the happiness of yielding and dreaming instead of resisting and doing, the sweetness of the fruit that is going rotten.

ELLIE. You dread it almost as much as I used to dread losing my dreams and having to fight and do things. But that is all over for me: my dreams are dashed to pieces. I should like to marry a very old, very rich man. I should like to marry you. I had much rather marry you than marry Mangan. Are you very rich?

CAPTAIN SHOTOVER. No. Living from hand to mouth. And I have a wife somewhere in Jamaica: a black one. My first wife. Unless she's dead.

ELLIE. What a pity! I feel so happy with you. [*She takes his hand, almost unconsciously, and pats it*]. I thought I should never feel happy again.

CAPTAIN SHOTOVER. Why?

ELLIE. Dont you know?

CAPTAIN SHOTOVER. No.

ELLIE. Heartbreak. I fell in love with Hector, and didnt know he was married.

CAPTAIN SHOTOVER. Heartbreak? Are you one of those who are so sufficient to themselves that they are only happy when they are stripped of everything, even of hope?

ELLIE [*gripping the hand*] It seems so; for I feel now as if there was nothing I could not do, because I want nothing.

[ 148 ]

CAPTAIN SHOTOVER. Thats the only real strength. Thats genius. Thats better than rum.

ELLIE [*throwing away his hand*] Rum! Why did you spoil it?

*Hector and Randall come in from the garden through the starboard door.*

HECTOR. I beg your pardon. We did not know there was anyone here.

ELLIE [*rising*] That means that you want to tell Mr Randall the story about the tiger. Come, Captain: I want to talk to my father; and you had better come with me.

CAPTAIN SHOTOVER [*rising*] Nonsense! the man is in bed.

ELLIE. Aha! Ive caught you. My real father has gone to bed; but the father you gave me is in the kitchen. You knew quite well all along. Come. [*She draws him out into the garden with her through the port door*].

HECTOR. Thats an extraordinary girl. She has the Ancient Mariner on a string like a Pekinese dog.

RANDALL. Now that they have gone, shall we have a friendly chat?

HECTOR. You are in what is supposed to be my house. I am at your disposal.

*Hector sits down in the draughtsman's chair, turning it to face Randall, who remains standing, leaning at his ease against the carpenter's bench.*

RANDALL. I take it that we may be quite frank. I mean about Lady Utterword.

HECTOR. You may. I have nothing to be frank about. I never met her until this afternoon.

RANDALL [*straightening up*] What! But you are her sister's husband.

HECTOR. Well, if you come to that, you are her husband's brother.

[ 149 ]

RANDALL. But you seem to be on intimate terms with her.

HECTOR. So do you.

RANDALL. Yes; but I am on intimate terms with her. I have known her for years.

HECTOR. It took her years to get to the same point with you that she got to with me in five minutes, it seems.

RANDALL [*vexed*] Really, Ariadne is the limit [*he moves away huffishly towards the windows*].

HECTOR [*coolly*] She is, as I remarked to Hesione, a very enterprising woman.

RANDALL [*returning, much troubled*] You see, Hushabye, you are what women consider a good-looking man.

HECTOR. I cultivated that appearance in the days of my vanity; and Hesione insists on my keeping it up. She makes me wear these ridiculous things [*indicating his Arab costume*] because she thinks me absurd in evening dress.

RANDALL. Still, you do keep it up, old chap. Now, I assure you I have not an atom of jealousy in my disposition—

HECTOR. The question would seem to be rather whether your brother has any touch of that sort.

RANDALL. What! Hastings! Oh, dont trouble about Hastings. He has the gift of being able to work sixteen hours a day at the dullest detail, and actually likes it. That gets him to the top wherever he goes. As long as Ariadne takes care that he is fed regularly, he is only too thankful to anyone who will keep her in good humour for him.

HECTOR. And as she has all the Shotover fascination, there is plenty of competition for the job, eh?

RANDALL [*angrily*] She encourages them. Her conduct is perfectly scandalous. I assure you, my dear

fellow, I havnt an atom of jealously in my composition;
but she makes herself the talk of every place she goes
to by her thoughtlessness. It's nothing more: she
doesnt really care for the men she keeps hanging
about her; but how is the world to know that? It's
not fair to Hastings. It's not fair to me.

HECTOR. Her theory is that her conduct is so
correct—

RANDALL. Correct! She does nothing but make
scenes from morning til night. You be careful, old
chap. She will get you into trouble: that is, she
would if she really cared for you.

HECTOR. Doesnt she?

RANDALL. Not a scrap. She may want your scalp to
add to her collection; but her true affection has been
engaged years ago. You had really better be careful.

HECTOR. Do you suffer much from this jealousy?

RANDALL. Jealousy? I jealous! My dear fellow,
havnt I told you that there is not an atom of—

HECTOR. Yes. And Lady Utterword told me she
never made scenes. Well, dont waste your jealousy on
my moustache. Never waste jealousy on a real man: it
is the imaginary hero that supplants us all in the long
run. Besides, jealousy does not belong to your easy
man-of-the-world pose, which you carry so well in
other respects.

RANDALL. Really, Hushabye, I think a man may be
allowed to be a gentleman without being accused of
posing.

HECTOR. It is a pose like any other. In this house we
know all the poses: our game is to find out the man
under the pose. The man under your pose is apparently Ellie's favorite, Othello.

RANDALL. Some of your games in this house are
damned annoying, let me tell you.

HECTOR. Yes: I have been their victim for many years. I used to writhe under them at first; but I became accustomed to them. At last I learned to play them.

RANDALL. If it's all the same to you, I had rather you didnt play them on me. You evidently dont quite understand my character, or my notions of good form.

HECTOR. Is it your notion of good form to give away Lady Utterword?

RANDALL [*a childishly plaintive note breaking into his huff*] I have not said a word against Lady Utterword. This is just the conspiracy over again.

HECTOR. What conspiracy?

RANDALL. You know very well, sir. A conspiracy to make me out to be pettish and jealous and childish and everything I am not. Everyone knows I am just the opposite.

HECTOR [*rising*] Something in the air of the house has upset you. It often does have that effect. [*He goes to the garden door and calls Lady Utterword with commanding emphasis*] Ariadne!

LADY UTTERWORD [*at some distance*] Yes.

RANDALL. What are you calling her for? I want to speak—

LADY UTTERWORD [*arriving breathless*] Yes. You really are a terribly commanding person. Whats the matter?

HECTOR. I do not know how to manage your friend Randall. No doubt you do.

LADY UTTERWORD. Randall: have you been making yourself ridiculous, as usual? I can see it in your face. Really, you are the most pettish creature.

RANDALL. You know quite well, Ariadne, that I have not an ounce of pettishness in my disposition. I have made myself perfectly pleasant here. I have remained absolutely cool and imperturbable in the face of a burglar. Imperturbability is almost too strong a point of mine. But [*putting his foot down with a stamp, and walking angrily up and down the room*] I insist on being treated with a certain consideration. I will not allow Hushabye to take liberties with me. I will not stand your encouraging people as you do.

HECTOR. The man has a rooted delusion that he is your husband.

LADY UTTERWORD. I know. He is jealous. As if he had any right to be! He compromises me everywhere. He makes scenes all over the place. Randall: I will not allow it. I simply will not allow it. You had no right to discuss me with Hector. I will not be discussed by men.

HECTOR. Be reasonable, Ariadne. Your fatal gift of beauty forces men to discuss you.

LADY UTTERWORD. Oh indeed! what about your fatal gift of beauty?

HECTOR. How can I help it?

LADY UTTERWORD. You could cut off your moustache: I cant cut off my nose. I get my whole life messed up with people falling in love with me. And then Randall says I run after men.

RANDALL. I—

LADY UTTERWORD. Yes you do: you said it just now. Why cant you think of something else than women? Napoleon was quite right when he said that women are the occupation of the idle man. Well, if ever there was an idle man on earth, his name is Randall Utterword.

RANDALL. Ariad—

LADY UTTERWORD [*overwhelming him with a torrent of words*] Oh yes you are: it's no use denying it. What have you ever done? What good are you? You are as much trouble in the house as a child of three. You couldnt live without your valet.

RANDALL. This is—

LADY UTTERWORD. Laziness! You are laziness incarnate. You are selfishness itself. You are the most uninteresting man on earth. You cant even gossip about anything but yourself and your grievances and your ailments and the people who have offended you. [*Turning to Hector*] Do you know what they call him, Hector?

HECTOR ⎱ [*speaking* ⎰ Please dont tell me.
RANDALL ⎰ *together*] ⎱ I'll not stand it—

LADY UTTERWORD. Randall the Rotter: that is his name in good society.

RANDALL [*shouting*] I'll not bear it, I tell you. Will you listen to me, you infernal— [*he chokes*].

LADY UTTERWORD. Well: go on. What were you going to call me? An infernal what? Which unpleasant animal is it to be this time?

RANDALL [*foaming*] There is no animal in the world so hateful as a woman can be. You are a maddening devil. Hushabye: you will not believe me when I tell you that I have loved this demon all my life; but God knows I have paid for it [*he sits down in the draughtsman's chair, weeping*].

LADY UTTERWORD [*standing over him with triumphant contempt*] Cry-baby!

HECTOR [*gravely, coming to him*] My friend: the Shotover sisters have two strange powers over men. They can make them love; and they can make them cry. Thank your stars that you are not married to one of them.

LADY UTTERWORD [*haughtily*] And pray, Hector—

HECTOR [*suddenly catching her round the shoulders; swinging her right round him and away from Randall;*

*and gripping her throat with the other hand*] Ariadne; if you attempt to start on me, I'll choke you: do you hear? The cat-and-mouse game with the other sex is a good game; but I can play your head off at it. [*He throws her, not at all gently, into the big chair, and proceeds, less fiercely but firmly*] It is true that Napoleon said that woman is the occupation of the idle man. But he added that she is the relaxation of the warrior. Well, *I* am the warrior. So take care.

LADY UTTERWORD [*not in the least put out, and rather pleased by his violence*] My dear Hector: I have only done what you asked me to do.

HECTOR. How do you make that out, pray?

LADY UTTERWORD. You called me in to manage Randall, didnt you? You said you couldnt manage him yourself.

HECTOR. Well, what if I did? I did not ask you to drive the man mad.

LADY UTTERWORD. He isnt mad. Thats the way to manage him. If you were a mother, youd understand.

HECTOR. Mother! What are you up to now?

LADY UTTERWORD. It's quite simple. When the children got nerves and were naughty, I smacked them just enough to give them a good cry and a healthy nervous shock. They went to sleep and were quite good afterwards. Well, I cant smack Randall: he is too big; so when he gets nerves and is naughty, I just rag him til he cries. He will be all right now. Look: he is half asleep already [*which is quite true*].

RANDALL [*waking up indignantly*] I'm not. You are most cruel, Ariadne. [*Sentimentally*] But I suppose I must forgive you, as usual [*he checks himself in the act of yawning*].

LADY UTTERWORD [*to Hector*] Is the explanation satisfactory, dread warrior?

HECTOR. Some day I shall kill you, if you go too far. I thought you were a fool.

LADY UTTERWORD [*laughing*] Everybody does, at first. But I am not such a fool as I look. [*She rises complacently*]. Now, Randall: go to bed. You will be a good boy in the morning.

RANDALL [*only very faintly rebellious*] I'll go to bed when I like. It isnt ten yet.

LADY UTTERWORD. It is long past ten. See that he goes to bed at once, Hector. [*She goes into the garden*].

HECTOR. Is there any slavery on earth viler than this slavery of men to women?

RANDALL [*rising resolutely*] I'll not speak to her tomorrow. I'll not speak to her for another week. I'll give her such a lesson. I'll go straight to bed without bidding her goodnight. [*He makes for the door leading to the hall*].

HECTOR. You are under a spell, man. Old Shotover sold himself to the devil in Zanzibar. The devil gave him a black witch for a wife; and these two demon daughters are their mystical progeny. I am tied to Hesione's apron-string; but I'm her husband; and if I did go stark staring mad about her, at least we became man and wife. But why should you let yourself be dragged about and beaten by Ariadne as a toy donkey is dragged about and beaten by a child? What do you get by it? Are you her lover?

RANDALL. You must not misunderstand me. In a higher sense—in a Platonic sense—

HECTOR. Psha! Platonic sense! She makes you her servant; and when pay-day comes round, she bilks you: that is what you mean.

RANDALL [*feebly*] Well, if I dont mind, I dont see what business it is of yours. Besides, I tell you I am going to punish her. You shall see: *I* know how to deal

[ 156 ]

with women. I'm really very sleepy. Say goodnight to Mrs Hushabye for me, will you, like a good chap. Goodnight. [*He hurries out*].

HECTOR. Poor wretch! Oh women! women! women! [*He lifts his fists in invocation to heaven*] Fall. Fall and crush. [*He goes out into the garden*].

# [ACT III]

*In the garden, Hector, as he comes out through the glass door of the poop, finds Lady Utterword lying voluptuously in the hammock on the east side of the flagstaff, in the circle of light cast by the electric arc, which is like a moon in its opal globe. Beneath the head of the hammock, a campstool. On the other side of the flagstaff, on the long garden seat, Captain Shotover is asleep, with Ellie beside him, leaning affectionately against him on his right hand. On his left is a deck chair. Behind them in the gloom, Hesione is strolling about with Mangan. It is a fine still night, moonless.*

LADY UTTERWORD. What a lovely night! It seems made for us.

HECTOR. The night takes no interest in us. What are we to the night? [*He sits down moodily in the deck chair*].

ELLIE [*dreamily, nestling against the Captain*] Its beauty soaks into my nerves. In the night there is peace for the old and hope for the young.

HECTOR. Is that remark your own?

ELLIE. No. Only the last thing the Captain said before he went to sleep.

CAPTAIN SHOTOVER. I'm not asleep.

HECTOR. Randall is. Also Mr Mazzini Dunn. Mangan too, probably.

MANGAN. No.

HECTOR. Oh, you are there. I thought Hesione would have sent you to bed by this time.

MRS HUSHABYE [*coming to the back of the garden seat, into the light, with Mangan*] I think I shall. He keeps telling me he has a presentiment that he is going to die. I never met a man so greedy for sympathy.

MANGAN [*plaintively*] But I have a presentiment. I really have. And you wouldnt listen.

MRS HUSHABYE. I was listening for something else. There was a sort of splendid drumming in the sky. Did none of you hear it? It came from a distance and then died away.

MANGAN. I tell you it was a train.

MRS HUSHABYE. And *I* tell you, Alf, there is no train at this hour. The last is nine fortyfive.

MANGAN. But a goods train.

MRS HUSHABYE. Not on our little line. They tack a truck on to the passenger train. What can it have been, Hector?

HECTOR. Heaven's threatening growl of disgust at us useless futile creatures. [*Fiercely*] I tell you, one of two things must happen. Either out of that darkness some new creation will come to supplant us as we have supplanted the animals, or the heavens will fall in thunder and destroy us.

LADY UTTERWORD [*in a cool instructive manner, wallowing comfortably in her hammock*] We have not supplanted the animals, Hector. Why do you ask heaven to destroy this house, which could be made quite comfortable if Hesione had any notion of how to live? Dont you know what is wrong with it?

HECTOR. We are wrong with it. There is no sense in us. We are useless, dangerous, and ought to be abolished.

LADY UTTERWORD. Nonsense! Hastings told me the very first day he came here, nearly twentyfour years ago, what is wrong with the house.

CAPTAIN SHOTOVER. What! The numskull said there was something wrong with my house!

LADY UTTERWORD. I said Hastings said it; and he is not in the least a numskull.

CAPTAIN SHOTOVER. Whats wrong with my house?

LADY UTTERWORD. Just what is wrong with a ship, papa. Wasnt it clever of Hastings to see that?

CAPTAIN SHOTOVER. The man's a fool. Theres nothing wrong with a ship.

LADY UTTERWORD. Yes there is.

MRS HUSHABYE. But what is it? Dont be aggravating, Addy.

LADY UTTERWORD. Guess.

HECTOR. Demons. Daughters of the witch of Zanzibar. Demons.

LADY UTTERWORD. Not a bit. I assure you, all this house needs to make it a sensible, healthy, pleasant house, with good appetites and sound sleep in it, is horses.

MRS HUSHABYE. Horses! What rubbish!

LADY UTTERWORD. Yes: horses. Why have we never been able to let this house? Because there are no proper stables. Go anywhere in England where there are natural, wholesome, contented, and really nice English people; and what do you always find? That the stables are the real centre of the household; and that if any visitor wants to play the piano the whole room has to be upset before it can be opened, there are so many things piled on it. I never lived until I learned to ride; and I shall never ride really well because I didnt begin as a child. There are only two classes in good society in England: the equestrian classes and the neurotic classes. It isnt mere convention: everybody can see that the people who hunt are the right people and the people who dont are the wrong ones.

CAPTAIN SHOTOVER. There is some truth in this. My ship made a man of me; and a ship is the horse of the sea.

LADY UTTERWORD. Exactly how Hastings explained your being a gentleman.

CAPTAIN SHOTOVER. Not bad for a numskull. Bring the man here with you next time: I must talk to him.

LADY UTTERWORD. Why is Randall such an obvious rotter? He is well bred; he has been at a public school and a university; he has been in the Foreign Office; he knows the best people and has lived all his life among them. Why is he so unsatisfactory, so contemptible? Why cant he get a valet to stay with him longer than a few months? Just because he is too lazy and pleasure-loving to hunt and shoot. He strums the piano, and sketches, and runs after married women, and reads literary books and poems. He actually plays the flute; but I never let him bring it into my house. If he would only—[*she is interrupted by the melancholy strains of a flute coming from an open window above. She raises herself indignantly in the hammock*]. Randall: you have not gone to bed. Have you been listening? [*The flute replies pertly:*]

How vulgar! Go to bed instantly, Randall: how dare you? [*The window is slammed down. She subsides*]. How can anyone care for such a creature!

MRS HUSHABYE. Addy: do you think Ellie ought to marry poor Alfred merely for his money?

MANGAN [*much alarmed*] Whats that? Mrs Hushabye: are my affairs to be discussed like this before everybody?

LADY UTTERWORD. I dont think Randall is listening now.

MANGAN. Everybody is listening. It isnt right.

MRS HUSHABYE. But in the dark, what does it matter? Ellie doesnt mind. Do you, Ellie?

ELLIE. Not in the least. What is your opinion, Lady Utterword? You have so much good sense.

MANGAN. But it isnt right. It— [*Mrs Hushabye puts her hand on his mouth*]. Oh, very well.

LADY UTTERWORD. How much money have you, Mr Mangan?

MANGAN. Really— No: I cant stand this.

LADY UTTERWORD. Nonsense, Mr. Mangan! It all turns on your income, doesnt it?

MANGAN. Well, if you come to that, how much money has she?

ELLIE. None.

LADY UTTERWORD. You are answered, Mr Mangan. And now, as you have made Miss Dunn throw her cards on the table, you cannot refuse to shew your own.

MRS HUSHABYE. Come, Alf! out with it! How much?

MANGAN [*baited out of all prudence*] Well, if you want to know, I have no money and never had any.

MRS HUSHABYE. Alfred: you musnt tell naughty stories.

MANGAN. I'm not telling you stories. I'm telling you the raw truth.

LADY UTTERWORD. Then what do you live on, Mr Mangan?

MANGAN. Travelling expenses. And a trifle of commission.

CAPTAIN SHOTOVER. What more have any of us but travelling expenses for our life's journey?

MRS HUSHABYE. But you have factories and capital and things?

MANGAN. People think I have. People think I'm an industrial Napoleon. Thats why Miss Ellie wants to marry me. But I tell you I have nothing.

ELLIE. Do you mean that the factories are like Marcus's tigers? That they dont exist?

MANGAN. They exist all right enough. But theyre not mine. They belong to syndicates and shareholders and all sorts of lazy good-for-nothing capitalists. I get money from such people to start the factories. I find people like Miss Dunn's father to work them, and keep a tight hand so as to make them pay. Of course I make them keep me going pretty well; but it's a dog's life; and I dont own anything.

MRS HUSHABYE. Alfred, Alfred: you are making a poor mouth of it to get out of marrying Ellie.

MANGAN. I'm telling the truth about my money for the first time in my life; and it's the first time my word has ever been doubted.

LADY UTTERWORD. How sad! Why dont you go in for politics, Mr Mangan?

MANGAN. Go in for politics! Where have you been living? I am in politics.

LADY UTTERWORD. I'm sure I beg your pardon. I never heard of you.

MANGAN. Let me tell you, Lady Utterword, that the Prime Minister of this country asked me to join the Government without even going through the nonsense of an election, as the dictator of a great public department.

LADY UTTERWORD. As a Conservative or a Liberal?

MANGAN. No such nonsense. As a practical business man. [*They all burst out laughing*]. What are you all laughing at?

MRS HUSHABYE. Oh, Alfred, Alfred!

ELLIE. You! who have to get my father to do everything for you!

MRS HUSHABYE. You! who are afraid of your own workmen!

HECTOR. You! with whom three women have been playing cat and mouse all the evening!

LADY UTTERWORD. You must have given an immense sum to the party funds, Mr Mangan.

MANGAN. Not a penny out of my own pocket. The syndicate found the money: they knew how useful I should be to them in the Government.

LADY UTTERWORD. This is most interesting and unexpected, Mr Mangan. And what have your administrative achievements been, so far?

MANGAN. Achievements? Well, I dont know what you call achievements; but Ive jolly well put a stop to the games of the other fellows in the other departments. Every man of them thought he was going to save the country all by himself, and do me out of the credit and out of my chance of a title. I took good care that if they wouldnt let me do it they shouldnt do it themselves either. I may not know anything about my own machinery; but I know how to stick a ramrod into the other fellow's. And now they all look the biggest fools going.

HECTOR. And in heaven's name, what do you look like?

MANGAN. I look like the fellow that was too clever for all the others, dont I? If that isnt a triumph of practical business, what is?

HECTOR. Is this England, or is it a madhouse?

LADY UTTERWORD. Do you expect to save the country, Mr Mangan?

MANGAN. Well, who else will? Will your Mr Randall save it?

LADY UTTERWORD. Randall the rotter! Certainly not.

MANGAN. Will your brother-in-law save it with his moustache and his fine talk.

HECTOR. Yes, if they will let me.

MANGAN [*sneering*] Ah! Will they let you?

HECTOR. No. They prefer you.

MANGAN. Very well then, as youre in a world where I'm appreciated and youre not, youd best be civil to me, hadnt you? Who else is there but me?

LADY UTTERWORD. There is Hastings. Get rid of your ridiculous sham democracy; and give Hastings the necessary powers, and a good supply of bamboo to bring the British native to his senses: he will save the country with the greatest ease.

CAPTAIN SHOTOVER. It had better be lost. Any fool can govern with a stick in his hand. *I* could govern that way. It is not God's way. The man is a numskull.

LADY UTTERWORD. The man is worth all of you rolled into one. What do you say, Miss Dunn?

ELLIE. I think my father would do very well if people did not put upon him and cheat him and despise him because he is so good.

MANGAN [*contemptuously*] I think I see Mazzini Dunn getting into parliament or pushing his way into the Government. Weve not come to that yet, thank God! What do you say, Mrs Hushabye?

MRS HUSHABYE. Oh, *I* say it matters very little which of you governs the country so long as we govern you.

HECTOR. We? Who is we, pray?

MRS HUSHABYE. The devil's granddaughters, dear. The lovely women.

HECTOR [*raising his hands as before*] Fall, I say; and deliver us from the lures of Satan!

ELLIE. There seems to be nothing real in the world

except my father and Shakespear. Marcus's tigers are false; Mr Mangan's millions are false; there is nothing really strong and true about Hesione but her beautiful black hair; and Lady Utterword's is too pretty to be real. The one thing that was left to me was the Captain's seventh degree of concentration; and that turns out to be—

CAPTAIN SHOTOVER. Rum.

LADY UTTERWORD [*placidly*] A good deal of my hair is quite genuine. The Duchess of Dithering offered me fifty guineas for this [*touching her forehead*] under the impression that it was a transformation; but it is all natural except the color.

MANGAN [*wildly*] Look here: I'm going to take off all my clothes [*he begins tearing off his coat*].

| | | |
|---|---|---|
| LADY UTTERWORD. | [*in consternation*] | Mr Mangan! |
| CAPTAIN SHOTOVER. | | Whats that? |
| HECTOR. | | Ha! ha! Do. Do. |
| ELLIE. | | Please dont. |

MRS HUSHABYE [*catching his arm and stopping him*] Alfred: for shame! Are you mad?

MANGAN. Shame! What shame is there in this house? Let's all strip stark naked. We may as well do the thing thoroughly when we're about it. Weve stripped ourselves morally naked: well, let us strip ourselves physically naked as well, and see how we like it. I tell you I cant bear this. I was brought up to be respectable. I dont mind the women dyeing their hair and the men drinking: it's human nature. But it's not human nature to tell everybody about it. Every time one of you opens your mouth I go like this [*he cowers as if to avoid a missile*] afraid of what will come next. How are we to have any self-respect if we dont keep it up that we're better than we really are?

LADY UTTERWORD. I quite sympathize with you, Mr Mangan. I have been through it all; and I know by experience that men and women are delicate plants and must be cultivated under glass. Our family habit of throwing stones in all directions and letting the air in is not only unbearably rude, but positively dangerous. Still, there is no use catching physical colds as well as moral ones; so please keep your clothes on.

MANGAN. I'll do as I like: not what you tell me. Am I a child or a grown man? I wont stand this mothering tyranny. I'll go back to the city, where I'm respected and made much of.

MRS HUSHABYE. Goodbye, Alf. Think of us sometimes in the city. Think of Ellie's youth!

ELLIE. Think of Hesione's eyes and hair!

CAPTAIN SHOTOVER. Think of this garden in which you are not a dog barking to keep the truth out!

HECTOR. Think of Lady Utterword's beauty! her good sense! her style!

LADY UTTERWORD. Flatterer. Think, Mr Mangan, whether you can really do any better for yourself elsewhere: that is the essential point, isnt it?

MANGAN [surrendering] All right: all right. I'm done. Have it your own way. Only let me alone. I dont know whether I'm on my head or my heels when you all start on me like this. I'll stay. I'll marry her. I'll do anything for a quiet life. Are you satisfied now?

ELLIE. No. I never really intended to make you marry me, Mr Mangan. Never in the depths of my soul. I only wanted to feel my strength: to know that you could not escape if I chose to take you.

MANGAN [indignantly] What! Do you mean to say you are going to throw me over after my acting so handsome?

LADY UTTERWORD. I should not be too hasty, Miss

Dunn. You can throw Mr Mangan over at any time up to the last moment. Very few men in his position go bankrupt. You can live very comfortably on his reputation for immense wealth.

ELLIE. I cannot commit bigamy, Lady Utterword.

| | | |
|---|---|---|
| MRS HUSHABYE. | | Bigamy! Whatever on earth are you talking about, Ellie? |
| LADY UTTERWORD. | [*exclaiming all together*] | Bigamy! What do you mean, Miss Dunn? |
| MANGAN. | | Bigamy! Do you mean to say youre married already? |
| HECTOR. | | Bigamy! This is some enigma. |

ELLIE. Only half an hour ago I became Captain Shotover's white wife.

MRS HUSHABYE. Ellie! What nonsense! Where?

ELLIE. In heaven, where all true marriages are made.

LADY UTTERWORD. Really, Miss Dunn! Really, papa!

MANGAN. He told me *I* was too old! And him a mummy!

HECTOR [*quoting Shelley*]

"Their altar the grassy earth outspread,
And their priest the muttering wind."

ELLIE. Yes: I, Ellie Dunn, give my broken heart and my strong sound soul to its natural captain, my spiritual husband and second father.

*She draws the Captain's arm through hers, and pats his hand. The Captain remains fast asleep.*

MRS HUSHABYE. Oh, thats very clever of you, petti-kins. Very clever. Alfred: you could never have lived up to Ellie. You must be content with a little share of me.

MANGAN [*sniffing and wiping his eyes*] It isnt kind—[*his emotion chokes him*].

LADY UTTERWORD. You are well out of it, Mr Mangan. Miss Dunn is the most conceited young woman I have met since I came back to England.

MRS HUSHABYE. Oh, Ellie isnt conceited. Are you, pettikins?

ELLIE. I know my strength now, Hesione.

MANGAN. Brazen, I call you. Brazen.

MRS HUSHABYE. Tut, tut, Alfred: dont be rude. Dont you feel how lovely this marriage night is, made in heaven? Arnt you happy, you and Hector? Open your eyes: Addy and Ellie look beautiful enough to please the most fastidious man: we live and love and have not a care in the world. We women have managed all that for you. Why in the name of common sense do you go on as if you were two miserable wretches?

CAPTAIN SHOTOVER. I tell you happiness is no good. You can be happy when you are only half alive. I am happier now I am half dead than ever I was in my prime. But there is no blessing on my happiness.

ELLIE [*her face lighting up*] Life with a blessing! that is what I want. Now I know the real reason why I couldnt marry Mr Mangan: there would be no blessing on our marriage. There is a blessing on my broken heart. There is a blessing on your beauty, Hesione. There is a blessing on your father's spirit. Even on the lies of Marcus there is a blessing; but on Mr Mangan's money there is none.

MANGAN. I dont understand a word of that.

ELLIE. Neither do I. But I know it means something.

MANGAN. Dont say there was any difficulty about the blessing. I was ready to get a bishop to marry us.

MRS HUSHABYE. Isnt he a fool, pettikins?

HECTOR [*fiercely*] Do not scorn the man. We are all fools.

*Mazzini, in pyjamas and a richly colored silk dressing-gown, comes from the house, on Lady Utterword's side.*

MRS HUSHABYE. Oh! here comes the only man who ever resisted me. Whats the matter, Mr Dunn? Is the house on fire?

MAZZINI. Oh no: nothing's the matter; but really it's impossible to go to sleep with such an interesting conversation going on under one's window, and on such a beautiful night too. I just had to come down and join you all. What has it been all about?

MRS HUSHABYE. Oh, wonderful things, soldier of freedom.

HECTOR. For example, Mangan, as a practical business man, has tried to undress himself and has failed ignominiously; whilst you, as an idealist, have succeeded brilliantly.

MAZZINI. I hope you dont mind my being like this, Mrs Hushabye. [*He sits down on the campstool*].

MRS HUSHABYE. On the contrary, I could wish you always like that.

LADY UTTERWORD. Your daughter's match is off, Mr Dunn. It seems that Mr Mangan, whom we all supposed to be a man of property, owns absolutely nothing.

MAZZINI. Well of course I knew that, Lady Utterword. But if people believe in him and are always giving him money, whereas they dont believe in me and never give me any, how can I ask poor Ellie to depend on what I can do for her?

MANGAN. Dont you run away with this idea that I have nothing. I—

HECTOR. Oh, dont explain. We understand. You have a couple of thousand pounds in exchequer bills, 50,000 shares worth tenpence a dozen, and half a dozen tabloids of cyanide of potassium to poison yourself with when you are found out. Thats the reality of your millions.

MAZZINI. Oh no, no, no. He is quite honest: the businesses are genuine and perfectly legal.

HECTOR [*disgusted*] Yah! Not even a great swindler!

MANGAN. So you think. But Ive been too many for some honest men, for all that.

LADY UTTERWORD. There is no pleasing you, Mr Mangan. You are determined to be neither rich nor poor, honest nor dishonest.

MANGAN. There you go again. Ever since I came into this silly house I have been made to look like a fool, though I'm as good a man in this house as in the city.

ELLIE [*musically*] Yes: this silly house, this strangely happy house, this agonizing house, this house without foundations. I shall call it Heartbreak House.

MRS HUSHABYE. Stop, Ellie; or I shall howl like an animal.

MANGAN [*breaks into a low snivelling*]!!!

MRS HUSHABYE. There! you have set Alfred off.

ELLIE. I like him best when he is howling.

CAPTAIN SHOTOVER. Silence! [*Mangan subsides into silence*]. I say, let the heart break in silence.

HECTOR. Do you accept that name for your house?

CAPTAIN SHOTOVER. It is not my house: it is only my kennel.

HECTOR. We have been too long here. We do not live in this house: we haunt it.

LADY UTTERWORD [*heart torn*] It is dreadful to

think how you have been here all these years while I have gone round the world. I escaped young; but it has drawn me back. It wants to break my heart too. But it shant. I have left you and it behind. It was silly of me to come back. I felt sentimental about papa and Hesione and the old place. I felt them calling to me.

MAZZINI. But what a very natural and kindly and charming human feeling, Lady Utterword!

LADY UTTERWORD. So I thought, Mr Dunn. But I know now that it was only the last of my influenza. I found that I was not remembered and not wanted.

CAPTAIN SHOTOVER. You left because you did not want us. Was there no heartbreak in that for your father? You tore yourself up by the roots; and the ground healed up and brought forth fresh plants and forgot you. What right had you to come back and probe old wounds?

MRS HUSHABYE. You were a complete stranger to me at first, Addy; but now I feel as if you had never been away.

LADY UTTERWORD. Thank you, Hesione; but the influenza is quite cured. The place may be Heartbreak House to you, Miss Dunn, and to this gentleman from the city who seems to have so little self-control; but to me it is only a very ill-regulated and rather untidy villa without any stables.

HECTOR. Inhabited by—?

ELLIE. A crazy old sea captain and a young singer who adores him.

MRS HUSHABYE. A sluttish female, trying to stave off a double chin and an elderly spread, vainly wooing a born soldier of freedom.

MAZZINI. Oh, really, Mrs Hushabye—

MANGAN. A member of His Majesty's Government

that everybody sets down as a nincompoop: dont forget him, Lady Utterword.

LADY UTTERWORD. And a very fascinating gentleman whose chief occupation is to be married to my sister.

HECTOR. All heartbroken imbeciles.

MAZZINI. Oh no. Surely, if I may say so, rather a favorable specimen of what is best in our English culture. You are very charming people, most advanced, unprejudiced, frank, humane, unconventional, democratic, free-thinking, and everything that is delightful to thoughtful people.

MRS HUSHABYE. You do us proud, Mazzini.

MAZZINI. I am not flattering, really. Where else could I feel perfectly at ease in my pyjamas? I sometimes dream that I am in very distinguished society, and suddenly I have nothing on but my pyjamas! Sometimes I havent even pyjamas. And I always feel overwhelmed with confusion. But here, I dont mind in the least: it seems quite natural.

LADY UTTERWORD. An infallible sign that you are not now in really distinguished society, Mr Dunn. If you were in my house, you would feel embarrassed.

MAZZINI. I shall take particular care to keep out of your house, Lady Utterword.

LADY UTTERWORD. You will be quite wrong, Mr Dunn. I should make you very comfortable; and you would not have the trouble and anxiety of wondering whether you should wear your purple and gold or your green and crimson dressing-gown at dinner. You complicate life instead of simplifying it by doing these ridiculous things.

ELLIE. Your house is not Heartbreak House: is it, Lady Utterword?

HECTOR. Yet she breaks hearts, easy as her house is.

That poor devil upstairs with his flute howls when she twists his heart, just as Mangan howls when my wife twists his.

LADY UTTERWORD. That is because Randall has nothing to do but have his heart broken. It is a change from having his head shampooed. Catch anyone breaking Hastings' heart!

CAPTAIN SHOTOVER. The numskull wins, after all.

LADY UTTERWORD. I shall go back to my numskull with the greatest satisfaction when I am tired of you all, clever as you are.

MANGAN [*huffily*] I never set up to be clever.

LADY UTTERWORD. I forgot you, Mr Mangan.

MANGAN. Well, I dont see that quite, either.

LADY UTTERWORD. You may not be clever, Mr Mangan; but you are successful.

MANGAN. But I dont want to be regarded merely as a successful man. I have an imagination like anyone else. I have a presentiment—

MRS HUSHABYE. Oh, you are impossible, Alfred. Here I am devoting myself to you; and you think of nothing but your ridiculous presentiment. You bore me. Come and talk poetry to me under the stars. [*She drags him away into the darkness*].

MANGAN [*tearfully, as he disappears*] Yes: it's all very well to make fun of me; but if you only knew—

HECTOR [*impatiently*] How is all this going to end?

MAZZINI. It wont end, Mr Hushabye. Life doesnt end: it goes on.

ELLIE. Oh, it cant go on for ever. I'm always expecting something. I dont know what it is; but life must come to a point sometime.

LADY UTTERWORD. The point for a young woman of your age is a baby.

HECTOR. Yes, but, damn it, I have the same feeling; and *I* cant have a baby.

LADY UTTERWORD. By deputy, Hector.

HECTOR. But I have children. All that is over and done with for me: and yet I too feel that this cant last. We sit here talking, and leave everything to Mangan and to chance and to the devil. Think of the powers of destruction that Mangan and his mutual admiration gang wield! It's madness: it's like giving a torpedo to a badly brought up child to play at earthquakes with.

MAZZINI. I know. I used often to think about that when I was young.

HECTOR. Think! Whats the good of thinking about it? Why didnt you do something?

MAZZINI. But I did. I joined societies and made speeches and wrote pamphlets. That was all I could do. But, you know, though the people in the societies thought they knew more than Mangan, most of them wouldnt have joined if they had known as much. You see they had never had any money to handle or any men to manage. Every year I expected a revolution, or some frightful smash-up: it seemed impossible that we could blunder and muddle on any longer. But nothing happened, except, of course, the usual poverty and crime and drink that we are used to. Nothing ever does happen. It's amazing how well we get along, all things considered.

LADY UTTERWORD. Perhaps somebody cleverer than you and Mr Mangan was at work all the time.

MAZZINI. Perhaps so. Though I was brought up not to believe in anything, I often feel that there is a great deal to be said for the theory of an overruling Providence, after all.

LADY UTTERWORD. Providence! I meant Hastings.

MAZZINI. Oh, I beg your pardon, Lady Utterword.

CAPTAIN SHOTOVER. Every drunken skipper trusts to Providence. But one of the ways of Providence with drunken skippers is to run them on the rocks.

MAZZINI. Very true, no doubt, at sea. But in politics, I assure you, they only run into jellyfish. Nothing happens.

CAPTAIN SHOTOVER. At sea nothing happens to the sea. Nothing happens to the sky. The sun comes up from the east and goes down to the west. The moon grows from a sickle to an arc lamp, and comes later and later until she is lost in the light as other things are lost in the darkness. After the typhoon, the flying-fish glitter in the sunshine like birds. It's amazing how they get along, all things considered. Nothing happens, except something not worth mentioning.

ELLIE. What is that, O Captain, my captain?

CAPTAIN SHOTOVER [*savagely*] Nothing but the smash of the drunken skipper's ship on the rocks, the splintering of her rotten timbers, the tearing of her rusty plates, the drowning of the crew like rats in a trap.

ELLIE. Moral: dont take rum.

CAPTAIN SHOTOVER [*vehemently*] That is a lie, child. Let a man drink ten barrels of rum a day, he is not a drunken skipper until he is a drifting skipper. Whilst he can lay his course and stand on his bridge and steer it, he is no drunkard. It is the man who lies drinking in his bunk and trusts to Providence that I call the drunken skipper, though he drank nothing but the waters of the River Jordan.

ELLIE. Splendid! And you havnt had a drop for an hour. You see you dont need it: your own spirit is not dead.

CAPTAIN SHOTOVER. Echoes: nothing but echoes. The last shot was fired years ago.

HECTOR. And this ship that we are all in? This soul's prison we call England?

CAPTAIN SHOTOVER. The captain is in his bunk, drinking bottled ditch-water; and the crew is gambling in the forecastle. She will strike and sink and split. Do you think the laws of God will be suspended in favor of England because you were born in it?

HECTOR. Well, I dont mean to be drowned like a rat in a trap. I still have the will to live. What am I to do?

CAPTAIN SHOTOVER. Do? Nothing simpler. Learn your business as an Englishman.

HECTOR. And what may my business as an Englishman be, pray?

CAPTAIN SHOTOVER. Navigation. Learn it and live; or leave it and be damned.

ELLIE. Quiet, quiet: youll tire yourself.

MAZZINI. I thought all that once, Captain; but I assure you nothing will happen.

*A dull distant explosion is heard.*

HECTOR [*starting up*] What was that?

CAPTAIN SHOTOVER. Something happening [*he blows his whistle*]. Breakers ahead!

*The light goes out.*

HECTOR [*furiously*] Who put that light out? Who dared put that light out?

NURSE GUINNESS [*running in from the house to the middle of the esplanade*] I did, sir. The police have telephoned to say we'll be summoned if we dont put that light out: it can be seen for miles.

HECTOR. It shall be seen for a hundred miles [*he dashes into the house*].

NURSE GUINNESS. The rectory is nothing but a heap of bricks, they say. Unless we can give the rector a bed he has nowhere to lay his head this night.

CAPTAIN SHOTOVER. The Church is on the rocks,

breaking up. I told him it would unless it headed for God's open sea.

NURSE GUINNESS. And you are all to go down to the cellars.

CAPTAIN SHOTOVER. Go there yourself, you and all the crew. Batten down the hatches.

NURSE GUINNESS. And hide beside the coward I married! I'll go on the roof first. [*The lamp lights up again*]. There! Mr Hushabye's turned it on again.

THE BURGLAR [*hurrying in and appealing to Nurse Guinness*] Here: wheres the way to that gravel pit? The boot-boy says theres a cave in the gravel pit. Them cellars is no use. Wheres the gravel pit, Captain?

NURSE GUINNESS. Go straight on past the flagstaff until you fall into it and break your dirty neck. [*She pushes him contemptuously towards the flagstaff, and herself goes to the foot of the hammock and waits there, as it were by Ariadne's cradle*].

*Another and louder explosion is heard. The burglar stops and stands trembling.*

ELLIE [*rising*] That was nearer.

CAPTAIN SHOTOVER. The next one will get us. [*He rises*]. Stand by, all hands, for judgement.

THE BURGLAR. Oh my Lordy God! [*He rushes away frantically past the flagstaff into the gloom*].

MRS HUSHABYE [*emerging panting from the darkness*] Who was that running away? [*She comes to Ellie*]. Did you hear the explosions? And the sound in the sky: it's splendid: it's like an orchestra: it's like Beethoven.

ELLIE. By thunder, Hesione: it is Beethoven.

*She and Hesione throw themselves into one another's arms in wild excitement. The light increases.*

MAZZINI [*anxiously*] The light is getting brighter.

NURSE GUINNESS [*looking up at the house*] It's Mr

Hushabye turning on all the lights in the house and tearing down the curtains.

RANDALL. [*rushing in in his pyjamas, distractedly waving a flute*] Ariadne: my soul, my precious, go down to the cellars: I beg and implore you, go down to the cellars!

LADY UTTERWORD [*quite composed in her hammock*] The governor's wife in the cellars with the servants! Really, Randall!

RANDALL. But what shall I do if you are killed?

LADY UTTERWORD. You will probably be killed, too, Randall. Now play your flute to shew that you are not afraid; and be good. Play us Keep the home fires burning.

NURSE GUINNESS [*grimly*] Theyll keep the home fires burning for us: them up there.

RANDALL [*having tried to play*] My lips are trembling. I cant get a sound.

MAZZINI. I hope poor Mangan is safe.

MRS HUSHABYE. He is hiding in the cave in the gravel pit.

CAPTAIN SHOTOVER. My dynamite drew him there. It is the hand of God.

HECTOR [*returning from the house and striding across to his former place*] There is not half light enough. We should be blazing to the skies.

ELLIE [*tense with excitement*] Set fire to the house, Marcus.

MRS HUSHABYE. My house! No.

HECTOR. I thought of that; but it would not be ready in time.

CAPTAIN SHOTOVER. The judgement has come. Courage will not save you; but it will shew that your souls are still alive.

MRS HUSHABYE. Sh-sh! Listen: do you hear it now? It's magnificent.

*The all turn away from the house and look up, listening.*

HECTOR [*gravely*] Miss Dunn: you can do no good here. We of this house are only moths flying into the candle. You had better go down to the cellar.

ELLIE [*scornfully*] I dont think.

MAZZINI. Ellie, dear, there is no disgrace in going to the cellar. An officer would order his soldiers to take cover. Mr Hushabye is behaving like an amateur. Mangan and the burglar are acting very sensibly; and it is they who will survive.

ELLIE. Let them. I shall behave like an amateur. But why should you run any risk?

MAZZINI. Think of the risk those poor fellows up there are running!

NURSE GUINNESS. Think of them, indeed, the murdering blackguards! What next?

*A terrific explosion shakes the earth. They reel back into their seats, or clutch the nearest support. They hear the falling of the shattered glass from the windows.*

MAZZINI. Is anyone hurt?

HECTOR. Where did it fall?

NURSE GUINNESS [*in hideous triumph*] Right in the gravel pit: I seen it. Serve un right! I seen it [*she runs away towards the gravel pit, laughing harshly*].

HECTOR. One husband gone.

CAPTAIN SHOTOVER. Thirty pounds of good dynamite wasted.

MAZZINI. Oh, poor Mangan!

HECTOR. Are you immortal that you need pity him? Our turn next.

*They wait in silence and intense expectation. Hesione and Ellie hold each other's hand tight.*

*A distant explosion is heard.*

MRS HUSHABYE [*relaxing her grip*] Oh! they have passed us.

LADY UTTERWORD. The danger is over, Randall. Go to bed.

CAPTAIN SHOTOVER. Turn in, all hands. The ship is safe. [*He sits down and goes asleep*].

ELLIE [*disappointedly*] Safe!

HECTOR [*disgustedly*] Yes, safe. And how damnably dull the world has become again suddenly! [*He sits down*].

MAZZINI [*sitting down*] I was quite wrong, after all. It is we who have survived; and Mangan and the burglar—

HECTOR. —the two burglars—

LADY UTTERWORD. —the two practical men of business—

MAZZINI. —both gone. And the poor clergyman will have to get a new house.

MRS HUSHABYE. But what a glorious experience! I hope theyll come again tomorrow night.

ELLIE [*radiant at the prospect*] Oh, I hope so.

*Randall at last succeeds in keeping the home fires burning on his flute.*

# "G.B.S." Explains

(A letter to the Editor of *The Observer*,
London, 4 January 1920)

Sir,—In your issue of December 23 you announced, under the heading "Mr. Bernard Shaw on the Peace," that I had contributed an article to "Die Neue Freie Presse" of Vienna. The same news appeared as "G.B.S.'s Outburst" in the "Globe," as "An Arraignment of the British Government" in the "Westminster Gazette," as "G.B.S.'s Message to Vienna" in the "Daily Chronicle," as "Bitter Attack on Britain" in the "Evening Standard," as "Mere Shavian Hot Air" in the "Sunday Chronicle," as "Bernard Shaw's Abuse of Britain" in the "Yorkshire Post," as "More Shavian Ravings" in the "People," as "Bitter Article on British Militarism" in the "Liverpool Post and Mercury," as "Humiliating the Enemy" in the "Newcastle Daily Journal," as "G.B.S. and Peace Revenge" in the "Pall Mall Gazette," as "A G.B.S. Plea for Germany" in the "Sunday Express," and in the "Manchester Guardian" under your own heading.

Now, as these papers are read by their subscribers only, whilst THE OBSERVER is read by everybody, will you allow me to explain in your columns that I have sent nothing to "Die Neue Freie Presse"? Absolutely nothing. What has happened is that some months ago I published a volume of plays entitled "Heartbreak House," which was noticed prominently in all the papers cited above. "Die Neue Freie Presse" has apparently quoted several of its most admired passages, notably a favourite one about President Wilson. And nobody has recognised it.

Such is literary fame. The literary staffs of our news-papers never write on politics; and the political staffs never read books. Moral: To obtain political pub-licity always print your views in German.—Yours, etc.,

G. BERNARD SHAW

# Bernard Shaw on "Heartbreak House"

(*Sunday Herald*, London, 23 October 1921)

I must protest against the practice of asking an author to say a few words about his own play. It is enough to have to write a play without having also to talk about it. Besides, I never say a few words. I always say a great many.

An author should wrap himself up in dignified silence, and leave his play to the judgment of the public, after intimating that he has not read any of the criticisms.

Unfortunately, though I can be dignified on extreme provocation, I cannot be silent. And I read all the notices of my plays.

I have no way of measuring the execution I have done except by the shrieks of the wounded. The people who are not wounded are counted up for me on the box office returns; so I need not worry about them.

I must admit that this has been a specially slaugh-terous occasion. A performance of "Heartbreak House," properly played as it is at the Court, is certainly stupendous value for money. The spectator gets, in acting and in drama, three nights' enter-tainment for the price of one.

[ 183 ]

Nobody can make head or tail of Hector Hushabye, liar, boaster, hero, stylist, Athos and D'Artagnan rolled into a single passionately sincere humbug; and, what is worse, you cannot trust him for a moment not to hold up the mirror to your own silly side.

Even Mr. Nicholson, though he can give charm to Mazzini Dunn's poverty, cannot give it to yours. The house is not Heartbreak House at first: the fly walks into the parlour with the happiest anticipations, and is kept amused until it gets fixed there as by a spell.

Then the heartbreak begins, and gets worse until the house breaks out through the windows, and becomes all England with all England's heart broken.

In vain do the tortured spectators beg for the house without the heartbreak, or to be at least allowed to go home. They are held ruthlessly on the rack until the limit of human endurance is reached after three hours of torment, unable to tear themselves away, though the doors (by County Council regulation) will all open outward at a touch, and the freedom of the street is only twenty steps off.

Why do people stand it? You might as well ask me why did I write it? I am not an unamiable man: I like pleasing people.

I should like to have everyone count the hours spent at my plays as the happiest of their lives. Yet I am mysteriously impelled, like Garibaldi, to offer them starvation, wounds, and death; and they seem impelled to embrace their doom, and even to find a strange joy in their anguish.

The players, too, expert in the art of pleasing, have to do terrible things, like Inquisitors, in spite of themselves. Will the public ever forgive them? The effects are as mad as the cause.

Look at this bundle of printed descriptions of the

play. The same man reviles it in one breath for having no action at all, and in the next for being so intolerably full of action that he nearly died of exhaustion.

Here you may read that the acting is wonderful: there, that it was unbearable. Those who can walk familiarly in high places and see the light beyond the shadow of death are delighted: the rest have only two cries—a cry of rage and a cry for mercy.

The only thoroughly bad criticisms are those in which the sufferer tries to account for the play by some silly theory about the author or about the drama or about human nature.

I am not an explicable phenomenon: neither is "Heartbreak House" nor the playgoers, who so curiously hang on to every word of it for three hours, and do not know whether in "that silly house, that strangely happy house, that agonising house," the happiness or the agony is worst or best.

These things are not to be explained; and I am no more responsible for them than the audience. They happen; and things do not happen in this world for nothing—at least not outside Parliament.

If people must have these experiences, why, they must; and that is all about it. There is no external compulsion to face the ordeal: nobody need go to the Court Theatre unless he feels that his life will be incomplete if he misses the chance. And so it will.

But at least I can warn him that the nearest cinema will prove a less strenuous adventure.

# Heartbreak House

(A letter to the Editor of the *Daily News*,
London, 24 October 1921)

Sir,—In reference to Mr. E. A. Baughan's article on
my play in your issue of Saturday last, may I remon-
strate mildly with your sub-editor? He decorated
the article with the heading, "Why 'Heartbreak
House' is a Failure." Now, the word "failure" has
several connotations, one of which is a commercial
one. If Mr. Selfridge presented Mr. Baughan with a
necktie which did not suit his complexion, and Mr.
Baughan thereupon wrote an article for you on Mr.
Selfridge's bad taste, and your sub-editor headed it
"Failure of Selfridges," the "Daily News" would have
to pay damages on an imagination-staggering scale.

It is no doubt greatly to Mr. J. B. Fagan's credit
that the Court Theatre is so conspicuously an artistic
enterprise that your sub-editor forgets that it has a
commercial side also. But it has; and the consequences of an announcement of failure, if understood
as an announcement that Mr. Fagan is insolvent in
respect of his production of "Heartbreak House,"
may have very annoying consequences, quite apart
from its effect on the playgoing public. I am sure that
this was not intended either by Mr. Baughan or by
your sub-editor, and that they will be anxious to
disclaim any knowledge of the box-office returns,
which, by the way, are open to their inspection, if Mr.
Baughan thinks he can stand them. I am afraid our
playgoers are going to let him down again; but it is
too soon for him to despair.

I must not demur to Mr. Baughan's opinion of my
play: he always goes on like that about me. I feel that

I have darkened his life; and I can only say that I would write the sort of plays he likes for him if I could: it is not ill will, but sheer natural incapacity that restrains me. But he has made a practical suggestion, which I am bound to acknowledge. In the old days, when even the humblest actor in the theatre had what was called a benefit, which meant that he was allowed to sell a handful of tickets to his friends if he could, he was also allowed to enlarge his part for the occasion (so tradition alleges) in this fashion: "My Lord, the carriage waits; and I will take this opportunity of observing that the man who would raise his hand to a woman, save in the way of kindness, is unworthy the name of Briton." At this cue the band would strike up the sailors' hornpipe, and the hero of the benefit would dance it. The play would then resume its normal course.

As I understand Mr. Baughan, he desires that at the Court Theatre Mr. Brember Wills, in the character of Captain Shotover, shall say: "Your father has washed himself; and I will take this opportunity of observing that the war was caused by Germany's natural and unscrupulous desire for expansion at the cost of weaker nations, as she thought, and by the necessity of earning a dividend for the vast capital sunk by herself and Austria in armaments" (cue for the National Anthem).

I must confess that the suggestion appeals enormously to my sense of humour. I believe it would draw all London. I shall go straight down to the theatre, and ask Mr. Brember Wills, as a personal favour to myself and Mr. Baughan, to try it.

G. BERNARD SHAW

# Mr. Shaw's Characteristic
# Speech at Matinee

(*Daily News*, London, 25 November 1921)

There was a crowded and enthusiastic house at the matinee at the Court Theatre, yesterday, of Mr. Bernard Shaw's "Heartbreak House," to which the critics had been invited for the purpose of writing a second and revised notice.

At the close of the performance, which caused constant laughter and applause, there were persistent cries of "Author."

In response, Mr. Fagan appeared apologetically in front of the curtain, and said that Mr. Shaw seemed to have left the theatre.

Mr. Shaw knew better. He stepped smiling to the front of a box, and made this characteristic little speech:

"I am afraid that only half the house can see me, but that is as it should be. An author should never be seen. His place is not on the stage. There are so many people there who are much more attractive.

"It is the business of the author to get out of the way.

"I have enjoyed myself immensely. (Laughter.) I think the performance was an excellent one. (Applause.) I am perfectly certain you have never seen a play like it before.

"Plays like this, with all the work we have put into it, should be seen at least a dozen times. (Laughter.)

"We will keep it going as long as we can. Come again!"

A daring step was then taken. The critics, who could be recognised, explained Mr. Fagan, by "their lofty brows and sackcloth and ashes concealed under furcoats," were invited to a tea party on the stage, presided over by Mr. Shaw himself.

A genial gathering assembled—to the delight of the gallery, who had the opportunity of seeing an author at bay, supported by the actors and actresses of the company and subjected to a running fire of questions.

This dialogue followed:

First Critic (hostile): What is the meaning of the play?

Second Critic (sympathetic): Don't tell him! Any explanation would spoil it.

First Critic (persisting): What is the meaning of the play?

Mr. Shaw (with a gesture of dismay): How can I tell you? I am the author. (Laughter.) But there's the play. If the meaning isn't clear . . .

Second Critic: It's perfectly clear. (Hear, hear.)

Third Critic: How do you explain the failure—or threatened failure—of the play?

Mr. Shaw: I suppose people don't like it.

Mr. Fagan: It isn't the play's fault. It's the public's. (Hear, hear.)

Mr. Shaw: Perhaps some people say, "It's all right . . . there's no need to go at once . . . it's a Shaw play . . . it will run for six months. . . . We'll go in March. But, that won't do. If they want to see it they must come at once. We can't play to a house that's coming in March.

Fourth Critic: Can't you say a few kind words about critics?

Mr. Shaw: I've been one myself. (Laughter.)

And so on—till the stage had to be got ready for the

evening performance, and author and critics were swept away smiling.

## Shaw on the Play's Reception

(*Sunday Express*, London, 11 December 1921)

The incident of the intervention of the Editor of the "Sunday Express" to force the critics to reconsider their verdict on a play, and to save it from what he believed to be unmerited damnation, is unprecedented in my experience, and, as far as I know, in the history of the theatre. I was much touched by it; and I cannot refuse to say a word in his columns as to as much of what has actually happened as the public can conceivably be concerned to know.

To begin, let nobody suppose that the fact that the play concluded its run of seven weeks yesterday is the fault of the Press. If the Press could kill a playwright I should have been a dead man twenty years ago. As a matter of fact I have never had a better Press for a new play; and I cannot recollect one as good. It took the Press a quarter of a century to discover that such a simple little play as "Arms and the Man" is a classic; and in due time the merits of "Heartbreak House" will be proclaimed, if only for the purpose of disparaging its successors. And meanwhile the majority of the notices have ranged from being reasonably favourable to the verge of extravagance in their eulogy.

On the other hand, the sufferers suffered as they have never suffered before. "Heartbreak House" went far higher over their heads than usual; and an unlucky accident behind the scenes on the first night prolonged their agony beyond all endurance.

To men in a desperate hurry to get back to their newspapers and write for the morrow's paper this was extremely trying. It is greatly to the credit of the Press that only two of the representatives of the big dailies broke down under the strain. But these two made a pitiable hullabaloo, which set up many echoes. It undoubtedly affected the box-office for a night or two. But on the ultimate result it had no effect at all. When the victims were persuaded by the Editor of the "Sunday Express" to venture again, they pleaded a speeding-up of the play (almost wholly imaginary) as an excuse for some recanting and hedging as to its attractions; and that, too, affected business for a few nights. But it was the public who decided the fate of the production, which would have been just the same had every paper in London raved about its beauties and its importance as if it were the Washington Conference.

The truth is "Heartbreak House" has done as well as my old successes at the Court Theatre during the memorable management of Mr. J. E. Vedrenne and Mr. Harley Granville-Barker seventeen years ago. That management began by producing what are now called highbrow plays for little runs of sixteen matinées, using the theatre for ordinary commercial purposes at night. When at last it ventured to put the highbrow plays in the evening bill, it was for short runs of from three to six weeks. The public was forewarned that if it did not come within that period it would be too late.

But the plays were not buried at the end of their first few weeks. They were revived again and again, always for short unlimited runs, and thereby nursed into popularity. Plays which began by drawing ten pounds at their first trial were revived later on to full houses. Compared to such beginnings, the beginning of "Heartbreak House" has been a delicious success. And the question will be asked accordingly "Why not apply the old system to it? Why does not Mr. Fagan do to-day what Messrs. Vedrenne and Barker did in 1904?"

The answer is a highly compound one; but the rough commercial side of it is that the expense of running a theatre is very much greater than it was, while prices of admission remain what they were, the increase paid by the public going to the Government as entertainment tax. Nobody dares to raise highbrow prices, because many of the old highbrow purchasers of stalls are now going to the gallery; and the brows of the people who made fortunes out of the war will require building up for some years before they can find any pleasure in such stuff as "Heartbreak House," or feel sure that they are doing the right thing unless they are in a very large and dashingly bediamonded crowd.

Besides, the old experiment did not really pay. It is true that for some years Messrs. Vedrenne and Barker could say that they kept their theatre and their theatre kept them. Not until, in pushing the experiment to a breaking test, they took a larger theatre, and finally had three theatres at work in the West End simultaneously, had they to wind up, solvent, but solvent at the cost of their last penny. We used to say that the experiment did pay its way within the limits of the little Court Theatre. But this statement would not have stood a strict commercial examination. If the incessant work of production done by myself, and to a much greater extent by Mr. Granville-Barker, who had to produce all the plays except mine, and was often left to produce the revivals of these, had been debited in the accounts at the rates then current for such work, and if Mr. Vedrenne had measured the work of managing a new play every three weeks against the usual allowance of one every three months or so, the balance would have shown a heavy deficit every time. And the attempt to make things more remunerative by extending the enterprise finally proved that its limits were not the limits of the Court Theatre, but of the culture of London.

Mr. Granville-Barker's final conclusion, after pushing his experiment to the utmost in every available direction, was that he could keep a classical theatre going if he could have the building free of rent and rates and taxes. This calculation was based on prewar expenses and pre-war rating and taxation. I very much doubt whether it was quite valid then. I am sure it is not valid now. Not that it matters, for there is not the slightest prospect of any British Government or municipality providing a site and theatre and exempting it from rates as an artistic institution.

The London County Council has just decided that theatrical art is not art at all, and that though the screever who depicts Admiral Lord Beatty in coloured chalk on the pavement is an artist, Sir Johnston Forbes-Robertson can claim the same rank only in virtue of his having exhibited at the Royal Academy. His Hamlet does not count. The County Council schools gave the children Shakespeare, and the auditors promptly surcharged the cost because Shakespeare is not educational, having been born in Stratford-on-Avon instead of in Athens.

Private benefactors cannot give such an endowment. Lord Howard de Walden, Lord Lytton, Lord Latham, Lord Willoughby de Broke, Sir Carl Meyer,

Miss Horniman, and others have given money and work to keep theatrical and musical art alive at the top as well as kicking at the bottom; but the situation remains desperate. In short, England is not Germany. We have municipal morgues and national race-courses, but no municipal theatres and no national one.

And so "Heartbreak House" has the shutters up. It has done just as much business—or as little, as I should prefer to put it—as plays of its kind have ever done, or are likely to do, under existing conditions.

The performances have been extraordinarily successful with that section of the public which is within their range. But that section is not large enough to fill a theatre for more than three or four weeks. And how are we who do the work to live on that? Am I to ask a first-rate company to work devotedly for me at a difficult and very nervous job for two months and get three weeks' salary for it? Am I to put in a month's work as producer, to say nothing of writing the play, for three weeks' fees?

And what is the manager to do? A successful play must not only pay its own way, but pay for several unsuccessful ones as well; and that cannot be done in three weeks. Mr. Fagan cannot, with all his devotion to drama for the intelligentsia, carry on on such terms. I cannot carry on. The artists who filled "Heartbreak House" with real people for us cannot carry on. They must fall back on more popular work or starve. I must fall back on Russia, from which I have just been notified of a credit of two shillings (representing heaven knows how many million roubles); on Germany and Austria and Italy, from which I receive mountains of marks and crowns and lire, which amount to a few shillings more; on Spain and Sweden; on America, which tolerated "Heartbreak

House" for nearly four months; and, above all, on alternative and more lucrative methods of employing my pen.

Twenty years ago I made a desperate effort to persuade several of our ablest writers of fiction to do something for the stage. They knew better. No one who is not dæmoniacally urged by an irresistible inward force, as I suppose Barrie, Galsworthy, Drinkwater, Dunsany, and the rest are, practises my trade when he has already mastered the trade of Fielding and Dickens.

One funny illustration of the way in which the public fail to connect literary and artistic work with the necessary bread and butter is the budget of letters and paragraphs in which I have been asked why I did not discuss "Heartbreak House" with the critics at the "Sunday Express" matinée.

Let me answer by a well-worn theatrical story. Charles Mathews once presented a hotel waiter with an order for the theatre as a supplementary tip. Next morning he asked him how he liked the play. "Oh, the play was all right, sir," said the waiter, "but who is to pay me for my time?"

And that is just what the critics would say if, after finishing work for which they are paid, they were asked to amuse an audience by discussing their notices with the authors and painters and composers they criticise—if, indeed, an audience could be got together for so dismal an entertainment. Having been a critic myself, I know what I should have said to such a proposal, and I have no reason to suppose that the time of Mr. John Francis Hope, Mr. Desmond McCarthy, Mr. Walkley, Mr. Courtney, Mr. William Archer, Mr. St. John Ervine, Mr. Baughan, Mr. O'Carroll, Mr. Archibald Haddon, and the rest is any less valuable than mine was, or that they would stand being told, like naughty schoolboys, to do their task over again. Such things are not done. As it was, some of them took the opportunity to give the play another lift, and for this I am sincerely grateful to them; but they know too well how little a play can be made or unmade by the Press.

Like all the great pushes of the war, "Heartbreak House" nearly succeeded. The congregation at the Court (for the same people come again and again to this sort of play) contributed about five-sixths of the cost of running the play, and would apparently have gone on doing so for years without any appreciable diminution of its enthusiasm. But as the odd sixth would finally have sent Mr. Fagan further down the King's-road to the Fulham Workhouse, he had at last to admit that my forecast was right, and that the British public had advanced very little since the time when nothing that I and Mr. Archer could do by our championship of Ibsen could, after the first great shock of "A Doll's House," keep a play of his on the London stage longer than a fortnight without loss.

To meet that loss an endowed theatre is needed; yet the vain appeal of the Shakespeare Memorial National Theatre has shown that you can get money in England for sport, for religion, for party politics, for charity, and even for nothing discoverable (as in the case of the Prince of Wales' Fund), but not for art, least of all the art of the theatre. We are in that respect barbarians, which means, not that we are indifferent to high art, but that we actively dislike it. We stay away from the Court Theatre just as we stay away from Mr. Goossens' extraordinarily interesting and important orchestral concerts, because we would be unhappy there. You cannot say that Mr. Goossens' concerts are a failure when you hear the audience wildly encoring Bach's Organ Fugue in C minor, scored by Elgar, incomparably the greatest master of the orchestra in the world, as well as England's one star of the first magnitude in composition; but count the empty seats, and find out what the whole costs, and what the band costs, and you will see that some-body must be losing a lot of money for the sake of English culture. And instead of feeling grateful to him you will dismiss him from your thoughts as an eccen-tric fool; and he will carefully conceal his name until some horse of his rehabilitates it by winning the Derby.

As for me, I am wondering whether I can pay my taxes at the end of the month without selling out. If I can it will certainly not be by writing for the classical end of the British stage.

# Augustus Does His Bit:
# A True-to-Life Farce

WITH

*Statement for the Drama Editor of the*
Evening Standard

Composition begun 12 August 1916; completed 23 August 1916. Published in *Heartbreak House, Great Catherine, & Playlets of the War*, 1919. First presented by the Stage Society at the Royal Court Theatre, London, on 21 January 1917; repeated on 22 January.

Lord Augustus Highcastle   *F. B. J. Sharp*
Horatio Floyd Beamish   *Charles Rock*
A Lady   *Lalla Vandervelde*

Period—1916

Scene—*The Mayor's Parlor in the Town Hall of Little Pifflington*

I wish to express my gratitude for certain good offices which Augustus secured for me in January 1917. I had been invited to visit the theatre of war in Flanders by the Commander-in-Chief: an invitation which was, under the circumstances, a summons to duty. Thus I had occasion to spend some days in procuring the necessary passports and other official facilities for my journey. It happened just then that the Stage Society gave a performance of this little play. It opened the heart of every official to me. I have always been treated with distinguished consideration in my contacts with bureaucracy during the war; but on this occasion I found myself *persona grata* in the highest degree. There was only one word when the formalities were disposed of; and that was "We are up against Augustus all day." The shewing-up of Augustus scandalized one or two innocent and patriotic critics who regarded the prowess of the British army as inextricably bound up with Highcastle prestige. But our Government departments knew better: their problem was how to win the war with Augustus on their backs, well-meaning, brave, patriotic, but obstructively fussy, self-important, imbecile, and disastrous.

Save for the satisfaction of being able to laugh at Augustus in the theatre, nothing, as far as I know, came of my dramatic reduction of him to absurdity. Generals, admirals, Prime Ministers and Controllers, not to mention Emperors, Kaisers and Tsars, were scrapped remorselessly at home and abroad, for their sins or services, as the case might be. But Augustus stood like the Eddystone in a storm, and stands so to this day. He gave us his word that he was indispensable; and we took it.

*The Mayor's parlor in the Town Hall of Little Piffling-*
*ton. Lord Augustus Highcastle, a distinguished member*
*of the governing class, in the uniform of a colonel, and*
*very well preserved at forty-five, is comfortably seated*
*at a writing table with his heels on it, reading The*
*Morning Post. The door faces him, a little to his left,*
*at the other side of the room. The window is behind him.*
*In the fireplace, a gas stove. On the table a bell button*
*and a telephone. Portraits of past Mayors, in robes and*
*gold chains, adorn the walls. An elderly clerk with a*
*short white beard and whiskers, and a very red nose,*
*shuffles in.*

AUGUSTUS [*hastily putting aside his paper and replacing his feet on the floor*] Hullo! Who are you?

THE CLERK. The staff [*a slight impediment in his
speech adds to the impression of incompetence produced
by his age and appearance*].

AUGUSTUS. You the staff! What do you mean, man?

THE CLERK. What I say. There aint anybody else.

AUGUSTUS. Tush! Where are the others?

THE CLERK. At the front.

AUGUSTUS. Quite right. Most proper. Why arnt you
at the front?

THE CLERK. Over age. Fiftyseven.

AUGUSTUS. But you can still do your bit. Many an
older man is in the G.R.'s, or volunteering for home
defence.

THE CLERK. I have volunteered.

AUGUSTUS. Then why are you not in uniform?

THE CLERK. They said they wouldnt have me if I
was given away with a pound of tea. Told me to go
home and not be an old silly. [*A sense of unbearable*

*wrong, till now only smouldering in him, bursts into flame*]. Young Bill Knight, that I took with me, got two and sevenpence. I got nothing. Is it justice? This country is going to the dogs, if you ask me.

AUGUSTUS [*rising indignantly*] I do not ask you, sir; I will not allow you to say such things in my presence. Our statesmen are the greatest known to history. Our generals are invincible. Our army is the admiration of the world. [*Furiously*] How dare you tell me that the country is going to the dogs!

THE CLERK. Why did they give young Bill Knight two and sevenpence, and not give me even my tram fare? Do you call that being great statesmen? As good as robbing me, I call it.

AUGUSTUS. Thats enough, Leave the room. [*He sits down and takes up his pen, settling himself to work. The clerk shuffles to the door. Augustus adds, with cold politeness*] Send me the Secretary.

THE CLERK. I'm the Secretary. I cant leave the room and send myself to you at the same time, can I?

AUGUSTUS. Dont be insolent. Where is the gentleman I have been corresponding with: Mr Horatio Floyd Beamish?

THE CLERK [*returning and bowing*] Here. Me.

AUGUSTUS. You! Ridiculous. What right have you to call yourself by a pretentious name of that sort?

THE CLERK. You may drop the Horatio Floyd. Beamish is good enough for me.

AUGUSTUS. Is there nobody else to take my instructions?

THE CLERK. It's me or nobody. And for two pins I'd chuck it. Dont you drive me too far. Old uns like me is up in the world now.

AUGUSTUS. If we were not at war, I should discharge you on the spot for disrespectful behaviour.

But England is in danger; and I cannot think of my personal dignity at such a moment. [*Shouting at him*] Dont you think of yours, either, worm that you are; or I'll have you arrested under the Defence of the Realm Act, double quick.

THE CLERK. What do I care about the realm? They done me out of two and seven—

AUGUSTUS. Oh, damn your two and seven! Did you receive my letters?

THE CLERK. Yes.

AUGUSTUS. I addressed a meeting here last night— went straight to the platform from the train. I wrote to you that I should expect you to be present and report yourself. Why did you not do so?

THE CLERK. The police wouldnt let me on the platform.

AUGUSTUS. Did you tell them who you were?

THE CLERK. They knew who I was. Thats why they wouldnt let me up.

AUGUSTUS. This is too silly for anything. This town wants waking up. I made the best recruiting speech I ever made in my life; and not a man joined.

THE CLERK. What did you expect? You told them our gallant fellows is falling at the rate of a thousand a day in the big push. Dying for Little Pifflington, you says. Come and take their places, you says. That aint the way to recruit.

AUGUSTUS. But I expressly told them their widows would have pensions.

THE CLERK. I heard you. Would have been all right if it had been the widows you wanted to get round.

AUGUSTUS [*rising angrily*] This town is inhabited by dastards. I say it with a full sense of responsibility, dastards! They call themselves Englishmen; and they are afraid to fight.

[ 205 ]

THE CLERK. Afraid to fight! You should see them on a Saturday night.

AUGUSTUS. Yes: they fight one another; but they wont fight the Germans.

THE CLERK. They got grudges again one another: how can they have grudges again the Huns that they never saw? Theyve no imagination: thats what it is. Bring the Huns here; and theyll quarrel with them fast enough.

AUGUSTUS [*returning to his seat with a grunt of disgust*] Mf! Theyll have them here if theyre not careful. [*Seated*] Have you carried out my orders about the war saving?

THE CLERK. Yes.

AUGUSTUS. The allowance of petrol has been reduced by three quarters?

THE CLERK. It has.

AUGUSTUS. And you have told the motor-car people to come here and arrange to start munition work now that their motor business is stopped?

THE CLERK. It aint stopped. Theyre busier than ever.

AUGUSTUS. Busy at what?

THE CLERK. Making small cars.

AUGUSTUS. New cars!

THE CLERK. The old cars only do twelve miles to the gallon. Everybody has to have a car that will do thirtyfive now.

AUGUSTUS. Cant they take the train?

THE CLERK. There aint no trains now. Theyve tore up the rails and sent them to the front.

AUGUSTUS. Psha!

THE CLERK. Well, we have to get about somehow.

AUGUSTUS. This is perfectly monstrous. Not in the least what I intended.

THE CLERK. Hell—

AUGUSTUS. Sir!

THE CLERK [*explaining*] Hell, they says, is paved with good intentions.

AUGUSTUS [*springing to his feet*] Do you mean to insinuate that hell is paved with my good intentions—with the good intentions of His Majesty's Government?

THE CLERK. I dont mean to insinuate anything until the Defence of the Realm Act is repealed. It aint safe.

AUGUSTUS. They told me that this town had set an example to all England in the matter of economy. I came down here to promise the Mayor a knighthood for his exertions.

THE CLERK. The Mayor! Where do *I* come in?

AUGUSTUS. You dont come in. You go out. This is a fool of a place. I'm greatly disappointed. Deeply disappointed. [*Flinging himself back into his chair*] Disgusted.

THE CLERK. What more can we do? Weve shut up everything. The picture gallery is shut. The museum is shut. The theatres and picture shows is shut: I havnt seen a movy picture for six months.

AUGUSTUS. Man, man: do you want to see picture shows when the Hun is at the gate?

THE CLERK [*mournfully*] I dont now, though it drove me melancholy mad at first. I was on the point of taking a pennorth of rat poison—

AUGUSTUS. Why didnt you?

THE CLERK. Because a friend advised me to take to drink instead. That saved my life, though it makes me very poor company in the mornings, as [*hiccuping*] perhaps youve noticed.

AUGUSTUS. Well, upon my soul! You are not ashamed to stand there and confess yourself a disgusting drunkard.

THE CLERK. Well, what of it? We're at war now; and everything's changed. Besides, I should lose my job here if I stood drinking at the bar. I'm a respectable man and must buy my drink and take it home with me. And they wont serve me with less than a quart. If youd told me before the war that I could get through a quart of whisky in a day, I shouldnt have believed you. Thats the good of war: it brings out powers in a man that he never suspected himself capable of. You said so yourself in your speech last night.

AUGUSTUS. I did not know that I was talking to an imbecile. You ought to be ashamed of yourself. There must be an end of this drunken slacking. I'm going to establish a new order of things here. I shall come down every morning before breakfast until things are properly in train. Have a cup of coffee and two rolls for me here every morning at half-past ten.

THE CLERK. You cant have no rolls. The only baker that baked rolls was a Hun; and he's been interned.

AUGUSTUS. Quite right, too. And was there no Englishman to take his place?

THE CLERK. There was. But he was caught spying; and they took him up to London and shot him.

AUGUSTUS. Shot an Englishman!

THE CLERK. Well, it stands to reason if the Germans wanted a spy they wouldnt employ a German that everybody would suspect, dont it?

AUGUSTUS [*rising again*] Do you mean to say, you scoundrel, that an Englishman is capable of selling his country to the enemy for gold?

THE CLERK. Not as a general thing I wouldnt say it; but theres men here would sell their own mothers for two coppers if they got the chance.

AUGUSTUS. Beamish: it's an ill bird that fouls its own nest.

THE CLERK. It wasnt me that let Little Pifflington get foul. *I* dont belong to the governing classes. I only tell you why you cant have no rolls.

AUGUSTUS [*intensely irritated*] Can you tell me where I can find an intelligent being to take my orders?

THE CLERK. One of the street sweepers used to teach in the school until it was shut up for the sake of economy. Will he do?

AUGUSTUS. What! You mean to tell me that when the lives of the gallant fellows in our trenches, and the fate of the British Empire, depend on our keeping up the supply of shells, you are wasting money on sweeping the streets?

THE CLERK. We have to. We dropped it for a while; but the infant death rate went up something frightful.

AUGUSTUS. What matters the death rate of Little Pifflington in a moment like this? Think of our gallant soldiers, not of your squalling infants.

THE CLERK. If you want soldiers you must have children. You cant buy em in boxes, like toy soldiers.

AUGUSTUS. Beamish: the long and the short of it is, you are no patriot. Go downstairs to your office; and have that gas stove taken away and replaced by an ordinary grate. The Board of Trade has urged on me the necessity for economizing gas.

THE CLERK. Our orders from the Minister of Munitions is to use gas instead of coal, because it saves material. Which is it to be?

AUGUSTUS [*bawling furiously at him*] Both! Dont criticize your orders: obey them. Yours not to reason why: yours but to do and die. Thats war. [*Cooling down*] Have you anything else to say?

THE CLERK. Yes: I want a rise.

AUGUSTUS [*reeling against the table in his horror*] A rise! Horatio Floyd Beamish: do you know that we are at war?

THE CLERK [*feebly ironical*] I have noticed something about it in the papers. Heard you mention it once or twice, now I come to think of it.

AUGUSTUS. Our gallant fellows are dying in the trenches; and you want a rise!

THE CLERK. What are they dying for? To keep me alive, aint it? Well, whats the good of that if I'm dead of hunger by the time they come back?

AUGUSTUS. Everybody else is making sacrifices without a thought of self; and you—

THE CLERK. Not half, they aint. Wheres the baker's sacrifice? Wheres the coal merchant's? Wheres the butcher's? Charging me double: thats how they sacrifice themselves. Well, I want to sacrifice myself that way too. Just double next Saturday: double and not a penny less; or no secretary for you [*he stiffens himself shakily, and makes resolutely for the door*].

AUGUSTUS [*looking after him contemptuously*] Go: miserable pro-German.

THE CLERK [*rushing back and facing him*] Who are you calling a pro-German?

AUGUSTUS. Another word, and I charge you under the Act with discouraging me. Go

*The clerk blenches and goes out, cowed.*

*The telephone rings.*

AUGUSTUS [*taking up the telephone receiver*] Hallo . . . Yes: who are you? . . . oh, Blueloo, is it? . . . Yes: theres nobody in the room: fire away . . . What? . . . A spy! . . . A woman! . . . Yes: I brought it down with me. Do you suppose I'm such a fool as to let it out of my hands? Why, it gives a list of all our anti-aircraft emplacements from Ramsgate to Skegness.

The Germans would give a million for it—what? . . .
But how could she possibly know about it? I havnt
mentioned it to a soul, except, of course, dear Lucy
. . . . Oh, Toto and Lady Popham and that lot: they
dont count: theyre all right. I mean that I havnt
mentioned it to any Germans. . . . Pooh! Dont you
be nervous, old chap. I know you think me a fool: but
I'm not such a fool as all that. If she tries to get it out
of me I'll have her in the Tower before you ring up
again. [*The clerk returns*]. Sh-sh! Somebody's just
come in: ring off. Goodbye. [*He hangs up the receiver*].

THE CLERK. Are you engaged? [*His manner is
strangely softened*].

AUGUSTUS. What business is that of yours? However,
if you will take the trouble to read the society papers
for this week, you will see that I am engaged to the
Honorable Lucy Popham, youngest daughter of—

THE CLERK. That aint what I mean. Can you see a
female?

AUGUSTUS. Of course I can see a female as easily as a
male. Do you suppose I'm blind?

THE CLERK. You dont seem to follow me, somehow.
Theres a female downstairs: what you might call a
lady. She wants to know can you see her if I let her up.

AUGUSTUS. Oh, you mean am I disengaged. Tell
the lady I have just received news of the greatest importance which will occupy my entire attention for the
rest of the day, and that she must write for an appoint-
ment.

THE CLERK. I'll ask her to explain her business to me.
*I* aint above talking to a handsome young female when
I get the chance [*going*].

AUGUSTUS. Stop. Does she seem to be a person of
consequence?

THE CLERK. A regular marchioness, if you ask me.

AUGUSTUS. Hm! Beautiful, did you say?

THE CLERK. A human chrysanthemum, sir, believe me.

AUGUSTUS. It will be extremely inconvenient for me to see her; but the country is in danger; and we must not consider our own comfort. Think how our gallant fellows are suffering in the trenches! Shew her up. [*The clerk makes for the door, whistling the latest popular love ballad*]. Stop whistling instantly, sir. This is not a casino.

THE CLERK. Aint it? You just wait til you see her. [*He goes out*].

*Augustus produces a mirror, a comb, and a pot of moustache pomade from the drawer of the writing-table, and sits down before the mirror to put some touches to his toilet.*

*The clerk returns, devotedly ushering a very attractive lady, brilliantly dressed, She has a dainty wallet hanging from her wrist. Augustus hastily covers up his toilet apparatus with The Morning Post, and rises in an attitude of pompous condescension.*

THE CLERK [*to Augustus*] Here she is. [*To the lady*] May I offer you a chair, lady? [*He places a chair at the writing-table opposite Augustus, and steals out on tiptoe*].

AUGUSTUS. Be seated, madam.

THE LADY [*sitting down*] Are you Lord Augustus Highcastle?

AUGUSTUS [*sitting also*] Madam: I am.

THE LADY [*with awe*] The great Lord Augustus?

AUGUSTUS. I should not dream of describing myself so, madam; but no doubt I have impressed my countrymen—and [*bowing gallantly*] may I say my countrywomen—as having some exceptional claims to their consideration.

THE LADY [*emotionally*] What a beautiful voice you have!

AUGUSTUS. What you hear, madam, is the voice of my country, which now takes a sweet and noble tone even in the harsh mouth of high officialism.

THE LADY. Please go on. You express yourself so wonderfully.

AUGUSTUS. It would be strange indeed if, after sitting on thirty-seven Royal Commissions, mostly as chairman, I had not mastered the art of public expression. Even the Radical papers have paid me the high compliment of declaring that I am never more impressive than when I have nothing to say.

THE LADY. I never read the Radical papers. All I can tell you is that what we women admire in you is not the politician, but the man of action, the heroic warrior, the *beau sabreur*.

AUGUSTUS [*gloomily*] Madam, I beg! Please! My military exploits are not a pleasant subject, unhappily.

THE LADY. Oh, I know, I know. How shamefully you have been treated! What ingratitude! But the country is with you. The women are with you. Oh, do you think all our hearts did not throb and all our nerves thrill when we heard how, when you were ordered to occupy that terrible quarry in Hulluch, and you swept into it at the head of your men like a sea-god riding on a tidal wave, you suddenly sprang over the top shouting "To Berlin! Forward!"; dashed at the German army single-handed; and were cut off and made prisoner by the Huns?

AUGUSTUS. Yes, madam; and what was my reward? They said I had disobeyed orders, and sent me home. Have they forgotten Nelson in the Baltic? Has any British battle ever been won except by a bold individual initiative? I say nothing of professional jealousy:

it exists in the army as elsewhere; but it is a bitter thought to me that the recognition denied me by my own country—or rather by the Radical cabal in the Cabinet which pursues my family with rancorous class hatred—that this recognition, I say, came to me at the hands of an enemy—of a rank Prussian.

THE LADY. You dont say so!

AUGUSTUS. How else should I be here instead of starving to death in Ruhleben? Yes, madam: the Colonel of the Pomeranian regiment which captured me, after learning what I had done, and conversing for an hour with me on European politics and military strategy, declared that nothing would induce him to deprive my country of my services, and set me free. I offered, of course, to procure the release in exchange of a German officer of equal quality; but he would not hear of it. He was kind enough to say he could not believe that a German officer answering to that description existed. [*With emotion*] I had my first taste of the ingratitude of my own country as I made my way back to our lines. A shot from our front trench struck me in the head. I still carry the flattened projectile as a trophy [*he throws it on the table: the noise it makes testifies to its weight*]. Had it penetrated to the brain I might never have sat on another Royal Commission. Fortunately we have strong heads, we Highcastles. Nothing has ever penetrated to our brains.

THE LADY. How thrilling! How simple! And how tragic! But you will forgive England? Remember: England! Forgive her.

AUGUSTUS [*with gloomy magnanimity*] It will make no difference whatever to my services to my country. Though she slay me, yet will I, if not exactly trust her, at least take my part in her government. I am ever at my country's call. Whether it be the embassy in a leading European capital, a governor-generalship in the tropics, or my humble mission here to make Little Pifflington do its bit, I am always ready for the sacrifice. Whilst England remains England, wherever there is a public job to be done you will find a Highcastle sticking to it. And now, madam, enough of my tragic personal history. You have called on business. What can I do for you?

THE LADY. You have relatives at the Foreign Office, have you not?

AUGUSTUS [*haughtily*] Madam: the Foreign Office is staffed by my relatives exclusively.

THE LADY. Has the Foreign Office warned you that you are being pursued by a female spy who is determined to obtain possession of a certain list of gun emplacements—

AUGUSTUS [*interrupting her somewhat loftily*] All that is perfectly well known to this department, madam.

THE LADY [*surprised and rather indignant*] Is it? Who told you? Was it one of your German brothers-in-law?

AUGUSTUS [*injured, remonstrating*] I have only three German brothers-in-law, madam. Really, from your tone, one would suppose that I had several. Pardon my sensitiveness on that subject; but reports are continually being circulated that I have been shot as a traitor in the courtyard of the Ritz Hotel simply because I have German brothers-in-law. [*With feeling*] If you had a German brother-in-law, madam, you would know that nothing else in the world produces so strong an anti-German feeling. Life affords no keener pleasure than finding a brother-in-law's name in the German casualty list.

THE LADY. Nobody knows that better than I. Wait until you hear what I have come to tell you: you will understand me as no one else could. Listen. This spy, this woman—

AUGUSTUS [*all attention*] Yes?

THE LADY. She is a German. A Hun.

AUGUSTUS. Yes, yes. She would be. Continue.

THE LADY. She is my sister-in-law.

AUGUSTUS [*deferentially*] I see you are well connected, madam. Proceed.

THE LADY. Need I add that she is my bitterest enemy?

AUGUSTUS. May I—[*he proffers his hand. They shake, fervently. From this moment onward Augustus becomes more and more confidential, gallant, and charming*].

THE LADY. Quite so. Well, she is an intimate friend of your brother at the War Office, Hungerford Highcastle: Blueloo as you call him: I dont know why.

AUGUSTUS [*explaining*] He was originally called The Singing Oyster, because he sang drawing-room ballads with such an extraordinary absence of expression. He was then called the Blue Point for a season or two. Finally he became Blueloo.

THE LADY. Oh, indeed: I didnt know. Well, Blueloo is simply infatuated with my sister-in-law; and he has rashly let out to her that this list is in your possession. He forgot himself because he was in a towering rage at its being entrusted to you: his language was terrible. He ordered all the guns to be shifted at once.

AUGUSTUS. What on earth did he do that for?

THE LADY. I cant imagine. But this I know. She made a bet with him that she would come down here and obtain possession of that list and get clean away into the street with it. He took the bet on condition that she brought it straight back to him at the War Office.

AUGUSTUS. Good heavens! And you mean to tell me that Blueloo was such a dolt as to believe that she could succeed? Does he take me for a fool?

THE LADY. Oh, impossible! He is jealous of your intellect. The bet is an insult to you: dont you feel that? After what you have done for our country—

AUGUSTUS. Oh, never mind that. It is the idiocy of the thing I look at. He'll lose his bet; and serve him right!

THE LADY. You feel sure you will be able to resist the siren? I warn you she is very fascinating.

AUGUSTUS. You need have no fear, madam. I hope she will come and try it on. Fascination is a game that two can play at. For centuries the younger sons of the Highcastles have had nothing to do but fascinate attractive females when they were not sitting on Royal Commissions or on duty at Knightsbridge barracks. By Gad, madam, if the siren comes here she will meet her match.

THE LADY. I feel that. But if she fails to seduce you—

AUGUSTUS [*blushing*] Madam!

THE LADY [*continuing*]—from your allegiance—

AUGUSTUS. Oh, that!

THE LADY.—she will resort to fraud, to force, to anything. She will burgle your office: she will have you attacked and garotted at night in the street.

AUGUSTUS. Pooh! I'm not afraid.

THE LADY. Oh, your courage will only tempt you into danger. She may get the list after all. It is true that the guns are moved. But she would win her bet.

AUGUSTUS [*cautiously*] You did not say that the guns were moved. You said that Blueloo had ordered them to be moved.

THE LADY. Well, that is the same thing, isnt it?

AUGUSTUS. Not quite—at the War Office. No doubt those guns will be moved: possibly even before the end of the war.

THE LADY. Then you think they are there still! But

if the German War Office gets the list—and she will copy it before she gives it back to Blueloo, you may depend on it—all is lost.

AUGUSTUS [*lazily*] Well, I should not go as far as that. [*Lowering his voice*] Will you swear to me not to repeat what I am going to say to you; for if the British public knew that I had said it, I should be at once hounded down as a pro-German.

THE LADY. I will be silent as the grave. I swear it.

AUGUSTUS [*again taking it easily*] Well, our people have for some reason made up their minds that the German War Office is everything that our War Office is not—that it carries promptitude, efficiency, and organization to a pitch of completeness and perfection that must be, in my opinion, destructive to the happiness of the staff. My own view—which you are pledged, remember, not to betray—is that the German War Office is no better than any other War Office. I found that opinion on my observation of the characters of my brothers-in-law: one of whom, by the way, is on the German general staff. I am not at all sure that this list of gun emplacements would receive the smallest attention. You see, there are always so many more important things to be attended to. Family matters, and so on, you understand.

THE LADY. Still, if a question were asked in the House of Commons—

AUGUSTUS. The great advantage of being at war, madam, is that nobody takes the slightest notice of the House of Commons. No doubt it is sometimes necessary for a Minister to soothe the more seditious members of that assembly by giving a pledge or two; but the War Office takes no notice of such things.

THE LADY [*staring at him*] Then you think this list of gun emplacements doesnt matter!!

[ 218 ]

AUGUSTUS. By no means, madam. It matters very much indeed. If this spy were to obtain possession of the list, Blueloo would tell the story at every dinner-table in London; and—

THE LADY. And you might lose your post. Of course.

AUGUSTUS [*amazed and indignant*] I lose my post! What are you dreaming about, madam? How could I possibly be spared? There are hardly Highcastles enough at present to fill half the posts created by this war. No: Blueloo would not go that far. He is at least a gentleman. But I should be chaffed; and, frankly, I dont like being chaffed.

THE LADY. Of course not. Who does? It would never do. Oh never, never.

AUGUSTUS. I'm glad you see it in that light. And now, as a measure of security, I shall put that list in my pocket. [*He begins searching vainly from drawer to drawer in the writing-table*]. Where on earth—? What the dickens did I—? Thats very odd: I— Where the deuce—? I thought I had put it in the— Oh, here it is! No: this is Lucy's last letter.

THE LADY [*elegiacally*] Lucy's Last Letter! What a title for a picture play!

AUGUSTUS [*delighted*] Yes: it is, isnt it? Lucy appeals to the imagination like no other woman. By the way [*handing over the letter*] I wonder could you read it for me? Lucy is a darling girl; but I really cant read her writing. In London I get the office typist to decipher it and make me a typed copy; but here there is nobody.

THE LADY [*puzzling over it*] It is really almost illegible. I think the beginning is meant for "Dearest Gus."

AUGUSTUS [*eagerly*] Yes: that is what she usually calls me. Please go on.

THE LADY [*trying to decipher it*] "What a"—"what a"—oh yes: "what a forgetful old"—something—"you are!" I cant make out the word.

AUGUSTUS [*greatly interested*] Is it blighter? That is a favorite expression of hers.

THE LADY. I think so. At all events it begins with a B. [*Reading*] "What a forgetful old"—[*she is interrupted by a knock at the door*].

AUGUSTUS [*impatiently*] Come in. [*The clerk enters, clean shaven and in khaki, with an official paper and an envelope in his hand*]. What is this ridiculous mummery, sir?

THE CLERK [*coming to the table and exhibiting his uniform to both*] Theyve passed me. The recruiting officer come for me. Ive had my two and seven.

AUGUSTUS [*rising wrathfully*] I shall not permit it. What do they mean by taking my office staff? Good God! they will be taking our hunt servants next. [*Confronting the clerk*] What did the man mean? What did he say?

THE CLERK. He said that now you was on the job we'd want another million men, and he was going to take the old-age pensioners or anyone he could get.

AUGUSTUS. And did you dare knock at my door and interrupt my business with this lady to repeat this man's ineptitudes?

THE CLERK. No. I come because the waiter from the hotel brought this paper. You left it on the coffee-room breakfast-table this morning.

THE LADY [*intercepting it*] It is the list. Good heavens!

THE CLERK [*proffering the envelope*] He says he thinks this is the envelope belonging to it.

THE LADY [*snatching the envelope also*] Yes! Addressed to you. Lord Augustus! [*Augustus comes back to the table to look at it*] Oh, how imprudent! Everybody would guess its importance with your name on it. Fortunately I have some letters of my own here [*opening her wallet*]. Why not hide it in one of my envelopes? then no one will dream that the enclosure is of any political value. [*Taking out a letter, she crosses the room towards the window, whispering to Augustus as she passes him*] Get rid of that man.

AUGUSTUS [*haughtily approaching the clerk, who humorously makes a paralytic attempt to stand at attention*] Have you any further business here, pray?

THE CLERK. Am I to give the waiter anything; or will you do it yourself?

AUGUSTUS. Which waiter is it? The English one?

THE CLERK. No: the one that calls hisself a Swiss. Shouldnt wonder if he'd made a copy of that paper.

AUGUSTUS. Keep your impertinent surmises to yourself, sir. Remember that you are in the army now; and let me have no more of your civilian insubordination. Attention! Left turn! Quick march!

THE CLERK [*stolidly*] I dunno what you mean.

AUGUSTUS. Go to the guard-room and report yourself for disobeying orders. Now do you know what I mean?

THE CLERK. Now look here. I aint going to argue with you—

AUGUSTUS. Nor I with you. Out with you.

*He seizes the clerk, and rushes him through the door. The moment the lady is left alone, she snatches a sheet of official paper from the stationery rack; folds it so that it resembles the list; compares the two to see that they look exactly alike; whips the list into her wallet; and substitutes the fascimile for it. Then she listens for the return of Augustus. A crash is heard, as of the clerk falling downstairs.*

*Augustus returns and is about to close the door when the voice of the clerk is heard from below:*

THE CLERK. I'll have the law of you for this, I will.

AUGUSTUS [*shouting down to him*] Theres no more law for you, you scoundrel. Youre a soldier now. [*He shuts the door and comes to the lady*]. Thank heaven, the war has given us the upper hand of these fellows at last. Excuse my violence; but discipline is absolutely necessary in dealing with the lower middle classes.

THE LADY. Serve the insolent creature right! Look! I have found you a beautiful envelope for the list, an unmistakeable lady's envelope. [*She puts the sham list into her envelope and hands it to him*].

AUGUSTUS. Excellent. Really very clever of you. [*Slyly*] Come: would you like to have a peep at the list [*beginning to take the blank paper from the envelope*]?

THE LADY [*on the brink of detection*] No no. Oh, please, no.

AUGUSTUS. Why? It wont bite you [*drawing it out further*].

THE LADY [*snatching at his hand*] Stop. Remember: if there should be an inquiry, you must be able to swear that you never shewed that list to a mortal soul.

AUGUSTUS. Oh, that is a mere form. If you are really curious—

THE LADY. I am not. I couldnt bear to look at it. One of my dearest friends was blown to pieces by an aircraft gun; and since then I have never been able to think of one without horror.

AUGUSTUS. You mean it was a real gun, and actually went off. How sad! how sad! [*He pushes the sham list back into the envelope, and pockets it*].

THE LADY. Ah! [*great sigh of relief*]. And now, Lord Augustus, I have taken up too much of your valuable time  Goodbye.

[ 222 ]

AUGUSTUS. What! Must you go?

THE LADY. You are so busy.

AUGUSTUS. Yes; but not before lunch, you know. I
never can do much before lunch. And I'm no good at
all in the afternoon. From five to six is my real working time. Must you really go?

THE LADY. I must, really. I have done my business
very satisfactorily. Thank you ever so much [*she
proffers her hand*].

AUGUSTUS [*shaking it affectionately as he leads her to
the door, but first pressing the bell button with his left
hand*] Goodbye. Goodbye. So sorry to lose you. Kind
of you to come; but there was no real danger. You
see, my dear little lady, all this talk about war saving,
and secrecy, and keeping the blinds down at night,
and so forth, is all very well; but unless it's carried out
with intelligence, believe me, you may waste a pound
to save a penny; you may let out all sorts of secrets
to the enemy; you may guide the Zeppelins right
on to your own chimneys. Thats where the ability of
the governing class comes in. Shall the fellow call a
taxi for you?

THE LADY. No, thanks: I prefer walking. Goodbye.
Again, many, many thanks.

*She goes out. Augustus returns to the writing-table
smiling, and takes another look at himself in the mirror.
The clerk returns with his head bandaged, carrying a
poker.*

THE CLERK. What did you ring for? [*Augustus hastily
drops the mirror*]. Dont you come nigh me or I'll split
your head with this poker, thick as it is.

AUGUSTUS. It does not seem to me an exceptionally
thick poker. I rang for you to shew the lady out.

THE CLERK. She's gone. She run out like a rabbit.
I ask myself, why was she in such a hurry?

THE LADY'S VOICE [*from the street*] Lord Augustus. Lord Augustus.

THE CLERK. She's calling you.

AUGUSTUS [*running to the window and throwing it up*] What is it? Wont you come up?

THE LADY. Is the clerk there?

AUGUSTUS. Yes. Do you want him?

THE LADY. Yes.

AUGUSTUS. The lady wants you at the window.

THE CLERK [*rushing to the window and putting down the poker*] Yes, maam? Here I am, maam. What is it, maam?

THE LADY. I want you to witness that I got clean away into the street. I am coming up now.

   *The two men stare at one another.*

THE CLERK. Wants me to witness that she got clean away into the street!

AUGUSTUS. What on earth does she mean?

   *The lady returns.*

THE LADY. May I use your telephone?

AUGUSTUS. Certainly. Certainly. [*Taking the receiver down*] What number shall I get you?

THE LADY. The War Office, please.

AUGUSTUS. The War Office!?

THE LADY. If you will be so good.

AUGUSTUS. But—Oh, very well. [*Into the receiver*] Hallo. This is the Town Hall Recruiting Office. Give me Colonel Bogey, sharp.

   *A pause.*

THE CLERK [*breaking the painful silence*] I dont think I'm awake. This is a dream of a movy picture, this is.

AUGUSTUS [*his ear at the receiver*] Shut up, will you? [*Into the telephone*] What? . . . [*To the lady*] Whom do you want to get on to?

THE LADY. Blueloo.

AUGUSTUS [*into the telephone*] Put me through to
Lord Hungerford Highcastle. . . . I'm his brother,
idiot. . . . That you, Blueloo? Lady here at Little
Pifflington wants to speak to you. Hold the line. [*To
the lady*] Now, madam [*he hands her the receiver*].

THE LADY [*sitting down in Augustus's chair to speak
into the telephone*] Is that Blueloo? . . . Do you recognize my voice? . . . Ive won our bet. . . .

AUGUSTUS. Your bet!

THE LADY [*into the telephone*] Yes: I have the list in my
wallet. . . .

AUGUSTUS. Nothing of the kind, madam. I have it
here in my pocket. [*He takes the envelope from his
pocket; draws out the paper; and unfolds it*].

THE LADY [*continuing*] Yes: I got clean into the street
with it. I have a witness. I could have got to London
with it. Augustus wont deny it. . . .

AUGUSTUS [*contemplating the blank paper*] Theres
nothing written on this. Where is the list of guns?

THE LADY [*continuing*] Oh, it was quite easy. I said
I was my sister-in-law and that I was a Hun. He
lapped it up like a kitten. . . .

AUGUSTUS. You dont mean to say that—

THE LADY [*continuing*] I got hold of the list for a
moment and changed it for a piece of paper out of
his stationery rack: it was quite easy [*she laughs; and
it is clear that Blueloo is laughing too*].

AUGUSTUS. What!

THE CLERK [*laughing slowly and laboriously, with
intense enjoyment*] Ha ha! Ha ha ha! Ha! [*Augustus
rushes at him: he snatches up the poker and stands on
guard*]. No you dont.

THE LADY [*still at the telephone, waving her disengaged hand behind her impatiently at them to stop
making a noise*] Sh-sh-sh-sh-sh!!! [*Augustus, with a*

*shrug, goes up the middle of the room. The lady resumes her conversation with the telephone*] What? . . . Oh yes: I'm coming up by the 12.35: why not have tea with me at Rumpelmeister's . . . Rum-pel-meis-ter's. You know: they call it Robinson's now. . . . Right. Ta ta. [*She hangs up the receiver, and is passing round the table on her way towards the door when she is confronted by Augustus*].

AUGUSTUS. Madam: I consider your conduct most unpatriotic. You make bets and abuse the confidence of the hardworked officials who are doing their bit for their country whilst our gallant fellows are perishing in the trenches—

THE LADY. Oh, the gallant fellows are not all in the trenches, Augustus. Some of them have come home for a few days hardearned leave; and I am sure you wont grudge them a little fun at your expense.

THE CLERK. Hear! Hear!

AUGUSTUS [*amiably*] Ah, well! For my country's sake—!

# Statement for the Drama Editor
## of the *Evening Standard*

(Incorporated with revision into the drama column
on 16 December 1916. From the holograph
manuscript in the University of
Texas Library at Austin.)

Augustus is only a sketch, and a very trifling one at
that, written for Madame Vandervelde, the wife of
the Belgian Socialist minister, to be performed at a
matinée in aid of the Belgians.

It was suggested by the recent appeal of the Government to the dramatic authors & variety theatre managers for didactic sketches inculcating war saving.
Augustus is my patriotic response to that appeal.

You can use this information; but do not quote it
as from me—at least do not insert it as a contribution from me, or you will get me into trouble with all
your competitors.

G.B.S.

# Annajanska,
# The Bolshevik Empress:
# A Revolutionary Romancelet

Composition begun 4 December 1917; completed 7 December 1917. Published in *Heartbreak House, Great Catherine, & Playlets of the War*, 1919. First presented, under the title *Annajanska, The Wild Grand Duchess*, at the Coliseum, London, in a variety bill on 21 January 1918.

General Strammfest    *Randle Ayrton*
Lieutenant Schneidekind    *Henry Miller*
Grand Duchess Annajanska
                           *Lillah McCarthy*
First Soldier    *Drelincourt Odlum*
Second Soldier    (*Not named*)

Period—1917

Scene—*The General's Office in a Military Station on the East Front of Beotia*

Annajanska is frankly a bravura piece. The modern variety theatre demands for its "turns" little plays called sketches, to last twenty minutes or so, and to enable some favorite performer to make a brief but dazzling appearance on some barely passable dramatic pretext. Miss Lillah McCarthy and I, as author and actress, have helped to make one another famous on many serious occasions, from Man and Superman to Androcles; and Mr Charles Ricketts has not disdained to snatch moments from his painting and sculpture to design some wonderful dresses for us. We three unbent as Mrs Siddons, Sir Joshua Reynolds, and Dr Johnson might have unbent, to devise a "turn" for the Coliseum variety theatre. Not that we would set down the art of the variety theatre as something to be condescended to, or our own art as elephantine. We should rather crave indulgence as three novices fresh from the awful legitimacy of the highbrow theatre.

Well, Miss McCarthy and Mr Ricketts justified themselves easily in the glamor of the footlights, to the strains of Tchaikovsky's 1812. I fear I did not. I have received only one compliment on my share; and that was from a friend who said "it is the only one of your works that is not too long". So I have made it a page or two longer, according to my own precept: EMBRACE YOUR REPROACHES: THEY ARE OFTEN GLORIES IN DISGUISE.

*The General's Office in a military station on the east front in Beotia. An office table with a telephone, writing materials, official papers, etc., is set across the room. At the end of the table, a comfortable chair for the General. Behind the chair, a window. Facing it at the other end of the table, a plain wooden bench. At the side of the table, with its back to the door, a common chair, with a typewriter before it. Beside the door, which is opposite the end of the bench, a rack for caps and coats. There is nobody in the room.*

*General Strammfest enters, followed by Lieutenant Schneidekind. They hang up their cloaks and caps. Schneidekind takes a little longer than Strammfest, who comes to the table.*

STRAMMFEST. Schneidekind.

SCHNEIDEKIND. Yes, sir.

STRAMMFEST. Have you sent my report yet to the government [*he sits down*].

SCHNEIDEKIND [*coming to the table*] Not yet, sir. Which government do you wish it sent to? [*He sits down*].

STRAMMFEST. That depends. Whats the latest? Which of them do you think is most likely to be in power tomorrow morning?

SCHNEIDEKIND. Well, the provisional government was going strong yesterday. But today they say that the prime minister has shot himself, and that the extreme left fellow has shot all the others.

STRAMMFEST. Yes: thats all very well; but these fellows always shoot themselves with blank cartridge.

SCHNEIDEKIND. Still, even the blank cartridge

means backing down. I should send the report to the Maximilianists.

STRAMMFEST. Theyre no stronger than the Oppido-shavians; and in my own opinion the Moderate Red Revolutionaries are as likely to come out on top as either of them.

SCHNEIDEKIND. I can easily put a few carbon sheets in the typewriter and send a copy each to the lot.

STRAMMFEST. Waste of paper. You might as well send reports to an infant school. [*He throws his head on the table with a groan*].

SCHNEIDEKIND. Tired out, sir?

STRAMMFEST. O Schneidekind, Schneidekind, how can you bear to live?

SCHNEIDEKIND. At my age, sir, I ask myself how can I bear to die?

STRAMMFEST. You are young, young and heartless. You are excited by the revolution: you are attached to abstract things like liberty. But my family has served the Panjandrums of Beotia faithfully for seven centuries. The Panjandrums have kept our place for us at their courts, honored us, promoted us, shed their glory on us, made us what we are. When I hear you young men declaring that you are fighting for civilization, for democracy, for the overthrow of militarism, I ask myself how can a man shed his blood for empty words used by vulgar tradesmen and common laborers: mere wind and stink. [*He rises, exalted by his theme*]. A king is a splendid reality, a man raised above us like a god. You can see him; you can kiss his hand; you can be cheered by his smile and terrified by his frown. I would have died for my Panjandrum as my father died for his father. Your toiling millions were only too honored to receive the toes of our boots in the proper spot for them when they displeased their betters. And now what is left in life for me? [*He relapses into his chair discouraged*] My Panjandrum is deposed and transported to herd with convicts. The army, his pride and glory, is paraded to hear seditious speeches from penniless rebels, with the colonel actually forced to take the chair and introduce the speaker. I myself am made Commander-in-Chief by my own solicitor: a Jew, Schneidekind! a Hebrew Jew! It seems only yesterday that these things would have been the ravings of a madman: today they are the commonplaces of the gutter press. I live now for three objects only: to defeat the enemy, to restore the Panjandrum, and to hang my solicitor.

SCHNEIDEKIND. Be careful, sir: these are dangerous views to utter nowadays. What if I were to betray you?

STRAMMFEST. What!

SCHNEIDEKIND. I wont, of course; my own father goes on just like that; but suppose I did?

STRAMMFEST [*chuckling*] I should accuse you of treason to the Revolution, my lad; and they would immediately shoot you, unless you cried and asked to see your mother before you died, when they would probably change their minds and make you a brigadier. Enough. [*He rises and expands his chest*]. I feel the better for letting myself go. To business. [*He takes up a telegram; opens it; and is thunderstruck by its contents*]. Great heaven! [*He collapses into his chair*]. This is the worst blow of all.

SCHNEIDEKIND. What has happened? Are we beaten?

STRAMMFEST. Man: do you think that a mere defeat could strike me down as this news does: I, who have been defeated thirteen times since the war began? O, my master, my master, my Panjandrum! [*he is convulsed with sobs*].

SCHNEIDEKIND. They have killed him?

STRAMMFEST. A dagger has been struck through his heart.

SCHNEIDEKIND. Good God!

STRAMMFEST.—and through mine, through mine.

SCHNEIDEKIND [*relieved*] Oh: a metaphorical dagger. I thought you meant a real one. What has happened?

STRAMMFEST. His daughter, the Grand Duchess Annajanska, she whom the Panjandrina loved beyond all her other children, has—has—[*he cannot finish*].

SCHNEIDEKIND. Committed suicide?

STRAMMFEST. No. Better if she had. Oh, far far better.

SCHNEIDEKIND [*in hushed tones*] Left the Church?

STRAMMFEST [*shocked*] Certainly not. Do not blaspheme, young man.

SCHNEIDEKIND. Asked for the vote?

STRAMMFEST. I would have given it to her with both hands to save her from this.

SCHNEIDEKIND. Save her from what? Dash it, sir, out with it.

STRAMMFEST. She has joined the Revolution.

SCHNEIDEKIND. But so have you, sir. Weve all joined the Revolution. She doesnt mean it any more than we do.

STRAMMFEST. Heaven grant you may be right! But that is not the worst. She has eloped with a young officer. Eloped, Schneidekind, eloped!

SCHNEIDEKIND [*not particularly impressed*] Yes, sir.

STRAMMFEST. Annajanska, the beautiful, the innocent, my master's daughter! [*He buries his face in his hands*].

*The telephone rings.*

SCHNEIDEKIND [*taking the receiver*] Yes: G.H.Q. Yes. . . . Dont bawl: I'm not a general. Who is speaking? . . . Why didnt you say so? dont you know your duty? Next time you will lose your stripe. . . . Oh, theyve made you a colonel, have they? Well, theyve made me a fieldmarshal: now what have you to say? . . . Look here: what did you ring up for? I cant spend the day here listening to your cheek. . . . What! the Grand Duchess! [*Strammfest starts*]. Where did you catch her?

STRAMMFEST [*snatching the telephone and listening for the answer*] Speak louder, will you: I am a General. . . . I know that, you dolt. Have you captured the officer that was with her? . . . Damnation! You shall answer for this: you let him go: he bribed you. . . . You must have seen him: the fellow is in the full dress court uniform of the Panderobajensky Hussars. I give you twelve hours to catch him or . . . whats that you say about the devil? Are you swearing at me, you . . . Thousand thunders! [*To Schneidekind*] The swine says that the Grand Duchess is a devil incarnate. [*Into the telephone*] Filthy traitor: is that the way you dare speak of the daughter of our anointed Panjandrum? I'll—

SCHNEIDEKIND [*pulling the telephone from his lips*] Take care, sir.

STRAMMFEST. I wont take care: I'll have him shot. Let go that telephone.

SCHNEIDEKIND. But for her own sake sir—

STRAMMFEST. Eh?

SCHNEIDEKIND. For her own sake they had better send her here. She will be safe in your hands.

STRAMMFEST [*yielding the receiver*] You are right. Be civil to him. I should choke [*he sits down*].

SCHNEIDEKIND [*into the telephone*] Hullo. Never mind all that: it's only a fellow here who has been fooling with the telephone. I had to leave the room for a moment. Wash out; and send the girl along.

We'll jolly soon teach her to behave herself here. . . . Oh, youve sent her already. Then why the devil didnt you say so, you—[*he hangs up the telephone angrily*]. Just fancy: they started her off this morning: and all this is because the fellow likes to get on the telephone and hear himself talk now that he is a colonel. [*The telephone rings again. He snatches the receiver furiously*] Whats the matter now? . . . [*To the General*] It's our own people downstairs. [*Into the receiver*] Here! do you suppose Ive nothing else to do than to hang on to the telephone all day? . . . Whats that? Not men enough to hold her! What do you mean? [*To the General*] She is there, sir.

STRAMMFEST. Tell them to send her up. I shall have to receive her without even rising, without kissing her hand, to keep up appearances before the escort. It will break my heart.

SCHNEIDEKIND [*into the receiver*] Send her up. . . . Tcha! [*He hangs up the receiver*]. He says she is half way up already: they couldnt hold her.

*The Grand Duchess bursts into the room, dragging with her two exhausted soldiers hanging on desperately to her arms. She is enveloped from head to foot by a fur-lined cloak, and wears a fur cap.*

SCHNEIDEKIND [*pointing to the bench*] At the word Go, place your prisoner on the bench in a sitting posture; and take your seats right and left of her. Go.

*The two soldiers make a supreme effort to force her to sit down. She flings them back so that they are forced to sit on the bench to save themselves from falling backwards over it, and she is herself dragged into sitting between them. The second soldier, holding on tight to the Grand Duchess with one hand, produces papers with the other, and waves them towards Schneidekind, who takes*

*them from him and passes them on to the General. He*
*opens them and reads them with a grave expression.*

SCHNEIDEKIND. Be good enough to wait, prisoner,
until the General has read the papers on your case.

THE GRAND DUCHESS [*to the soldiers*] Let go. [*To
Strammfest*] Tell them to let go, or I'll upset the
bench backwards and bash our three heads on the
floor.

FIRST SOLDIER. No, little mother. Have mercy on
the poor.

STRAMMFEST [*growling over the edge of the paper he
is reading*] Hold your tongue.

THE GRAND DUCHESS [*blazing*] Me, or the soldier?

STRAMMFEST [*horrified*] The soldier, madam.

THE GRAND DUCHESS. Tell him to let go.

STRAMMFEST. Release the lady.

*The soldiers take their hands off her. One of them
wipes his fevered brow. The other sucks his wrist.*

SCHNEIDEKIND [*fiercely*] 'ttention!

*The two soldiers sit up stiffly.*

THE GRAND DUCHESS, Oh, let the poor man suck
his wrist. It may be poisoned. I bit it.

STRAMMFEST [*shocked*] You bit a common soldier!

THE GRAND DUCHESS. Well, I offered to cauterize it
with the poker in the office stove. But he was afraid,
What more could I do?

SCHNEIDEKIND. Why did you bite him, prisoner?

THE GRAND DUCHESS. He would not let go.

STRAMMFEST. Did he let go when you bit him?

THE GRAND DUCHESS. No. [*Patting the soldier on the
back*] You should give the man a cross for his devotion. I could not go on eating him; so I brought him
along with me.

STRAMMFEST. Prisoner—

THE GRAND DUCHESS. Dont call me prisoner,

General Strammfest. My grandmother dandled you on her knee.

STRAMMFEST [*bursting into tears*] O God, yes. Believe me, my heart is what it was then.

THE GRAND DUCHESS. Your brain also is what it was then. I will not be addressed by you as prisoner.

STRAMMFEST. I may not, for your own sake, call you by your rightful and most sacred titles. What am I to call you?

THE GRAND DUCHESS. The Revolution has made us comrades. Call me comrade.

STRAMMFEST. I had rather die.

THE GRAND DUCHESS. Then call me Annajanska; and I will call you Peter Piper, as grandmamma did.

STRAMMFEST [*painfully agitated*] Schneidekind: you must speak to her: I cannot—[*he breaks down*].

SCHNEIDEKIND [*officially*] The Republic of Beotia has been compelled to confine the Panjandrum and his family, for their own safety, within certain bounds. You have broken those bounds.

STRAMMFEST [*taking the word from him*] You are—I must say it—a prisoner. What am I to do with you?

THE GRAND DUCHESS. You should have thought of that before you arrested me.

STRAMMFEST. Come, come, prisoner! do you know what will happen to you if you compel me to take a sterner tone with you?

THE GRAND DUCHESS. No. But I know what will happen to you.

STRAMMFEST. Pray what, prisoner?

THE GRAND DUCHESS. Clergyman's sore throat.

*Schneidekind splutters: drops a paper; and conceals his laughter under the table.*

STRAMMFEST [*thunderously*] Lieutenant Schneidekind.

SCHNEIDEKIND [*in a stifled voice*] Yes, sir. [*The table vibrates visibly*].

STRAMMFEST. Come out of it, you fool: youre upsetting the ink.

*Schneidekind emerges, red in the face with suppressed mirth.*

STRAMMFEST. Why dont you laugh? Dont you appreciate Her Imperial Highness's joke?

SCHNEIDEKIND [*suddenly becoming solemn*] I dont want to, sir.

STRAMMFEST. Laugh at once, sir. I order you to laugh.

SCHNEIDEKIND [*with a touch of temper*] I really cant, sir. [*He sits down decisively*].

STRAMMFEST [*growling at him*] Yah! [*He turns impressively to the Grand Duchess*] Your Imperial Highness desires me to address you as comrade?

THE GRAND DUCHESS [*rising and waving a red handkerchief*] Long live the Revolution, comrade!

STRAMMFEST [*rising and saluting*] Proletarians of all lands, unite. Lieutenant Schneidekind: you will rise and sing the Marseillaise.

SCHNEIDEKIND [*rising*] But I cannot, sir. I have no voice, no ear.

STRAMMFEST. Then sit down; and bury your shame in your typewriter [*Schneidekind sits down*]. Comrade Annajanska: you have eloped with a young officer.

THE GRAND DUCHESS [*astounded*] General Strammfest: you lie.

STRAMMFEST. Denial, comrade, is useless. It is through that officer that your movements have been traced. [*The Grand Duchess is suddenly enlightened, and seems amused. Strammfest continues in a forensic manner*] He joined you at the Golden Anchor in Hakonsburg. You gave us the slip there; but the officer was traced to Potterdam, where you rejoined him and went alone to Premsylople. What have you done with that unhappy young man? Where is he?

THE GRAND DUCHESS [*pretending to whisper an important secret*] Where he has always been.

STRAMMFEST [*eagerly*] Where is that?

THE GRAND DUCHESS [*impetuously*] In your imagination. I came alone. I am alone. Hundreds of officers travel every day from Hakonsburg to Potterdam. What do I know about them?

STRAMMFEST. They travel in khaki. They do not travel in full dress court uniform as this man did.

SCHNEIDEKIND. Only officers who are eloping with grand duchesses wear court uniform: otherwise the grand duchesses could not be seen with them.

STRAMMFEST. Hold your tongue [*Schneidekind, in high dudgeon, folds his arms and retires from the conversation. The General returns to his paper and to his examination of the Grand Duchess*] This officer travelled with your passport. What have you to say to that?

THE GRAND DUCHESS. Bosh! How could a man travel with a woman's passport?

STRAMMFEST. It is quite simple, as you very well know. A dozen travellers arrive at the boundary. The official collects their passports. He counts twelve persons; then counts the passports. If there are twelve, he is satisfied.

THE GRAND DUCHESS. Then how do you know that one of the passports was mine?

STRAMMFEST. A waiter at the Potterdam Hotel looked at the officer's passport when he was in his bath. It was your passport.

THE GRAND DUCHESS. Stuff! Why did he not have me arrested?

STRAMMFEST. When the waiter returned to the hotel

with the police the officer had vanished; and you were there with your own passport. They knouted him.

THE GRAND DUCHESS. Oh! Strammfest: send these men away. I must speak to you alone.

STRAMMFEST [*rising in horror*] No: this is the last straw: I cannot consent. It is impossible, utterly, eternally impossible, that a daughter of the Imperial House should speak to anyone alone, were it even her own husband.

THE GRAND DUCHESS. You forget that there is an exception. She may speak to a child alone. [*She rises*] Strammfest: you have been dandled on my grandmother's knee. By that gracious action the dowager Panjandrina made you a child forever. So did Nature, by the way. I order you to speak to me alone. Do you hear? I order you. For seven hundred years no member of your family has ever disobeyed an order from a member of mine. Will you disobey me?

STRAMMFEST. There is an alternative to obedience. The dead cannot disobey. [*He takes out his pistol and places the muzzle against his temple*].

SCHNEIDEKIND [*snatching the pistol from him*] For God's sake, General—

STRAMMFEST [*attacking him furiously to recover the weapon*] Dog of a subaltern, restore that pistol, and my honor.

SCHNEIDEKIND [*reaching out with the pistol to the Grand Duchess*] Take it: quick: he is as strong as a bull.

THE GRAND DUCHESS [*snatching it*] Aha! Leave the room, all of you except the General. At the double! lightning! electricity! [*she fires shot after shot, spattering bullets about the ankles of the soldiers. They fly precipitately. She turns to Schneidekind, who has by this time been flung on the floor by the General*] You too. [*He scrambles up*]. March [*He flies to the door*].

SCHNEIDEKIND [*turning at the door*] For your own sake, comrade—

THE GRAND DUCHESS [*indignantly*] Comrade! You!!! Go. [*She fires two more shots. He vanishes*].

STRAMMFEST [*making an impulsive movement towards her*] My Imperial Mistress—

THE GRAND DUCHESS. Stop. I have one bullet left, if you attempt to take this from me [*putting the pistol to her temple*].

STRAMMFEST [*recoiling, and covering his eyes with his hands*] No no: put it down: put it down. I promise everything: I swear anything; put it down, I implore you.

THE GRAND DUCHESS [*throwing it on the table*] There!

STRAMMFEST [*uncovering his eyes*] Thank God!

THE GRAND DUCHESS [*gently*] Strammfest: I am your comrade. Am I nothing more to you?

STRAMMFEST [*falling on his knee*] You are, God help me, all that is left to me of the only power I recognize on earth [*he kisses her hand*].

THE GRAND DUCHESS [*indulgently*] Idolater! When will you learn that our strength has never been in ourselves, but in your illusions about us? [*She shakes off her kindliness, and sits down in his chair*] Now tell me, what are your orders? And do you mean to obey them?

STRAMMFEST [*starting like a goaded ox, and blundering fretfully about the room*] How can I obey six different dictators, and not one gentleman among the lot of them? One of them orders me to make peace with the foreign enemy. Another orders me to offer all the neutral countries 48 hours to choose between adopting his views on the single tax and being instantly invaded and annihilated. A third orders me to go to a damned Socialist Conference and explain that Beotia will allow no annexations and no indemnities, and merely wishes to establish the Kingdom of Heaven on Earth throughout the universe. [*He finishes behind Schneidekind's chair*].

THE GRAND DUCHESS. Damn their trifling!

STRAMMFEST. I thank Your Imperial Highness from the bottom of my heart for that expression. Europe thanks you.

THE GRAND DUCHESS. M'yes; but—[*rising*] Strammfest: you know that your cause—the cause of the dynasty—is lost.

STRAMMFEST. You must not say so. It is treason, even from you. [*He sinks, discouraged, into the chair, and covers his face with his hand*].

THE GRAND DUCHESS. Do not deceive yourself, General: never again will a Panjandrum reign in Beotia. [*She walks slowly across the room, brooding bitterly, and thinking aloud*]. We are so decayed, so out of date, so feeble, so wicked in our own despite, that we have come at last to will our own destruction.

STRAMMFEST. You are uttering blasphemy.

THE GRAND DUCHESS. All great truths begin as blasphemies. All the king's horses and all the king's men cannot set up my father's throne again. If they could, you would have done it, would you not?

STRAMMFEST. God knows I would!

THE GRAND DUCHESS. You really mean that? You would keep the people in their hopeless squalid misery? you would fill those infamous prisons again with the noblest spirits in the land? you would thrust the rising sun of liberty back into the sea of blood from which it has risen? And all because there was in the middle of the dirt and ugliness and horror a little patch of court splendor in which you could stand with a few orders on your uniform, and yawn day after day and night after night in unspeakable boredom until your grave yawned wider still, and you fell into it because you had nothing better to do. How can you be so stupid, so heartless?

STRAMMFEST. You must be mad to think of royalty in such a way. I never yawned at court. The dogs yawned; but that was because they were dogs: they had no imagination, no ideals, no sense of honor and dignity to sustain them.

THE GRAND DUCHESS. My poor Strammfest: you were not often enough at court to tire of it. You were mostly soldiering; and when you came home to have a new order pinned on your breast, your happiness came through looking at my father and mother and at me, and adoring us. Was that not so?

STRAMMFEST. Do you reproach me with it? I am not ashamed of it.

THE GRAND DUCHESS. Oh, it was all very well for you, Strammfest. But think of me, of me! standing there for you to gape at, and knowing that I was no goddess, but only a girl like any other girl! It was cruelty to animals: you could have stuck up a wax doll or a golden calf to worship; it would not have been bored.

STRAMMFEST. Stop; or I shall renounce my allegiance to you. I have had women flogged for such seditious chatter as this.

THE GRAND DUCHESS. Do not provoke me to send a bullet through your head for reminding me of it.

STRAMMFEST. You always had low tastes. You are no true daughter of the Panjandrums: you are a changeling, thrust into the Panjandrina's bed by some profligate nurse. I have heard stories of your childhood: of how—

THE GRAND DUCHESS. Ha, ha! Yes: they took me to the circus when I was a child. It was my first moment of happiness, my first glimpse of heaven. I ran away and joined the troupe. They caught me and dragged me back to my gilded cage; but I had tasted freedom; and they never could make me forget it.

STRAMMFEST. Freedom! To be the slave of an acrobat! to be exhibited to the public! to—

THE GRAND DUCHESS. Oh, I was trained to that. I had learnt that part of the business at court.

STRAMMFEST. You had not been taught to strip yourself half naked and turn head over heels—

THE GRAND DUCHESS. Man: I wanted to get rid of my swaddling clothes and turn head over heels. I wanted to, I wanted to, I wanted to. I can do it still. Shall I do it now?

STRAMMFEST. If you do, I swear I will throw myself from the window so that I may meet your parents in heaven without having my medals torn from my breast by them.

THE GRAND DUCHESS. Oh, you are incorrigible. You are mad, infatuated. You will not believe that we royal divinities are mere common flesh and blood even when we step down from our pedestals and tell you ourselves what a fool you are. I will argue no more with you: I will use my power. At a word from me your men will turn against you: already half of them do not salute you; and you dare not punish them: you have to pretend not to notice it.

STRAMMFEST. It is not for you to taunt me with that if it is so.

THE GRAND DUCHESS [haughtily] Taunt! I condescend to taunt! To taunt a common General! You forget yourself, sir.

STRAMMFEST [*dropping on his knee submissively*] Now at last you speak like your royal self.

THE GRAND DUCHESS. Oh, Strammfest, Strammfest, they have driven your slavery into your very bones. Why did you not spit in my face?

STRAMMFEST [*rising with a shudder*] God forbid!

THE GRAND DUCHESS. Well, since you will be my slave, take your orders from me. I have not come here to save our wretched family and our bloodstained crown. I am come to save the Revolution.

STRAMMFEST. Stupid as I am, I have come to think that I had better save that than save nothing. But what will the Revolution do for the people? Do not be deceived by the fine speeches of the revolutionary leaders and the pamphlets of the revolutionary writers. How much liberty is there where they have gained the upper hand? Are they not hanging, shooting, imprisoning as much as ever we did? Do they ever tell the people the truth? No: if the truth does not suit them they spread lies instead, and make it a crime to tell the truth.

THE GRAND DUCHESS. Of course they do. Why should they not?

STRAMMFEST [*hardly able to believe his ears*] Why should they not!

THE GRAND DUCHESS. Yes: why should they not? We did it. You did it, whip in hand: you flogged women for teaching children to read.

STRAMMFEST. To read sedition. To read Karl Marx.

THE GRAND DUCHESS. Pshaw! How could they learn to read the Bible without learning to read Karl Marx? Why do you not stand to your guns and justify what you did, instead of making silly excuses. Do you suppose *I* think flogging a woman worse than flogging a man? I, who am a woman myself!

STRAMMFEST. I am at a loss to understand your Imperial Highness. You seem to me to contradict yourself.

THE GRAND DUCHESS. Nonsense! I say that if the people cannot govern themselves, they must be governed by somebody. If they will not do their duty without being half forced and half humbugged, somebody must force them and humbug them. Some energetic and capable minority must always be in power. Well, I am on the side of the energetic minority whose principles I agree with. The Revolution is as cruel as we were; but its aims are my aims. Therefore I stand for the Revolution.

STRAMMFEST. You do not know what you are saying. This is pure Bolshevism. Are you, the daughter of a Panjandrum, a Bolshevist?

THE GRAND DUCHESS. I am anything that will make the world less like a prison and more like a circus.

STRAMMFEST. Ah! You still want to be a circus star.

THE GRAND DUCHESS. Yes, and be billed as the Bolshevik Empress. Nothing shall stop me. You have your orders, General Strammfest: save the Revolution.

STRAMMFEST. What Revolution? Which Revolution? No two of your rabble of revolutionists mean the same thing by the Revolution. What can save a mob in which every man is rushing in a different direction?

THE GRAND DUCHESS. I will tell you. The war can save it.

STRAMMFEST. The war?

THE GRAND DUCHESS. Yes, the war. Only a great common danger and a great common duty can unite us and weld these wrangling factions into a solid commonwealth.

STRAMMFEST. Bravo! War sets everything right: I

have always said so. But what is a united people without a united army? And what can *I* do? I am only a
soldier. I cannot make speeches: I have won no
victories: they will not rally to my call [*again he sinks
into his chair with his former gesture of discouragement*].

THE GRAND DUCHESS. Are you sure they will not
rally to mine?

STRAMMFEST. Oh, if only you were a man and a
soldier!

THE GRAND DUCHESS. Suppose I find you a man
and a soldier?

STRAMMFEST [*rising in a fury*] Ah! the scoundrel
you eloped with! You think you will shove this fellow
into an army command, over my head. Never.

THE GRAND DUCHESS. You promised everything.
You swore anything. [*She marches as if in front of a
regiment*]. I know that this man alone can rouse the
army to enthusiasm.

STRAMMFEST. Delusion! Folly! He is some circus
acrobat; and you are in love with him.

THE GRAND DUCHESS. I swear I am not in love with
him. I swear I will never marry him.

STRAMMFEST. Then who is he?

THE GRAND DUCHESS. Anybody in the world but you
would have guessed long ago. He is under your very eyes.

STRAMMFEST [*staring past her right and left*] Where?

THE GRAND DUCHESS. Look out of the window.

*He rushes to the window, looking for the officer. The
Grand Duchess takes off her cloak and appears in the
uniform of the Panderobajensky Hussars.*

STRAMMFEST [*peering through the window*] Where is
he? I can see no one.

THE GRAND DUCHESS. Here, silly.

STRAMMFEST [*turning*] You! Great Heavens! The
Bolshevik Empress!

# Back to Methuselah:
# A Metabiological Pentateuch

WITH

*Preface: The Infidel Half Century*

*A Glimpse of the Domesticity of
Franklyn Barnabas*

*Postscript: After Twenty-five Years*

*Birmingham as a Home of Dramatic Art*

*The Serial Play*

*Bernard Shaw Piqued*

*Letters to the Editor of* The Times,
*25 and 28 February 1924*

*Shaw Has Become a Prophet*

Composition begun 19 March 1918; completed 27 May 1920. Published 1921. Revised text in Collected Edition, 1930. Further revised for World's Classics Edition, 1945. (As this text was the last to be revised by Shaw in his lifetime, it is used in the present edition as the definitive text). First presented by the Theatre Guild at the Garrick Theatre, New York, on 27 February 1922 (Parts I and II), 6 March 1922 (Parts III and IV), and 13 March 1922 (Part V).

Part I: IN THE BEGINNING

Adam    *George Gaul*
Eve    *Ernita Lascelles*
The Serpent    *Margaret Wycherly*
Cain    *Dennis King*

Period—4004 B.C.

ACT 1    *The Garden of Eden. Afternoon*

ACT 2    *An Oasis in Mesopotamia a Few Centuries Later. Morning*

Part II: THE GOSPEL OF THE BROTHERS BARNABAS

Franklyn Barnabas    *Albert Bruning*
Conrad Barnabas    *Moffat Johnston*
The Parlormaid    *Margaret Wycherly*
Reverend William Haslam    *Stanley Howlett*
Cynthia ("Savvy") Barnabas
                    *Eleanor Woodruff*
Joyce Burge    *A. P. Kaye*
Lubin    *Claude King*

Period—Shortly after World War I.

Scene—*Franklyn Barnabas' Study, Hampstead Heath. A Fine Afternoon in Spring*

Part III: THE THING HAPPENS

Burge-Lubin (President of the British Islands)
*A. P. Kaye*
Barnabas (The Accountant-General)
*Moffat Johnston*
The Voice of the Telephone Operator
(*Not named*)
Confucius (Chief Secretary)   *Claude King*
Negress (The Minister of Health)
*Mary Lawton*
The Archbishop of York   *Stanley Howlett*
Mrs Lutestring (The Domestic Minister)
*Margaret Wycherly*

Period—A.D. 2170

Scene—*The Official Parlor of the President of the British Islands. A Summer Afternoon*

Part IV: THE TRAGEDY OF AN ELDERLY GENTLEMAN

The Elderly Gentleman (Joseph Popham Bolge Bluebin Barlow, O.M.)   *Albert Bruning*
Fusima   *Ernita Lascelles*
Zozim   *Claude King*
Zoo Ennistymon   *Eleanor Woodruff*
General Aufsteig (Cain Adamson Charles Napoleon, Emperor of Turania)   *George Gaul*
The Oracle   *Margaret Wycherly*

Ambrose Badger Bluebin, Prime Minister of the British Islands (The British Envoy) *A. P. Kaye*

Molly Badger Bluebin    *Shirley King*

Ethel Badger Bluebin    *Martha Bryan-Allen*

Period—A.D. 3000. Ireland.

ACT I    *Burrin Pier on the South Shore of Galway Bay. A Summer Day*

ACT II    *A Courtyard before the Temple in Galway*

ACT III    *Inside the Temple*

Part V: AS FAR AS THOUGHT CAN REACH

Strephon    *Dennis King*

Chloe    *Eleanor Woodruff*

He-Ancient    *Moffat Johnston*

Acis    *Walter Abel*

She-Ancient    *Margaret Wycherly*

Amaryllis (The Newly Born)    *Martha Bryan-Allen*

Ecrasia    *Clelia Benjamin*

Arjillax    *Stanley Howlett*

Martellus    *Claude King*

Pygmalion    *A. P. Kaye*

Ozymandias    *George Gaul*

Cleopatra-Semiramis    *Ernita Lascelles*

The Ghost of Adam    *George Gaul*

The Ghost of Eve    *Ernita Lascelles*

The Ghost of Cain    *Dennis King*

The Ghost of the Serpent    *Margaret Wycherly*

The Ghost of Lilith    *Mary Lawton*

Period—A.D. 31,920

Scene—*A Sunlit Glade beside a little Classic Temple. A Summer Afternoon*

# Preface: The Infidel Half Century

---

*Contents*

---

THE DAWN OF DARWINISM

One day early in the eighteen hundred and sixties, I,
being then a small boy, was with my nurse, buying

something in the shop of a petty newsagent, book-seller, and stationer in Camden Street, Dublin, when there entered an elderly man, weighty and solemn, who advanced to the counter, and said pompously, "Have you the works of the celebrated Buffoon?"

My own works were at that time unwritten, or it is possible that the shop assistant might have misunder-stood him so far as to produce a copy of Man and Superman. As it was, she knew quite well what he wanted; for this was before the Education Act of 1870 had produced shop assistants who know how to read and know nothing else. The celebrated Buffoon was not a humorist, but the famous natural-ist Buffon. Every literate child at that time knew Buffon's Natural History as well as Esop's Fables. And no living child had heard the name that has since obliterated Buffon's in the popular consciousness: the name of Darwin.

Ten years elapsed. The celebrated Buffoon was forgotten; I had doubled my years and my length; and I had discarded the religion of my forefathers. One day the richest and consequently most dogmatic of my uncles came into a restaurant where I was dining, and found himself, much against his will, in conversation with the most questionable of his nephews. By way of making myself agreeable, I spoke of modern thought and Darwin. He said, "Oh, thats the fellow who wants to make out that we all have tails like monkeys." I tried to explain that what Darwin had insisted on in this connection was that some monkeys have no tails. But my uncle was as impervious to what Darwin really said as any Neo-Darwinian nowadays. He died impenitent, and did not mention me in his will.

Twenty years elapsed. If my uncle had been alive,

he would have known all about Darwin, and known it all wrong. In spite of the efforts of Grant Allen to set him right, he would have accepted Darwin as the discoverer of Evolution, of Heredity, and of modification of species by Selection. For the pre-Darwinian age had come to be regarded as a Dark Age in which men still believed that the book of Genesis was a standard scientific treatise, and that the only additions to it were Galileo's demonstration of Leonardo da Vinci's simple remark that the earth is a moon of the sun, Newton's theory of gravitation, Sir Humphry Davy's invention of the safety-lamp, the discovery of electricity, the application of steam to industrial purposes, and the penny post. It was just the same in other subjects. Thus Nietzsche, by the two or three who had come across his writings, was supposed to have been the first man to whom it occurred that mere morality and legality and urbanity lead nowhere, as if Bunyan had never written Badman. Schopenhauer was credited with inventing the distinction between the Covenant of Grace and the Covenant of Works which troubled Cromwell on his deathbed. People talked as if there had been no dramatic or descriptive music before Wagner; no impressionist painting before Whistler; whilst as to myself, I was finding that the surest way to produce an effect of daring innovation and originality was to revive the ancient attraction of long rhetorical speeches; to stick closely to the methods of Molière; and to lift characters bodily out of the pages of Charles Dickens.

## THE ADVENT OF THE NEO-DARWINIANS

This particular sort of ignorance does not always or often matter. But in Darwin's case it did matter. If

Darwin had really led the world at one bound from the book of Genesis to Heredity, to Modification of Species by Selection, and to Evolution, he would have been a philosopher and a prophet as well as an eminent professional naturalist, with geology as a hobby. The delusion that he had actually achieved this feat did no harm at first, because if people's views are sound, about evolution or anything else, it does not make two straws difference whether they call the revealer of their views Tom or Dick. But later on such apparently negligible errors have awkward consequences. Darwin was given an imposing reputation as discoverer and founder of Evolution when he had really only sidetracked it by shewing that many of its developments can be accounted for by what he called Natural Selection, meaning that instead of being evolved to fulfil some vital purpose they were the aimless and promiscuous results of external material pressures and accidents leading to the survival of the fittest to survive under such circumstances. With, of course, the extinction of the unfit. Of this he gave many examples.

As the vogue of Evolution, begun by Goethe and maintained by Darwin's grandfather, faded out in 1830, neither Darwin nor his contemporaries seem to have been aware of it. The next generation accepted Natural Selection as the only method of biological development, and thereby came into conflict with the old Creative Evolutionists and with Darwin himself: a schism which obliged them to distinguish themselves as Neo-Darwinians.

Before ten more years had elapsed, the Neo-Darwinians were dominating biological Science. It was 1906; I was fifty; I had published my own view of evolution in a play called Man and Superman;

and I found that most people were unable to understand how I could be an Evolutionist and not a Neo-Darwinian, or why I derided Neo-Darwinism as a mischievous heresy, and would fall on its professors slaughterously in public discussions. It was in the hope of making me clear the matter up that the Fabian Society, which was then organizing a series of lectures on Prophets of the Nineteenth Century, asked me to deliver a lecture on the prophet Darwin. I did so; and scraps of that lecture, which was never published, variegate these pages.

## POLITICAL INADEQUACY OF THE HUMAN ANIMAL

Ten more years elapsed. Neo-Darwinism in politics had produced a European catastrophe of a magnitude so appalling, and a scope so unpredictable, that as I write these lines in 1920, it is still far from certain whether our civilization will survive it. The circumstances of this catastrophe, the boyish cinema-fed romanticism which made it possible to impose it on the people as a crusade, and especially the ignorance and errors of the victors of Western Europe when its violent phase had passed and the time for reconstruction arrived, confirmed a doubt which had grown steadily in my mind during my forty years public work as a Socialist: namely, whether the human animal, as he exists at present, is capable of solving the social problems raised by his own aggregation, or, as he calls it, his civilization.

## COWARDICE OF THE IRRELIGIOUS

Another observation I had made was that good-natured unambitious men are cowards when they have no religion. They are dominated and exploited not only by greedy and often half-witted and half-alive weaklings who will do anything for cigars, champagne, motor cars, and the more childish and selfish uses of money, but by able and sound administrators who can do nothing else with them than dominate and exploit them. Government and exploitation become synonymous under such circumstances; and the world is finally ruled by the childish, the brigands, and the blackguards. Those who refuse to stand in with them are persecuted and occasionally executed when they give any trouble to the exploiters. They fall into poverty when they lack lucrative specific talents. At the present moment one half of Europe, having knocked the other half down, is trying to kick it to death, and may succeed: a procedure which is, logically, sound Neo-Darwinism. And the good-natured majority are looking on in helpless horror, or allowing themselves to be persuaded by the news-papers of their exploiters that the kicking is not only a sound commercial investment, but an act of divine justice of which they are the ardent instruments.

But if Man is really incapable of organizing a big civilization, and cannot organize even a village or a tribe any too well, what is the use of giving him a religion ? A religion may make him hunger and thirst for righteousness; but will it endow him with the practical capacity to satisfy that appetite ? Good intentions do not carry with them a grain of political science, which is a very complicated one, quite beyond the normal parliament man to whom political science is as remote and distasteful as the differential calculus, and to whom such an elementary but vital point as the law of economic rent is a *pons asinorum* never to be approached, much less crossed. As to the common voter, he is mostly so hard at work all day earning a living that he cannot keep awake for five minutes over a book.

## IS THERE ANY HOPE IN EDUCATION?

The usual answer is that we must educate our masters: that is, ourselves. We must teach citizenship and political science at school. But must we? There is no must about it, the hard fact being that we must *not* teach political science or citizenship at school. The schoolmaster who attempted it would soon find himself penniless in the streets without pupils, if not in the dock pleading to a pompously worded indictment for sedition against the exploiters. Our schools teach the morality of feudalism corrupted by commercialism, and hold up the military conqueror, the robber baron, and the profiteer, as models of the illustrious and the successful. In vain do the prophets who see through this imposture preach and teach a better gospel: the individuals whom they convert are doomed to pass away in a few years; and the new generations are dragged back in the schools to the morality of the fifteenth century, and think themselves Liberal when they are defending the ideas of Henry VII, and gentlemanly when they are opposing to them the ideas of Richard III. Thus the educated man is a greater nuisance than the uneducated one: indeed it is the inefficiency and sham of the educational side of our schools (to which, except under compulsion, children would not be sent by their parents at all if they did not act as prisons in which the immature are kept from worrying the mature) that save us from being dashed on the rocks of false doctrine instead of drifting down the midstream of mere ignorance.

There is no way out through our present public schools.

## HOMEOPATHIC EDUCATION

Our education, however, is not all false. It must teach mathematics and grammar honestly; and this involves a training in logic. Why does not such training provoke our scholars to detect falsehood? The answer is that it sometimes does. Voltaire was a pupil of the Jesuits; Samuel Butler was a public schoolboy who had had his Latin grammar beaten into him by his father, a hopelessly conventional and erroneous country parson. But then Voltaire was Voltaire, and Butler was Butler: that is, their minds were so abnormally strong that they could throw off the doses of poison that paralyze ordinary minds. When the doctors inoculate you and the homeopathists drug you, they give you an infinitesimally attenuated dose. If they gave you the virus at full strength it would overcome your resistance and produce its direct effect. The doses of false doctrine given at public schools and universities are so big that they overwhelm the resistance that a tiny dose would provoke. The normal student is corrupted beyond redemption, and will drive the genius who resists out of the country if he can. Byron and Shelley had to fly to Italy, whilst Castlereagh and Eldon ruled the roost at home. Rousseau was hunted from frontier to frontier; Karl Marx starved in exile in a Soho lodging; Ruskin's articles were refused by the magazines (he was too rich to be otherwise persecuted); whilst mindless forgotten nonentities governed the land; sent men to the prison or the gallows for blasphemy and sedition (meaning the truth about Church and State); and sedulously stored up the social disease and corruption which explode from time to time in mechanized world wars that have neither the romance of chivalry nor the solid gains of conquest.

Homeopathic education has not yet been officially tried, and would obviously be a delicate matter if it were. A body of schoolmasters inciting their pupils to infinitesimal peccadilloes with the object of provoking them to exclaim "Get thee behind me, Satan," or telling them white lies about history for the sake of being contradicted, insulted, and refuted, would certainly do less harm than our present educational allopaths do; but then nobody will advocate homeopathic education. Allopathy has produced the poisonous illusion that it enlightens instead of darkening. The suggestion may, however, explain why, whilst most people's minds succumb to inculcation and environment, a few react vigorously: honest and decent people coming from thievish slums, and sceptics and realists from country parsonages.

## THE DIABOLICAL EFFICIENCY OF TECHNICAL EDUCATION

But meanwhile—and here comes the horror of it— our technical instruction is honest and efficient. The public schoolboy who is carefully blinded, duped, and corrupted as to the nature of a society based on profiteering, and is taught to honor parasitic idleness and luxury, learns to shoot and ride and keep fit with all the assistance and guidance that can be procured for him by the most anxiously sincere desire that he may do these things well, and if possible superlatively well. In the army he learns to fly; to drop bombs; to use machine-guns to the utmost of his capacity.

The discovery of high explosives is rewarded and dignified: instruction in the manufacture of the weapons, battleships, submarines, and land batteries by which they are applied destructively, is quite genuine: the instructors know their business, and really mean the learners to succeed. The result is that powers of destruction that could hardly without uneasiness be entrusted to infinite wisdom and infinite benevolence are placed in the hands of romantic schoolboy patriots who, however generous by nature, are by education ignoramuses, dupes, snobs, and sportsmen to whom fighting is a religion and killing an accomplishment; whilst political power is left to militarist imperialists in chronic terror of invasion and subjugation, pompous tufthunting fools, commercial adventurers to whom the organization by the nation of its own industrial services would mean checkmate, financial parasites on the money market, stupid people who cling to the *status quo* merely because they are used to it, rich party Yesmen to whom the House of Commons is only a fashionable club, and Anarchist Bohemians and freebooters who want liberties without duties. Place and power are obtainable by heredity, by simple purchase, by keeping newspapers and pretending that they are organs of public opinion, by the wiles of seductive women, and by prostituting ambitious talent to the service of the profiteers, who call the tune because, having secured all the spare plunder, they alone can afford to pay the piper.

Under such circumstances neither the rulers nor the ruled can understand high politics. They do not even know that there is such a branch of knowledge as political science; but between them they can coerce and enslave with the deadliest efficiency, even to the wiping out of civilization, because their education as slayers has been honestly and thoroughly carried out. The commonplace sound people submit, and compel the rest to submit, because they have been taught to do so as an article of religion and a point of honor. Those in whom natural enlightenment has reacted against artificial education submit because they are compelled; but they would resist, and finally resist effectively, if they were not cowards. And they are cowards because they have neither an officially accredited and established religion nor a generally recognized point of honor, and are all at sixes and sevens with their various private speculations, sending their children perforce to the schools where they will be corrupted for want of any other schools. The rulers are equally intimidated by the immense extension and cheapening of the means of slaughter and destruction. The old British caution which maintained a balance of Power through command of the sea is intensified into a terror that sees security in nothing short of absolute military mastery of the entire globe: that is, in an impossibility that will yet seem possible in detail to soldiers and to parochial and insular patriotic civilians.

## FLIMSINESS OF CIVILIZATION

This situation has occurred so often before, always with the same result of a collapse of civilization (Professor Flinders Petrie has let out the secret of previous collapses), that the rich are instinctively crying "Let us eat and drink; for tomorrow we die," and the poor, "How long, O Lord, how long?" But the pitiless reply still is that God helps those who help themselves. This does not mean that if Man cannot find the remedy no remedy will be found. The power that produced Man when the monkey was not up to the mark, can produce a higher creature than Man if Man does not come up to the mark. We must beware; for Man is not yet an ideal creature. At his present best many of his ways are so unpleasant that they are unmentionable in polite society, and so painful that he is compelled to pretend that pain is often a good. Nature, also called Providence, holds no brief for the human experiment: it must stand or fall by its results. If Man will not serve, Nature will try another experiment.

What hope is there then of human improvement? According to the Neo-Darwinists, to the Mechanists, no hope whatever, because improvement can come only through some senseless accident which must, on the statistical average of accidents, be presently wiped out by some other equally senseless accident.

## CREATIVE EVOLUTION

But this dismal creed does not discourage those who believe that the impulse that produces evolution is creative. They have observed the simple fact that the will to do anything can and does, at a certain pitch of intensity set up by conviction of its necessity, create and organize new tissue to do it with. To them therefore mankind is by no means played out yet. If the weight lifter, under the trivial stimulus of an athletic competition, can "put up a muscle," it seems reasonable to believe that an equally earnest and convinced philosopher could "put up a brain." Both are directions of vitality to a certain end. Evolution shews us this direction of vitality doing all sorts of things: providing the centipede with a hundred legs, and ridding the fish of any legs at all; building lungs and arms for the land and gills and fins for the sea; enabling the mammal to gestate its young inside its body, and the fowl to incubate hers outside it; offering us, we may say, our choice of any sort of bodily contrivance to maintain our activity and increase our resources.

## VOLUNTARY LONGEVITY

Among other matters apparently changeable at will is the duration of individual life. Weismann, a very clever and suggestive biologist who was unhappily stultified by Neo-Darwinism, pointed out that as certain living organisms, though they multiply by splitting into living halves, never die, death is neither natural nor inevitable.

Besides, life varies widely in duration. Nobody can explain why a parrot should live ten times as long as a dog, and a turtle centuries longer than a wasp. Even within the same species we find Man's average lifetime varying from generation to generation and from individual to individual. Luigi Cornaro lived sixty years longer than Raphael or Mozart. Even our oldest men do not live long enough: they are, for all the purposes of high civilization, mere children when they die; and our Prime Ministers, though rated as mature, divide their time between the golf course and the Treasury Bench in parliament.

Conceivably, however, the same power that has taken us thus far can take us farther. If Man now fixes the term of his life at three score and ten years he can fix it at three hundred or three thousand, or even until a sooner-or-later-inevitable accident makes an end. Surely our ruinous world-wars should convince him of the necessity for at least outliving his taste for golf and cigars if the race is to be saved.

This is not fantastic speculation: it is deductive biology, if there is such a science as biology.

Here, then, is an alternative to the scrapping of our species as a political failure, and its replacement by a new experiment in creative evolution. And so, to make the suggestion more entertaining than it would be to most people in the form of a biological treatise, I have written Back to Methuselah as a contribution to the modern Bible.

Many people, however, can read treatises and cannot read Bibles. Darwin could not read Shakespear. Some who can read both, like to learn the history of their ideas. Some are so entangled in the current confusion of Creative Evolution with Circumstantial Selection by their historical ignorance that they are puzzled by any distinction between the two. For all their sakes I must give here a little history of the conflict between the view of Evolution taken by the Darwinians (though not altogether by Darwin himself) and called Natural Selection, and that which is emerging, under the title of Creative Evolution, as the genuinely scientific religion for which all wise men are now anxiously looking.

### THE EARLY EVOLUTIONISTS

Empedocles, in the fifth century B.C., was an Evolutionist; and there is no reason to assume that he was the first. Our contemporary Joseph Needham will certainly not be the last. Erasmus Darwin, the grandfather of Charles, wrote, as his declaration of faith, "The world has been evolved, not created: it has arisen little by little from a small beginning, and has increased through the activity of the elemental forces embodied in itself, and so has rather grown than come into being at an almighty word. What a sublime idea of the infinite might of the great Architect, the Cause of all causes, the Father of all fathers, the Ens Entium! For if we would compare the Infinite, it would surely require a greater Infinite to cause the causes of effects than to produce the effects themselves." In this, published in the year 1794, you have nineteenth-century Evolution precisely defined. And Erasmus Darwin was by no means its only apostle. It was in the air then. A German biologist named Treviranus, whose book was published in 1802, wrote, "In every living being there exists a capacity for endless diversity of form. Each possesses the power of adapting its organization to the variations of the external world; and it is this power, called into activity by cosmic changes, which has enabled the simple zoophytes of the primitive world to climb to higher and higher stages of organization, and has brought endless variety into nature." There you have your evolution of Man from the amœba all complete whilst Nelson was still alive on the seas. And in 1809, before the battle of Waterloo, a French soldier named Lamarck, who had beaten his musket into a microscope and turned zoologist, declared that species were an illusion produced by the shortness of our individual lives, and that they were constantly changing and melting into one another and into new forms as surely as the hand of a clock is continually moving, though it moves so slowly that it looks stationary to us. We have since come to think that its industry is less continuous: that the clock stops for a long time, and then is suddenly "put on" by a mysterious finger. But never mind that just at present.

## THE ADVENT OF THE NEO-LAMARCKIANS

I call special attention to Lamarck, who, whilst making many ingenious suggestions as to the reaction of external causes on life and habit, such as changes of climate, food supply, geological upheavals and so forth, really held as his fundamental proposition that living organisms change because they want to. If you have no eyes, and want to see, and keep trying to see, you will finally get eyes. If, like a mole or a subterranean fish, you have eyes and dont want to see, you will lose your eyes. If you like eating the tender tops of trees enough to make you concentrate all your energies on the stretching of your neck, you will finally get a long neck, like the giraffe. This seems absurd to inconsiderate people at the first blush; but it is within the personal experience of all of us that it is just by this process that a child tumbling about on the floor becomes an adult walking erect; and that a man sprawling on the road with a bruised chin, or supine on the ice with a bashed occiput, becomes a bicyclist and a skater. The process is not continuous, as it would be if mere practice had anything to do with it; for though you may improve at each bicycling lesson *during* the lesson, when you begin your next lesson you do not begin at the point at which you left off: you relapse apparently to the beginning. Finally, you succeed quite suddenly, and never relapse again. More miraculous still, you at once exercise the new power unconsciously. Although you are adapting your front wheel to your balance so elaborately and actively that the accidental locking of your handle bars for a second will throw you off; though five minutes before you could not do it at all, yet now you do it as unconsciously as you grow your finger nails. You

have a new faculty, and must have created some new
bodily tissue as its organ. And you have done it
solely by willing. For here there can be no question
of Circumstantial Selection, or of the survival of the
fittest. The man who is learning how to ride a bicycle
has no advantage over the non-cyclist in the struggle
for existence: quite the contrary. He has acquired a
new habit, an automatic unconscious habit, solely
because he wanted to, and kept trying until it was
added unto him.

## HOW ACQUIREMENTS ARE INHERITED

But when your son tries to skate or bicycle in his
turn, he does not pick up the accomplishment where
you left it, any more than he is born six feet high
with a beard and a tall hat. The set-back that occurred
between your lessons occurs again. The race learns
exactly as the individual learns. Your son relapses,
not to the very beginning, but to a point which no
mortal method of measurement can distinguish from
the beginning. Now this is odd; for certain other
habits of yours, equally acquired (to the Evolutionist,
of course, all habits are acquired), equally unconscious,
equally automatic, are transmitted without any
perceptible relapse. For instance, the very first act of
your son when he enters the world as a separate
individual is to yell with indignation: that yell which
Shakespear thought the most tragic and piteous of all
sounds. In the act of yelling he begins to breathe:
another habit, and not even a necessary one, as the
object of breathing can be achieved in other ways,
as by deep sea fishes. He circulates his blood by pump-
ing it with his heart. He demands a meal, and proceeds at once to perform the most elaborate chemical

operations on the food he swallows. He manufactures teeth; discards them; and replaces them with fresh ones. Compared to these habitual feats, walking, standing upright, and bicycling are the merest trifles; yet it is only by going through the wanting, trying process that he can stand, walk, or cycle, whereas in the other and far more difficult and complex habits he not only does not consciously want nor consciously try, but actually consciously objects very strongly. Take that early habit of cutting the teeth: would he do that if he could help it? Take that later habit of decaying and eliminating himself by death—equally an acquired habit, remember—how his consciousness abhors it! Yet it has become so automatic that he does it in spite of himself, even to his own destruction.

We have here a routine which, given time enough for it to operate, will finally produce the most elaborate forms of organized life on Lamarckian lines without the intervention of Circumstantial Selection at all. If you can turn a pedestrian into a cyclist, and a cyclist into a pianist or violinist, without the intervention of Circumstantial Selection, you can turn an amœba into a man, or a man into a superman, without it. All of which is rank heresy to the Neo-Darwinian, who imagines that if you stop Circumstantial Selection, you not only stop development but inaugurate a rapid and disastrous degeneration.

Let us fix the Lamarckian evolutionary process well in our minds. You are alive; and you want to be more alive. You want an extension of consciousness and of power. You want, consequently, additional organs, or additional uses of your existing organs: that is, additional habits. You get them because you want them badly enough to keep trying for them until they come. Nobody knows how: nobody knows why:

all we know is that the thing actually takes place. We relapse miserably from effort to effort until the old organ is modified or the new one created, when suddenly the impossible becomes possible and the habit is formed. The moment we form it we want to get rid of the consciousness of it so as to economize our consciousness for fresh conquests of life; for all consciousness means preoccupation and obstruction. If we had to think about breathing or digesting or circulating our blood we should have no attention to spare for anything else, as we find to our cost when anything goes wrong with these operations. We want to be unconscious of them just as we wanted to acquire them; and we finally win what we want. But we win unconsciousness of our habits at the cost of losing our control of them; and we also build one habit and its corresponding functional modification of our organs on another, and so become dependent on our old habits. Consequently we have to persist in them even when they hurt us. We cannot stop breathing to avoid an attack of asthma, nor to escape drowning. We can lose a habit and discard an organ when we no longer need them, just as we acquired them; but this process is slow and broken by relapses; and relics of the organ and the habit long survive their utility. And if other and still indispensable habits and modifications have been built on the ones we wish to discard, we must provide a new foundation for them before we demolish the old ones. This is also a slow process and a very curious one.

## THE MIRACLE OF CONDENSED RECAPITULATION

The relapses between the efforts to acquire a habit are important because, as we have seen, they recur not only from effort to effort in the case of the individual, but from generation to generation in the case of the race. This relapsing from generation to generation is an invariable characteristic of the evolutionary process. For instance, Raphael, though descended from eight uninterrupted generations of painters, had to learn to paint apparently as if no Sanzio had ever handled a brush before. But he had also to learn to breathe, and digest, and circulate his blood. Although his father and mother were fully grown adults when he was conceived, he was not conceived or even born fully grown: he had to go back and begin as a speck of protoplasm, and to struggle through an embryonic lifetime, during part of which he was indistinguishable from an embryonic dog, and had neither a skull nor a backbone. When he at last acquired these articles, he was for some time doubtful whether he was a bird or a fish. He had to compress untold centuries of development into nine months before he was human enough to break loose as an independent being. And even then he was still so incomplete that his parents might well have exclaimed "Good Heavens! have you learnt nothing from our experience that you come into the world in this ridiculously elementary state? Why cant you talk and walk and paint and behave decently?" To that question Baby Raphael had no answer. All he could have said was that this is how evolution or transformation happens. The time may come when the same force that compressed the development of millions of years into nine months may pack many more millions into even a shorter space; so that Raphaels may be born painters as they are now born breathers and blood circulators. But they will still begin as specks of protoplasm, and acquire the faculty of painting in their mother's womb at quite a late stage of their embryonic life. They must recapitulate the history of mankind in their own persons, however briefly they may condense it.

Nothing was so astonishing and significant in the discoveries of the embryologists, nor anything so absurdly little appreciated, as this recapitulation, as it is now called: this power of hurrying up into months a process which was once so long and tedious that the mere contemplation of it is unendurable by men whose span of life is three-score-and-ten. It widened human possibilities to the extent of enabling us to hope that the most prolonged and difficult operations of our minds may yet become instantaneous, or, as we call it, instinctive. It also directed our attention to examples of this packing up of centuries into seconds which were staring us in the face in all directions. As I write these lines the newspapers are occupied by the exploits of a child of eight, who has just defeated twenty adult chess players in twenty games played simultaneously, and has been able afterwards to reconstruct all the twenty games without any apparent effort of memory. Most people, including myself, play chess (when they play it at all) from hand to mouth, and can hardly recall the last move but one, or foresee the next but two. Also, when I have to make an arithmetical calculation, I have to do it step by step with pencil and paper, slowly, reluctantly, and with so little confidence in the result that I dare not act on it without "proving" the sum by a further calculation involving more ciphering. But there are men who can neither read, write, nor cipher, to whom the answer to such sums as I can do is instantly obvious without any conscious calculation at all; and the result is infallible. Yet some of these natural arithmeticians have but a small vocabulary; are at a loss when they have to find words for any but the simplest everyday occasions; and cannot for the life of them describe mechanical operations which they perform daily in the course of their trade; whereas to me the whole vocabulary of English literature, from Shakespear to the latest edition of the Encyclopædia Britannica, is so completely and instantaneously at my call that I have never had to consult even a thesaurus except once or twice when for some reason I wanted a third or fourth synonym. Again, though I have tried and failed to draw recognizable portraits of persons I have seen every day for years, Sir Bernard Partridge, having seen a man once, will, without more strain than is involved in eating a sandwich, draw him to the life. The keyboard of a piano is a device I have never been able to master; yet Mr Cyril Scott uses it as easily as I use a knife and fork; and to Sir Edward Elgar an orchestral score was as instantaneously intelligible at sight as a page of Shakespear is to me. One man cannot, after trying for years, finger the flute fluently. Another will take up a flute with a newly invented arrangement of keys on it, and play it at once with hardly a mistake. We find people to whom writing is so difficult that they prefer to sign their name with a mark, and beside them men who master systems of shorthand and improvise new systems of their own as easily as they learnt the alphabet. These contrasts are to be seen on all hands, and have nothing to do with variations in general intelligence, nor even in the specialized intelligence proper to the faculty in question: for example, no composer or dramatic poet has ever pretended to be able to perform all the parts he writes for the singers, actors, and players

who are his executants. One might as well expect
Napoleon to be a fencer, or the Astronomer Royal to
know how many beans make five any better than his
bookkeeper. Even exceptional command of language
does not imply the possession of ideas to express:
Mezzofanti, the master of fifty-eight languages, had
less to say in them than Shakespear with his little
Latin and less Greek; and public life is the paradise
of voluble windbags.

All these are cases in which a long, laborious, conscious, detailed process of acquirement has been
condensed into an instinctive and unconscious inborn
one. Factors which formerly had to be considered
one by one in succession are integrated into what
seems a single simple factor. Chains of hardly soluble
problems have coalesced in one problem which solves
itself the moment it is raised. What is more, they
have been pushed back (or forward, if you like) from
post-natal to pre-natal ones. The child in the womb
may take some time over them; but it is a miracu-
lously shortened time.

The time phenomena involved are curious, and
suggest that we are either wrong about our history
or else that we enormously exaggerate the periods
required for the pre-natal acquirement of habits. In
the nineteenth century we talked very glibly about
geological periods, and flung millions of eons about
in the most lordly manner in our reaction against
Archbishop Ussher's chronology. We had a craze
for big figures, and positively liked to believe that the
progress made by the child in the womb in a month
was represented in prehistoric time by ages and ages.
We insisted that Evolution advanced more slowly
than any snail ever crawled, and that Nature does not
proceed by leaps and bounds. This was all very well

as long as we were dealing with such acquired habits as breathing or digestion. It was possible to believe that dozens of epochs had gone to the slow building up of these habits. But when we have to consider the case of a man born not only as an accomplished metabolist, but with such aptitudes that he is a stenographer or pianist at least five sixths ready-made as soon as he can control his hands intelligently, or a playwright, painter, sculptor, poet or philosopher while still adolescent, we are forced to suspect that acquirements can be assimilated and stored as congenital qualifications in a shorter time than we think; so that, as between Lyell and Archbishop Ussher, the laugh may not be with Lyell quite so uproariously as it seemed fifty years ago.

## HEREDITY AN OLD STORY

It is evident that the evolutionary process is a hereditary one, or, to put it less drily, that human life is continuous and immortal. The Evolutionists took heredity for granted. So did everybody. The human mind has been soaked in heredity as long back as we can trace its thought. Hereditary peers, hereditary monarchs, hereditary castes and trades and classes were the best known of social institutions, and in some cases of public nuisances. Pedigree men counted pedigree dogs and pedigree horses among their most cherished possessions. Far from being unconscious of heredity, or sceptical, men were insanely credulous about it: they not only believed in the transmission of qualities and habits from generation to generation, but expected the son to begin mentally where the father left off.

[ 279 ]

This belief in heredity led naturally to the practice of Intentional Selection. Good blood and breeding were eagerly sought after in human marriage. In dealing with plants and animals, selection with a view to the production of new varieties and the improvement and modification of species has been practised ever since men began to cultivate them. My pre-Darwinian uncle knew as well as Darwin that the race-horse and the dray-horse are not separate creations from the Garden of Eden, but adaptations by deliberate human selection of the medieval war-horse to modern racing and industrial haulage. He knew that there are nearly two hundred different sorts of dogs, all capable of breeding with one another and of producing cross varieties unknown to Adam. He knew that the same thing is true of pigeons. He knew that gardeners had spent their lives trying to breed black tulips and green carnations and unheard-of orchids, and had actually produced flowers just as strange to Eve. His quarrel with the Evolutionists was not a quarrel with the evidence for Evolution: he had accepted enough of it to prove Evolution ten times over before he ever heard of it. What he repudiated was cousinship with the ape, and the implied suspicion of a rudimentary tail, because it was offensive to his sense of his own dignity, and because he thought that apes were ridiculous, and tails diabolical when associated with the erect posture. Also he believed that Evolution was a heresy which involved the destruction of Christianity, of which, as a member of the Protestant Episcopal Irish Church, he conceived himself a pillar. But this was only his ignorance; for a man may deny his descent from an ape and be eligible as a churchwarden without being any the less a convinced Evolutionist.

## DISCOVERY ANTICIPATED BY DIVINATION

What is more, the religious folk can claim to be among the pioneers of Evolutionism. Weismann, Neo-Darwinist though he was, devoted a long passage in his History of Evolution to the Nature Philosophy of Lorenz Oken, published in 1809. Oken defined natural science as "the science of the everlasting transmutations of the Holy Ghost in the world." His religion had started him on the right track, and not only led him to think out a whole scheme of Evolution in abstract terms, but guided his aim in a significantly good scientific shot which brought him within the scope of Weismann. He not only defined the original substance from which all forms of life have developed as protoplasm, or, as he called it, primitive slime (*Urschleim*), but actually declared that this slime took the form of vesicles out of which the universe was built. Here was the modern cell morphology guessed by a religious thinker long before the microscope and the scalpel forced it on the vision of mere laboratory workers who could not think and had no religion. Lorenz Oken *thought* very hard to find out what was happening to the Holy Ghost, and thereby made a contribution of extraordinary biological importance. The man who was scientific enough to see that the Holy Ghost is a scientific fact got easily in front of the laboratory researchers who sinned against it.

The metaphysical side of Evolution was thus no novelty when Darwin arrived. Had Oken never lived, there would still have been millions of persons trained from their childhood to believe that we are continually urged upwards by a force called the Will of God. In 1819 Schopenhauer published his treatise on The World as Will, which is the metaphysical complement to Lamarck's natural history, as it demonstrates that the driving force behind Evolution is a will-to-live, and to live, as Christ said long before, more abundantly. And the earlier philosophers, from Plato to Leibniz, had kept the human mind open for the thought of the universe as one idea behind all its physically apprehensible transformations.

## CORRECTED DATES FOR THE DISCOVERY OF EVOLUTION

All this, remember, is the state of things in the pre-Darwin period, which so many of us still think of as a pre-evolutionary period. Evolutionism was the rage before Queen Victoria came to the throne. To fix this chronology, let me repeat the story told by Weismann of the July revolution in Paris in 1830, when the French got rid of Charles the Tenth. Goethe was then still living; and a French friend of his called on him and found him wildly excited. "What do you think of the great event?" said Goethe. "The volcano is in eruption; and all is in flames. There can no longer be discussion with closed doors." The Frenchman replied that no doubt it was a terrible business; but what could they expect with such a ministry and such a king? "Stuff!" said Goethe: "I am not thinking of these people at all, but of the open rupture in the French Academy between Cuvier and St Hilaire. It is of the utmost importance to science." The rupture Goethe meant was about Evolution, Cuvier contending that there were four species, and St Hilaire that there was only one.

From 1830 to 1859, when Darwin published his

Origin of Species, there was a slump in Evolutionism. Nobody who knew the theory was adding anything to it. This slump not only heightened the general impression of entire novelty when Darwin brought the subject to the front again but prevented him from realizing how much had been done before, even by his own grandfather, to whom he was accused of being unjust. His insistence on the godless part played in organic development by circumstances delighted the sceptical intelligentsia. Nowadays, when we are turning in weary disgust and disillusion from Neo-Darwinism and Mechanism to Vitalism and Creative Evolution, it is difficult to credit this. Let me therefore try to bring back something of the atmosphere of that time by describing a scene, very characteristic of its superstitions, in which I took what was then considered an unspeakably shocking part.

## DEFYING THE LIGHTNING: A FRUSTRATED EXPERIMENT

One evening in 1878 or thereabouts, I, being then in my earliest twenties, was at a bachelor party of young men of the professional class in the house of a rising young London physician. We fell to talking about religious revivals; and an anecdote was related of an "infidel" who, having incautiously scoffed at the mission of Messrs Moody and Sankey, a then famous firm of American evangelists, was subsequently carried home on a shutter, slain by divine vengeance as a blasphemer. A timid minority, without quite venturing to question the truth of the incident—for they naturally did not care to run the risk of going home on shutters themselves—nevertheless shewed a certain disposition to cavil at those who exulted in it; and something approaching to an argument began. At last it was alleged by the most evangelical of the disputants that Charles Bradlaugh, the most formidable atheist on the Secularist platform, had taken out his watch publicly and challenged the Almighty to strike him dead in five minutes if he really existed and disapproved of atheism. The leader of the cavillers, with great heat, repudiated this as a gross calumny, declaring that Bradlaugh had repeatedly and indignantly contradicted it, and implying that the atheist champion was far too pious a man to commit such a blasphemy. This exquisite confusion of ideas roused my sense of comedy. It was clear to me that the challenge attributed to Charles Bradlaugh was a scientific experiment of a quite simple, straightforward, and proper kind to ascertain whether the expression of atheistic opinions really did involve any personal risk. It was certainly the method taught in the Bible, Elijah having confuted the prophets of Baal in precisely that way, with every circumstance of bitter mockery of their god when he failed to send down fire from heaven. Accordingly I said that if the question at issue were whether the penalty of questioning the theology of Messrs Moody and Sankey was to be struck dead on the spot by an incensed deity, nothing could effect a more convincing settlement of it than the very obvious experiment attributed to Mr Bradlaugh, and that consequently if he had not tried it, he ought to have tried it. The omission, I added, was one which could easily be remedied there and then, as I happened to share Mr Bradlaugh's views as to the absurdity of the belief in these violent interferences with the order of nature by a short-tempered and thin-skinned supernatural deity. Therefore—and at that point I took out my watch.

The effect was electrical. Neither sceptics nor devotees were prepared to abide the result of the experiment. In vain did I urge the pious to trust in the accuracy of their deity's aim with a thunderbolt, and the justice of his discrimination between the innocent and the guilty. In vain did I appeal to the sceptics to accept the logical outcome of their scepticism: it soon appeared that when thunderbolts were in question there were no sceptics. Our host, seeing that his guests would vanish precipitately if the impious challenge were uttered, leaving him alone with a solitary infidel under sentence of extermination in five minutes, interposed and forbade the experiment, pleading at the same time for a change of subject. I of course complied, but could not refrain from remarking that though the dreadful words had not been uttered, yet, as the thought had been formulated in my mind, it was very doubtful whether the consequences could be averted by sealing my lips. However, the rest appeared to feel that the game would be played according to the rules, and that it mattered very little what I thought so long as I said nothing. Only the leader of the evangelical party, I thought, was a little preoccupied until five minutes had elapsed and the weather was still calm.

## IN QUEST OF THE FIRST CAUSE

Another reminiscence. In those days we thought in terms of time and space, of cause and effect, as we still do; but we do not now demand from a religion that it shall explain the universe completely in terms of cause and effect, and present the world to us as a manufactured article and as the private property of its Manufacturer. We did then. We were invited to pity the delusion of certain heathens who held that the world is supported by an elephant who is supported by a tortoise. Mahomet decided that the mountains are great weights to keep the world from being blown away into space. But we refuted these orientals by asking triumphantly what the tortoise stands on? Freethinkers asked which came first: the owl or the egg. Nobody thought of saying that the ultimate problem of existence, being clearly insoluble and even unthinkable on causation lines, could not be a causation problem. To pious people this would have been flat atheism, because they assumed that God must be a Cause, and sometimes called him The Great First Cause. To the Rationalists it would have been a renunciation of reason. Here and there a man would confess that he stood as with a dim lantern in a dense fog, and could see but a little way in any direction into infinity. But he did not really believe that infinity was infinite or that the eternal was also sempiternal: he assumed that all things, known and unknown, were caused.

Hence it was that I found myself one day towards the end of the eighteen-seventies in a cell in the old Brompton Oratory arguing with Father Addis, who had been called by one of his flock to attempt my conversion to Roman Catholicism. The universe exists, said the father: somebody must have made it. If that somebody exists, said I, somebody must have made him. I grant that for the sake of argument, said the Oratorian. I grant you a maker of God. I grant you a maker of the maker of God. I grant you as long a line of makers as you please; but an infinity of makers is unthinkable and extravagant: it is no harder to believe in number one than in number fifty thousand or fifty million; so why not accept number one and stop there, since no attempt to get behind him will remove your logical difficulty? By your leave, said I, it is as easy for me to believe that the universe made itself as that a maker of the universe made himself: in fact much easier; for the universe visibly exists and makes itself as it goes along, whereas a maker for it is a hypothesis.

Of course we two could get no further on these lines. He rose, very sensible and friendly, and said that we were like two men working a saw, he pushing it forward and I pushing it back, and cutting nothing. But when we had dropped the subject and were walking through the refectory, he returned to it for a moment to say that he should go mad if he lost his belief. I, glorying in the robust callousness of youth and the comedic spirit, felt quite comfortable and said so; though I was touched, too, by his evident sincerity.

These two anecdotes are superficially trivial and even comic; but there is an abyss of horror beneath them. They reveal a condition so utterly irreligious that religion means nothing but belief in a nursery bogey, and its inadequacy is demonstrated by a toy logical dilemma, neither the bogey nor the dilemma having anything to do with religion, or being serious enough to impose on or confuse any properly educated child over the age of six. One hardly knows which is the more appalling: the abjectness of the credulity or the flippancy of the scepticism. The result was inevitable. All who were strongminded enough not to be terrified by the bogey were left stranded in empty contemptuous negation, and argued, when

they argued at all, as I argued with Father Addis.
But their position was not intellectually comfortable.
A member of parliament expressed their discomfort
when, objecting to the admission of Charles Bradlaugh into parliament, he said "Hang it all, a man
should believe in something or somebody." It was
easy to throw the bogey into the dustbin; but none
the less the world, our corner of the universe, did not
look like a pure accident: it presented evidences of
design in every direction. There was mind and
purpose behind it. As the anti-Bradlaugh member
would have put it, there must be somebody behind
the something: no atheist could get over that.

## PALEY'S WATCH

Paley had put the argument in an apparently unanswerable form. If you found a watch, full of
mechanism exquisitely adapted to produce a series of
operations all leading to the fulfilment of one central
purpose of measuring for mankind the march of the
day and night, could you believe that it was not the
work of a cunning artificer who had designed and
contrived it all to that end? And here was a far
more wonderful thing than a watch, a man with all
his organs ingeniously contrived, cords and levers,
girders and kingposts, circulating systems of pipes and
valves, dialysing membranes, retorts, carburettors,
pumps, glands, ventilators, inlets and outlets, telephone transmitters in his ears, light recorders and
lenses in his eyes: was it conceivable that this was the
work of chance? that no artificer had wrought here?
that there was no purpose in this, no design, no
guiding intelligence? The thing was incredible. In
vain did Helmholtz declare that "the eye has every

possible defect that can be found in an optical instrument, and even some peculiar to itself," and that "if an optician tried to sell me an instrument which had all these defects I should think myself quite justified in blaming his carelessness in the strongest terms, and sending him back his instrument." To discredit the optician's skill was not to get rid of the optician. The eye might not be so cleverly made as Paley thought, but it was made somehow, by somebody.

And then my argument with Father Addis began all over again. It was easy enough to say that every man makes his own eyes: indeed the embryologists had actually caught him doing it. But what about the very evident purpose that prompted him to do it? Why did he want to see, if not to extend his consciousness and his knowledge and his power? That purpose was at work everywhere, and must be something bigger than the individual eye-making man. Only the stupidest muckrakers could fail to see this, and even to know it as part of their own consciousness. Yet to admit it seemed to involve letting the bogey come back, so inextricably had we managed to mix up belief in the bogey's existence with belief in the existence of design in the universe.

## THE IRRESISTIBLE CRY OF ORDER, ORDER!

Our scornful young scientific and philosophic lions of today must not blame the Church of England for this confusion of thought. In 1562 the Church, in convocation in London "for the avoiding of diversities of opinions and for the establishment of consent touching true religion," proclaimed in their first utterance, and as an Article of Religion, that God is " without body, parts, or passions," or, as we say, an *Élan Vital* or Life Force. Unfortunately neither parents, parsons, nor pedagogues could be induced to adopt that article. St John might say that "God is spirit" as pointedly as he pleased; our Sovereign Lady Elizabeth might ratify the Article again and again; serious divines might feel as deeply as they could that a God with body, parts, and passions could be nothing but an anthropomorphic idol: no matter: people at large could not conceive a God who was not anthropomorphic: they stood by the Old Testament legends of a God whose parts had been seen by one of the patriarchs, and finally set up as against the Church a God who, far from being without body, parts, or passions, was composed of nothing else, and of very evil passions too. They imposed this idol in practice on the Church itself, in spite of the First Article, and thereby homeopathically produced the atheist, whose denial of God was simply a denial of the idol and a demonstration against an unbearable and most unchristian idolatry. The idol was, as Shelley had been expelled from Oxford for pointing out, an almighty fiend, with a petty character and unlimited power, spiteful, cruel, jealous, vindictive, and physically violent. The most sadistic schoolmasters, the most tyrannical parents, fell far short in their attempts to imitate it. But it was not its social vices that brought it low. What made it scientifically intolerable was that it was ready at a moment's notice to upset the whole order of the universe on the most trumpery provocation, whether by stopping the sun in the valley of Ajalon or sending an atheist home dead on a shutter (the shutter was indispensable because it marked the utter unpreparedness of the atheist, who, unable to save himself by a deathbed repentance, was subsequently roasted through all

eternity in blazing brimstone). It was this disorderli-
ness, this refusal to obey its own laws of nature, that
created a scientific need for its destruction. Science
could stand a cruel and unjust god; for nature was
full of suffering and injustice. But a disorderly god
was impossible. In the Middle Ages a compromise
had been made by which two different orders of truth,
religious and scientific, had been recognized, in order
that a schoolman might say that two and two make
four without being burnt for heresy. But the nineteenth century, steeped in a meddling, presumptuous,
reading-and-writing, socially and politically powerful
ignorance inconceivable by Thomas Aquinas or even
Roger Bacon, was incapable of so convenient an
arrangement; and science was strangled by bigoted
ignoramuses claiming infallibility for their interpreta-
tion of the Bible, which was regarded, not as a literature nor even as a book, but partly as an oracle which
answered and settled all questions, and partly as a
talisman to be carried by soldiers in their breast
pockets or placed under the pillows of persons who
were afraid of ghosts. The tract shops exhibited in
their windows bullet-dinted testaments, mothers' gifts
to their soldier sons whose lives had been saved by it;
for the muzzle-loaders of those days could not drive a
projectile through so many pages.

### THE MOMENT AND THE MAN

This superstition of a continual capricious disorder
in nature, of a lawgiver who was also a lawbreaker,
made atheists in all directions among clever and light-
minded people. But atheism did not account for
Paley's watch. Atheism accounted for nothing; and
it was the business of science to account for everything

[ 291 ]

that was plainly accountable. Science had no use for mere negation: what was desired by it above all things just then was a demonstration that the evidences of design could be explained without resort to the hypothesis of a personal designer. If only some genius, whilst admitting Paley's facts, could knock the brains out of Paley by the discovery of a method whereby watches could happen without watchmakers, that genius was assured of such a welcome from the thought of his day as no natural philosopher had ever enjoyed before.

The time being thus ripe, the genius appeared; and his name was Charles Darwin. And now, what did Darwin really discover?

Here, I am afraid, I shall require once more the assistance of the giraffe, or, as he was called in the days of the celebrated Buffoon, the camelopard (by children, cammyleopard). I do not remember how this animal imposed himself illustratively on the Evolution controversy; but there was no getting away from him then; and I am old-fashioned enough to be unable to get away from him now. How did he come by his long neck? Lamarck would have said, by wanting to get at the tender leaves high up on the tree, and trying until he succeeded in wishing the necessary length of neck into existence. Another answer was also possible: namely, that some pre-historic stockbreeder, wishing to produce a natural curiosity, selected the longest-necked animals he could find, and bred from them until at last an animal with an abnormally long neck was evolved by intentional selection, just as the race-horse or the fantail pigeon has been evolved. Both these explanations, you will observe, involve consciousness, will, design, purpose, either on the part of the animal itself or on

the part of a superior intelligence controlling its
destiny. Darwin pointed out that a third explanation, involving neither will nor purpose nor design
either in the animal or anyone else, was on the cards.
If your neck is too short to reach your food, you die.
That may be the simple explanation of the fact that
all the surviving animals that feed on foliage have
necks or trunks long enough to reach it. So bang
goes your belief that the necks must have been
designed to reach the food. But Lamarck did not
believe that the necks were so designed in the beginning: he believed that the long necks were evolved
by wanting and trying. Not necessarily, said Darwin.
Consider the effect on the giraffes of the natural
multiplication of their numbers, as insisted on by
Malthus. Suppose the average height of the foliage-
eating animals is four feet, and that they increase in
numbers until a time comes when all the trees are
eaten away to within four feet of the ground. Then
the animals who happen to be an inch or two short
of the average will die of starvation. All the animals
who happen to be an inch or so above the average
will be better fed and stronger than the others. They
will secure the strongest and tallest mates; and their
progeny will survive whilst the average ones and the
sub-average ones will die out. This process, by which
the species gains, say, an inch in reach, will repeat
itself until the giraffe's neck is so long that he can
always find food enough within his reach, at which
point, of course, the selective process stops and the
length of the giraffe's neck stops with it. Otherwise,
he would grow until he could browse off the trees in
the moon. And this, mark you, without the intervention of any stock-breeder, human or divine, and
without will, purpose, design, or even consciousness

beyond the blind will to satisfy hunger. It is true that this blind will, being in effect a will to live, gives away the whole case; but still, as compared to the open-eyed intelligent wanting and trying of Lamarck, the Darwinian process may be described as a chapter of accidents. As such, it seems simple, because you do not at first realize all that it involves. But when its whole significance dawns on you, your heart sinks into a heap of sand within you. There is a hideous fatalism about it, a ghastly and damnable reduction of beauty and intelligence, of strength and purpose, of honor and aspiration, to such casually picturesque changes as an avalanche may make in a mountain landscape, or a railway accident in a human figure. To call this Natural Selection is a blasphemy, possible to many for whom Nature is nothing but a casual aggregation of inert and dead matter, but eternally impossible to the spirits and souls of the righteous. If it be no blasphemy, but a truth of science, then the stars of heaven, the showers and dew, the winter and summer, the fire and heat, the mountains and hills, may no longer be called to exalt the Lord with us by praise: their work is to modify all things by blindly starving and murdering everything that is not lucky enough to survive in the universal struggle for hogwash.

### THE BRINK OF THE BOTTOMLESS PIT

Thus did the neck of the giraffe reach out across the whole heavens and make men believe that what they saw there was a gloaming of the gods. For if this sort of selection could turn an antelope into a giraffe, it could conceivably turn a pond full of amœbas into the French Academy. Though Lamarck's way, the way of life, will, aspiration, and achievement, remained still possible, this newly shewn way of hunger, death, stupidity, delusion, chance, and bare survival was also possible: was indeed most certainly the way in which many apparently intelligently designed transformations had actually come to pass. Had I not preluded with the apparently idle story of my revival of the controversial methods of Elijah, I should be asked how it was that the explorer who opened up this gulf of despair, far from being stoned or crucified as the destroyer of the honor of the race and the purpose of the world, was hailed as Deliverer, Savior, Prophet, Redeemer, Enlightener, Rescuer, Hope Giver, and Epoch Maker; whilst poor Lamarck was swept aside as a crude and exploded guesser hardly worthy to be named as his erroneous forerunner. In the light of my anecdote, the explanation is obvious. The first thing the gulf did was to swallow up Paley, and the Disorderly Designer, and Shelley's Almighty Fiend, and all the rest of the pseudo-religious rubbish that had blocked every upward and onward path since the hopes of men had turned to Science as their true Savior. It seemed such a convenient grave that nobody at first noticed that it was nothing less than the bottomless pit, now become a very real terror. For though Darwin left a path round it for his soul, his followers presently dug it right into the crater.

Yet for the moment, there was nothing but wild rejoicing. We had been so oppressed by the notion that everything that happened in the world was the arbitrary personal act of an arbitrary personal god of dangerously jealous and cruel personal character, so that even the relief of the pains of childbed and the operating table by chloroform was objected to as an interference with his arrangements which he would

probably resent, that we just jumped at Darwin.
When Napoleon was asked what would happen when
he died, he said that Europe would express its intense
relief with a great "Ouf!" Well, when Darwin killed
the god who objected to chloroform, everybody who
had ever thought about it said "Ouf!" Paley was
buried fathoms deep with his watch, now fully
accounted for without any divine artificer at all. We
were so glad to be rid of both that we never gave a
thought to the consequences. When a prisoner sees
the door of his dungeon open, he dashes for it without
stopping to think where he shall get his dinner outside.
The moment we found that we could do without
Shelley's almighty fiend intellectually, he went into
the gulf that seemed only a dustbin with a suddenness
that made our own lives one of the most astonishing
periods in history. If I had told that uncle of mine
that within thirty years from the date of our conversation I should be exposing myself to suspicions of the
grossest superstition by questioning the sufficiency of
Darwin; maintaining the reality of the Holy Ghost;
and declaring that the phenomenon of the Thought
becoming Flesh was occurring daily, he would have
regarded me as the most extravagant madman our
family had ever produced. Yet it was so. In 1906 I
might have vituperated Jehovah more heartily than
ever Shelley did without eliciting a protest in any
circle of thinkers, or shocking any public audience
accustomed to modern discussion; but when I
described Darwin as "an intelligent and industrious
pigeon fancier," that blasphemous levity, as it seemed,
was received with horror and indignation. The tide
has now turned; and every puny whipster may say
what he likes about Darwin; but anyone who wants
to know what it was to be a Lamarckian during the

last quarter of the nineteenth century has only to read Mr Festing Jones's memoir of Samuel Butler to learn how completely even a man of genius could isolate himself by antagonizing Darwin on the one hand and the Church on the other.

## WHY DARWIN CONVERTED THE CROWD

I am well aware that in describing the effect of Darwin's discovery on naturalists and on persons capable of serious reflection on the nature and attributes of God, I am leaving the vast mass of the British public out of account. I have pointed out elsewhere that the British nation does not consist of atheists and Plymouth Brothers; and I am not now going to pretend that it ever consisted of Darwinians and Lamarckians. The average citizen is irreligious and unscientific: you talk to him about cricket and golf, market prices and party politics, not about evolution and relativity, transubstantiation and predestination. Nothing will knock into his head the fateful distinction between Evolution as promulgated by Erasmus Darwin, and Circumstantial (so-called Natural) Selection as revealed by his grandson. Yet the doctrine of Charles reached him, though the doctrine of Erasmus had passed over his head. Why did not Erasmus Darwin popularize the word Evolution as effectively as Charles ?

The reason was, I think, that Circumstantial Selection is easier to understand, more visible and concrete, than Lamarckian evolution. Evolution as a philosophy and physiology of the will is a mystical process, which can be apprehended only by a trained, apt, and comprehensive thinker. Though the phenomena of use and disuse, of wanting and trying, of the manufacture of weight lifters and wrestlers from men of ordinary strength, are familiar enough as facts, they are extremely puzzling as subjects of thought, and lead you into metaphysics the moment you try to account for them. But pigeon fanciers, dog fanciers, gardeners, stock breeders, or stud grooms, can understand Circumstantial Selection, because it is their business to produce transformation by imposing on flowers and animals a Selection From Without. All that Darwin had to say to them was that the mere chapter of accidents is always doing on a huge scale what they themselves are doing on a very small scale. There is hardly a laborer attached to an English country house who has not taken a litter of kittens or puppies to the bucket, and drowned all of them except the one he thinks the most promising. Such a man has nothing to learn about the survival of the fittest except that it acts in more ways than he has yet noticed; for he knows quite well, as you will find if you are not too proud to talk to him, that this sort of selection occurs naturally (in Darwin's sense) too: that, for instance, a hard winter will kill off a weakly child as the bucket kills off a weakly puppy. Then there is the farm laborer. Shakespear's Touchstone, a court-bred fool, was shocked to find in the shepherd a natural philosopher, and opined that he would be damned for the part he took in the sexual selection of sheep. As to the production of new species by the selection of variations, that is no news to your gardener. Now if you are familiar with these three processes: the survival of the fittest, sexual selection, and variation leading to new kinds, there is nothing to puzzle you in Darwinism.

That was the secret of Darwin's popularity. He never puzzled anybody. If very few of us have read

The Origin of Species from end to end, it is not because it overtaxes our mind, but because we take in the whole case and are prepared to accept it long before we have come to the end of the innumerable instances and illustrations of which the book mainly consists. Darwin becomes tedious in the manner of a man who insists on continuing to prove his innocence after he has been acquitted. You assure him that there is not a stain on his character, and beg him to leave the court; but he will not be content with enough evidence to acquit him: he will have you listen to all the evidence that exists in the world. Darwin's industry was enormous. His patience, his perseverance, his conscientiousness reached the human limit. But he never got deeper beneath or higher above his facts than an ordinary man could follow him. He was not conscious of having raised a stupendous issue, because, though it arose instantly, it was not his business. He was conscious of having discovered a process of transformation and modification which accounted for a great deal of natural history. But he did not put it forward as accounting for the whole of natural history. He included it under the heading of Evolution, though it was only pseudo-evolution at best; but he revealed it as *a* method of evolution, not as *the* method of evolution. He did not pretend that it excluded other methods, or that it was the chief method. Though he demonstrated that many transformations which had been taken as functional adaptations (the current phrase for Lamarckian evolution) either certainly were or conceivably might be due to Circumstantial Selection, he was careful not to claim that he had superseded Lamarck or disproved Functional Adaptation. In short, he was not a Darwinian, but an honest naturalist working away at his job with so little preoccupation with theological speculation that he never quarrelled with the theistic Unitarianism into which he was born, and remained to the end the engagingly simple and socially easy-going soul he had been in his boyhood, when his elders doubted whether he would ever be of much use in the world.

## HOW WE RUSHED DOWN A STEEP PLACE

Not so the rest of us intellectuals. We all began going to the devil with the utmost cheerfulness. Everyone who had a mind to change, changed it. Only Samuel Butler, on whom Darwin had acted homeopathically, reacted against him furiously; ran up the Lamarckian flag to the top-gallant peak; declared with penetrating accuracy that Darwin had "banished mind from the universe"; and even attacked Darwin's personal character, unable to bear the fact that the author of so abhorrent a doctrine was an amiable and upright man. Nobody would listen to him. He was so completely submerged by the flowing tide of Darwinism that when Darwin wanted to clear up the misunderstanding on which Butler was basing his personal attacks, Darwin's friends, very foolishly and snobbishly, persuaded him that Butler was too ill-conditioned and negligible to be answered. That they could not recognize in Butler a man of genius mattered little: what did matter was that they could not understand the provocation under which he was raging. They actually regarded the banishment of mind from the universe as a glorious enlightenment and emancipation for which he was ignorantly ungrateful. Even now, when Butler's eminence is unchallenged, and his biographer, Mr Festing Jones, is enjoying a vogue like that of Boswell

or Lockhart, his memoirs shew him rather as a
shocking example of the bad controversial manners
of our country parsonages than as a prophet who
tried to head us back when we were gaily dancing
to our damnation across the rainbow bridge which
Darwinism had thrown over the gulf which separates
life and hope from death and despair. We were
intellectually intoxicated with the idea that the world
could make itself without design, purpose, skill, or
intelligence: in short, without life. We completely
overlooked the difference between the modification
of species by adaptation to their environment and the
appearance of new species: we just threw in the word
"variations" or the word "sports" (fancy a man of
science talking of an unknown factor as a sport instead
of as $x$!) and left them to "accumulate" and account
for the difference between a cockatoo and a hippo-
potamus. Such phrases set us free to revel in demonstrating to the Vitalists and Bible worshippers that if
we once admit the existence of any kind of force,
however unintelligent, and stretch out the past to
unlimited time for such force to operate accidentally
in, that force may conceivably, by the action of Circumstantial Selection, produce a world in which every
function has an organ perfectly adapted to perform
it, and therefore presents every appearance of having
been designed, like Paley's watch, by a conscious and
intelligent artificer for the purpose. We took a per-
verse pleasure in arguing, without the least suspicion
that we were reducing ourselves to absurdity, that all
the books in the British Museum library might have
been written word for word as they stand on the
shelves if no human being had ever been conscious,
just as the trees stand in the forest doing wonderful
things without consciousness.

And the Darwinians went far beyond denying consciousness to trees. Weismann insisted that the chick breaks out of its eggshell automatically; that the butterfly, springing into the air to avoid the pounce of the lizard, "does not wish to avoid death; knows nothing about death," what has happened being simply that a flight instinct evolved by Circumstantial Selection reacts promptly to a visual impression produced by the lizard's movement. His proof is that the butterfly immediately settles again on the flower, and repeats the performance every time the lizard springs, thus shewing that it learns nothing from experience, and—Weismann concludes—is not conscious of what it does.

It should hardly have escaped so curious an observer that when the cat jumps up on the dinner table, and you put it down, it instantly jumps up again, and finally establishes its right to a place on the cloth by convincing you that if you put it down a hundred times it will jump up a hundred and one times; so that if you desire its company at dinner you can have it only on its own terms. If Weismann really thought that cats act thus without any consciousness or any purpose, immediate or ulterior, he must have known very little about cats. But a thoroughgoing Weismannite, if any such still survive from those mad days, would contend that I am not at present necessarily conscious of what I am doing; that my writing of these lines, and your reading of them, are effects of Circumstantial Selection; that I need know no more about Darwinism than a butterfly knows of a lizard's appetite; and that the proof that I actually am doing it unconsciously is that as I have spent forty years in writing in this fashion without, as far as I can see, producing any visible effect on public opinion, I must be incapable of learning from experience, and am therefore a mere automaton. And the Weismannite demonstration of this would of course be an equally unconscious effect of Circumstantial Selection.

## DARWINISM NOT FINALLY REFUTABLE

Do not too hastily say that this is inconceivable. To Circumstantial Selection all mechanical and chemical reactions are possible, provided you accept the geologists' estimates of the great age of the earth, and therefore allow time enough for the circumstances to operate. It is true that mere survival of the fittest in the struggle for existence plus sexual selection fail as hopelessly to account for Darwin's own life work as for my conquest of the bicycle; but who can prove that there are not other soulless factors, unnoticed or undiscovered, which only require imagination enough to fit them to the evolution of an automatic Jesus or Shakespear? When a man tells you that you are a product of Circumstantial Selection solely, you cannot finally disprove it. You can only tell him out of the depths of your inner conviction that he is a fool and a liar. But as this, though British, is uncivil, it is wiser to offer him the counter-assurance that you are the product of Lamarckian evolution, formerly called Functional Adaptation and now Creative Evolution, and challenge him to disprove *that*, which he can no more do than you can disprove Circumstantial Selection, both forces being conceivably able to produce anything if you only give them rope enough. You may also defy him to act for a single hour on the assumption that he may safely cross Oxford Street in a state of unconsciousness, trusting to his dodging reflexes to react automatically and promptly enough

[ 303 ]

to the visual impression produced by a motor bus, and the audible impression produced by its hooter. But if you allow yourself to defy him to explain any particular action of yours by Circumstantial Selection, he should always be able to find some explanation that will fit the case if only he is ingenious enough and goes far enough to find it. Darwin found several such explanations in his controversies. Anybody who really wants to believe that the universe has been produced by Circumstantial Selection co-operating with a force as inhuman as we conceive magnetism to be can find a logical excuse for his belief if he tries hard enough.

## TRAUMATIC SELECTION

The stultification and damnation which ensued are illustrated by a comparison of the ease and certainty with which Butler's mind moved to humane and inspiring conclusions with the grotesque stupidities and cruelties of the idle and silly controversy which arose among the Darwinians as to whether acquired habits can be transmitted from parents to offspring. Consider, for example, how Weismann set to work on that subject. An Evolutionist with a live mind would first have dropped the popular expression "acquired habits," because to an Evolutionist there are no other habits and can be no others, a man being only an amœba with acquirements. He would then have considered carefully the process by which he himself had acquired his habits. He would have assumed that the habits with which he was born must have been acquired by a similar process. He would have known what a habit is: that is, an action voluntarily attempted until it has become more or less automatic and involuntary; and it would never have occurred to him that injuries or accidents coming from external sources against the will of the victim could possibly establish a habit; that, for instance, a family could acquire a habit of being killed in railway accidents.

And yet Weismann began to investigate the point by behaving like the farmer's wife in the old catch. He got a colony of mice, and cut off their tails. Then he waited to see whether their children would be born without tails. They were not, as Butler could have told him beforehand. He then cut off the children's tails, and waited to see whether the grandchildren would be born with at least rather short tails. They were not, as I could have told him beforehand. So with the patience and industry on which men of science pride themselves, he cut off the grandchildren's tails too, and waited, full of hope, for the birth of curtailed great grandchildren. But their tails were quite up to the mark, as any fool could have told him beforehand. Weismann then gravely drew the inference that acquired habits cannot be transmitted. And yet Weismann was not a born imbecile. He was an exceptionally clever and studious man, not without roots of imagination and philosophy in him which Darwinism killed as weeds. How was it that he did not see that he was not experimenting with habits or characteristics at all? How had he overlooked the glaring fact that his experiment had been tried for many generations in China on the feet of Chinese women without producing the smallest tendency on their part to be born with abnormally small feet? He must have known about the bound feet even if he knew nothing of the mutilations, the clipped ears and docked tails, practised by dog fanciers and horse breeders on many generations of the unfortunate animals they deal in. Such amazing blindness and stupidity on the part of a man who was naturally neither blind nor stupid is a telling illustration of what Darwin unintentionally did to the minds of his disciples by turning their attention so exclusively towards the part played in Evolution by accident and violence operating with entire callousness to suffering and sentiment.

A vital conception of Evolution would have taught Weismann that biological problems are not to be solved by assaults on mice. The scientific form of his experiment would have been something like this. First, he should have procured a colony of mice highly susceptible to hypnotic suggestion. He should then have hypnotized them into an urgent conviction that the fate of the musque world depends on the disappearance of its tail, just as some ancient and forgotten experimenter seems to have convinced the cats of the Isle of Man. Having thus made the mice desire to lose their tails with a life-or-death intensity, he would very soon have seen a few mice born with little or no tail. These would be recognized by the other mice as superior beings, and privileged in the division of food and in sexual selection. Ultimately the tailed mice would be put to death as monsters by their fellows, and the miracle of the tailless mouse completely achieved.

The objection to this experiment is not that it seems too funny to be taken seriously, and is not cruel enough to overawe the mob, but simply that it is impossible because the human experimenter cannot get at the mouse's mind. And that is what is wrong with all the barren cruelties of the laboratories. Darwin's followers did not think of this. Their only idea of investigation was to imitate "Nature" by perpetrating violent and senseless cruelties, and watch

the effect of them with a paralyzing fatalism which
forbade the smallest effort to use their minds instead
of their knives and eyes, and establish an abominable tradition that the man who hesitates to be as
cruel as Circumstantial Selection itself is a traitor to
science. For Weismann's experiment upon the mice
was a mere joke compared to the atrocities committed
by other Darwinians in their attempts to prove that
mutilations could not be transmitted. Granted that
the worst of these experiments may not have been
experiments at all, but cruelties committed by cruel
men attracted to the laboratory as a secret refuge
left by law and public superstition for the amateur
of passionate torture. But there is no reason to suspect
Weismann of Sadism. Cutting off the tails of
several generations of mice is not voluptuous enough
to tempt a scientific Nero. It was a mere piece of
one-eyedness; and it was Darwin who put out
Weismann's humane and sensible eye. He blinded
many another eye and paralyzed many another will
also. Ever since he set up Circumstantial Selection
as the creator and ruler of the universe, the scientific
world has been the very citadel of stupidity and
cruelty. Fearful as the tribal god of the Hebrews
was, nobody ever shuddered as they passed even his
meanest and narrowest little Bethel or his proudest
war-consecrating cathedral as we shudder now when
we pass a physiological laboratory. If we dreaded
and mistrusted the priest, we could at least keep him
out of the house; but what of the modern Darwinist
surgeon whom we dread and mistrust ten times more,
but into whose hands we must all give ourselves from
time to time? Miserably as religion had been debased,
it did at least still proclaim that our relation to one
another was that of a fellowship in which we were

all equal and members one of another before the judgment-seat of our common father. Darwinism proclaimed that our true relation is that of competitors and combatants in a struggle for mere survival, and that every act of pity or loyalty to the old fellowship is a vain and mischievous attempt to lessen the severity of the struggle and preserve inferior varieties from the efforts of Nature to weed them out. Even in Socialist Societies which existed solely to substitute the law of fellowship for the law of competition, and the method of providence and wisdom for the method of rushing violently down a steep place into the sea, I found myself regarded as a blasphemer and an ignorant sentimentalist because whenever the Neo-Darwinian doctrine was preached there I made no attempt to conceal my intellectual contempt for its blind coarseness and shallow logic, or my natural abhorrence of its sickening inhumanity.

## THE GREATEST OF THESE IS SELF-CONTROL

As there is no place in Darwinism for free will, or any other sort of will, the Neo-Darwinists held that there is no such thing as self-control. Yet self-control is just the one quality of survival value which Circumstantial Selection must invariably and inevitably develop in the long run. Uncontrolled qualities may be selected for survival and development for certain periods and under certain circumstances. For instance, since it is the ungovernable gluttons who strive the hardest to get food and drink, their efforts would develop their strength and cunning in a period of such scarcity that the utmost they could do would not enable them to over-eat themselves. But a change of circumstances involving a plentiful supply of food would destroy them. We see this very thing happening often enough in the case of a healthy and vigorous poor man who becomes a millionaire by one of the accidents of our competitive commerce, and immediately proceeds to dig his grave with his teeth. But the self-controlled man survives all such changes of circumstance, because he adapts himself to them, and eats neither as much as he can hold nor as little as he can scrape along on, but as much as is good for him. What *is* self-control? It is nothing but a highly developed vital sense, dominating and regulating the mere appetites. To overlook the very existence of this supreme sense; to miss the obvious inference that it is the quality that distinguishes the fittest to survive; to omit, in short, the highest moral claim of Evolutionary Selection: all this, which the Neo-Darwinians did in the name of Natural Selection, shewed the most pitiable want of mastery of their own subject, the dullest lack of observation of the forces upon which Natural Selection works.

## THE HUMANITARIANS AND THE PROBLEM OF EVIL

The humanitarians were as delighted as anybody with Darwinism at first. They had been perplexed by the Problem of Evil and the Cruelty of Nature. They were Shelleyists, but not atheists. Those who believed in God were at a terrible disadvantage with the athiest. They could not deny the existence of natural facts so cruel that to attribute them to the will of a god is to make that god a demon. Belief in Jehovah was hard for any thoughtful person without belief in the Devil as well. The painted Devil, with his horns, his barbed tail, and his abode of burning brimstone, was an incredible bogey; but the evil attributed to him was real enough; and the atheists argued that the author of evil, if he exists, must be strong enough to overcome God, else God is morally responsible for everything he permits the Devil to do. Neither conclusion delivered us from the horror of attributing the cruelty of nature to the workings of an evil will, or could reconcile it with our impulses towards justice, mercy, and a higher life.

A complete deliverance was offered by the discovery of Circumstantial Selection: that is to say, of a method by which horrors having every appearance of being elaborately planned by some intelligent contriver are only accidents without any moral significance at all. Suppose a watcher from the stars saw a frightful accident produced by two crowded trains at full speed crashing into one another! How could he conceive that a catastrophe brought about by such elaborate machinery, such ingenious preparation, such skilled direction, such vigilant industry, was quite unintentional? Would he not conclude that the signalmen were devils?

Well, Circumstantial Selection is largely a theory of collisions: that is, a theory of the innocence of much apparently designed devilry. In this way Darwin brought intense relief as well as an enlarged knowledge of facts to the humanitarians. He destroyed the omnipotence of God for them; but he also exonerated God from a hideous charge of cruelty. Granted that the comfort was shallow, and that deeper reflection was bound to shew that worse than all conceivable devil-deities is a blind, deaf, dumb, heartless, senseless mob of forces that strike as a tree does when it is blown down by the wind, or as the tree itself is struck by lightning. This did not occur to the humanitarians at the moment: people do not reflect deeply when they are in the first happiness of escape from an intolerably oppressive situation.

Happily for our uneasy souls the problem of evil yields easily to Creative Evolution. If the driving power behind Evolution is omnipotent only in the sense that there seems no limit to its final achievement; and if it must meanwhile struggle with matter and circumstance by the method of trial and error, then the world must be full of its unsuccessful experiments. Christ may meet a tiger, or a High Priest arm-in-arm with a Roman Governor, and be the unfittest to survive under the circumstances. Mozart may have a genius that prevails against Emperors and Archbishops, and a lung that succumbs to some obscure and noxious property of foul air. If all our calamities are either accidents or sincerely repented mistakes, there is no malice in the Cruelty of Nature and no Problem of Evil in the Victorian sense at all. The theology of the women who told us that they became atheists when they sat by the cradles of their children and saw them strangled by the hand of God is succeeded by the theology of Blanco Posnet, with his "It was early days when He made the croup, I guess. It was the best He could think of then; but when it turned out wrong on His hands He made you and me to fight the croup for Him."

## WHY DARWIN PLEASED THE SOCIALISTS

The Humanitarians were not alone among the agitators in their welcome to Darwin. He had the luck to please everybody who had an axe to grind. The Militarists were as enthusiastic as the Humanitarians, the Socialists as the Capitalists. The Socialists

were specially encouraged by Darwin's insistence on
the influence of environment. Perhaps the strongest
moral bulwark of Capitalism is the belief in the
efficacy of individual righteousness. Robert Owen
made desperate efforts to convince England that her
criminals, her drunkards, her ignorant and stupid
masses, were the victims of circumstance: that if we
would only establish his new moral world we should
find that the masses born into an educated and
moralized community would be themselves educated
and moralized. The stock reply to this is to be
found in Lewes's Life of Goethe. Lewes scorned
the notion that circumstances govern character. He
pointed to the variety of character in the governing
rich class to prove the contrary. Similarity of circumstance can hardly be carried to a more desolating
dead level than in the case of the individuals who are
born and bred in English country houses, and sent
first to Eton or Harrow, and then to Oxford or
Cambridge, to have their minds and habits formed.
Such a routine would destroy individuality if anything
could. Yet individuals come out from it as different
as Pitt from Fox. There was no more effective retort
to the Socialist than to tell him to reform himself
before he pretends to reform society. If you were
rich, how pleasant it was to feel that you owed your
riches to the superiority of your own character!
The industrial revolution had turned numbers of
greedy dullards into monstrously rich men. Nothing
could be more humiliating and threatening to them
than the view that the falling of a shower of gold into
their pockets was as pure an accident as the falling
of a shower of hail on their umbrellas, and happened
alike to the just and unjust. Nothing could be more
flattering and fortifying to them than the assumption

that they were rich because they were virtuous.

Now Darwinism made a clean sweep of all such self-righteousness. It more than justified Robert Owen by discovering in the environment of an organism an influence on it more potent than Owen had ever claimed. It implied that street arabs are produced by slums and not by original sin: that prostitutes are produced by starvation wages and not by feminine concupiscence. It threw the authority of science on the side of the Socialist who said that he who would reform himself must first reform society. It suggested that if we want healthy and wealthy citizens we must have healthy and wealthy towns; and that these can exist only in healthy and wealthy countries. It led straight to the conclusion that the type of character which remains indifferent to the welfare of its neighbors as long as its own personal appetites are satisfied is the disastrous type, and the type which is deeply concerned about its environment the only possible type for a permanently prosperous community. It shewed that the surprising changes which Robert Owen had produced in factory children by a change in their circumstances which does not seem any too generous to us nowadays were as nothing to the changes—changes not only of habits but of species, not only of species but of orders—which might conceivably be the work of environment acting on individuals without any character or intellectual consciousness whatever. No wonder the Socialists received Darwin with open arms.

### DARWIN AND KARL MARX

Besides, the Socialists had an evolutionary prophet of their own, Karl Marx, who discredited Manchester as Darwin discredited the Garden of Eden. To him civilization was an organism evolving irresistibly by circumstantial selection; and he published the first volume of his Das Kapital in 1867. The revolt against anthropomorphic idolatry, which was, as we have seen, the secret of Darwin's success, had been accompanied by a revolt against the conventional respectability which covered not only the brigandage and piracy of feudal robber barons, but the hypocrisy, inhumanity, snobbery, and greed of the bourgeoisie, who were deeply corrupted by an essentially diabolical identification of success in life with big profits. The moment Marx shewed that the relation of the bourgeoisie to society was grossly immoral and disastrous, and that the whited wall of starched shirt fronts concealed and defended the most infamous of all tyrannies and the basest of all robberies, he became an inspired prophet in the mind of every generous soul whom his book reached. He had said and proved what they wanted to have proved; and they would hear nothing against him. Now Marx was by no means infallible: his economics, half borrowed, and half home-made by a literary amateur, were not, when strictly followed up, even favourable to Socialism. His theory of civilization had been promulgated already in Buckle's History of Civilization, a book as epoch-making in the minds of its readers as Das Kapital. There was nothing about Socialism in the widely read first volume of Das Kapital: every reference it made to workers and capitalists shewed that Marx had never breathed industrial air, and had dug his case out of bluebooks in the British Museum. Compared to Darwin, he seemed to have no power of observation: there was not a fact in Das Kapital that had not been taken out of a book, nor a discussion that had not been opened by somebody else's pamphlet. No matter: he exposed the bourgeoisie and made an end of its moral prestige. That was enough: like Darwin he had for the moment the World Will by the ear. Marx had, too, what Darwin had not: implacability and a fine Jewish literary gift, with terrible powers of hatred, invective, irony, and all the bitter qualities bred, first in the oppression of a rather pampered young genius (Marx was the spoilt child of a well-to-do family) by a social system utterly uncongenial to him, and later on by exile and poverty. Thus Marx and Darwin between them toppled over two closely related idols, and became the prophets of two new creeds.

## WHY DARWIN PLEASED THE PROFITEERS ALSO

But how, at this rate, did Darwin succeed with the profiteers too? It is not easy to make the best of both worlds when the two are at war, as the proletariat and the proprietors were and are over their shares in the national income. But Darwin kept a foot in each camp easily. He got his main postulate, the pressure of population on the available means of subsistence, from the treatise of Malthus on Population, just as he got his other postulate of a practically unlimited time for that pressure to operate from the geologist Lyell, who made an end of Archbishop Ussher's Biblical estimate of the age of the earth as 4004 B.C. plus A.D. The treatise of Ricardo on the Law of Diminishing Return presented profit and rent as natural perquisites for which no man was responsible nor could avert. Long before Darwin published a line, the disciples of Malthus and Ricardo were preaching the fatalistic Wages Fund doctrine, and assuring the workers that Trade Unionism is a vain defiance of the inexorable laws of political economy. The Neo-Darwinians were presently assuring us that temperance legislation is a vain defiance of Natural Selection, and that the right way to deal with drunkenness is to flood the country with cheap gin and let the fittest survive. Cobdenism is, after all, nothing but the abandonment of trade to Circumstantial Selection.

It is hardly possible to exaggerate the importance of this preparation for Darwinism by a vast political and clerical propaganda of its moral atmosphere. Never in history, as far as we know, had there been such a determined, richly subsidized, politically organized attempt to persuade the human race that all progress, all prosperity, all salvation, individual and social, depend on an unrestrained conflict for food and money, on the suppression and elimination of the weak by the strong, on Free Trade, Free Contract, Free Competition, Natural Liberty, *Laisser-faire*: in short, on "doing the other fellow down" with impunity. Even the proletariat sympathized, though to them Capitalist liberty meant only wage slavery without the legal safeguards of chattel slavery. People were tired of governments and kings and priests and providences, and wanted to find out how Nature would arrange matters if she were let alone. And they found it out to their cost in the days when Lancashire used up nine generations of wage slaves in one generation of their masters, who, becoming richer and richer, had their uneasy consciences soothed when Bastiat proved convincingly that Nature had arranged Economic Harmonies which would settle social questions far better than theocracies or aristocracies or mobocracies, the real *deus ex machina* being unrestrained plutocracy.

## THE POETRY AND PURITY OF MATERIALISM

Thus the stars in their courses fought for Darwin. Every faction drew a moral from him; every catholic hater of faction founded a hope on him; every black-guard felt justified by him; and every saint felt en-couraged by him. The notion that any harm could come of so splendid an enlightenment seemed as silly as the notion that the atheists would steal all our spoons. The physicists went further than the Dar-winians. Tyndall declared that he saw in Matter the promise and potency of all forms of life, and with his Irish graphic lucidity made a picture of a world of magnetic atoms, each atom with a positive and a negative pole, arranging itself by attraction and repulsion in orderly crystalline structure. Such a picture is dangerously fascinating to thinkers oppressed by the bloody disorders of the living world. Craving for purer subjects of thought, they find in the con-templation of crystals and magnets a happiness more dramatic and less childish than the happiness found by the mathematicians in abstract numbers, because they see in the crystals beauty and movement without the corrupting appetites of fleshly vitality. In such materialism as that of Lucretius and Tyndall there is a nobility which produces poetry: the poet Davidson found his highest inspiration in it. Even its pessimism as it faces the cooling of the sun and the return of the ice-caps does not degrade the pessimist: for example, the Quincy Adamses, with their insistence on modern democratic degradation as an inevitable result of solar shrinkage, are not dehumanized as the vivisectionists are. Perhaps nobody is at heart fool enough to believe that life is at the mercy of temperature: Dante was not troubled by the objection that Brunetto could not have lived in the fire nor Ugolino in the ice.

But the physicists found their intellectual vision of the world incommunicable to those who were not born with it. It came to the public simply as Materialism; and Materialism lost its peculiar purity and dignity when it entered into the Darwinian reaction against Bible fetichism. Between the two of them religion was knocked to pieces; and where there had been God, a cause, a faith that the universe was ordered, and therefore a sense of moral responsibility as part of that order, there was now an utter void. Chaos had come again.

The first effect was exhilarating: we had the runaway child's sense of freedom before it gets hungry and lonely and frightened. Not that we desired God back again. We printed the verses in which William Blake, the most religious of our great poets, called the anthropomorphic idol Old Nobodaddy, and gibed at him in terms which the printer had to leave us to guess from dashes and asterisks. It did not occur to us that Old Nobodaddy, instead of being a ridiculous fiction, might be a real imposter, and that he could not have impersonated anybody if there had not been Somebodaddy to impersonate. We did not see the significance of the fact that on the last occasion on which God had been "expelled with a pitchfork," men so different as Voltaire and Robespierre had said, the one that if God did not exist it would be necessary to invent him, and the other that after an honest attempt to dispense with a Supreme Being in practical politics, some such hypothesis had been found quite indispensable, and could not be replaced by a sham Goddess of Reason. If these two opinions were quoted at all, they were quoted as jokes at the expense of Nobodaddy. We were quite sure for the moment that whatever lingering superstition might have daunted these men of the eighteenth century, we Darwinians could do without God, and had made a good riddance of Him.

## THE VICEROYS OF THE KING OF KINGS

Now in politics it is much easier to do without God than to do without his viceroys and vicars and lieutenants; and we begin to miss the lieutenants long before we begin to miss their principal. Roman Catholics do what their confessors advise without troubling God; and Royalists are content to worship the King and ask the policeman. But God's trustiest lieutenants often lack official credentials. They may be professed atheists who are also men of honor and high public spirit. The old belief that it matters dreadfully to God whether a man thinks himself an atheist or not, and that the extent to which it matters can be stated with exactness as one single damn, was an error; for the divinity is in the honor and public spirit, not in the mouthed *credo* or *non credo*. The consequences of this error became grave when the fitness of a man for public trust was tested, not by his honor and public spirit, but by asking him whether he belonged to the Church of England. Darwin destroyed this test; but when it was dropped, there remained no test at all; and the door to public trust was open to the man who had no sense of God because he had no sense of anything beyond his own business interests and personal appetites and ambitions. As a result, the people who did not feel in the least inconvenienced by being no longer governed by Nobodaddy soon found themselves very acutely inconvenienced by being governed by fools and commercial adventurers. They had forgotten not only God but Goldsmith, who had warned them that "honor sinks where commerce long prevails."

The lieutenants of God are not always persons: some of them are legal and parliamentary fictions. One of them is Public Opinion. The pre-Darwinian statesmen and publicists were not restrained directly by God; but they restrained themselves by setting up an image of a Public Opinion which would not tolerate any attempt to tamper with British liberties. Their favorite way of putting it was that any Government which proposed such and such an infringement of such and such a British liberty would be hurled from office in a week. Compulsory military service was the stock instance of this in England.

All this had no foundation on the facts. There was no limit to what the British people would put up with. It was this very helplessness of the people that forced their rulers to pretend that they were not helpless, and that the certainty of a sturdy and unconquerable popular resistance forbade any trifling with Magna Carta or the Petition of Rights or the authority of parliament. Now the reality behind this fiction was the divine sense that liberty is a need vital to human growth. Accordingly, though it was difficult enough to effect a political reform, yet, once parliament had passed it, its wildest opponent had no hope that the Government would cancel it, or shelve it, or be bought off from executing it. From Walpole to Campbell-Bannerman there was no Prime Minister to whom such renaguing or trafficking would ever have occurred, though there were plenty who employed corruption unsparingly to procure the votes of members of parliament for their policy.

## POLITICAL OPPORTUNISM IN EXCELSIS

The moment Nobodaddy was slain by Darwin, Public Opinion, as divine deputy, lost its sanctity. Politicians no longer told themselves that the British public would never suffer this or that: they allowed themselves to know that for their own personal purposes, which are limited to their ten or twenty years on the front benches in parliament, the British Public can be humbugged and coerced into believing and suffering everything that it pays their rulers to impose on them, and that any excuse for an un-popular step will serve if it can be kept in countenance for three days: that is, until the terms of the excuse are forgotten. With its last ideal gone, policy died and was succeeded by unprincipled opportunism. All Governments became like the tramp who walks always with the wind and ends as a pauper, or the stone that rolls down the hill and ends as an avalanche: their way was the way to destruction.

## THE BETRAYAL OF WESTERN CIVILIZATION

Within sixty years from the publication of Darwin's Origin of Species political opportunism had brought parliaments into contempt; created a popular de-mand for direct action by the organized industries ("Syndicalism"); and wrecked the centre of Europe in a paroxysm of that chronic terror of one another, that cowardice of the irreligious, which, masked in the bravado of militarist patriotism, had ridden the Powers like a nightmare since the Franco-Prussian war of 1870–71. The sturdy old cosmopolitan Liberal-ism evaporated. Ordinances for the government of our Crown Colonies contain, as a matter of course, prohibitions of all criticism, spoken or written of their ruling officials, which would have scandalized George III and elicited Liberal pamphlets from Catherine II. Statesmen are afraid of the suburbs, of the newspapers, of the profiteers, of the diplomatists, of the militarists, of the country houses, of the trade unions, of everything ephemeral on earth except the revolutions they are provoking; and they would be afraid of these if they were not too ignorant of society and history to appreciate the risk, and to know that a revolution always seems hopeless and impossible the day before it breaks out, and indeed never does break out until it seems hopeless and impossible; for rulers who think it possible take care to insure the risk by ruling reasonably. This brings about a condition fatal to all political stability: namely, that you never know where to have the politicians. If the fear of God was in them it might be possible to come to some general understanding as to what God disapproves of; and Europe might pull together on that basis. But the present panic, in which Prime Ministers drift from election to election, either fighting or running away from everybody who shakes a fist at them, makes a European civilization impossible; for peace and prosperity depend on the loyalty of States to civilization. Every meaner consideration should have given way to this loyalty. What actually happened was that France and England made an alliance with Russia to defend themselves against Germany; Germany made an alliance with Turkey to defend herself against the three; whilst the United States held aloof as long as they could, and the other States either did the same or joined in the fray through compulsion, bribery, or their judgment as to which side their bread was buttered.

In 1918 the surrender of Germany on terms which the victors never dreamt of observing did not change the situation. If the Western Powers had selected their allies in the Lamarckian manner intelligently, purposely, and vitally, *ad majorem Dei gloriam*, as good Europeans, there would have been a durable League of Nations and no war. But because the selection relied on was purely circumstantial opportunist selection, so that the alliances were mere marriages of convenience, they have turned out, not merely as badly as might have been expected, but far worse than the blackest pessimist had ever imagined possible. How it will all end we do not yet know. When wolves combine to kill a horse, the death of the horse only sets them fighting one another for the choicest morsels.

## THE HOMEOPATHIC REACTION AGAINST DARWINISM

Throughout all this godless welter of the infidel century, Darwinism has been acting not only directly but homeopathically, its poison rallying our vital forces not only to resist it and cast it out, but to achieve a new Reformation and put a credible and healthy religion in its place. Samuel Butler was the pioneer of the reaction as far as the casting out was concerned; but the issue was confused by the physiologists, who were divided on the question into Mechanists and Vitalists. The Mechanists said that life is nothing but physical and chemical action; that they have demonstrated this in many cases of so-called vital phenomena; and that there is no reason to doubt that with improved methods they will presently be able to demonstrate it in all of them. The Vitalists said that a dead body and a live one are physically and chemically identical, and that the difference can be accounted for only by the existence of a Vital Force. This seems simple; but the Anti-Mechanists objected to be called Vitalists (obviously the right name for them) on two contradictory grounds. First, that vitality is scientifically inadmissible, because it cannot be isolated and experimented with in the laboratory. Second, that force, being by definition anything that can alter the speed or direction of matter in motion (briefly, that can overcome inertia), is essentially a mechanistic conception. Here we had the new Vitalism only half extricated from the upstart Mechanism, objecting to be called either, and unable to give a clear lead to the new direction.

These professional faction fights are ephemeral, and need not trouble us here. The old Vitalist, who was essentially a Materialist, has evolved into the Neo-Vitalist, who is, as every genuine scientist must be, finally a metaphysician. And as the Neo-Vitalist turns from the disputes of his youth to the future of his science, he will cease to boggle at the name Vitalist, or at the inevitable, ancient, popular, and quite correct use of the term Force to denote metaphysical as well as physical overcomers of inertia.

Since the discovery of Evolution as the method of the Life Force, the religion of metaphysical Vitalism has been gaining the definiteness and concreteness needed to make it assimilable by the educated critical man. But it has always been with us. The popular religions, disgraced by their Opportunist cardinals and bishops, have been kept in credit by canonized saints whose secret was their conception of themselves as the instruments and vehicles of divine power and aspiration: a conception which at moments becomes an actual experience of ecstatic possession by that power. And above and below all have been millions of humble and obscure persons, sometimes totally illiterate, sometimes unconscious of having any religion at all, sometimes believing in their simplicity that the gods and temples and priests of their district stood for their instinctive righteousness, who have kept sweet the tradition that good people follow a light that shines within and above and ahead of them, that bad people care only for themselves, and that the good are saved and blessed and the bad damned and miserable. Protestantism was a movement towards the pursuit of a light called an inner light because every man must see it with his own eyes and not take any priest's word for it or any Church's account of it. In short, there is no question of a new religion, but rather of redistilling the eternal spirit of religion and thus extricating it from the sludgy residue of temporalities and legends that are making belief impossible, though they are the stock-in-trade of all the Churches and all the Schools.

## RELIGION AND ROMANCE

It is the adulteration of religion by the romance of miracles and paradises and torture chambers that makes it reel at the impact of every advance in science, instead of being clarified by it. If you take an English village lad, and teach him that religion means believing that the stories of Noah's Ark and the Garden of Eden are literally true on the authority of God himself, and if that boy becomes an artisan and goes into the town among the sceptical city proletariat, then, when the jibes of his mates set him thinking, and he sees that these stories cannot be literally true, and learns that no candid prelate now pretends to believe them, he does not make any fine distinctions: he declares at once that religion is a fraud, and parsons and teachers hypocrites and liars. He becomes indifferent to religion if he has little intellectual conscience, and indignantly hostile to it if he has a good deal.

The same revolt against wantonly false teaching is happening daily in the professional classes whose recreation is reading and whose intellectual sport is controversy. They banish the Bible from their houses, and sometimes put into the hands of their unfortunate children Ethical and Rationalist tracts of the deadliest dullness, compelling these wretched infants to sit out the discourses of Secularist lecturers (I have delivered some of them myself), who wearied them at a length now abandoned in the Church of England. Our minds have reacted so violently towards provable logical theorems and demonstrable mechanical or chemical facts that we have become incapable of metaphysical truth, and try to cast out incredible and silly lies by credible and clever ones, calling in Satan to cast out Satan, and getting more into his clutches than ever in the process. Thus the world is kept sane less by the saints than by the vast mass of the indifferent, who neither act nor react in the matter. Butler's preaching of the gospel of Laodicea was a piece of common sense founded on his observation of this.

But indifference will not guide nations through civilization to the establishment of the perfect city of God. An indifferent statesman is a contradiction in terms; and a statesman who is indifferent on principle, a Laisser-faire or Muddle-Through doctrinaire, plays the deuce with us in the long run. Our statesmen must get a religion by hook or crook; and while we are ruled by Adult Suffrage it must be a religion capable of vulgarization. The thought first put into words by the Mills when they said "There is no God; but this is a family secret," and long held unspoken by aristocratic statesmen and diplomatists, will not serve now; for the revival of civilization after the war cannot be effected by artificial breathing: the driving force of an undeluded popular consent is indispensable, and will be impossible until the statesman can appeal to the vital instincts of the people in terms of a common religion.

## THE DANGER OF REACTION

And here arises the danger that when we realize this we shall run back in terror to our old superstitions. We jumped out of the frying-pan into the fire; and we are just as likely to jump back again, now that we feel hotter than ever. History records very little in the way of mental activity on the part of the mass of mankind except a series of stampedes from affirmative errors into negative ones and back again. It must therefore be said very precisely and clearly that the bankruptcy of Darwinism does not mean that Nobodaddy was Somebodaddy *with* "body, parts, and passions" after all; that the world was made in the year 4004 B.C.; that damnation means an eternity of blazing brimstone; that the Immaculate Conception means that sex is sinful and that Christ was parthenogenetically brought forth by a virgin descended in like manner from a line of virgins right back to Eve; that the Trinity is an anthropomorphic monster with three heads which are yet only one head; that in Rome the bread and wine on the altar become flesh and blood, and in England, in a still more mystical manner, they do and they do not; that the Bible is an infallible scientific manual, an accurate historical chronicle, and a complete guide to conduct; that we may lie and cheat and murder and then wash ourselves innocent in the blood of the Lamb on Sunday at the cost of a *credo* and a penny in the plate; and so on and so forth. Civilization cannot be saved by people not only crude enough to believe these things, but irreligious enough to believe that such belief constitutes a religion. The education of children cannot safely be left in their hands. If dwindling sects like the Church of England, the Church of Rome, the Greek Church, and the rest, persist in trying to cramp the human mind within the limits of these grotesque perversions of natural truths and poetic metaphors, then they must be ruthlessly banished from the schools to free the soul that is hidden in every dogma. The real Class War will be a war of intellectual classes; and its conquest will be the souls of the children.

## A TOUCHSTONE FOR DOGMA

The test of a dogma is its universality. Any doctrine that the British churchgoer, the Brahman, the Jainist, the Buddhist, the Mussulman cannot hold in common, however varied their rituals, is an obstruction to the fellowship of the Holy Ghost. The only frontier to the currency of a sound dogma as such is the frontier of capacity for understanding it.

This does not mean that we should throw away legend and parable and drama: they are the natural vehicles of dogma; but woe to the Churches and rulers who substitute the legend for the dogma, the parable for the history, the drama for the religion!

Better by far declare the throne of God empty than set a liar and a fool on it. What are called wars of religion are always wars to destroy religion by affirming the historical truth or material substantiality of some legend, and killing those who refuse to accept it as historical or substantial. But who has ever refused to accept a good legend with delight *as* a legend? The legends, the parables, the dramas, are among the choicest treasures of mankind. No one is ever tired of stories of miracles. In vain did Mahomet repudiate the miracles ascribed to him: in vain did Christ furiously scold those who asked him to give them an exhibition as a conjurer: in vain did the saints declare that God chose them not for their powers but for their weaknesses; that the humble might be exalted, and the proud rebuked. People will have their miracles, their stories, their heroes and heroines and saints and martyrs and divinities to exercise their gifts of affection, admiration, wonder, and worship, and their Judases and devils to enable them to be angry and yet feel that they do well to be angry. Every one of these legends is the common heritage of the human race; and there is only one inexorable condition attached to their healthy enjoyment, which is that no one shall believe them literally. The reading of stories and delighting in them made Don Quixote a gentleman: the believing them literally made him a madman who slew lambs instead of feeding them. In England today good books of Eastern religious legends are read eagerly; and Protestants and Atheists read legends of the saints with pleasure. Sceptical Freethinkers read the Bible: indeed they seem to be its only readers now except the parsons at the Church lecterns. This is because the imposition of the legends as literal truths at once changes them from legends into falsehoods. The feeling against the Bible has become so strong at last that educated people will not tolerate even the chronicles of King David, which may be historical, and are certainly more candid than the official biographies of our contemporary monarchs.

## WHAT TO DO WITH THE LEGENDS

What we should do, then, is to pool our legends and make a delightful stock of religious folk-lore on an honest basis for all children. With our minds freed from pretence and falsehood we could enter into the heritage of all the faiths. China would share her sages with Spain, and Spain her saints with China. The Belfast Orangemen who gives his son a thrashing if the boy is so tactless as to ask how the evening and the morning could be the first day before the sun was created, or to betray an innocent calf-love for the Virgin Mary, would buy him a bookful of legends of the creation and of mothers of God from all parts of the world, and be very glad to find his laddie as interested in such things as in marbles or Police and Robbers. That would be better than beating all good feeling towards religion out of the child, and blackening his mind by teaching him that the worshippers of the holy virgins, whether of the Parthenon or St Peter's, are fire-doomed heathens and idolaters. All the sweetness of religion is conveyed to children by the hands of storytellers and image-makers. Without their fictions the truths of religion would for the multitude be neither intelligible nor even apprehensible; and the prophets would prophesy and the philosophers cerebrate in vain. And nothing stands between the people and the fictions

[ 330 ]

except the silly falsehood that the fictions are literal truths, and that there is nothing in religion but fiction.

## A LESSON FROM SCIENCE TO THE CHURCHES

Let the Churches ask themselves why there is no revolt against the dogmas of mathematics though there is one against the dogmas of religion. It is not that the mathematical dogmas are more comprehensible. The law of inverse squares is as incomprehensible to the common man as the Athanasian creed. It is not that science is free from legends, witchcraft, miracles, biographic boostings of quacks as heroes and saints, and of barren scoundrels as explorers and discoverers. On the contrary, the inconography and hagiology of Scientism are as copious as they are mostly squalid. But no student of science has yet been taught that specific gravity consists in the belief that Archimedes jumped out of his bath and ran naked through the streets of Syracuse shouting Eureka, Eureka, or that the law of inverse squares must be discarded if anyone can prove that Newton was never in an orchard in his life. When some unusually conscientious or enterprising bacteriologist reads the pamphlets of Jenner, and discovers that they might have been written by an ignorant but curious and observant nurserymaid, and could not possibly have been written by any person with a scientifically trained mind, he does not feel that the whole edifice of science has collapsed and crumbled, and that there is no such thing as smallpox. It may come to that yet; for hygiene, as it forces its way into our schools, is being taught as falsely as religion is taught there; but in mathematics and physics the faith is still kept pure, and you may take the law and leave the legends without suspicion of heresy. Accordingly, the tower of the mathematician stands unshaken whilst the temple of the priest rocks to its foundation.

## THE RELIGIOUS ART OF THE TWENTIETH CENTURY

Creative Evolution is already a religion, and is indeed now unmistakeably the religion of the twentieth century, newly arisen from the ashes of pseudo-Christianity, of mere scepticism, and of the soulless affirmations and blind negations of the Mechanists and Neo-Darwinians. But it cannot become a popular religion until it has its legends, its parables, its miracles. And when I say popular I do not mean apprehensible by villagers only. I mean apprehensible by Cabinet Ministers as well. It is unreasonable to look to the professional politician and administrator for light and leading in religion. He is neither a philosopher nor a prophet: if he were, he would be philosophizing and prophesying, and not neglecting both for the drudgery of practical government. Not being an expert, he must take religion as he finds it; and before he can take it, he must have been told stories about it in his childhood and had before him all his life an elaborate iconography of it produced by writers, painters, sculptors, temple architects, and artists of all the higher sorts. Even if, as sometimes happens, he is a bit of an amateur in metaphysics as well as a professional politician, he must still govern according to the popular iconography, and not according to his own interpretations if these happen to be heterodox.

It will be seen then that the revival of religion on a scientific basis does not mean the death of art, but a glorious rebirth of it. Indeed art has never been great when it was not providing an iconography for a live religion. And it has never been quite contemptible except when imitating the iconography after the religion had become a superstition. Italian painting from Giotto to Carpaccio is all religious painting; and it moves us deeply and has real greatness. Compare with it the attempts of our painters a century ago to achieve the effects of the old masters by imitation when they should have been illustrating a faith of their own. Contemplate, if you can bear it, the dull daubs of Hilton and Haydon, who knew so much more about drawing and scumbling and glazing and perspective and anatomy and "marvellous fore-shortening" than Giotto, the latchet of whose shoe they were nevertheless not worthy to unloose. Compare Mozart's Magic Flute, Beethoven's Ninth Symphony, and Wagner's Ring cycle, all of them reachings-forward to the new Vitalist art, with the dreary pseudo-sacred oratorios and cantatas produced for no better reason than that Handel made splendid thunder in that way. Compare Flaxman and Thor-waldsen and Gibson with Phidias and Praxiteles, Stevens with Michael Angelo, Bouguereau's Virgin with Cimabue's, or the best operatic Christs of Scheffer and Müller with the worst Christs that the worst painters could paint before the end of the fifteenth century, and you must feel that until we have a great religious movement we cannot hope for a great artistic one. The disillusioned Raphael could paint a mother and child, but not a queen of Heaven as much less skilful men had done in the days of his great-grandfathers; yet he could reach forward to the twentieth century and paint a Transfiguration of the Son of Man as they could not. Also, please note, he could decorate a house of pleasure for a plutocrat very beautifully with voluptuous pictures of Cupid and Psyche; for this simple sort of Vitalism is always with us, and, like portrait painting, keeps the artist supplied with subject matter in the intervals between the ages of faith; so that your sceptical Rembrandts and Velasquezs are at least not compelled to paint shop fronts for want of anything else to paint in which they can really believe.

## THE ARTIST-PROPHETS

And there are always great anticipations. Michael Angelo painted the Superman three hundred years before Nietzsche wrote Thus Spake Zoroaster. As a painter of prophets and sibyls he is greatest among the very greatest in his craft, because we aspire to a world of prophets and sibyls. Beethoven never heard of radio-activity nor of electrons dancing in vortices of inconceivable energy; but pray can anyone explain the last movement of his Hammerklavier Sonata, Opus 106, otherwise than as a musical picture of these whirling electrons? His contemporaries said he was mad, partly perhaps because the movement was so hard to play; but we, who can make a pianola play it to us over and over until it is as familiar as Pop Goes the Weasel, know that it is sane and methodical. As such, it must represent something; and as all Beethoven's serious compositions represent some process within himself, some nerve storm or soul storm, and the storm here is clearly one of physical movement, I should much like to know what other storm than the atomic storm could have driven him to this oddest of all those many expressions of cyclonic energy which have given him the same distinction among musicians that Michael Angelo has among draughtsmen.

In Beethoven's day the business of art was held to be "the sublime and beautiful." In our day it has fallen to be the imitative and voluptuous. In both periods the word passionate has been freely employed; but in the eighteenth century passion meant irresistible impulse of the loftiest kind: for example, a passion for astronomy or for truth. For us it has come to mean concupiscence and nothing else. One might say to the art of Europe what Antony said to the corpse of Cæsar: "Are all thy conquests, glories, triumphs, spoils, shrunk to this little measure?" But in fact it is the mind of Europe that has shrunk, being, as we have seen, wholly preoccupied with a busy spring-cleaning to get rid of its superstitions before readjusting itself to the creative conception of Evolution.

## EVOLUTION IN THE THEATRE

On the stage (and here I come at last to my own particular function in the matter), Comedy, as a destructive, derisory, critical, negative art, kept the theatre open when sublime tragedy perished. From Molière to Oscar Wilde we had a line of comedic playwrights who, if they had nothing fundamentally positive to say, were at least in revolt against falsehood and imposture, and were not only, as they claimed, "chastening morals by ridicule," but, in Johnson's phrase, clearing our minds of cant, and thereby shewing an uneasiness in the presence of error which is the surest symptom of intellectual vitality. Meanwhile the name of Tragedy was assumed by plays in which everyone was killed in the last act, just as, in spite of Molière, plays in which everyone was married in the last act called themselves comedies. Now neither tragedies nor comedies can be produced according to a prescription which gives only the last moments of the last act.

Ever since Shakespear, playwrights have been struggling with their lack of positive religion. Many of them were forced to become mere pandars and sensation-mongers because, though they had higher ambitions, they could find no better subject matter. From Congreve to Sheridan they were so sterile in spite of their wit that they did not achieve between them the output of Molière's single lifetime; and they were all (not without reason) ashamed of their profession, and preferred to be regarded as mere men of fashion with a rakish hobby. Goldsmith's was the only saved soul in that pandemonium. Consider the great exception of Goethe. He is Olympian: the other giants are infernal in everything but their veracity and their repudiation of the irreligion of their time: that is, they are bitter and hopeless. It is not a question of mere dates. Goethe was an Evolutionist in 1830: many modern playwrights, even young ones, are still untouched by Creative Evolution. Even Ibsen was Darwinized to the extent of exploiting heredity on the stage much as the ancient Athenian playwrights exploited the Eumenides. Evolution as a poetic aspiration is plain enough in his Emperor or Galilean; but it is one of Ibsen's distinctions that nothing was valid for him but science; and he left that vision of the future which his Roman seer calls "the third Empire" behind him when he settled down to his serious grapple with realities in those plays of nineteenth century life with which he overcame Europe, and broke the dusty windows of every dry-rotten theatre in it from Moscow to Manchester.

## MY OWN PART IN THE MATTER

In my own activities as a playwright I found this state of things intolerable. The fashionable theatre prescribed one serious subject: clandestine adultery: the dullest of all subjects for a serious author, whatever it may be for audiences who read the police intelligence and skip the reviews and leading articles. I tried slum-landlordism, doctrinaire Free Love (pseudo-Ibsenism), prostitution, militarism, marriage, history, current politics, natural Christianity, national and individual character, paradoxes of conventional society, husband-hunting, questions of conscience, professional delusions and impostures, all worked into a series of comedies of manners in the classic fashion, which was then very much out of fashion, the mechanical tricks of Parisian "construction" being held obligatory in the theatre. But this, though it occupied me and established me professionally, did not constitute me an iconographer of the religion of my time, fulfilling my natural function as an artist. I knew that civilization needs a religion as a matter of life or death; and as the conception of Creative Evolution developed I saw that we were at last within reach of a faith which complied with the first condition of all the religions that have ever taken hold of humanity: namely, that it must be, first and fundamentally, a science of metabiology. This was a crucial point with me; for I had seen Bible fetichism, after standing up to all the rationalistic batteries of Hume, Voltaire, and the rest, collapse before the onslaught of much less gifted Evolutionists, solely because they discredited it as a biological document; so that from that moment it lost its hold, and left literate Christendom faithless. My own Irish eighteenth-centuryism made it impossible for me to believe anything until I could conceive it as a scientific hypothesis, even though the abominations, quackeries, impostures, venalities, credulities, and delusions of the camp followers of science, and the brazen lies and priestly pretensions of the pseudo-scientific cure-mongers, all sedulously inculcated by modern "secondary education," were so monstrous that I was sometimes forced to make a verbal distinction between science and knowledge lest I should mislead my readers. But I never forgot that without knowledge even wisdom is more dangerous than mere opportunist ignorance, and that somebody must take the Garden of Eden in hand and weed it properly.

Accordingly, in 1901, I took the legend of Don Juan in its Mozartian form and made it a dramatic parable of Creative Evolution. But being then at the height of my invention and comedic talent, I decorated it too brilliantly and lavishly. I surrounded it with a comedy of which it formed only one act, and that act was so completely episodical (it was a dream which did not affect the action of the piece) that the comedy could be detached and played by itself. Also I supplied the published work with an imposing framework consisting of a preface, an appendix called The Revolutionist's Handbook, and a final display of aphoristic fireworks. The effect was so vertiginous, apparently, that nobody noticed the new religion in the centre of the intellectual whirlpool. Now I protest I did not cut these cerebral capers in mere inconsiderate exuberance. I did it because the worst convention of the criticism of the theatre current at that time was that intellectual seriousness is out of place on the stage; that the theatre is a place of shallow amusement; that people go there to be soothed after the enormous intellectual strain of a day in the city: in short, that a playwright is a person whose business it is to make unwholesome confectionery out of cheap emotions. My answer to this was to put all my intellectual goods in the shop window under the sign of Man and Superman. That part of my design succeeded. By good luck and acting, the comedy triumphed on the stage; and the book was a good deal discussed. But as its tale of a husband huntress obscured its evolutionary doctrine I try again with this cycle of plays that keep to the point all through. I abandon the legend of Don Juan with its erotic associations, and go back to the legend of the Garden of Eden. I exploit the external interest of the philosopher's stone which enables men to live for ever. I am not, I hope, under more illusion than is humanly inevitable as to my contribution to the scriptures of Creative Evolution. It is my hope that a hundred parables by younger hands will soon leave mine as far behind as the religious pictures of the fifteenth century left behind the first attempts of the early Christians at iconography. In that hope I withdraw and ring up the curtain.

AYOT SAINT LAWRENCE, 1921
*Revised, 1944*

[The 1944 Postscript appears, as Shaw directed, after the end of the play (see pages 685–703).]

# PART I

## IN THE BEGINNING

# ⌈ACT I⌉

---

*The Garden of Eden. Afternoon. An immense serpent is sleeping with her head buried in a thick bed of Johnswort, and her body coiled in apparently endless rings through the branches of a tree, which is already well grown; for the days of creation have been longer than our reckoning. She is not yet visible to anyone unaware of her presence, as her colors of green and brown make a perfect camouflage. Near her head a low rock shews above the Johnswort.*

*The rock and tree are on the border of a glade in which lies a dead fawn all awry, its neck being broken. Adam, crouching with one hand on the rock, is staring in consternation at the dead body. He has not noticed the serpent on his left hand. He turns his face to his right and calls excitedly.*

---

ADAM. Eve! Eve!

EVE'S VOICE. What is it, Adam?

ADAM. Come here. Quick. Something has happened.

EVE [*running in*] What? Where? [*Adam points to the fawn*]. Oh! [*She goes to it; and he is emboldened to go with her*]. What is the matter with its eyes?

ADAM. It is not only its eyes. Look. [*He kicks it*].

EVE. Oh dont! Why doesnt it wake?

ADAM. I dont know. It is not asleep.

EVE. Not asleep?

ADAM. Try.

EVE [*trying to shake it and roll it over*] It is stiff and cold.

ADAM. Nothing will wake it.

EVE. It has a queer smell. Pah! [*She dusts her hands, and draws away from it*]. Did you find it like that?

ADAM. No. It was playing about; and it tripped and went head over heels. It never stirred again. Its neck is wrong [*he stoops to lift the neck and shew her*].

EVE. Dont touch it. Come away from it.

*They both retreat, and contemplate it from a few steps' distance with growing repulsion.*

EVE. Adam.

ADAM. Yes?

EVE. Suppose you were to trip and fall, would you go like that?

ADAM. Ugh! [*He shudders and sits down on the rock*].

EVE [*throwing herself on the ground beside him, and grasping his knee*] You must be careful. Promise me you will be careful.

ADAM. What is the good of being careful? We have to live here for ever. Think of what for ever means! Sooner or later I shall trip and fall. It may be tomorrow; it may be after as many days as there are leaves in the garden and grains of sand by the river. No matter: some day I shall forget and stumble.

EVE. I too.

ADAM [*horrified*] Oh no, no. I should be alone. Alone for ever. You must never put yourself in danger of stumbling. You must not move about. You must sit still. I will take care of you and bring you what you want.

EVE [*turning away from him with a shrug, and hugging her ankles*] I should soon get tired of that. Besides, if it happened to you, *I* should be alone. I could not sit still then. And at last it would happen to me too.

[ 341 ]

ADAM. And then?

EVE. Then we should be no more. There would be only the things on all fours, and the birds, and the snakes.

ADAM. That must not be.

EVE. Yes: that must not be. But it might be.

ADAM. No. I tell you it must not be. I know that it must not be.

EVE. We both know it. How do we know it?

ADAM. There is a voice in the garden that tells me things.

EVE. The garden is full of voices sometimes. They put all sorts of thoughts into my head.

ADAM. To me there is only one voice. It is very low; but it is so near that it is like a whisper from within myself. There is no mistaking it for any voice of the birds or beasts, nor for your voice.

EVE. It is strange that I should hear voices from all sides and you only one from within. But I have some thoughts that come from within me and not from the voices. The thought that we must not cease to be comes from within.

ADAM [*despairingly*] But we shall cease to be. We shall fall like the fawn and be broken. [*Rising and moving about in his agitation*] I cannot bear this knowledge. I will not have it. It must not be, I tell you. Yet I do not know how to prevent it.

EVE. That is just what I feel; but it is very strange that you should say so: there is no pleasing you. You change your mind so often.

ADAM [*scolding her*] Why do you say that? How have I changed my mind?

EVE. You say we must not cease to exist. But you used to complain of having to exist always and for ever. You sometimes sit for hours brooding and silent, hating me in your heart. When I ask you what I have done to you, you say you are not thinking of me, but of the horror of having to be here for ever. But I know very well that what you mean is the horror of having to be here with me for ever.

ADAM. Oh! That is what you think, is it? Well, you are wrong. [*He sits down again, sulkily*]. It is the horror of having to be with myself for ever. I like you; but I do not like myself. I want to be different; to be better; to begin again and again; to shed myself as a snake sheds its skin. I am tired of myself. And yet I must endure myself, not for a day or for many days, but for ever. That is a dreadful thought. That is what makes me sit brooding and silent and hateful. Do you never think of that?

EVE. No: I do not think about myself: what is the use? I am what I am: nothing can alter that. I think about you.

ADAM. You should not. You are always spying on me. I can never be alone. You always want to know what I have been doing. It is a burden. You should try to have an existence of your own, instead of occupying yourself with my existence.

EVE. I have to think about you. You are lazy: you are dirty: you neglect yourself: you are always dreaming: you would eat bad food and become disgusting if I did not watch you and occupy myself with you. And now some day, in spite of all my care, you will fall on your head and become dead.

ADAM. Dead? What word is that?

EVE [*pointing to the fawn*] Like that. I call it dead.

ADAM [*rising and approaching it slowly*] There is something uncanny about it.

EVE [*joining him*] Oh! It is changing into little white worms.

[ 343 ]

ADAM. Throw it into the river. It is unbearable.

EVE. I dare not touch it.

ADAM. Then I must, though I loathe it. It is poisoning the air. [*He gathers its hooves in his hand and carries it away in the direction from which Eve came, holding it as far from him as possible*].

*Eve looks after them for a moment; then, with a shiver of disgust, sits down on the rock, brooding. The body of the serpent becomes visible, glowing with wonderful new colors. She rears her head slowly from the bed of Johnswort, and speaks into Eve's ear in a strange seductively musical whisper.*

THE SERPENT. Eve.

EVE [*startled*] Who is that?

THE SERPENT. It is I. I have come to shew you my beautiful new hood. See [*she spreads a magnificent amethystine hood*]!

EVE [*admiring it*] Oh! But who taught you to speak?

THE SERPENT. You and Adam. I have crept through the grass, and hidden, and listened to you.

EVE. That was wonderfully clever of you.

THE SERPENT. I am the most subtle of all the creatures of the field.

EVE. Your hood is most lovely. [*She strokes it and pets the serpent*]. Pretty thing! Do you love your godmother Eve?

THE SERPENT. I adore her. [*She licks Eve's neck with her double tongue*].

EVE [*petting her*] Eve's wonderful darling snake. Eve will never be lonely now that her snake can talk to her.

THE SERPENT. I can talk of many things. I am very wise. It was I who whispered the word to you that you did not know. Dead. Death. Die.

EVE [*shuddering*] Why do you remind me of it? I

forgot it when I saw your beautiful hood. You must not remind me of unhappy things.

THE SERPENT. Death is not an unhappy thing when you have learnt how to conquer it.

EVE. How can I conquer it?

THE SERPENT. By another thing, called birth.

EVE. What? [*Trying to pronounce it*] B-birth?

THE SERPENT. Yes, birth.

EVE. What is birth?

THE SERPENT. The serpent never dies. Some day you shall see me come out of this beautiful skin, a new snake with a new and lovelier skin. That is birth.

EVE. I have seen that. It is wonderful.

THE SERPENT. If I can do that, what can I not do? I tell you I am very subtle. When you and Adam talk, I hear you say "Why?" Always "Why?" You see things; and you say "Why?" But I dream things that never were; and I say "Why not?" I made the word dead to describe my old skin that I cast when I am renewed. I call that renewal being born.

EVE. Born is a beautiful word.

THE SERPENT. Why not be born again and again as I am, new and beautiful every time?

EVE. I! It does not happen: that is why.

THE SERPENT. That is how; but it is not why. Why not?

EVE. But I should not like it. It would be nice to be new again; but my old skin would lie on the ground looking just like me; and Adam would see it shrivel up and—

THE SERPENT. No. He need not. There is a second birth.

EVE. A second birth?

THE SERPENT. Listen. I will tell you a great secret.

[ 345 ]

I am very subtle; and I have thought and thought and thought. And I am very wilful, and must have what I want; and I have willed and willed and willed. And I have eaten strange things: stones and apples that you are afraid to eat.

EVE. You dared!

THE SERPENT. I dared everything. And at last I found a way of gathering together a part of the life in my body—

EVE. What is the life?

THE SERPENT. That which makes the difference between the dead fawn and the live one.

EVE. What a beautiful word! And what a wonderful thing! Life is the loveliest of all the new words.

THE SERPENT. Yes: it was by meditating on Life that I gained the power to do miracles.

EVE. Miracles? Another new word.

THE SERPENT. A miracle is an impossible thing that is nevertheless possible. Something that never could happen, and yet does happen.

EVE. Tell me some miracle that you have done.

THE SERPENT. I gathered a part of the life in my body, and shut it into a tiny white case made of the stones I had eaten.

EVE. And what good was that?

THE SERPENT. I shewed the little case to the sun, and left it in its warmth. And it burst; and a little snake came out; and it became bigger and bigger from day to day until it was as big as I. That was the second birth.

EVE. Oh! That is too wonderful. It stirs inside me. It hurts.

THE SERPENT. It nearly tore me asunder. Yet I am alive, and can burst my skin and renew myself as before. Soon there will be as many snakes in Eden as there are scales on my body. Then death will not matter: this snake and that snake will die; but the snakes will live.

EVE. But the rest of us will die sooner or later, like the fawn. And then there will be nothing but snakes, snakes, snakes everywhere.

THE SERPENT. That must not be. I worship you, Eve. I must have something to worship. Something quite different to myself, like you. There must be something greater than the snake.

EVE. Yes: it must not be. Adam must not perish. You are very subtle: tell me what to do.

THE SERPENT. Think. Will. Eat the dust. Lick the white stone: bite the apple you dread. The sun will give life.

EVE. I do not trust the sun. I will give life myself. I will tear another Adam from my body if I tear my body to pieces in the act.

THE SERPENT. Do. Dare it. Everything is possible: everything. Listen. I am old. I am the old serpent, older than Adam, older than Eve. I remember Lilith, who came before Adam and Eve. I was her darling as I am yours. She was alone: there was no man with her. She saw death as you saw it when the fawn fell; and she knew then that she must find out how to renew herself and cast the skin like me. She had a mighty will: she strove and strove and willed and willed for more moons than there are leaves on all the trees of the garden. Her pangs were terrible: her groans drove sleep from Eden. She said it must never be again: that the burden of renewing life was past bearing: that it was too much for one. And when she cast the skin, lo! there was not one new Lilith but two: one like herself, the other like Adam. You were the one: Adam was the other.

EVE. But why did she divide into two, and make us different?

THE SERPENT. I tell you the labor is too much for one. Two must share it.

EVE. Do you mean that Adam must share it with me? He will not. He cannot bear pain, nor take trouble with his body.

THE SERPENT. He need not. There will be no pain for him. He will implore you to let him do his share. He will be in your power through his desire.

EVE. Then I will do it. But how? How did Lilith work this miracle?

THE SERPENT. She imagined it.

EVE. What is imagined?

THE SERPENT. She told it to me as a marvellous story of something that never happened to a Lilith that never was. She did not know then that imagination is the beginning of creation. You imagine what you desire; you will what you imagine; and at last you create what you will.

EVE. How can I create out of nothing?

THE SERPENT. Everything must have been created out of nothing. Look at that thick roll of hard flesh on your strong arm! That was not always there: you could not climb a tree when I first saw you. But you willed and tried and willed and tried; and your will created out of nothing the roll on your arm until you had your desire, and could draw yourself up with one hand and seat yourself on the bough that was above your head.

EVE. That was practice.

THE SERPENT. Things wear out by practice: they do not grow by it. Your hair streams in the wind as if it were trying to stretch itself further and further. But it does not grow longer for all its practice in streaming, because you have not willed it so. When Lilith told me what she had imagined in our silent language (for there were no words then) I bade her desire it and will it; and then, to our great wonder, the thing she had desired and willed created itself in her under the urging of her will. Then I too willed to renew myself as two instead of one; and after many days the miracle happened, and I burst from my skin with another snake interlaced with me; and now there are two imaginations, two desires, two wills to create with.

EVE. To desire, to imagine, to will, to create. That is too long a story. Find me one word for it all: you, who are so clever at words.

THE SERPENT. In one word, to conceive. That is the word that means both the beginning in imagination and the end in creation.

EVE. Find me a word for the story Lilith imagined and told you in your silent language: the story that was too wonderful to be true, and yet came true.

THE SERPENT. A poem.

EVE. Find me another word for what Lilith was to me.

THE SERPENT. She was your mother.

EVE. And Adam's mother?

THE SERPENT. Yes.

EVE [about to rise] I will go and tell Adam to conceive.

THE SERPENT [laughs]!!!

EVE [jarred and startled] What a hateful noise! What is the matter with you? No one has ever uttered such a sound before.

THE SERPENT. Adam cannot conceive.

EVE. Why?

THE SERPENT. Lilith did not imagine him so. He can imagine: he can will: he can desire: he can gather his life together for a great spring towards creation:

[ 349 ]

he can create all things except one; and that one is his own kind.

EVE. Why did Lilith keep this from him?

THE SERPENT. Because if he could do it he could do without Eve.

EVE. That is true. It is I who must conceive.

THE SERPENT. Yes. By that he is tied to you.

EVE. And I to him?

THE SERPENT. Yes, until you create another Adam.

EVE. I had not thought of that. You are very subtle. But if I create another Eve he may turn to her and do without me. I will not create any Eves, only Adams.

THE SERPENT. They cannot renew themselves without Eves. Sooner or later you will die like the fawn; and the new Adams will be unable to create without new Eves. You can imagine such an end; but you cannot desire it, therefore cannot will it, therefore cannot create Adams only.

EVE. If I am to die like the fawn, why should not the rest die too? What do I care?

THE SERPENT. Life must not cease. That comes before everything. It is silly to say you do not care. You do care. It is that care that will prompt your imagination; inflame your desires; make your will irresistible; and create out of nothing.

EVE [*thoughtfully*] There can be no such thing as nothing. The garden is full, not empty.

THE SERPENT. That is true. Darling Eve: this is a great thought. Yes: there is no such thing as nothing, only things we cannot see. The chameleon eats the air.

EVE. I have another thought: I must tell it to Adam. [*Calling*] Adam! Adam! Coo-ee!

ADAM'S VOICE. Coo-ee!

EVE. This will please him, and cure his fits of melancholy.

THE SERPENT. Do not tell him yet. I have not told
you the great secret.

EVE. What more is there to tell? It is I who have
to do the miracle.

THE SERPENT. No: he, too, must desire and will.
But he must give his desire and his will to you.

EVE. How?

THE SERPENT. That is the great secret. Hush! he
is coming.

ADAM [*returning*] Is there another voice in the garden
besides our voices and the Voice? I heard a new
voice.

EVE [*rising and running to him*] Only think, Adam!
Our snake has learnt to speak by listening to us.

ADAM [*delighted*] Is it so? [*He goes past her to the stone,
and fondles the serpent*].

THE SERPENT [*responding affectionately*] It is so, dear
Adam.

EVE. But I have more wonderful news than that.
Adam: we need not live for ever.

ADAM [*dropping the snake's head in his excitement*]
What! Eve: do not play with me about this. If only
there may be an end some day, and yet no end!
If only I can be relieved of the horror of having to
endure myself for ever! If only the care of this
terrible garden may pass on to some other gardener!
If only the sentinel set by the Voice can be relieved!
If only the rest and sleep that enable me to bear it
from day to day could grow after many days into an
eternal rest, an eternal sleep, then I could face my
days, however long they may last. Only, there must
be some end, some end: I am not strong enough to
bear eternity.

THE SERPENT. You need not live to see another summer; and yet there shall be no end.

ADAM. That cannot be.

THE SERPENT. It can be.

EVE. It shall be.

THE SERPENT. It is. Kill me; and you will find another snake in the garden tomorrow. You will find more snakes than there are fingers on your hands.

EVE. I will make other Adams, other Eves.

ADAM. I tell you you must not make up stories about this. It cannot happen.

THE SERPENT. I can remember when you were yourself a thing that could not happen. Yet you are.

ADAM [struck] That must be true. [He sits down on the stone].

THE SERPENT. I will tell Eve the secret; and she will tell it to you.

ADAM. The secret! [He turns quickly towards the serpent, and in doing so puts his foot on something sharp]. Oh!

EVE. What is it?

ADAM [rubbing his foot] A thistle. And there, next to it, a briar. And nettles, too! I am tired of pulling these things up to keep the garden pleasant for us for ever.

THE SERPENT. They do not grow very fast. They will not overrun the whole garden for a long time: not until you have laid down your burden and gone to sleep for ever. Why should you trouble yourself? Let the new Adams clear a place for themselves.

ADAM. That is very true. You must tell us your secret. You see, Eve, what a splendid thing it is not to have to live for ever.

EVE [throwing herself down discontentedly and plucking at the grass] That is so like a man. The moment you find we need not last for ever, you talk as if we were going to end today. You must clear away some of those horrid things, or we shall be scratched and stung whenever we forget to look where we are stepping.

ADAM. Oh yes, some of them, of course. But only some. I will clear them away tomorrow.

THE SERPENT [*laughs*]!!!

ADAM. That is a funny noise to make. I like it.

EVE. I do not. Why do you make it again?

THE SERPENT. Adam has invented something new. He has invented tomorrow. You will invent things every day now that the burden of immortality is lifted from you.

EVE. Immortality? What is that?

THE SERPENT. My new word for having to live for ever.

EVE. The serpent has made a beautiful word for being. Living.

ADAM. Make me a beautiful word for doing things tomorrow; for that surely is a great and blessed invention.

THE SERPENT. Procrastination.

EVE. That is a sweet word. I wish I had a serpent's tongue.

THE SERPENT. That may come too. Everything is possible.

ADAM [*springing up in sudden terror*] Oh!

EVE. What is the matter now?

ADAM. My rest! My escape from life!

THE SERPENT. Death. That is the word.

ADAM. There is a terrible danger in this procrastination.

EVE. What danger?

ADAM. If I put off death until tomorrow, I shall

never die. There is no such day as tomorrow, and never can be.

THE SERPENT. I am very very subtle; but Man is deeper in his thought than I am. The woman knows that there is no such thing as nothing: the man knows that there is no such day as tomorrow. I do well to worship them.

ADAM. If I am to overtake death, I must appoint a real day, not a tomorrow. When shall I die?

EVE. You may die when I have made another Adam. Not before. But then, as soon as you like. [*She rises, and passing behind him, strolls off carelessly to the tree and leans against it, stroking a ring of the snake*].

ADAM. There need be no hurry even then.

EVE. I see you will put it off until tomorrow.

ADAM. And you? Will you die the moment you have made a new Eve?

EVE. Why should I? Are you eager to be rid of me? Only just now you wanted me to sit still and never move lest I should stumble and die like the fawn. Now you care no longer.

ADAM. It does not matter so much now.

EVE [*angrily to the snake*] This death that you have brought into the garden is an evil thing. He wants me to die.

THE SERPENT [*to Adam*] Do you want her to die?

ADAM. No. It is I who am to die. Eve must not die before me. I should be lonely.

EVE. You could get one of the new Eves.

ADAM. That is true. But they might not be quite the same. They could not: I feel sure of that. They would not have the same memories. They would be— I want a word for them.

THE SERPENT. Strangers.

ADAM. Yes: that is a good hard word. Strangers.

[ 354 ]

EVE. When there are new Adams and new Eves we shall live in a garden of strangers. We shall need each other. [*She comes quickly behind him and turns up his face to her*]. Do not forget that, Adam. Never forget it.

ADAM. Why should I forget it? It is I who have thought of it.

EVE. I, too, have thought of something. The fawn stumbled and fell and died. But you could come softly up behind me and [*she suddenly pounces on his shoulders and throws him forward on his face*] throw me down so that I should die. I should not dare to sleep if there were no reason why you should not make me die.

ADAM [*scrambling up in horror*] Make you die!!! What a frightful thought!

THE SERPENT. Kill, kill, kill, kill. That is the word.

EVE. The new Adams and Eves might kill us. I shall not make them. [*She sits on the rock and pulls him down beside her, clasping him to her with her right arm*].

THE SERPENT. You must. For if you do not there will be an end.

ADAM. No: they will not kill us: they will feel as I do. There is something against it. The Voice in the garden will tell them that they must not kill, as it tells me.

THE SERPENT. The voice in the garden is your own voice.

ADAM. It is; and it is not. It is something greater than me: I am only a part of it.

EVE. The Voice does not tell me not to kill you. Yet I do not want you to die before me. No voice is needed to make me feel that.

ADAM [*throwing his arm round her shoulder with an expression of anguish*] Oh no: that is plain without any voice. There is something that holds us together, something that has no word—

[ 355 ]

THE SERPENT. Love. Love. Love.

ADAM. That is too short a word for so long a thing.

THE SERPENT [*laughs*]! ! !

EVE [*turning impatiently to the snake*] That heart-biting sound again! Do not do it. Why do you do it?

THE SERPENT. Love may soon be too long a word for so short a thing. But when it is short it will be very sweet.

ADAM [*ruminating*] You puzzle me. My old trouble was heavy; but it was simple. These wonders that you promise to do may tangle up my being before they bring me the gift of death. I was troubled with the burden of eternal being; but I was not confused in my mind. If I did not know that I loved Eve, at least I did not know that she might cease to love me, and come to love some other Adam and desire my death. Can you find a name for that knowledge?

THE SERPENT. Jealousy. Jealousy. Jealousy.

ADAM. A hideous word.

EVE [*shaking him*] Adam: you must not brood. You think too much.

ADAM [*angrily*] How can I help brooding when the future has become uncertain? Anything is better than uncertainty. Life has become uncertain. Love is uncertain. Have you a word for this new misery?

THE SERPENT. Fear. Fear. Fear.

ADAM. Have you a remedy for it?

THE SERPENT. Yes. Hope. Hope. Hope.

ADAM. What is hope?

THE SERPENT. As long as you do not know the future you do not know that it will not be happier than the past. That is hope.

ADAM. It does not console me. Fear is stronger in me than hope. I must have certainty. [*He rises threateningly*]. Give it to me; or I will kill you when next I catch you asleep.

EVE [*throwing her arms round the serpent*] My beautiful snake. Oh no. How can you even think such a horror?

ADAM. Fear will drive me to anything. The serpent gave me fear. Let it now give me certainty or go in fear of me.

THE SERPENT. Bind the future by your will. Make a vow.

ADAM. What is a vow?

THE SERPENT. Choose a day for your death; and resolve to die on that day. Then death is no longer uncertain but certain. Let Eve vow to love you until your death. Then love will be no longer uncertain.

ADAM. Yes: that is splendid: that will bind the future.

EVE [*displeased, turning away from the serpent*] But it will destroy hope.

ADAM [*angrily*] Be silent, woman. Hope is wicked. Happiness is wicked. Certainty is blessed.

THE SERPENT. What is wicked? You have invented a word.

ADAM. Whatever I fear to do is wicked. Listen to me, Eve; and you, snake, listen too, that your memory may hold my vow. I will live a thousand sets of the four seasons—

THE SERPENT. Years. Years.

ADAM. I will live a thousand years; and then I will endure no more: I will die and take my rest. And I will love Eve all that time and no other woman.

EVE. And if Adam keeps his vow I will love no other man until he dies.

THE SERPENT. You have both invented marriage. And what he will be to you and not to any other woman is husband; and what you will be to him and not to any other man is wife.

[ 357 ]

ADAM [*instinctively moving his hand towards her*]
Husband and wife.

EVE [*slipping her hand into his*] Wife and husband.

THE SERPENT [*laughs*]! ! !

EVE [*snatching herself loose from Adam*] Do not make
that odious noise, I tell you.

ADAM. Do not listen to her: the noise is good: it
lightens my heart. You are a jolly snake. But you
have not made a vow yet. What vow do you make?

THE SERPENT. I make no vows. I take my chance.

ADAM. Chance? What does that mean?

THE SERPENT. It means that I fear certainty as you
fear uncertainty. It means that nothing is certain
but uncertainty. If I bind the future I bind my will.
If I bind my will I strangle creation.

EVE. Creation must not be strangled. I tell you I
will create, though I tear myself to pieces in the act.

ADAM. Be silent, both of you. I will bind the future.
I will be delivered from fear. [*To Eve*] We have made
our vows; and if you must create, you shall create
within the bounds of those vows. You shall not listen
to that snake any more. Come [*he seizes her by the
hair to drag her away*].

EVE. Let me go, you fool. It has not yet told me the
secret.

ADAM [*releasing her*] That is true. What is a fool?

EVE. I do not know: the word came to me. It is what
you are when you forget and brood and are filled
with fear. Let us listen to the snake.

ADAM. No: I am afraid of it. I feel as if the ground
were giving way under my feet when it speaks. Do
you stay and listen to it.

THE SERPENT [*laughs*]! ! !

ADAM [*brightening*] That noise takes away fear.
Funny. The snake and the woman are going to

whisper secrets. [*He chuckles and goes away slowly, laughing his first laugh*].

EVE. Now the secret. The secret. [*She sits on the rock and throws her arms round the serpent, who begins whispering to her*].

*Eve's face lights up with intense interest, which increases until an expression of overwhelming repugnance takes its place. She buries her face in her hands.*

# ⌈ACT II⌉

*A few centuries later. Morning. An oasis in Meso-
potamia. Close at hand the end of a log house abuts on
a kitchen garden. Adam is digging in the middle of the
garden. On his right, Eve sits on a stool in the shadow
of a tree by the doorway, spinning flax. Her wheel,
which she turns by hand, is a large disc of heavy wood,
practically a fly-wheel. At the opposite side of the
garden is a thorn brake with a passage through it barred
by a hurdle.*

*The two are scantily and carelessly dressed in rough
linen and leaves. They have lost their youth and attractive grace; and Adam has an unkempt beard and jag-
gedly cut hair; but they are strong and in the prime of
life. Adam looks worried, like a farmer. Eve, better
humored (having given up worrying), sits and spins and
thinks.*

A MAN'S VOICE. Hallo, mother!

EVE [*looking across the garden towards the hurdle*] Here
is Cain.

ADAM [*uttering a grunt of disgust*]! ! ! [*He goes on
digging without raising his head*].

*Cain kicks the hurdle out of his way, and strides into
the garden. In pose, voice, and dress he is insistently warlike. He is equipped with huge spear and broad brass-
bound leather shield; his casque is a tiger's head with
bull's horns; he wears a scarlet cloak with gold brooch
over a lion's skin with the claws dangling; his feet are
in sandals with brass ornaments; his shins are in brass*

*greaves; and his bristling military moustache glistens with oil. To his parents he has the self-assertive, not-quite-at-ease manner of a revolted son who knows that he is not forgiven nor approved of.*

CAIN [*to Adam*] Still digging? Always dig, dig, dig. Sticking in the old furrow. No progress! no advanced ideas! no adventures! What should I be if I had stuck to the digging you taught me?

ADAM. What are you now, with your shield and spear, and your brother's blood crying from the ground against you?

CAIN. I am the first murderer: you are only the first man. Anybody could be the first man: it is as easy as to be the first cabbage. To be the first murderer one must be a man of spirit.

ADAM. Begone. Leave us in peace. The world is wide enough to keep us apart.

EVE. Why do you want to drive him away? He is mine. I made him out of my own body. I want to see my work sometimes.

ADAM. You made Abel also. He killed Abel. Can you bear to look at him after that?

CAIN. Whose fault was it that I killed Abel? Who invented killing? Did *I*? No: he invented it himself. I followed your teaching. I dug and dug and dug. I cleared away the thistles and briars. I ate the fruits of the earth. I lived in the sweat of my brow, as you do. I was a fool. But Abel was a discoverer, a man of ideas, of spirit: a true Progressive. He was the discoverer of blood. He was the inventor of killing. He found out that the fire of the sun could be brought down by a dewdrop. He invented the altar to keep the fire alive. He changed the beasts he killed into meat by the fire on the altar. He kept himself alive by eating meat. His meal cost him a day's glorious health-giving sport and an hour's amusing play with the fire. You learnt nothing from him: you drudged and drudged and drudged, and dug and dug and dug, and made me do the same. I envied his happiness, his freedom. I despised myself for not doing as he did instead of what you did. He became so happy that he shared his meal with the Voice that had whispered all his inventions to him. He said that the Voice was the voice of the fire that cooked his food, and that the fire that could cook could also eat. It was true: I saw the fire consume the food on his altar. Then I, too, made an altar, and offered my food on it, my grains, my roots, my fruit. Useless: nothing happened. He laughed at me; and then came my great idea: why not kill him as he killed the beasts? I struck; and he died, just as they did. Then I gave up your old silly drudging ways, and lived as he had lived, by the chase, by the killing, and by the fire. Am I not better than you? stronger, happier, freer?

ADAM. You are not stronger: you are shorter in the wind: you cannot endure. You have made the beasts afraid of us; and the snake has invented poison to protect herself against you. I fear you myself. If you take a step towards your mother with that spear of yours I will strike you with my spade as you struck Abel.

EVE. He will not strike me. He loves me.

ADAM. He loved his brother. But he killed him.

CAIN. I do not want to kill women. I do not want to kill my mother. And for her sake I will not kill you, though I could send this spear through you without coming within reach of your spade. But for her, I could not resist the sport of trying to kill you, in spite of my fear that you would kill me. I have striven with a boar and with a lion as to which of us should kill the other. I have striven with a man: spear to spear and shield to shield. It is terrible; but there is no joy like it. I call it fighting. He who has never fought has never lived. That is what has brought me to my mother today.

ADAM. What have you to do with one another now? She is the creator, you the destroyer.

CAIN. How can I destroy unless she creates? I want her to create more and more men: aye, and more and more women, that they may in turn create more men. I have imagined a glorious poem of many men, of more men than there are leaves on a thousand trees. I will divide them into two great hosts. One of them I will lead; and the other will be led by the man I fear most and desire to fight and kill most. And each host shall try to kill the other host. Think of that! all those multitudes of men fighting, fighting, killing, killing! The four rivers running with blood! The shouts of triumph! the howls of rage! the curses of despair! the shrieks of torment! That will be life indeed: life lived to the very marrow: burning, overwhelming life. Every man who has not seen it, heard it, felt it, risked it, will feel a humbled fool in the presence of the man who has.

EVE. And I! I am to be a mere convenience to make men for you to kill!

ADAM. Or to kill you, you fool.

CAIN. Mother: the making of men is your right, your risk, your agony, your glory, your triumph. You make my father here your mere convenience, as you call it, for that. He has to dig for you, sweat for you, plod for you, like the ox who helps him to tear up the ground or the ass who carries his burdens for him. No woman shall make me live my father's life. I will hunt: I will fight and strive to the very bursting of my sinews. When I have slain the boar at the risk of my life, I will throw it to my woman to cook, and give her a morsel of it for her pains. She shall have no other food; and that will make her my slave. And the man that slays me shall have her for his booty. Man shall be the master of Woman, not her baby and her drudge.

*Adam throws down his spade, and stands looking darkly at Eve.*

EVE. Are you tempted, Adam? Does this seem a better thing to you than love between us?

CAIN. What does he know of love? Only when he has fought, when he has faced terror and death, when he has striven to the spending of the last rally of his strength, can he know what it is to rest in love in the arms of a woman. Ask that woman whom you made, who is also my wife, whether she would have me as I was in the days when I followed the ways of Adam, and was a digger and a drudge?

EVE [*angrily throwing down her distaff*] What! You dare come here boasting about that good-for-nothing Lua, the worst of daughters and the worst of wives! You her master! You are more her slave than Adam's ox or your own sheepdog. Forsooth, when you have slain the boar at the risk of your life, you will throw her a morsel of it for her pains! Ha! Poor wretch: do you think I do not know her, and know you, better than that? Do you risk your life when you trap the ermine and the sable and the blue fox to hang on her lazy shoulders and make her look more like an animal than a woman? When you have to snare the little tender birds because it is too much trouble for her to chew honest food, how much of a great warrior do you feel then? You slay the tiger at the risk of your life; but who gets the striped skin you have run that risk for? She takes it to lie on, and flings you the carrion flesh you cannot eat. You fight because you think that your fighting makes her admire and desire you. Fool: she makes you fight because you bring her the ornaments and the treasures of those you have slain, and because she is courted and propitiated with power and gold by the people who fear you. You say that *I* make a mere convenience of Adam: I who spin and keep the house, and bear and rear children, and am a woman and not a pet animal to please men and prey on them! What are you, you poor slave of a painted face and a bundle of skunk's fur? You were a man-child when I bore you. Lua was a woman-child when I bore her. What have you made of yourselves?

CAIN [*letting his spear fall into the crook of his shield arm, and twirling his moustache*] There is something higher than man. There is hero and superman.

EVE. Superman! You are no superman: you are Anti-man: you are to other men what the stoat is to the rabbit; and she is to you what the leech is to the stoat. You despise your father; but when he dies the world will be the richer because he lived. When you die, men will say, "He was a great warrior; but it would have been better for the world if he had never been born." And of Lua they will say nothing; but when they think of her they will spit.

CAIN. She is a better sort of woman to live with than you. If Lua nagged at me as you are nagging, and as you nag at Adam, I would beat her black and blue from head to foot. I have done it too, slave as you say I am.

EVE. Yes, because she looked at another man. And then you grovelled at her feet, and cried, and begged her to forgive you, and were ten times more her slave than ever; and she, when she had finished screaming and the pain went off a little, she forgave you, did she not?

CAIN. She loved me more than ever. That is the true nature of woman.

EVE [*now pitying him maternally*] Love! You call that love! You call that the nature of woman! My boy: this is neither man nor woman nor love nor life. You have no real strength in your bones nor sap in your flesh.

CAIN. Ha! [*he seizes his spear and swings it muscularly*].

EVE. Yes: you have to twirl a stick to feel your strength: you cannot taste life without making it bitter and boiling hot: you cannot love Lua until her face is painted, nor feel the natural warmth of her flesh until you have stuck a squirrel's fur on it. You can feel nothing but a torment, and believe nothing but a lie. You will not raise your head to look at all the miracles of life that surround you; but you will run ten miles to see a fight or a death.

ADAM. Enough said. Let the boy alone.

CAIN. Boy! Ha! ha!

EVE [*to Adam*] You think, perhaps, that his way of life may be better than yours after all. You are still tempted. Well, will you pamper me as he pampers his woman? Will you kill tigers and bears until I have a heap of their skins to lounge on? Shall I paint my face and let my arms waste into pretty softness, and eat partridges and doves, and the flesh of kids whose milk you will steal for me?

ADAM. You are hard enough to bear with as you are. Stay as you are; and I will stay as I am.

CAIN. You neither of you know anything about life. You are simple country folk. You are the nurses and valets of the oxen and dogs and asses you have tamed to work for you. I can raise you out of that. I have a plan. Why not tame men and women to work for us? Why not bring them up from childhood never to know any other lot, so that they may believe that we are gods, and that they are here only to make life glorious for us?

ADAM [*impressed*] That is great thought, certainly.

EVE [*contemptuously*] Great thought!

ADAM. Well, as the serpent used to say, why not?

EVE. Because I would not have such wretches in my house. Because I hate creatures with two heads, or with withered limbs, or that are distorted and perverted and unnatural. I have told Cain already that he is not a man and that Lua is not a woman: they are monsters. And now you want to make still more unnatural monsters, so that you may be utterly lazy and worthless, and that your tamed human animals may find work a blasting curse. A fine dream, truly! [*To Cain*] Your father is a fool skin deep; but you are a fool to your very marrow; and your baggage of a wife is worse.

ADAM. Why am I a fool? How am I a greater fool than you?

EVE. You said there would be no killing because the Voice would tell our children that they must not kill. Why did it not tell Cain that?

CAIN. It did; but I am not a child to be afraid of a Voice. The Voice thought I was nothing but my brother's keeper. It found that I was myself, and that it was for Abel to be himself also, and look to himself. He was not my keeper any more than I was his: why did he not kill me? There was no more to prevent him than there was to prevent me: it was man to man; and I won. I was the first conqueror.

ADAM. What did the Voice say to you when you thought all that?

CAIN. Why, it gave me right. It said that my deed was as a mark on me, a burnt-in mark such as Abel put on his sheep, that no man should slay me. And here I stand unslain, whilst the cowards who have never slain, the men who are content to be their brothers' keepers instead of their masters, are despised and rejected, and slain like rabbits. He who bears the brand of Cain shall rule the earth. When he falls, he shall be avenged sevenfold: the Voice has said it; so beware how you plot against me, you and all the rest.

ADAM. Cease your boasting and bullying, and tell the truth. Does not the Voice tell you that as no man dare slay you for murdering your brother, you ought to slay yourself?

CAIN. No.

ADAM. Then there is no such thing as divine justice, unless you are lying.

CAIN. I am not lying: I dare all truths. There is divine justice. For the Voice tells me that I must offer myself to every man to be killed if he can kill me. Without danger I cannot be great. That is how I pay for Abel's blood. Danger and fear follow my steps everywhere. Without them courage would have no sense. And it is courage, courage, courage, that raises the blood of life to crimson splendor.

ADAM [*picking up his spade and preparing to dig again*] Take yourself off then. This splendid life of yours does not last for a thousand years; and I must last for a thousand years. When you fighters do not get killed in fighting one another or fighting the beasts, you die from mere evil in yourselves. Your flesh ceases to grow like man's flesh: it grows like a fungus on a tree. Instead of breathing, you sneeze, or cough up your insides, and wither and perish. Your bowels become rotten; your hair falls from you; your teeth blacken and drop out; and you die before your time, not because you will, but because you must. I will dig, and live.

CAIN. And pray, what use is this thousand years of life to you, you old vegetable? Do you dig any better because you have been digging for hundreds of years? I have not lived as long as you; but I know all there is to be known of the craft of digging. By quitting it I have set myself free to learn nobler crafts of which you know nothing. I know the craft of fighting and of hunting: in a word, the craft of killing. What certainty have you of your thousand years? I could kill both of you; and you could no more defend yourselves than a couple of sheep. I spare you; but others may kill you. Why not live bravely, and die early and make room for others? Why, I—I! that know many more crafts than either of you, am tired of myself when I am not fighting or hunting. Sooner than face a thousand years of it I should kill myself, as the Voice sometimes tempts me to do already.

ADAM. Liar: you denied just now that it called on you to pay for Abel's life with your own.

CAIN. The Voice does not speak to me as it does to you. I am a man: you are only a grown-up child. One does not speak to a child as to a man. And a man does not listen and tremble in silence. He replies: he makes the Voice respect him: in the end he dictates what the Voice shall say.

ADAM. May your tongue be accurst for such blasphemy!

EVE. Keep a guard on your own tongue; and do not curse my son. It was Lilith who did wrong when she shared the labor of creation so unequally between man and wife. If you, Cain, had had the trouble of making Abel, or had had to make another man to replace him when he was gone, you would not have killed him: you would have risked your own life to save his. That is why all this empty talk of yours, which tempted Adam just now when he threw down his spade and listened to you for a while, went by me like foul wind that has passed over a dead body. That is why there is enmity between Woman the creator and Man the destroyer. I know you: I am your mother. You are idle: you are selfish. It is long and hard and painful to create life: it is short and easy to steal the life others have made. When you dug, you made the earth live and bring forth as I live and bring forth. It was for that that Lilith set you free from the travail of women, not for theft and murder.

CAIN. The Devil thank her for it! I can make better use of my time than to play the husband to the clay beneath my feet.

ADAM. Devil? What new word is that?

CAIN. Hearken to me, old fool. I have never in my soul listened willingly when you have told me of the Voice that whispers to you. There must be two Voices: one that gulls and despises you, and another that trusts and respects me. I call yours the Devil. Mine I call the Voice of God.

ADAM. Mine is the Voice of Life: yours the Voice of Death.

CAIN. Be it so. For it whispers to me that death is not really death: that it is the gate of another life: a life infinitely splendid and intense: a life of the soul alone: a life without clods or spades, hunger or fatigue—

EVE. Selfish and idle, Cain. I know.

CAIN. Selfish, yes: a life in which no man is his

brother's keeper, because his brother can keep himself. But am I idle? In rejecting your drudgery, have I not embraced evils and agonies of which you know nothing? The arrow is lighter in the hand than the spade; but the energy that drives it through the breast of a fighter is as fire to water compared with the strength that drives the spade into the harmless dirty clay. My strength is as the strength of ten because my heart is pure.

ADAM. What is that word? What is pure?

CAIN. Turned from the clay. Turned upward to the sun, to the clear clean heavens.

ADAM. The heavens are empty, child. The earth is fruitful. The earth feeds us. It gives us the strength by which we made you and all mankind. Cut off from the clay which you despise, you would perish miserably.

CAIN. I revolt against the clay. I revolt against the food. You say it gives us strength: does it not also turn into filth and smite us with diseases? I revolt against these births that you and mother are so proud of. They drag us down to the level of the beasts. If that is to be the last thing as it has been the first, let mankind perish. If I am to eat like a bear, if Lua is to bring forth cubs like a bear, then I had rather be a bear than a man; for the bear is not ashamed: he knows no better. If you are content, like the bear, I am not. Stay with the woman who gives you children: I will go to the woman who gives me dreams. Grope in the ground for your food: I will bring it from the skies with my arrows, or strike it down as it roams the earth in the pride of its life. If I must have food or die, I will at least have it at as far a remove from the earth as I can. The ox shall make it something nobler than grass before it comes to me.

And as the man is nobler than the ox, I shall some day let my enemy eat the ox; and then I will slay and eat him?

ADAM. Monster! You hear this, Eve?

EVE. So that is what comes of turning your face to the clean clear heavens! Man-eating! Child-eating! For that is what it would come to, just as it came to lambs and kids when Abel began with sheep and goats. You are a poor silly creature after all. Do you think I never have these thoughts: I! who have the labor of the child-bearing: I! who have the drudgery of preparing the food? I thought for a moment that perhaps this strong brave son of mine, who could imagine something better, and could desire what he imagined, might also be able to will what he desired until he created it. And all that comes of it is that he wants to be a bear and eat children. Even a bear would not eat a man if it could get honey instead.

CAIN. I do not want to be a bear. I do not want to eat children. I do not know what I want, except that I want to be something higher and nobler than this stupid old digger whom Lilith made to help you to bring me into the world, and whom you despise now that he has served your turn.

ADAM [in sullen rage] I have half a mind to shew you that my spade can split your undutiful head open, in spite of your spear.

CAIN. Undutiful! Ha! ha! [Flourishing his spear] Try it, old everybody's father. Try a taste of fighting.

EVE. Peace, peace, you two fools. Sit down and be quiet; and listen to me. [Adam, with a weary shrug, throws down his spade. Cain, with a laughing one, throws down his shield and spear. Both sit on the ground]. I hardly know which of you satisfies me least, you with your dirty digging, or he with his dirty killing. I cannot think it was for either of these cheap ways of life that Lilith set you free. [*To Adam*] You dig roots and coax grains out of the earth: why do you not draw down a divine sustenance from the skies? He steals and kills for his food; and makes up idle poems of life after death; and dresses up his terror-ridden life with fine words and his disease-ridden body with fine clothes, so that men may glorify and honor him instead of cursing him as murderer and thief. All you men, except only Adam, are my sons, or my sons' sons, or my sons' sons' sons: you all come to see me: you all shew off before me: all your little wisdoms and accomplishments are trotted out before mother Eve. The diggers come: the fighters and killers come: they are both very dull; for they either complain to me of the last harvest, or boast to me of the last fight; and one harvest is just like another, and the last fight only a repetition of the first. Oh, I have heard it all a thousand times. They tell me too of their last-born: the clever thing the darling child said yesterday, and how much more wonderful or witty or quaint it is than any child that ever was born before. And I have to pretend to be surprised, delighted, interested; though the last child is like the first, and has said and done nothing that did not delight Adam and me when you and Abel said it. For you were the first children in the world, and filled us with such wonder and delight as no couple can ever again feel while the world lasts. When I can bear no more, I go to our old garden, that is now a mass of nettles and thistles, in the hope of finding the serpent to talk to. But you have made the serpent our enemy: she has left the garden, or is dead: I never see her now. So I have to come back and listen to Adam saying the same thing for the ten-thousandth time, or to receive a

visit from the last great-great-grandson who has
grown up and wants to impress me with his importance. Oh, it is dreary, dreary! And there is yet nearly
seven hundred years of it to endure.

CAIN. Poor mother! You see, life is too long. One
tires of everything. There is nothing new under the
sun.

ADAM [*to Eve, grumpily*] Why do you live on, if you
can find nothing better to do than complain?

EVE. Because there is still hope.

CAIN. Of what?

EVE. Of the coming true of your dreams and mine.
Of newly created things. Of better things. My sons
and my sons' sons are not all diggers and fighters.
Some of them will neither dig nor fight: they are
more useless than either of you: they are weaklings
and cowards: they are vain; yet they are dirty and
will not take the trouble to cut their hair. They
borrow and never pay; but one gives them what they
want, because they tell beautiful lies in beautiful
words. They can remember their dreams. They
can dream without sleeping. They have not will
enough to create instead of dreaming; but the serpent
said that every dream could be willed into creation
by those strong enough to believe in it. There are
others who cut reeds of different lengths and blow
through them, making lovely patterns of sound in the
air; and some of them can weave the patterns together, sounding three reeds at the same time, and
raising my soul to things for which I have no words.
And others make little mammoths out of clay, or
make faces appear on flat stones, and ask me to create
women for them with such faces. I have watched
those faces and willed; and then I have made a
woman-child that has grown up quite like them.

And others think of numbers without having to count on their fingers, and watch the sky at night, and give names to the stars, and can foretell when the sun will be covered with a black saucepan lid. And there is Tubal, who made this wheel for me which has saved me so much labor. And there is Enoch, who walks on the hills, and hears the Voice continually, and has given up his will to do the will of the Voice, and has some of the Voice's greatness. When they come, there is always some new wonder, or some new hope: something to live for. They never want to die, because they are always learning and always creating either things or wisdom, or at least dreaming of them. And then you, Cain, come to me with your stupid fighting and destroying, and your foolish boasting; and you want me to tell you that it is all splendid, and that you are heroic, and that nothing but death or the dread of death makes life worth living. Away with you, naughty child; and do you, Adam, go on with your work and not waste your time listening to him.

CAIN. I am not, perhaps, very clever; but—

EVE [*interrupting him*] Perhaps not; but do not begin to boast of that. It is no credit to you.

CAIN. For all that, mother, I have an instinct which tells me that death plays its part in life. Tell me this: who invented death?

*Adam springs to his feet. Eve drops her distaff. Both shew the greatest consternation.*

CAIN. What is the matter with you both?

ADAM. Boy: you have asked us a terrible question.

EVE. You invented murder. Let that be enough for you.

CAIN. Murder is not death. You know what I mean. Those whom I slay would die if I spared them. If I

[ 375 ]

am not slain, yet I shall die. Who put this upon me? I say, who invented death?

ADAM. Be reasonable, boy. Could you bear to live for ever? You think you could, because you know that you will never have to make your thought good. But I have known what it is to sit and brood under the terror of eternity, of immortality. Think of it, man: to have no escape! to be Adam, Adam, Adam through more days than there are grains of sand by the two rivers, and then be as far from the end as ever! I, who have so much in me that I hate and long to cast off! Be thankful to your parents who enabled you to hand on your burden to new and better men, and won for you an eternal rest; for it was we who invented death.

CAIN [*rising*] You did well: I, too, do not want to live for ever. But if you invented death, why do you blame me, who am a minister of death?

ADAM. I do not blame you. Go in peace. Leave me to my digging, and your mother to her spinning.

CAIN. Well, I will leave you to it, though I have shewn you a better way. [*He picks up his shield and spear*]. I will go back to my brave warrior friends and their splendid women. [*He strides to the thorn brake*]. When Adam delved and Eve span, who was then the gentle man? [*He goes away roaring with laughter, which ceases as he cries from the distance*] Goodbye, mother.

ADAM [*grumbling*] He might have put the hurdle back, lazy hound! [*He replaces the hurdle across the passage*].

EVE. Through him and his like, death is gaining on life. Already most of our grandchildren die before they have sense enough to know how to live.

ADAM. No matter. [*He spits on his hands, and takes*

*up the spade again*]. Life is still long enough to learn to dig, short as they are making it.

EVE [*musing*] Yes, to dig. And to fight. But is it long enough for the other things, the great things? Will they live long enough to eat manna?

ADAM. What is manna?

EVE. Food drawn down from heaven, made out of the air, not dug dirtily from the earth. Will they learn all the ways of all the stars in their little time? It took Enoch two hundred years to learn to interpret the will of the Voice. When he was a mere child of eighty, his babyish attempts to understand the Voice were more dangerous than the wrath of Cain. If they shorten their lives, they will dig and fight and kill and die; and their baby Enochs will tell them that it is the will of the Voice that they should dig and fight and kill and die for ever.

ADAM. If they are lazy and have a will towards death I cannot help it. I will live my thousand years: if they will not, let them die and be damned.

EVE. Damned? What is that?

ADAM. The state of them that love death more than life. Go on with your spinning; and do not sit there idle while I am straining my muscles for you.

EVE [*slowly taking up her distaff*] If you were not a fool you would find something better for both of us to live by than this spinning and digging.

ADAM. Go on with your work, I tell you; or you shall go without bread.

EVE. Man need not always live by bread alone. There is something else. We do not yet know what it is; but some day we shall find out; and then we will live on that alone; and there shall be no more digging nor spinning, nor fighting nor killing.

*She spins resignedly. He digs impatiently.*

# PART II

## THE GOSPEL OF
## THE BROTHERS BARNABAS

*In the first years after the war of 1914–18 an impressive-looking gentleman of 50 is writing in a well-furnished study. He is dressed in black. His coat is a frock-coat; his tie is white; and his waistcoat, though it is not quite a clergyman's waistcoat, and his collar, though it buttons in front instead of behind, combine with the prosperity indicated by his surroundings, and his air of personal distinction, to suggest the clerical dignitary. Still, he is clearly neither dean nor bishop; he is rather too starkly intellectual for a popular Free Church enthusiast; and he is not careworn enough to be a great headmaster.*

*The study windows, which have broad comfortable window seats, overlook Hampstead Heath towards London. Consequently, it being a fine afternoon in spring, the room is sunny. As you face these windows, you have on your right the fireplace, with a few logs smouldering in it, and a couple of comfortable library chairs on the hearthrug; beyond it and beside it the door; before you the writing-table, at which the clerical gentleman sits a little to your left facing the door with his right profile presented to you; on your left a settee; and on your right a couple of Chippendale chairs. There is also an upholstered square stool in the middle of the room, against the writing-table. The walls are covered with bookshelves above and lockers beneath.*

*The door opens; and another gentleman, shorter than the clerical one, within a year or two of the same age, dressed in a well-worn tweed lounge suit, with a short beard and much less style in his bearing and carriage, looks in.*

---

THE CLERICAL GENTLEMAN [*familiar and by no means cordial*] Hallo! I didnt expect you until the five o'clock train.

THE TWEEDED GENTLEMAN [*coming in very slowly*] I have something on my mind. I thought I'd come early.

THE CLERICAL GENTLEMAN [*throwing down his pen*] What is on your mind?

THE TWEEDED GENTLEMAN [*sitting down on the stool, heavily preoccupied with his thought*] I have made up my mind at last about the time. I make it three hundred years.

THE CLERICAL GENTLEMAN [*sitting up energetically*] Now that is extraordinary. Most extraordinary. The very last words I wrote when you interrupted me were "at least three centuries." [*He snatches up his manuscript, and points to it*]. Here it is: [*reading*] "the term of human life must be extended to at least three centuries."

THE TWEEDED GENTLEMAN. How did you arrive at it?

*A parlor maid opens the door, ushering in a young clergyman.*

THE PARLOR MAID. The Reverend Mr Haslam.

*She goes. The visitor is so unwelcome that his host forgets to rise; and the two brothers stare at the intruder, unable to conceal their dismay. Haslam, who has nothing clerical about him except his collar, and wears a snuff-colored suit, smiles with a frank schoolboyishness that makes it impossible to be unkind to him, and explodes into obviously unpremeditated speech.*

[ 379 ]

HASLAM. I'm afraid I'm an awful nuisance. I'm the rector; and I suppose one ought to call on people.

THE TWEEDED GENTLEMAN [*in ghostly tones*] We're not Church people, you know.

HASLAM. Oh, I dont mind that, if you dont. The Church people here are mostly as dull as ditch water. I have heard such a lot about you! and there are so jolly few people to talk to! I thought you perhaps wouldnt mind. Do you mind? for of course I'll go like a shot if I'm in the way.

THE CLERICAL GENTLEMAN [*rising, disarmed*] Sit down, Mr—er?

HASLAM. Haslam.

THE CLERICAL GENTLEMAN. Mr Haslam.

THE TWEEDED GENTLEMAN [*rising and offering him the stool*] Sit down. [*He retreats towards the Chippendale chairs*].

HASLAM [*sitting down on the stool*] Thanks awfully.

THE CLERICAL GENTLEMAN [*resuming his seat*] This is my brother Conrad, Professor of Biology at Jarrowfields University: Dr Conrad Barnabas. My name is Franklyn: Franklyn Barnabas. I was in the Church myself for some years.

HASLAM [*sympathizing*] Yes: one cant help it. If theres a living in the family, or one's governor knows a patron, one gets shoved into the Church by one's parents.

CONRAD [*sitting down on the furthest Chippendale with a snort of amusement*] Mp!

FRANKLYN. One gets shoved out of it, sometimes, by one's conscience.

HASLAM. Oh yes; but where is a chap like me to go? I'm afraid I'm not intellectual enough to split straws when theres a job in front of me, and nothing better for me to do. I daresay the Church was a bit thick for you; but it's good enough for me. It will last my time, anyhow [*he laughs good-humoredly*].

FRANKLYN [*with renewed energy*] There again! You see, Con. It will last his time. Life is too short for men to take it seriously.

HASLAM. Thats a way of looking at it, certainly.

FRANKLYN. I was not shoved into the Church, Mr Haslam: I felt it to be my vocation to walk with God, like Enoch. After twenty years of it I realized that I was walking with my own ignorance and self-conceit, and that I was not within a hundred and fifty years of the experience and wisdom I was pretending to.

HASLAM. Now I come to think of it, old Methuselah must have had to think twice before he took on anything for life. If I thought I was going to live nine hundred and sixty years, I dont think I should stay in the Church.

FRANKLYN. If men lived even a third of that time, the Church would be very different from the thing it is.

CONRAD. If I could count on nine hundred and sixty years I could make myself a real biologist, instead of what I am now: a child trying to walk. Are you sure you might not become a good clergyman if you had a few centuries to do it in?

HASLAM. Oh, theres nothing much the matter with me: it's quite easy to be a decent parson. It's the Church that chokes me off. I couldnt stick it for nine hundred years. I should chuck it. You know, sometimes, when the bishop, who is the most priceless of fossils, lets off something more than usually out-of-date, the bird starts in my garden.

FRANKLYN. The bird?

HASLAM. Oh yes. Theres a bird there that keeps on singing "Stick it or chuck it: stick it or chuck it"

[ 381 ]

—just like that—for an hour on end in the spring. I wish my father had found some other shop for me.

*The parlor maid comes back.*

THE PARLOR MAID. Any letters for the post, sir?

FRANKLYN. These. [*He proffers a basket of letters. She comes to the table and takes them*].

HASLAM [*to the maid*] Have you told Mr Barnabas yet?

THE PARLOR MAID [*flinching a little*] No, sir.

FRANKLYN. Told me what?

HASLAM. She is going to leave you?

FRANKLYN. Indeed? I'm sorry. Is it our fault, Mr Haslam?

HASLAM. Not a bit. She is jolly well off here.

THE PARLOR MAID [*reddening*] I have never denied it, sir: I couldnt ask for a better place. But I have only one life to live; and I maynt get a second chance. Excuse me, sir; but the letters must go to catch the post. [*She goes out with the letters*].

*The two brothers look inquiringly at Haslam.*

HASLAM. Silly girl! Going to marry a village woodman and live in a hovel with him and a lot of kids tumbling over one another, just because the fellow has poetic-looking eyes and a moustache.

CONRAD [*demurring*] She said it was because she had only one life.

HASLAM. Same thing, poor girl! The fellow persuaded her to chuck it; and when she marries him she'll have to stick it. Rotten state of things, I call it.

CONRAD. You see, she hasnt time to find out what life really means. She has to die before she knows.

HASLAM [*agreeably*] Thats it.

FRANKLYN. She hasnt time to form a well-instructed conscience.

HASLAM [*still more cheerfully*] Quite.

[ 382 ]

FRANKLYN. It goes deeper. She hasnt time to form a genuine conscience at all. Some romantic points of honor and a few conventions. A world without conscience: that is the horror of our condition.

HASLAM [*beaming*] Simply fatuous. [*Rising*] Well, I suppose I'd better be going. It's most awfully good of you to put up with my calling.

CONRAD [*in his former low ghostly tone*] You neednt go, you know, if you are really interested.

HASLAM [*fed up*] Well, I'm afraid I ought to—I really must get back—I have something to do in the—

FRANKLYN [*smiling benignly and rising to proffer his hand*] Goodbye.

CONRAD [*gruffly, giving him up as a bad job*] Goodbye.

HASLAM. Goodbye. Sorry—er—

*As the rector moves to shake hands with Franklyn, feeling that he is making a frightful mess of his departure, a vigorous sunburnt young lady with hazel hair cut to the level of her neck, like an Italian youth in a Gozzoli picture, comes in impetuously. She seems to have nothing on but her short skirt, her blouse, her stockings, and a pair of Norwegian shoes: in short, she is a Simple-Lifer.*

THE SIMPLE-LIFER [*swooping on Conrad and kissing him*] Hallo, Nunk. Youre before your time.

CONRAD. Behave yourself. Theres a visitor.

*She turns quickly and sees the rector. She instinctively switches at her Gozzoli fringe with her fingers, but gives it up as hopeless.*

FRANKLYN. Mr Haslam, our new rector. [*To Haslam*] My daughter Cynthia.

CONRAD. Usually called Savvy, short for Savage.

SAVVY. I usually call Mr Haslam Bill, short for William. [*She strolls to the hearthrug, and surveys them calmly from that commanding position*].

FRANKLYN. You know him?

SAVVY. Rather. Sit down, Bill.

FRANKLYN. Mr Haslam is going, Savvy. He has an engagement.

SAVVY. I know. I'm the engagement.

CONRAD. In that case, would you mind taking him into the garden while I talk to your father?

SAVVY [*to Haslam*] Tennis?

HASLAM. Rather!

SAVVY. Come on. [*She dances out. He runs out boyishly after her*].

FRANKLYN [*leaving his table and beginning to walk up and down the room discontentedly*] Savvy's manners jar on me. They would have horrified her grandmother.

CONRAD [*obstinately*] They are happier manners than Mother's manners.

FRANKLYN. Yes: they are franker, wholesomer, better in a hundred ways. And yet I squirm at them. I cannot get it out of my head that Mother was a well-mannered woman, and that Savvy has no manners at all.

CONRAD. There wasnt any pleasure in Mother's fine manners. That makes a biological difference.

FRANKLYN. But there was beauty in Mother's manners, grace in them, style in them: above all, decision in them. Savvy is such a cub.

CONRAD. So she ought to be, at her age.

FRANKLYN. There it comes again! Her age! her age!

CONRAD. You want her to be fully grown at eighteen. You want to force her into a stuck-up, artificial, premature self-possession before she has any self to possess. You just let her alone: she is right enough for her years.

FRANKLYN. I have let her alone; and look at the result! Like all the other young people who have been let alone, she becomes a Socialist. That is, she becomes hopelessly demoralized.

CONRAD. Well, arnt you a Socialist?

FRANKLYN. Yes; but that is not the same thing. You and I were brought up in the old bourgeois morality. We were taught bourgeois manners and bourgeois points of honor. Bourgeois manners may be snobbish manners: there may be no pleasure in them, as you say; but they are better than no manners. Many bourgeois points of honor may be false; but at least they exist. The women know what to expect and what is expected of them. Savvy doesnt. She is a Bohemian and nothing else. She has to improvize her manners and her conduct as she goes along. It's often charming, no doubt; but sometimes she puts her foot in it frightfully; and then I feel she must be blaming me for not teaching her better.

CONRAD. Well, you have something better to teach her now, at all events.

FRANKLYN. Yes: but it is too late. She doesnt trust me now. She doesnt talk about such things to me. She doesnt read anything I write. She never comes to hear me lecture. I am out of it as far as Savvy is concerned. [*He resumes his seat at the writing-table*].

CONRAD. I must have a talk to her.

FRANKLYN. Perhaps she will listen to you. You are not her father.

CONRAD. I sent her my last book. I can break the ice by asking her what she made of it.

FRANKLYN. When she heard you were coming, she asked me whether all the leaves were cut, in case it fell into your hands. She hasnt read a word of it.

CONRAD [*rising indignantly*] What!

FRANKLYN [*inexorably*] Not a word of it.

CONRAD [*beaten*] Well, I suppose it's only natural.

[ 385 ]

Biology is a dry subject for a girl; and I am a pretty dry old codger. [*He sits down again resignedly*].

FRANKLYN. Brother: if that is so; if biology as you have worked at it, and religion as I have worked at it, are dry subjects like the old stuff they taught under these names, and we two are dry old codgers, like the other preachers and professors, then the Gospel of the Brothers Barnabas is a delusion. Unless this withered thing religion, and this dry thing science, come alive again in our hands, alive and intensely interesting, we may just as well go out and dig the garden until it is time to dig our graves. [*The parlor maid returns. Franklyn is impatient at the interruption*]. Well? what is it now?

THE PARLOR MAID. Mr Joyce Burge on the telephone, sir. He wants to speak to you.

FRANKLYN [*astonished*] Mr Joyce Burge!

THE PARLOR MAID. Yes, sir.

FRANKLYN [*to Conrad*] What on earth does this mean? I havnt heard from him nor exchanged a word with him for years. I resigned the chairmanship of the Liberal Association and shook the dust of party politics from my feet before he was Prime Minister in the Coalition. Of course, he dropped me like a hot potato.

CONRAD. Well, now that the Coalition has chucked him out, and he is only one of the half-dozen leaders of the Opposition, perhaps he wants to pick you up again.

THE PARLOR MAID [*warningly*] He is holding the line, sir.

FRANKLYN. Yes: all right [*he hurries out*].

*The parlor maid goes to the hearthrug to make up the fire. Conrad rises and strolls to the middle of the room, where he stops and looks quizzically down at her.*

CONRAD. So you have only one life to live, eh?

THE PARLOR MAID [*dropping on her knees in consternation*] I meant no offence, sir.

CONRAD. You didnt give any. But you know you could live a devil of a long life if you really wanted to.

THE PARLOR MAID [*sitting down on her heels*] Oh, dont say that, sir. It's so unsettling.

CONRAD. Why? Have you been thinking about it?

THE PARLOR MAID. It would never have come into my head if you hadnt put it there, sir. Me and cook had a look at your book.

CONRAD. What!

> You and cook
> Had a look
> At my book!

And my niece wouldnt open it! The prophet is without honor in his own family. Well, what do you think of living for several hundred years? Are you going to have a try for it?

THE PARLOR MAID. Well, of course youre not in earnest, sir. But it does set one thinking, especially when one is going to be married.

CONRAD. What has that to do with it? He may live as long as you, you know.

THE PARLOR MAID. Thats just it, sir. You see, he must take me for better for worse, til death do us part. Do you think he would be so ready to do that, sir, if he thought it might be for several hundred years?

CONRAD. Thats true. And what about yourself?

THE PARLOR MAID. Oh, I tell you straight out, sir, I'd never promise to live with the same man as long as that. I wouldnt put up with my own children as long as that. Why, cook figured it out, sir, that when

[ 387 ]

you were only 200, you might marry your own great-great-great-great-great-great-grandson and not even know who he was.

CONRAD. Well, why not? For all you know, the man you are going to marry may be your great-great-great-great-great-great-grandmothers' great-great-great-great-great-great-grandson.

THE PARLOR MAID. But do you think it would ever be thought respectable, sir?

CONRAD. My good girl, all biological necessities have to be made respectable whether we like it or not; so you neednt worry yourself about that.

*Franklyn returns and crosses the room to his chair, but does not sit down. The parlor maid goes out.*

CONRAD. Well, what does Joyce Burge want?

FRANKLYN. Oh, a silly misunderstanding. I have promised to address a meeting in Middlesborough; and some fool has put it into the papers that I am "coming to Middlesborough," without any explanation. Of course, now that we are on the eve of a general election, political people think I am coming there to contest the parliamentary seat. Burge knows that I have a following, and thinks I could get into the House of Commons and head a group there. So he insists on coming to see me. He is staying with some people at Dollis Hill, and can be here in five or ten minutes, he says.

CONRAD. But didnt you tell him that it's a false alarm?

FRANKLYN. Of course I did; but he wont believe me.

CONRAD. Called you a liar, in fact?

FRANKLYN. No: I wish he had: any sort of plain speaking is better than the nauseous sham good fellowship our democratic public men get up for shop use. He pretends to believe me, and assures me his visit is quite disinterested; but why should he come if he has no axe to grind? These chaps never believe anything they say themselves; and naturally they cannot believe anything anyone else says.

CONRAD [*rising*] Well, I shall clear out. It was hard enough to stand the party politicians before the war; but now that they have managed to half kill Europe between them, I cant be civil to them, and I dont see why I should be.

FRANKLYN. Wait a bit. We have to find out how the world will take our new gospel. [*Conrad sits down again*]. Party politicians are still unfortunately an important part of the world. Suppose we try it on Joyce Burge.

CONRAD. How can you? You can tell things only to people who can listen. Joyce Burge has talked so much that he has lost the power of listening. He doesnt listen even in the House of Commons.

*Savvy rushes in breathless, followed by Haslam, who remains timidly just inside the door.*

SAVVY [*running to Franklyn*] I say! Who do you think has just driven up in a big car?

FRANKLYN. Mr Joyce Burge, perhaps.

SAVVY [*disappointed*] Oh, they know, Bill. Why didnt you tell us he was coming? I have nothing on.

HASLAM. I'd better go, hadnt I?

CONRAD. You just wait here, both of you. When you start yawning, Joyce Burge will take the hint, perhaps.

SAVVY [*to Franklyn*] May we?

FRANKLYN. Yes, if you promise to behave yourself.

SAVVY [*making a wry face*] That will be a treat, wont it?

THE PARLOR MAID [*entering and announcing*] Mr Joyce Burge. [*Haslam hastily moves to the fireplace;*

*and the parlor maid goes out and shuts the door when the visitor has passed in*].

FRANKLYN [*hurrying past Savvy to his guest with the false cordiality he has just been denouncing*] Oh! Here you are. Delighted to see you. [*He shakes Burge's hand, and introduces Savvy*] My daughter.

SAVVY [*not daring to approach*] Very kind of you to come.

*Joyce Burge stands fast and says nothing; but he screws up his cheeks into a smile at each introduction, and makes his eyes shine in a very winning manner. He is a well-fed man turned fifty, with broad forehead, and grey hair which, his neck being short, falls almost to his collar.*

FRANKLYN. Mr Haslam, our rector.

*Burge conveys an impression of shining like a church window; and Haslam seizes the nearest library chair on the hearth, and swings it round for Burge between the stool and Conrad. He then retires to the window seat at the other side of the room, and is joined by Savvy. They sit there, side by side, hunched up with their elbows on their knees and their chins on their hands, providing Burge with a sort of Strangers' Gallery during the ensuing sitting.*

FRANKLYN. I forget whether you know my brother Conrad. He is a biologist.

BURGE [*suddenly bursting into energetic action and shaking hands heartily with Conrad*] By reputation only, but very well, of course. How I wish I could have devoted myself to biology! I have always been interested in rocks and strata and volcanoes and so forth: they throw such a light on the age of the earth. [*With conviction*] There is nothing like biology. "The cloud-capped towers, the solemn binnacles, the gorgeous temples, the great globe itself: yea, all that it inherit shall dissolve, and, like this influential pageant faded, leave not a rack behind." Thats biology, you know: good sound biology. [*He sits down. So do the others, Franklyn on the stool, and Conrad on his Chippendale*]. Well, my dear Barnabas, what do you think of the situation? Dont you think the time has come for us to make a move?

FRANKLYN. The time has always come to make a move.

BURGE. How true! But what is the move to be? You are a man of enormous influence. We know that. Weve always known it. We have to consult you whether we like it or not. We—

FRANKLYN [*interrupting firmly*] I never meddle in party politics now.

SAVVY. It's no use saying you have no influence, daddy. Heaps of people swear by you.

BURGE [*shining at her*] Of course they do. Come! let me prove to you what we think of you. Shall we find you a first-rate constituency to contest at the next election? One that wont cost you a penny. A metropolitan seat. What do you say to the Strand?

FRANKLYN. My dear Burge, I am not a child. Why do you go on wasting your party funds on the Strand? You know you cannot win it.

BURGE. We cannot win it; but you—

FRANKLYN. Oh, please!

SAVVY. The Strand's no use, Mr Burge. I once canvassed for a Socialist there. Cheese it.

BURGE. Cheese it!

HASLAM [*spluttering with suppressed laughter*] Priceless!

SAVVY. Well, I suppose I shouldnt say cheese it to a Right Honorable. But the Strand, you know! Come off it.

FRANKLYN. You must excuse my daughter's shocking manners, Burge; but I agree with her that popular democratic statesmen soon come to believe that everyone they speak to is an ignorant dupe and a born fool into the bargain.

BURGE [*laughing genially*] You old aristocrat, you! But believe me, the instinct of the people is sound—

CONRAD [*cutting in sharply*] Then why are you in the Opposition instead of in the Government?

BURGE [*shewing signs of temper under this heckling*] I deny that I am in the Opposition morally. The Government does not represent the country. I was chucked out of the Coalition by a Tory conspiracy. The people want me back. I dont want to go back.

FRANKLYN [*gently remonstrant*] My dear Burge: of course you do.

BURGE [*turning on him*] Not a bit of it. I want to cultivate my garden. I am not interested in politics: I am interested in roses. I havnt a scrap of ambition. I went into politics because my wife shoved me into them, bless her! But I want to serve my country. What else am I for? I want to save my country from the Tories. They dont represent the people. The man they have made Prime Minister has never represented the people; and you know it. Lord Dunreen is the bitterest old Tory left alive. What has he to offer to the people?

FRANKLYN [*cutting in before Burge can proceed—as he evidently intends—to answer his own question*] I will tell you. He has ascertainable beliefs and principles to offer. The people know where they are with Lord Dunreen. They know what he thinks right and what he thinks wrong. With your followers they never know where they are. With you they never know where they are.

BURGE [*amazed*] With me!

FRANKLYN. Well, where are you? What are you?

BURGE. Barnabas: you must be mad. You ask me what I am?

FRANKLYN. I do.

BURGE. I am, if I mistake not, Joyce Burge, pretty well known throughout Europe, and indeed throughout the world, as the man who—unworthily perhaps, but not quite unsuccessfully—held the helm when the ship of State weathered the mightiest hurricane that has ever burst with earth-shaking violence on the land of our fathers.

FRANKLYN. I know that. I know who you are. And the earth-shaking part of it to me is that though you were placed in that enormously responsible position, neither I nor anyone else knows what your beliefs are, or even whether you have either beliefs or principles. What we did know was that your Government was formed largely of men who regarded you as a robber of henroosts, and whom you regarded as enemies of the people.

BURGE [*adroitly, as he thinks*] I agree with you. I agree with you absolutely. I dont believe in coalition governments.

FRANKLYN. Precisely. Yet you formed two.

BURGE. Why? Because we were at war. That is what you fellows never would realize. The Hun was at the gate. Our country, our lives, the honor of our wives and mothers and daughters, the tender flesh of our innocent babes, were at stake. Was that a time to argue about principles?

FRANKLYN. I should say it was the time of all others to confirm the resolution of our own men and gain the confidence and support of public opinion throughout the world by a declaration of principle. Do you

[ 393 ]

think the Hun would ever have come to the gate if he had known that it would be shut in his face on principle? Did he not hold his own against you until America boldly affirmed the democratic principle and came to our rescue? Why did you let America snatch that honor from England?

BURGE. Barnabas: America was carried away by words, and had to eat them at the Peace Conference. Beware of platform eloquence: it is the bane of popular speakers like you.

FRANKLYN ⎫ [exclaiming ⎧ Well!
SAVVY ⎬ all ⎨ I like that!
HASLAM ⎭ together] ⎩ Priceless!

BURGE [continuing remorselessly] Come down to facts. It wasnt principle that won the war: it was the British fleet and the blockade. America found the talk: I found the shells. You cannot win wars by principles; but you can win elections by them. There I am with you. You want the next election to be fought on principles: that is what it comes to, doesnt it?

FRANKLYN. I dont want it to be fought at all? An election is a moral horror, as bad as a battle except for the blood: a mud bath for every soul concerned in it. You know very well that it will not be fought on principle.

BURGE. On the contrary it will be fought on nothing else. I believe a program is a mistake. I agree with you that principle is what we want.

FRANKLYN. Principle without program, eh?

BURGE. Exactly. There it is in three words.

FRANKLYN. Why not in one word? Platitudes. That is what principle without program means.

BURGE [puzzled but patient, trying to get at Franklyn's drift in order to ascertain his price] I have not made myself clear. Listen. I am agreeing with you. I

am on your side. I am accepting your proposal.
There isnt going to be any more coalition. This time
there wont be a Tory in the Cabinet. Every candidate
will have to pledge himself to Free Trade, slightly
modified by consideration for our Overseas Domin-
ions; to Disestablishment; to Reform of the House of
Lords; to a revised scheme of Taxation of Land
Values; and to doing whatever is necessary to keep
Ireland and India quiet. Does that satisfy you?

FRANKLYN. It does not even interest me. Suppose
your friends do commit themselves to all this! What
does it prove about them except that they are hopelessly out of date even in party politics? that they
have learnt nothing and forgotten nothing since
1885? What is it to me that they hate the Church
and hate the landed gentry? that they are jealous of
the nobility, and have shipping shares instead of manu-
facturing businesses in the Midlands? I can find you
hundreds of the most sordid rascals, or the most densely
stupid reactionaries, with all these qualifications.

BURGE. Personal abuse proves nothing. Do you
suppose the Tories are all angels because they are all
members of the Church of England?

FRANKLYN. No; but they stand together as members of the Church of England, whereas your people,
in attacking the Church, are all over the shop. The
supporters of the Church are of one mind about
religion: its enemies are of a dozen minds. The
Churchmen are a phalanx: your people are a mob
in which atheists are jostled by Plymouth Brethren,
and Positivists by Pillars of Fire. You have with you
all the crudest unbelievers and all the crudest fanatics.

BURGE. We stand, as Cromwell did, for liberty of
conscience, if that is what you mean.

FRANKLYN. How can you talk such rubbish over the

[ 395 ]

graves of your conscientious objectors? All law limits liberty of conscience: if a man's conscience allows him to steal your watch or to shirk military service, how much liberty do you allow it? Liberty of conscience is not my point.

BURGE [*testily*] I wish you would come to your point. Half the time you are saying that you must have principles; and when I offer you principles you say they wont work.

FRANKLYN. You have not offered me any principles. Your party shibboleths are not principles. If you get into power again you will find yourself at the head of a rabble of Socialists and anti-Socialists, of Jingo Imperialists and Little Englanders, of cast-iron Materialists and ecstatic Quakers, of Christian Scientists and Compulsory Inoculationists, of Syndicalists and Bureaucrats: in short, of men differing fiercely and irreconcilably on every principle that goes to the root of human society and destiny; and the impossibility of keeping such a team together will force you to sell the pass again to the solid Conservative Opposition.

BURGE [*rising in wrath*] Sell the pass again! You accuse me of having sold the pass!

FRANKLYN. When the terrible impact of real warfare swept your parliamentary sham warfare into the dustbin, you had to go behind the backs of your followers and make a secret agreement with the leaders of the Opposition to keep you in power on condition that you dropped all legislation of which they did not approve. And you could not even hold them to their bargain; for they presently betrayed the secret and forced the coalition on you.

BURGE. I solemnly declare that this is a false and monstrous accusation.

FRANKLYN. Do you deny that the thing occurred? Were the uncontradicted reports false? Were the published letters forgeries?

BURGE. Certainly not. But *I* did not do it. I was not Prime Minister then. It was that old dotard, that played-out old humbug Lubin. He was Prime Minister then, not I.

FRANKLYN. Do you mean to say you did not know?

BURGE [*sitting down again with a shrug*] Oh, I had to be told. But what could I do? If we had refused we might have had to go out of office.

FRANKLYN. Precisely.

BURGE. Well, could we desert the country at such a crisis? The Hun was at the gate. Everyone has to make sacrifices for the sake of the country at such moments. We had to rise above party; and I am proud to say we never gave party a second thought. We stuck to—

CONRAD. Office?

BURGE [*turning on him*] Yes, sir, to office: that is, to responsibility, to danger, to heart-sickening toil, to abuse and misunderstanding, to a martyrdom that made us envy the very soldiers in the trenches. If you had had to live for months on aspirin and bromide of potassium to get a wink of sleep, you wouldnt talk about office as if it were a catch.

FRANKLYN. Still, you admit that under our parliamentary system Lubin could not have helped himself?

BURGE. On that subject my lips are closed. Nothing will induce me to say one word against the old man. I never have; and I never will. Lubin is old: he has never been a real statesman: he is as lazy as a cat on a hearthrug: you cant get him to attend to anything:

he is good for nothing but getting up and making speeches with a peroration that goes down with the back benches. But I say nothing against him. I gather that you do not think much of me as a statesman; but at all events I can get things done. I can hustle: even you will admit that. But Lubin! Oh my stars, Lubin!! If you only knew—

*The parlor maid opens the door and announces a visitor.*

THE PARLOR MAID. Mr Lubin.

BURGE [*bounding from his chair*] Lubin! Is this a conspiracy?

*They all rise in amazement, staring at the door. Lubin enters: a man at the end of his sixties, a York-shireman with the last traces of Scandinavian flax still in his white hair, undistinguished in stature, unassuming in his manner, and taking his simple dignity for granted, but wonderfully comfortable and quite self-assured in contrast to the intellectual restlessness of Franklyn and the mesmeric self-assertiveness of Burge. His presence suddenly brings out the fact that they are unhappy men, ill at ease, square pegs in round holes, whilst he flourishes like a primrose.*

*The parlor maid withdraws.*

LUBIN [*coming to Franklyn*] How do you do, Mr Barnabas? [*He speaks very comfortably and kindly, much as if he were the host, and Franklyn an embarrassed but welcome guest*]. I had the pleasure of meeting you once at the Mansion House. I think it was to celebrate the conclusion of the hundred years peace with America.

FRANKLYN [*shaking hands*] It was long before that: a meeting about Venezuela, when we were on the point of going to war with America.

LUBIN [*not at all put out*] Yes: you are quite right.

I knew it was something about America. [*He pats Franklyn's hand*]. And how have you been all this time? Well, eh?

FRANKLYN [*smiling to soften the sarcasm*] A few vicissitudes of health naturally in so long a time.

LUBIN. Just so. Just so. [*Looking round at Savvy*] The young lady is—?

FRANKLYN. My daughter, Savvy.

*Savvy comes from the window between her father and Lubin.*

LUBIN [*taking her hand affectionately in both his*] And why has she never come to see us?

BURGE. I dont know whether you have noticed, Lubin, that I am present.

*Savvy takes advantage of this diversion to slip away to the settee, where she is stealthily joined by Haslam, who sits down on her left.*

LUBIN [*seating himself in Burge's chair with ineffable comfortableness*] My dear Burge: if you imagine that it is possible to be within ten miles of your energetic presence without being acutely aware of it, you do yourself the greatest injustice. How are you? And how are your good newspaper friends? [*Burge makes an explosive movement; but Lubin goes on calmly and sweetly*] And what are you doing here with my old friend Barnabas, if I may ask?

BURGE [*sitting down in Conrad's chair, leaving him standing uneasily in the corner*] Well, just what you are doing, if you want to know. I am trying to enlist Mr Barnabas's valuable support for my party.

LUBIN. Your party, eh? The newspaper party?

BURGE. The Liberal Party. The party of which I have the honor to be leader.

LUBIN. Have you now? Thats very interesting; for I thought *I* was the leader of the Liberal Party.

However, it is very kind of you to take it off my hands, if the party will let you.

BURGE. Do you suggest that I have not the support and confidence of the party?

LUBIN. I don't suggest anything, my dear Burge. Mr Barnabas will tell you that we all think very highly of you. The country owes you a great deal. During the war, you did very creditably over the munitions; and if you were not quite so successful with the peace, nobody doubted that you meant well.

BURGE. Very kind of you, Lubin. Let me remark that you cannot lead a progressive party without getting a move on.

LUBIN. You mean you cannot. I did it for ten years without the least difficulty. And very comfortable, prosperous, pleasant years they were.

BURGE. Yes; but what did they end in?

LUBIN. In you, Burge. You dont complain of that, do you?

BURGE [*fiercely*] In plague, pestilence, and famine; battle, murder, and sudden death.

LUBIN [*with an appreciative chuckle*] The Nonconformist can quote the prayer-book for his own purposes, I see. How you enjoyed yourself over that business, Burge! Do you remember the Knock-Out Blow?

BURGE. It came off: dont forget that. Do you remember fighting to the last drop of your blood?

LUBIN [*unruffled, to Franklyn*] By the way, I remember your brother Conrad—a wonderful brain and a dear good fellow—explaining to me that I couldnt fight to the last drop of my blood, because I should be dead long before I came to it. Most interesting, and quite true. He was introduced to me at a meeting where the suffragettes kept disturbing me. They had to be carried out kicking and making a horrid disturbance.

CONRAD. No: it was later, at a meeting to support the Franchise Bill which gave them the vote.

LUBIN [*discovering Conrad's presence for the first time*] Youre right: it was. I knew it had something to do with women. My memory never deceives me. Thank you. Will you introduce me to this gentleman, Barnabas?

CONRAD [*not at all affably*] I am the Conrad in question. [*He sits down in dudgeon on the vacant Chippendale*].

LUBIN. Are you? [*Looking at him pleasantly*] Yes: of course you are. I never forget a face. But [*with an arch turn of his eyes to Savvy*] your pretty niece engaged all my powers of vision.

BURGE. I wish youd be serious, Lubin. God knows we have passed through times terrible enough to make any man serious.

LUBIN. I do not think I need to be reminded of that. In peace time I used to keep myself fresh for my work by banishing all worldly considerations from my mind on Sundays; but war has no respect for the Sabbath; and there have been Sundays within the last few years on which I have had to play as many as sixty-six games of bridge to keep my mind off the news from the front.

BURGE [*scandalized*] Sixty-six games of bridge on Sunday!!!

LUBIN. You probably sang sixty-six hymns. But as I cannot boast either your admirable voice or your spiritual fervor, I had to fall back on bridge.

FRANKLYN. If I may go back to the subject of your visit, it seems to me that you may both be completely superseded by the Labor Party.

BURGE. But I am in the truest sense myself a Labor leader. I—[*he stops, as Lubin has risen with a half-suppressed yawn, and is already talking calmly, but without a pretence of interest*].

LUBIN. The Labor Party! Oh no, Mr Barnabas. No, no, no, no, no. [*He moves in Savvy's direction*]. There will be no trouble about that. Of course we must give them a few seats: more, I quite admit, than we should have dreamt of leaving to them before the war; but—[*by this time he has reached the sofa where Savvy and Haslam are seated. He sits down between them; takes her hand; and drops the subject of Labor*]. Well, my dear young lady? What is the latest news? Whats going on? Have you seen Shoddy's new play? Tell me all about it, and all about the latest books, and all about everything.

SAVVY. You have not met Mr Haslam. Our Rector.

LUBIN [*who has quite overlooked Haslam*] Never heard of him. Is he any good?

FRANKLYN. I was introducing him. This is Mr Haslam.

HASLAM. How d'ye do?

LUBIN. I beg your pardon, Mr Haslam. Delighted to meet you. [*To Savvy*] Well, now, how many books have you written.

SAVVY [*rather overwhelmed but attracted*] None. I dont write.

LUBIN. You dont say so! Well, what do you do? Music? Skirt-dancing?

SAVVY. I dont do anything.

LUBIN. Thank God! You and I were born for one another. Who is your favorite poet, Sally?

SAVVY. Savvy.

LUBIN. Savvy! I never heard of him. Tell me all about him. Keep me up to date.

SAVVY. It's not a poet. *I* am Savvy, not Sally.

LUBIN. Savvy! Thats a funny name, and very pretty. Savvy. It sounds Chinese. What does it mean?

CONRAD. Short for Savage.

LUBIN [*patting her hand*] La belle Sauvage.

HASLAM [*rising and surrendering Savvy to Lubin by crossing to the fireplace*] I suppose the Church is out of it as far as progressive politics are concerned.

BURGE. Nonsense! That notion about the Church being unprogressive is one of those shibboleths that our party must drop. The Church is all right essentially. Get rid of the establishment; get rid of the bishops; get rid of the candlesticks; get rid of the 39 articles; and the Church of England is just as good as any other Church; and I dont care who hears me say so.

LUBIN. It doesnt matter a bit who hears you say so, my dear Burge. [*To Savvy*] Who did you say your favorite poet was?

SAVVY. I dont make pets of poets. Who's yours?

LUBIN. Horace.

SAVVY. Horace who?

LUBIN. Quintus Horatius Flaccus: the noblest Roman of them all, my dear.

SAVVY. Oh, if he is dead, that explains it. I have a theory that all the dead people we feel especially interested in must have been ourselves. You must be Horace's reincarnation.

LUBIN [*delighted*] That is the very most charming and penetrating and intelligent thing that has ever been said to me. Barnabas: will you exchange daughters with me? I can give you your choice of two.

FRANKLYN. Man proposes. Savvy disposes.

LUBIN. What does Savvy say?

BURGE. Lubin: I came here to talk politics.

LUBIN. Yes: you have only one subject, Burge. I came here to talk to Savvy. Take Burge into the next room, Barnabas; and let him rip.

BURGE [*half-angry, half-indulgent*] No; but really, Lubin, we are at a crisis—

LUBIN. My dear Burge, life is a disease; and the only difference between one man and another is the stage of the disease at which he lives. You are always at the crisis: I am always in the convalescent stage. I enjoy convalescence. It is the part that makes the illness worth while.

SAVVY [*half-rising*] Perhaps I'd better run away. I am distracting you.

LUBIN [*making her sit down*] Not at all, my dear. You are only distracting Burge. Jolly good thing for him to be distracted by a pretty girl. Just what he needs.

BURGE. I sometimes envy you, Lubin. The great movement of mankind, the giant sweep of the ages, passes you by and leaves you standing.

LUBIN. It leaves me sitting, and quite comfortable, thank you. Go on sweeping. When you are tired of it, come back; and you will find England where it was, and me in my accustomed place, with Miss Savvy telling me all sorts of interesting things.

SAVVY [*who has been growing more and more restless*] Dont let him shut you up, Mr Burge. You know, Mr Lubin, I am frightfully interested in the Labor movement, and in Theosophy, and in reconstruction after the war, and all sorts of things. I daresay the flappers in your smart set are tremendously flattered when you sit beside them and are nice to them as you are being nice to me; but I am not smart; and I am no use as a flapper. I am dowdy and serious.

I want you to be serious. If you refuse, I shall go and sit beside Mr Burge, and ask him to hold my hand.

LUBIN. He wouldnt know how to do it, my dear. Burge has a reputation as a profligate—

BURGE [*starting*] Lubin: this is monstrous. I—

LUBIN [*continuing*]—but he is really a model of domesticity. His name is coupled with all the most celebrated beauties; but for him there is only one woman; and that is not you, my dear, but his very charming wife.

BURGE. You are destroying my character in the act of pretending to save it. Have the goodness to confine yourself to your own character and your own wife. Both of them need all your attention.

LUBIN. I have the privilege of my age and of my transparent innocence. I have not to struggle with your volcanic energy.

BURGE [*with an immense sense of power*] No, by George!

FRANKLYN. I think I shall speak both for my brother and myself, and possibly also for my daughter, if I say that since the object of your visit and Mr Joyce Burge's is to some extent political, we should hear with great interest something about your political aims, Mr Lubin.

LUBIN [*assenting with complete good humor, and becoming attentive, clear, and businesslike in his tone*] By all means, Mr Barnabas. What we have to consider first, I take it, is what prospect there is of our finding you beside us in the House after the next election.

FRANKLYN. When I speak of politics, Mr Lubin, I am not thinking of elections, or available seats, or party funds, or the registers, or even, I am sorry to have to add, of parliament as it exists at present. I had much rather you talked about bridge than about electioneering: it is the more interesting game of the two.

BURGE. He wants to discuss principles, Lubin.

LUBIN [*very cool and clear*] I understand Mr Barnabas quite well. But elections are unsettled things: principles are settled things.

CONRAD [*impatiently*] Great Heavens!—

LUBIN [*interrupting him with quiet authority*] One moment, Dr Barnabas. The main principles on which modern civilized society is founded are pretty well understood among educated people. That is what our dangerously half-educated masses and their pet demagogues—if Burge will excuse that expression—

BURGE. Dont mind me. Go on. I shall have something to say presently.

LUBIN. —that is what our dangerously half-educated people do not realize. Take all this fuss about the Labor Party, with its imaginary new principles and new politics. The Labor members will find that the immutable laws of political economy take no more notice of their ambitions and aspirations than the law of gravitation. I speak, if I may say so, with knowledge; for I have made a special study of the Labor question.

FRANKLYN [*with interest and some surprise*] Indeed?

LUBIN. Yes. It occurred quite at the beginning of my career. I was asked to deliver an address to the students at the Working Men's College; and I was strongly advised to comply, as Gladstone and Morley and others were doing that sort of thing at the moment. It was rather a troublesome job, because I had not gone into political economy at the time. As you know, at the university I was a classical scholar; and my profession was the Law. But I looked up the text-books, and got up the case most carefully. I found that the correct view is that all this Trade Unionism and Socialism and so forth is founded on the ignorant delusion that wages and the production and distri-bution of wealth can be controlled by legislation or by any human action whatever. They obey fixed scientific laws, which have been ascertained and settled finally by the highest economic authorities. Naturally I do not at this distance of time remember the exact process of reasoning; but I can get up the case again at any time in a couple of days; and you may rely on me absolutely, should the occasion arise, to deal with all these ignorant and unpractical people in a conclusive and convincing way, except, of course, as far as it may be advisable to indulge and flatter them a little so as to let them down without creating ill feeling in the working-class electorate. In short, I can get that lecture up again almost at a moment's notice.

SAVVY. But, Mr Lubin, I have had a university education too; and all this about wages and dis-tribution being fixed by immutable laws of political economy is obsolete rot.

FRANKLYN [*shocked*] Oh, my dear! That is not polite.

LUBIN. No, no, no. Dont scold her. She mustnt be scolded. [*To Savvy*] I understand. You are a disciple of Karl Marx.

SAVVY. No, no. Karl Marx's economics are all rot.

LUBIN [*at last a little taken aback*] Dear me!

SAVVY. You must excuse me, Mr Lubin; but it's like hearing a man talk about the Garden of Eden.

CONRAD. Why shouldnt he talk about the Garden of Eden? It was a first attempt at biology anyhow.

LUBIN [*recovering his self-possession*] I am sound on the Garden of Eden. I have heard of Darwin.

SAVVY. But Darwin is all rot.

LUBIN. What! Already!

SAVVY. It's no good your smiling at me like a Cheshire cat, Mr Lubin; and I am not going to sit here mumchance like an old-fashioned goody goody wife while you men monopolize the conversation and pay out the very ghastliest exploded drivel as the latest thing in politics. I am not giving you my own ideas, Mr Lubin, but just the regular orthodox science of today. Only the most awful old fossils think that Socialism is bad economics and that Darwin invented Evolution. Ask Papa. Ask Uncle. Ask the first person you meet in the street. [*She rises and crosses to Haslam*]. Give me a cigaret, Bill, will you?

HASLAM. Priceless. [*He complies*].

FRANKLYN. Savvy has not lived long enough to have any manners, Mr Lubin; but that is where you stand with the younger generation. Dont smoke, dear.

*Savvy, with a shrug of rather mutinous resignation, throws the cigaret into the fire. Haslam, on the point of lighting one for himself, changes his mind.*

LUBIN [*shrewd and serious*] Mr Barnabas: I confess I am surprised; and I will not pretend that I am convinced. But I am open to conviction. I may be wrong.

BURGE [*in a burst of irony*] Oh no. Impossible! Impossible!

LUBIN. Yes, Mr Barnabas, though I do not possess Burge's genius for being always wrong, I have been in that position once or twice. I could not conceal from you, even if I wished to, that my time has been so completely filled by my professional work as a lawyer, and later on by my duties as leader of the House of Commons in the days when Prime Ministers were also leaders——

BURGE [*stung*] Not to mention bridge and smart society.

LUBIN. —not to mention my continual and trying efforts to make Burge behave himself, that I have not been able to keep my academic reading up to date. I have kept my classics brushed up out of sheer love for them; but my economics and my science, such as they were, may possibly be a little rusty. Yet I think I may say that if you and your brother will be so good as to put me on the track of the necessary documents, I will undertake to put the case to the House or to the country to your entire satisfaction. You see, as long as you can shew these troublesome half-educated people who want to turn the world upside down that they are talking nonsense, it really does not matter very much whether you do it in terms of what Miss Barnabas calls obsolete rot or in terms of what her granddaughter will probably call unmitigated tosh. I have no objection whatever to denounce Karl Marx. Anything I can say against Darwin will please a large body of sincerely pious voters. If it will be easier to carry on the business of the country on the understanding that the present state of things is to be called Socialism, I have no objection in the world to call it Socialism. There is the precedent of the Emperor Constantine, who saved the society of his own day by agreeing to call his Imperialism Christianity. Mind: I must not go ahead of the electorate. You must not call a voter a Socialist until—

FRANKLYN. Until he is a Socialist. Agreed.

LUBIN. Oh, not at all. You need not wait for that. You must not call him a Socialist until he wishes to be called a Socialist: that is all. Surely you would not say that I must not address my constituents as gentlemen until they are gentlemen. I address them as gentlemen because they wish to be so addressed. [*He rises from the sofa and goes to Franklyn, placing a reassuring hand on his shoulder*]. Do not be afraid of Socialism, Mr Barnabas. You need not tremble for your property or your position or your dignity. England will remain what England is, no matter what new political names may come into vogue. I do not intend to resist the transition to Socialism. You may depend on me to guide it, to lead it, to give suitable expression to its aspirations, and to steer it clear of Utopian absurdities. I can honestly ask for your support on the most advanced Socialist grounds no less than on the soundest Liberal ones.

BURGE. In short, Lubin, youre incorrigible. You dont believe anything is going to change. The millions are still to toil—the people—my people—for I am a man of the people—

LUBIN [*interrupting him contemptuously*] Dont be ridiculous, Burge. You are a country solicitor, further removed from the people, more foreign to them, more jealous of letting them up to your level, than any duke or any archbishop.

BURGE [*hotly*] I deny it. You think I have never been poor. You think I have never cleaned my own boots. You think my fingers have never come out through the soles when I was cleaning them. You think—

LUBIN. I think you fall into the very common mistake of supposing that it is poverty that makes the proletarian and money that makes the gentleman. You are quite wrong. You never belonged to the people: you belonged to the impecunious. Impecuniosity and broken boots are the lot of the unsuccessful middle class, and the commonplaces of the early struggles of the professional and younger son class. I defy you to find a farm laborer in England with broken boots. Call a mechanic one of the poor, and he'll punch your head. When you talk to your constituents about the toiling millions, they dont consider that you are referring to them. They are all third cousins of somebody with a title or a park. I am a Yorkshireman, my friend. I know England; and you dont. If you did you would know——

BURGE. What do you know that I dont know?

LUBIN. I know that we are taking up too much of Mr Barnabas's time. [*Franklyn rises*]. May I take it, my dear Barnabas, that I may count on your support if we succeed in forcing an election before the new register is in full working order?

BURGE [*rising also*] May the party count on your support? I say nothing about myself. Can the party depend on you? Is there any question of yours that I have left unanswered?

CONRAD. We havnt asked you any, you know.

BURGE. May I take that as a mark of confidence?

CONRAD. If I were a laborer in your constituency, I should ask you a biological question.

LUBIN. No you wouldnt, my dear Doctor. Laborers never ask questions.

BURGE. Ask it now. I have never flinched from being heckled. Out with it. Is it about the land?

CONRAD. No.

BURGE. Is it about the Church?

CONRAD. No.

BURGE. Is it about the House of Lords?

CONRAD. No.

BURGE. Is it about Proportional Representation?

CONRAD. No.

BURGE. Is it about Free Trade?

CONRAD. No.

BURGE. Is it about the priest in the school?

CONRAD. No.

BURGE. Is it about Ireland?

CONRAD. No.

BURGE. Is it about Germany?

CONRAD. No.

BURGE. Well, is it about Republicanism? Come! I won't flinch. Is it about the Monarchy?

CONRAD. No.

BURGE. Well, what the devil is it about, then?

CONRAD. You understand that I am asking the question in the character of a laborer who earned thirteen shillings a week before the war and earns thirty now, when he can get it?

BURGE. Yes: I understand that. I am ready for you Out with it.

CONRAD. And whom you propose to represent in parliament?

BURGE. Yes, yes, yes. Come on.

CONRAD. The question is this. Would you allow your son to marry my daughter, or your daughter to marry my son?

BURGE [taken aback] Oh, come! Thats not a political question.

CONRAD. Then, as a biologist, I dont take the slightest interest in your politics; and I shall not walk across the street to vote for you or anyone else at the election. Good evening.

LUBIN. Serve you right, Burge! Dr Barnabas: you have my assurance that my daughter shall marry the man of her choice, whether he be lord or laborer. May *I* count on your support?

BURGE [hurling the epithet at him] Humbug!

SAVVY. Stop. [They all stop short in the movement of

*leave-taking to look at her*]. Daddy: are you going to let them off like this? How are they to know anything if nobody ever tells them? If you dont, I will.

CONRAD. You cant. You didnt read my book; and you know nothing about it. You just hold your tongue.

SAVVY. I just wont, Nunk. I shall have a vote when I am thirty; and I ought to have it now. Why are these two ridiculous people to be allowed to come in and walk over us as if the world existed only to play their silly parliamentary game?

FRANKLYN [*severely*] Savvy: you really must not be uncivil to our guests.

SAVVY. I'm sorry. But Mr Lubin didnt stand on much ceremony with me, did he? And Mr Burge hasnt addressed a single word to me. I'm not going to stand it. You and Nunk have a much better program than either of them. It's the only one we are going to vote for; and they ought to be told about it for the credit of the family and the good of their own souls. You just tip them a chapter from the gospel of the brothers Barnabas, Daddy.

*Lubin and Burge turn inquiringly to Franklyn, suspecting a move to form a new party.*

FRANKLYN. It is quite true, Mr Lubin, that I and my brother have a little program of our own which—

CONRAD [*interrupting*] It's not a little program: it's an almighty big one. It's not our own: it's the program of the whole of civilization.

BURGE. Then why split the party before you have put it to us? For God's sake let us have no more splits. I am here to learn. I am here to gather your opinions and represent them. I invite you to put your views before me. I offer myself to be heckled. You have asked me only an absurd non-political question.

[ 413 ]

FRANKLYN. Candidly, I fear our program will be thrown away on you. It would not interest you.

BURGE [*with challenging audacity*] Try. Lubin can go if he likes; but I am still open to new ideas, if only I can find them.

FRANKLYN [*to Lubin*] Are you prepared to listen, Mr Lubin; or shall I thank you for your very kind and welcome visit, and say good evening?

LUBIN [*sitting down resignedly on the settee, but involuntarily making a movement which looks like the stifling of a yawn*] With pleasure, Mr Barnabas. Of course you know that before I can adopt any new plank in the party platform, it will have to reach me through the National Liberal Federation, which you can approach through your local Liberal and Radical Association.

FRANKLYN. I could recall to you several instances of the addition to your party program of measures of which no local branch of your Federation had ever dreamt. But I understand that you are not really interested. I will spare you, and drop the subject.

LUBIN [*waking up a little*] You quite misunderstand me. Please do not take it in that way. I only—

BURGE [*talking him down*] Never mind the Federation: *I* will answer for the Federation. Go on, Barnabas: go on. Never mind Lubin [*he sits down in the chair from which Lubin first displaced him*].

FRANKLYN. Our program is only that the term of human life shall be extended to three hundred years.

LUBIN [*softly*] Eh?

BURGE [*explosively*] What!

SAVVY. Our election cry is "Back to Methuselah!"

HASLAM. Priceless!

*Lubin and Burge look at one another.*

CONRAD. No. We are not mad.

SAVVY. Theyre not joking either. They mean it.

LUBIN [*cautiously*] Assuming that, in some sense which I am for the moment unable to fathom, you are in earnest, Mr Barnabas, may I ask what this has to do with politics?

FRANKLYN. The connection is very evident. You are now, Mr Lubin, within immediate reach of your seventieth year. Mr Joyce Burge is your junior by about eleven years. You will go down to posterity as one of a European group of immature statesmen and monarchs who, doing the very best for your respective countries of which you were capable, succeeded in all-but-wrecking the civilization of Europe, and did, in effect, wipe out of existence many millions of its inhabitants.

BURGE. Less than a million.

FRANKLYN. That was our loss alone.

BURGE. Oh, if you count foreigners—!

HASLAM. God counts foreigners, you know.

SAVVY [*with intense satisfaction*] Well said, Bill.

FRANKLYN. I am not blaming you. Your task was beyond human capacity. What with our huge armaments, our terrible engines of destruction, our systems of coercion manned by an irresistible police, you were called on to control powers so gigantic that one shudders at the thought of their being entrusted even to an infinitely experienced and benevolent God, much less to mortal men whose whole life does not last a hundred years.

BURGE. We won the war: dont forget that.

FRANKLYN. No: the soldiers and sailors won it, and left you to finish it. And you were so utterly incompetent that the multitudes of children slain by hunger in the first years of peace made us all wish we were at war again.

[ 415 ]

CONRAD. It's no use arguing about it. It is now absolutely certain that the political and social problems raised by our civilization cannot be solved by mere human mushrooms who decay and die when they are just beginning to have a glimmer of the wisdom and knowledge needed for welfare government.

LUBIN. Quite an interesting idea, Doctor. Extravagant. Fantastic. But quite interesting. When I was young I used to feel my human limitations very acutely.

BURGE. God knows I have often felt that I could not go on if it had not been for the sense that I was only an instrument in the hands of a Power above us.

CONRAD. I'm glad you both agree with us, and with one another.

LUBIN. I have not gone so far as that, I think. After all, we have had many very able political leaders even within your recollection and mine.

FRANKLYN. Have you read the recent biographies —Dilke's, for instance—which revealed the truth about them?

LUBIN. I did not discover any new truth revealed in these books, Mr Barnabas.

FRANKLYN. What! Not the truth that England was governed all that time by a little woman who knew her own mind?

SAVVY. Hear, hear!

LUBIN. That often happens. Which woman do you mean?

FRANKLYN. Queen Victoria, to whom your Prime Ministers stood in the relation of naughty children whose heads she knocked together when their tempers and quarrels became intolerable. Within thirteen years of her death Europe became a hell.

BURGE. Quite true. That was because she was

[ 416 ]

piously brought up, and regarded herself as an instrument. If a statesman remembers that he is only an instrument, and feels quite sure that he is rightly interpreting the divine purpose, he will come out all right, you know.

FRANKLYN. The Kaiser felt like that. Did he come out all right?

BURGE. Well, let us be fair, even to the Kaiser. Let us be fair.

FRANKLYN. Were you fair to him when you won an election on the program of hanging him?

BURGE. Stuff! I am the last man alive to hang anybody; but the people wouldnt listen to reason. Besides, I knew the Dutch wouldnt give him up.

SAVVY. Oh, dont start arguing about poor old Bill. Stick to our point. Let these two gentlemen settle the question for themselves. Mr Burge: do you think Mr Lubin is fit to govern England?

BURGE. No. Frankly, I dont.

LUBIN [*remonstrant*] Really!

CONRAD. Why?

BURGE. Because he has no conscience: thats why.

LUBIN. [*shocked and amazed*] Oh!

FRANKLYN. Mr Lubin: do you consider Joyce Burge qualified to govern England?

LUBIN [*with dignified emotion, wounded, but without bitterness*] Excuse me, Mr Barnabas; but before I answer that question I want to say this. Burge: we have had differences of opinion; and your newspaper friends have said hard things of me. But we worked together for years; and I hope I have done nothing to justify you in the amazing accusation you have just brought against me. Do you realize that you said that I have no conscience?

BURGE. Lubin: I am very accessible to an appeal to

my emotions; and you are very cunning in making such appeals. I will meet you to this extent. I dont mean that you are a bad man. I dont mean that I dislike you, in spite of your continual attempts to discourage and depress me. But you have a mind like a looking-glass. You are very clear and smooth and lucid as to what is standing in front of you. But you have no foresight and no hindsight. You have no vision and no memory. You have no continuity; and a man without continuity can have neither conscience nor honor from one day to another. The result is that you have always been a damned bad minister; and you have sometimes been a damned bad friend. Now you can answer Barnabas's question and take it out of me to your heart's content. He asked you was I fit to govern England.

LUBIN [*recovering himself*] After what has just passed I sincerely wish I could honestly say yes, Burge. But it seems to me that you have condemned yourself out of your own mouth. You represent something which has had far too much influence and popularity in this country since Joseph Chamberlain set the fashion; and that is mere energy without intellect and without knowledge. Your mind is not a trained mind: it has not been stored with the best information, nor cultivated by intercourse with educated minds at any of our great seats of learning. As I happen to have enjoyed that advantage, it follows that you do not understand my mind. Candidly, I think that disqualifies you. The peace found out your weaknesses.

BURGE. Oh! What did it find out in you?

LUBIN. You and your newspaper confederates took the peace out of my hands. The peace did not find me out because it did not find me in.

FRANKLYN. Come! Confess, both of you! You were

only flies on the wheel. The war went England's way; but the peace went its own way, and not England's way nor any of the ways you had so glibly appointed for it. Your peace treaty was a scrap of paper before the ink dried on it. The statesmen of Europe were incapable of governing Europe. What they needed was a couple of hundred years training and experience: what they had actually had was a few years at the bar or in a counting-house or on the grouse moors and golf courses. And now we are waiting, with monster cannons trained on every city and seaport, and huge aeroplanes ready to spring into the air and drop bombs every one of which will obliterate a whole street, and poison gases that will strike multitudes dead with a breath, until one of you gentlemen rises in his helplessness to tell us, who are as helpless as himself, that we are at war again.

CONRAD. Aha! What consolation will it be for us then that you two are able to tell off one another's defects so cleverly in your afternoon chat?

BURGE [*angrily*] If you come to that, what consolation will it be that you two can sit there and tell both of us off? you, who have had no responsibility! you, who havnt lifted a finger, as far as I know, to help us through this awful crisis which has left me ten years older than my proper age! Can you tell me a single thing you did to help us during the whole infernal business?

CONRAD. We're not blaming you: you hadnt lived long enough. No more had we. Cant you see that three-score-and-ten, though it may be long enough for a very crude sort of village life, isnt long enough for a complicated civilization like ours? Flinders Petrie has counted nine attempts at civilization made by people exactly like us; and every one of them failed just as ours is failing. They failed because the

citizens and statesmen died of old age or over-eating
before they had grown out of schoolboy games and
savage sports and cigars and champagne. The signs
of the end are always the same: Democracy, Socialism,
and Votes for Women. We shall go to smash within
the lifetime of men now living unless we recognize
that we must live longer.

LUBIN. I am glad you agree with me that Socialism
and Votes for Women are signs of decay.

FRANKLYN. Not at all: they are only the difficulties
that overtax your capacity. If you cannot organize
Socialism you cannot organize civilized life; and you
will relapse into barbarism accordingly.

SAVVY. Hear, hear!

BURGE. A useful point. We cannot put back the clock.

HASLAM. *I* can. Ive often done it.

LUBIN. Tut tut! My dear Burge: what are you
dreaming of? Mr Barnabas: I am a very patient man.
But will you tell me what earthly use or interest
there is in a conclusion that cannot be realized? I
grant you that if we could live three hundred years we
should all be, perhaps wiser, certainly older. You
will grant me in return, I hope, that if the sky falls we
shall all catch larks.

FRANKLYN. Your turn now, Conrad. Go ahead.

CONRAD. I dont think it's any good. I dont think
they want to live longer than usual.

LUBIN. Although I am a mere child of 69, I am old
enough to have lost the habit of crying for the moon.

BURGE. Have you discovered the elixir of life or have
you not? If not, I agree with Lubin that you are
wasting our time.

CONRAD. Is your time of any value?

BURGE [*unable to believe his ears*] My time of any
value! What do you mean?

LUBIN [*smiling comfortably*] From your high scientific point of view, I daresay, none whatever, Professor. In any case I think a little perfectly idle discussion would do Burge good. After all, we might as well hear about the elixir of life as read novels, or whatever Burge does when he is not playing golf on Walton Heath. What is your elixir, Dr Barnabas? Lemons? Sour milk? Or what is the latest?

BURGE. We were just beginning to talk seriously; and now you snatch at the chance of talking rot. [*He rises*]. Good evening. [*He turns to the door*].

CONRAD [*rudely*] Die as soon as you like. Good evening.

BURGE [*hesitating*] Look here. I took sour milk twice a day until Metchnikoff died. He thought it would keep him alive for ever; and he died of it.

CONRAD. You might as well have taken sour beer.

BURGE. You believe in lemons?

CONRAD. I wouldnt eat a lemon for ten pounds.

BURGE [*sitting down again*] What do you recommend?

CONRAD [*rising with a gesture of despair*] Whats the use of going on, Frank? Because I am a doctor, and because they think I have a bottle to give them that will make them live for ever, they are listening to me for the first time with their mouths open and their eyes shut. Thats their notion of science.

SAVVY. Steady, Nunk! Hold the fort.

CONRAD [*growls and sits down*]!!!!

LUBIN. You volunteered the consultation, Doctor. I may tell you that, far from sharing the credulity as to science which is now the fashion, I am prepared to demonstrate that during the last fifty years, though the Church has often been wrong, and even the Liberal Party has not been infallible, the men of science have always been wrong.

CONRAD. Yes: the fellows you call men of science. The people who make money by it, and their medical hangers-on. But has anybody been right?

LUBIN. The poets and story tellers, especially the classical poets and story tellers, have been, in the main, right. I will ask you not to repeat this as my opinion outside; for the vote of the medical profession and its worshippers is not to be trifled with.

FRANKLYN. You are quite right: the poem is our real clue to biological science. The most scientific document we possess at present is, as your grandmother would have told you quite truly, the story of the Garden of Eden.

BURGE [*pricking up his ears*] Whats that? If you can establish that, Barnabas, I am prepared to hear you out with my very best attention. I am listening. Go on.

FRANKLYN. Well, you remember, dont you, that in the Garden of Eden Adam and Eve were not created mortal, and that natural death, as we call it, was not a part of life, but a later and quite separate invention?

BURGE. Now you mention it, thats true. Death came afterwards.

LUBIN. What about accidental death? That was always possible.

FRANKLYN. Precisely. Adam and Eve were hung up between two frightful possibilities. One was the extinction of mankind by their accidental death. The other was the prospect of living for ever. They could bear neither. They decided that they would just take a short turn of a thousand years, and meanwhile hand on their work to a new pair. Consequently, they had to invent natural birth and natural death, which are, after all, only modes of perpetuating life without putting on any single creature the terrible burden of immortality.

[ 422 ]

LUBIN. I see. The old must make room for the new.

BURGE. Death is nothing but making room. Thats all there is in it or ever has been in it.

FRANKLYN. Yes; but the old must not desert their posts until the new are ripe for them. They desert them now two hundred years too soon.

SAVVY. I believe the old people are the new people reincarnated, Nunk. I suspect I am Eve. I am very fond of apples; and they always disagree with me.

CONRAD. You are Eve, in a sense. The Eternal Life persists; only It wears out Its bodies and minds and gets new ones, like new clothes. You are only a new hat and frock on Eve.

FRANKLYN. Yes. Bodies and minds ever better and better fitted to carry out Its eternal pursuit.

LUBIN [*with quiet scepticism*] What pursuit, may one ask, Mr Barnabas?

FRANKLYN. The pursuit of omnipotence and omniscience. Greater power and greater knowledge: these are what we are all pursuing even at the risk of our lives and the sacrifice of our pleasures. Evolution is that pursuit and nothing else. It is the path to godhead. A man differs from a microbe only in being further on the path.

LUBIN. And how soon do you expect this modest end to be reached?

FRANKLYN. Never, thank God! As there is no limit to power and knowledge there can be no end. "The power and the glory, world without end": have those words meant nothing to you?

BURGE [*pulling out an old envelope*] I should like to make a note of that. [*He does so*].

CONRAD. There will always be something to live for.

BURGE [*pocketing his envelope and becoming more and*

*more businesslike*] Right: I have got that. Now what about sin? What about the Fall? How do you work them in?

CONRAD. I dont work in the Fall. The Fall is outside Science. But I daresay Frank can work it in for you.

BURGE [*to Franklyn*] I wish you would, you know. It's important. Very important.

FRANKLYN. Well, consider it this way. It is clear that when Adam and Eve were immortal it was necessary that they should make the earth an extremely comfortable place to live in.

BURGE. True. If you take a house on a ninety-nine years lease, you spend a good deal of money on it. If you take it for three months you generally have a bill for dilapidations to pay at the end of them.

FRANKLYN. Just so. Consequently, when Adam had the Garden of Eden on a lease for ever, he took care to make it what the house agents call a highly desirable country residence. But the moment he invented death, and became a tenant for life only, the place was no longer worth the trouble. It was then that he let the thistles grow. Life was so short that it was no longer worth his while to do anything thoroughly well.

BURGE. Do you think that is enough to constitute what an average elector would consider a Fall? Is it tragic enough?

FRANKLYN. That is only the first step of the Fall. Adam did not fall down that step only: he fell down a whole flight. For instance, before he invented birth he dared not have lost his temper; for if he had killed Eve he would have been lonely and barren to all eternity. But when he invented birth, and anyone who was killed could be replaced, he could afford

[ 424 ]

to let himself go. He undoubtedly invented wife-beating; and that was another step down. One of his sons invented meat-eating. The other was horrified at the innovation. With the ferocity which is still characteristic of bulls and other vegetarians, he slew his beefsteak-eating brother, and thus invented murder. That was a very steep step. It was so exciting that all the others began to kill one another for sport, and thus invented war, the steepest step of all. They even took to killing animals as a means of killing time, and then, of course, ate them to save the long and difficult labor of agriculture. I ask you to contemplate our fathers as they came crashing down all the steps of this Jacob's ladder that reached from paradise to a hell on earth in which they had multiplied the chances of death from violence, accident, and disease until they could hardly count on three score and ten years of life, much less the thousand that Adam had been ready to face! With that picture before you, will you now ask me where was the Fall? You might as well stand at the foot of Snowdon and ask me where is the mountain. The very children see it so plainly that they compress its history into a two line epic:

Old Daddy Long Legs wouldnt say his prayers:
Take him by the hind legs and throw him downstairs.

LUBIN [*still immovably sceptical*] And what does Science say to this fairy tale, Doctor Barnabas? Surely Science knows nothing of Genesis, nor of Adam and Eve.

CONRAD. Then it isnt Science: thats all. Science has to account for everything; and everything includes the Bible.

FRANKLYN. The Book of Genesis is a part of nature like any other part of nature. The fact that the tale of the Garden of Eden has survived and held the imagination of men spellbound for centuries, whilst hundreds of much more plausible and amusing stories have gone out of fashion and perished like last year's popular song, is a scientific fact; and Science is bound to explain it. You tell me that Science knows nothing of it. Then Science is more ignorant than the children at any village school.

CONRAD. Of course if you think it more scientific to say that what we are discussing is not Adam and Eve and Eden, but the phylogeny of the blastoderm—

SAVVY. You neednt swear, Nunk.

CONRAD. Shut up, you: I am not swearing. [*To Lubin*] If you want the professional humbug of re-writing the Bible in words of four syllables, and pretending it's something new, I can humbug you to your heart's content. I can call Genesis Phylogenesis. Let the Creator say, if you like, "I will establish an antipathetic symbiosis between thee and the female, and between thy blastoderm and her blastoderm." Nobody will understand you; and Savvy will think you are swearing. The meaning is the same.

HASLAM. Priceless. But it's quite simple. The one version is poetry: the other is science.

FRANKLYN. The one is classroom jargon: the other is inspired human language.

LUBIN [*calmly reminiscent*] One of the few modern authors into whom I have occasionally glanced is Rousseau, who was a sort of Deist like Burge—

BURGE [*interrupting him forcibly*] Lubin: has this stupendously important communication which Professor Barnabas has just made to us: a communication for which I shall be indebted to him all my life long: has this, I say, no deeper effect on you than to set you pulling my leg by trying to make out that I am an infidel?

LUBIN. It's very interesting and amusing, Burge; and I think I see a case in it. I think I could undertake to argue it in an ecclesiastical court. But important is hardly a word I should attach to it.

BURGE. Good God! Here is this professor: a man utterly removed from the turmoil of our political life: devoted to pure learning in its most abstract phases; and I solemnly declare he is the greatest politician, the most inspired party leader, in the kingdom. I take off my hat to him. I, Joyce Burge, give him best. And you sit there purring like an Angora cat, and can see nothing in it!

CONRAD [opening his eyes widely] Hallo! What have I done to deserve this tribute?

BURGE. Done! You have put the Liberal Party into power for the next thirty years, Doctor: thats what youve done.

CONRAD. God forbid!

BURGE. It's all up with the Church now. Thanks to you, we go to the country with one cry and one only: Back to the Bible! Think of the effect on the Nonconformist vote. You gather that in with one hand; and you gather in the modern scientific sceptical professional vote with the other. The village atheist and the first cornet in the local Salvation Army band meet on the village green and shake hands. You take your school children, your Bible class under the ¦Cowper-Temple clause, into the museum. You shew the kids the Piltdown skull; and you say, "Thats Adam. Thats Eve's husband." You take the spectacled science student from the laboratory in

Owens College; and when he asks you for a truly scientific history of Evolution, you put into his hand The Pilgrim's Progress. You— [*Savvy and Haslam explode into shrieks of merriment*]. What are you two laughing at?

SAVVY. Oh, go on, Mr Burge. Dont stop.

HASLAM. Priceless!

FRANKLYN. Would thirty years of office for the Liberal Party seem so important to you, Mr Burge, if you had another two and a half centuries to live?

BURGE [*decisively*] No. You will have to drop that part of it. The constituencies wont swallow it.

LUBIN [*seriously*] I am not so sure of that, Burge. I am not sure that it may not prove the only point they will swallow.

BURGE. It will be no use to us even if they do. It's not a party point. It's as good for the other side as for us.

LUBIN. Not necessarily. If we get in first with it, it will be associated in the public mind with our party. Suppose I put it forward as a plank in our program that we advocate the extension of human life to three hundred years! Dunreen, as leader of the opposite party, will be bound to oppose me: to denounce me as a visionary and so forth. By doing so he will place himself in the position of wanting to rob the people of two hundred and thirty years of their natural life. The Unionists will become the party of Premature Death; and we shall become the Longevity party.

BURGE [*shaken*] You really think the electorate would swallow it?

LUBIN. My dear Burge: is there anything the electorate will not swallow if it is judiciously put to them? But we must make sure of our ground. We must have the support of the men of science. Is there serious agreement among them, Doctor, as to the possibility of such an evolution as you have described?

CONRAD. Yes. Ever since the reaction against Darwin set in at the beginning of the present century, all scientific opinion worth counting has been converging rapidly upon Creative Evolution.

FRANKLYN. Poetry has been converging on it: philosophy has been converging on it: religion has been converging on it. It is going to be the religion of the twentieth century: a religion that has its intellectual roots in philosophy and science just as medieval Christianity had its intellectual roots in Aristotle.

LUBIN. But surely any change would be so extremely gradual that—

CONRAD. Dont deceive yourself. It's only the politicians who improve the world so gradually that nobody can see the improvement. The notion that Nature does not proceed by jumps is only one of the budget of plausible lies that we call classical education. Nature always proceeds by jumps. She may spend twenty thousand years making up her mind to jump; but when she makes it up at last, the jump is big enough to take us into a new age.

LUBIN [impressed] Fancy my being leader of the party for the next three hundred years!

BURGE. What!!!

LUBIN. Perhaps hard on some of the younger men. I think in fairness I shall have to step aside to make room after another century or so: that is, if Mimi can be persuaded to give up Downing Street.

BURGE. This is too much. Your colossal conceit blinds you to the most obvious necessity of the political situation.

LUBIN. You mean my retirement. I really cannot see that it is a necessity. I could not see it when I was almost an old man—or at least an elderly one. Now that it appears that I am a young man, the case for it breaks down completely. [*To Conrad*] May I ask are there any alternative theories? Is there a scientific Opposition?

CONRAD. Well, some authorities hold that the human race is a failure, and that a new form of life, better adapted to high civilization, will supersede us as we have superseded the ape and the elephant.

BURGE. The superman: eh?

CONRAD. No. Some being quite different from us.

LUBIN. Is that altogether desirable?

FRANKLYN. I fear so. However that may be, we may be quite sure of one thing. We shall not be let alone. The force behind evolution, call it what you like, is determined to solve the problem of civilization; and if it cannot do it through us, it will produce more capable agents. You and I are not God's last word: God can still create. If you cannot do His work He will produce some being who can.

BURGE [*with zealous reverence*] What do we know about Him, Barnabas? What does anyone know about Him?

CONRAD. We know this about Him with absolute certainty. The power my brother calls God proceeds by the method of Trial and Error; and if we turn out to be one of the errors, we shall go the way of the mastodon and the megatherium and all the other scrapped experiments.

LUBIN [*rising and beginning to walk up and down the room with his considering cap on*] I admit that I am impressed, gentlemen. I will go so far as to say that your theory is likely to prove more interesting than even Welsh Disestablishment. But as practical politicians—hm! Eh, Burge?

CONRAD. We are not practical politicians. We are out to get something done. Practical politicians are people who have mastered the art of using parliament to prevent anything being done.

FRANKLYN. When we get matured statesmen and citizens—

LUBIN [*stopping short*] Citizens! Oh! Are the citizens to live three hundred years as well as the statesmen?

CONRAD. Of course.

LUBIN. I confess this had not occurred to me [*he sits down abruptly, evidently very unfavourably affected by this new light*].

*Savvy and Haslam look at one another with unspeakable feelings.*

BURGE. Do you think it would be wise to go quite so far at first? Surely it would be more prudent to begin with the best men.

FRANKLYN. You need not be anxious about that. It will begin with the best men.

LUBIN. I am glad to hear you say so. You see, we must put this into a practical parliamentary shape.

BURGE. We shall have to draft a Bill: that is the long and the short of it. Until you have your Bill drafted you dont know what you are really doing: that is my experience.

LUBIN. A Bill! Nonsense! we cannot dream of doing anything. We should interest the electorate in this as a sort of religious aspiration and personal hope, using it at the same time to remove its prejudices against those of us who are getting on in years. But it would be in the last degree upsetting to enable everyone to live longer than usual. Take the mere question of the manufacture of the specific, whatever it may be! There are forty millions of people in the country. Let me assume for the sake of illustration that each person would have to consume, say, five ounces a day of the elixir. That would be—let me see—five times three hundred and sixty-five is—um—twenty-five— thirty-two—eighteen—eighteen hundred and twenty- five ounces a year: just two ounces over the hundred- weight.

BURGE. Two million tons a year, in round numbers, of stuff that everyone would clamor for: that men would trample down women and children in the streets to get at. You couldnt produce it. There would be blue murder. It's out of the question. We must keep the actual secret to ourselves.

CONRAD [staring at them] The actual secret! What on earth are you talking about?

BURGE. The stuff. The powder. The bottle. The tabloid. Whatever it is. You said it wasnt lemons.

CONRAD. My good sir: I have no powder, no bottle, no tabloid. I am not a quack: I am a biologist. This is a thing thats going to happen.

LUBIN [completely let down] Going to happen! Oh! Is that all? [He looks at his watch].

BURGE. Going to happen! What do you mean? Do you mean that you cant make it happen?

CONRAD. No more than I could have made you happen.

FRANKLYN. We can put it into men's heads that there is nothing to prevent its happening but their own will to die before their work is done, and their own ignorance of the splendid work there is for them to do.

CONRAD. Spread that knowledge and that convic- tion; and as surely as the sun will rise tomorrow, the thing will happen.

FRANKLYN. We dont know where or when or to whom it will happen. It may happen first to someone in this room.

HASLAM. It wont happen to me: thats jolly sure.

CONRAD. It might happen to anyone. It might happen to the parlormaid. How do we know?

SAVVY. The parlormaid! Oh, thats nonsense, Nunk.

LUBIN [*once more quite comfortable*] I think Miss Savvy has delivered the final verdict.

BURGE. Do you mean to say that you have nothing more practical to offer than the mere wish to live longer? Why, if people could live by merely wishing to, we should all be living for ever already! Everybody would like to live for ever. Why dont they?

CONRAD. Pshaw! Everybody would like to have a million of money. Why havnt they? Because the men who would like to be millionaires wont save sixpence even with the chance of starvation staring them in the face. The men who want to live for ever wont cut off a glass of beer or a pipe of tobacco, though they believe the teetotallers and non-smokers live longer. That sort of liking is not willing. See what they do when they know they must.

FRANKLYN. Do not mistake mere idle fancies for the tremendous miracle-working force of Will nerved to creation by a conviction of Necessity. I tell you men capable of such willing, and realizing its necessity, will do it reluctantly, under inner compulsion, as all great efforts are made. They will hide what they are doing from themselves: they will take care not to know what they are doing. They will live three hundred years, not because they would like to, but because the soul deep down in them will know that they must, if the world is to be saved.

LUBIN [*turning to Franklyn and patting him almost paternally*] Well, my dear Barnabas, for the last thirty years the post has brought me at least once a week a plan from some crank or other for the establishment

of the millennium. I think you are the maddest of all
the cranks; but you are much the most interesting.
I am conscious of a very curious mixture of relief and
disappointment in finding that your plan is all moon-
shine, and that you have nothing practical to offer us.
But what a pity! It is such a fascinating idea! I
think you are too hard on us practical men; but there
are men in every Government, even on the Front
Bench, who deserve all you say. And now, before
dropping the subject, may I put just one question to
you? An idle question, since nothing can come of
it, but still—

FRANKLYN. Ask your question.

LUBIN. Why do you fix three hundred years as the
exact figure?

FRANKLYN. Because we must fix some figure. Less
would not be enough: and more would be more than
we dare as yet face.

LUBIN. Pooh! I am quite prepared to face three
thousand, not to say three million.

CONRAD. Yes, because you dont believe you will be
called on to make good your word.

FRANKLYN [*gently*] Also, perhaps, because you have
never been troubled much by visions of the future.

BURGE [*with intense conviction*] The future does not
exist for Henry Hopkins Lubin.

LUBIN. If by the future you mean the millennial
delusions which you use as a bunch of carrots to lure
the uneducated British donkey to the polling booth
to vote for you, it certainly does not.

BURGE. I can see the future not only because, if I
may say so in all humility, I have been gifted with a
certain power of spiritual vision, but because I have
practised as a solicitor. A solicitor has to advise
families. He has to think of the future and know the

past. His office is the real modern confessional. Among other things he has to make people's wills for them. He has to shew them how to provide for their daughters after their deaths. Has it occurred to you, Lubin, that if you live three hundred years, your daughters will have to wait a devilish long time for their money?

FRANKLYN. The money may not wait for them. Few investments flourish for three hundred years.

SAVVY. And what about before your death? Suppose they didnt get married! Imagine a girl living at home with her mother and on her father for three hundred years! Theyd murder her if she didnt murder them first.

LUBIN. By the way, Barnabas, is your daughter to keep her good looks all the time?

FRANKLYN. Will it matter? Can you conceive the most hardened flirt going on flirting for three centuries? At the end of half the time we shall hardly notice whether it is a woman or a man we are speaking to.

LUBIN [*not quite relishing this ascetic prospect*] Hm! [*He rises*]. Ah, well: you must come and tell my wife and my young people all about it; and you will bring your daughter with you, of course. [*He shakes hands with Savvy*]. Goodbye. [*He shakes hands with Franklyn*]. Goodbye, Doctor. [*He shakes hands with Conrad*]. Come on, Burge: you must really tell me what line you are going to take about the Church at the election?

BURGE. Havnt you heard? Havnt you taken in the revelation that has been vouchsafed to us? The line I am going to take is Back to Methuselah.

LUBIN [*decisively*] Dont be ridiculous, Burge. You dont suppose, do you, that our friends here are in earnest, or that our very pleasant conversation has had anything to do with practical politics! They have just been pulling our legs very wittily. Come along. [*He goes out, Franklyn politely going with him, but shaking his head in mute protest*].

BURGE [*shaking Conrad's hand*] It's beyond the old man, Doctor. No spiritual side to him: only a sort of classical side that goes down with his own set. Besides, he's done, gone, past, burnt out, burst up; thinks he is our leader and is only our rag and bottle department. But you may depend on me. I will work this stunt of yours in. I see its value. [*He begins moving towards the door with Conrad*]. Of course I cant put it exactly in your way; but you are quite right about our needing something fresh; and I believe an election can be fought on the death rate and on Adam and Eve as scientific facts. It will take the Opposition right out of its depth. And if we win there will be an O.M. for somebody when the first honors list comes around [*by this time he has talked himself out of the room and out of earshot, Conrad accompanying him*].

*Savvy and Haslam, left alone seize each other in an ecstasy of amusement, and jazz to the settee, where they sit down again side by side.*

HASLAM [*caressing her*] Darling! What a priceless humbug old Lubin is!

SAVVY. Oh, sweet old thing! I love him. Burge is a flaming fraud if you like.

HASLAM. Did you notice one thing? It struck me as rather curious.

SAVVY. What?

HASLAM. Lubin and your father have both survived the war. But their sons were killed in it.

SAVVY [*sobered*] Yes. Jim's death killed mother.

HASLAM. And they never said a word about it!

SAVVY. Well, why should they? The subject didnt come up. *I* forgot about it too; and I was very fond of Jim.

HASLAM. *I* didnt forget it, because I'm of military age; and if I hadnt been a parson I'd have had to go out and be killed too. To me the awful thing about their political incompetence was that they had to kill their own sons. It was the war casualty lists and the starvation afterwards that finished me up with politics and the Church and everything else except you.

SAVVY. Oh, I was just as bad as any of them. I sold flags in the street in my best clothes; and—hsh! [*she jumps up and pretends to be looking for a book on the shelves behind the settee*].

*Franklyn and Conrad return, looking weary and glum.*

CONRAD. Well, thats how the gospel of the brothers Barnabas is going to be received! [*He drops into Burge's chair*].

FRANKLYN [*going back to his seat at the table*] It's no use. Were you convinced, Mr Haslam?

HASLAM. About our being able to live three hundred years? Frankly, no.

CONRAD. [*to Savvy*] Nor you, I suppose?

SAVVY. Oh, I dont know. I thought I was for a moment. I can believe, in a sort of way, that people might live for three hundred years. But when you came down to tin tacks, and said that the parlormaid might, then I saw how absurd it was.

FRANKLYN. Just so. We had better hold our tongues about it, Con. We should only be laughed at, and lose the little credit we earned on false pretences in the days of our ignorance.

[ 437 ]

CONRAD. I daresay. But Creative Evolution doesnt stop while people are laughing. Laughing may even lubricate its job.

SAVVY. What does that mean?

CONRAD. It means that the first man to live three hundred years maynt have the slightest notion that he is going to do it, and may be the loudest laugher of the lot.

SAVVY. Or the first woman?

CONRAD [assenting] Or the first woman.

HASLAM. Well, it wont be one of us, anyhow.

FRANKLYN. How do you know?

*This is unanswerable. None of them have anything more to say.*

# PART III

# THE THING HAPPENS

*A summer afternoon in the year 2170 A.D. The official parlor of the President of the British Islands. A board table, long enough for three chairs at each side besides the presidential chair at the head and an ordinary chair at the foot, occupies the breadth of the room. On the table, opposite every chair, a small switchboard with a dial. There is no fireplace. The end wall is a silvery screen nearly as large as a pair of folding doors. The door is on your left as you face the screen; and there is a row of thick pegs, padded and covered with velvet, beside it.*

*A stoutish middle-aged man, good-looking and breezily genial, dressed in a silk smock, stockings, handsomely ornamented sandals, and a gold fillet round his brows, comes in. He is like Joyce Burge, yet also like Lubin, as if Nature had made a composite photograph of the two men. He takes off his fillet and hangs it on a peg; then sits down in the presidential chair at the head of the table, which is at the end farthest from the door. He puts a peg into his switchboard; turns the pointer on the dial; puts another peg in; and presses a button. Immediately the silvery screen vanishes; and in its place appears, in reverse from right to left, another office similarly furnished, with a thin, unamiable man similarly dressed, but in duller colors, turning over some documents at the table. His gold fillet is hanging up on a similar peg beside the door. He is rather like Conrad Barnabas, but younger and much more commonplace.*

BURGE-LUBIN. Hallo, Barnabas!

BARNABAS [*without looking round*] What number?

BURGE-LUBIN. Five double x three two gamma. Burge-Lubin.

*Barnabas puts a plug in number five; turns his pointer to double x; puts another plug in 32; presses a button and looks round at Burge-Lubin, who is now visible to him as well as audible.*

BARNABAS [*curtly*] Oh! That you, President?

BURGE-LUBIN. Yes. They told me you wanted me to ring you up. Anything wrong?

BARNABAS [*harsh and querulous*] I wish to make a protest.

BURGE-LUBIN [*good-humored and mocking*] What! Another protest! Whats wrong now?

BARNABAS. If you only knew all the protests I havnt made, you would be surprised at my patience. It is you who are always treating me with the grossest want of consideration.

BURGE-LUBIN. What have I done now?

BARNABAS. You have put me down to go to the Record Office today to receive that American fellow, and do the honors of a ridiculous cinema show. That is not the business of the Accountant General: it is the business of the President. It is an outrageous waste of my time, and an unjustifiable shirking of your duty at my expense. I refuse to go. You must go.

BURGE-LUBIN. My dear boy, nothing would give me greater pleasure than to take the job off your hands—

BARNABAS. Then do it. Thats all I want [*he is about to switch off*].

BURGE-LUBIN. Dont switch off. Listen. This American has invented a method of breathing under water.

[ 440 ]

BARNABAS. What do I care? I dont want to breathe under water.

BURGE-LUBIN. You may, my dear Barnabas, at any time. You know you never look where you are going when you are immersed in your calculations. Some day you will walk into the Serpentine. This man's invention may save your life.

BARNABAS [*angrily*] Will you tell me what that has to do with your putting your ceremonial duties on to my shoulders? I will not be trifled [*he vanishes and is replaced by the blank screen*]—

BURGE-LUBIN [*indignantly holding down his button*] Dont cut us off, please: we have not finished. I am the President, speaking to the Accountant General. What are you dreaming of?

A WOMAN'S VOICE. Sorry. [*The screen shews Barnabas as before*].

BURGE-LUBIN. Since you take it that way, I will go in your place. It's a pity, because, you see, this American thinks you are the greatest living authority on the duration of human life; and—

BARNABAS [*interrupting*] The American thinks! What do you mean? I am the greatest living authority on the duration of human life. Who dares dispute it?

BURGE-LUBIN. Nobody, dear lad, nobody. Dont fly out at me. It is evident that you have not read the American's book.

BARNABAS. Dont tell me that you have, or that you have read any book except a novel for the last twenty years; for I wont believe you.

BURGE-LUBIN. Quite right, dear old fellow: I havnt read it. But I have read what The Times Literary Supplement says about it.

BARNABAS. I dont care two straws what it says about it. Does it say anything about me?

BURGE-LUBIN. Yes.

BARNABAS. Oh, does it? What?

BURGE-LUBIN. It points out that an extraordinary number of first-rate persons like you and me have died by drowning during the last two centuries, and that when this invention of breathing under water takes effect, your estimate of the average duration of human life will be upset.

BARNABAS [alarmed] Upset my estimate! Gracious Heavens! Does the fool realize what that means? Do you realize what that means?

BURGE-LUBIN. I suppose it means that we shall have to amend the Act.

BARNABAS. Amend my Act! Monstrous!

BURGE-LUBIN. But we must. We cant ask people to go on working until they are forty-three unless our figures are unchallengeable. You know what a row there was over those last three years, and how nearly the too-old-at-forty people won.

BARNABAS. They would have made the British Islands bankrupt if theyd won. But you dont care for that: you care for nothing but being popular.

BURGE-LUBIN. Oh, well: I shouldnt worry if I were you; for most people complain that there is not enough work for them, and would be only too glad to stick on instead of retiring at forty-three, if only they were asked as a favor instead of having to.

BARNABAS. Thank you: I need no consolation. [He rises determinedly and puts on his fillet].

BURGE-LUBIN. Are you off? Where are you going to?

BARNABAS. To that cinema tomfoolery, of course. I shall put this American impostor in his place. [He goes out].

BURGE-LUBIN [calling after him] God bless you, dear old chap! [With a chuckle, he switches off; and the *screen becomes blank. He presses a button and holds it down while he calls*] Hallo!

A WOMAN'S VOICE. Hallo!

BURGE-LUBIN [*formally*] The President respectfully solicits the privilege of an interview with the Chief Secretary, and holds himself entirely at his honor's august disposal.

A CHINESE VOICE. He is coming.

BURGE-LUBIN. Oh! That you, Confucius? So good of you. Come along [*he releases the button*].

*A man in a yellow gown, presenting the general appearance of a Chinese sage, enters.*

BURGE-LUBIN [*jocularly*] Well, illustrious Sage-&-Onions, how are your poor sore feet?

CONFUCIUS [*gravely*] I thank you for your kind inquiries. I am well.

BURGE-LUBIN. Thats right. Sit down and make yourself comfortable. Any business for me today?

CONFUCIUS [*sitting down on the first chair round the corner of the table to the President's right*] None.

BURGE-LUBIN. Have you heard the result of the by-election?

CONFUCIUS. A walk-over. Only one candidate.

BURGE-LUBIN. Any good?

CONFUCIUS. He was released from the County Lunatic Asylum a fortnight ago. Not mad enough for the lethal chamber: not sane enough for any place but the division lobby. A very popular speaker.

BURGE-LUBIN. I wish the people would take a serious interest in politics.

CONFUCIUS. I do not agree. The Englishman is not fitted by nature to understand politics. Ever since the public services have been manned by Chinese, the country has been well and honestly governed. What more is needed?

BURGE-LUBIN. What I cant make out is that China is one of the worst governed countries on earth.

CONFUCIUS. No. It was badly governed twenty years ago; but since we forbade any Chinaman to take part in our public services, and imported natives of Scotland for that purpose, we have done well. Your information here is always twenty years out of date.

BURGE-LUBIN. People dont seem to be able to govern themselves. I cant understand it. Why should it be so?

CONFUCIUS. Justice is impartiality. Only strangers are impartial.

BURGE-LUBIN. It ends in the public services being so good that the Government has nothing to do but think.

CONFUCIUS. Were it otherwise, the Government would have too much to do to think.

BURGE-LUBIN. Is that any excuse for the English people electing a parliament of lunatics?

CONFUCIUS. The English people always did elect parliaments of lunatics. What does it matter if your permanent officials are honest and competent?

BURGE-LUBIN. You do not know the history of this country. What would my ancestors have said to the menagerie of degenerates that is still called the House of Commons? Confucius: you will not believe me; and I do not blame you for it; but England once saved the liberties of the world by inventing parliamentary government, which was her peculiar and supreme glory.

CONFUCIUS. I know the history of your country perfectly well. It proves the exact contrary.

BURGE-LUBIN. How do you make that out?

CONFUCIUS. The only power your parliament ever

had was the power of withholding supplies from the king.

BURGE-LUBIN. Precisely. That great Englishman Simon de Montfort—

CONFUCIUS. He was not an Englishman: he was a Frenchman. He imported parliaments from France.

BURGE-LUBIN [*surprised*] You dont say so!

CONFUCIUS. The king and his loyal subjects killed Simon for forcing his French parliament on them. The first thing British parliaments always did was to grant supplies to the king for life with enthusiastic expressions of loyalty, lest they should have any real power, and be expected to do something.

BURGE-LUBIN. Look here, Confucius: you know more history than I do, of course; but democracy—

CONFUCIUS. An institution peculiar to China. And it was never really a success there.

BURGE-LUBIN. But the Habeas Corpus Act!

CONFUCIUS. The English always suspended it when it threatened to be of the slightest use.

BURGE-LUBIN. Well, trial by jury: you cant deny that we established that?

CONFUCIUS. All cases that were dangerous to the governing classes were tried in the Star Chamber or by Court Martial except when the prisoner was not tried at all, but executed after calling him names enough to make him unpopular.

BURGE-LUBIN. Oh, bother! You may be right in these little details; but in the large we have managed to hold our own as a great race. Well, people who could do nothing couldnt have done that, you know.

CONFUCIUS. I did not say you could do nothing. You could fight. You could eat. You could drink. Until the twentieth century you could produce children. You could play games. You could work

when you were forced to. But you could not govern
yourselves.

BURGE-LUBIN. Then how did we get our reputation
as the pioneers of liberty?

CONFUCIUS. By your steadfast refusal to be governed
at all. A horse that kicks everyone who tries to harness
and guide him may be a pioneer of liberty; but he
is not a pioneer of government. In China he would
be shot.

BURGE-LUBIN. Stuff! Do you imply that the admin-
istration of which I am president is no Government?

CONFUCIUS. I do. *I* am the Government.

BURGE-LUBIN. You! You!! You fat yellow lump
of conceit!

CONFUCIUS. Only an Englishman could be so
ignorant of the nature of government as to suppose
that a capable statesman cannot be fat, yellow, and
conceited. Many Englishmen are slim, red-nosed,
and modest. Put them in my place, and within a year
you will be back in the anarchy and chaos of the
nineteenth and twentieth centuries.

BURGE-LUBIN. Oh, if you go back to the Dark Ages
I have nothing more to say. But we did not perish.
We extricated ourselves from that chaos. We are
now the best governed country in the world. How
did we manage that if we are such fools as you
pretend?

CONFUCIUS. You did not do it until the slaughter and
ruin produced by your anarchy forced you at last to
recognize two inexorable facts. First, that government
is absolutely necessary to civilization, and that you
could not maintain civilization by merely doing down
your neighbor, as you called it, and cutting off the
head of your king whenever he happened to be a
logical Scot and tried to take his position seriously.

Second, that government is an art of which you are congenitally incapable. Accordingly, you imported educated negresses and Chinese to govern you. Since then you have done very well.

BURGE-LUBIN. So have you, you old humbug. All the same, I dont know how you stand the work you do. You seem to me positively to like public business. Why wont you let me take you down to the coast some week-end and teach you marine golf?

CONFUCIUS. It does not interest me. I am not a barbarian.

BURGE-LUBIN. You mean that I am?

CONFUCIUS. That is evident.

BURGE-LUBIN. How?

CONFUCIUS. People like you. They like cheerful good-natured barbarians. They have elected you President five times in succession. They will elect you five times more. I like you. You are better company than a dog or a horse because you can speak.

BURGE-LUBIN. Am I a barbarian because you like me.

CONFUCIUS. Surely. Nobody likes me: I am held in awe. Capable persons are never liked. I am not likeable; but I am indispensable.

BURGE-LUBIN. Oh, cheer up, old man: theres nothing so disagreeable about you as all that. I dont dislike you; and if you think I'm afraid of you, you jolly well dont know Burge-Lubin: thats all.

CONFUCIUS. You are brave: yes. It is a form of stupidity.

BURGE-LUBIN. You may not be brave: one doesnt expect it from a Chink. But you have the devil's own cheek.

CONFUCIUS. I have the assured certainty of the man who sees and knows. Your genial bluster, your cheery self-confidence, are pleasant, like the open air. But

[ 447 ]

they are blind: they are vain. I seem to see a great dog wag his tail and bark joyously. But if he leaves my heel he is lost.

BURGE-LUBIN. Thank you for a handsome compliment. I have a big dog; and he is the best fellow I know. If you knew how much uglier you are than a chow, you wouldnt start these comparisons, though. [*Rising*] Well, if you have nothing for me to do, I am going to leave your heel for the rest of the day and enjoy myself. What would you recommend me to do with myself?

CONFUCIUS. Give yourself up to contemplation; and great thoughts will come to you.

BURGE-LUBIN. Will they? If you think I am going to sit here on a fine day like this with my legs crossed waiting for great thoughts, you exaggerate my taste for them. I prefer marine golf. [*Stopping short*] Oh, by the way, I forgot something. I have a word or two to say to the Minister of Health. [*He goes back to his chair*].

CONFUCIUS. Her number is—

BURGE-LUBIN. I know it.

CONFUCIUS [*rising*] I cannot understand her attraction for you. For me a woman who is not yellow does not exist, save as an official. [*He goes out*].

*Burge-Lubin operates his switchboard as before. The screen vanishes; and a dainty room with a bed, a wardrobe, and a dressing-table with a mirror and a switch on it, appears. Seated at it a handsome negress is trying on a brilliant head scarf. Her dressing-gown is thrown back from her shoulders to her chair. She is in corset, knickers, and silk stockings.*

BURGE-LUBIN [*horrified*] I beg your pardon.

*The startled negress snatches the peg out of her switchboard and vanishes.*

THE NEGRESS'S VOICE. Who is it?

BURGE-LUBIN. Me. The President. Burge-Lubin. I had no idea your bedroom switch was in. I beg your pardon.

*The negress reappears. She has pulled the dressing-gown perfunctorily over her shoulders, and continues her experiments with the scarf, not at all put out, and rather amused by Burge's prudery.*

THE NEGRESS. Stupid of me. I was talking to another lady this morning; and I left the peg in.

BURGE-LUBIN. But I am so sorry.

THE NEGRESS [*sunnily: still busy with the scarf*] Why? It was my fault.

BURGE-LUBIN [*embarrassed*] Well—er—er— But I suppose you were used to it in Africa.

THE NEGRESS. Your delicacy is very touching, Mr President. It would be funny if it were not so unpleasant, because, like all white delicacy, it is in the wrong place. How do you think this suits my complexion?

BURGE-LUBIN. How can any really vivid color go wrong with a black satin skin? It is our women's wretched pale faces that have to be matched and lighted. Yours is always right.

THE NEGRESS. Yes: it is a pity your white beauties have all the same ashy faces, the same colorless drab, the same age. But look at their beautiful noses and little lips! They are physically insipid: they have no beauty: you cannot love them; but how elegant!

BURGE-LUBIN. Cant you find an official pretext for coming to see me? Isnt it ridiculous that we have never met? It's so tantalizing to see you and talk to you, and to know all the time that you are two hundred miles away, and that I cant touch you?

THE NEGRESS. I cannot live on the East Coast: it

is hard enough to keep my blood warm here. Besides, my friend, it would not be safe. These distant flirtations are very charming; and they teach self-control.

BURGE-LUBIN. Damn self-control! I want to hold you in my arms—to— [*the negress snatches out the peg from the switchboard and vanishes. She is still heard laughing*]. Black devil! [*He snatches out his peg furiously: her laugh is no longer heard*]. Oh, these sex episodes! Why can I not resist them? Disgraceful! *Confucius returns.*

CONFUCIUS. I forgot. There is something for you to do this morning. You have to go to the Record Office to receive the American barbarian.

BURGE-LUBIN. Confucius: once for all, I object to this Chinese habit of describing white men as barbarians.

CONFUCIUS [*standing formally at the end of the table with his hands palm to palm*] I make a mental note that you do not wish the Americans to be described as barbarians.

BURGE-LUBIN. Not at all. The Americans are barbarians. But we are not. I suppose the particular barbarian you are speaking of is the American who has invented a means of breathing under water.

CONFUCIUS. He says he has invented such a method. For some reason which is not intelligible in China, Englishmen always believe any statement made by an American inventor, especially one who has never invented anything. Therefore you believe this person and have given him a public reception. Today the Record Office is entertaining him with a display of the cinematographic records of all the eminent Englishmen who have lost their lives by drowning since the cinema was invented. Why not go to see it if you are at a loss for something to do?

BURGE-LUBIN. What earthly interest is there in looking at a moving picture of a lot of people merely because they were drowned? If they had had any sense, they would not have been drowned, probably.

CONFUCIUS. That is not so. It has never been noticed before; but the Record Office has just made two remarkable discoveries about the public men and women who have displayed extraordinary ability during the past century. One is that they retained unusual youthfulness up to an advanced age. The other is that they all met their death by drowning.

BURGE-LUBIN. Thats funny. Can you explain it?

CONFUCIUS. It cannot be explained. It is not reasonable. Therefore I do not believe it.

*The Accountant General rushes in, looking ghastly. He staggers to the middle of the table.*

BURGE-LUBIN. Whats the matter? Are you ill?

BARNABAS [*choking*] No. I— [*he collapses into the middle chair*]. I must speak to you in private.

*Confucius calmly withdraws.*

BURGE-LUBIN. What on earth is it? Have some oxygen.

BARNABAS. I have had some. Go to the Record Office. You will see men fainting there again and again, and being revived with oxygen, as I have been. They have seen with their own eyes as I have.

BURGE-LUBIN. Seen what?

BARNABAS. Seen the Archbishop of York.

BURGE-LUBIN. Well, why shouldnt they see the Archbishop of York? What are they fainting for? Has he been murdered?

BARNABAS. No: he has been drowned.

BURGE-LUBIN. Good God! Where? When? How? Poor fellow!

BARNABAS. Poor fellow! Poor thief! Poor swindler!

Poor robber of his country's Exchequer! Poor fellow indeed! Wait til I catch him.

BURGE-LUBIN. How can you catch him when he is dead? Youre mad.

BARNABAS. Dead! Who said he was dead?

BURGE-LUBIN. You did. Drowned.

BARNABAS [*exasperated*] Will you listen to me? Was old Archbishop Haslam, the present man's last predecessor but four, drowned or not?

BURGE-LUBIN. I dont know. Look him up in the Encyclopedia Britannica.

BARNABAS. Yah! Was Archbishop Stickit, who wrote Stickit on the Psalms, drowned or not?

BURGE-LUBIN. Yes, mercifully. He deserved it.

BARNABAS. Was President Dickenson drowned? Was General Bullyboy drowned?

BURGE-LUBIN. Who is denying it?

BARNABAS. Well, weve had moving pictures of all four put on the screen today for this American; and they and the Archbishop are the same man. Now tell me I am mad.

BURGE-LUBIN. I do tell you you are mad. Stark raving mad.

BARNABAS. Am I to believe my own eyes or am I not?

BURGE-LUBIN. You can do as you please. All I can tell you is that *I* dont believe your eyes if they cant see any difference between a live archbishop and two dead ones. [*The apparatus rings, he holds the button down*]. Yes?

THE WOMAN'S VOICE. The Archbishop of York, to see the President.

BARNABAS [*hoarse with rage*] Have him in. I'll talk to the scoundrel.

BURGE-LUBIN [*releasing the button*] Not while you are in this state.

BARNABAS [*reaching furiously for his button and holding it down*] Send the Archbishop in at once.

BURGE-LUBIN. If you lose your temper, Barnabas, remember that we shall be two to one.

*The Archbishop enters. He has a white band round his throat, set in a black stock. He wears a sort of kilt of black ribbons, and soft black boots that button high up on his calves. His costume does not differ otherwise from that of the President and the Accountant General; but its color scheme is black and white. He is older than the Reverend Bill Haslam was when he wooed Miss Savvy Barnabas; but he is recognizably the same man. He does not look a day over fifty, and is very well preserved even at that; but his boyishness of manner is quite gone: he now has complete authority and self-possession: in fact the President is a little afraid of him; and it seems quite natural and inevitable that he should speak first.*

THE ARCHBISHOP. Good day, Mr President.

BURGE-LUBIN. Good day, Mr Archbishop. Be seated.

THE ARCHBISHOP [*sitting down between them*] Good day, Mr Accountant General.

BARNABAS [*malevolently*] Good day to you. I have a question to put to you, if you dont mind.

THE ARCHBISHOP [*looking curiously at him, jarred by his uncivil tone*] Certainly. What is it?

BARNABAS. What is your definition of a thief?

THE ARCHBISHOP. Rather an old-fashioned word, is it not?

BARNABAS. It survives officially in my department.

THE ARCHBISHOP. Our departments are full of survivals. Look at my tie! my apron! my boots! They are all mere survivals; yet it seems that without them I cannot be a proper Archbishop.

BARNABAS. Indeed! Well, in my department the

[ 453 ]

word thief survives, because in the community the thing thief survives. And a very despicable and dishonorable thing he is, too.

THE ARCHBISHOP [*coolly*] I daresay.

BARNABAS. In my department, sir, a thief is a person who lives longer than the statutory expectation of life entitles him to, and goes on drawing public money when, if he were an honest man, he would be dead.

THE ARCHBISHOP. Then let me say, sir, that your department does not understand its own business. If you have miscalculated the duration of human life, that is not the fault of the persons whose longevity you have miscalculated. And if they continue to work and produce, they pay their way, even if they live two or three centuries.

BARNABAS. I know nothing about their working and producing. That is not the business of my department. I am concerned with their expectation of life; and I say that no man has any right to go on living and drawing money when he ought to be dead.

THE ARCHBISHOP. You do not comprehend the relation between income and production.

BARNABAS. I understand my own department.

THE ARCHBISHOP. That is not enough. Your department is part of a synthesis which embraces all the departments.

BURGE-LUBIN. Synthesis! This is an intellectual difficulty. This is a job for Confucius. I heard him use that very word the other day; and I wondered what on earth he meant. [*Switching on*] Hallo! Put me through to the Chief Secretary.

CONFUCIUS'S VOICE. You are speaking to him.

BURGE-LUBIN. An intellectual difficulty, old man. Something we dont understand. Come and help us out.

THE ARCHBISHOP. May I ask how the question has arisen?

BARNABAS. Ah! You begin to smell a rat, do you? You thought yourself pretty safe. You—

BURGE-LUBIN. Steady, Barnabas. Dont be in a hurry.

*Confucius enters.*

THE ARCHBISHOP [*rising*] Good morning, Mr Chief Secretary.

BURGE-LUBIN [*rising in instinctive imitation of the Archbishop*] Honor us by taking a seat, O sage.

CONFUCIUS. Ceremony is needless. [*He bows to the company, and takes the chair at the foot of the table*].

*The President and the Archbishop resume their seats.*

BURGE-LUBIN. We wish to put a case to you, Confucius. Suppose a man, instead of conforming to the official estimate of his expectation of life, were to live for more than two centuries and a half, would the Accountant General be justified in calling him a thief?

CONFUCIUS. No. He would be justified in calling him a liar.

THE ARCHBISHOP. I think not, Mr Chief Secretary. What do you suppose my age is?

CONFUCIUS. Fifty.

BURGE-LUBIN. You dont look it. Forty-five; and young for your age.

THE ARCHBISHOP. My age is two hundred and eighty-three.

BARNABAS [*morosely triumphant*] Hmp! Mad, am I?

BURGE-LUBIN. Youre both mad. Excuse me, Archbishop; but this is getting a bit—well—

THE ARCHBISHOP [*to Confucius*] Mr Chief Secretary: will you, to oblige me, assume that I have lived nearly three centuries? As a hypothesis?

BURGE-LUBIN. What is a hypothesis?

CONFUCIUS. It does not matter. I understand. [*To

*the Archbishop*] Am I to assume that you have lived in your ancestors, or by metempsychosis—

BURGE-LUBIN. Met—Emp—Sy—Good Lord! What a brain, Confucius! What a brain!

THE ARCHBISHOP. Nothing of that kind. Assume in the ordinary sense that I was born in the year 1887, and that I have worked continuously in one profession or another since the year 1910. Am I a thief?

CONFUCIUS. I do not know. Was that one of your professions?

THE ARCHBISHOP. No. I have been nothing worse than an Archbishop, a President, and a General.

BARNABAS. Has he or has he not robbed the Exchequer by drawing five or six incomes when he was entitled only to one? Answer me that.

CONFUCIUS. Certainly not. The hypothesis is that he has worked continuously since 1910. We are now in the year 2170. What is the official lifetime?

BARNABAS. Seventy-eight. Of course it's an average; and we dont mind a man here and there going on to ninety, or even, as a curiosity, becoming a centenarian. But I say that a man who goes beyond that is a swindler.

CONFUCIUS. Seventy-eight into two hundred and eighty-three goes more than three and a half times. Your department owes the Archbishop two and a half educations and three and a half retiring pensions.

BARNABAS. Stuff! How can that be?

CONFUCIUS. At what age do your people begin to work for the community?

BURGE-LUBIN. Three. They do certain things every day when they are three. Just to break them in, you know. But they become self-supporting, or nearly so, at thirteen.

CONFUCIUS. And at what age do they retire?

BARNABAS. Forty-three.

CONFUCIUS. That is, they do thirty years' work; and they receive maintenance and education, without working, for thirteen years of childhood and thirty-five years of superannuation, forty-eight years in all, for each thirty years' work. The Archbishop has given you 260 years' work, and has received only one education and no superannuation. You therefore owe him over 300 years of leisure and nearly eight educations. You are thus heavily in his debt. In other words, he has effected an enormous national economy by living so long; and you, by living only seventy-eight years, are profiting at his expense. He is the benefactor: you are the thief. [*Half rising*] May I now withdraw and return to my serious business, as my own span is comparatively short?

BURGE-LUBIN. Dont be in a hurry, old chap. [*Confucius sits down again*]. This hypothecary, or whatever you call it, is put up seriously. I dont believe it; but if the Archbishop and the Accountant General are going to insist that it's true, we shall have either to lock them up or to see the thing through.

BARNABAS. It's no use trying these Chinese subtleties on me. I'm a plain man; and though I dont understand metaphysics, and dont believe in them, I understand figures; and if the Archbishop is only entitled to seventy-eight years, and he takes 283, I say he takes more than he is entitled to. Get over that if you can.

THE ARCHBISHOP. I have not taken 283 years: I have taken 23 and given 260.

CONFUCIUS. Do your accounts shew a deficiency or a surplus?

BARNABAS. A surplus. Thats what I cant make out. Thats the artfulness of these people.

BURGE-LUBIN. That settles it. Whats the use of
arguing? The Chink says you are wrong; and theres
an end of it.

BARNABAS. I say nothing against the Chink's
arguments. But what about my facts?

CONFUCIUS. If your facts include a case of a man
living 283 years, I advise you to take a few weeks at
the seaside.

BARNABAS. Let there be an end of this hinting that
I am out of my mind. Come and look at the cinema
record. I tell you this man is Archbishop Haslam,
Archbishop Stickit, President Dickenson, General
Bullyboy and himself into the bargain: all five of them.

THE ARCHBISHOP. I do not deny it. I never have
denied it. Nobody has ever asked me.

BURGE-LUBIN. But damn it, man—I beg your
pardon, Archbishop; but really, really—

THE ARCHBISHOP. Dont mention it. What were you
going to say?

BURGE-LUBIN. Well, you were drowned four times
over. You are not a cat, you know.

THE ARCHBISHOP. That is very easy to understand.
Consider my situation when I first made the amazing
discovery that I was destined to live three hundred
years! I—

CONFUCIUS [interrupting him] Pardon me. Such a
discovery was impossible. You have not made it yet.
You may live a million years if you have already lived
two hundred. There is no question of three hundred
years. You have made a slip at the very beginning of
your fairy tale, Mr Archbishop.

BURGE-LUBIN. Good, Confucius! [To the Arch-
bishop] He has you there. I dont see how you can
get over that.

THE ARCHBISHOP. Yes: it is quite a good point.

But if the Accountant General will go to the British Museum library, and search the catalogue, he will find under his own name a curious and now forgotten book, dated 1924, entitled The Gospel of the Brothers Barnabas. That gospel was that men must live three hundred years if civilization is to be saved. It shewed that this extension of individual human life was possible, and how it was likely to come about. I married the daughter of one of the brothers.

BARNABAS. Do you mean to say you claim to be a connexion of mine?

THE ARCHBISHOP. I claim nothing. As I have by this time perhaps three or four million cousins of one degree or another. I have ceased to call on the family.

BURGE-LUBIN. Gracious heavens! Four million relatives! Is that calculation correct, Confucius?

CONFUCIUS. In China it might be forty millions if there were no checks on population.

BURGE-LUBIN. This is a staggerer. It brings home to one—but [recovering] it isnt true, you know. Let us keep sane.

CONFUCIUS [to the Archbishop] You wish us to understand that the illustrious ancestors of the Accountant General communicated to you a secret by which you could attain the age of three hundred years.

THE ARCHBISHOP. No. Nothing of the kind. They simply believed that mankind could live any length of time it knew to be absolutely necessary to save civilization from extinction. I did not share their belief: at least I was not conscious of sharing it: I thought I was only amused by it. To me my father-in-law and his brother were a pair of clever cranks who had talked one another into a fixed idea which had become a monomania with them. It was not until I got into serious difficulties with the pension authorities after turning seventy that I began to suspect the truth.

CONFUCIUS. The truth?

THE ARCHBISHOP. Yes, Mr Chief Secretary: the truth. Like all revolutionary truths, it began as a joke. As I shewed no signs of ageing after forty-five, my wife used to make fun of me by saying that I was certainly going to live three hundred years. She was sixty-eight when she died; and the last thing she said to me, as I sat by her bedside holding her hand, was "Bill: you really dont look fifty. I wonder—" She broke off, and fell asleep wondering, and never awoke. Then I began to wonder too. That is the explanation of the three hundred years, Mr Secretary.

CONFUCIUS. It is very ingenious, Mr Archbishop. And very well told.

BURGE-LUBIN. Of course you understand that *I* dont for a moment suggest the very faintest doubt of your absolute veracity, Archbishop. You know that, dont you?

THE ARCHBISHOP. Quite, Mr President. Only you dont believe me: that is all. I do not expect you to. In your place I should not believe. You had better have a look at the films. [*Pointing to the Accountant General*] He believes.

BURGE-LUBIN. But the drowning? What about the drowning? A man might get drowned once, or even twice if he was exceptionally careless. But he couldnt be drowned four times. He would run away from water like a mad dog.

THE ARCHBISHOP. Perhaps Mr Chief Secretary can guess the explanation of that.

CONFUCIUS. To keep your secret, you had to die.

BURGE-LUBIN. But dash it all, man, he isnt dead.

CONFUCIUS. It is socially impossible not to do what

everybody else does. One must die at the usual time.

BARNABAS. Of course. A simple point of honor.

CONFUCIUS. Not at all. A simple necessity.

BURGE-LUBIN. Well, I'm hanged if I see it. I should jolly well live for ever if I could.

THE ARCHBISHOP. It is not so easy as you think. You, Mr Chief Secretary, have grasped the difficulties of the position. Let me remind you, Mr President, that I was over eighty before the 1969 Act for the Redistribution of Income entitled me to a handsome retiring pension. Owing to my youthful appearance I was prosecuted for attempting to obtain public money on false pretences when I claimed it. I could prove nothing; for the register of my birth had been blown to pieces by a bomb dropped on a village church years before in the first of the big modern wars. I was ordered back to work as a man of forty, and had to work for fifteen years more, the retiring age being then fifty-five.

BURGE-LUBIN. As late as fifty-five! How did people stand it?

THE ARCHBISHOP. They made difficulties about letting me go even then, I still looked so young. For some years I was in continual trouble. The industrial police rounded me up again and again, refusing to believe that I was over age. They began to call me The Wandering Jew. You see how impossible my position was. I foresaw that in twenty years more my official record would prove me to be seventy-five; my appearance would make it impossible to believe that I was more than forty-five; and my real age would be one hundred and seventeen. What was I to do? Bleach my hair? Hobble about on two sticks? Mimic the voice of a centenarian? Better have killed myself.

BARNABAS. You ought to have killed yourself. As

an honest man you were entitled to no more than an honest man's expectation of life.

THE ARCHBISHOP. I did kill myself. It was quite easy. I left a suit of clothes by the seashore during the bathing season, with documents in the pockets to identify me. I then turned up in a strange place, pretending I had lost my memory, and forgotten my name and age and everything about myself. Under treatment I recovered my health, but not my memory. I have had several careers since I began this routine of life and death. I have been an archbishop three times. When I persuaded the authorities to knock down all our towns and rebuild them from the foundations, or move them, I went into the artillery, and became a general. I have been President.

BURGE-LUBIN. Dickenson?

THE ARCHBISHOP. Yes.

BURGE-LUBIN. But they found Dickenson's body: its ashes are buried in St Paul's.

THE ARCHBISHOP. They almost always found the body. During the bathing season there are plenty of bodies. I have been cremated again and again. At first I used to attend my own funeral in disguise, because I had read about a man doing that in an old romance by an author named Bennett, from whom I remember borrowing five pounds in 1912. But I got tired of that. I would not cross the street now to read my latest epitaph.

*The Chief Secretary and the President look very glum. Their incredulity is vanquished at last.*

BURGE-LUBIN. Look here. Do you chaps realize how awful this is? Here we are sitting calmly in the presence of a man whose death is overdue by two centuries. He may crumble into dust before our eyes at any moment.

BARNABAS. Not he. He'll go on drawing his pension until the end of the world.

THE ARCHBISHOP. Not quite that. My expectation of life is only three hundred years.

BARNABAS. You will last out my time anyhow: thats enough for me.

THE ARCHBISHOP [*coolly*] How do you know?

BARNABAS [*taken aback*] How do I know!

THE ARCHBISHOP. Yes: how do you know? I did not begin even to suspect until I was nearly seventy. I was only vain of my youthful appearance. I was not quite serious about it until I was ninety. Even now I am not sure from one moment to another, though I have given you my reason for thinking that I have quite unintentionally committed myself to a lifetime of three hundred years.

BURGE-LUBIN. But how do you do it? Is it lemons? Is it Soya beans? Is it—

THE ARCHBISHOP. I do not do it. It happens. It may happen to anyone. It may happen to you.

BURGE-LUBIN [*the full significance of this for himself dawning on him*] Then we three may be in the same boat with you, for all we know?

THE ARCHBISHOP. You may. Therefore I advise you to be very careful how you take any step that will make my position uncomfortable.

BURGE-LUBIN. Well, I'm dashed! One of my secretaries was remarking only this morning how well and young I am looking? Barnabas: I have an absolute conviction that I am one of the—the—shall I say one of the victims?—of this strange destiny.

THE ARCHBISHOP. Your great-great-great-great-great-great-grandfather formed the same conviction when he was between sixty and seventy. I knew him.

BURGE-LUBIN [*depressed*] Ah! But he died.

THE ARCHBISHOP. No.

BURGE-LUBIN [*hopefully*] Do you mean to say he is still alive.

THE ARCHBISHOP. No. He was shot. Under the influence of his belief that he was going to live three hundred years he became a changed man. He began to tell people the truth; and they disliked it so much that they took advantage of certain clauses of an Act of Parliament he had himself passed during the Four Years War, and had purposely forgotten to repeal afterwards. They took him to the Tower of London and shot him.

*The apparatus rings.*

CONFUCIUS [*answering*] Yes? [*He listens*].

A WOMAN'S VOICE. The Domestic Minister has called.

BURGE-LUBIN [*not quite catching the answer*] Who does she say has called?

CONFUCIUS. The Domestic Minister.

BARNABAS. Oh, dash it! That awful woman!

BURGE-LUBIN. She certainly is a bit of a terror. I dont exactly know why; for she is not at all bad-looking.

BARNABAS [*out of patience*] For Heaven's sake, dont be frivolous.

THE ARCHBISHOP. He cannot help it, Mr Accountant General. Three of his sixteen great-great-great-grandfathers married Lubins.

BURGE-LUBIN. Tut tut! I am not frivolling. *I* did not ask the lady here. Which of you did?

CONFUCIUS. It is her official duty to report person-ally to the President once a quarter.

BURGE-LUBIN. Oh, that! Then I suppose it's my official duty to receive her. Theyd better send her in. You dont mind, do you? She will bring us back to real life. I dont know how you fellows feel; but I'm just going dotty.

CONFUCIUS [*into the telephone*] The President will receive the Domestic Minister at once.

*They watch the door in silence for the entrance of the Domestic Minister.*

BURGE-LUBIN [*suddenly, to the Archbishop*] I suppose you have been married over and over again.

THE ARCHBISHOP. Once. You do not make vows until death when death is three hundred years off.

*They relapse into uneasy silence. The Domestic Minister enters. She is a handsome woman, apparently in the prime of life, with elegant, tense, well held-up figure, and the walk of a goddess. Her expression and deportment are grave, swift, decisive, awful, unanswerable. She wears a Dianesque tunic instead of a blouse, and a silver coronet instead of a gold fillet. Her dress otherwise is not markedly different from that of the men, who rise as she enters, and incline their heads with instinctive awe. She comes to the vacant chair between Barnabas and Confucius.*

BURGE-LUBIN [*resolutely genial and gallant*] Delighted to see you, Mrs Lutestring.

CONFUCIUS. We are honored by your celestial presence.

BARNABAS. Good day, madam.

THE ARCHBISHOP. I have not had the pleasure of meeting you before. I am the Archbishop of York.

MRS LUTESTRING. Surely we have met, Mr Archbishop. I remember your face. We— [*she checks herself suddenly*] Ah no: I remember now: it was someone else. [*She sits down*].

*They all sit down.*

THE ARCHBISHOP [*also puzzled*] Are you sure you are mistaken? I also have some association with your face, Mrs Lutestring. Something like a door opening continually and revealing you. And a smile of welcome when you recognized me. Did you ever open a door for me, I wonder?

MRS LUTESTRING. I often opened a door for the person you have just reminded me of. But he has been dead many years.

*The rest, except the Archbishop, look at one another quickly.*

CONFUCIUS. May I ask how many years?

MRS LUTESTRING [*struck by his tone, looks at him for a moment with some displeasure; then replies*] It does not matter. A long time.

BURGE-LUBIN. You mustnt rush to conclusions about the Archbishop, Mrs Lutestring. He is an older bird than you think. Older than you, at all events.

MRS LUTESTRING [*with a melancholy smile*] I think not, Mr President. But the subject is a delicate one. I had rather not pursue it.

CONFUCIUS. There is a question which has not been asked.

MRS LUTESTRING [*very decisively*] If it is a question about my age, Mr Chief Secretary, it had better not be asked. All that concerns you about my personal affairs can be found in the books of the Accountant General.

CONFUCIUS. The question I was thinking of will not be addressed to you. But let me say that your sensitiveness on the point is very strange, coming from a woman so superior to all common weaknesses as we know you to be.

MRS LUTESTRING. I may have reasons which have nothing to do with common weaknesses, Mr Chief Secretary. I hope you will respect them.

CONFUCIUS [*after bowing to her in assent*] I will now put my question. Have you, Mr Archbishop, any ground for assuming, as you seem to do, that what has happened to you has not happened to other people as well?

BURGE-LUBIN. Yes, by George! I never thought of that.

THE ARCHBISHOP. I have never met any case but my own.

CONFUCIUS. How do you know?

THE ARCHBISHOP. Well, no one has ever told me that they were in this extraordinary position.

CONFUCIUS. That proves nothing. Did you ever tell anybody that you were in it? You never told us. Why did you never tell us?

THE ARCHBISHOP. I am surprised at the question, coming from so astute a mind as yours, Mr Secretary. When you reach the age I reached before I discovered what was happening to me, I was old enough to know and fear the ferocious hatred with which human animals, like all other animals, turn upon any unhappy individual who has the misfortune to be unlike themselves in every respect: to be unnatural, as they call it. You will still find, among the tales of that twentieth-century classic, Wells, a story of a race of men who grew twice as big as their fellows, and another story of a man who fell into the hands of a race of blind men. The big people had to fight the little people for their lives; and the man with eyes would have had his eyes put out by the blind had he not fled to the desert, where he perished miserably. Wells's teaching, on that and other matters, was not lost on me. By the way, he lent me five pounds once which I never repaid; and it still troubles my conscience.

CONFUCIUS. And were you the only reader of Wells?

If there were others like you, had they not the same reason for keeping the secret?

THE ARCHBISHOP. That is true. But I should know. You short-lived people are so childish. If I met a man of my own age I should recognize him at once. I have never done so.

MRS LUTESTRING. Would you recognize a woman of your age, do you think?

THE ARCHBISHOP. I— [*He stops and turns upon her with a searching look, startled by the suggestion and the suspicion it rouses*].

MRS LUTESTRING. What is your age, Mr Archbishop?

BURGE-LUBIN. Two hundred and eighty-three, he says. That is his little joke. Do you know, Mrs Lutestring, he had almost talked us into believing him when you came in and cleared the air with your robust common sense.

MRS LUTESTRING. Do you really feel that, Mr President? I hear the note of breezy assertion in your voice. I miss the note of conviction.

BURGE-LUBIN [*jumping up*] Look here. Let us stop talking damned nonsense. I dont wish to be disagreeable; but it's getting on my nerves. The best joke wont bear being pushed beyond a certain point. That point has been reached. I—I'm rather busy this morning. We all have our hands pretty full. Confucius here will tell you that I have a heavy day before me.

BARNABAS. Have you anything more important than this thing, if it's true?

BURGE-LUBIN. Oh, if, if, if it's true! But it isnt true.

BARNABAS. Have you anything at all to do?

BURGE-LUBIN. Anything to do! Have you forgotten, Barnabas, that I happen to be President, and that the weight of the entire public business of this country is on my shoulders?

BARNABAS. Has he anything to do, Confucius?

CONFUCIUS. He has to be President.

BARNABAS. That means he has nothing to do.

BURGE-LUBIN [*sulkily*] Very well, Barnabas. Go on making a fool of yourself. [*He sits down*]. Go on.

BARNABAS. I am not going to leave this room until we get to the bottom of this swindle.

MRS LUTESTRING [*turning with deadly gravity on the Accountant General*] This what, did you say?

CONFUCIUS. These expressions cannot be sustained. You obscure the discussion in using them.

BARNABAS [*glad to escape from her gaze by addressing Confucius*] Well, this unnatural horror. Will that satisfy you?

CONFUCIUS. That is in order. But we do not commit ourselves to the implications of the word horror.

THE ARCHBISHOP. By the word horror the Accountant General means only something unusual.

CONFUCIUS. I notice that the honorable Domestic Minister, on learning the advanced age of the venerable prelate, shews no sign of surprise or incredulity.

BURGE-LUBIN. She doesnt take it seriously. Who would? Eh, Mrs Lutestring?

MRS LUTESTRING. I take it very seriously indeed, Mr President. I see now that I was not mistaken at first. I have met the Archbishop before.

THE ARCHBISHOP. I felt sure of it. This vision of a door opening to me, and a woman's face welcoming me, must be a reminiscence of something that really happened; though I see it now as an angel opening the gate of heaven.

MRS LUTESTRING. Or a parlormaid opening the door of the house of the young woman you were in love with?

THE ARCHBISHOP [*making a wry face*] Is that the reality? How these things grow in our imagination! But may I say, Mrs Lutestring, that the transfiguration of a parlormaid to an angel is not more amazing than her transfiguration to the very dignified and able Domestic Minister I am addressing. I recognize the angel in you. Frankly, I do not recognize the parlormaid.

BURGE-LUBIN. Whats a parlormaid?

MRS LUTESTRING. An extinct species. A woman in a black dress and white apron, who opened the house door when people knocked or rang, and was either your tyrant or your slave. I was a parlormaid in the house of one of the Accountant General's remote ancestors. [*To Confucius*] You asked me my age, Mr Chief Secretary, I am two hundred and seventy-four.

BURGE-LUBIN [*gallantly*] You dont look it. You really dont look it.

MRS LUTESTRING [*turning her face gravely towards him*] Look again, Mr President.

BURGE-LUBIN [*looking at her bravely until the smile fades from his face, and he suddenly covers his eyes with his hands*] Yes: you do look it. I am convinced. It's true. Now call up the Lunatic Asylum, Confucius; and tell them to send an ambulance for me.

MRS LUTESTRING [*to the Archbishop*] Why have you given away your secret? our secret?

THE ARCHBISHOP. They found it out. The cinema records betrayed me. But I never dreamt that there were others. Did you?

MRS LUTESTRING. I knew one other. She was a cook. She grew tired, and killed herself.

THE ARCHBISHOP. Dear me! However, her death simplifies the situation, as I have been able to convince these gentlemen that the matter had better go no further.

MRS LUTESTRING. What! When the President knows! It will be all over the place before the end of the week.

BURGE-LUBIN [*injured*] Really, Mrs Lutestring! You speak as if I were a notoriously indiscreet person. Barnabas: have I such a reputation?

BARNABAS [*resignedly*] It cant be helped. It's constitutional.

CONFUCIUS. It is utterly unconstitutional. But, as you say, it cannot be helped.

BURGE-LUBIN [*solemnly*] I deny that a secret of State has ever passed my lips—except perhaps to the Minister of Health, who is discretion personified. People think, because she is a negress—

MRS LUTESTRING. It does not matter much now. Once, it would have mattered a great deal. But my children are all dead.

THE ARCHBISHOP. Yes: the children must have been a terrible difficulty. Fortunately for me, I had none.

MRS LUTESTRING. There was one daughter who was the child of my very heart. Some years after my first drowning I learnt that she had lost her sight. I went to her. She was an old woman of ninety-six, blind. She asked me to sit and talk with her because my voice was like the voice of her dead mother.

BURGE-LUBIN. The complications must be frightful. Really I hardly know whether I do want to live much longer than other people.

MRS LUTESTRING. You can always kill yourself, as cook did; but that was influenza. Long life is complicated, and even terrible; but it is glorious all the same. I would no more change places with an ordinary woman than with a mayfly that lives only a day.

THE ARCHBISHOP. What set you thinking of it first?

MRS LUTESTRING. Conrad Barnabas's book. Your wife told me it was more wonderful than Napoleon's Book of Fate and Old Moore's Almanac, which cook and I used to read. I was very ignorant: it did not seem so impossible to me as to an educated woman. Yet I forgot all about it, and married and drudged as a poor man's wife, and brought up children, and looked twenty years older than I really was, until one day, long after my husband died and my children were out in the world working for themselves, I noticed that I looked twenty years younger than I really was. The truth came to me in a flash.

BURGE-LUBIN. An amazing moment. Your feelings must have been beyond description. What was your first thought?

MRS LUTESTRING. Pure terror. I saw that the little money I had laid up would not last, and that I must go out and work again. They had things called Old Age Pensions then: miserable pittances for worn-out old laborers to die on. I thought I should be found out if I went on drawing it too long. The horror of facing another lifetime of drudgery, of missing my hard-earned rest and losing my poor little savings, drove everything else out of my mind. You people nowadays can have no conception of the dread of poverty that hung over us then, or of the utter tiredness of forty years' unending overwork and striving to make a shilling do the work of a pound.

THE ARCHBISHOP. I wonder you did not kill yourself. I often wonder why the poor in those evil old times did not kill themselves. They did not even kill other people.

MRS LUTESTRING. You never kill yourself, because

you always may as well wait until tomorrow. And you have not energy nor conviction enough to kill the others. Besides, how can you blame them when you would do as they do if you were in their place?

BURGE-LUBIN. Devilish poor consolation, that.

MRS LUTESTRING. There were other consolations in those days for people like me. We drank preparations of alcohol to relieve the strain of living and give us an artificial happiness.

| BURGE-LUBIN | [*all together,* | Alcohol! |
| CONFUCIUS | *making* | Pfff. . . .! |
| BARNABAS | *wry faces*] | Disgusting. |

MRS LUTESTRING. A little alcohol would improve your temper and manners, and make you much easier to live with, Mr Accountant General.

BURGE-LUBIN [*laughing*] By George, I believe you! Try it, Barnabas.

MRS LUTESTRING. You, Mr President, were born intoxicated with your own well-fed natural exuberance. You cannot imagine what alcohol was to an underfed poor woman. I had carefully arranged my little savings so that I could get drunk, as we called it, once a week; and my only pleasure was looking forward to that poor little debauch. That is what saved me from suicide. I could not bear to miss my next carouse. But when I stopped working, and lived on my pension, the fatigue of my life's drudgery began to wear off, because, you see, I was not really old. I recuperated. I looked younger and younger. And at last I was rested enough to have courage and strength to begin life again. Besides, political changes were making it easier: life was a little better worth living for the nine-tenths of the people who used to be mere drudges. After that, I never turned back nor faltered. My only regret now is that I shall die when

I am three hundred or thereabouts. There was only one thing that made life hard; and that is gone now.

CONFUCIUS. May we ask what that was?

MRS LUTESTRING. Perhaps you will all be offended if I tell you.

BURGE-LUBIN. Offended! My dear lady: do you suppose, after such a stupendous revelation, that anything short of a blow from a sledge-hammer could produce the smallest impression on any of us?

MRS LUTESTRING. Well, you see, it has been so hard on me never to meet a grown-up person. You are all such children. And I never was very fond of children, except that one girl who woke up the mother passion in me. I have been very lonely sometimes.

BURGE-LUBIN [*again gallant*] But surely, Mrs Lutestring, that has been your own fault. If I may say so, a lady of your attractions need never have been lonely.

MRS LUTESTRING. Why?

BURGE-LUBIN. Why! Well—. Well, er—. Well, er er—. Well! [*he gives it up*].

THE ARCHBISHOP. He means that you might have married. Curious, how little they understand our position.

MRS LUTESTRING. I did marry. I married again on my hundred and first birthday. But of course I had to marry an elderly man: a man over sixty. He was a great painter. On his deathbed he said to me "It has taken me fifty years to learn my trade, and to paint all the foolish pictures a man must paint and get rid of before he comes through them to the great things he ought to paint. And now that my foot is at last on the threshold of the temple I find that it is also the threshold of my tomb." That man would have been the greatest painter of all time if he could have lived as long as I. I saw him die of old age whilst he was still, as he said himself, a gentleman amateur, like all modern painters.

BURGE-LUBIN. But why had you to marry an elderly man? Why not marry a young one? or shall I say a middle-aged one? If my own affections were not already engaged; and if, to tell the truth, I were not a little afraid of you—for you are a very superior woman, as we all acknowledge—I should esteem myself happy in—er—er—

MRS LUTESTRING. Mr President: have you ever tried to take advantage of the innocence of a little child for the gratification of your senses?

BURGE-LUBIN. Oh! Oh!! Hang it all, what do you take me for? What right have you to ask me such a question?

MRS LUTESTRING. I am at present in my two hundred and seventy-fifth year. You suggest that I should take advantage of the innocence of a child of thirty, and marry it.

THE ARCHBISHOP. Can you shortlived people not understand that as the confusion and immaturity and primitive animalism in which we live for the first hundred years of our life is worse in this matter of sex than in any other, you are intolerable to us in that relation?

BURGE-LUBIN. Do you mean to say, Mrs Lutestring, that you regard me as a child?

MRS LUTESTRING. Do you expect me to regard you as a completed soul? Oh, you may well be afraid of me. There are moments when your levity, your ingratitude, your shallow jollity, make my gorge rise so against you that if I could not remind myself that you are a child I should be tempted to doubt your right to live at all.

[ 475 ]

CONFUCIUS. Do you grudge us the few years we have? you who have three hundred!

BURGE-LUBIN. You accuse me of levity! Must I remind you, madam, that I am the President, and that you are only the head of a department?

BARNABAS. Ingratitude too! You draw a pension for three hundred years when we owe you only seventy-eight; and you call us ungrateful!

MRS LUTESTRING. I do. When I think of the blessings that have been showered on you, and contrast them with the poverty! the humiliations! the anxieties! the heartbreak! the insolence and tyranny that were the daily lot of mankind when I was learning to suffer instead of learning to live! when I see how lightly you take it all! how you quarrel over the crumpled leaves in your beds of roses! how you are so dainty about your work that unless it is made either interesting or delightful to you you leave it to negresses and Chinamen, I ask myself whether even three hundred years of thought and experience can save you from being superseded by the Power that created you and put you on your trial.

BURGE-LUBIN. My dear lady: our Chinese and colored friends are perfectly happy. They are twenty times better off here than they would be in China or Liberia. They do their work admirably; and in doing it they set us free for higher employments.

THE ARCHBISHOP [*who has caught the infection of her indignation*] What higher employments are you capable of? you that are superannuated at seventy and dead at eighty!

MRS LUTESTRING. You are not really doing higher work. You are supposed to make the decisions and give the orders; but the negresses and the Chinese make up your minds for you and tell you what orders to give, just as my brother, who was a sergeant in the Guards, used to prompt his officers in the old days. When I want to get anything done at the Health Ministry I do not come to you: I go to the black lady who has been the real president during your present term of office, or to Confucius, who goes on for ever while presidents come and presidents go.

BURGE-LUBIN. This is outrageous. This is treason to the white race. And let me tell you, madam, that I have never in my life met the Minister of Health, and that I protest against the vulgar color prejudice which disparages her great ability and her eminent services to the State. My relations with her are purely telephonic, gramophonic, photophonic, and, may I add, platonic.

THE ARCHBISHOP. There is no reason why you should be ashamed of them in any case, Mr President. But let us look at the position impersonally. Can you deny that what is happening is that the English people have become a Joint Stock Company admitting Asiatics and Africans as shareholders?

BARNABAS. Nothing like it. I know all about the old joint stock companies. The shareholders did no work.

THE ARCHBISHOP. That is true; but we, like them, get our dividends whether we work or not. We work partly because we know there would be no dividends if we did not, and partly because if we refuse we are regarded as mentally deficient and put into a lethal chamber. But in the twentieth century the idle shareholders were so rich, as it was called, that they had become the most intellectually lazy and fat-headed people on the face of the earth. There is a good deal of that fat still clinging to us.

BURGE-LUBIN. As President, I must not listen to

unpatriotic criticisms of our national character, Mr Archbishop.

THE ARCHBISHOP. As Archbishop, Mr President, it is my official duty to criticize the national character unsparingly. At the canonization of Saint Henrik Ibsen, you yourself unveiled the monument to him which bears on its pedestal the noble inscription, "I came not to call sinners, but the righteous, to repentance." The proof of what I say is that our routine work, and what may be called our ornamental and figure-head work, is being more and more sought after by the English; whilst the thinking, organizing, calculating, directing work is done by yellow brains, brown brains, and black brains, just as it was done in my early days by Jewish brains, Scottish brains, Italian brains, German brains. The only white men who still do serious work are those who, like the Accountant General, have no capacity for enjoyment, and no social gifts to make them welcome outside their offices.

BARNABAS. I had gifts enough to find you out, anyhow.

THE ARCHBISHOP. But not enough to grasp the significance of your discovery. If you were to kill me as I stand here, you would have to appoint an Indian to succeed me. I take precedence today not as an Englishman, but as a man with more than a century and a half of fully adult experience. We are letting all the power slip into the hands of the colored people. In another hundred years we shall be simply their household pets.

BURGE-LUBIN [reacting buoyantly] Not the least danger of it. I grant you we leave the most troublesome part of the labor of the nation to them. And a good job too: why should we drudge at it? But think of the activities of our leisure! Is there a jollier place on earth to live in than England out of office hours? And to whom do we owe that? To ourselves, not to the niggers. The nigger and the Chink are all right from Tuesday to Friday; but from Friday to Tuesday they are simply nowhere; and the real life of England is from Friday to Tuesday.

THE ARCHBISHOP. That is terribly true. In devising brainless amusements; in pursuing them with enormous vigor, and taking them with eager seriousness, our English people are the wonder of the world. They always were. And it is just as well; for otherwise their sensualities would become morbid and destroy them. What appals me is that their amusements should amuse them. They are the amusements of boys and girls. They are pardonable up to the age of fifty or sixty: after that they are ridiculous. I tell you, what is wrong with us is that we are a non-adult race; and the Irish and the Scots, and the niggers and Chinks, as you call them, though their lifetime is as short as ours, or shorter, yet do somehow contrive to grow up a little before they die. We die in boyhood: the maturity that should make us the greatest of all nations lies beyond the grave for us. Either we shall go under as greybeards with golf clubs in our hands, or we must will to live longer.

MRS LUTESTRING. Yes: that is it. I could not have expressed it in words; but you have expressed it for me. I felt, even when I was an ignorant domestic slave, that we had the possibility of becoming a great nation within us; but our faults and follies drove me to cynical hopelessness. We all ended then like that. It is the highest creatures who take the longest to mature, and are the most helpless during their immaturity. I know now that it took me a whole century to grow up. I began my serious life when I was a hundred and twenty. Asiatics cannot control me: I am not a child in their hands, as you are, Mr President. Neither, I am sure, is the Archbishop. They respect me. You are not grown up enough even for that, though you were kind enough to say that I frighten you.

BURGE-LUBIN. Honestly, you do. And will you think me very rude if I say that if I must choose between a white woman old enough to be my great-grandmother and a black woman of my own age, I shall probably find the black woman more sympathetic?

MRS LUTESTRING. And more attractive in color, perhaps?

BURGE-LUBIN. Yes. Since you ask me, more—well, not more attractive: I do not deny that you have an excellent appearance—but I will say, richer. More Venetian. Tropical. "The shadowed livery of the burnished sun."

MRS LUTESTRING. Our women, and their favorite story writers, begin already to talk about men with golden complexions.

CONFUCIUS [*expanding into a smile all across both face and body*]. A-a-a-a——h!

BURGE-LUBIN. Well, what of it, madam? Have you read a very interesting book by the librarian of the Biological Society suggesting that the future of the world lies with the Mulatto?

MRS LUTESTRING [*rising*] Mr Archbishop: if the white race is to be saved, our destiny is apparent.

THE ARCHBISHOP. Yes: our duty is pretty clear.

MRS LUTESTRING. Have you time to come home with me and discuss the matter?

THE ARCHBISHOP [*rising*] With pleasure.

BARNABAS [*rising also and rushing past Mrs Lutestring to the door, where he turns to bar her way*] No you dont. Burge: you understand, dont you?

BURGE-LUBIN. No. What is it?

BARNABAS. These two are going to marry.

BURGE-LUBIN. Why shouldnt they, if they want to?

BARNABAS. They dont want to. They will do it in cold blood because their children will live three hundred years. It mustnt be allowed.

CONFUCIUS. You cannot prevent it. There is no law that gives you power to interfere with them.

BARNABAS. If they force me to it I will obtain legislation against marriages above the age of seventy-eight.

THE ARCHBISHOP. There is not time for that before we are married, Mr Accountant General. Be good enough to get out of the lady's way.

BARNABAS. There is time to send the lady to the lethal chamber before anything comes of your marriage. Dont forget that.

MRS LUTESTRING. What nonsense, Mr Accountant General! Good afternoon, Mr President. Good afternoon, Mr Chief Secretary. [*They rise and acknowledge her salutation with bows. She walks straight at the Accountant General, who instinctively shrinks out of her way as she leaves the room*].

THE ARCHBISHOP. I am surprised at you, Mr Barnabas. Your tone was like an echo from the Dark Ages. [*He follows the Domestic Minister*].

*Confucius, shakes his head and clucking with his tongue in deprecation of this painful episode, moves to the chair just vacated by the Archbishop and stands behind it with folded palms, looking at the President. The Accountant General shakes his fist after the departed visitors, and bursts into savage abuse of them.*

BARNABAS. Thieves! Cursed thieves! Vampires! What are you going to do, Burge?

BURGE-LUBIN. Do?

BARNABAS. Yes, do. There must be dozens of these people in existence. Are you going to let them do what the two who have just left us mean to do, and crowd us off the face of the earth?

BURGE-LUBIN [*sitting down*] Oh, come, Barnabas! What harm are they doing? Arnt you interested in them? Dont you like them?

BARNABAS. Like them! I hate them. They are monsters, unnatural monsters. They are poison to me.

BURGE-LUBIN. What possible objection can there be to their living as long as they can? It does not shorten our lives, does it?

BARNABAS. If I have to die when I am seventy-eight, I dont see why another man should be privileged to live to be two hundred and seventy-eight. It does shorten my life, relatively. It makes us ridiculous. If they grew to be twelve feet high they would make us all dwarfs. They talked to us as if we were children. There is no love lost between us: their hatred of us came out soon enough. You heard what the woman said, and how the Archbishop backed her up?

BURGE-LUBIN. But what can we do to them?

BARNABAS. Kill them.

BURGE-LUBIN. Nonsense!

BARNABAS. Lock them up. Sterilize them somehow, anyhow.

BURGE-LUBIN. But what reason could we give?

BARNABAS. What reason can you give for killing a snake? Nature tells you to do it.

BURGE-LUBIN. My dear Barnabas, you are out of your mind.

[ 482 ]

BARNABAS. Havnt you said that once too often already this morning?

BURGE-LUBIN. I dont believe you will carry a single soul with you.

BARNABAS. I understand. I know you. You think you are one of them.

CONFUCIUS. Mr Accountant General: you may be one of them.

BARNABAS. How dare you accuse me of such a thing? I am an honest man, not a monster. I won my place in public life by demonstrating that the true expectation of human life is seventy-eight point six. And I will resist any attempt to alter or upset it to the last drop of my blood if need be.

BURGE-LUBIN. Oh, tut tut! Come, come! Pull yourself together. How can you, a descendant of the great Conrad Barnabas, the man who is still remembered by his masterly Biography of a Black Beetle, be so absurd?

BARNABAS. You had better go and write the autobiography of a jackass. I am going to raise the country against this horror, and against you, if you shew the slightest sign of weakness about it.

CONFUCIUS [*very impressively*] You will regret it if you do.

BARNABAS. What is to make me regret it?

CONFUCIUS. Every mortal man and woman in the community will begin to count on living for three centuries. Things will happen which you do not foresee: terrible things. The family will dissolve: parents and children will be no longer the old and the young: brothers and sisters will meet as strangers after a hundred years of separation: the ties of blood will lose their innocence. The imaginations of men, let loose over the possibilities of three centuries of life,

[ 483 ]

will drive them mad and wreck human society. This discovery must be kept a dead secret. [*He sits down*].

BARNABAS. And if I refuse to keep the secret?

CONFUCIUS. I shall have you safe in a lunatic asylum the day after you blab.

BARNABAS. You forget that I can produce the Archbishop to prove my statement.

CONFUCIUS. So can I. Which of us do you think he will support when I explain to him that your object in revealing his age is to get him killed?

BARNABAS [*desperate*] Burge: are you going to back up this yellow abomination against me? Are we public men and members of the Government? or are we damned blackguards?

CONFUCIUS [*unmoved*] Have you ever known a public man who was not what vituperative people called a damned blackguard when some inconsiderate person wanted to tell the public more than was good for it?

BARNABAS. Hold your tongue, you insolent heathen. Burge: I spoke to you.

BURGE-LUBIN. Well, you know, my dear Barnabas, Confucius is a very long-headed chap. I see his point.

BARNABAS. Do you? Then let me tell you that, except officially, I will never speak to you again. Do you hear?

BURGE-LUBIN [*cheerfully*] You will. You will.

BARNABAS. And dont you ever dare speak to me again. Do you hear? [*He turns to the door*].

BURGE-LUBIN. I will. I will. Goodbye, Barnabas. God bless you.

BARNABAS. May you live forever, and be the laughing-stock of the whole world! [*he dashes out in a fury*].

BURGE-LUBIN [*laughing indulgently*] He will keep the secret all right. I know Barnabas. You neednt worry.

CONFUCIUS [*troubled and grave*] There are no secrets except the secrets that keep themselves. Consider. There are those films at the Record Office. We have no power to prevent the Master of the Records from publishing this discovery made in his department. We cannot silence the American—who can silence an American?—nor the people who were there today to receive him. Fortunately, a film can prove nothing but a resemblance.

BURGE-LUBIN. Thats very true. After all, the whole thing is confounded nonsense, isnt it?

CONFUCIUS [*raising his head to look at him*] You have decided not to believe it now that you realize its inconveniences. That is the English method. It may not work in this case.

BURGE-LUBIN. English be hanged! It's common sense. You know, those two people got us hypnotized: not a doubt of it. They must have been kidding us. They were, werent they?

CONFUCIUS. You looked into that woman's face; and you believed.

BURGE-LUBIN. Just so. Thats where she had me. I shouldnt have believed her a bit if she'd turned her back to me.

CONFUCIUS [*shakes his head slowly and repeatedly*] ? ? ?

BURGE-LUBIN. You really think—? [*he hesitates*].

CONFUCIUS. The Archbishop has always been a puzzle to me. Ever since I learnt to distinguish between one English face and another I have noticed what the woman pointed out: that the English face is not an adult face, just as the English mind is not an adult mind.

BURGE-LUBIN. Stow it, John Chinaman. If ever there was a race divinely appointed to take charge of the non-adult races and guide them and train them

[ 485 ]

and keep them out of mischief until they grow up to be capable of adopting our institutions, that race is the English race. It is the only race in the world that has that characteristic. Now!

CONFUCIUS. That is the fancy of a child nursing a doll. But it is ten times more childish of you to dispute the highest compliment ever paid to you.

BURGE-LUBIN. You call it a compliment to class us as grown-up children.

CONFUCIUS. Not grown-up children, children at fifty, sixty, seventy. Your maturity is so late that you never attain to it. You have to be governed by races which are mature at forty. That means that you are potentially the most highly developed race on earth, and would be actually the greatest if you could live long enough to attain to maturity.

BURGE-LUBIN [grasping the idea at last] By George, Confucius, youre right! I never thought of that. That explains everything. We are just a lot of schoolboys; theres no denying it. Talk to an Englishman about anything serious, and he listens to you curiously for a moment just as he listens to a chap playing classical music. Then he goes back to his marine golf, or motoring, or flying, or women, just like a bit of stretched elastic when you let it go. [Soaring to the height of his theme] Oh, youre quite right. We are only in our infancy. I ought to be in a perambulator, with a nurse shoving me along. It's true: it's absolutely true. But some day we'll grow up; and then, by Jingo! we'll shew em.

CONFUCIUS. The Archbishop is an adult. When I was a child I was dominated and intimidated by people whom I now know to have been weaker and sillier than I, because there was some mysterious quality in their mere age that overawed me. I confess

[ 486 ]

that, though I have kept up appearances, I have always been afraid of the Archbishop. It is this that convinced me. It was this in the woman's face that convinced you. Their new departure in the history of the race is no fraud. It does not even surprise me.

BURGE-LUBIN. Oh, come! Not surprise you! It's your pose never to be surprised at anything; but if you are not surprised at this you are not human.

CONFUCIUS. I am staggered, just as a man may be staggered by an explosion for which he has himself laid the charge and lighted the fuse. But I am not surprised, because, as a philosopher and a student of evolutionary biology, I have come to regard some such development as this as inevitable. If I had not thus prepared myself to be credulous, no mere evidence of films and well-told tales would have persuaded me to believe. As it is, I do believe.

BURGE-LUBIN. Well, that being settled, what the devil is to happen next? Whats the next move for us?

CONFUCIUS. We do not make the next move. The next move will be made by the Archbishop and the woman.

BURGE-LUBIN. Their marriage?

CONFUCIUS. More than that. They have made the momentous discovery that they are not alone in the world.

BURGE-LUBIN. You think there are others?

CONFUCIUS. There must be many others. Each of them believes that he or she is the only one to whom the miracle has happened. But the Archbishop knows better now. He will advertize in terms which only the longlived people will understand. He will bring them together and organize them. They will hasten from all parts of the earth. They will become a great Power.

BURGE-LUBIN [*a little alarmed*] I say, will they? I suppose they will. I wonder is Barnabas right after all? Ought we to allow it?

CONFUCIUS. Nothing that we can do will stop it. We cannot in our souls really want to stop it: the vital force that has produced this change would paralyse our opposition to it, if we were mad enough to oppose. But we will not oppose. You and I may be of the elect, too.

BURGE-LUBIN. Yes: thats what gets us every time. What the deuce ought we to do? Something must be done about it, you know.

CONFUCIUS. Let us sit still, and meditate in silence on the vistas before us.

BURGE-LUBIN. By George, I believe youre right. Let us.

*They sit meditating, the Chinaman naturally, the President with visible effort and intensity. He is positively glaring into the future when the voice of the Negress is heard.*

THE NEGRESS. Mr President.

BURGE-LUBIN [*joyfully*] Yes. [*Taking up a peg*] Are you at home?

THE NEGRESS. No. Omega, zero, x squared.

*The President rapidly puts the peg in the switchboard; works the dial; and presses the button. The screen becomes transparent; and the Negress, brilliantly dressed, appears on what looks like the bridge of a steam yacht in glorious sea weather. The installation with which she is communicating is beside the binnacle.*

CONFUCIUS [*looking round, and recoiling with a shriek of disgust*] Ach! Avaunt! Avaunt! [*He rushes from the room*].

BURGE-LUBIN. What part of the coast is that?

THE NEGRESS. Fishguard Bay. Why not run over and

join me for the afternoon? I am disposed to be approachable at last.

BURGE-LUBIN. But Fishguard! Two hundred and seventy miles!

THE NEGRESS. There is a lightning express on the Irish Air Service at half-past sixteen. They will drop you by a parachute in the bay. The dip will do you good. I will pick you up and dry you and give you a first-rate time.

BURGE-LUBIN. Delightful. But a little risky, isnt it?

THE NEGRESS. Risky! I thought you were afraid of nothing.

BURGE-LUBIN. I am not exactly afraid; but——

THE NEGRESS [*offended*] But you think it is not good enough. Very well [*she raises her hand to take the peg out of her switchboard*].

BURGE-LUBIN [*imploringly*] No: stop: let me explain: hold the line just one moment. Oh, please.

THE NEGRESS [*waiting with her hand poised over the peg*] Well?

BURGE-LUBIN. The fact is, I have been behaving very recklessly for some time past under the impression that my life would be so short that it was not worth bothering about. But I have just learnt that I may live—well, much longer than I expected. I am sure your good sense will tell you that this alters the case. I——

THE NEGRESS [*with suppressed rage*] Oh, quite. Pray dont risk your precious life on my account. Sorry for troubling you. Goodbye. [*She snatches out her peg and vanishes*].

BURGE-LUBIN [*urgently*] No: please hold on. I can convince you—— [*a loud buzz-uzz-uzz*]. Engaged! Who is she calling up now? [*He presses the button and calls*] The Chief Secretary. Say I want to see him again, just for a moment.

CONFUCIUS'S VOICE. Is the woman gone?

BURGE-LUBIN. Yes, yes: it's all right. Just a moment, if— [*Confucius returns*] Confucius: I have some important business at Fishguard. The Irish Air Service can drop me in the bay by parachute. I suppose it's quite safe, isnt it?

CONFUCIUS. Nothing is quite safe. The air service is as safe as any other travelling service. The parachute is safe. But the water is not safe.

BURGE-LUBIN. Why? They will give me an unsinkable tunic, wont they?

CONFUCIUS. You will not sink; but the sea is very cold. You may get rheumatism for life.

BURGE-LUBIN. For life! That settles it: I wont risk it.

CONFUCIUS. Good. You have at last become prudent: you are no longer what you call a sportsman: you are a sensible coward, almost a grown-up man. I congratulate you.

BURGE-LUBIN [*resolutely*] Coward or no coward, I will not face three hundred years of rheumatism for any woman that ever was born. [*He rises and goes to the rack for his fillet*] I am going home. [*He cocks the fillet rakishly*] Good evening.

CONFUCIUS. So early? If the Minister of Health rings you up, what shall I tell her?

BURGE-LUBIN. Tell her to go to the devil. [*He goes out*].

CONFUCIUS [*shaking his head, shocked at the President's impoliteness*] No. No, no, no, no, no. Oh, these English! these crude young civilizations! Their manners! Hogs. Hogs.

# PART IV

## TRAGEDY OF AN
## ELDERLY GENTLEMAN

# [ ACT I ]

---

*Burrin pier on the south shore of Galway Bay in Ireland, a region of stone-capped hills and granite fields. It is a fine summer day in the year 3000 A.D. On an ancient stone stump, about three feet thick and three feet high, used for securing ships by ropes to the shore, and called a bollard or holdfast, an elderly gentleman sits facing the land, with his head bowed and his face in his hands, sobbing. His sunburnt skin contrasts with his white whiskers and eyebrows. He wears a black frock-coat, a white waistcoat, lavender trousers, a brilliant silk cravat with a jewelled pin stuck in it, a tall hat of grey felt, and patent leather boots with white spats. His starched linen cuffs protrude from his coat sleeves; and his collar, also of starched white linen, is Gladstonian. On his right, three or four full sacks, lying side by side on the flags, suggest that the pier, unlike many remote Irish piers, is occasionally useful as well as romantic. On his left, behind him, a flight of stone steps descends out of sight to the sea level.*

*A woman in a silk tunic and sandals, wearing little else except a cap with the number 2 on it in gold, comes up the steps from the sea, and stares in astonishment at the sobbing man. Her age cannot be guessed: her face is firm and chiselled like a young face; but her expression is unyouthful in its severity and determination.*

---

THE WOMAN. What is the matter?

*The elderly gentleman looks up; hastily pulls himself together; takes out a silk handkerchief and dries his tears lightly with a brave attempt to smile through them; and tries to rise gallantly, but sinks back.*

THE WOMAN. Do you need assistance?

THE ELDERLY GENTLEMAN. No. Thank you very much. No. Nothing. The heat. [*He punctuates with sniffs, and dabs with his handkerchief at his eyes and nose*]. Hay fever.

THE WOMAN. You are a foreigner, are you not?

THE ELDERLY GENTLEMAN. No. You must not regard me as a foreigner. I am a Briton.

THE WOMAN. You come from some part of the British Commonwealth?

THE ELDERLY GENTLEMAN [*amiably pompous*] From its capital, madam.

THE WOMAN. From Baghdad?

THE ELDERLY GENTLEMAN. Yes. You may not be aware, madam, that these islands were once the centre of the British Commonwealth, during a period now known as The Exile. They were its headquarters a thousand years ago. Few people know this interesting circumstance now; but I assure you it is true. I have come here on a pious pilgrimage to one of the numerous lands of my fathers. We are of the same stock, you and I. Blood is thicker than water. We are cousins.

THE WOMAN. I do not understand. You say you have come here on a pious pilgrimage. Is that some new means of transport?

THE ELDERLY GENTLEMAN [*again shewing signs of distress*] I find it very difficult to make myself understood here. I was not referring to a machine, but to a—a—a sentimental journey.

[ 492 ]

THE WOMAN. I am afraid I am as much in the dark as before. You said also that blood is thicker than water. No doubt it is; but what of it?

THE ELDERLY GENTLEMAN. Its meaning is obvious.

THE WOMAN. Perfectly. But I assure you I am quite aware that blood is thicker than water.

THE ELDERLY GENTLEMAN [*sniffing: almost in tears again*] We will leave it at that, madam.

THE WOMAN [*going nearer to him and scrutinizing him with some concern*] I am afraid you are not well. Were you not warned that it is dangerous for shortlived people to come to this country? There is a deadly disease called discouragement, against which short-lived people have to take very strict precautions. Intercourse with us puts too great a strain on them.

THE ELDERLY GENTLEMAN [*pulling himself together huffily*] It has no effect on me, madam. I fear my conversation does not interest you. If not, the remedy is in your own hands.

THE WOMAN [*looking at her hands, and then looking inquiringly at him*] Where?

THE ELDERLY GENTLEMAN [*breaking down*] Oh, this is dreadful. No understanding, no intelligence, no sympathy— [*his sobs choke him*].

THE WOMAN. You see, you are ill.

THE ELDERLY GENTLEMAN [*nerved by indignation*] I am not ill. I have never had a day's illness in my life.

THE WOMAN. May I advise you?

THE ELDERLY GENTLEMAN. I have no need of a lady doctor, thank you, madam.

THE WOMAN [*shaking her head*] I am afraid I do not understand. I said nothing about a butterfly.

THE ELDERLY GENTLEMAN. Well, *I* said nothing about a butterfly.

[ 493 ]

THE WOMAN. You spoke of a lady doctor. The word is known here only as the name of a butterfly.

THE ELDERLY GENTLEMAN [*insanely*] I give up. I can bear this no longer. It is easier to go out of my mind at once. [*He rises and dances about, singing*]

> I'd be a butterfly, born in a bower,
> Making apple dumplings without any flour.

THE WOMAN [*smiling gravely*] It must be at least a hundred and fifty years since I last laughed. But if you do that any more I shall certainly break out like a primary of sixty. Your dress is so extraordinarily ridiculous.

THE ELDERLY GENTLEMAN [*halting abruptly in his antics*] My dress ridiculous! I may not be dressed like a Foreign Office clerk; but my clothes are perfectly in fashion in my native metropolis, where yours —pardon my saying so—would be considered extremely unusual and hardly decent.

THE WOMAN. Decent? There is no such word in our language. What does it mean?

THE ELDERLY GENTLEMAN. It would not be decent for me to explain. Decency cannot be discussed without indecency.

THE WOMAN. I cannot understand you at all. I fear you have not been observing the rules laid down for shortlived visitors.

THE ELDERLY GENTLEMAN. Surely, madam, they do not apply to persons of my age and standing. I am not a child, not an agricultural laborer.

THE WOMAN [*severely*] They apply to you very strictly. You are expected to confine yourself to the society of children under sixty. You are absolutely forbidden to approach fully adult natives under any circumstances. You cannot converse with persons of my

[ 494 ]

age for long without bringing on a dangerous attack of discouragement. Do you realize that you are already shewing grave symptoms of that very distressing and usually fatal complaint?

THE ELDERLY GENTLEMAN. Certainly not, madam. I am fortunately in no danger of contracting it. I am quite accustomed to converse intimately and at the greatest length with the most distinguished persons. If you cannot discriminate between hay fever and imbecility, I can only say that your advanced years carry with them the inevitable penalty of dotage.

THE WOMAN. I am one of the guardians of this district; and I am responsible for your welfare—

THE ELDERLY GENTLEMAN. The Guardians! Do you take me for a pauper?

THE WOMAN. I do not know what a pauper is. You must tell me who you are, if it is possible for you to express yourself intelligibly—

THE ELDERLY GENTLEMAN [*snorts indignantly*]!

THE WOMAN [*continuing*]—and why you are wandering here alone without a nurse.

THE ELDERLY GENTLEMAN [*outraged*] Nurse!

THE WOMAN. Shortlived visitors are not allowed to go about here without nurses. Do you not know that rules are meant to be kept?

THE ELDERLY GENTLEMAN. By the lower classes, no doubt. But to persons in my position there are certain courtesies which are never denied by well-bred people; and—

THE WOMAN. There are only two human classes here: the shortlived and the normal. The rules apply to the shortlived, and are for their own protection. Now tell me at once who you are.

THE ELDERLY GENTLEMAN [*impressively*] Madam, I am a retired gentleman, formerly Chairman of the

All-British Synthetic Egg and Vegetable Cheese Trust in Baghdad, and now President of the British Historical and Archæological Society, and a Vice-President of the Travellers' Club.

THE WOMAN. All that does not matter.

THE ELDERLY GENTLEMAN [*again snorting*] Hm! Indeed!

THE WOMAN. Have you been sent here to make your mind flexible?

THE ELDERLY GENTLEMAN. What an extraordinary question! Pray do you find my mind noticeably stiff?

THE WOMAN. Perhaps you do not know that you are on the west coast of Ireland, and that it is the practice among natives of the Eastern Island to spend some years here to acquire mental flexibility. The climate has that effect.

THE ELDERLY GENTLEMAN [*haughtily*] I was born, not in the Eastern Island, but, thank God, in dear old British Baghdad; and I am not in need of a mental health resort.

THE WOMAN. Then why are you here?

THE ELDERLY GENTLEMAN. Am I trespassing? I was not aware of it.

THE WOMAN. Trespassing? I do not understand the word.

THE ELDERLY GENTLEMAN. Is this land private property? If so, I make no claim. I proffer a shilling in satisfaction of damage (if any), and am ready to withdraw if you will be good enough to shew me the nearest way. [*He offers her a shilling*].

THE WOMAN [*taking it and examining it without much interest*] I do not understand a single word of what you have just said.

THE ELDERLY GENTLEMAN. I am speaking the plainest English. Are you the landlord?

THE WOMAN [*shaking her head*] There is a tradition in this part of the country of an animal with a name like that. It used to be hunted and shot in the barbarous ages. It is quite extinct now.

THE ELDERLY GENTLEMAN [*breaking down again*] It is a dreadful thing to be in a country where nobody understands civilized institutions. [*He collapses on the bollard, struggling with his rising sobs*]. Excuse me. Hay fever.

THE WOMAN [*taking a tuning-fork from her girdle and holding it to her ear; then speaking into space on one note, like a chorister intoning a psalm*] Burrin Pier Galway please send someone to take charge of a discouraged shortliver who has escaped from his nurse male harmless babbles unintelligibly with moments of sense distressed hysterical foreign dress very funny has curious fringe of white sea-weed under his chin.

THE ELDERLY GENTLEMAN. This is a gross impertinence. An insult.

THE WOMAN [*replacing her tuning-fork and addressing the elderly gentleman*] These words mean nothing to me. In what capacity are you here? How did you obtain permission to visit us?

THE ELDERLY GENTLEMAN [*importantly*] Our Prime Minister, Mr Badger Bluebin, has come to consult the oracle. He is my son-in-law. We are accompanied by his wife and daughter: my daughter and granddaughter. I may mention that General Aufsteig, who is one of our party, is really the Emperor of Turania travelling incognito. I understand he has a question to put to the oracle informally. I have come solely to visit the country.

THE WOMAN. Why should you come to a place where you have no business?

THE ELDERLY GENTLEMAN. Great Heavens, madam,

can anything be more natural? I shall be the only member of the Travellers' Club who has set foot on these shores. Think of that! My position will be unique.

THE WOMAN. Is that an advantage? We have a person here who has lost both legs in an accident. His position is unique. But he would much rather be like everyone else.

THE ELDERLY GENTLEMAN. This is maddening. There is no analogy whatever between the two cases.

THE WOMAN. They are both unique.

THE ELDERLY GENTLEMAN. Conversation in this place seems to consist of ridiculous quibbles. I am heartily tired of them.

THE WOMAN. I conclude that your Travellers' Club is an assembly of persons who wish to be able to say that they have been in some place where nobody else has been.

THE ELDERLY GENTLEMAN. Of course if you wish to sneer at us—

THE WOMAN. What is sneer?

THE ELDERLY GENTLEMAN [*with a wild sob*] I shall drown myself.

*He makes desperately for the edge of the pier, but is confronted by a man with the number one on his cap, who comes up the steps and intercepts him. He is dressed like the woman, but a slight moustache proclaims his sex.*

THE MAN [*to the elderly gentleman*] Ah, here you are. I shall really have to put a collar and lead on you if you persist in giving me the slip like this.

THE WOMAN. Are you this stranger's nurse?

THE MAN. Yes. I am very tired of him. If I take my eyes off him for a moment, he runs away and talks to everybody.

THE WOMAN [*after taking out her tuning-fork and*

*sounding it, intones as before*] Burrin Pier. Wash out. [*She puts up the fork, and addresses the man*]. I sent a call for someone to take care of him. I have been trying to talk to him; but I can understand very little of what he says. You must take better care of him: he is badly discouraged already. If I can be of any further use, Fusima, Gort, will find me. [*She goes away*].

THE ELDERLY GENTLEMAN. Any further use! She has been of no use to me. She spoke to me without any introduction, like any improper female. And she has made off with my shilling.

THE MAN. Please speak slowly: I cannot follow. What is a shilling? What is an introduction? Improper female doesnt make sense.

THE ELDERLY GENTLEMAN. Nothing seems to make sense here. All I can tell you is that she was the most impenetrably stupid woman I have ever met in the whole course of my life.

THE MAN. That cannot be. She cannot appear stupid to you. She is a secondary, and getting on for a tertiary at that.

THE ELDERLY GENTLEMAN. What is a tertiary? Everybody here keeps talking to me about primaries and secondaries and tertiaries as if people were geological strata.

THE MAN. The primaries are in their first century. The secondaries are in their second century. I am still classed as a primary [*he points to his number*]; but I may almost call myself a secondary, as I shall be ninety-five next January. The tertiaries are in their third century. Did you not see the number two on her badge? She is an advanced secondary.

THE ELDERLY GENTLEMAN. That accounts for it. She is in her second childhood.

THE MAN. Her second childhood! She is in her fifth childhood.

THE ELDERLY GENTLEMAN [*again resorting to the bollard*] Oh! I cannot bear these unnatural arrangements.

THE MAN [*impatient and helpless*] You shouldnt have come among us. This is no place for you.

THE ELDERLY GENTLEMAN. No place for me! May I ask why? I am a Vice-President of the Travellers' Club. I have been everywhere: I hold the record in the Club for civilized countries.

THE MAN. What is a civilized country?

THE ELDERLY GENTLEMAN. It is—well, it is a civilized country. [*Desperately*] I dont know: I—I—I—I shall go mad if you keep on asking me to tell you things that everybody knows. Countries where you can travel comfortably. Where there are good hotels. Excuse me; but, though you say you are ninety-four, you are worse company than a child of five with your eternal questions. Why not call me Daddy at once?

THE MAN. I did not know your name was Daddy.

THE ELDERLY GENTLEMAN. My name is Joseph Popham Bolge Bluebin Barlow, O.M.

THE MAN. That is five men's names. Daddy is shorter. And O.M. will not do here. It is our name for certain wild creatures, descendants of the aboriginal inhabitants of this coast. They used to be called the O'Mulligans. We will stick to Daddy.

THE ELDERLY GENTLEMAN. People will think I am your father.

THE MAN [*shocked*] Sh-sh! People here never allude to such relationships. It is not quite delicate, is it? What does it matter whether you are my father or not?

[ 500 ]

THE ELDERLY GENTLEMAN. My worthy nonagenarian friend: your faculties are totally decayed. Could you not find me a guide of my own age?

THE MAN. A young person?

THE ELDERLY GENTLEMAN. Certainly not. I cannot go about with a young person.

THE MAN. Why?

THE ELDERLY GENTLEMAN. Why! Why!! Why!!! Have you no moral sense?

THE MAN. I shall have to give you up. I cannot understand you.

THE ELDERLY GENTLEMAN. But you meant a young woman, didnt you?

THE MAN. I meant simply somebody of your own age. What difference does it make whether the person is a man or a woman?

THE ELDERLY GENTLEMAN. I could not have believed in the existence of such scandalous insensibility to the elementary decencies of human intercourse.

THE MAN. What are decencies?

THE ELDERLY GENTLEMAN [shrieking] Everyone asks me that.

THE MAN [taking out a tuning-fork and using it as the woman did] Zozim on Burrin Pier to Zoo Ennistymon I have found the discouraged shortliver he has been talking to a secondary and is much worse I am too old he is asking for someone of his own age or younger come if you can. [He puts up his fork and turns to the Elderly Gentleman]. Zoo is a girl of fifty, and rather childish at that. So perhaps she may make you happy.

THE ELDERLY GENTLEMAN. Make me happy! A bluestocking of fifty! Thank you.

THE MAN. Bluestocking? The effort to make out your meaning is fatiguing. Besides, you are talking too much to me: I am old enough to discourage you. Let us be silent until Zoo comes. [*He turns his back on the Elderly Gentleman, and sits down on the edge of the pier, with his legs dangling over the water*].

THE ELDERLY GENTLEMAN. Certainly. I have no wish to force my conversation on any man who does not desire it. Perhaps you would like to take a nap. If so, pray do not stand on ceremony.

THE MAN. What is a nap?

THE ELDERLY GENTLEMAN [*exasperated, going to him and speaking with great precision and distinctness*] A nap, my friend, is a brief period of sleep which overtakes superannuated persons when they endeavour to entertain unwelcome visitors or to listen to scientific lectures. Sleep. Sleep. [*Bawling into his ear*] Sleep.

THE MAN. I tell you I am nearly a secondary. I never sleep.

THE ELDERLY GENTLEMAN [*awestruck*] Good Heavens!

*A young woman with the number one on her cap arrives by land. She looks no older than Savvy Barnabas, whom she somewhat resembles, looked a thousand years before. Younger, if anything.*

THE YOUNG WOMAN. Is this the patient?

THE MAN [*scrambling up*] This is Zoo. [*To Zoo*] Call him Daddy.

THE ELDERLY GENTLEMAN [*vehemently*] No.

THE MAN [*ignoring the interruption*] Bless you for taking him off my hands! I have had as much of him as I can bear. [*He goes down the steps and disappears*].

THE ELDERLY GENTLEMAN [*ironically taking off his hat and making a sweeping bow from the edge of the pier in the direction of the Atlantic Ocean*] Good afternoon, sir; and thank you very much for your extraordinary politeness, your exquisite consideration for my feelings, your courtly manners. Thank you from the bottom of my heart. [*Clapping his hat on again*] Pig! Ass!

ZOO [*laughs very heartily at him*]!!!

THE ELDERLY GENTLEMAN [*turning sharply on her*] Good afternoon, madam. I am sorry to have had to put your friend in his place; but I find that here as elsewhere it is necessary to assert myself if I am to be treated with proper consideration. I had hoped that my position as a guest would protect me from insult.

ZOO. Putting my friend in his place. That is some poetic expression, is it not? What does it mean?

THE ELDERLY GENTLEMAN. Pray, is there no one in these islands who understands plain English?

ZOO. Well, nobody except the oracles. They have to make a special historical study of what we call the dead thought.

THE ELDERLY GENTLEMAN. Dead thought! I have heard of the dead languages, but never of the dead thought.

ZOO. Well, thoughts die sooner than languages. I understand your language; but I do not always understand your thought. The oracles will understand you perfectly. Have you had your consultation yet?

THE ELDERLY GENTLEMAN. I did not come to consult the oracle, madam. I am here simply as a gentleman travelling for pleasure in the company of my daughter, who is the wife of the British Prime Minister, and of General Aufsteig, who, I may tell you in confidence, is really the Emperor of Turania, the greatest military genius of the age.

ZOO. Why should you travel for pleasure! Can you not enjoy yourself at home?

[ 503 ]

THE ELDERLY GENTLEMAN. I wish to see the world.

ZOO. It is too big. You can see a bit of it anywhere.

THE ELDERLY GENTLEMAN [*out of patience*] Damn it, madam, you dont want to spend your life looking at the same bit of it! [*Checking himself*] I beg your pardon for swearing in your presence.

ZOO. Oh! That is swearing, is it? I have read about that. It sounds quite pretty. Dammitmaddam, dammitmaddam, dammitmaddam, dammitmaddam. Say it as often as you please: I like it.

THE ELDERLY GENTLEMAN [*expanding with intense relief*] Bless you for those profane but familiar words! Thank you, thank you. For the first time since I landed in this terrible country I begin to feel at home. The strain which was driving me mad relaxes: I feel almost as if I were at the club. Excuse my taking the only available seat: I am not so young as I was. [*He sits on the bollard*]. Promise me that you will not hand me over to one of these dreadful tertiaries or secondaries or whatever you call them.

ZOO. Never fear. They had no business to give you in charge of Zozim. You see he is just on the verge of becoming a secondary; and these adolescents will give themselves the airs of tertiaries. You naturally feel more at home with a flapper like me [*She makes herself comfortable on the sacks*].

THE ELDERLY GENTLEMAN. Flapper? What does that mean?

ZOO. It is an archaic word which we still use to describe a female who is no longer a girl and is not yet quite adult.

THE ELDERLY GENTLEMAN. A very agreeable age to associate with, I find. I am recovering rapidly. I have a sense of blossoming like a flower. May I ask your name?

ZOO. Zoo.

THE ELDERLY GENTLEMAN. Miss Zoo.

ZOO. Not Miss Zoo. Zoo.

THE ELDERLY GENTLEMAN. Precisely. Er—Zoo what?

ZOO. No. Not Zoo What. Zoo. Nothing but Zoo.

THE ELDERLY GENTLEMAN [*puzzled*] Mrs Zoo, perhaps.

ZOO. No. Zoo. Cant you catch it? Zoo.

THE ELDERLY GENTLEMAN. Of course. Believe me, I did not really think you were married; you are obviously too young; but here it is so hard to feel sure—er—

ZOO [*hopelessly puzzled*] What?

THE ELDERLY GENTLEMAN. Marriage makes a difference, you know. One can say things to a married lady that would perhaps be in questionable taste to anyone without that experience.

ZOO. You are getting out of my depth: I dont understand a word you are saying. Married and questionable taste convey nothing to me. Stop, though. Is married an old form of the word mothered?

THE ELDERLY GENTLEMAN. Very likely. Let us drop the subject. Pardon me for embarrassing you. I should not have mentioned it.

ZOO. What does embarrassing mean?

THE ELDERLY GENTLEMAN. Well, really! I should have thought that so natural and common a condition would be understood as long as human nature lasted. To embarrass is to bring a blush to the cheek.

ZOO. What is a blush?

THE ELDERLY GENTLEMAN [*amazed*] Dont you blush? ? ?

ZOO. Never heard of it. We have a word flush, meaning a rush of blood to the skin. I have noticed it in my babies, but not after the age of two.

THE ELDERLY GENTLEMAN. Your babies!!! I fear
I am treading on very delicate ground; but your
appearance is extremely youthful; and if I may ask
how many—?

ZOO. Only four as yet. It is a long business with us.
I specialize in babies. My first was such a success
that they made me go on. I—

THE ELDERLY GENTLEMAN. In Heaven's name,
madam, how old are you?

ZOO. Fifty-six.

THE ELDERLY GENTLEMAN. My knees are trembling. I fear I am really ill.

ZOO. I noticed that you are not strong on your legs
yet. You have many of the ways and weaknesses of a
baby. No doubt that is why I feel called on to mother
you. You certainly are a very silly little Daddy.

THE ELDERLY GENTLEMAN. My name, I repeat, is
Joseph Popham Bolge Bluebin Barlow, O.M.

ZOO. An unnecessarily long name. I cannot call you
all that. What did your mother call you?

THE ELDERLY GENTLEMAN. You bring back the
bitterest struggles of my childhood. I was sensitive
on the point. Children suffer greatly from absurd
nicknames. My mother thoughtlessly called me Iddy
Toodles. I was called Iddy until I went to school,
when I made my first stand for children's rights by
insisting on being called at least Joe. At fifteen I
refused to answer to anything shorter than Joseph.
At eighteen I discovered that the name Joseph was
supposed to indicate an unmanly prudery because of
some old story about a Joseph who rejected the
advances of his employer's wife: very properly in my
opinion. I then became Popham to my family and
intimate friends, and Mister Barlow to the rest of the
world. My mother slipped back into Iddy when her

faculties began to fail her, poor woman; but I could
not resent that, at her age.

ZOO. Do you mean to say that your mother bothered
about you after you were ten?

THE ELDERLY GENTLEMAN. Naturally, madam. She
was my mother. What would you have had her do?

ZOO. Go on to the next, of course. After eight or nine
children become quite uninteresting, except to themselves. I shouldnt know my two eldest if I met them.

THE ELDERLY GENTLEMAN [*collapsing*] I am dying.
Let me die. I wish to die.

ZOO [*going to him quickly and supporting him*] Hold up.
Sit up straight. Whats the matter?

THE ELDERLY GENTLEMAN [*faintly*] My spine, I
think. Shock. Concussion.

ZOO [*maternally*] Pow wow wow! What is there to
shock you? [*Shaking him playfully*] There! Sit up;
and be good.

THE ELDERLY GENTLEMAN [*still feebly*] Thank you.
I am better now.

ZOO [*resuming her seat on the sacks*] But what was all
the rest of that long name for? There was a lot more
of it. Blops Booby or something.

THE ELDERLY GENTLEMAN [*impressively*] Bolge
Bluebin, madam: a historical name. Let me inform
you that I can trace my family back for more than a
thousand years, from the Eastern Empire to its ancient
seat in these islands, to a time when two of my
ancestors, Joyce Bolge and Hengist Horsa Bluebin,
wrestled with one another for the prime ministership
of the British Empire, and occupied that position
successively with a glory of which we can in these
degenerate days form but a faint conception. When
I think of these mighty men, lions in war, sages in
peace, not babblers and charlatans like the pigmies

[ 507 ]

who now occupy their places in Baghdad, but strong silent men, ruling an empire on which the sun never set, my eyes fill with tears: my heart bursts with emotion: I feel that to have lived but to the dawn of manhood in their day, and then died for them, would have been a nobler and happier lot than the ignominious ease of my present longevity.

ZOO. Longevity! [*she laughs*].

THE ELDERLY GENTLEMAN. Yes, madam, relative longevity. As it is, I have to be content and proud to know that I am descended from both those heroes.

ZOO. You must be descended from every Briton who was alive in their time. Dont you know that?

THE ELDERLY GENTLEMAN. Do not quibble, madam. I bear their names, Bolge and Bluebin; and I hope I have inherited something of their majestic spirit. Well, they were born in these islands. I repeat, these islands were then, incredible as it now seems, the centre of the British Empire. When that centre shifted to Baghdad, and the Englishman at last returned to the true cradle of his race in Mesopotamia, the western islands were cast off, as they had been before by the Roman Empire. But it was to the British race, and in these islands, that the greatest miracle in history occurred.

ZOO. Miracle?

THE ELDERLY GENTLEMAN. Yes: the first man to live three hundred years was an Englishman. The first, that is, since the contemporaries of Methuselah.

ZOO. Oh, that!

THE ELDERLY GENTLEMAN. Yes, that, as you call it so flippantly. Are you aware, madam, that at that immortal moment the English race had lost intellectual credit to such an extent that they habitually spoke of one another as fatheads? Yet England is now a sacred grove to which statesmen from all over the earth come to consult English sages who speak with the experience of two and a half centuries of life. The land that once exported cotton shirts and hardware now exports nothing but wisdom. You see before you, madam, a man utterly weary of the week-end riverside hotels of the Euphrates, the minstrels and pierrots on the sands of the Persian Gulf, the toboggans and funiculars of the Hindoo Koosh. Can you wonder that I turn, with a hungry heart, to the mystery and beauty of these haunted islands, thronged with spectres from a magic past, made holy by the footsteps of the wise men of the West. Consider this island on which we stand, the last foothold of man on this side of the Atlantic: this Ireland, described by the earliest bards as an emerald gem set in a silver sea! Can I, a scion of the illustrious British race, ever forget that when the Empire transferred its seat to the East, and said to the turbulent Irish race which it had oppressed but never conquered, "At last we leave you to yourselves; and much good may it do you," the Irish as one man uttered the historic shout "No: we'll be damned if you do," and emigrated to the countries where there was still a Nationalist question, to India, Persia, and Corea, to Morocco, Tunis, and Tripoli. In these countries they were ever foremost in the struggle for national independence; and the world rang continually with the story of their sufferings and wrongs. And what poem can do justice to the end, when it came at last? Hardly two hundred years had elapsed when the claims of nationality were so universally conceded that there was no longer a single country on the face of the earth with a national grievance or a national movement. Think of the position of the

Irish, who had lost all their political faculties by disuse except that of nationalist agitation, and who owed their position as the most interesting race on earth solely to their sufferings! The very countries they had helped to set free boycotted them as intolerable bores. The communities which had once idolized them as the incarnation of all that is adorable in the warm heart and witty brain, fled from them as from a pestilence. To regain their lost prestige, the Irish claimed the city of Jerusalem, on the ground that they were the lost tribes of Israel; but on their approach the Jews abandoned the city and redistributed themselves throughout Europe. It was then that these devoted Irishmen, not one of whom had ever seen Ireland, were counselled by an English Archbishop, the father of the oracles, to go back to their own country. This had never once occurred to them, because there was nothing to prevent them and nobody to forbid them. They jumped at the suggestion. They landed here: here in Galway Bay, on this very ground. When they reached the shore the older men and women flung themselves down and passionately kissed the soil of Ireland, calling on the young to embrace the earth that had borne their ancestors. But the young looked gloomily on, and said "There is no earth, only stone." You will see by looking round you why they said that: the fields here are of stone: the hills are capped with granite. They all left for England next day; and no Irishman ever again confessed to being Irish, even to his own children; so that when that generation passed away the Irish race vanished from human knowledge. And the dispersed Jews did the same lest they should be sent back to Palestine. Since then the world, bereft of its Jews and its Irish, had been a tame dull place.

Is there no pathos for you in this story? Can you not understand now why I am come to visit the scene of this tragic effacement of a race of heroes and poets?

ZOO. We still tell our little children stories like that, to help them to understand. But such things do not happen really. That scene of the Irish landing here and kissing the ground might have happened to a hundred people. It couldnt have happened to a hundred thousand: you know that as well as I do. And what a ridiculous thing to call people Irish because they live in Ireland! you might as well call them Airish because they live in air. They must be just the same as other people. Why do you shortlivers persist in making up silly stories about the world and trying to act as if they were true? Contact with truth hurts and frightens you: you escape from it into an imaginary vacuum in which you can indulge your desires and hopes and loves and hates without any contradiction by the solid facts of life. You love to throw dust in your own eyes.

THE ELDERLY GENTLEMAN. It is my turn now, madam, to inform you that I do not understand a single word you are saying. I should have thought that the use of a vacuum for removing dust was a mark of civilization rather than of savagery.

ZOO [*giving him up as hopeless*] Oh, Daddy, Daddy: I can hardly believe that you are human, you are so stupid. It was well said of your people in the olden days "Dust thou art; and to dust thou shalt return."

THE ELDERLY GENTLEMAN [*nobly*] My body is dust, madam: not my soul. What does it matter what my body is made of? the dust of the ground, the particles of the air, or even the slime of the ditch? The important thing is that when my Creator took it, whatever it was, He breathed into its nostrils the

[ 511 ]

breath of life; and Man became a living soul. Yes, madam, a living soul. I am not the dust of the ground: I am a living soul. That is an exalting, a magnificent thought. It is also a great scientific fact. I am not interested in the chemicals and the microbes: I leave them to the chumps and noodles, to the blockheads and the muckrakers who are incapable of their own glorious destiny, and unconscious of their own divinity. They tell me there are leucocytes in my blood, and sodium and carbon in my flesh. I thank them for the information, and tell them that there are blackbeetles in my kitchen, washing soda in my laundry, and coal in my cellar. I do not deny their existence; but I keep them in their proper place, which is not, if I may be allowed to use an antiquated form of expression, the temple of the Holy Ghost. No doubt you think me behind the times; but I rejoice in my enlightenment; and I recoil from your ignorance, your blindness, your imbecility. Humanly I pity you. Intellectually I despise you.

ZOO. Bravo, Daddy! You have the root of the matter in you. You will not die of discouragement after all.

THE ELDERLY GENTLEMAN. I have not the smallest intention of doing so, madam. I am no longer young; and I have moments of weakness; but when I approach this subject the divine spark in me kindles and glows. The corruptible becomes incorruptible; and the mortal Bolge Bluebin Barlow puts on immortality. On this ground I am your equal, even if you survive me by ten thousand years.

ZOO. Yes; but what do we know about this breath of life that puffs you up so exaltedly? Just nothing. So let us shake hands as cultivated Agnostics, and change the subject.

THE ELDERLY GENTLEMAN. Cultivated fiddlesticks,

madam! You cannot change this subject until the heavens and the earth pass away. I am not an Agnostic: I am a gentleman. When I believe a thing I say I believe it: when I dont believe it I say I dont believe it. I do not shirk my responsibilities by pretending that I know nothing and therefore can believe nothing. We can disclaim neither our knowledge nor our ignorance. We must proceed on assumptions of some sort or we cannot form a human society.

ZOO. The assumptions must be scientific, Daddy. We must live by science in the long run.

THE ELDERLY GENTLEMAN. I have learnt to fear the discoveries we owe to science. Any fool can make a discovery. Every baby has to discover more in the first years of its life than Roger Bacon ever discovered in his laboratory. When I was seven years old I discovered the sting of the wasp. But I do not ask you to worship me on that account. I assure you, madam, the merest mediocrities can discover the most surprising facts about the physical universe as soon as they are civilized enough to have time to study these things, and to invent instruments and apparatus for research. But what is the consequence? Their discoveries discredit the simple stories of our religion. At first we had no idea of astronomical space. We believed the sky to be only the ceiling of a room as large as the earth, with another room on top of it. Death was to us a going upstairs into that room, or, if we did not obey the priests, going downstairs into the coal cellar. We founded our religion, our morality, our laws, our lessons, our poems, our prayers, on that simple belief. Well, the moment men became astronomers and made telescopes, their belief perished. When they could no longer believe in the sky, they found that they could no longer believe in their

Deity, because they had always thought of him as living in the sky. When the priests themselves ceased to believe in their Deity and began to believe in astronomy, they changed their name and their dress, and called themselves doctors and men of science. They set up a new religion in which there was no Deity, but only wonders and miracles, with scientific instruments and apparatus as the wonder workers. Instead of worshipping the greatness and wisdom of the Deity, men gaped foolishly at the million billion miles of space and worshipped the astronomer as infallible and omniscient. They built temples for his telescopes. Then they looked into their own bodies with microscopes, and found there, not the soul they had formerly believed in, but millions of micro-organisms; so they gaped at these as foolishly as at the millions of miles, and built microscope temples in which horrible sacrifices were offered. They even gave their own bodies to be sacrificed by the micro-scope man, who was worshipped, like the astronomer, as infallible and omniscient. Thus our discoveries, instead of increasing our wisdom, only destroyed the little childish wisdom we had. But I shall shock you if I proceed. My opinions on this subject are so advanced! so intellectually daring! that I have never ventured to confess to them lest I should be imprison-ed for blasphemy, or even burnt alive.

ZOO. Indeed! What opinions?

THE ELDERLY GENTLEMAN [*after looking cautiously round*] I do not approve of microscopes. I never have.

ZOO. You call that advanced! Oh, Daddy, that is pure obscurantism.

THE ELDERLY GENTLEMAN. Call it so if you will, madam; but I maintain that it is dangerous to shew too much to people who do not know what they are looking at. I think that a man who is sane as long as he looks at the world through his own eyes is very likely to become a dangerous madman if he takes to looking at the world through telescopes and microscopes. Even when he is telling fairy stories about giants and dwarfs, the giants had better not be too big nor the dwarfs too small and too malicious. Before the microscope came, our fairy stories only made the children's flesh creep pleasantly, and did not frighten grown-up persons at all. But the microscope men terrified themselves and everyone else out of their wits with the invisible monsters they saw: poor harmless little things that die at the touch of a ray of sunshine, and are themselves the victims of all the diseases they are supposed to produce! Whatever the scientific people may say, imagination without microscopes was kindly and often courageous, because it worked on things of which it had some real knowledge. But imagination with microscopes, working on a terrifying spectacle of millions of grotesque creatures of whose nature it had no knowledge, became a cruel, terror-stricken, persecuting delirium. Are you aware, madam, that a general massacre of men of science took place in the twenty-first century of the pseudo-Christian era, when all their laboratories were demolished, and all their apparatus destroyed?

ZOO. Yes: the shortlived are as savage in their advances as in their relapses. But when Science crept back, it had been taught its place. The mere collectors of anatomical or chemical facts were not supposed to know more about Science than the collector of used postage stamps about international trade or literature. The scientific terrorist who was afraid to use a spoon or a tumbler until he had dipt it in some poisonous acid to kill the microbes, was no longer given titles, pensions, and monstrous powers over the bodies of other people: he was sent to a mental hospital. But all that is an old story: the extension of life to three hundred years has provided the human race with capable leaders, and made short work of such childish stuff.

THE ELDERLY GENTLEMAN [*pettishly*] You attribute every advance in civilization to your inordinately long lives. Let me tell you that this question was familiar to men who died before they had reached my own age?

ZOO. Yes: an ancient writer whose name has come down to us in several forms, such as Shakespear, Shelley, Sheridan, and Shoddy, has a remarkable passage about your dispositions being horridly shaken by thoughts beyond the reaches of your souls. But that does not come to much, does it?

THE ELDERLY GENTLEMAN. At all events, madam, I may remind you, if you come to capping ages, that whatever your secondaries and tertiaries may be, you are younger than I am.

ZOO. Yes, Daddy; but it is not the number of years we have behind us, but the number we have before us, that makes us careful and responsible and determined to find out the truth about everything. What does it matter to you whether anything is true or not? your flesh is as grass: you come up like a flower, and wither in your second childhood. A lie will last your time: it will not last mine. If I knew I had to die in twenty years it would not be worth my while to educate myself: I should not bother about anything but having a little pleasure while I lasted.

THE ELDERLY GENTLEMAN. Young woman: you are mistaken. Shortlived as we are, we—the best of us,

I mean—regard civilization and learning, art and science, as an ever-burning torch, which passes from the hand of one generation to the hand of the next, each generation fanning it to a farther reaching glow. We may be insects; but like the coral insect we build islands which become continents; like the bee we store sustenance for future communities. The individual perishes; but the race is immortal. The acorn of today is the oak of the next millennium. I throw my stone on the cairn and die; but later comers add another stone and yet another; and lo! a mountain. I—

ZOO [*interrupts him by laughing heartily at him*] !!!!!!

THE ELDERLY GENTLEMAN. May I ask what I have said that calls for this merriment?

ZOO. Oh, Daddy, Daddy, Daddy, you are a funny little man, with your torches and your coral insects and bees and acorns and stones and mountains.

THE ELDERLY GENTLEMAN. Metaphors, madam. Metaphors merely.

ZOO. Images, images, images. I was talking about men, not about images.

THE ELDERLY GENTLEMAN. I was illustrating—not, I hope, quite infelicitously—the great march of Progress. I was shewing you how, shortlived as we orientals are, mankind gains in stature from generation to generation, from epoch to epoch, from barbarism to civilization, from civilization to perfection.

ZOO. I see. The father grows to be six feet high, and hands on his six feet to his son, who adds another six feet and becomes twelve feet high, and hands his twelve feet on to his son, who is full-grown at eighteen feet, and so on. In a thousand years you would all be three or four miles high. At that rate your ancestors

Bilge and Bluebeard, who you call giants, must have been about quarter of an inch high.

THE ELDERLY GENTLEMAN. I am not here to bandy quibbles and paradoxes with a girl who blunders over the greatest names in history. I am in earnest. I am treating a solemn theme seriously. I never said that the son of a man six feet high would be twelve feet high.

ZOO. You didnt mean that?

THE ELDERLY GENTLEMAN. Most certainly not.

ZOO. Then you didnt mean anything. Now listen to me, you little ephemeral thing. I knew quite well what you meant by your torch handed on from generation to generation. But every time that torch is handed on, it dies down to the tiniest spark; and the man who gets it can rekindle it only by his own light. You are little taller than Bilge or Bluebeard; and you are no wiser. Their wisdom, such as it was, perished with them: so did their strength, if their strength ever existed outside your imagination. I do not know how old you are: you look about five hundred—

THE ELDERLY GENTLEMAN. Five hundred! Really, madam—

ZOO [continuing]; but I know, of course, that you are an ordinary shortliver. Well, your wisdom is only such wisdom as a man can have before he has had experience enough to distinguish his wisdom from his folly, his destiny from his delusions, his—

THE ELDERLY GENTLEMAN. In short, such wisdom as your own.

ZOO. No, no, no, no. How often must I tell you that we are made wise not by the recollections of our past, but by the responsibilities of our future. I shall be more reckless when I am a tertiary than I am today. If you cannot understand that, at least you must admit that I have learnt from tertiaries. I have seen

[ 518 ]

their work and lived under their institutions. Like all young things I rebelled against them; and in their hunger for new lights and new ideas they listened to me and encouraged me to rebel. But my ways did not work; and theirs did; and they were able to tell me why. They have no power over me except that power: they refuse all other power; and the consequence is that there are no limits to their power except the limits they set themselves. You are a child governed by children, who make so many mistakes and are so naughty that you are in continual rebellion against them; and as they can never convince you that they are right they can govern you only by beating you, imprisoning you, torturing you, killing you if you disobey them without being strong enough to kill or torture them.

THE ELDERLY GENTLEMAN. That may be an unfortunate fact. I condemn it and deplore it. But our minds are greater than the facts. We know better. The greatest ancient teachers, followed by the galaxy of Christs who arose in the twentieth century, not to mention such comparatively modern spiritual leaders as Blitherinjam, Tosh, and Spiffkins, all taught that punishment and revenge, coercion and militarism, are mistakes, and that the golden rule—

ZOO [interrupting] Yes, yes, yes, Daddy: we long-lived people know that quite well. But did any of their disciples ever succeed in governing you for a single day on their Christlike principles? It is not enough to know what is good: you must be able to do it. They couldnt do it because they did not live long enough to find out how to do it, or to outlive the childish passions that prevented them from really wanting to do it. You know very well that they could only keep order—such as it was—by the very coercion

[ 519 ]

and militarism they were denouncing and deploring. They had actually to kill one another for preaching their own gospel, or be killed themselves.

THE ELDERLY GENTLEMAN. The blood of the martyrs, madam, is the seed of the Church.

ZOO. More images, Daddy! The blood of the short-lived falls on stony ground.

THE ELDERLY GENTLEMAN [*rising, very testy*] You are simply mad on the subject of longevity. I wish you would change it. It is rather personal and in bad taste. Human nature is human nature, longlived or short-lived, and always will be.

ZOO. Then you give up the idea of progress?

THE ELDERLY GENTLEMAN. I do nothing of the sort. I stand for progress and for freedom broadening down from precedent to precedent.

ZOO. You are certainly a true Briton.

THE ELDERLY GENTLEMAN. I am proud of it. But in your mouth I feel that the compliment hides some insult; so I do not thank you for it.

ZOO. All I meant was that though Britons some-times say quite clever things and deep things as well as silly and shallow things, they always forget them ten minutes after they have uttered them.

THE ELDERLY GENTLEMAN. Leave it at that, madam: leave it at that. [*He sits down again*]. Even a Pope is not expected to be continually pontificating. Our flashes of inspiration shew that our hearts are in the right place.

ZOO. Of course. You cannot keep your heart in any place but the right place.

THE ELDERLY GENTLEMAN. Tcha!

ZOO. But you can keep your hands in the wrong place. In your neighbors' pockets, for example. So, you see, it is your hands that really matter.

THE ELDERLY GENTLEMAN [*exhausted*] Well, a woman must have the last word. I will not dispute it with you.

ZOO. Good. Now let us go back to the really interesting subject of our discussion. You remember? The slavery of the shortlived to images and metaphors.

THE ELDERLY GENTLEMAN [*aghast*] Do you mean to say, madam, that after having talked my head off, and reduced me to despair and silence by your intolerable loquacity, you actually propose to begin all over again? I shall leave you at once.

ZOO. You must not. I am your nurse; and you must stay with me.

THE ELDERLY GENTLEMAN. I absolutely decline to do anything of the sort [*he rises and walks away with marked dignity*].

ZOO [*using her tuning-fork*] Zoo on Burrin Pier to Oracle Police at Ennistymon have you got me? . . . What? . . . I am picking you up now but you are flat to my pitch. . . . Just a shade sharper. . . . Thats better: still a little more. . . . Got you: right. Isolate Burrin Pier quick.

THE ELDERLY GENTLEMAN [*is heard to yell*] Oh!

ZOO [*still intoning*] Thanks. . . . Oh nothing serious I am nursing a shortliver and the silly creature has run away he has discouraged himself very badly by gadding about and talking to secondaries and I must keep him strictly to heel.

*The Elderly Gentleman returns, indignant.*

ZOO. Here he is you can release the Pier thanks. Goodbye. [*She puts up her tuning-fork*].

THE ELDERLY GENTLEMAN. This is outrageous. When I tried to step off the pier on to the road, I received a shock, followed by an attack of pins and needles which ceased only when I stepped back on to the stones.

ZOO. Yes: there is an electric hedge there. It is a very old and very crude method of keeping animals from straying.

THE ELDERLY GENTLEMAN. We are perfectly familiar with it in Baghdad, madam; but I little thought I should live to have it ignominiously applied to myself. I consider that in using it on me you have taken a very great liberty.

ZOO. What is a liberty?

THE ELDERLY GENTLEMAN [*exasperated*] I shall not explain, madam. I believe you know as well as I do. [*He sits down on the bollard in dudgeon*].

ZOO. No: even you can tell me things I do not know. Havnt you noticed that all the time you have been here we have been asking you questions?

THE ELDERLY GENTLEMAN. Noticed it! It has almost driven me mad. Do you see my white hair? It was hardly grey when I landed: there were patches of its original auburn still distinctly discernible.

ZOO. That is one of the symptoms of discouragement. But have you noticed something much more important to yourself: that is, that you have never asked us any questions, although we know so much more than you do?

THE ELDERLY GENTLEMAN. I am not a child, madam. I believe I have had occasion to say that before. And I am an experienced traveller. I know that what the traveller observes must really exist, or he could not observe it. But what the natives tell him is invariably pure fiction.

ZOO. Not here, Daddy. With us life is too long for telling lies. They all get found out. Youd better ask me questions while you have the chance.

THE ELDERLY GENTLEMAN. If I have occasion to consult the oracle I shall address myself to a proper one: to a tertiary: not to a primary flapper playing at being an oracle. If you are a nurserymaid, attend to your duties; and do not presume to ape your elders.

ZOO [*rising ominously and reddening*] You silly—

THE ELDERLY GENTLEMAN [*thundering*] Silence! Do you hear? Hold your tongue.

ZOO. Something very disagreeable is happening to me. I feel hot all over. I have a horrible impulse to injure you. What have you done to me?

THE ELDERLY GENTLEMAN [*triumphant*] Aha! I have made you blush. Now you know what blushing means. Blushing with shame!

ZOO. Whatever you are doing, it is something so utterly evil that if you do not stop I will kill you.

THE ELDERLY GENTLEMAN [*apprehending his danger*] Doubtless you think it safe to threaten an old man—

ZOO [*fiercely*] Old! You are a child: an evil child. We kill evil children here. We do it even against our own wills by instinct. Take care.

THE ELDERLY GENTLEMAN [*rising with crestfallen courtesy*] I did not mean to hurt your feelings. I— [*swallowing the apology with an effort*] I beg your pardon. [*He takes off his hat, and bows*].

ZOO. What does that mean?

THE ELDERLY GENTLEMAN. I withdraw what I said.

ZOO. How can you withdraw what you said?

THE ELDERLY GENTLEMAN. I can say no more than that I am sorry.

ZOO. You have reason to be. That hideous sensation you gave me is subsiding; but you have had a very narrow escape. Do not attempt to kill me again; for at the first sign in your voice or face I shall strike you dead.

THE ELDERLY GENTLEMAN. *I* attempt to kill you! I never dreamt of such a thing. Surely you cannot believe that I am a murderer.

ZOO. I know you are a murderer. It is not merely that you threw words at me as if they were stones, meaning to hurt me. It was the instinct to kill that you roused in me. I did not know it was in my nature: never before has it wakened and sprung out at me, warning me to kill or be killed. I must now reconsider my whole political position. I am no longer a Conservative.

THE ELDERLY GENTLEMAN [*dropping his hat*] Gracious Heavens! you have lost your senses. I am at the mercy of a madwoman: I might have known it from the beginning. I can bear no more of this. [*Offering his chest for the sacrifice*] Kill me at once; and much good may my death do you!

ZOO. It would be useless unless all the other shortlivers were killed at the same time. Besides, it is a measure which should be taken politically and constitutionally, not privately. However, I am prepared to discuss it with you.

THE ELDERLY GENTLEMAN. I could hardly do so impartially. Had we not rather discuss your intention of withdrawing from the Conservative party? How the Conservatives have tolerated your opinions so far is more than I can imagine: I can only conjecture that you have contributed very liberally to the party funds. [*He picks up his hat, and sits down again*].

ZOO. Do not babble so senselessly: our chief political controversy is the most momentous in the world for you and your like.

THE ELDERLY GENTLEMAN [*interested*] Indeed? Pray, may I ask what it is? I am a keen politician, and may perhaps be of some use. [*He puts on his hat, cocking it slightly*].

ZOO. We have two great parties: the Conservative party and the Colonization party. The Colonizers are of opinion that we should increase our numbers and colonize. The Conservatives hold that we should stay as we are, confined to these islands, a race apart, wrapped up in the majesty of our wisdom on a soil held as holy ground for us by an adoring world, with our sacred frontier traced beyond dispute by the sea. They contend that it is our destiny to rule the world, and that even when we were shortlived we did so. They say that our power and our peace depend on our remoteness, our exclusiveness, our separation, and the restriction of our numbers. Five minutes ago that was my political faith. Now I do not think there should be any shortlived people at all. [*She throws herself again carelessly on the sacks*].

THE ELDERLY GENTLEMAN. Am I to infer that you deny my right to live because I allowed myself— perhaps injudiciously—to give you a slight scolding?

ZOO. Is it worth living for so short a time? Are you any good to yourself?

THE ELDERLY GENTLEMAN [*stupent*] Well, upon my soul!

ZOO. It is such a very little soul! You only encourage the sin of pride in us, and keep us looking down at you instead of up to something higher than ourselves.

THE ELDERLY GENTLEMAN. Is not that a selfish view, madam? Think of the good you do us by your oracular counsels!

ZOO. What good have our counsels ever done you? You come to us for advice when you know you are in difficulties. But you never know you are in difficulties until twenty years after you have made the mistakes that led to them; and then it is too late. You cannot understand our advice: you often do more mischief by trying to act on it than if you had been left to your own childish devices. If you were not childish you would not come to us at all: you would learn from experience that your consultations of the oracle are never of any real help to you. You draw wonderful imaginary pictures of us, and write fictitious tales and poems about our beneficent operations in the past, our wisdom, our justice, our mercy: stories in which we often appear as sentimental dupes of your prayers and sacrifices; but you do it only to conceal from yourselves the truth that you are incapable of being helped by us. Your Prime Minister pretends that he has come to be guided by the oracle; but we are not deceived: we know quite well that he has come here so that when he goes back he may have the authority and dignity of one who has visited the holy islands and spoken face to face with the ineffable ones. He will pretend that all the measures he wishes to take for his own purposes have been enjoined on him by the oracle.

THE ELDERLY GENTLEMAN. But you forget that the answers of the oracle cannot be kept secret or misrepresented. They are written and promulgated. The Leader of the Opposition can obtain copies. All the nations know them. Secret diplomacy has been totally abolished.

ZOO. Yes: you publish documents; but they are garbled or forged. And even if you published our real answers it would make no difference, because the shortlived cannot interpret the plainest writings. Your scriptures command you in the plainest terms to do exactly the contrary of everything your own laws and chosen rulers command and execute. You cannot defy Nature. It is a law of Nature that there is a fixed relation between conduct and length of life.

THE ELDERLY GENTLEMAN. I have never heard of any such law, madam.

ZOO. Well, you are hearing of it now.

THE ELDERLY GENTLEMAN. Let me tell you that we shortlivers, as you call us, have lengthened our lives very considerably.

ZOO. How?

THE ELDERLY GENTLEMAN. By saving time. By enabling men to cross the ocean in an afternoon, and to see and speak to one another when they are thousands of miles apart. We hope shortly to organize their labor, and press natural forces into their service, so scientifically that the burden of labor will cease to be perceptible, leaving common men more leisure than they will know what to do with.

ZOO. Daddy: the man whose life is lengthened in this way may know more than a savage; but the difference between such men living seventy years and those living three hundred would be all the greater; for to a shortliver increase of years is only increase of sorrow; but to a longliver every extra year is a prospect continually forcing him to stretch his faculties to the utmost to face it. Therefore I say that we who live three hundred years can be of no use to you who live less than a hundred, and that our true destiny is not to advise and govern you, but to supplant and supersede you. In that faith I now declare myself a Colonizer and an Exterminator.

THE ELDERLY GENTLEMAN. Oh, steady! steady! Pray! pray! Reflect, I implore you. It is possible to colonize without exterminating the natives. Would

you treat us less mercifully than our barbarous forefathers treated the Redskin and the Negro? Are we
not, as Britons, entitled at least to some reserva-
tions?

ZOO. What is the use of prolonging the agony? You
would perish slowly in our presence, no matter what
we did to preserve you. You were almost dead when
I took charge of you today, merely because you had
talked for a few minutes to a secondary. Besides, we
have our own experience to go upon. Have you never
heard that our children occasionally revert to the
ancestral type, and are born shortlived?

THE ELDERLY GENTLEMAN [*eagerly*] Never. I hope
you will not be offended if I say that it would be a
great comfort to me if I could be placed in charge of
one of those normal individuals.

ZOO. Abnormal, you mean. What you ask is impossible: we weed them all out.

THE ELDERLY GENTLEMAN. When you say that you
weed them out, you send a cold shiver down my spine.
I hope you dont mean that you—that you—that you
assist Nature in any way?

ZOO. Why not? Have you not heard the saying of
the Chinese sage Dee Ning, that a good garden needs
weeding? But it is not necessary for us to interfere.
We are naturally rather particular as to the conditions
on which we consent to live. One does not mind the
accidental loss of an arm or a leg or an eye: after
all, no one with two legs is unhappy because he has
not three; so why should a man with one be unhappy
because he has not two? But infirmities of mind and
temper are quite another matter. If one of us has
no self-control, or is too weak to bear the strain of
our truthful life without wincing, or is tormented
by depraved appetites and superstitions, or is unable

to keep free from pain and depression, he naturally becomes discouraged, and refuses to live.

THE ELDERLY GENTLEMAN. Good Lord! Cuts his throat, do you mean?

ZOO. No: why should he cut his throat? He simply dies. He wants to. He is out of countenance, as we call it.

THE ELDERLY GENTLEMAN. Well!!! But suppose he is depraved enough not to want to die, and to settle the difficulty by killing all the rest of you?

ZOO. Oh, he is one of the thoroughly degenerate short-livers whom we occasionally produce. He emigrates.

THE ELDERLY GENTLEMAN. And what becomes of him then?

ZOO. You shortlived people always think very highly of him. You accept him as what you call a great man.

THE ELDERLY GENTLEMAN. You astonish me; and yet I must admit that what you tell me accounts for a great deal of the little I know of the private life of our great men. We must be very convenient to you as a dumping place for your failures.

ZOO. I admit that.

THE ELDERLY GENTLEMAN. Good. Then if you carry out your plan of colonization, and leave no shortlived countries in the world, what will you do with your undesirables?

ZOO. Kill them. Our tertiaries are not at all squeamish about killing.

THE ELDERLY GENTLEMAN. Gracious Powers!

ZOO [*glancing up at the sun*] Come. It is just sixteen o'clock; and you have to join your party at half-past in the temple in Galway.

THE ELDERLY GENTLEMAN [*rising*] Galway! Shall I at last be able to boast of having seen that magnificent city?

ZOO. You will be disappointed: we have no cities. There is a temple of the oracle: that is all.

THE ELDERLY GENTLEMAN. Alas! and I came here to fulfil two long-cherished dreams. One was to see Galway. It has been said, "See Galway and die." The other was to contemplate the ruins of London.

ZOO. Ruins! We do not tolerate ruins. Was London a place of any importance?

THE ELDERLY GENTLEMAN [*amazed*] What! London! It was the mightiest city of antiquity. [*Rhetorically*] Situate just where the Dover Road crosses the Thames, it—

ZOO [*curtly interrupting*] There is nothing there now. Why should anybody pitch on such a spot to live? The nearest houses are at a place called Strand-on-the-Green: it is very old. Come. We shall go across the water. [*She goes down the steps*].

THE ELDERLY GENTLEMAN. Sic transit gloria mundi!

ZOO [*from below*] What did you say?

THE ELDERLY GENTLEMAN [*despairingly*] Nothing. You would not understand. [*He goes down the steps*].

# [ACT II]

*A courtyard before the columned portico of a temple. The temple door is in the middle of the portico. A veiled and robed woman of majestic carriage passes along behind the columns towards the entrance. From the opposite direction a man of compact figure, clean-shaven, saturnine, and self-centred: in short, very like Napoleon I, wearing a military uniform of Napoleonic cut, marches with measured steps; places his hand in his lapel in the traditional manner; and fixes the woman with his eye. She stops, her attitude expressing haughty amazement at his audacity. He is on her right: she on his left.*

NAPOLEON [*impressively*] I am the Man of Destiny.

THE VEILED WOMAN [*unimpressed*] How did you get in here?

NAPOLEON. I walked in. I go on until I am stopped. I never am stopped. I tell you I am the Man of Destiny.

THE VEILED WOMAN. You will be a man of very short destiny if you wander about here without one of our children to guide you. I suppose you belong to the Baghdad envoy.

NAPOLEON. I came with him; but I do not belong to him. I belong to myself. Direct me to the oracle if you can. If not, do not waste my time.

THE VEILED WOMAN. Your time, poor creature, is short. I will not waste it. Your envoy and his party will be here presently. The consultation of the oracle is arranged for them, and will take place according to the prescribed ritual. You can wait here until they come [*she turns to go into the temple*].

NAPOLEON. I never wait. [*She stops*]. The prescribed ritual is, I believe, the classical one of the pythoness on her tripod, the intoxicating fumes arising from the abyss, the convulsions of the priestess as she delivers the message of the God, and so on. That sort of thing does not impose on me: I use it myself to impose on simpletons. I believe that what is, is. I know that what is not, is not. The antics of a woman sitting on a tripod and pretending to be drunk do not interest me. Her words are put into her mouth, not by a god, but by a man three hundred years old, who has had the capacity to profit by his experience. I wish to speak to that man face to face, without mummery or imposture.

THE VEILED WOMAN. You seem to be an unusually sensible person. But there is no old man. I am the oracle on duty today. I am on my way to take my place on the tripod, and go through the usual mummery, as you rightly call it, to impress your friend the envoy. As you are superior to that kind of thing, you may consult me now. [*She leads the way into the middle of the courtyard*]. What do you want to know?

NAPOLEON [*following her*] Madam: I have not come all this way to discuss matters of State with a woman. I must ask you to direct me to one of your oldest and ablest men.

THE ORACLE. None of our oldest and ablest men or women would dream of wasting their time on you. You would die of discouragement in their presence.

NAPOLEON. You can keep this idle fable of discouragement for people credulous enough to be intimidated by it, madam. I do not believe in metaphysical forces.

THE ORACLE. No one asks you to. A field is something physical, is it not? Well, I have a field.

NAPOLEON. I have several million fields. I am Emperor of Turania.

THE ORACLE. You do not understand. I am not speaking of an agricultural field. Do you not know that every mass of matter in motion carries with it an invisible gravitational field, every magnet an invisible magnetic field, and every living organism a mesmeric field? Even you have a perceptible mesmeric field. Feeble as it is, it is the strongest I have yet observed in a shortliver.

NAPOLEON. By no means feeble, madam. I understand you now; and I may tell you that the strongest characters blench in my presence, and submit to my domination. But I do not call that a physical force.

THE ORACLE. What else do you call it, pray? Our physicists deal with it. Our mathematicians express its measurements in algebraic equations.

NAPOLEON. Do you mean that they could measure mine?

THE ORACLE. Yes: by a figure infinitely near to zero. Even in us the force is negligible during our first century of life. In our second century it develops quickly, and becomes dangerous to shortlivers who venture into its field. If I were not veiled and robed in insulating material you could not endure my presence; and I am still a young woman: one hundred and seventy if you wish to know exactly.

NAPOLEON [*folding his arms*] I am not intimidated: no woman alive, old or young, can put me out of countenance. Unveil, madam. Disrobe. You will move this temple as easily as shake me.

THE ORACLE. Very well [*she throws back her veil*].

NAPOLEON [*shrieking, staggering, and covering his*

*eyes*] No. Stop. Hide your face again. [*Shutting his eyes and distractedly clutching at his throat and heart*] Let me go. Help! I am dying.

THE ORACLE. Do you still wish to consult an older person?

NAPOLEON. No, no. The veil, the veil, I beg you.

THE ORACLE [*replacing the veil*] So.

NAPOLEON. Ouf! One cannot always be at one's best. Twice before in my life I have lost my nerve and behaved like a poltroon. But I warn you not to judge my quality by these involuntary moments.

THE ORACLE. I have no occasion to judge of your quality. You want my advice. Speak quickly; or I shall go about my business.

NAPOLEON [*After a moment's hesitation, sinks respectfully on one knee*] I—

THE ORACLE. Oh, rise, rise. Are you so foolish as to offer me this mummery which even you despise?

NAPOLEON [*rising*] I knelt in spite of myself. I compliment you on your impressiveness, madam.

THE ORACLE [*impatiently*] Time! time! time! time!

NAPOLEON. You will not grudge me the necessary time, madam, when you know my case. I am a man gifted with a certain specific talent in a degree altogether extraordinary. I am not otherwise a very extraordinary person: my family is not influential; and without this talent I should cut no particular figure in the world.

THE ORACLE. Why cut a figure in the world?

NAPOLEON. Superiority will make itself felt, madam. But when I say I possess this talent I do not express myself accurately. The truth is that my talent possesses me. It is genius. It drives me to exercise it. I m u s t exercise it. I am great when I exercise it. At other moments I am nobody.

THE ORACLE. Well, exercise it. Do you need an oracle to tell you that?

NAPOLEON. Wait. This talent involves the shedding of human blood.

THE ORACLE. Are you a surgeon, or a dentist?

NAPOLEON. Psha! You do not appreciate me, madam. I mean the shedding of oceans of blood, the death of millions of men.

THE ORACLE. They object, I suppose.

NAPOLEON. Not at all. They adore me.

THE ORACLE. Indeed!

NAPOLEON. I have never shed blood with my own hand. They kill each other: they die with shouts of triumph on their lips. Those who die cursing do not curse me. My talent is to organize this slaughter; to give mankind this terrible joy which they call glory; to let loose the devil in them that peace has bound in chains.

THE ORACLE. And you? Do you share their joy?

NAPOLEON. Not at all. What satisfaction is it to me to see one fool pierce the entrails of another with a bayonet? I am a man of princely character, but of simple personal tastes and habits. I have the virtues of a laborer: industry and indifference to personal comfort. But I must rule, because I am so superior to other men that it is intolerable to me to be mis-ruled by them. Yet only as a slayer can I become a ruler. I cannot be great as a writer: I have tried and failed. I have no talent as a sculptor or painter; and as lawyer, preacher, doctor, or actor, scores of second-rate men can do as well as I, or better. I am not even a diplomatist: I can only play my trump card of force. What I can do is to organize war. Look at me! I seem a man like other men, because nine-tenths of me is common humanity. But the other tenth is a faculty for seeing things as they are that no other man possesses.

THE ORACLE. You mean that you have no imagination?

NAPOLEON [*forcibly*] I mean that I have the only imagination worth having: the power of imagining things as they are, even when I cannot see them. You feel yourself my superior, I know: nay, you are my superior: have I not bowed my knee to you by instinct? Yet I challenge you to a test of our respective powers. Can you calculate what the mathematicians call vectors, without putting a single algebraic symbol on paper? Can you launch ten thousand men across a frontier and a chain of mountains and know to a mile exactly where they will be at the end of seven weeks? The rest is nothing: I got it all from the books at my military school. Now this great game of war, this playing with armies as other men play with bowls and skittles, is one which I must go on playing, partly because a man must do what he can and not what he would like to do, and partly because, if I stop, I immediately lose my power and become a beggar in the land where I now make men drunk with glory.

THE ORACLE. No doubt then you wish to know how to extricate yourself from this unfortunate position?

NAPOLEON. It is not generally considered unfortunate, madam. Supremely fortunate rather.

THE ORACLE. If you think so, go on making them drunk with glory. Why trouble me with their folly and your vectors?

NAPOLEON. Unluckily, madam, men are not only heroes: they are also cowards. They desire glory; but they dread death.

THE ORACLE. Why should they? Their lives are too

short to be worth living. That is why they think your game of war worth playing.

NAPOLEON. They do not look at it quite in that way. The most worthless soldier wants to live for ever. To make him risk being killed by the enemy I have to convince him that if he hesitates he will inevitably be shot at dawn by his own comrades for cowardice.

THE ORACLE. And if his comrades refuse to shoot him?

NAPOLEON. They will be shot too, of course.

THE ORACLE. By whom?

NAPOLEON. By their comrades.

THE ORACLE. And if they refuse?

NAPOLEON. Up to a certain point they do not refuse.

THE ORACLE. But when that point is reached, you have to do the shooting yourself, eh?

NAPOLEON. Unfortunately, madam, when that point is reached, they shoot me.

THE ORACLE. Mf! It seems to me they might as well shoot you first as last. Why dont they?

NAPOLEON. Because their love of fighting, their desire for glory, their shame of being branded as dastards, their instinct to test themselves in terrible trials, their fear of being killed or enslaved by the enemy, their belief that they are defending their hearths and homes, overcome their natural cowardice, and make them willing not only to risk their own lives but to kill everyone who refuses to take that risk. But if war continues too long, there comes a time when the soldiers, and also the taxpayers who are supporting and munitioning them, reach a condition which they describe as being fed up. The troops have proved their courage, and want to go home and enjoy in peace the glory it has earned them. Besides, the risk of death for each soldier becomes a certainty if the fighting goes on for ever: he hopes to escape for six months, but knows he cannot escape for six years. The risk of bankruptcy for the citizen becomes a certainty in the same way. Now what does this mean for me?

THE ORACLE. Does that matter in the midst of such calamity?

NAPOLEON. Psha! madam: it is the only thing that matters: the value of human life is the value of the greatest living man. Cut off that infinitesimal layer of grey matter which distinguishes my brain from that of the common man, and you cut down the stature of humanity from that of a giant to that of a nobody. I matter supremely: my soldiers do not matter at all: there are plenty more where they came from. If you kill me, or put a stop to my activity (it is the same thing), the nobler part of human life perishes. You must save the world from that catastrophe, madam. War has made me popular, powerful, famous, historically immortal. But I foresee that if I go on to the end it will leave me execrated, dethroned, imprisoned, perhaps executed. Yet if I stop fighting I commit suicide as a great man and become a common one. How am I to escape the horns of this tragic dilemma? Victory I can guarantee: I am invincible. But the cost of victory is the demoralization, the depopulation, the ruin of the victors no less than of the vanquished. How am I to satisfy my genius by fighting until I die? that is my question to you.

THE ORACLE. Were you not rash to venture into these sacred islands with such a question on your lips? Warriors are not popular here, my friend.

NAPOLEON. If a soldier were restrained by such a consideration, madam, he would no longer be a soldier. Besides [*he exhibits a pistol*], I have not come unarmed.

THE ORACLE. What is that thing?

NAPOLEON. It is an instrument of my profession, madam. I raise this hammer; I point the barrel at you; I pull this trigger that is against my forefinger; and you fall dead.

THE ORACLE. Give it to me [*she puts out her hand to take it from him*].

NAPOLEON [*retreating a step*] Pardon me, madam. I never trust my life in the hands of a person over whom I have no control.

THE ORACLE [*sternly*] Give it to me [*she raises her hand to her veil*].

NAPOLEON [*dropping the pistol and covering his eyes*] Quarter! Kamerad! Take it, madam [*he kicks it towards her*]: I surrender.

THE ORACLE. Give me that thing. Do you expect me to stoop for it?

NAPOLEON [*taking his hands from his eyes with an effort*] A poor victory, madam [*he picks up the pistol and hands it to her*]: there was no vector strategy needed to win it. [*Making a pose of his humiliation*] But enjoy your triumph: you have made me—ME! Cain Adamson Charles Napoleon! Emperor of Turania! cry for quarter.

THE ORACLE. The way out of your difficulty, Cain Adamson, is very simple.

NAPOLEON [*eagerly*] Good. What is it?

THE ORACLE. To die before the tide of glory turns. Allow me [*she shoots him*].

*He falls with a shriek. She throws the pistol away and goes haughtily into the temple.*

NAPOLEON [*scrambling to his feet*] Murderess! Monster! She-devil! Unnatural, inhuman wretch!

You deserve to be hanged, guillotined, broken on the wheel, burnt alive. No sense of the sacredness of human life! No thought for my wife and children! Bitch! Sow! Wanton! [*He picks up the pistol*]. And missed me at five yards! Thats a woman all over.

*He is going away whence he came when Zoo arrives and confronts him at the head of a party consisting of the British Envoy, the Elderly Gentleman, the Envoy's wife, and her daughter, aged about eighteen. The Envoy, a typical politician, looks like an imperfectly reformed criminal disguised by a good tailor. The dress of the ladies is coeval with that of the Elderly Gentleman, and suitable for public official ceremonies in western capitals at the nineteenth fin de siècle.*

*They file in under the portico. Zoo immediately comes out imperiously to Napoleon's right, whilst the Envoy's wife hurries effusively to his left. The Envoy meanwhile passes along behind the columns to the door, followed by his daughter. The Elderly Gentleman stops just where he entered, to see why Zoo has swooped so abruptly on the Emperor of Turania.*

ZOO [*to Napoleon, severely*] What are you doing here by yourself? You have no business to go about here alone. What was that noise just now? What is that in your hand?

*Napoleon glares at her in speechless fury; pockets the pistol; and takes out a whistle.*

THE ENVOY'S WIFE. Arnt you coming with us to the oracle, sire?

NAPOLEON. To hell with the oracle, and with you too [*he turns to go*]!

THE ENVOY'S WIFE ⎱
ZOO            ⎰ [*together*] ⎰ Oh, sire!!
                                  Where are you
                                     going?

NAPOLEON. To fetch the police [*He goes out past Zoo,*

*almost jostling her, and blowing piercing blasts on his whistle*].

ZOO [*whipping out her tuning-fork and intoning*] Hallo Galway Central. [*The whistling continues*]. Stand by to isolate. [*To the Elderly Gentleman, who is staring after the whistling Emperor*] How far has he gone?

THE ELDERLY GENTLEMAN. To that curious statue of a fat old man.

ZOO [*quickly, intoning*] Isolate the Falstaff monument isolate hard. Paralyze—[*the whistling stops*]. Thank you. [*She puts up her tuning-fork*]. He shall not move a muscle until I come to fetch him.

THE ENVOY'S WIFE. Oh! he will be frightfully angry! Did you hear what he said to me?

ZOO. Much we care for his anger!

THE DAUGHTER [*coming forward between her mother and Zoo*] Please, madam, whose statue is it? and where can I buy a picture postcard of it? It is so funny. I will take a snapshot when we are coming back; but they come out so badly sometimes.

ZOO. They will give you pictures and toys in the temple to take away with you. The story of the statue is too long. It would bore you [*she goes past them across the courtyard to get rid of them*].

THE WIFE [*gushing*] Oh no, I assure you.

THE DAUGHTER [*copying her mother*] We should be so interested.

ZOO. Nonsense! All I can tell you about it is that a thousand years ago, when the whole world was given over to you shortlived people, there was a war called the War to end War. In the war which followed it the capital cities of the world were wiped out of existence; and that was the end of pseudo-Christian civilization. The last civilized thing that happened was that the statesmen discovered that cowardice was a great patriotic virtue; and a public monument was erected to its first preacher, an ancient and very fat sage called Sir John Falstaff. Well [*pointing*], thats Falstaff.

THE ELDERLY GENTLEMAN [*coming from the portico to his granddaughter's right*] Great Heavens! And at the base of this monstrous poltroon's statue the War God of Turania is now gibbering impotently.

ZOO. Serve him right! War God indeed!

THE ENVOY [*coming between his wife and Zoo*] I dont know any history: a modern Prime Minister has something better to do than sit reading books; but—

THE ELDERLY GENTLEMAN [*interrupting him encouragingly*] You make history, Ambrose.

THE ENVOY. Well, perhaps I do; and perhaps history makes me. I hardly recognize myself in the newspapers sometimes, though I suppose leading articles are the materials of history, as you might say. Of course I am all for peace, and dont hold with the race of armaments in principle; still, we must keep ahead or be wiped out.

ZOO. You will wipe yourselves out just as you did before. You will then begin all over again as half-starved ignorant savages, and fight with boomerangs and poisoned arrows until you work up to high explosives once more, with the same result. That is, unless we have sense enough to make an end of this ridiculous game by destroying you.

THE ENVOY [*aghast*] Destroying us!

THE ELDERLY GENTLEMAN. I told you, Ambrose. I warned you.

THE ENVOY. But—

ZOO [*impatiently*] I wonder what Zozim is doing. He ought to be here to receive you.

THE ELDERLY GENTLEMAN. Do you mean that

rather insufferable young man whom you found boring me on the pier?

ZOO. Yes. He has to dress-up in a Druid's robe, and put on a wig and a long false beard, to impress you silly people. *I* have to put on a purple mantle. I have no patience with such mummery; but you expect it from us; so I suppose it must be kept up. Will you wait here until Zozim comes, please [*she turns to enter the temple*].

THE ENVOY. My good lady, is it worth while dressing-up and putting on false beards for us if you tell us beforehand that it is all humbug?

ZOO. One would not think so; but if you wont believe in anyone who is not dressed-up, why, we must dress-up for you. It was you who invented all this nonsense, not we.

THE ELDERLY GENTLEMAN. But do you expect us to be impressed after this?

ZOO. I dont expect anything. I know, as a matter of experience, that you will be impressed. The oracle will frighten you out of your wits. [*she goes into the temple*].

THE WIFE. These people treat us as if we were dirt beneath their feet. I wonder at you putting up with it, Amby. It would serve them right if we went home at once: wouldnt it, Eth?

THE DAUGHTER. Yes, mamma. But perhaps they wouldnt mind.

THE ENVOY. No use talking like that, Molly. Ive got to see this oracle. The folks at home wont know how we have been treated: all theyll know is that Ive stood face to face with the oracle and had the straight tip from her. I hope this Zozim chap is not going to keep us waiting much longer; for I feel as nervous as I did before my maiden speech in parliament; and thats the honest truth.

THE ELDERLY GENTLEMAN. I never thought I should want to see that man again; but now I wish he would take charge of us instead of Zoo. She was charming at first; quite charming; but she turned into a fiend because I had a few words with her. You would not believe: she very nearly killed me. You heard what she said just now. She belongs to a party here which wants to have us all killed.

THE WIFE [*terrified*] Us! But we have done nothing: we have been as nice to them as nice could be. Oh, Amby, come away, come away: there is something dreadful about this place and these people.

THE ENVOY. There is, and no mistake. But youre safe with me: you ought to have sense enough to know that.

THE ELDERLY GENTLEMAN. I am sorry to say, Molly, that it is not merely us four poor weak creatures they want to kill, but the entire race of Man, except themselves.

THE ENVOY. Not so poor neither, Poppa. Nor so weak, if you are going to take in all the Powers. If it comes to killing, two can play at that game, longlived or shortlived.

THE ELDERLY GENTLEMAN. No, Ambrose; we should have no chance. We are worms beside these fearful people: mere worms.

*Zozim comes from the temple, robed majestically, and wearing a wreath of mistletoe in his flowing white wig. His false beard reaches almost to his waist. He carries a staff with a curiously carved top.*

ZOZIM [*in the doorway, impressively*] Hail, strangers!

ALL [*reverently*] Hail!

ZOZIM. Are ye prepared?

THE ENVOY. We are.

ZOZIM [*unexpectedly becoming conversational, and*

*strolling down carelessly to the middle of the group between the two ladies*] Well, I'm sorry to say the oracle is not. She was delayed by some member of your party who got loose; and as the show takes a bit of arranging, you will have to wait a few minutes. The ladies can go inside and look round the entrance hall and get pictures and things if they want them.

THE WIFE ⎫                    ⎧ Thank you. ⎫ [*They go*
THE DAUGHTER ⎬ [*together*] ⎨ I should *like* ⎬ *into the*
                      ⎭                    ⎩ to, very much. ⎭ *temple*].

THE ELDERLY GENTLEMAN [*in dignified rebuke of Zozim's levity*] Taken in this spirit, sir, the show, as you call it, becomes almost an insult to our common sense.

ZOZIM. Quite, I should say. You need not keep it up with me.

THE ENVOY [*suddenly making himself very agreeable*] Just so: just so. We can wait as long as you please. And now, if I may be allowed to seize the opportunity of a few minutes friendly chat—?

ZOZIM. By all means, if only you will talk about things I can understand.

THE ENVOY. Well, about this colonizing plan of yours. My father-in-law here has been telling me something about it; and he has just now let out that you want not only to colonize us, but to—to—to—well, shall we say to supersede us. Now why supersede us? Why not live and let live? Theres not a scrap of ill-feeling on our side. We should welcome a colony of immortals—we may almost call you that—in the British Middle East. No doubt the Turanian Empire, with its Mahometan traditions, overshadows us now. We have had to bring the Emperor with us on this expedition, though of course you know as well as I do that he has imposed himself on my party just

[ 545 ]

to spy on me. I dont deny that he has the whip hand of us to some extent, because if it came to a war none of our generals could stand up against him. I give him best at that game: he is the finest soldier in the world. Besides, he is an emperor and an autocrat; and I am only an elected representative of the British democracy. Not that our British democrats wont fight: they will fight the heads off all the Turanians that ever walked; but then it takes so long to work them up to it, while he has only to say the word and march. But you people would never get on with him. Believe me, you would not be as comfortable in Turania as you would be with us. We understand you. We like you. We are easy-going people; and we are rich people. That will appeal to you. Turania is a poor place when all is said. Five-eighths of it is desert. They dont irrigate as we do. Besides—now I am sure this will appeal to you and to all right-minded men—we are Christians.

ZOZIM. The old uns prefer Mahometans.

THE ENVOY [*shocked*] What!

ZOZIM [*distinctly*] They prefer Mahometans. Whats wrong with that?

THE ENVOY. Well, of all the disgraceful—

THE ELDERLY GENTLEMAN [*diplomatically interrupting his scandalized son-in-law*] There can be no doubt, I am afraid, that by clinging too long to the obsolete features of the old pseudo-Christian Churches we allowed the Mahometans to get ahead of us at a very critical period of the development of the Eastern world. When the Mahometan Reformation took place, it left its followers with the enormous advantage of having the only established religion in the world in whose articles of faith any intelligent and educated person could believe.

[ 546 ]

THE ENVOY. But what about our Reformation? Dont give the show away, Poppa. We followed suit, didnt we?

THE ELDERLY GENTLEMAN. Unfortunately, Ambrose, we could not follow suit very rapidly. We had not only a religion to deal with, but a Church.

ZOZIM. What is a Church?

THE ENVOY. Not know what a Church is! Well!

THE ELDERLY GENTLEMAN. You must excuse me; but if I attempted to explain you would only ask me what a bishop is; and that is a question that no mortal man can answer. All I can tell you is that Mahomet was a truly wise man; for he founded a religion without a Church; consequently when the time came for a Reformation of the mosques there were no bishops and deans to obstruct it. Our bishops and deans prevented us for two hundred years from following suit; and we have never recovered the start we lost then. I can only plead that we did reform our Church at last. No doubt we had to make a few compromizes as a matter of good taste; but there is now very little in our Articles of Religion that is not accepted as at least allegorically true by our Higher Criticism.

THE ENVOY [*encouragingly*] Besides, does it matter? Why, *I* have never read the Articles in my life; and I am Prime Minister! Come! if my services in arranging for the reception of a colonizing party would be acceptable, they are at your disposal. And when I say a reception I mean a reception. Royal honors, mind you! A salute of a hundred and one guns! The streets lined with troops! The Guards turned out at the Palace! Dinner at the Guildhall!

ZOZIM. Discourage me if I know what youre talking about! I wish Zoo would come: she understands these things. All I can tell you is that the general opinion among the Colonizers is in favour of beginning in a country where the people are of a different color from us; so that we can make short work without any risk of mistakes.

THE ENVOY. What do you mean by short work? I hope—

ZOZIM [*with obviously feigned geniality*] Oh, nothing, nothing, nothing. We are thinking of trying North America: thats all. You see, the Red Men of that country used to be white. They passed through a period of sallow complexions, followed by a period of no complexions at all, into the red characteristic of their climate. Besides, several cases of long life have occurred in North America.

THE ELDERLY GENTLEMAN. But have you considered the possibility of your colony turning red?

ZOZIM. That wont matter. We are not particular about our pigmentation. The old books mention redfaced Englishmen: they appear to have been common objects at one time.

THE ELDERLY GENTLEMAN [*very persuasively*] But do you think you would be popular in North America? It seems to me, if I may say so, that on your own shewing you need a country in which society is organized in a series of highly exclusive circles, in which the privacy of private life is very jealously guarded, and in which no one presumes to speak to anyone else without an introduction following a strict examination of social credentials. It is only in such a country that persons of special tastes and attainments can form a little world of their own, and protect themselves absolutely from intrusion by common persons. I think I may claim that our British society has developed this exclusiveness to perfection. If you

[ 548 ]

would pay us a visit and see the working of our caste system, our club system, our guild system, you would admit that nowhere else in the world, least of all, perhaps, in North America, which has a regrettable tradition of social promiscuity, could you keep yourselves so entirely to yourselves.

ZOZIM [*good-naturedly embarrassed*] Look here. There is no good discussing this. I had rather not explain; but it wont make any difference to our Colonizers what sort of shortlivers they come across. We shall arrange all that. Never mind how. Let us join the ladies.

THE ELDERLY GENTLEMAN [*throwing off his diplomatic attitude and abandoning himself to despair*] We understand you only too well, sir. Well, kill us. End the lives you have made miserably unhappy by opening up to us the possibility that any of us may live three hundred years. I solemnly curse that possibility. To you it may be a blessing, because you do live three hundred years. To us, who live less than a hundred, whose flesh is as grass, it is the most unbearable burden our poor tortured humanity has ever groaned under.

THE ENVOY. Hullo, Poppa! Steady! How do you make that out?

ZOZIM. What is three hundred years? Short enough, if you ask me. Why, in the old days you people lived on the assumption that you were going to last out for ever and ever and ever. Immortal, you thought yourselves. Were you any happier then?

THE ELDERLY GENTLEMAN. As President of the Baghdad Historical Society I am in a position to inform you that the communities which took this monstrous pretension seriously were the most wretched of which we have any record. My Society has printed an editio princeps of the works of the father of history, Thucyderodotus Macollybuckle. Have you read his account of what was blasphemously called the Perfect City of God, and the attempt made to reproduce it in the northern part of these islands by Jonhobsnoxius, called the Leviathan? Those misguided people sacrificed the fragment of life that was granted to them to an imaginary immortality. They crucified the prophet who told them to take no thought for the morrow, and that here and now was their Australia: Australia being a term signifying paradise, or an eternity of bliss. They tried to produce a condition of death in life: to mortify the flesh, as they called it.

ZOZIM. Well, you are not suffering from that, are you? You have not a mortified air.

THE ELDERLY GENTLEMAN. Naturally we are not absolutely insane and suicidal. Nevertheless we impose on ourselves abstinences and disciplines and studies that are meant to prepare us for living three centuries. And we seldom live one. My childhood was made unnecessarily painful, my boyhood unnecessarily laborious, by ridiculous preparations for a length of days which the chances were fifty thousand to one against my ever attaining. I have been cheated out of the natural joys and freedoms of my life by this dream to which the existence of these islands and their oracles gives a delusive possibility of realization. I curse the day when long life was invented, just as the victims of Jonhobsnoxius cursed the day when eternal life was invented.

ZOZIM. Pooh! You could live three centuries if you chose.

THE ELDERLY GENTLEMAN. That is what the fortunate always say to the unfortunate. Well, I do not choose. I accept my three score and ten years. If they are filled with usefulness, with justice, with mercy, with good-will: if they are the lifetime of a soul that never loses its honor and a brain that never loses its eagerness, they are enough for me, because these things are infinite and eternal, and can make ten of my years as long as thirty of yours. I shall not conclude by saying live as long as you like and be damned to you, because I have risen for the moment far above any ill-will to you or to any fellow-creature: but I am your equal before that eternity in which the difference between your lifetime and mine is as the difference between one drop of water and three in the eyes of the Almighty Power from which we have both proceeded.

ZOZIM [*impressed*] You spoke that piece very well, Daddy. I couldnt talk like that if I tried. It sounded fine. Ah! here come the ladies.

*To his relief, they have just appeared on the threshold of the temple.*

THE ELDERLY GENTLEMAN [*passing from exaltation to distress*] It means nothing to him: in this land of discouragement the sublime has become the ridiculous. [*Turning on the hopelessly puzzled Zozim*] "Behold, thou hast made my days as it were a span long; and mine age is even as nothing in respect of thee."

THE WIFE ⎱ ⎰ Poppa, Poppa: dont
          ⎪ [*running* ⎰ look like that.
THE DAUGHTER ⎰ *to him*] ⎱ Oh, granpa, whats the
          ⎭          ⎩ matter?

ZOZIM [*with a shrug*] Discouragement!

THE ELDERLY GENTLEMAN [*throwing off the women with a superb gesture*] Liar! [*Recollecting himself, he adds, with noble courtesy, raising his hat and bowing*] I beg your pardon, sir; but I am NOT discouraged.

*A burst of orchestral music, through which a powerful gong sounds, is heard from the temple. Zoo, in a purple robe, appears in the doorway.*

ZOO. Come. The oracle is ready.

*Zozim motions them to the threshold with a wave of his staff. The Envoy and the Elderly Gentleman take off their hats and go into the temple on tiptoe, Zoo leading the way. The Wife and Daughter, frightened as they are, raise their heads uppishly and follow flatfooted, sustained by a sense of their Sunday clothes and social consequence. Zozim remains in the portico, alone.*

ZOZIM [*taking off his wig, beard, and robe, and bundling them under his arm*] Ouf! [*He goes home*].

# [ACT III]

*Inside the temple. A gallery overhanging an abyss. Dead silence. The gallery is brightly lighted; but beyond is a vast gloom, continually changing in intensity. A shaft of violet light shoots upwards; and a very harmonious and silvery carillon chimes. When it ceases the violet ray vanishes.*

*Zoo comes along the gallery, followed by the Envoy's daughter, his wife, the Envoy himself, and the Elderly Gentleman. The two men are holding their hats with the brims near their noses, as if prepared to pray into them at a moment's notice. Zoo halts: they all follow her example. They contemplate the void with awe. Organ music of the kind called sacred in the nineteenth century begins. Their awe deepens. The violet ray, now a diffused mist, rises again from the abyss.*

THE WIFE [*to Zoo, in a reverent whisper*] Shall we kneel?

ZOO [*loudly*] Yes, if you want to. You can stand on your head if you like. [*She sits down carelessly on the gallery railing, with her back to the abyss*].

THE ELDERLY GENTLEMAN [*jarred by her callousness*] We desire to behave in a becoming manner.

ZOO. Very well. Behave just as you feel. It doesnt matter how you behave. But keep your wits about you when the pythoness ascends, or you will forget the questions you have come to ask her.

THE ENVOY ⎫ ⎧ [*very nervous, takes out*
⎪ [*simul-* ⎪ *a paper to refresh his*
⎬ *taneously*] ⎨ *memory*] Ahem!
THE DAUGHTER ⎪ ⎪ [*alarmed*] The python-
⎭ ⎩ ess? Is she a snake?

THE ELDERLY GENTLEMAN. Tch-ch! The priestess of the oracle. A sybil. A prophetess. Not a snake.

THE WIFE. How awful!

ZOO. I'm glad you think so.

THE WIFE. Oh dear! Dont you think so?

ZOO. No. This sort of thing is got up to impress you, not to impress me.

THE ELDERLY GENTLEMAN. I wish you would let it impress us, then, madam. I am deeply impressed; and your levity jars on me unbearably.

ZOO. You just wait. All this business with colored lights and chords on that old organ is only tomfoolery. Wait til you see the pythoness.

*The Envoy's wife falls on her knees, and takes refuge in prayer.*

THE DAUGHTER [*trembling*] Are we really going to see a woman who has lived three hundred years?

ZOO. Stuff! Youd drop dead if a tertiary as much as looked at you. The oracle is only a hundred and seventy; and youll find it hard enough to stand her.

THE DAUGHTER [*piteously*] Oh! [*she falls on her knees*].

THE ENVOY. Whew! Stand by me, Poppa. This is a little more than I bargained for. Are you going to kneel; or how?

THE ELDERLY GENTLEMAN. Perhaps it would be in better taste.

*The two men kneel.*

*The vapour of the abyss thickens; and a distant roll of thunder seems to come from its depths. The pythoness, seated on her tripod, rises slowly from it. She has*

*discarded the insulating robe and veil in which she con-*
*versed with Napoleon, and is now draped in voluminous*
*folds of a single piece of grey-white stuff. Something*
*supernatural about her terrifies the beholders, who throw*
*themselves on their faces. Her outline flows and waves:*
*she is almost distinct at moments, and again vague and*
*shadowy: above all, she is larger than life-size, not*
*enough to be measured by the flustered congregation, but*
*enough to affect them with a dreadful sense of her super-*
*naturalness.*

ZOO. Get up, get up. Do pull yourselves together,
you people.

*The Envoy and his family, by shuddering negatively,*
*intimate that it is impossible. The Elderly Gentleman*
*manages to get on his hands and knees.*

ZOO. Come on, Daddy: you are not afraid. Speak to
her. She wont wait here all day for you, you know.

THE ELDERLY GENTLEMAN [*rising very deferentially*
*to his feet*] Madam; you will excuse my very natural
nervousness in addressing, for the first time in my
life, a—a—a—a goddess. My friend and relative the
Envoy is unhinged. I throw myself upon your indulgence—

ZOO [*interrupting him intolerantly*] Dont throw yourself on anything belonging to her or you will go right
through her and break your neck. She isnt solid,
like you.

THE ELDERLY GENTLEMAN. I was speaking figura-
tively—

ZOO. You have been told not to do it. Ask her what
you want to know; and be quick about it.

THE ELDERLY GENTLEMAN [*stooping and taking the*
*prostrate Envoy by the shoulders*] Ambrose: you must
make an effort. You cannot go back to Baghdad
without the answers to your questions.

THE ENVOY [*rising to his knees*] I shall be only too glad to get back alive on any terms. If my legs would support me I'd just do a bunk straight for the ship.

THE ELDERLY GENTLEMAN. No, no. Remember: your dignity—

THE ENVOY. Dignity be damned! I'm terrified. Take me away, for God's sake.

THE ELDERLY GENTLEMAN [*producing a brandy flask and taking the cap off*] Try some of this. It is still nearly full, thank goodness!

THE ENVOY [*clutching it and drinking eagerly*] Ah! Thats better. [*He tries to drink again. Finding that he has emptied it, he hands it back to his father-in-law upside down*].

THE ELDERLY GENTLEMAN [*taking it*] Great heavens! He has swallowed half-a-pint of neat brandy. [*Much perturbed, he screws the cap on again, and pockets the flask*].

THE ENVOY [*staggering to his feet; pulling a paper from his pocket; and speaking with boisterous confidence*] Get up, Molly. Up with you, Eth.

*The two women rise to their knees.*

THE ENVOY. What I want to ask is this. [*He refers to the paper*]. Ahem! Civilization has reached a crisis. We are at the parting of the ways. We stand on the brink of the Rubicon. Shall we take the plunge? Already a leaf has been torn out of the book of the Sybil. Shall we wait until the whole volume is consumed? On our right is the crater of the volcano: on our left the precipice. One false step, and we go down to annihilation dragging the whole human race with us. [*He pauses for breath*].

THE ELDERLY GENTLEMAN [*recovering his spirits under the familiar stimulus of political oratory*] Hear, hear!

[ 556 ]

ZOO. What are you raving about? Ask your question while you have the chance? What is it you want to know?

THE ENVOY [*patronizing her in the manner of a Premier debating with a very young member of the Opposition*] A young woman asks me a question. I am always glad to see the young taking an interest in politics. It is an impatient question; but it is a practical question, an intelligent question. She asks why we seek to lift a corner of the veil that shrouds the future from our feeble vision.

ZOO. I dont. I ask you to tell the oracle what you want, and not keep her sitting there all day.

THE ELDERLY GENTLEMAN [*warmly*] Order, order!

ZOO. What does "Order, order!" mean?

THE ENVOY. I ask the august oracle to listen to my voice—

ZOO. You people seem never to tire of listening to your voices; but it doesnt amuse us. What do you want?

THE ENVOY. I want, young woman, to be allowed to proceed without unseemly interruptions.

*A low roll of thunder comes from the abyss.*

THE ELDERLY GENTLEMAN. There! Even the oracle is indignant. [*To the Envoy*] Do not allow yourself to be put down by this lady's rude clamor, Ambrose. Take no notice. Proceed.

THE ENVOY'S WIFE. I cant bear this much longer, Amby. Remember: *I* havnt had any brandy.

THE DAUGHTER [*trembling*] There are serpents curling in the vapour. I am afraid of the lightning. Finish it, Papa; or I shall die.

THE ENVOY [*sternly*] Silence. The destiny of British civilization is at stake. Trust me. I am not afraid. As I was saying—where was I?

zoo. I dont know. Does anybody?

THE ELDERLY GENTLEMAN [*tactfully*] You were just coming to the election, I think.

THE ENVOY [*reassured*] Just so. The election. Now what we want to know is this: ought we to dissolve in August, or put it off until next spring?

zoo. Dissolve? In what? [*Thunder*]. Oh! My fault this time. That means that the oracle understands you, and desires me to hold my tongue.

THE ENVOY [*fervently*] I thank the oracle.

THE WIFE [*to Zoo*] Serve you right!

THE ELDERLY GENTLEMAN. Before the oracle replies, I should like to be allowed to state a few of the reasons why, in my opinion, the Government should hold on until the spring. In the first—

*Terrific lightning and thunder. The Elderly Gentleman is knocked flat; but as he immediately sits up again dazedly it is clear that he is none the worse for the shock. The ladies cower in terror. The Envoy's hat is blown off; but he seizes it just as it quits his temples, and holds it on with both hands. He is recklessly drunk, but quite articulate, as he seldom speaks in public without taking stimulants beforehand.*

THE ENVOY [*taking one hand from his hat to make a gesture of stilling the tempest*] Thats enough. We know how to take a hint. I'll put the case in three words. I am the leader of the Potterbill party. My party is in power. I am Prime Minister. The Opposition— the Rotterjacks—have won every bye-election for the last six months. They—

THE ELDERLY GENTLEMAN [*scrambling heatedly to his feet*] Not by fair means. By bribery, by misrepresentation, by pandering to the vilest prejudices [*muttered thunder*]—I beg your pardon [*he is silent*].

THE ENVOY. Never mind the bribery and lies. The

[ 558 ]

oracle knows all about that. The point is that though our five years will not expire until the year after next, our majority will be eaten away at the bye-elections by about Easter. We cant wait: we must start some question that will excite the public, and go to the country on it. But some of us say do it now. Others say wait til the spring. We cant make up our minds one way or the other. Which would you advise?

ZOO. But what is the question that is to excite your public?

THE ENVOY. That doesnt matter. I dont know yet. We will find a question all right enough. The oracle can foresee the future: we cannot. [*Thunder*]. What does that mean? What have I done now?

ZOO [*severely*] How often must you be told that we cannot foresee the future? There is no such thing as the future until it is the present.

THE ELDERLY GENTLEMAN. Allow me to point out, madam, that when the Potterbill party sent to consult the oracle fifteen years ago, the oracle prophesied that the Potterbills would be victorious at the General Election; and they were. So it is evident that the oracle can foresee the future, and is sometimes willing to reveal it.

THE ENVOY. Quite true. Thank you, Poppa. I appeal now, over your head, young woman, direct to the August Oracle, to repeat the signal favour conferred on my illustrious predecessor, Sir Fuller Eastwind, and to answer me exactly as he was answered.

*The oracle raises her hands to command silence.*

ALL. Sh-sh-sh!

*Invisible trombones utter three solemn blasts in the manner of Die Zauberflöte.*

THE ELDERLY GENTLEMAN. May I—

ZOO [*quickly*] Hush. The oracle is going to speak.

THE ORACLE. Go home, poor fool.

*She vanishes; and the atmosphere changes to prosaic daylight. Zoo comes off the railing; throws off her robe; makes a bundle of it, and tucks it under her arm. The magic and mystery are gone. The women rise to their feet. The Envoy's party stare at one another helplessly.*

ZOO. The same reply, word for word, that your illustrious predecessor, as you call him, got fifteen years ago. You asked for it; and you got it. And just think of all the important questions you might have asked. She would have answered them, you know. It is always like that. I will go and arrange to have you sent home: you can wait for me in the entrance hall [*she goes out*].

THE ENVOY. What possessed me to ask for the same answer old Eastwind got?

THE ELDERLY GENTLEMAN. But it was not the same answer. The answer to Eastwind was an inspiration to our party for years. It won us the election.

THE ENVOY'S DAUGHTER. I learnt it at school, grandpa. It wasnt the same at all. I can repeat it. [*She quotes*] "When Britain was cradled in the west, the east wind hardened her and made her great. Whilst the east wind prevails Britain shall prosper. The east wind shall wither Britain's enemies in the day of contest. Let the Rotterjacks look to it."

THE ENVOY. The old man invented that. I see it all. He was a doddering old ass when he came to consult the oracle. The oracle naturally said "Go home, poor fool." There was no sense in saying that to me; but as that girl said, I asked for it. What else could the poor old chap do but fake up an answer fit for publication? There were whispers about it; but nobody believed them. I believe them now.

THE ELDERLY GENTLEMAN. Oh, I cannot admit that Sir Fuller Eastwind was capable of such a fraud.

THE ENVOY. He was capable of anything: I knew his private secretary. And now what are we going to say? You dont suppose I am going back to Baghdad to tell the British Empire that the oracle called me a fool, do you?

THE ELDERLY GENTLEMAN. Surely we must tell the truth, however painful it may be to our feelings.

THE ENVOY. I am not thinking of my feelings: I am not so selfish as that, thank God. I am thinking of the country: of our party. The truth, as you call it, would put the Rotterjacks in for the next twenty years. It would be the end of me politically. Not that I care for that: I am only too willing to retire if you can find a better man. Dont hesitate on my account.

THE ELDERLY GENTLEMAN. No, Ambrose: you are indispensable. There is no one else.

THE ENVOY. Very well, then. What are you going to do?

THE ELDERLY GENTLEMAN. My dear Ambrose, you are the leader of the party, not I. What are you going to do?

THE ENVOY. I am going to tell the exact truth: thats what I'm going to do. Do you take me for a liar?

THE ELDERLY GENTLEMAN [*puzzled*] Oh. I beg your pardon. I understood you to say—

THE ENVOY [*cutting him short*] You understood me to say that I am going back to Baghdad to tell the British electorate that the oracle repeated to me, word for word, what it said to Sir Fuller Eastwind fifteen years ago. Molly and Ethel can bear me out. So must you, if you are an honest man. Come on.

*He goes out, followed by his wife and daughter.*

THE ELDERLY GENTLEMAN [*left alone and shrinking*

*into an old and desolate figure*] What am I to do ? I am a most perplexed and wretched man. [*He falls on his knees, and stretches his hands in entreaty over the abyss*]. I invoke the oracle. I cannot go back and connive at a blasphemous lie. I implore guidance.

*The pythoness walks in on the gallery behind him, and touches him on the shoulder. Her size is now natural. Her face is hidden by her hood. He flinches as if from an electric shock; turns to her; and cowers, covering his eyes in terror.*

THE ELDERLY GENTLEMAN. No: not close to me. I'm afraid I cant bear it.

THE ORACLE [*with grave pity*] Come: look at me. I am my natural size now: what you saw there was only a foolish picture of me thrown on a cloud by a lantern. How can I help you ?

THE ELDERLY GENTLEMAN. They have gone back to lie about your answer. I cannot go with them. I cannot live among people to whom nothing is real. I have become incapable of it through my stay here. I implore to be allowed to stay.

THE ORACLE. My friend: if you stay with us you will die of discouragement.

THE ELDERLY GENTLEMAN. If I go back I shall die of disgust and despair. I take the nobler risk. I beg of you, do not cast me out.

*He catches her robe and holds her.*

THE ORACLE. Take care. I have been here one hundred and seventy years. Your death does not mean to me what it means to you.

THE ELDERLY GENTLEMAN. It is the meaning of life, not of death, that makes banishment so terrible to me.

THE ORACLE. Be it so, then. You may stay.

*She offers him her hands. He grasps them and raises*

*himself a little by clinging to her. She looks steadily into his face. He stiffens; a little convulsion shakes him; his grasp relaxes; and he falls dead.*

THE ORACLE [*looking down at the body*] Poor short-lived thing! What else could I do for you?

# PART V

# AS FAR AS
# THOUGHT CAN REACH

---

*Summer afternoon in the year 31,920 A.D. A sunlit glade
at the southern foot of a thickly wooded hill. On the west
side of it, the steps and columned porch of a dainty little
classic temple. Between it and the hill, a rising path to the
wooded heights begins with rough steps of stones in the
moss. On the opposite side, a grove. In the middle of the
glade, an altar in the form of a low marble table as long
as a man, set parallel to the temple steps and pointing to
the hill. Curved marble benches radiate from it into the
foreground; but they are not joined to it: there is plenty
of space to pass between the altar and the benches.*

*A dance of youths and maidens is in progress. The
music is provided by a few fluteplayers seated together
on the steps of the temple. There are no children; and none
of the dancers seems younger than eighteen. Some of the
youths have beards. Their dress, like the architecture of
the temple and the design of the altar and curved seats,
resembles Grecian of the fourth century* B.C., *freely
handled. They move with perfect balance and remarkable
grace, racing through a figure like a farandole. They
neither romp nor hug in our manner.*

*At the first full close they clap their hands to stop the
musicians, who recommence with a saraband, during
which a strange figure appears on the path beyond the
temple. He is deep in thought, with his eyes closed and
his feet feeling automatically for the rough irregular steps
as he slowly descends them. Except for a sort of linen kilt*

[ 564 ]

*consisting mainly of a girdle carrying a sporran and a few minor pockets, he is naked. In physical hardihood and uprightness he seems to be in the prime of life; and his eyes and mouth shew no signs of age; but his face, though fully and firmly fleshed, bears a network of lines, varying from furrows to hairbreadth reticulations, as if Time had worked over every inch of it incessantly through whole geologic periods. His head is finely domed and utterly bald. Except for his eyelashes he is quite hairless. He is unconscious of his surroundings, and walks right into one of the dancing couples, separating them. He wakes up and stares about him. The couple stop indignantly. The rest stop. The music stops. The youth whom he has jostled accosts him without malice, but without anything that we should call manners.*

---

THE YOUTH. Now, then, ancient sleepwalker: why dont you keep your eyes open and mind where you are going?

THE ANCIENT [*mild, bland, and indulgent*] I did not know there was a nursery here, or I should not have turned my face in this direction. Such accidents cannot always be avoided. Go on with your play: I will turn back.

THE YOUTH. Why not stay with us and enjoy life for once in a way? We will teach you to dance.

THE ANCIENT. No, thank you. I danced when I was a child like you. Dancing is a very crude attempt to get into the rhythm of life. It would be painful to me to go back from that rhythm to your babyish gambols: in fact I could not do it if I tried. But at your age it is pleasant; and I am sorry I disturbed you.

THE YOUTH. Come! own up: arnt you very unhappy? It's dreadful to see you ancients going about by yourselves, never noticing anything, never dancing, never laughing, never singing, never getting anything out of life. None of us are going to be like that when we grow up. It's a dog's life.

THE ANCIENT. Not at all. You repeat that old phrase without knowing that there was once a creature on earth called a dog. Those who are interested in extinct forms of life will tell you that it loved the sound of its own voice and bounded about when it was happy, just as you are doing here. It is you, my children, who are living the dog's life.

THE YOUTH. The dog must have been a good sensible creature; it set you a very wise example. You should let yourself go occasionally and have a good time.

THE ANCIENT. My children: be content to let us ancients go our ways and enjoy ourselves in our own fashion.

*He turns to go.*

THE MAIDEN. But wait a moment. Why will you not tell us how you enjoy yourself? You must have secret pleasures that you hide from us, and that you never get tired of. I get tired of all our dances and all our tunes. I get tired of all my partners.

THE YOUTH [*suspiciously*] Do you? I shall bear that in mind.

*They all look at one another as if there were some sinister significance in what she has said.*

THE MAIDEN. We all do: what is the use of pretending we dont? It is natural

SEVERAL YOUNG PEOPLE. No, no. We dont. It is not natural.

THE ANCIENT. You are older than he is, I see. You are growing up.

THE MAIDEN. How do you know? I do not look so much older, do I?

[ 566 ]

THE ANCIENT. Oh, I was not looking at you. Your looks do not interest me.

THE MAIDEN. Thank you.

*They all laugh.*

THE YOUTH. You old fish! I believe you dont know the difference between a man and a woman.

THE ANCIENT. It has long ceased to interest me in the way it interests you. And when anything no longer interests us we no longer know it.

THE MAIDEN. You havnt told me how I shew my age. That is what I want to know. As a matter of fact I am older than this boy here: older than he thinks. How did you find that out?

THE ANCIENT. Easily enough. You are ceasing to pretend that these childish games—this dancing and singing and mating—do not become tiresome and unsatisfying after a while. And you no longer care to pretend that you are younger than you are. These are the signs of adolescence. And then, see these fantastic rags with which you have draped yourself. [*He takes up a piece of her draperies in his hand*]. It is rather badly worn here. Why do you not get a new one?

THE MAIDEN. Oh, I did not notice it. Besides, it is too much trouble. Clothes are a nuisance. I think I shall do without them some day, as you ancients do.

THE ANCIENT. Signs of maturity. Soon you will give up all these toys and games and sweets.

THE YOUTH. What! And be as miserable as you?

THE ANCIENT. Infant: one moment of the ecstasy of life as we live it would strike you dead. [*He stalks gravely out through the grove*].

*They stare after him, much damped.*

THE YOUTH [*to the musicians*] Let us have another dance.

*The musicians shake their heads; get up from their seats on the steps; and troop away into the temple. The others follow them, except the Maiden, who sits down on the altar.*

A MAIDEN [*as she goes*] There! The ancient has put them out of countenance. It is your fault, Strephon, for provoking him. [*She leaves, much disappointed*].

A YOUTH. Why need you have cheeked him like that? [*He goes, grumbling*].

STREPHON [*calling after him*] I thought it was understood that we are always to cheek the ancients on principle.

ANOTHER YOUTH. Quite right too! There would be no holding them if we didnt. [*He goes*].

THE MAIDEN. Why dont you really stand up to them? *I* did.

ANOTHER YOUTH. Sheer, abject, pusillanimous, dastardly cowardice. Thats why. Face the filthy truth. [*He goes*].

ANOTHER YOUTH [*turning on the steps as he goes out*] And dont you forget, infant, that one moment of the ecstasy of life as I live it would strike you dead. Haha!

STREPHON [*now the only one left, except the Maiden*] Arnt you coming, Chloe?

THE MAIDEN [*shakes her head*]!

THE YOUTH [*hurrying back to her*] What is the matter?

THE MAIDEN [*tragically pensive*] I dont know.

THE YOUTH. Then there is something the matter. Is that what you mean?

THE MAIDEN. Yes. Something is happening to me. I dont know what.

THE YOUTH. You no longer love me. I have seen it for a month past.

THE MAIDEN. Dont you think all that is rather silly?

We cannot go on as if this kind of thing, this dancing and sweethearting, were everything.

THE YOUTH. What is there better? What else is there worth living for?

THE MAIDEN. Oh, stuff! Dont be frivolous.

THE YOUTH. Something horrible is happening to you. You are losing all heart, all feeling. [*He sits on the altar beside her and buries his face in his hands*]. I am bitterly unhappy.

THE MAIDEN. Unhappy! Really, you must have a very empty head if there is nothing in it but a dance with one girl who is no better than any of the other girls.

THE YOUTH. You did not always think so. You used to be vexed if I as much as looked at another girl.

THE MAIDEN. What does it matter what I did when I was a baby? Nothing existed for me then except what I tasted and touched and saw; and I wanted all that for myself, just as I wanted the moon to play with. Now the world is opening out for me. More than the world: the universe. Even little things are turning out to be great things, and becoming intensely interesting. Have you ever thought about the properties of numbers?

THE YOUTH [*sitting up, markedly disenchanted*] Numbers!!! I cannot imagine anything drier or more repulsive.

THE MAIDEN. They are fascinating, just fascinating. I want to get away from our eternal dancing and music, and just sit down by myself and think about numbers.

THE YOUTH [*rising indignantly*] Oh, this is too much. I have suspected you for some time past. We have all suspected you. The girls swear you have deceived us as to your age. You are getting flat-chested; you are bored with us; and you talk to the ancients when you get the chance. Tell me the truth: how old are you?

THE MAIDEN. Just twice your age, my poor boy.

THE YOUTH. Twice my age! Do you mean to say you are four?

THE MAIDEN. Very nearly four.

THE YOUTH [*collapsing on the altar with a groan*] Oh!

THE MAIDEN. My poor Strephon: I pretended I was only two for your sake. I was two when you were born. I saw you break from your shell; and you were such a charming child! You ran round and talked to us all so prettily, and were so handsome and well grown, that I lost my heart to you at once. But now I seem to have lost it altogether: bigger things are taking possession of me. Still, we were very happy in our childish way for the first year, werent we?

STREPHON. I was happy until you began cooling towards me.

THE MAIDEN. Not towards you, but towards all the trivialities of our life here. Just think. I have hundreds of years to live: perhaps thousands. Do you suppose I can spend centuries dancing; listening to flutes ringing changes on a few tunes and a few notes; raving about the beauty of a few pillars and arches; making jingles with words; lying about with your arms round me, which is really neither comfortable nor convenient; everlastingly choosing colors for dresses, and putting them on, and washing; making a business of sitting together at fixed hours to absorb our nourishment; taking little poisons with it to make us delirious enough to imagine we are enjoying ourselves; and then having to pass the nights in shelters lying in cots and losing half our lives in a state of unconsciousness. Sleep is a shameful thing:

[ 570 ]

I have not slept at all for weeks past. I have stolen out at night when you were all lying insensible—quite disgusting, I call it—and wandered about the woods, thinking, thinking, thinking; grasping the world; taking it to pieces; building it up again; devising methods; planning experiments to test the methods; and having a glorious time. Every morning I have come back here with greater and greater reluctance; and I know that the time will soon come—perhaps it has come already—when I shall not come back at all.

STREPHON. How horribly cold and uncomfortable!

THE MAIDEN. Oh, dont talk to me of comfort! Life is not worth living if you have to bother about comfort. Comfort makes winter a torture, spring an illness, summer an oppression, and autumn only a respite. The ancients could make life one long frowsty comfort if they chose. But they never lift a finger to make themselves comfortable. They will not sleep under a roof. They will not clothe themselves: a girdle with a few pockets hanging to it to carry things about in is all they wear: they will sit down on the wet moss or in a gorse bush when there is dry heather within two yards of them. Two years ago, when you were born, I did not understand this. Now I feel that I would not put myself to the trouble of walking two paces for all the comfort in the world.

STREPHON. But you dont know what this means to me. It means that you are dying to me: yes, just dying. Listen to me [*he puts his arm around her*].

THE MAIDEN [*extricating herself*] Dont. We can talk quite as well without touching one another.

STREPHON [*horrified*] Chloe! Oh, this is the worst symptom of all! The ancients never touch one another.

THE MAIDEN. Why should they?

STREPHON. Oh, I dont know. But dont you want to touch me? You used to.

THE MAIDEN. Yes: that is true: I used to. We used to think it would be nice to sleep in one another's arms; but we never could go to sleep because our weight stopped our circulations just above the elbows. Then somehow my feeling began to change bit by bit. I kept a sort of interest in your head and arms long after I lost interest in your whole body. And now that has gone.

STREPHON. You no longer care for me at all, then?

THE MAIDEN. Nonsense! I care for you much more seriously than before; though perhaps not so much for you in particular. I mean I care more for everybody. But I dont want to touch you unnecessarily; and I certainly dont want you to touch me.

STREPHON [rising decisively] That finishes it. You dislike me.

THE MAIDEN [impatiently] I tell you again, I do not dislike you; but you bore me when you cannot understand; and I think I shall be happier by myself in future. You had better get a new companion. What about the girl who is to be born today?

STREPHON. I do not want the girl who is to be born today. How do I know what she will be like? I want you.

THE MAIDEN. You cannot have me. You must recognize facts and face them. It is no use running after a woman twice your age. I cannot make my childhood last to please you. The age of love is sweet; but it is short; and I must pay nature's debt. You no longer attract me; and I no longer care to attract you. Growth is too rapid at my age: I am maturing from week to week.

STREPHON. You are maturing, as you call it—I call it ageing—from minute to minute. You are going much further than you did when we began this conversation.

THE MAIDEN. It is not the ageing that is so rapid. It is the realization of it when it has actually happened. Now that I have made up my mind to the fact that I have left childhood behind me, it comes home to me in leaps and bounds with every word you say.

STREPHON. But your vow. Have you forgotten that? We all swore together in that temple: the temple of love. You were more earnest than any of us.

THE MAIDEN [*with a grim smile*] Never to let our hearts grow cold! Never to become as the ancients! Never to let the sacred lamp be extinguished! Never to change or forget! To be remembered for ever as the first company of true lovers faithful to this vow so often made and broken by past generations! What folly!

STREPHON. Folly!! You blaspheme: it was a beautiful and holy compact; and I will keep it whilst I live. Are you going to break it?

THE MAIDEN. Dear child: it has broken itself. The change has come in spite of my childish vow. [*She rises*]. Do you mind if I go into the woods for a walk by myself? This chat of ours seems to me an unbearable waste of time. I have so much to think of.

STREPHON [*again collapsing on the altar and covering his eyes with his hands*] My heart is broken. [*He weeps*].

THE MAIDEN [*with a shrug*] I have luckily got through my childhood without that experience. It shews how wise I was to choose a lover half my age. [*She goes towards the grove, and is disappearing among the trees, when another youth, older and manlier than Strephon, with crisp hair and firm arms, comes from the temple, and calls to her from the threshold*].

THE TEMPLE YOUTH. I say, Chloe. Is there any sign of the Ancient yet? The hour of birth is overdue. The baby is kicking like mad. She will break her shell prematurely.

THE MAIDEN [*looks across to the hill path; then points up it, and says*] She is coming, Acis.

*The Maiden turns away through the grove and is lost to sight among the trees.*

ACIS [*coming to Strephon*] Whats the matter? Has Chloe been unkind?

STREPHON. She has grown up in spite of all her promises. She deceived us about her age. She is four.

ACIS. Four! I am sorry, Strephon. I am getting on for three myself; and I know what old age is. I hate to say "I told you so"; but she was getting a little hard set and flat-chested and thin on the top, wasnt she?

STREPHON [*breaking down*] Dont.

ACIS. You must pull yourself together. This is going to be a busy day. First the birth. Then the Festival of the Artists.

STREPHON [*rising*] What is the use of being born if we have to decay into unnatural, heartless, loveless, joyless monsters in four short years? What use are the artists if they cannot bring their beautiful creations to life? I have a great mind to die and have done with it all. [*He moves away to the corner of the curved seat farthest from the temple, and throws himself moodily into it*].

*An Ancient woman has descended the hill path during Strephon's lament, and has heard most of it. She is like the He-Ancient, equally bald, and equally without sexual charm, but intensely interesting and rather terrifying. Her sex is discoverable only by her voice, as her breasts are manly, and her figure otherwise not very different.*

[ 574 ]

*She wears no clothes, but has draped herself rather perfunctorily with a ceremonial robe, and carries two implements like long slender saws. She comes to the altar between the two young men.*

THE SHE-ANCIENT [*to Strephon*] Infant: you are only at the beginning of it all. [*To Acis*] Is the child ready to be born?

ACIS. More than ready, Ancient. Shouting and kicking and cursing. We have called to her to be quiet and wait until you come; but of course she only half understands, and is very impatient.

THE SHE-ANCIENT. Very well. Bring her out into the sun.

ACIS [*going quickly into the temple*] All ready. Come along.

*Joyous processional music strikes up in the temple.*

THE SHE-ANCIENT [*going close to Strephon*] Look at me.

STREPHON [*sulkily, keeping his face averted*] Thank you; but I dont want to be cured. I had rather be miserable in my own way than callous in yours.

THE SHE-ANCIENT. You like being miserable? You will soon grow out of that. [*She returns to the altar*].

*The procession, headed by Acis, emerges from the temple. Six youths carry on their shoulders a burden covered with a gorgeous but light pall. Before them certain official maidens carry a new tunic, ewers of water, silver dishes pierced with holes, cloths, and immense sponges. The rest carry wands with ribbons, and strew flowers. The burden is deposited on the altar, and the pall removed. It is a huge egg.*

THE SHE-ANCIENT [*freeing her arms from her robe, and placing her saws on the altar ready to her hand in a business-like manner*] A girl, I think you said?

ACIS. Yes.

THE TUNIC BEARER. It is a shame. Why cant we have more boys?

SEVERAL YOUTHS [*protesting*] Not at all. More girls. We want new girls.

A GIRL'S VOICE FROM THE EGG. Let me out. Let me out. I want to be born. I want to be born. [*The egg rocks*].

ACIS [*snatching a wand from one of the others and whacking the egg with it*] Be quiet, I tell you. Wait. You will be born presently.

THE EGG. No, no: at once, at once. I want to be born: I want to be born. [*Violent kicking within the egg, which rocks so hard that it has to be held on the altar by the bearers*].

THE SHE-ANCIENT. Silence. [*The music stops; and the egg behaves itself*].

*The She-Ancient takes her two saws, and with a couple of strokes rips the egg open. The Newly Born, a pretty girl who would have been guessed as seventeen in our day, sits up in the broken shell, exquisitely fresh and rosy, but with filaments of spare albumen clinging to her here and there.*

THE NEWLY BORN [*as the world bursts on her vision*] Oh! Oh!! Oh!!! Oh!!!! [*She continues this ad libitum during the following remonstrances*].

ACIS. Hold your noise, will you?

*The washing begins. The Newly Born shrieks and struggles.*

A YOUTH. Lie quiet, you clammy little devil.

A MAIDEN. You must be washed, dear. Now quiet, quiet, quiet: be good.

ACIS. Shut your mouth, or I'll shove the sponge in it.

THE MAIDEN. Shut your eyes. Itll hurt if you dont.

ANOTHER MAIDEN. Dont be silly. One would think nobody had ever been born before.

THE NEWLY BORN [*yells*]!!!!!!

ACIS. Serve you right! You were told to shut your eyes.

THE YOUTH. Dry her off quick. I can hardly hold her. Shut it, will you; or I'll smack you.

*The dressing begins. The Newly Born chuckles with delight.*

THE MAIDEN. Your arms go here, dear. Isnt it pretty? Youll look lovely.

THE NEWLY BORN [*rapturously*] Oh! Oh!! Oh!!! Oh!!!!

ANOTHER YOUTH. No: the other arm: youre putting it on back to front. You are a silly little beast.

ACIS. Here! Thats it. Now youre clean and decent. Up with you! Oopsh! [*He hauls her up to her feet. She cannot walk at first, but masters it after a few steps*]. Now then: march. Here she is, Ancient: put her through the catechism.

THE SHE-ANCIENT. What name have you chosen for her?

ACIS. Amaryllis.

THE SHE-ANCIENT [*to the Newly Born*] Your name is Amaryllis.

THE NEWLY BORN. What does it mean?

A YOUTH. Love.

A MAIDEN. Mother.

ANOTHER YOUTH. Lilies.

THE NEWLY BORN [*to Acis*] What is your name?

ACIS. Acis.

THE NEWLY BORN. I love you, Acis. I must have you all to myself. Take me in your arms.

ACIS. Steady, young one. I am three years old.

THE NEWLY BORN. What has that to do with it? I love you; and I must have you or I will go back into my shell again.

ACIS. You cant. It's broken. Look here [*pointing to Strephon, who has remained in his seat without looking round at the birth, wrapped up in his sorrow*]! Look at this poor fellow!

THE NEWLY BORN. What is the matter with him?

ACIS. When he was born he chose a girl two years old for his sweetheart. He is two years old now himself; and already his heart is broken because she is four. That means that she has grown up like this Ancient here, and has left him. If you choose me, we shall have only a year's happiness before I break your heart by growing up. Better choose the youngest you can find.

THE NEWLY BORN. I will not choose anyone but you. You must not grow up. We will love one another for ever. [*They all laugh*]. What are you laughing at?

THE SHE-ANCIENT. Listen, child—

THE NEWLY BORN. Do not come near me, you dreadful old creature. You frighten me.

ACIS. Just give her another moment. She is not quite reasonable yet. What can you expect from a child less than five minutes old?

THE NEWLY BORN. I think I feel a little more reasonable now. Of course I was rather young when I said that; but the inside of my head is changing very rapidly. I should like to have things explained to me.

ACIS [*to the She-Ancient*] Is she all right, do you think?

*The She-Ancient looks at the Newly Born critically; feels her bumps like a phrenologist; grips her muscles and shakes her limbs; examines her teeth; looks into her eyes for a moment; and finally relinquishes her with an air of having finished her job.*

THE SHE-ANCIENT. She will do. She may live.

*They all wave their hands and shout for joy.*

THE NEWLY-BORN [*indignant*] I may live! Suppose there had been anything wrong with me?

THE SHE-ANCIENT. Children with anything wrong do not live here, my child. Life is not cheap with us. But you would not have felt anything.

THE NEWLY BORN. You mean that you would have murdered me!

THE SHE-ANCIENT. That is one of the funny words the newly born bring with them out of the past. You will forget it tomorrow. Now listen. You have four years of childhood before you. You will not be very happy; but you will be interested and amused by the novelty of the world; and your companions here will teach you how to keep up an imitation of happiness during your four years by what they call arts and sports and pleasures. The worst of your troubles is already over.

THE NEWLY BORN. What! In five minutes?

THE SHE-ANCIENT. No: you have been growing for two years in the egg. You began by being several sorts of creatures that no longer exist, though we have fossils of them. Then you became human; and you passed in fifteen months through a development that once cost human beings twenty years of awkward stumbling immaturity after they were born. They had to spend fifty years more in the sort of childhood you will complete in four years. And then they died of decay. But you need not die until your accident comes.

THE NEWLY BORN. What is my accident?

THE SHE-ANCIENT. Sooner or later you will fall and break your neck; or a tree will fall on you; or you will be struck by lightning. Something or other must make an end of you someday.

[ 579 ]

THE NEWLY BORN. But why should any of these things happen to me?

THE SHE-ANCIENT. There is no why. They do. Everything happens to everybody sooner or later if there is time enough. And with us there is eternity.

THE NEWLY BORN. Nothing need happen. I never heard such nonsense in all my life. I shall know how to take care of myself.

THE SHE-ANCIENT. So you think.

THE NEWLY BORN. I dont think: I know. I shall enjoy life for ever and ever.

THE SHE-ANCIENT. If you should turn out to be a person of infinite capacity, you will no doubt find life infinitely interesting. However, all you have to do now is to play with your companions. They have many pretty toys, as you see: a temple, pictures, images, flowers, bright fabrics, music: above all, themselves; for the most amusing child's toy is another child. At the end of four years, your mind will change: you will become wise; and then you will be entrusted with power.

THE NEWLY BORN. But I want power now.

THE SHE-ANCIENT. No doubt you do; so that you could play with the world by tearing it to pieces.

THE NEWLY BORN. Only to see how it is made. I should put it all together again much better than before.

THE SHE-ANCIENT. There was a time when children were given the world to play with because they promised to improve it. They did not improve it; and they would have wrecked it had their power been as great as that which you will wield when you are no longer a child. Until then your young companions will instruct you in whatever is necessary. You are not forbidden to speak to the ancients; but you had better not do so, as most of them have long ago exhausted all the interest there is in observing children and conversing with them [*She turns to go*]

THE NEWLY BORN. Wait. Tell me some things that I ought to do and ought not to do. I feel the need of education.

*They all laugh at her, except the She-Ancient.*

THE SHE-ANCIENT. You will have grown out of that by tomorrow. Do what you please. [*She goes away up the hill path*].

*The officials take their paraphernalia and the fragments of the egg back into the temple.*

ACIS. Just fancy: that old girl has been going for seven hundred years and hasnt had her fatal accident yet; and she is not a bit tired of it all.

THE NEWLY BORN. How could anyone ever get tired of life?

ACIS. They do. That is, of the same life. They manage to change themselves in a wonderful way. You meet them sometimes with a lot of extra heads and arms and legs: they make you split laughing at them. Most of them have forgotten how to speak: the ones that attend to us have to brush up their knowledge of the language once a year or so. Nothing makes any difference to them that I can see. They never enjoy themselves. I dont know how they can stand it. They dont even come to our festival of the arts. That old one who saw you out of your shell has gone off to moodle about doing nothing; though she knows that this is Festival Day.

THE NEWLY BORN. What is Festival Day?

ACIS. Two of our greatest sculptors are bringing us their latest masterpieces; and we are going to crown them with flowers and sing dithyrambs to them and dance round them.

THE NEWLY BORN. How jolly! What is a sculptor?

ACIS. Listen here, young one. You must find out things for yourself, and not ask questions. For the first day or two you must keep your eyes and ears open and your mouth shut. Children should be seen and not heard.

THE NEWLY BORN. Who are you calling a child? I am fully quarter of an hour old. [*She sits down on the curved bench near Strephon with her maturest air*].

VOICES IN THE TEMPLE [*all expressing protest, disappointment, disgust*] Oh! Oh! Scandalous. Shameful. Disgraceful. What filth! Is this a joke? Why theyre ancients! Ss-s-s-sss! Are you mad, Arjillax? This is an outrage. An insult. Yah! etc. etc. etc. [*The malcontents appear on the steps, grumbling*].

ACIS. Hullo: whats the matter? [*He goes to the steps of the temple*].

*The two sculptors issue from the temple. One has a beard two feet long: the other is beardless. Between them comes a handsome nymph with marked features, dark hair richly waved, and authoritative bearing.*

THE AUTHORITATIVE NYMPH [*swooping down to the centre of the glade with the sculptors, between Acis and the Newly Born*] Do not try to browbeat me, Arjillax, merely because you are clever with your hands. Can you play the flute?

ARJILLAX [*the bearded sculptor on her right*] No, Ecrasia: I cannot. What has that to do with it? [*He is half derisive, half impatient, wholly resolved not to take her seriously in spite of her beauty and imposing tone*].

ECRASIA. Well, have you ever hesitated to criticize our best flute players, and to declare whether their music is good or bad? Pray have I not the same right to criticize your busts, though I cannot make images any more than you can play?

[ 582 ]

ARJILLAX. Any fool can play the flute, or play anything else, if he practises enough; but sculpture is a creative art, not a mere business of whistling into a pipe. The sculptor must have something of the god in him. From his hand comes a form which reflects a spirit. He does not make it to please you, nor even to please himself, but because he must. You must take what he gives you, or leave it if you are not worthy of it.

ECRASIA [*scornfully*] Not worthy of it! Ho! May I not leave it because it is not worthy of me?

ARJILLAX. Of you! Hold your silly tongue, you conceited humbug. What do you know about it?

ECRASIA. I know what every person of culture knows: that the business of the artist is to create beauty. Until today your works have been full of beauty; and I have been the first to point that out.

ARJILLAX. Thank you for nothing. People have eyes, havnt they, to see what is as plain as the sun in the heavens without your pointing it out?

ECRASIA. You were very glad to have it pointed out. You did not call me a conceited humbug then. You stifled me with caresses. You modelled me as the genius of art presiding over the infancy of your master here [*indicating the other sculptor*], Martellus.

MARTELLUS [*a silent and meditative listener, shudders and shakes his head, but says nothing*].

ARJILLAX [*quarrelsomely*] I was taken in by your talk.

ECRASIA. I discovered your genius before anyone else did. Is that true, or is it not?

ARJILLAX. Everybody knew I was an extraordinary person. When I was born my beard was three feet long.

ECRASIA. Yes; and it has shrunk from three feet to

[ 583 ]

two. Your genius seems to have been in the last foot of your beard; for you have lost both.

MARTELLUS [*with a short sardonic cachinnation*] Ha! My beard was three and a half feet long when I was born; and a flash of lightning burnt it off and killed the ancient who was delivering me. Without a hair on my chin I became the greatest sculptor in ten generations.

ECRASIA. And yet you come to us today with empty hands. We shall actually have to crown Arjillax here because no other sculptor is exhibiting.

ACIS [*returning from the temple steps to behind the curved seat on the right of the tree*] Whats the row, Ecrasia? Why have you fallen out with Arjillax?

ECRASIA. He has insulted us! outraged us! profaned his art! You know how much we hoped from the twelve busts he placed in the temple to be unveiled today. Well, go in and look at them. That is all I have to say. [*She sweeps to the curved seat, and sits down just where Acis is leaning over it*].

ACIS. I am no great judge of sculpture. Art is not my line. What is wrong with the busts?

ECRASIA. Wrong with them! Instead of being ideally beautiful nymphs and youths, they are horribly realistic studies of—but I really cannot bring my lips to utter it.

*The Newly Born, full of curiosity, runs to the temple, and peeps in.*

ACIS. Oh, stow it, Ecrasia. Your lips are not so squeamish as all that. Studies of what?

THE NEWLY BORN [*from the temple steps*] Ancients.

ACIS [*surprised but not scandalized*] Ancients!

ECRASIA. Yes, ancients. The one subject that is by the universal consent of all connoisseurs absolutely excluded from the fine arts. [*To Arjillax*] How can you defend such a proceeding?

ARJILLAX. If you come to that, what interest can you find in the statues of smirking nymphs and posturing youths you stick up all over the place?

ECRASIA. You did not ask that when your hand was still skilful enough to model them.

ARJILLAX. Skilful! You high-nosed idiot, I could turn such things out by the score with my eyes bandaged and one hand tied behind me. But what use would they be? They would bore me; and they would bore you if you had any sense. Go in and look at my busts. Look at them again and yet again until you receive the full impression of the intensity of mind that is stamped on them; and then go back to the pretty-pretty confectionery you call sculpture, and see whether you can endure its vapid emptiness. [*He mounts the altar impetuously*] Listen to me, all of you; and do you, Ecrasia, be silent if you are capable of silence.

ECRASIA. Silence is the most perfect expression of scorn. Scorn! That is what I feel for your revolting busts.

ARJILLAX. Fool: the busts are only the beginning of a mighty design. Listen.

ACIS. Go ahead, old sport. We are listening.

*Martellus stretches himself on the sward beside the altar. The Newly Born sits on the temple steps with her chin on her hands, ready to devour the first oration she has ever heard. The rest sit or stand at ease.*

ARJILLAX. In the records which generations of children have rescued from the stupid neglect of the ancients, there has come down to us a fable which, like many fables, is not a thing that was done in the past, but a thing that is to be done in the future. It is a legend of a supernatural being called the Archangel Michael.

THE NEWLY BORN. Is this a story? I want to hear a story. [*She runs down the steps and sits on the altar at Arjillax's feet*].

ARJILLAX. The Archangel Michael was a mighty sculptor and painter. He found in the centre of the world a temple erected to the goddess of the centre, called Mediterranea. This temple was full of silly pictures of pretty children, such as Ecrasia approves.

ACIS. Fair play, Arjillax! If she is to keep silent, let her alone.

ECRASIA. I shall not interrupt, Acis. Why should I not prefer youth and beauty to age and ugliness?

ARJILLAX. Just so. Well, the Archangel Michael was of my opinion, not yours. He began by painting on the ceiling the newly born in all their childish beauty. But when he had done this he was not satisfied; for the temple was no more impressive than it had been before, except that there was more strength and promise of greater things about his newly born ones than any other artist had attained to. So he painted all round these newly born a company of ancients, who were in those days called prophets and sybils, whose majesty was that of the mind alone at its intensest. And this painting was acknowledged through ages and ages to be the summit and masterpiece of art. Of course we cannot believe such a tale literally. It is only a legend. We do not believe in archangels; and the notion that thirty thousand years ago sculpture and painting existed, and had even reached the glorious perfection they have reached with us, is absurd. But what men cannot realize they can at least aspire to. They please themselves by pretending that it was realized in a golden age of the

[ 586 ]

past. This splendid legend endured because it lived as a desire in the hearts of the greatest artists. The temple of Mediterranea never was built in the past, nor did Michael the Archangel exist. But today the temple is here [*he points to the porch*]; and the man is here [*he slaps himself on the chest*]. I, Arjillax, am the man. I will place in your theatre such images of the newly born as must satisfy even Ecrasia's appetite for beauty; and I will surround them with ancients more august than any who walk through our woods.

MARTELLUS [*as before*] Ha!

ARJILLAX [*stung*] Why do you laugh, you who have come empty-handed, and, it seems, empty-headed?

ECRASIA [*rising indignantly*] Oh, shame! You dare disparage Martellus, twenty times your master.

ACIS. Be quiet, will you [*he seizes her shoulders and thrusts her back into her seat*].

MARTELLUS. Let him disparage his fill, Ecrasia. [*Sitting up*] My poor Arjillax, I too had this dream. I too found one day that my images of loveliness had become vapid, uninteresting, tedious, a waste of time and material. I too lost my desire to model limbs, and retained only my interest in heads and faces. I, too, made busts of ancients; but I had not your courage: I made them in secret, and hid them from you all.

ARJILLAX [*jumping down from the altar behind Martellus in his surprise and excitement*] You made busts of ancients! Where are they, man? Will you be talked out of your inspiration by Ecrasia and the fools who imagine she speaks with authority? Let us have them all set up beside mine in the theatre. I have opened the way for you; and you see I am none the worse.

MARTELLUS. Impossible. They are all smashed. [*He rises, laughing*].

ALL. Smashed!

ARJILLAX. Who smashed them?

MARTELLUS. I did. That is why I laughed at you just now. You will smash yours before you have completed a dozen of them. [*He goes to the end of the altar and sits down beside the Newly Born*].

ARJILLAX. But why?

MARTELLUS. Because you cannot give them life. A live ancient is better than a dead statue. [*He takes the Newly Born on his knee: she is flattered and voluptuously responsive*]. Anything alive is better than anything that is only pretending to be alive. [*To Arjillax*] Your disillusion with your works of beauty is only the beginning of your disillusion with images of all sorts. As your hand became more skilful and your chisel cut deeper, you strove to get nearer and nearer to truth and reality, discarding the fleeting fleshly lure, and making images of the mind that fascinates to the end. But how can so noble an inspiration be satisfied with any image, even an image of the truth? In the end the intellectual conscience that tore you away from the fleeting in art to the eternal must tear you away from art altogether, because art is false and life alone is true.

THE NEWLY BORN [*flings her arms round his neck and kisses him enthusiastically*].

MARTELLUS [*rises; carries her to the curved bench on his left; deposits her beside Strephon as if she were his overcoat; and continues without the least change of tone*] Shape it as you will, marble remains marble, and the graven image an idol. As I have broken my idols, and cast away my chisel and modelling tools, so will you too break these busts of yours.

ARJILLAX. Never.

MARTELLUS. Wait, my friend. I do not come empty-handed today, as you imagined. On the contrary, I bring with me such a work of art as you have never seen, and an artist who has surpassed both you and me further than we have surpassed all our competitors.

ECRASIA. Impossible. The greatest things in art can never be surpassed.

ARJILLAX. Who is this paragon whom you declare greater than I?

MARTELLUS. I declare him greater than myself, Arjillax.

ARJILLAX [*frowning*] I understand. Sooner than not drown me, you are willing to clasp me round the waist and jump overboard with me.

ACIS. Oh, stop squabbling. That is the worst of you artists. You are always in little squabbling cliques; and the worst cliques are those which consist of one man. Who is this new fellow you are throwing in one another's teeth?

ARJILLAX. Ask Martellus: do not ask me. I know nothing of him. [*He leaves Martellus, and sits down beside Ecrasia, on her left*].

MARTELLUS. You know him quite well. Pygmalion.

ECRASIA [*indignantly*] Pygmalion! That soulless creature! A scientist! A laboratory person!

ARJILLAX. Pygmalion produce a work of art! You have lost your artistic senses. The man is utterly incapable of modelling a thumb nail, let alone a human figure.

MARTELLUS. That does not matter: I have done the modelling for him.

ARJILLAX. What on earth do you mean?

MARTELLUS [*calling*] Pygmalion: come forth.

*Pygmalion, a square-fingered youth with his face laid out in horizontal blocks, and a perpetual smile of eager benevolent interest in everything, and expectation of equal interest from everybody else, comes from the temple to the centre of the group, who regard him for the most part with dismay, as dreading that he will bore them. Ecrasia is openly contemptuous.*

MARTELLUS. Friends: it is unfortunate that Pygmalion is constitutionally incapable of exhibiting anything without first giving a lecture about it to explain it; but I promise you that if you will be patient he will shew you the two most wonderful works of art in the world, and that they will contain some of my own very best workmanship. Let me add that they will inspire a loathing that will cure you of the lunacy of art for ever. [*He sits down next the Newly Born, who pouts and turns a very cold right shoulder to him, a demonstration utterly lost on him*].

*Pygmalion, with the smile of a simpleton, and the eager confidence of a fanatical scientist, climbs awkwardly on to the altar. They prepare for the worst.*

PYGMALION. My friends: I will omit the algebra—

ACIS. Thank God!

PYGMALION [*continuing*]—because Martellus has made me promise to do so. To come to the point, I have succeeded in making artificial human beings. Real live ones, I mean.

INCREDULOUS VOICES. Oh, come! Tell us another. Really, Pyg! Get out. You havnt. What a lie!

PYGMALION. I tell you I have. I will shew them to you. It has been done before. One of the very oldest documents we possess mentions a tradition of a biologist who extracted certain unspecified minerals from the earth and, as it quaintly expresses it, "breathed into their nostrils the breath of life." This is the only tradition from the primitive ages which we can regard as really scientific. There are later documents which specify the minerals with great precision, even to their atomic weights; but they are utterly unscientific, because they overlook the element of life which makes all the difference between a mere mixture of salts and gases and a living organism. These mixtures were made over and over again in the crude laboratories of the Silly-Clever Ages; but nothing came of them until the ingredient which the old chronicler called the breath of life was added by this very remarkable early experimenter. In my view he was the founder of biological science.

ARJILLAX. Is that all we know about him? It doesnt amount to very much, does it?

PYGMALION. There are some fragments of pictures and documents which represent him as walking in a garden and advising people to cultivate their gardens. His name has come down to us in several forms. One of them is Jove. Another is Voltaire.

ECRASIA. You are boring us to distraction with your Voltaire. What about your human beings?

ARJILLAX. Aye: come to them.

PYGMALION. I assure you that these details are intensely interesting. [*Cries of* No! They are not! Come to the human beings! Conspuez Voltaire! Cut it short, Pyg! *interrupt him from all sides*]. You will see their bearing presently. I promise you I will not detain you long. We know, we children of science, that the universe is full of forces and powers and energies of one kind and another. The sap rising in a tree, the stone holding together in a definite crystalline structure, the thought of a philosopher holding his brain in form and operation with an inconceivably powerful grip, the urge of evolution: all these forces can be used by us. For instance, I use the force of gravitation when I put a stone on my tunic to prevent it being blown away when I am bathing. By substituting appropriate machines for the stone we have made not only gravitation our slave, but also electricity and magnetism, atomic attraction, repulsion, polarization, and so forth. But hitherto the vital force has eluded us; so it has had to create machinery for itself. It has created and developed bony structure of the requisite strength, and clothed them with cellular tissue of such amazing sensitiveness that the organs it forms will adapt their action to all the normal variations in the air they breathe, the food they digest, and the circumstances about which they have to think. Yet, as these live bodies, as we call them, are only machines after all, it must be possible to construct them mechanically.

ARJILLAX. Everything is possible. Have you done it? that is the question.

PYGMALION. Yes. But that is a mere fact. What is interesting is the explanation of the fact. Forgive my saying so; but it is such a pity that you artists have no intellect.

ECRASIA [*sententiously*] I do not admit that. The artist divines by inspiration all the truths that the so-called scientist grubs up in his laboratory slowly and stupidly long afterwards.

ARJILLAX [*to Ecrasia, quarrelsomely*] What do you know about it? You are not an artist.

ACIS. Shut your heads, both of you. Let us have the artificial men. Trot them out, Pygmalion.

PYGMALION. It is a man and a woman. But I really must explain first.

ALL [*groaning*]!!!

PYGMALION. Yes: I—

ACIS. We want results, not explanations.

PYGMALION [*hurt*] I see I am boring you. Not one of you takes the least interest in science. Goodbye.

[*He descends from the altar and makes for the temple*].

SEVERAL YOUTHS AND MAIDENS [*rising and rushing to him*] No, no. Dont go. Dont be offended. We want to see the artificial pair. We will listen. We are tremendously interested. Tell us all about it.

PYGMALION [*relenting*] I shall not detain you two minutes.

ALL. Half an hour if you like. Please go on, Pygmalion. [*They rush him back to the altar, and hoist him on to it*]. Up you go.

*They return to their former places.*

PYGMALION. As I told you, lots of attempts were made to produce protoplasm in the laboratory. Why were these synthetic plasms, as they called them, no use?

ECRASIA. We are waiting for you to tell us.

THE NEWLY BORN [*modelling herself on Ecrasia, and trying to outdo her intellectually*] Clearly because they were dead.

PYGMALION. Not bad for a baby, my pet. But dead and alive are very loose terms. You are not half as much alive as you will be in another month or so. What was wrong with the synthetic protoplasm was that it could not fix and conduct the Life Force. It was like a wooden magnet or a lightning conductor made of silk: it would not take the current.

ACIS. Nobody but a fool would make a wooden magnet, and expect it to attract anything.

PYGMALION. He might if he were so ignorant as not to be able to distinguish between wood and soft iron. In those days they were very ignorant of the differences between things, because their methods of analysis were crude. They mixed up messes that were so like protoplasm that they could not tell the difference. But the difference was there, though their

[ 593 ]

analysis was too superficial and incomplete to detect it. You must remember that these poor devils were very little better than our idiots: we should never dream of letting one of them survive the day of its birth. Why, the Newly Born there already knows by instinct many things that their greatest physicists could hardly arrive at by forty years of strenuous study. Her simple direct sense of spacetime and quantity unconsciously solves problems which cost their most famous mathematicians years of prolonged and laborious calculations requiring such intense mental application that they frequently forgot to breathe when engaged in them, and almost suffocated themselves in consequence.

ECRASIA. Leave these obscure prehistoric abortions; and come back to your synthetic man and woman.

PYGMALION. When I undertook the task of making synthetic men, I did not waste my time on protoplasm. It was evident to me that if it were possible to make protoplasm in the laboratory, it must be equally possible to begin higher up and make fully evolved muscular and nervous tissues, bone, and so forth. Why make the seed when the making of the flower would be no greater miracle? I tried thousands of combinations before I succeeded in producing anything that would fix high-potential Life Force.

ARJILLAX. High what?

PYGMALION. High-po-tential. The Life Force is not so simple as you think. A high-potential current of it will turn a bit of dead tissue into a philosopher's brain. A low-potential current will reduce the same bit of tissue to a mass of corruption. Will you believe me when I tell you that, even in man himself, the Life Force used to slip suddenly down from its human level to that of a fungus, so that men found their flesh

[ 594 ]

no longer growing as flesh, but proliferating horribly in a lower form which was called cancer, until the lower form of life killed the higher, and both perished together miserably?

MARTELLUS. Keep off the primitive tribes, Pygmalion. They interest you; but they bore these young things.

PYGMALION. I am only trying to make you understand. There was the Life Force raging all round me: there was I, trying to make organs that would capture it as a battery captures electricity, and tissues that would conduct it and operate it. It was easy enough to make eyes more perfect than our own, and ears with a larger range of sound; but they could neither see nor hear, because they were not susceptible to the Life Force. But it was far worse when I discovered how to make them susceptible; for the first thing that happened was that they ceased to be eyes and ears and turned into heaps of maggots.

ECRASIA. Disgusting! Please stop.

ACIS. If you dont want to hear, go away. You go ahead, Pyg.

PYGMALION. I went ahead. You see, the lower potentials of the Life Force could make maggots, but not human eyes nor ears. I improved the tissue until it was susceptible to a higher potential.

ARJILLAX [*intensely interested*] Yes; and then?

PYGMALION. Then the eyes and ears turned into cancers.

ECRASIA. Oh, hideous!

PYGMALION. Not at all. That was a great advance. It encouraged me so much that I put aside the eyes and ears, and made a brain. It wouldnt take the Life Force at all until I had altered its constitution a dozen times; but when it did, it took a much higher

[ 595 ]

potential, and did not dissolve; and neither did the eyes and ears when I connected them up with the brain. I was able to make a sort of monster: a thing without arms or legs; and it really and truly lived for half-an-hour.

THE NEWLY BORN. Half-an-hour! What good was that? Why did it die?

PYGMALION. Its blood went wrong. But I got that right; and then I went ahead with a complete human body: arms and legs and all. He was my first man.

ARJILLAX. Who modelled him?

PYGMALION. I did.

MARTELLUS. Do you mean to say you tried your own hand before you sent for me?

PYGMALION. Bless you, yes, several times. My first man was the ghastliest creature: a more dreadful mixture of horror and absurdity than you who have not seen him can conceive.

ARJILLAX. If you modelled him, he must indeed have been a spectacle.

PYGMALION. Oh, it was not his shape. You see I did not invent that. I took actual measurements and moulds from my own body. Sculptors do that sometimes, you know; though they pretend they dont.

MARTELLUS. Hm!

ARJILLAX. Hah!

PYGMALION. He was all right to look at, at first, or nearly so. But he behaved in the most appalling manner; and subsequent developments were so disgusting that I really cannot describe them to you. He seized all sorts of things and swallowed them. He drank every fluid in the laboratory. I tried to explain to him that he must take nothing that he could not digest and assimilate completely; but of course he could not understand me. He assimilated a little of

what he swallowed; but the process left horrible
residues which he had no means of getting rid of.
His blood turned to poison; and he perished in torments, howling. I then perceived that I had produced
a prehistoric man; for there are certain traces in our
own bodies of arrangements which enabled the
earlier forms of mankind to renew their bodies by
swallowing flesh and grains and vegetables and all
sorts of unnatural and hideous foods, and getting rid
of what they could not digest.

ECRASIA. But what a pity he died! What a glimpse
of the past we have lost! He could have told us stories
of the Golden Age.

PYGMALION. Not he. He was a most dangerous
beast. He was afraid of me, and actually tried to kill
me by snatching up things and striking at me with
them. I had to give him two or three pretty severe
shocks before I convinced him that he was at my
mercy.

THE NEWLY BORN. Why did you not make a woman
instead of a man? She would have known how to
behave herself.

MARTELLUS. Why did you not make a man and a
woman? Their children would have been interesting.

PYGMALION. I intended to make a woman; but after
my experience with the man it was out of the question.

ECRASIA. Pray why?

PYGMALION. Well, it is difficult to explain if you
have not studied prehistoric methods of reproduction.
You see the only sort of men and women I could
make were men and women just like us as far as their
bodies were concerned. That was how I killed the
poor beast of a man. I hadnt provided for his horrible
prehistoric methods of feeding himself. Suppose the

woman had reproduced in some prehistoric way instead of being oviparous as we are? She couldnt have done it with a modern female body. Besides, the experiment might have been painful.

ECRASIA. Then have you nothing to shew us at all?

PYGMALION. Oh yes I have. I am not so easily beaten as that. I set to work again for months to find out how to make a digestive system that would deal with waste products and a reproductive system capable of internal nourishment and incubation.

ECRASIA. Why did you not find out how to make them like us?

STREPHON [*crying out in his grief for the first time*] Why did you not make a woman whom you could love? That was the secret you needed.

THE NEWLY BORN. Oh yes. How true! How great of you, darling Strephon! [*She kisses him impulsively*].

STREPHON [*passionately*] Let me alone.

MARTELLUS. Control your reflexes, child.

THE NEWLY BORN. My what!

MARTELLUS. Your reflexes. The things you do without thinking. Pygmalion is going to shew you a pair of human creatures who are all reflexes and nothing else. Take warning by them.

THE NEWLY BORN. But wont they be alive, like us?

PYGMALION. That is a very difficult question to answer, my dear. I confess I thought at first I had created living creatures; but Martellus declares they are only automata. But then Martellus is a mystic: *I* am a man of science. He draws a line between an automaton and a living organism. I cannot draw that line to my own satisfaction.

MARTELLUS. Your artificial men have no self-control. They only respond to stimuli from without.

PYGMALION. But they are conscious. I have taught

them to talk and read; and now they tell lies. That is
so very lifelike.

MARTELLUS. Not at all. If they were alive they
would tell the truth. You can provoke them to tell
any silly lie; and you can foresee exactly the sort of
lie they will tell. Give them a clip below the knee,
and they will jerk their foot forward. Give them a
clip on their appetites or vanities or any of their lusts
and greeds, and they will boast and lie, and affirm
and deny, and hate and love without the slightest
regard to the facts that are staring them in the face,
or to their own obvious limitations. That proves that
they are automata.

PYGMALION [*unconvinced*] I know, dear old chap;
but there really is some evidence that we are descended
from creatures quite as limited and absurd as these.
After all, the baby there is three-quarters an automaton. Look at the way she has been going on!

THE NEWLY BORN [*indignantly*] What do you mean?
How have I been going on?

ECRASIA. If they have no regard for truth, they can
have no real vitality.

PYGMALION. Truth is sometimes so artificial: so
relative, as we say in the scientific world, that it is
very hard to feel quite sure that what is false and even
ridiculous to us may not be true to them.

ECRASIA. I ask you again, why did you not make
them like us? Would any true artist be content with
less than the best?

PYGMALION. I couldnt. I tried. I failed. I am convinced that what I am about to shew you is the very
highest living organism that can be produced in the
laboratory. The best tissues we can manufacture will
not take as high potentials as the natural product:
that is where Nature beats us. You dont seem to

understand, any of you, what an enormous triumph
it was to produce consciousness at all.

ACIS. Cut the cackle; and come to the synthetic
couple.

SEVERAL YOUTHS AND MAIDENS. Yes, yes. No
more talking. Let us have them. Dry up, Pyg; and
fetch them along. Come on: out with them! The
synthetic couple: the synthetic couple.

PYGMALION [*waving his hands to appease them*] Very
well, very well. Will you please whistle for them?
They respond to the stimulus of a whistle.

*All who can, whistle like streetboys.*

ECRASIA [*makes a wry face and puts her fingers in her
ears*]!

PYGMALION. Sh-sh-sh! Thats enough: thats enough:
thats enough. [*Silence*]. Now let us have some music.
A dance tune. Not too fast.

*The flutists play a quiet dance.*

MARTELLUS. Prepare yourselves for something
ghastly.

*Two figures, a man and woman of noble appearance,
beautifully modelled and splendidly attired, emerge hand
in hand from the temple. Seeing that all eyes are fixed
on them, they halt on the steps, smiling with gratified
vanity. The woman is on the man's left.*

PYGMALION [*rubbing his hands with the purring satisfaction of a creator*] This way, please.

*The figures advance condescendingly and pose them-
selves centrally between the curved seats.*

PYGMALION. Now if you will be so good as to oblige
us with a little something. You dance so beautifully,
you know. [*He sits down next Martellus, and whispers
to him*] It is extraordinary how sensitive they are to
the stimulus of flattery.

*The Figures, with a gracious air, dance pompously,*

[ 600 ]

*but very passably. At the close they bow to one another.*
ON ALL HANDS [*clapping*] Bravo! Thank you. Wonderful! Splendid. Perfect.

*The Figures acknowledge the applause in an obvious condition of swelled head.*

THE NEWLY BORN. Can they make love?

PYGMALION. Yes: they can respond to every stimulus. They have all the reflexes. Put your arm round the man's neck, and he will put his arm round your body. He cannot help it.

THE FEMALE FIGURE [*frowning*] Round mine, you mean.

PYGMALION. Yours, too, of course, if the stimulus comes from you.

ECRASIA. Cannot he do anything original?

PYGMALION. No. But then, you know, I do not admit that any of us can do anything really original, though Martellus thinks we can.

ACIS. Can he answer a question?

PYGMALION. Oh yes. A question is a stimulus, you know. Ask him one.

ACIS [*to the Male Figure*] What do you think of what you see around you? Of us, for instance, and our ways and doings?

THE MALE FIGURE. I have not seen the newspaper today.

THE FEMALE FIGURE. How can you expect my husband to know what to think of you if you give him his breakfast without his paper?

MARTELLUS. You see. He is a mere automaton.

THE NEWLY BORN. Have they feelings?

PYGMALION. Of course they have. I tell you they have all the reflexes.

THE NEWLY BORN. But feelings are not reflexes.

PYGMALION. They are sensations. When the rays

of light enter their eyes and make a picture on their retinas, their brains become conscious of the picture and they act accordingly. When the waves of sound started by your speaking enter their ears they respond accordingly.

THE MALE FIGURE. We are part of a cosmic system. Free will is an illusion. We are the children of Cause and Effect. We are the Unalterable, the Irresistible, the Irresponsible, the Inevitable: in a word, the Determinist.

My name is Ozymandias, king of kings:
Look on my works, ye mighty; and despair.

*There is a general stir of curiosity at this.*

ACIS. What the dickens does he mean?

THE MALE FIGURE. Silence, base accident of Nature. This [*taking the hand of the Female Figure and introducing her*] is Cleopatra-Semiramis, consort of the king of kings, and therefore queen of queens. Ye are things hatched from eggs by the brainless sun and the blind fire; but the king of kings and queen of queens are not accidents of the egg: they are thought-out and hand-made to receive the sacred Life Force. There is one person of the king and one of the queen; but the Life Force of the king and queen is all one: the glory equal, the majesty co-eternal. Such as the king is so is the queen, the king thought-out and hand-made, the queen thought-out and hand-made. The actions of the king are caused, and therefore determined, from the beginning of the world to the end; and the actions of the queen are likewise. The king logical and predetermined and inevitable, and the queen logical and predetermined and inevitable. And yet they are not two logical and predetermined and inevitable, but one logical and predetermined and inevitable. Therefore confound not the persons, nor divide the substance; but worship us twain as one: two in one and one in two, lest by error ye fall into irretrievable damnation.

THE FEMALE FIGURE. And if any say unto you "Which one?" remember that though there is one person of the king and one of the queen, yet these two persons are not alike, but are woman and man; and that as woman was created after man, the skill and practice gained in making him were added to her, wherefore she is to be exalted above him in all personal respects, and—

THE MALE FIGURE. Peace, woman; for this is a damnable heresy. Both Man and Woman are what they are and must do what they must according to the eternal laws of Cause and Effect. Look to your words; for if they enter my ear and jar too repugnantly on my sensorium, who knows that the inevitable response to that stimulus may not be a message to my muscles to snatch up some heavy object and break you in pieces.

*The Female Figure picks up a stone and is about to throw it at her consort.*

ARJILLAX [*springing up and shouting to Pygmalion, who is fondly watching the Male Figure*] Look out, Pygmalion! Look at the woman!

*Pygmalion, seeing what is happening, hurls himself on the Female Figure and wrenches the stone out of her hand.*

*All spring up in consternation.*

ARJILLAX. She meant to kill him.

STREPHON. This is horrible.

THE FEMALE FIGURE [*wrestling with Pygmalion*] Let me go. Let me go, will you [*she bites his hand*].

PYGMALION [*releasing her and staggering*] Oh!

*A general shriek of horror echoes his exclamation. He*

[ 603 ]

*turns deadly pale, and supports himself against the end of the curved seat.*

THE FEMALE FIGURE [*to her consort*] You would stand there and let me be treated like this, you unmanly coward.

*Pygmalion falls dead.*

THE NEWLY BORN. Oh! Whats the matter? Why did he fall? What has happened to him?

*They look on anxiously as Martellus kneels down and examines the body of Pygmalion.*

MARTELLUS. She has bitten a piece out of his hand nearly as large as a finger nail: enough to kill ten men. There is no pulse, no breath.

ECRASIA. But his thumb is clinched.

MARTELLUS. No: it has just straightened out. See! He has gone. Poor Pygmalion!

THE NEWLY BORN. Oh! [*She weeps*].

STREPHON. Hush, dear: thats childish.

THE NEWLY BORN [*subsiding with a sniff*]!!

MARTELLUS [*rising*] Dead in his third year. What a loss to Science!

ARJILLAX. Who cares about Science? Serve him right for making that pair of horrors!

THE MALE FIGURE [*glaring*] Ha!

THE FEMALE FIGURE. Keep a civil tongue in your head, you.

THE NEWLY BORN. Oh, do not be so unkind, Arjillax. You will make water come out of my eyes again.

MARTELLUS [*contemplating the Figures*] Just look at these two devils. I modelled them out of the stuff Pygmalion made for them. They are masterpieces of art. And see what they have done! Does that convince you of the value of art, Arjillax?

STREPHON. They look dangerous. Keep away from them.

ECRASIA. No need to tell us that, Strephon. Pf! They poison the air.

THE MALE FIGURE. Beware, woman. The wrath of Ozymandias strikes like the lightning.

THE FEMALE FIGURE. You just say that again if you dare, you filthy creature.

ACIS. What are you going to do with them, Martellus? You are responsible for them, now that Pygmalion has gone.

MARTELLUS. If they were marble it would be simple enough: I could smash them. As it is, how am I to kill them without making a horrible mess?

THE MALE FIGURE [*posing heroically*] Ha! [*He declaims*]

> Come one: come all: this rock shall fly
> From its firm base as soon as I.

THE FEMALE FIGURE [*fondly*] My man! My hero husband! I am proud of you. I love you.

MARTELLUS. We must send out a message for an ancient.

ACIS. Need we bother an ancient about such a trifle? It will take less than half a second to reduce our poor Pygmalion to a pinch of dust. Why not calcine the two along with him?

MARTELLUS. No: the two automata are trifles; but the use of our powers of destruction is never a trifle. I had rather have the case judged.

*The He-Ancient emerges from the grove. The Figures are panic-stricken.*

THE HE-ANCIENT [*mildly*] Am I wanted? I feel called. [*Seeing the body of Pygmalion and immediately taking a sterner tone*] What! A child lost! A life wasted! How has this happened?

THE FEMALE FIGURE [*frantically*] I didnt do it. It

was not me. May I be struck dead if I touched him! It was he [*pointing to the Male Figure*].

ALL [*amazed at the lie*] Oh!

THE MALE FIGURE. Liar. You bit him. Everyone here saw you do it.

THE HE-ANCIENT. Silence. [*Going between the Figures*] Who made these two loathsome dolls?

THE MALE FIGURE [*trying to assert himself with his knees knocking*] My name is Ozymandias, king of—

THE HE-ANCIENT [*with a contemptuous gesture*] Pooh!

THE MALE FIGURE [*falling on his knees*] Oh dont, sir. Dont. She did it, sir: indeed she did.

THE FEMALE FIGURE [*howling lamentably*] Boohoo! oo! ooh!

THE HE-ANCIENT. Silence, I say.

*He knocks the Male Automaton upright by a very light flip under the chin. The Female Automaton hardly dares to sob. The immortals contemplate them with shame and loathing. The She-Ancient comes from the trees opposite the temple.*

THE SHE-ANCIENT. Somebody wants me. What is the matter? [*She comes to the left hand of the Female Figure, not seeing the body of Pygmalion*]. Pf! [*Severely*] You have been making dolls. You must not: they are not only disgusting: they are dangerous.

THE FEMALE FIGURE [*snivelling piteously*] I'm not a doll, mam. I'm only poor Cleopatra-Semiramis, queen of queens. [*Covering her face with her hands*] Oh, dont look at me like that, mam. I meant no harm. He hurt me: indeed he did.

THE HE-ANCIENT. The creature has killed that poor youth.

THE SHE-ANCIENT [*seeing the body of Pygmalion*] What! This clever child, who promised so well!

[ 606 ]

THE FEMALE FIGURE. He made me. I had as much right to kill him as he had to make me. And how was I to know that a little thing like that would kill him? I shouldnt die if he cut off my arm or leg.

ECRASIA. What nonsense!

MARTELLUS. It may not be nonsense. I daresay if you cut off her leg she would grow another, like the lobsters and the little lizards.

THE HE-ANCIENT. Did this dead boy make these two things?

MARTELLUS. He made them in his laboratory. I moulded their limbs. I am sorry. I was thoughtless: I did not foresee that they would kill and pretend to be persons they were not, and declare things that were false, and wish evil. I thought they would be merely mechanical fools.

THE MALE FIGURE. Do you blame us for our human nature?

THE FEMALE FIGURE. We are flesh and blood and not angels.

THE MALE FIGURE. Have you no hearts?

ARJILLAX. They are mad as well as mischievous. May we not destroy them?

STREPHON. We abhor them.

THE NEWLY BORN. We loathe them.

ECRASIA. They are noisome.

ACIS. I dont want to be hard on the poor devils; but they are making me feel uneasy in my inside. I never had such a sensation before.

MARTELLUS. I took a lot of trouble with them. But as far as I am concerned, destroy them by all means. I loathed them from the beginning.

ALL. Yes, yes: we all loathe them. Let us calcine them. Away with them! Make an end of them.

THE FEMALE FIGURE. Oh, dont be so cruel. I'm

not fit to die. I will never bite anyone again. I will tell the truth. I will do good. Is it my fault if I was not made properly? Kill him; but spare me.

THE MALE FIGURE. No! I have done no harm: she has. Kill her if you like: you have no right to kill me.

THE NEWLY BORN. Do you hear that? They want to have one another killed.

ARJILLAX. Monstrous! Kill them both.

THE HE-ANCIENT. Silence. These things are mere automata: they cannot help shrinking from death at any cost. You see that they have no self-control, and are merely shuddering through a series of reflexes. Let us see whether we cannot put a little more life into them. [*He takes the Male Figure by the hand, and places his disengaged hand on its head*]. Now listen. One of you two is to be destroyed. Which of you shall it be?

THE MALE FIGURE [*after a slight convulsion during which his eyes are fixed on the He-Ancient*] Spare her; and kill me.

STREPHON. Thats better.

THE NEWLY BORN. Much better.

THE SHE-ANCIENT [*handling the Female Automaton in the same manner*] Which of you shall we kill?

THE FEMALE FIGURE. Kill us both. How could either of us live without the other?

ECRASIA. The woman is more sensible than the man.

*The Ancients release the Automata.*

THE MALE FIGURE [*sinking to the ground*] I am discouraged. Life is too heavy a burden.

THE FEMALE FIGURE [*collapsing*] I am dying. I am glad. I am afraid to live.

THE NEWLY BORN. I think it would be nice to give the poor things a little music.

ARJILLAX. Why?

THE NEWLY BORN. I dont know. But it would.

*The Musicians play.*

THE FEMALE FIGURE. Ozymandias: do you hear that? [*She rises on her knees and looks raptly into space*] Queen of queens! [*She dies*].

THE MALE FIGURE [*crawling feebly towards her until he reaches her hand*] I knew I was really a king of kings. [*To the others*] Illusions, farewell: we are going to our thrones. [*He dies*].

*The music stops. There is dead silence for a moment.*

THE NEWLY BORN. That was funny.

STREPHON. It was. Even the Ancients are smiling.

THE NEWLY BORN. Just a little.

THE SHE-ANCIENT [*quickly recovering her grave and peremptory manner*] Take these two abominations away to Pygmalion's laboratory, and destroy them with the rest of the laboratory refuse. [*Some of them move to obey*]. Take care: do not touch their flesh: it is noxious: lift them by their robes. Carry Pygmalion into the temple; and dispose of his remains in the usual way.

*The three bodies are carried out as directed, Pygmalion into the temple by his bare arms and legs, and the two Figures through the grove by their clothes. Martellus superintends the removal of the Figures, Acis that of Pygmalion. Ecrasia, Arjillax, Strephon, and the Newly Born sit down as before, but on contrary benches; so that Strephon and the Newly Born now face the grove, and Ecrasia and Arjillax the temple. The Ancients remain standing at the altar.*

ECRASIA [*as she sits down*] Oh for a breeze from the hills!

STREPHON. Or the wind from the sea at the turn of the tide!

THE NEWLY BORN. I want some clean air.

[ 609 ]

THE HE-ANCIENT. The air will be clean in a moment. This doll flesh that children make decomposes quickly at best; but when it is shaken by such passions as the creatures are capable of, it breaks up at once and becomes horribly tainted.

THE SHE-ANCIENT. Let it be a lesson to you all to be content with lifeless toys, and not attempt to make living ones. What would you think of us ancients if we made toys of you children?

THE NEWLY BORN [*coaxingly*] Why do you not make toys of us? Then you would play with us; and that would be very nice.

THE SHE-ANCIENT. It would not amuse us. When you play with one another you play with your bodies, and that makes you supple and strong; but if we played with you we should play with your minds, and perhaps deform them.

STREPHON. You are a ghastly lot, you ancients. I shall kill myself when I am four years old. What do you live for?

THE HE-ANCIENT. You will find out when you grow up. You will not kill yourself.

STREPHON. If you make me believe that, I shall kill myself now.

THE NEWLY BORN. Oh no. I want you. I love you.

STREPHON. I love someone else. And she has gone old, old. Lost to me for ever.

THE HE-ANCIENT. How old?

STREPHON. You saw her when you barged into us as we were dancing. She is four.

THE NEWLY BORN. How I should have hated her twenty minutes ago! But I have grown out of that now.

THE HE-ANCIENT. Good. That hatred is called jealousy, the worst of our childish complaints.

[ 610 ]

*Martellus, dusting his hands and puffing, returns from the grove.*

MARTELLUS. Ouf! [*He sits down next the Newly Born*] That job's finished.

ARJILLAX. Ancients: I should like to make a few studies of you. Not portraits, of course: I shall idealize you a little. I have come to the conclusion that you ancients are the most interesting subjects after all.

MARTELLUS. What! Have those two horrors, whose ashes I have just deposited with peculiar pleasure in poor Pygmalion's dustbin, not cured you of this silly image-making?

ARJILLAX. Why did you model them as young things, you fool? If Pygmalion had come to me, I should have made ancients of them for him. Not that I should have modelled them any better. I have always said that no one can beat you at your best as far as hand-work is concerned. But this job required brains. That is where I should have come in.

MARTELLUS. Well, my brainy boy, you are welcome to try your hand. There are two of Pygmalion's pupils at the laboratory who helped him to manufacture the bones and tissues and all the rest of it. They can turn out a couple of new automatons; and you can model them as ancients if this venerable pair will sit for you.

ECRASIA [*decisively*] No. No more automata. They are too disgusting.

ACIS [*returning from the temple*] Well, thats done. Poor old Pyg!

ECRASIA. Only fancy, Acis! Arjillax wants to make more of those abominable things, and to destroy even their artistic character by making ancients of them.

THE NEWLY BORN. You wont sit for them, will you? Please dont.

THE HE-ANCIENT. Children, listen.

ACIS [*striding down the steps to the bench and seating himself next Ecrasia*] What! Even the Ancient wants to make a speech! Give it mouth, O Sage.

STREPHON. For heaven's sake dont tell us that the earth was once inhabited by Ozymandiases and Cleopatras. Life is hard enough for us as it is.

THE HE-ANCIENT. Life is not meant to be easy, my child; but take courage: it can be delightful. What I wanted to tell you is that ever since men existed, children have played with dolls.

ECRASIA. You keep using that word. What are dolls, pray?

THE SHE-ANCIENT. What you call works of art. Images. We call them dolls.

ARJILLAX. Just so. You have no sense of art; and you instinctively insult it.

THE HE-ANCIENT. Children have been known to make dolls out of rags, and to caress them with the deepest fondness.

THE SHE-ANCIENT. Eight centuries ago, when I was a child, I made a rag doll. The rag doll is the dearest of all.

THE NEWLY BORN [*eagerly interested*] Oh! Have you got it still?

THE SHE-ANCIENT. I kept it a full week.

ECRASIA. Even in your childhood, then, you did not understand high art, and adored your own amateur crudities.

THE SHE-ANCIENT. How old are you?

ECRASIA. Eight months.

THE SHE-ANCIENT. When you have lived as long as I have—

ECRASIA [*interrupting rudely*] I shall worship rag dolls, perhaps. Thank heaven, I am still in my prime.

THE HE-ANCIENT. You are still capable of thanking, though you do not know what you thank. You are a thanking little animal, a blaming little animal, a—

ACIS. A gushing little animal.

ARJILLAX. And, as she thinks, an artistic little animal.

ECRASIA [*nettled*] I am an animated being with a reasonable soul and human flesh subsisting. If your automata had been properly animated, Martellus, they would have been more successful.

THE SHE-ANCIENT. That is where you are wrong, my child. If those two loathsome things had been rag dolls, they would have been amusing and lovable. The Newly Born here would have played with them; and you would all have laughed and played with them too until you had torn them to pieces; and then you would have laughed more than ever.

THE NEWLY BORN. Of course we should. Isnt that funny?

THE HE-ANCIENT. When a thing is funny, search it for a hidden truth.

STREPHON. Yes; and take all the fun out of it.

THE SHE-ANCIENT. Do not be so embittered because your sweetheart has outgrown her love for you. The Newly Born will make amends.

THE NEWLY BORN. Oh yes: I will be more than she could ever have been.

STREPHON. Psha! Jealous!

THE NEWLY BORN. Oh no. I have grown out of that. I love her now because she loved you, and because you love her.

THE HE-ANCIENT. That is the next stage. You are getting on very nicely, my child.

MARTELLUS. Come! what is the truth that was hidden in the rag doll?

THE HE-ANCIENT. Well, consider why you are not content with the rag doll, and must have something more closely resembling a real living creature. As you grow up you make images and paint pictures. Those of you who cannot do that make stories about imaginary dolls. Or you dress yourselves up as dolls and act plays about them.

THE SHE-ANCIENT. And, to deceive yourself the more completely, you take them so very very seriously that Ecrasia here declares that the making of dolls is the holiest work of creation, and the words you put into the mouths of dolls the sacredest of scriptures and the noblest of utterances.

ECRASIA. Tush!

ARJILLAX. Tosh!

THE SHE-ANCIENT. Yet the more beautiful they become the further they retreat from you. You cannot caress them as you caress the rag doll. You cannot cry for them when they are broken or lost, or when you pretend they have been unkind to you, as you could when you played with rag dolls.

THE HE-ANCIENT. At last, like Pygmalion, you demand from your dolls the final perfection of resemblance to life. They must move and speak.

THE SHE-ANCIENT. They must love and hate.

THE HE-ANCIENT. They must think that they think.

THE SHE-ANCIENT. They must have soft flesh and warm blood.

THE HE-ANCIENT. And then, when you have achieved this as Pygmalion did; when the marble masterpiece is dethroned by the automaton and the homo by the homunculus; when the body and the brain, the reasonable soul and human flesh subsisting, as Ecrasia says, stand before you unmasked as mere machinery, and your impulses are shewn to be nothing but reflexes, you are filled with horror and loathing, and would give worlds to be young enough to play with your rag doll again, since every step away from it has been a step away from love and happiness. Is it not true?

THE SHE-ANCIENT. Speak, Martellus: you who have travelled the whole path.

MARTELLUS. It is true. With fierce joy I turned a temperature of a million degrees on those two things I had modelled, and saw them vanish in an instant into inoffensive dust.

THE SHE-ANCIENT. Speak, Arjillax: you who have advanced from imitating the lightly living child to the intensely living ancient. Is it true, so far?

ARJILLAX. Is it partly true: I cannot pretend to be satisfied now with modelling pretty children.

THE HE-ANCIENT. And you, Ecrasia: you cling to your highly artistic dolls as the noblest projections of the Life Force, do you not?

ECRASIA. Without art, the crudeness of reality would make the world unbearable.

THE NEWLY BORN [*anticipating the She-Ancient, who is evidently going to challenge her*] Now you are coming to me, because I am the latest arrival. But I dont understand your art and your dolls at all. I want to caress my darling Strephon, not to play with dolls.

ACIS. I am in my fourth year; and I have got on very well without your dolls. I had rather walk up a mountain and down again than look at all the statues Martellus and Arjillax ever made. You prefer a statue to an automaton, and a rag doll to a statue. So do I; but I prefer a man to a rag doll. Give me friends, not dolls.

THE HE-ANCIENT. Yet I have seen you walking over the mountains alone. Have you not found your best friend in yourself?

[ 615 ]

ACIS. What are you driving at, old one? What does all this lead to?

THE HE-ANCIENT. It leads, young man, to the truth that you can create nothing but yourself.

ACIS [*musing*] I can create nothing but myself. Ecrasia: you are clever. Do you understand it? I dont.

ECRASIA. It is as easy to understand as any other ignorant error. What artist is as great as his own works? He can create masterpieces; but he cannot improve the shape of his own nose.

ACIS. There! What have you to say to that, old one?

THE HE-ANCIENT. He can alter the shape of his own soul. He could alter the shape of his nose if the difference between a turned-up nose and a turned-down one were worth the effort. One does not face the throes of creation for trifles.

ACIS. What have you to say to that, Ecrasia?

ECRASIA. I say that if the ancients had thoroughly grasped the theory of fine art they would understand that the difference between a beautiful nose and an ugly one is of supreme importance: that it is indeed the only thing that matters.

THE SHE-ANCIENT. That is, they would understand something they could not believe, and that you do not believe.

ACIS. Just so, mam. Art is not honest: that is why I never could stand much of it. It is all make-believe. Ecrasia never really says things: she only rattles her teeth in her mouth.

ECRASIA. Acis: you are rude.

ACIS. You mean that I wont play the game of make-believe. Well, I dont ask you to play it with me; so why should you expect me to play it with you?

ECRASIA. You have no right to say that I am not

sincere. I have found a happiness in art that real life has never given me. I am intensely in earnest about art. There is a magic and mystery in art that you know nothing of.

THE SHE-ANCIENT. Yes, child: art is the magic mirror you make to reflect your invisible dreams in visible pictures. You use a glass mirror to see your face: you use works of art to see your soul. But we who are older use neither glass mirrors nor works of art. We have a direct sense of life. When you gain this you will put aside your mirrors and statues, your toys and your dolls.

THE HE-ANCIENT. Yet we too have our toys and our dolls. That is the trouble of the ancients.

ARJILLAX. What! The ancients have their troubles! It is the first time I ever heard one of them confess it.

THE HE-ANCIENT. Look at us. Look at me. This is my body, my blood, my brain; but it is not me. I am the eternal life, the perpetual resurrection; but [*striking his body*] this structure, this organism, this makeshift, can be made by a boy in a laboratory, and is held back from dissolution only by my use of it. Worse still, it can be broken by a slip of the foot, drowned by a cramp in the stomach, destroyed by a flash from the clouds. Sooner or later, its destruction is certain.

THE SHE-ANCIENT. Yes: this body is the last doll to be discarded. When I was a child, Ecrasia, I, too, was an artist, like your sculptor friends there, striving to create perfection in things outside myself. I made statues: I painted pictures: I tried to worship them.

THE HE-ANCIENT. I had no such skill; but I, like Acis, sought perfection in friends, in lovers, in nature, in things outside myself. Alas! I could not create it: I could only imagine it.

THE SHE-ANCIENT. I, like Arjillax, found out that my statues of bodily beauty were no longer even beautiful to me; and I pressed on and made statues and pictures of men and women of genius, like those in the old fable of Michael Angelo. Like Martellus, I smashed them when I saw that there was no life in them.

THE HE-ANCIENT. And I, like Acis, ceased to walk over the mountains with my friends, and walked alone; for I found that I had creative power over myself but none over my friends. And then I ceased to walk on the mountains; for I saw that the mountains were dead.

ACIS [*protesting vehemently*] No. I grant you about the friends perhaps; but the mountains are still the mountains, each with its name, its individuality, its upstanding strength and majesty, its beauty—

ECRASIA. What! Acis among the rhapsodists!

THE HE-ANCIENT. Mere metaphor, my poor boy: the mountains are corpses.

ALL THE YOUNG [*repelled*] Oh!

THE HE-ANCIENT. Yes. In the hardpressed heart of the earth, where the inconceivable heat of the sun still glows, the stone lives in fierce atomic convulsion, as we live in our slower way. When it is cast out to the surface it dies like a deep-sea fish: what you see is only its cold dead body. We have tapped that central heat as prehistoric man tapped water springs; but nothing has come up alive from those flaming depths: your landscapes, your mountains, are only the world's cast skins and decaying teeth on which we live like microbes.

ECRASIA. Ancient: you blaspheme against Nature and against Man.

THE SHE-ANCIENT. Child, child, how much enthusiasm will you have for man when you have endured

[ 618 ]

eight centuries of him, as I have, and seen him perish by an empty mischance that is yet a certainty? When I discarded my dolls as he discarded his friends and his mountains, it was to myself I turned as to the final reality. Here, and here alone, I could shape and create. When my arm was weak and I willed it to be strong, I could create a roll of muscle on it; and when I understood that, I understood that I could without any greater miracle give myself ten arms and three heads.

THE HE-ANCIENT. I also came to understand such miracles. For fifty years I sat contemplating this power in myself and concentrating my will.

THE SHE-ANCIENT. So did I; and for five more years I made myself into all sorts of fantastic monsters. I walked upon a dozen legs: I worked with twenty hands and a hundred fingers: I looked to the four quarters of the compass with eight eyes out of four heads. Children fled in amazement from me until I had to hide myself from them; and the ancients, who had forgotten how to laugh, smiled grimly when they passed.

THE HE-ANCIENT. We have all committed these follies. You will all commit them.

THE NEWLY-BORN. Oh, do grow a lot of arms and legs and heads for us. It would be so funny.

THE HE-ANCIENT. My child: I am just as well as I am. I would not lift my finger now to have a thousand heads.

THE SHE-ANCIENT. But what would I not give to have no head at all?

ALL THE YOUNG. Whats that? No head at all? Why? How?

THE HE-ANCIENT. Can you not understand?

ALL THE YOUNG [*shaking their heads*] No.

THE SHE-ANCIENT. One day, when I was tired of learning to walk forward with some of my feet and backwards with others and sideways with the rest all at once, I sat on a rock with my four chins resting on four of my palms, and four of my elbows resting on four of my knees. And suddenly it came into my mind that this monstrous machinery of heads and limbs was no more me than my statues had been me, and that it was only an automaton that I had enslaved.

MARTELLUS. Enslaved? What does that mean?

THE SHE-ANCIENT. A thing that must do what you command it is a slave; and its commander is its master. These are words you will learn when your turn comes.

THE HE-ANCIENT. You will also learn that when the master has come to do everything through the slave, the slave becomes his master, because his master cannot live without him.

THE SHE-ANCIENT. And so I perceived that I had made myself the slave of a slave.

THE HE-ANCIENT. When we discovered that, we shed our superfluous heads and legs and arms until we had our old shapes again, and no longer startled the children.

THE SHE-ANCIENT. But still I am the slave of this slave, my body. How am I to be delivered from it?

THE HE-ANCIENT. That, children, is the trouble of the ancients. For whilst we are tied to this tyrannous body we are subject to its death, and our destiny is not achieved.

THE NEWLY BORN. What is your destiny?

THE HE-ANCIENT. To be immortal.

THE SHE-ANCIENT. The day will come when there will be no people, only thought.

THE HE-ANCIENT. And that will be life eternal.

ECRASIA. I trust I shall meet my fatal accident before that day dawns.

ARJILLAX. For once, Ecrasia, I agree with you.

ECRASIA. No limbs, no contours, no exquisite lines and elegant shapes, no worship of beautiful bodies, no poetic embraces in which cultivated lovers pretend that their caressing hands are wandering over celestial hills and enchanted valleys, no—

ACIS [*interrupting her disgustedly*] What an inhuman mind you have, Ecrasia!

ECRASIA. Inhuman!

ACIS. Yes: inhuman. Why dont you fall in love with someone?

ECRASIA. I! I have been in love all my life. I burned with it even in the egg.

ACIS. Not a bit of it. You and Arjillax are just as hard as two stones.

ECRASIA. You did not always think so, Acis.

ACIS. Oh, I know. I offered you my love once, and asked for yours.

ECRASIA. And did I deny it to you, Acis?

ACIS. You didnt even know what love was.

ECRASIA. Oh! I adored you, you stupid oaf, until I found that you were a mere animal.

ACIS. And I made no end of a fool of myself about you until I discovered that you were a mere artist. You appreciated my contours! I was a masterpiece appealing to your tastes and your senses. Your tastes and senses had overlaid the direct impulse of life in you. And because I cared only for our life, and went straight to it, and was bored by your calling my limbs fancy names and mapping me into mountains and valleys and all the rest of it, you called me an animal. Well, I am an animal, if you call a live man an animal.

ECRASIA. You need not explain. You refused to be

[ 621 ]

refined. I did my best to lift your prehistoric impulses on to the plane of beauty, of imagination, of romance, of poetry, of art, of—

ACIS. These things are all very well in their way and in their proper places. But they are not love. They are an unnatural adulteration of love. Love is a simple thing and a deep thing: it is an act of life and not an illusion. Art is all illusion.

ARJILLAX. That is false. The statue comes to life always. The statues of today are the men and women of the next incubation. I hold up the marble figure before the mother and say "This is the model you must copy." We produce what we see. Let no man dare to create in art a thing that he would not have exist in life.

MARTELLUS. Yes: I have been through all that. But you yourself are making statues of ancients instead of beautiful nymphs and swains. And Ecrasia is right about the ancients being inartistic. They are damnably inartistic.

ECRASIA [*triumphant*] Ah! Our greatest artist vindicates me. Thanks, Martellus.

MARTELLUS. The body always ends by being a bore. Nothing remains beautiful and interesting except thought, because the thought is the life. Which is just what this old gentleman and this old lady seem to think too.

THE SHE-ANCIENT. Quite so.

THE HE-ANCIENT. Precisely.

THE NEWLY BORN [*to the He-Ancient*] But you cant be nothing. What do you want to be?

THE HE-ANCIENT. A vortex.

THE NEWLY BORN. A what?

THE SHE-ANCIENT. A vortex. I began as a vortex: why should I not end as one?

[ 622 ]

ECRASIA. Oh! That is what you old people are! Vorticists!

ACIS. If life is thought, can you live without a head?

THE HE-ANCIENT. Not now perhaps. But prehistoric men thought they could not live without tails. I can live without a tail. Why should I not live without a head?

THE NEWLY BORN. What is a tail?

THE HE-ANCIENT. A habit of which your ancestors managed to cure themselves.

THE SHE-ANCIENT. None of us now believe that all this machinery of flesh and blood is necessary. It dies.

THE HE-ANCIENT. It imprisons us on this petty planet and forbids us to range through the stars.

ACIS. But even a vortex is a vortex in something. You cant have a whirlpool without water; and you cant have a vortex without gas, or molecules or atoms or ions or electrons or something, not nothing.

THE HE-ANCIENT. No: the vortex is not the water nor the gas nor the atoms: it is a power over these things.

THE SHE-ANCIENT. The body was the slave of the vortex; but the slave has become the master; and we must free ourselves from that tyranny. It is this stuff [*indicating her body*], this flesh and blood and bone and all the rest of it, that is intolerable. Even pre-historic man dreamed of what he called an astral body, and asked who would deliver him from the body of this death.

ACIS [*evidently out of his depth*] I shouldnt think too much about it if I were you. You have to keep sane, you know.

*The two Ancients look at one another; shrug their shoulders; and address themselves to their departure.*

[ 623 ]

THE HE-ANCIENT. We are staying too long with you, children. We must go.

*All the young people rise rather eagerly.*

ARJILLAX. Dont mention it.

THE SHE-ANCIENT. It is tiresome for us, too. You see, children, we have to put things very crudely to you to make ourselves intelligible.

THE HE-ANCIENT. And I am afraid we do not quite succeed.

STREPHON. Very kind of you to come at all and talk to us, I'm sure.

MARTELLUS. Why do the other ancients never come and give us a turn?

THE SHE-ANCIENT. It is so difficult for them. They have forgotten how to speak; how to read; even how to think in your fashion. We do not communicate with one another in that way nor apprehend the world as you do.

THE HE-ANCIENT. I find it more and more difficult to keep up your language. Another century or two and it will be impossible. I shall have to be relieved by a younger shepherd.

ACIS. Of course we are always delighted to see you; but still, if it tires you so severely, we could manage pretty well by ourselves, you know.

THE SHE-ANCIENT. Tell me, Acis: do you ever think of yourself as having to live perhaps for thousands of years?

ACIS. Oh, dont talk about it. I have only four years of what any reasonable person would call living; and three and a half of them are already gone.

ECRASIA. You must not mind our saying so; but really you cannot call being an ancient living.

THE NEWLY BORN [*almost in tears*] Oh, this dreadful shortness of our lives! I cannot bear it.

[ 624 ]

STREPHON. I made up my mind on that subject long ago. When I am three years and fifty weeks old, I shall have my fatal accident. And it will not be an accident.

THE HE-ANCIENT. We are very tired of this subject. I must leave you.

THE NEWLY BORN. What is being tired?

THE SHE-ANCIENT. The tediousness of attending to children. Farewell.

*The two Ancients go away severally, she into the grove, he up to the hills behind the temple.*

ALL. Ouf! [*A great sigh of relief*].

ECRASIA. Dreadful people!

STREPHON. Bores!

MARTELLUS. Yet one would like to follow them; to enter into their life; to grasp their thought; to comprehend the universe as they must.

ARJILLAX. Getting old, Martellus?

MARTELLUS. Well, I have finished with the dolls; and I am no longer jealous of you. That looks like the end. Two hours sleep is enough for me. I am afraid I am beginning to find you all rather silly.

STREPHON. I know. My girl went off this morning. She hadnt slept for weeks. And she found mathematics more interesting than me.

MARTELLUS. There is a prehistoric saying that has come down to us from a famous woman teacher. She said "Leave women; and study mathematics." She was right: I am tired of women. I will study mathematics, which I have neglected too long. Farewell, children, my old playmates. I almost wish I could feel sentimental about parting from you; but the cold truth is that you bore me. Do not be angry with me: your turn will come. [*He passes away gravely into the grove*].

[ 625 ]

ARJILLAX. There goes a great spirit. What a sculptor he was! And now, nothing! It is as if he had cut off his hands.

THE NEWLY BORN. Oh, will you all leave me as he has left you?

ECRASIA. Never. We have sworn it.

STREPHON. What is the use of swearing? She swore. He swore. You have sworn. They have sworn.

ECRASIA. You speak like a grammar.

STREPHON. That is how one ought to speak, isnt it? We shall all be forsworn.

THE NEWLY BORN. Do not talk like that. You are saddening us; and you are chasing the light away. It is growing dark.

ACIS. Night is falling. The light will come back tomorrow.

THE NEWLY BORN. What is tomorrow?

ACIS. The day that never comes. [*He turns towards the temple*].

*All begin trooping into the temple.*

THE NEWLY BORN [*holding Acis back*] That is no answer. What—

ARJILLAX. Silence. Little children should be seen and not heard.

THE NEWLY BORN [*puts out her tongue at him*]!

ECRASIA. Ungraceful. You must not do that.

THE NEWLY BORN. I will do what I like. But there is something the matter with me. I want to lie down. I cannot keep my eyes open.

ECRASIA. You are falling asleep. You will wake up again.

THE NEWLY BORN [*drowsily*] What is sleep?

ACIS. Ask no questions; and you will be told no lies. [*He takes her by the ear, and leads her firmly towards the temple*].

[ 626 ]

THE NEWLY BORN. Ai! oi! ai! Dont. I want to be carried. [*She reels into the arms of Acis, who carries her into the temple*].

ECRASIA. Come, Arjillax: you at least are still an artist. I adore you.

ARJILLAX. Do you? Unfortunately for you, I am not still a child. I have grown out of cuddling. I can only appreciate your figure. Does that satisfy you?

ECRASIA. At what distance?

ARJILLAX. Arm's length or more.

ECRASIA. Thank you: not for me. [*She turns away from him*].

ARJILLAX. Ha! ha! [*He strides off into the temple*].

ECRASIA [*calling to Strephon, who is on the threshold of the temple, going in*] Strephon.

STREPHON. No. My heart is broken. [*He goes into the temple*].

ECRASIA. Must I pass the night alone? [*She looks round, seeking another partner; but they have all gone*]. After all, I can imagine a lover nobler than any of you. [*She goes into the temple*].

*It is now quite dark. A vague radiance appears near the temple and shapes itself into the ghost of Adam.*

A WOMAN'S VOICE [*in the grove*] Who is that?

ADAM. The ghost of Adam, the first father of mankind. Who are you?

THE VOICE. The ghost of Eve, the first mother of mankind.

ADAM. Come forth, wife; and shew yourself to me.

EVE [*appearing near the grove*] Here I am, husband. You are very old.

A VOICE [*in the hills*] Ha! ha! ha!

ADAM. Who laughs? Who dares laugh at Adam?

EVE. Who has the heart to laugh at Eve?

THE VOICE. The ghost of Cain, the first child, and

the first murderer. [*He appears between them; and as he does so there is a prolonged hiss*]. Who dares hiss at Cain, the lord of death?

A VOICE. The ghost of the serpent, that lived before Adam and before Eve, and taught them how to bring forth Cain. [*She becomes visible, coiled in the trees*].

A VOICE. There is one that came before the serpent.

THE SERPENT. That is the voice of Lilith, in whom the father and mother were one. Hail, Lilith!

*Lilith becomes visible between Cain and Adam.*

LILITH. I suffered unspeakably; I tore myself asunder; I lost my life, to make of my one flesh these twain, man and woman. And this is what has come of it. What do you make of it, Adam, my son?

ADAM. I made the earth bring forth by my labor, and the woman bring forth by my love. And this is what has come of it. What do you make of it, Eve, my wife?

EVE. I nourished the egg in my body and fed it with my blood. And now they let it fall as the birds do, and suffer not at all. What do you make of it, Cain, my first-born?

CAIN. I invented killing and conquest and mastery and the winnowing out of the weak by the strong. And now the strong have slain one another; the weak live for ever; and victory is deadlier than defeat. What do you make of it, snake?

THE SERPENT. I am justified. For I chose wisdom and the knowledge of good and evil; and now there is no evil; and wisdom and good are one. It is enough. [*She vanishes*].

CAIN. There is no place for me on earth any longer. You cannot deny that mine was a splendid game while it lasted. But now! Out, out, brief candle! [*He vanishes*].

EVE. The clever ones were always my favorites. The diggers and the fighters have dug themselves in with the worms. My clever ones have inherited the earth. All's well. [*She fades away*].

ADAM. I can make nothing of it, neither head nor tail. What is it all for? Why? Whither? Whence? We were well enough in the garden. And now the fools have killed all the animals; and they are dissatisfied because they cannot be bothered with their bodies! Foolishness, I call it. [*He disappears*].

LILITH. They have accepted the burden of eternal life. They have taken the agony from birth; and their life does not fail them even in the hour of their destruction. Their breasts are without milk: their bowels are gone: the very shapes of them are only ornaments for their children to admire and caress without understanding. Is this enough; or must I labor again? Shall I bring forth something that will sweep them away and make an end of them as they have swept away the beasts of the garden, and made an end of the crawling things and the flying things and of all them that refuse to live for ever? I had patience with them for many ages: they tried me very sorely. They did terrible things: they embraced death, and said that eternal life was a fable. I stood amazed at the malice and destructiveness of the things I had made: Mars blushed as he looked down on the shame of his sister planet: cruelty and hypocrisy became so hideous that the face of the earth was pitted with the graves of little children among which living skeletons crawled in search of horrible food. The pangs of another birth were already upon me when one man repented and lived three hundred years; and I waited to see what would come of that. And so much came of it that the horrors of that time

[ 629 ]

seem now but an evil dream. They have redeemed themselves from their vileness, and turned away from their sins. Best of all, they are still not satisfied: the impulse I gave them in that day when I sundered myself in twain and launched Man and Woman on the earth still urges them: after passing a million goals they press on to the goal of redemption from the flesh, to the vortex freed from matter, to the whirlpool in pure intelligence that, when the world began, was a whirlpool in pure force. And though all that they have done seems but the first hour of the infinite work of creation, yet I will not supersede them until they have forded this last stream that lies between flesh and spirit, and disentangled their life from the matter that has always mocked it. I can wait: waiting and patience mean nothing to the eternal. I gave the woman the greatest of gifts: curiosity. By that her seed has been saved from my wrath; for I also am curious; and I have waited always to see what they will do tomorrow. Let them feed that appetite well for me. I say, let them dread, of all things, stagnation; for from the moment I, Lilith, lose hope and faith in them, they are doomed. In that hope and faith I have let them live for a moment; and in that moment I have spared them many times. But mightier creatures than they have killed hope and faith, and perished from the earth; and I may not spare them for ever. I am Lilith: I brought life into the whirlpool of force, and compelled my enemy, Matter, to obey a living soul. But in enslaving Life's enemy I made him Life's master; for that is the end of all slavery; and now I shall see the slave set free and the enemy reconciled, the whirlpool become all life and no matter. And because these infants that call themselves ancients are reaching out towards that,

I will have patience with them still; though I know well that when they attain it they shall become one with me and supersede me, and Lilith will be only a legend and a lay that has lost its meaning. Of Life only is there no end; and though of its million starry mansions many are empty and many still unbuilt, and though its vast domain is as yet unbearably desert, my seed shall one day fill it and master its matter to its uttermost confines. And for what may be beyond, the eyesight of Lilith is too short. It is enough that there is a beyond. [*She vanishes*].

# A Glimpse of the
# Domesticity of Franklyn Barnabas

(Originally intended to be the second act of *The
Gospel of the Brothers Barnabas*. First published in
the Collected Edition, 1930, in *Short Stories,
Scraps and Shavings*)

If you have read Back to Methuselah you will remember Franklyn Barnabas, the ex-clergyman who, with
his gruff brother Conrad, the biologist, had come to
the conclusion that the duration of human life must be
extended to three hundred years, not in the least as all
the stupid people thought because people would
profit by a longer experience, but because it was not
worth their while to make any serious attempt to better
the world or their own condition when they had only
thirty or forty years of full maturity to enjoy before
they doddered away into decay and death. The
brothers Barnabas were in fact the first discoverers of
the staringly obvious truth that it is our expectation of
life, and not our experience of it, that determines our
conduct and character. Consequently the very vulgar
proposition that you cannot change human nature,
and therefore cannot make the revolutionary political
and economic changes which are now known to be
necessary to save our civilization from perishing like
all previous recorded ones, is valid only on the assumption that you cannot change the duration of human
life. If you can change that, then you can change
political conduct through the whole range which lies
between the plague-stricken city's policy of "Let us
eat and drink; for tomorrow we die" and the long-sighted and profound policies of the earthly paradises
of More, Morris, Wells, and all the other Utopians.

It was with this thesis of the Barnabases that I was concerned when I wrote Back to Methuselah; and though I got interested enough in Franklyn personally to go a little way into his domestic history, I had to discard my researches as both irrelevant and certain to sidetrack my main theme and confuse my biological drama with a domestic comedy.

Also I had amused myself by bringing Franklyn Barnabas into contact with a notable social philosopher of our day for the mere fun of caricaturing him. But this proved a hopeless enterprise; for, like all really great humorists, he had himself exploited his own possibilities so thoroughly in that direction that I could produce nothing but a manifestly inferior copy of a gorgeous original. Still, even a bad caricature may have some value when the original has dissolved into its elements for remanufacture by the Life Force. As we cannot now have a photograph of Shakespear, much less a portrait by a master, we cling to the in-human caricature by Droeshout as at least a corrective to the commonplace little bust of a commonplace little gent in the shrine in Stratford church; and so I think it possible that my thumbnail sketch, in-adequate and libellous as it is, may give a hint or two to some future great biographer as to what the original of Immenso Champernoon was like in the first half of his career, when, in defiance of the very order of nature, he began without a figure as a convivial immensity with vine leaves in his hair, deriding his own aspect, and in middle life slimmed into a Catholic saint, thereby justifying my reminder to those who took him too lightly of old, that Thomas Aquinas began as a comically fat man and ended as The Divine Doctor.

Until the other day I believed that my studies of the

Barnabas home out Hampstead way, with my Champernoon caricature, had perished in the waste-paper basket which has swallowed many discarded pages of my works. But they have just turned up in the course of a hunt for matter wherewith to complete a collected edition of my works; and, being much at a loss for padding for this particular volume of scraps of fiction, I looked through them and thought they might prove not only readable, but perhaps useful to married ladies with interesting husbands who attract husband stealers. Such ladies, if they are at all bearable, have all the trumps in their hands, and need never be beaten if they understand the game and play it with the requisite audacity and contempt for the danger.

Here, then, are a few scraps of the scenes which took place in the suburban villa in which the brothers Barnabas made their famous attempt to persuade our political leaders in the first years after the war to discard their obsolete party programs and raise the slogan of Back to Methuselah.

*Conrad Barnabas the biologist is in the library waiting for his brother Franklyn. Franklyn comes in presently looking worried and irritated. The conversation proceeds as follows.*

CONRAD. Anything wrong?

FRANKLYN. As usual.

CONRAD. Clara broken out again?

FRANKLYN. She left the house on Saturday saying that she would live with me no longer. My worthy brother-in-law wants to see me about her.

CONRAD. What! Immenso Champernoon! Dont say he's coming here.

FRANKLYN. He is.

CONRAD. Oh, Lord!

[ 634 ]

FRANKLYN. Perhaps if you start a discussion with him he may forget to talk about Clara. I really cannot stand any more of it. I have been a very good husband to her for twenty years, as husbands go; and now I sometimes regret that we did not separate at our first quarrel.

CONRAD. Well, Clara has been a fairly good wife to you, as wives go. She keeps the house very well.

FRANKLYN. A well-kept house is an excellent thing as far as it goes. But it is not an indispensable condition of life to me. Constitutionally I am an untidy irregular man. We all are, we Barnabases. You are.

CONRAD. But I knew better than to marry. You knew what you were doing, you know.

FRANKLYN. I dont think anyone knows quite what he is doing when he marries.

CONRAD. Widowers do. And they marry.

FRANKLYN. It suits them, perhaps. Besides, a married man forms married habits and becomes dependent on marriage, just as a sailor becomes dependent on the sea. But there are limits. I know a sailor who was torpedoed nine times, and yet went to sea again. But the tenth time finished him: he took a job in the docks. Well, Clara has torpedoed me nine times. If she is going to do it again she may find it once too often.

CONRAD. I cannot make out what you have to quarrel about. Whats wrong with her, or you?

FRANKLYN. If you want to know whats wrong with me, you must ask her. What is wrong with her is that she is a bluestocking.

CONRAD. Oh, come! Thats rather out of date, isnt it? I dont believe the women students at Cambridge know the meaning of the word. You dont object at this time of day to a woman cultivating her mind and being educated?

FRANKLYN. Not at all. Nobody ever does: among our set of people at any rate. A bluestocking is not an educated woman or a woman with a cultivated mind.

CONRAD. What else?

FRANKLYN. A bluestocking is a woman who has a mania for intellectual subjects without having a ray of intellect.

CONRAD. Oho! Thats not a bluestocking: it's a university professor. When a man is mentally incapable of abstract thought he takes to metaphysics; and they make him a professor. When he is incapable of conceiving quantity in the abstract he takes to mathematics; and they make him a professor. When he is incapable of distinguishing between a clockwork mouse and a real one he takes to biology; and they make him a professor. And so on. The fact is, these chaps are clockwork mice themselves. By tutoring them and coaching them and stuffing them with textbooks you wind them up, and they go. You feel safe with them because you always know how far they will go and how they will go. But Clara is not like that. She hasnt been wound up. She is not a fool.

FRANKLYN. Isnt she?

CONRAD. Well, not that sort of fool. These people have no minds at all: Clara has a very restless mind, not to say a fidgety one. What has she been worrying about now?

FRANKLYN. Indian religions. Theosophy. Yoga. Reincarnation. Karma. Anything from the East.

CONRAD. Damn the East! Are we never to look at home for our religion?

FRANKLYN. Amen. She calls Creative Evolution Western Materialism, cockney blasphemy, and all the rest of it. Says she wont live in the house with it.

[ 636 ]

CONRAD. But a woman doesnt leave her home for a thing like that. Whats the row, really?

FRANKLYN. Oh, what is the row always, in married life? It's not Creative Evolution, it's because I discuss Creative Evolution with Mrs Etteen and refuse to discuss it with Clara. How can I discuss it with a woman who tells me I dont understand it, and that the truth about it is all in the Vedantas or the Upanishads or the last number of the Theosophical Journal or some other nigger scripture?

CONRAD. Mrs Etteen? Who is she?

FRANKLYN. Oh—er—a lady.

CONRAD. Thank God I'm not married, and can discuss Creative Evolution with anyone I like.

FRANKLYN. And now I shall have to sit here and keep my temper while Immenso gasses about domestic virtue.

CONRAD. Why need you keep your temper? I tell you frankly, I intend to lose mine.

FRANKLYN. It wont make the smallest difference to Immenso.

THE PARLOR MAID [*announcing*] Mr Champernoon. [*She withdraws*].

*Immenso Chapernoon is a man of colossal mould, with the head of a cherub on the body of a Falstaff, which he carries with ease and not without grace. At forty or thereabouts his hair is still brown and curly. He is friendly, a little shy, and jokes frequently enough to be almost always either still enjoying the last or already anticipating the next. He is careless of his dress and person, in marked contrast to Franklyn, who, though untidy as to his papers, looks comparatively valeted and manicured.*

FRANKLYN. Conrad's here, Imm. You dont mind, do you?

CONRAD [*striving not to let Immenso's large and genial aspect disarm him*] I can go.

IMMENSO. Not at all. Delighted to see you, doctor. [*He sits down on the sofa, which groans beneath the burden*].

FRANKLYN. Well, what is the latest? Has Clara made up her mind to a separation, or has she discovered a new religion, or have you a treaty of good behaviour in your pocket which I am to sign?

IMMENSO. I really forget what she said.

CONRAD. You forget!

IMMENSO. The way I look at it is this. A man is not a balloon.

CONRAD. Some men are damned like one.

IMMENSO [*grinning genially*] Like all men of science you are the dupe of appearances. For instance, *I* am superficially like a balloon. I fancy that was in your mind when you introduced the subject of balloons.

CONRAD. It is just possible. But it was you who introduced the subject.

IMMENSO. Let me suggest an experiment. Procure a balloon; and place it on the lawn. Place me at the same time on the roof. Detach us both simultaneously from the lawn and from the roof. The balloon will immediately shoot up into the heavens and be lost. *I* will, on the contrary, descend to earth with destructive force, and probably make a considerable dent in it. In other words, you will not know where to find the balloon; and you will know where to find me. That is the essential difference.

FRANKLYN. Yes, yes; but what has it to do with Clara?

IMMENSO. This. The earth is my home. If my home were in the skies I could not be a married man. You conceive me at the altar trying to get married, with the bride, the bridesmaids, the best man, the pew opener, and the parson all holding me down. But they would have to let go sooner or later. And then up I would shoot. My head would strike the stars. My coat would be whitened in the milky way. And my wife would be that most pitiful of all widows, a grass widow. The natural occupation of the grass widow is to make hay whilst the sun shines. But my widow could not, because my bulk would obscure the sun. I should be a perpetual eclipse—

FRANKLYN. My dear Imm: I shall be delighted to hear your views on balloons, on grass, and on eclipses when we have nothing else to talk about. I have no doubt they will be extremely entertaining. But just at present I want to know what Clara intends to do, or intends me to do.

IMMENSO. But dont you see that that is just what I am coming to?

CONRAD. I'm damned if *I* do.

IMMENSO. If you ask me—

CONRAD. I dont. It would be much shorter to ask a policeman.

IMMENSO. You could not ask a better man. A policeman would tell you at once that the whole police system, like all other eternally stable systems, depends, not on the wandering policeman but on the fixed point policeman. Not on the rolling stone policeman, a human avalanche who gathers no moss, but on the monumental policeman whom you always know where to find.

FRANKLYN. Again I ask you, Imm, what message have you brought to me from Clara?

IMMENSO. Again I tell you, Frank, I bring to you the message of gravitation which saves me from the fate of the balloon, and of the fixed point policeman on whom Conrad depends for his knowledge of the way to Putney. That is important, because if you cant find the way to Putney you cant find the way to paradise.

FRANKLYN. Yes. You were about to say that Clara told you to tell me—?

IMMENSO. As a matter of detail she told me not to tell you. But what she said was that you could never live alone, because, as she put it, you are no anchorite.

FRANKLYN. Did you defend me from the monstrously false accusation which that implies?

IMMENSO. I pointed out that she was your anchor, and that if a man's anchor belied its own nature and swam away from him, it could hardly blame him for drifting.

FRANKLYN. And what did she say to that?

IMMENSO. She said there was no use talking to me. She said I was making puns of her distress.

FRANKLYN. And was that all?

IMMENSO. No. You may have noticed that when a woman says there is no use talking to a man, he can very seldom get a word in edgeways for the following half hour.

CONRAD. If she shut you up, she is a woman in a thousand.

IMMENSO. That is an almost perfect example of a modern scientific definition. It has the air of exactitude which arithmetic alone can give. Yet as, from the moment the population exceeds nine hundred and ninety-nine, every woman is a woman in a thousand, it means absolutely nothing whatever.

FRANKLYN. We make you a present of modern science, Imm: nobody here worships it any more than you do—[*Conrad is about to protest*]—no, Con: you sit quiet and say nothing. I shall sit quiet and say

[ 640 ]

nothing. When Imm is tired of playing with his own mind, he will perhaps have a human impulse, and relieve my anxiety to learn what Clara intends to do.

IMMENSO [*coloring at the implied reproach*] I am not inconsiderate, I hope. Certainly not intentionally so. But what Clara intends to do is her affair. What you intend to do is your affair. My only comment is that probably neither of you will do it. On the other hand I am deeply concerned, as a Christian, and may I say as a friend—if a brother-in-law may presume so far—with what you both ought to do.

FRANKLYN. And what is that.

IMMENSO. Anchor yourself to the hearthstone. Make that your fixed point. There must be fixed points in life or we shall become a community of balloons. Even for balloons there must be fixed gas works, a necessity quaintly met by the House of Commons. There must be irrevocable contracts. What is the first question we ask a man? His name. What is the second? His address. A man without a name is nobody. A man without an address is a vagabond. A man with two addresses is a libertine. A man with two solicitors and two bankers is a rogue. What is a marriage? Two persons with one name, one address. Not a changeable name, but one rooted in history, buried in parish registers to undergo a glorious resurrection in every generation; not a changeable address, but one hearthstone rooted in the solid earth of the motherland as a rock of ages, one certainty among all the uncertainties, one star among all the planets and meteors, one unshakable and unchangeable thing that is and was and ever shall be. You must have a root; and this matter of the root is also the root of the matter.

FRANKLYN. Marriage is not one of the certainties.

Are there any certainties? Everything passes away; everything gets broken; we get tired of everything. Including marriages.

IMMENSO. No. Nothing can pass unless it passes something. A bus passes Piccadilly Circus; but Piccadilly Circus remains. I get tired of Clara; but I remain. So does Clara, by the way. And though everything gets broken you cannot break the thinnest glass goblet without striking it against a fixed object. You cannot break it by striking it against a butterfly. Has Con here ever considered, as a curious point in entomology, that you cannot break a butterfly at all? Foolish people say you can break it on a wheel; but it has never been done. Whistler survived his stodgiest enemies.

CONRAD. We have now got from the hearthstone to the butterfly as the emblem of constancy.

IMMENSO. You are a bachelor, Con: it has been your dreadful fate to sip every flower and change every hour until Polly your passion requited. Has she ever done so? No: she eludes you in every form except that of the Polyglot bible, in which you find the words SUPER HANC PETRAM: Upon this rock will I build my Church. What is that rock? The hearthstone. Come back to the hearthstone, Frank.

FRANKLYN. Like a bad penny.

IMMENSO. Not at all. A bad penny is nailed to the counter. Now it is the chief glory and peculiar quality of the hearthstone that you cannot nail anything to it. Also that though you can stand by it you cannot fall by it without getting your head under the grate. You can stand by it; sit by it: you can even, when Clara is indiscreetly curious, lie by it; but you cannot be nailed to it nor fall by it nor inconvenience yourself in any way by it.

FRANKLYN. What are we to do with this fellow, Con ?

CONRAD. It's a pathological case. Theres a disease called echolalia. It sets stupid people gabbling rhymes: that is, words that echo each other. Imm here, being a clever chap, gabbles ideas that echo. He's by way of being a pundit, and is really only a punster.

IMMENSO. Be it so. You may say the same of Plato, of Shakespear. At all events, I keep to the point, which is the home.

FRANKLYN. Clara is the point.

IMMENSO. She is the point inasmuch as you have a tendency to stray from her. But the definition of a point is position without magnitude. Now Clara has both position and magnitude; and you will find that the more you attempt to destroy her position, the more oppressive her magnitude will become.

FRANKLYN. Imm: I know your trick of never arguing, but simply talking every idea out of my head except your own ideas. But it's no use your preaching the virtues of an imaginary world of irrevocable contracts to me. We are struggling out of a tyranny of sacred traditions, immutable laws, and irrevocable contracts into a freedom in which we may prove all things and hold fast to that which is good. If I find married life with Clara intolerable, I shall chuck it and chuck her; and thats all about it.

IMMENSO. Many men begin by chucking the woman they love. The saying that "each man slays the thing he loves" would be more true if it ran that "each man chucks the thing he loves"; but he usually chucks it under the chin. In any other sense you will find it difficult to chuck Clara.

CONRAD. Tell me this. Suppose Frank and Clara, instead of having at the outside-twenty-five years more to live, had two hundred and fifty! Suppose

[ 643 ]

that having brought up one family to the point at which that family naturally breaks up and the young people depart and make new families of their own, they were left to sit and stare at one another for two centuries, or to begin over again with another family, would you still admit no time limit to their contract? Does it occur to you that under such circumstances it might become unreasonable, or be considered indecent, or even declared illegal, for marriages to last for three centuries?

IMMENSO [*reflectively*] I see. You mean that when a tie has endured for, say, fifty years, it becomes so intimate, so sacred, that it establishes, in effect, a relation far closer than the relation of consanguinity, and should be placed on the list of degrees within which marriage is forbidden; that the two may become one flesh so completely that even as brother and sister they would be more remote from one another, and that consequently marriage between them would become unthinkable through its very perfection. That is an idea which commands my respect. When they made you a man of science, Con, they killed a poet, more's the pity!

CONRAD. I never meant any such infernal nonsense. I meant that only fools stick in the same groove for ever, and that the law of change is a biological law.

IMMENSO. Well, if you come to that, I must remind you—though without prejudice to my eternal and unchangeable derision, loathing, contempt, and utter disbelief in biology and all other ologies whatever except perhaps the doxology—that it is a biological law that Frank and Clara shall have only one life and can bring up only one family, and that they must make the best of it.

CONRAD. I deny that it is a biological law. It is nothing

but a bad habit. We can live as long as we like. Do you know what people really die of?

IMMENSO. Of reasonableness. They do not want to live for ever.

CONRAD. Of laziness, and want of conviction, and failure to make their lives worth living. That is why. That is sound scientific biology for you. I believe that we are on the brink of a generation that will live longer. Or else we are on the brink of destruction.

IMMENSO. The slain poet has his revenge. He rises from the dead as a scientific madman.

CONRAD. Gasbag!

IMMENSO. Oh, that this too too solid flesh would melt, thaw, and resolve itself into a gas! Call me a Jack Pudding, Con. That will not smell of the laboratory; but it will hit me in the stomach.

FRANKLYN. I am sorry to again make a digression. What does Clara want me to do? She sends me word that it is her firm intention never to cross my threshold again, and that I must see you about it. I have seen you; and I am as wise as I was before. There is no use asking you whether she gave you any message for me, as you will immediately proceed to deliver the message of the universe. Did she give you a letter?

IMMENSO [*producing a key*] She gave me this. She thinks it is her latchkey; but as a matter of fact I tried to open the door with it, and found it would not work; so I had to ring for admission in the usual course. But she undoubtedly believed that it was the key of this house when she gave it me. It is symbolically the key of your house. Actually, now that I look at it, I believe it is the key of mine. She has been staying with us for a few days. So if you will allow me I will keep it [*he replaces it in his pocket*].

FRANKLYN. Then she is in earnest about never crossing the threshold?

*Mrs Franklyn Barnabas (Clara) flounces in through the window. She is a very active lady of fifty or thereabouts, rather under than over, and is richly but hastily and untidily dressed.*

CLARA. I must apologize for entering unannounced by this way instead of through the front door as a stranger should. But Frank can hardly expect me to make a parade of our unhappy differences before the servants.

FRANKLYN. I never suggested for a moment that you should.

CLARA. And Imm took the wrong key: you know how incorrigibly careless he is. Give it back to me.

IMMENSO. Two wrongs will not make a right. I had better keep it.

CLARA. I see Con has come here to talk about me. I wish you would mind your own business, Con.

CONRAD. Damn silly business! I came here to talk about something serious.

CLARA [*smiling*] Dont be naughty, Con. But it serves me right for spoiling you. And the first thing I see when I come into the place is Savvy playing tennis with that young rector. I call it hypocrisy. She does not believe in the Thirty-nine Articles. What right has she to lead that young man on? One would think that she had seen enough of the tragedy of a marriage between two people of different religious beliefs in this house.

FRANKLYN. I quite agree.

CLARA [*flushing*] Do you indeed? Then I think thats a very nasty thing of you to say. You are always worse when you have been talking to Con behind my back. And Imm has been making mischief, I suppose, as usual.

IMMENSO [*bounding from his chair*] *I* make mischief!!!

CONRAD [*rising angrily*] How can Frank help talking about you to me when you make his life a hell?

FRANKLYN [*who has also risen*] You take offence at your own words. I am long past caring whether you find my remarks nasty or not.

CLARA. Have you all had tea?

*This simple question deflates the three men hopelessly.*

CONRAD. Tcha! [*he sits down angrily*].

FRANKLYN [*sitting down limply*] Have you had tea, Imm? I forgot to ask you.

IMMENSO [*sitting down ponderously*] I am banting. I have given up afternoon tea.

CLARA [*snatching her hat off carelessly and throwing it aside*] Who has been here while I have been away? [*She sits*]. What have you been doing? How much was the garden account on Saturday? I saw grapes at six and sixpence a pound not a patch on ours. Did you go through cook's books?

FRANKLYN. I know nothing whatever about it. Campbell will tell you about the garden. I told him not to bother me. I gave cook a cheque for what she asked, and sent her book to my solicitor to check.

CLARA. To your solicitor!

FRANKLYN. You have complained so much about the trouble of housekeeping that I have made up my mind to try another plan.

CLARA [*rising*] Well, did you ever! I shall talk to cook about letting you be so ridiculous: what right had she to ask you for a cheque? it is my house and my business. [*Making for the garden door*] Where is Campbell? [*She goes out*].

FRANKLYN [*slowly*] Why do the servants stay?

CONRAD. Why do you stay?

IMMENSO [*rising*] That raises the question, why do *I* stay? My work, it would appear, is done.

CONRAD. Running away, eh?

IMMENSO. Most moral victories have that appearance.

FRANKLYN. Well, off with you. You have the brother's privilege. You can run away from Clara.

*Clara returns, in a much better humor.*

CLARA. Imm: are you staying to dinner?

IMMENSO. It has not been suggested.

FRANKLYN. I took it as a matter of course, Imm, if you care to.

CLARA. Youd better. [*Immenso resumes his seat*]. Frank: only fancy! cook's become a Theosophist.

FRANKLYN. Indeed? Did she get that in before you complained about the cheque she got from me?

CLARA [*coaxing*] But dear Frank, what was she to do? She needed the money to keep the house going. You must not blame her.

FRANKLYN. I do not blame her.

CLARA. Well, then, what are you talking about? Come, darling: dont be cross. Dont worry about the house. Cook was very glad to see me back; and no wonder: she must have had a dreadful time of it. Dont make me feel that I am more welcome in the kitchen than I am here. Arnt you going to kiss me?

FRANKLYN. Yes, yes. [*He kisses her*] There, dear, there. You are perfectly welcome.

CLARA. Con looks very cheap. Shall I get you some ammoniated quinine, Con? You look just as you did when you were sickening for the influenza last year twelvemonths.

CONRAD. I am quite well.

CLARA. You always say that. It is really very hard that I cant go away for a week without everybody getting ill.

CONRAD. I tell you I am not ill.

CLARA. Well, if youre not, I must say you are not very
cordial in your manner. You know how glad I always
am to see you here. I think you might shew that you
are glad to see me.

CONRAD. Do you want me to kiss you?

CLARA. You may if you like. Nobody can say that I
bear malice [*She advances her cheek in his direction*].

CONRAD [*desperate*] Oh, very well. [*He gets up and
kisses her*].

CLARA. Thats better. Now you have quite a color. [*He
is, in fact, blushing slightly*].

*Savvy, Franklyn's daughter, looks in. She is rather
pleasant as a modern bright young thing; but she jars on
her father by her dowdiness and rowdiness. She fears
neither God nor man.*

SAVVY. Mamma: Campbell's here.

CLARA. What does he want?

SAVVY. Nothing. You said you wanted him. About
the grapes.

CLARA [*springing up*] Oh yes, of course. They were
six and sixpence at Covent Garden. You dont mind
my running away for a moment, do you: I promise to
come back in a jiffy. [*She hurries out*].

SAVVY. Has she given in? Or have you?

CONRAD. Stalemate, Savvy.

SAVVY. Does that mean that she is coming back?

FRANKLYN. Yes, dear. Yes.

SAVVY. I'm rather glad, you know. The house was
getting into a bit of a mess. [*She goes out*].

IMMENSO. I think you have summed up the situation
correctly in one word, Con.

CONRAD. Have I? What word?

IMMENSO. Stalemate. That is exactly what is wrong
with Frank.

FRANKLYN. What do you mean?

IMMENSO. My meaning is obvious. You are Clara's mate; and in the course of a too monotonous domestic routine you have become stale.

FRANKLYN. And Clara? Do you find her any fresher?

IMMENSO. Clara, with an instinct that amounts to genius, has recognized the situation. Finding herself stale, she takes herself off and then comes back and woos you afresh. What we have just witnessed here is a renewal of the honeymoon.

CONRAD. Tcha!

IMMENSO. Clara went away a stale mate, and returned a bride. Why dont you do the same, Frank? Why do you stick here in a groove, like a tram car? An Englishman's house is his castle; and when I am a frequent visitor it may be called the Elephant and Castle. But what is the Elephant and Castle? It is not a place at which tram cars stay: it is a point of continual departure and continual return. It is an ark which sends out doves every minute, and to which the doves return when the waters have abated. I shall write a book describing the adventures of a husband who leaves his wife every month only to return and woo her afresh, thus making himself a perpetual bridegroom, his wife a perpetual bride, and his life a perpetual honeymoon. Thus we reconcile the law of change and the irrevocable contract. Thus John Bull in his daily round of work, John Doin' as you may call him, becomes also Don Juan—

FRANKLYN. For heaven's sake, Imm, if you must make puns, make good ones, I—

*Clara returns, looking serious.*

CLARA. Frank: whats to be done? Campbell is thinking of turning Roman Catholic. He wants my advice about it.

FRANKLYN. What about the grapes?

CLARA. Do you think the grapes more important than the man's soul? I shall certainly not encourage him. And dont you encourage him either, Imm. You are always defending the Church of Rome; and I live in daily fear of your joining it just for an intellectual lark.

IMMENSO. I suggest to you, Clara, that Campbell's case is not a simple case of the grapes, but of the fox and the grapes. Now THE fox par excellence was George Fox the quaker. A Roman Catholic fox is therefore an absurdity. Campbell should turn quaker.

CLARA. I never know whether you are serious or not, Imm; and neither does anyone else; but Campbell would not join the Society of Friends: he is too cantankerous. I am greatly concerned about Campbell. He has the Keltic imagination: he is the most dreadful liar. And he has a Scottish philosophic subtlety that is almost Eastern. I advised him to read some Indian poetry. I will lend him the poems of Stupendranath Begorr.

IMMENSO. Stupendranath told me a curious thing about his uncle. He lost all his property by gambling in stocks, and had to live by getting married at the rate of two hundred a year.

CLARA. No man has a right to get married on two hundred a year. His wife must be a slave.

IMMENSO. I dont mean two hundred pounds a year: I mean two hundred marriages a year. Under our tolerant rule polygamy is unlimited in India. This gentleman conferred his high caste on the daughters of Indian snobs by marrying them. They made him handsome presents on each occasion; and these presents furnished him with a large income.

CLARA. But how could he support thousands of wives?

IMMENSO. He did not take them away with him. He left them on their parents' hands.

CLARA. And you approve of this! You advocate it! You support it!

IMMENSO. Not for a moment. I simply mention it.

CLARA. Then why do you mention it? It ought not to be mentioned. You would not mention it if you had not some sympathy with it.

CONRAD. If it is good enough for the British Empire it is good enough for you. You support the British Empire, dont you?

CLARA. Of course I support the British Empire. I am a Briton, I am proud to say. I believe we have a sacred mission to spread British ideas, British feelings, and British institutions over the whole world, because they are the best, the wholesomest, the cleanest, the freest. I would not have anyone in my house who questioned that for a moment. But if your silly story were true, it would mean that Stupendranath's vicious uncle, a black man, a gambler, and a bigamist, was imposing his abominable habits and customs on the British Government. I will write to the Secretary of State for India and have this man prosecuted.

FRANKLYN. My dear: you have been entertaining in our house for fully quarter of a century scores of people who spend their lives in trying to improve British institutions of one kind or another into something more reasonable. If they had been conventional patriots you would have called them dull and refused to invite them. What is the use of saying that you would not have such people in your house?

CLARA. Tell me this. Have I ever once—once during that quarter of a century, as you pompously call it to cover up the weakness of your argument—have I ever once invited or entertained Stupendranath's uncle or any of his shameless wives?

FRANKLYN. I did not say you had.

CLARA. Then what are you talking about?

FRANKLYN. I dont know. Ask Imm: he started this unfortunate subject.

IMMENSO. I cant help feeling that the future of British ideas depends on totally unreasonable people like Clara.

CLARA. Unreasonable! Pray why—

IMMENSO [*forcibly*] No, Clara: you may put down a husband because his domestic peace and comfort for the next week depends on his submission. But you cannot put down a brother. I can trample on you with impunity, because I can walk out afterwards to a comfortable home as long as I am careful to allow my own wife to trample on me. I say you are an utterly unreasonable woman; and I do not care a dump whether you like it or not. As it happens I am now defending you; and—

CLARA. You are a great fat fool, Imm; and I am perfectly capable of defending myself.

IMMENSO. The Roman conqueror had a slave to whisper to him "Remember that thou art mortal." The frankness of the British family relation provides me with a sister to remind me that I am a great fat fool. Why is England still England? Because there are so many people like Clara in it. She believes in her ideas, in her culture, in her morals, and backs them against the universe.

CONRAD. Does that give her any right to shove them down other people's throats with a bayonet?

IMMENSO. Yes: I should say it does. If the German shoves his ideas down our throats with music, and the French with wit, and the Italians with rhetorical paintings and romance, why should not we, being more handy with the bayonet than with any of these things, not carry on our propaganda with cold steel? By doing so we stake our lives and all our possessions on our ideas. Is not that more heroic than merely staking them on the success of an opera, an epigram, or a picture? What are we in India for, if not to lock up Stupendranath's uncle as a bigamist? When we put down the burning of widows and sent the car of Juggernaut to the jobmaster's scrap heap, we did India the only sort of service that could justify our interference with her. When we consented to tolerate Stupendranath's uncle we were hauling down the flag, and surrendering to the oriental. I grant you we have no right to govern India, because the Indians can govern themselves at least as well as we govern ourselves, which is not saying much. But we have a sacred right to persecute India. We have no right in the East except the right of the Crusader. The Catholic Englishman imposing British justice, British religion, and British institutions on the Hindoo is God's apostle. A Liberal Englishman undertaking to regulate oriental polygamy and idolatry is an officious meddler, an apostate, and, as Clara puts it, a fat fool.

CLARA. Nonsense! Why shouldnt the poor people have their own religions and their own institutions? I am sure they are just as respectable as ours. The Salvation Army killed Aunt Martha by playing under her window when she had worn her nerves to rags with neuralgia and morphia. And you justify such a thing!

FRANKLYN. Serve you right, Imm, for trying to take her part. You had better accept Clara as a true Briton and leave it at that. Why persist in expressing her views when you know very well that she hasnt got any?

CLARA. Dont be rude, Frank. It just comes to this, that when you men say things, they are views; but when I say a thing, you just say anything that comes handy for the sake of contradicting and shewing off your superior male intellects. What I say is that the Salvation Army is noisy. You say that it is as quiet as a church mouse; and you call that a view. It may be a view; but it's a lie; and you ought to be ashamed of pretending to believe it. I say that our institutions are a disgrace, right down from the silly humbugs in parliament to the borough council dustmen who never come when they are wanted and have to be cleaned up after for half a day when they do come. I say we are the most stupid, prejudiced, illiterate, drinking, betting, immoral, lazy, idle, unpunctual, good-for-nothing people on the face of the earth, as you would know if you had to keep the house and deal with them instead of sitting here airing your views. And I say that the Indians, and the Chinese, and the Japanese, and the Burmese are people with souls, and have the most wonderful ancient books of wisdom, and make far better brass work and pottery than Tottenham Court Road can. These may not be views; but they are facts. Imm there thinks he is ever so much wiser than Confucius or Lao-Tse; but when I read Lao-Tse and then try to read Imm's stuff afterwards it bores me to tears.

IMMENSO. Lao-Tse, being only a sage, cannot draw tears. For that, you need sage and onions.

CLARA. What a silly joke! You great baby.

*Savvy looks in again.*

SAVVY. Mrs Etteen's motor has just stopped at the gate. Look out. [*She vanishes*].

CLARA. I believe that woman has been here every day since I left.

[ 655 ]

FRANKLYN [*indignantly*] I have not seen Mrs Etteen for six weeks past. As you object to my seeing her; and I do not care two straws whether I see her or not, you can tell her that I am out, or busy, or anything you please: I will hide myself somewhere until she goes. [*He makes for the door*].

CLARA. No, Frank, you must stay. What—[*he goes out*]. Now that is a beastly thing of Frank to do. He will tell her next time he sees her that I drove him away.

CONRAD. Well, so you did.

CLARA. I did nothing of the sort. I asked him to stay. He makes himself ridiculous over her; and then people say that *I* make him ridiculous—that I am a jealous wife and all sorts of things. You shall just see how jealous I am.

*The parlor maid enters, followed by a slender lady, beautifully dressed, with an expression of delicate patience that almost suggests suffering. Her eyes, violet in color, have a softness and depth that make her romantically attractive. Age inscrutable, but certainly under fifty and possibly under forty.*

THE PARLOR MAID. Mrs Etteen. [*She withdraws*].

MRS ETTEEN [*approaching Clara and speaking with a deprecating shyness that gives a curious penetration to the audacity of what she says*] I am so disappointed to find you here.

CLARA. Pray why?

MRS ETTEEN. That silly Mrs Topham told me that you had deserted your husband; and as I have adored him for years, I just rushed to offer myself as an unworthy substitute.

CLARA. Well, I'm sure! Theres nothing like being candid, is there? Have you had tea?

MRS ETTEEN. Yes, thank you. Is this your famous brother, Mr Immenso Champernoon?

*Immenso, who has been sitting as if mesmerized, too shy to look at anyone, starts convulsively to his feet and presents himself for inspection with his hands hanging limply at his sides and his eyes directed to the carpet.*

CLARA. Yes: thats Immenso. He's no use to you: he's happily married. Imm: this is Mrs Etteen.

IMMENSO [*murmuring thunderously*] Ahooroo. Eh plea. [*He is understood to have said "How do you do? Very pleased." They shake hands*].

CLARA. Doctor Conrad Barnabas, Franklyn's brother. Unmarried. Fair game; so he wont interest you.

MRS ETTEEN. You are very naughty, Clara. How do you do, Doctor? I have read your book [*shaking hands*].

CONRAD. How do you do?

CLARA. I can be quite as candid as you, Rosie darling. Sure youve had tea?

MRS ETTEEN. Quite [*She sits down next to Immenso and turns her eyes full on him*]. Mr Champernoon: you are the wisest man in England when you are not talking glorious nonsense. Can you explain something to me?

IMMENSO [*trying to recover his assurance in the dangerous warmth of the violet eyes*] Explanation is not a difficult art. I should say that any fool can explain anything. Whether he can leave you any the wiser is another matter.

MRS ETTEEN. Would you believe that I have been married three times?

IMMENSO. Does that need an explanation? Have you not such a thing in your house as a mirror?

MRS ETTEEN. Oh! Gallant! You make me blush.

CLARA. You be careful, Imm. You are only mortal, like that Roman conqueror you were talking about.

MRS ETTEEN. I should be very proud to make a

conquest of you, Mr Champernoon; and, as it happens, what I am going to ask you is why I cannot.

IMMENSO [*rising rather heavily and moving to a distant seat*] Will you think me very boorish if I beg you to begin our acquaintance at the beginning and not at the end?

CLARA. Nothing doing, Rosie.

MRS ETTEEN. I know. But isnt it queer? I am not an ugly woman. I am not a very unamiable woman. I dont think I am an exceptionally stupid woman. I do think I am rather a fascinating woman: at least I always secure the attention of men. I have even infatuated more than one. And the upshot of it all is that I have had three husbands, and have been unable to keep one of them, though I have taken the greatest trouble to charm and please them. And here is Clara, who never cares what she does or says, who buys her clothes anywhere and flings them on anyhow, who bullies us and quarrels with us and rides roughshod over all our poor little susceptibilities, and yet keeps her wonderful husband without an effort, though we all want to take him from her.

CLARA. Whats the matter with my clothes? I dont get them anywhere: I get them from Valentino's, where you get yours; and I pay what I am asked. What more can I do? You dont expect me to spend my life bothering about my appearance, do you? I am not a professional husband stealer.

MRS ETTEEN. You dont need to steal husbands, dear. Youve got the best one in the market for nothing. But we poor pretty things dress and dress, and paint and paint, and dye and dye, and charm and charm, and all in vain. They wont stay with us even if we catch them once in a while. That is what I want you to explain to me, Mr Champernoon. It is so unjust.

IMMENSO [*tackling the subject ponderously and seriously*] I take it that a married life, to be permanent, must be part of nature's daily food. Now nature's daily food is not excessively agreeable. A man cannot live on Bath buns.

MRS ETTEEN. An elephant can.

IMMENSO. A very palpable hit, Mrs Etteen. I had, in fact, compared myself to an elephant just before you came in. And curiously enough, I live very largely on buns. But they are plain currant buns. An attempt to live on Bath buns would result in a surfeit of sweetness. If I call Clara a currant bun—

CLARA. I shall call you a sausage roll; so there!

IMMENSO. My sister, who has no illusions about me, will call me a sausage roll. But you, Mrs Etteen, will draw the moral that by laying yourself out to be exquisitely sweet, you may be making it impossible for a plain man to endure your charm for longer than a very brief honeymoon.

MRS ETTEEN. But why does the same thing not apply to very charming men? Franklyn Barnabas is the most charming man I know; but Clara does not get tired of him. What is your answer to that?

IMMENSO. My answer is that perhaps she does get tired of him.

CLARA. Now hold your tongue, Imm. That was not why I went away.

MRS ETTEEN. Oh! You did go away then?

CLARA. Now that Imm has been inconsiderate enough to let it out, you had better be told that Frank and I separated because he and his brother here have set up a new religion which I simply decline to entertain, and which I hope I have heard the last of.

MRS ETTEEN [*sadly*] The separation did not last very long, did it?

[ 659 ]

CLARA. Nearly a week. Do you call that nothing?

MRS ETTEEN. You see, he came back.

CLARA. He came back! What do you mean? *I* came back. You dont suppose he left me.

MRS ETTEEN. I hoped it. But why dont you get tired of him if what your brother says is true? Surely Franklyn is a Bath bun, if ever there was one.

IMMENSO. I should describe him rather as a Bath Oliver. A Bath Oliver has no sweetness; but it has a certain Cromwellian cleanness and plainness. Hence, no doubt, the name Oliver.

MRS ETTEEN. That is rather funny. But it leaves me lonely, and Clara triumphant. Doctor Conrad: has science nothing to say?

CONRAD. Yes. Science tells you that the trouble is that Frank is not an amoeba.

MRS ETTEEN. What is an amoeba?

CONRAD. Our common ancestor. An early form of life which you will find in the nearest ditch.

MRS ETTEEN. And where does Franklyn come in?

CONRAD. The amoeba can split himself into two amoebas, and the two can split themselves into four and so on. Well, Frank cannot split himself up into a dozen Franks so that there shall be a Frank for every woman who wants him. Theres only one of him; and Clara's got it. Hadnt you better make up your mind to that?

MRS ETTEEN. But Franklyn can split himself up. There is a place in America called Salt Lake City, where the Mormons live. All the best men there were amoebas. They divided themselves among a dozen or twenty women. Why should not Franklyn divide himself between Clara and me? Why should she have this treasure of a man all to herself?

CLARA. Youd better ask him. If he decides to give you a share you can have the lot.

MRS ETTEEN. Greedy!

CLARA. All or nothing for me, thank you.

MRS ETTEEN. You see what a wonderful man he is. She never gets tired of him.

CLARA. Yes I do. I get tired of him, and of the house, and of the children, and of Conrad, and of Imm; and so would you if you took on my job. But they belong here and I belong here; and you dont, darling; and thats what makes all the difference.

IMMENSO. I think that settles it, Mrs Etteen.

MRS ETTEEN. *I* dont. I have an absolute inner conviction that I belong to Franklyn and that Franklyn belongs to me. We must have been married to one another in a former existence. I feel that Clara is only accepting a fact, as all sensible women do. I began by accepting facts myself. But I now believe that the progress of the world depends on the people who refuse to accept facts and insist on the satisfaction of their instincts.

CLARA. It depends a good deal on the sort of instincts you have, doesnt it?

MRS ETTEEN. Oh, if you satisfy the lower instincts and starve the higher, experience pulls you up very short indeed. Besides, Clara, you dont mean that my admiration for Franklyn is a low instinct. You cannot blame me for sharing your own taste.

CLARA. Admire as much as you please. Women make me ill the way they slobber over Frank; and he never looks really contemptible except when he is encouraging them and purring and making sheep's eyes at them. But I suppose he is there to be admired, like my diamond cross. Mothers have the trouble of keeping children clean and fed and well-behaved for old maids and old bachelors to pet and admire; and I suppose wives must be content to keep husbands presentable for unattached females to flirt with. But there are limits.

MRS ETTEEN. If you will let me feed him and do all the troublesome part I will let you come and admire him as often as you like.

CLARA. Rosie: you have the devil's own cheek.

MRS ETTEEN. I! I am the greatest coward alive.

CLARA. But take care You think that the risk you run is only to be thrown out of the house as you deserve. But that isnt the risk you run at all. You can stay to dinner if you like: Imm is dining with us, and Conrad, and the rector. You can just trot over the house and look for Franklyn if you want to: he is somewhere about, waiting till you have gone. But some day, if you dont take care, you will be taken at your word. For two pins I would just throw over all this marriage business and leave you in possession. It is no sinecure for me, nor for any woman.

MRS ETTEEN [*rising, and not trying to conceal that she is wounded*] If he is waiting for me to go, I had better go. [*She goes to the door. It opens in her face; and Franklyn enters*].

FRANKLYN [*with a courteous air of delighted surprise*] What! You here, Mrs Etteen! How do you do?

MRS ETTEEN. Didnt you know? [*She turns and looks at Clara*].

CLARA. I had to tell her you were waiting for her to go, Frank. If Rosie wont be a lady and tell lies enough to make herself agreeable, she must not complain if the truth hits her harder than she bargains for. People with soft corns shouldnt stand on other people's toes.

*Mrs Etteen, greatly distressed, snatches out her handkerchief.*

CLARA. Sit down, Rosie; and dont be a fool: you can stay to dinner.

MRS ETTEEN [*struggling inarticulately with her tears*] I am so sorry—[*she cannot go on*].

CLARA. Frank: take her round the garden and talk to her. It is you that have upset her.

MRS ETTEEN. Oh no.

FRANKLYN. Come.

MRS ETTEEN [*taking his arm*] I am so ashamed—so sorry—[*She goes out into the garden on Franklyn's arm*].

CONRAD. You got the best of that, Clara.

CLARA. I should think so, indeed. I always get the best of it. She used to frighten me and fluster me. Thats the worst of the way women are brought up: we are trained never to tell the truth or to face the truth: all we know is how to play cat's cradle with one another; and of course the consequence is that the moment we are faced by anyone who just throws the truth in our faces, we get rattled and make fools of ourselves. Rosie played that game on me and nearly drove me mad. I dont know what I should have done if Frank hadnt taken me in hand and shewed me the trick of it. Then I played it on her. I can play her head off at it. When she tries to terrify me by putting a few of her cards on the table: I put the whole pack on the table, both hers and mine; and as I have the ace of trumps I win every time. She came here as a thief to steal Frank from me. Now she comes as a beggar: and I throw her a scrap of him occasionally. She is having her scrap now, in the garden, poor wretch!

CONRAD. Yes: that is what women are: dogs fighting one another for the best bones. And what are we men? The bones you fight for. You dont catch me getting married.

CLARA. Oh indeed! You are glad enough to come here and be taken care of and pet the children without any expense or responsibility, all the same. You cuckoo! [*She flings the epithet in his face and sweeps scornfully out of the room*].

CONRAD [*rising*] Damn her impudence! I will never enter this house again.

IMMENSO. That will not solve the problem. The bachelor solution is no solution. The bachelor is either a hermit or a cuckoo. Go and get married, Con. Better be a husband than a domestic parasite.

CONRAD. I shall go out of this house, anyhow. Good evening.

IMMENSO. I doubt if she will let you. However, you can try. Good evening.

CONRAD. I will jolly soon see whether she can stop me [*he leaves the room*].

*Immenso takes a paper and begins to read; putting his feet up, and making himself quite comfortable on the sofa.*

CLARA'S VOICE. Where are you going, Con?

CONRAD'S VOICE. I am going out of this house, never to darken your doors again: thats where I'm going.

CLARA'S VOICE. You are going to do nothing of the sort, because I have locked up all your things in your room.

## THE TWO VOICES SIMULTANEOUSLY

I tell you I am going. Give me the key of my room instantly. Do you suppose I am going to stay in a house where I

Now dont be ridiculous, Con: you know very well you brought it on yourself by saying that Rosie and I were two dogs am told to my face that I am a sponge, a parasite, a-a-a-a cuckoo ? I'm damned if I'll stand it. You can keep your house and your children and your unfortunate devil of a husband. I tell you I wont. What pleasure is it to you to have me if you grudge every morsel I eat and drink, and are jealous every time I talk to Savvy ? Youre as jealous as— fighting for a bone. If you go, what am I to say to Frank and Savvy ? Am I to tell them the nasty things you said about them ? And there is roast chicken being done expressly for you; and I have not the least intention of allowing you to waste it. So be good, and remember that we dine at half-past seven and that half-past-seven means half-past-seven and not eight as it usually—

*The voices fade out of hearing. Immenso, who at the first sound of them has looked up from his paper to listen, smiles broadly; crosses his shins; and settles himself to read until the rector comes to dinner.*

We may as well skip the dinner, as the presence of the rector puts a stop to domestic bickering without adding to the brilliancy of the general conversation. Readers of Back to Methuselah will remember the Reverend William Haslam as a very young man who had been shoved into a Church living, as he expressed it, by his father, who was a friend of the patron and a schoolfellow of the bishop. Being at this stage of his career a complete unbeliever, with only two passions, one for lawn tennis and the other for Savvy Barnabas, and being afflicted with perfect clearness of mind as to his unworthiness as a parson (being a hollow fraud, he calls it) he is not very interesting even in ordinary Hampstead society. In the presence of intellects like those of Champernoon and the Barnabases he is a mere cipher in a continuous collar. Nobody, himself least of all, has the faintest suspicion that he alone of all that gifted company is destined to survive three hundred years and be three times an archbishop.

For the present, then, it makes no difference to the dinner party when he slips away from it at the earliest possible moment with Savvy, and takes refuge in the library, where we may now have a look at them as they sit on the sofa, each with an arm round the other's ribs.

HASLAM. Look here, darling: hadnt you better tell your father that we're going to be married?

SAVVY. He wont care.

HASLAM. But he ought to know, you know.

SAVVY. Well, you can tell him if you like. I am not going to intrude my affairs on him when he doesnt even pretend to take any interest in them. I dont mind telling Nunky.

HASLAM. When is it to be? He may as well know the worst at once.

SAVVY. As soon as you like. Now that both Nunky and Papa have gone raving mad on this stunt of theirs about living for ever, life here is becoming unbearable. They expect a dress to last ten years because they expect me to last three hundred. Promise me that when we are married, I shall never hear the words Creative Evolution again.

HASLAM. I promise. I cant keep Adam and Eve out of the lessons in church; but I can keep Creative Evolution out of them. Oh, by the way! I am afraid you will have to come to church. Do you mind very much?

SAVVY. Not a bit. I had to do it in college, you know. Thatll be all right, Bill.

HASLAM. I always rip through pretty fast; and I never preach more than seven minutes: old Lady Mumford makes such an awful row if I do.

SAVVY. Does that matter?

HASLAM. I should think it does. Her big subscription just barely makes the two ends meet in the church accounts. Consequently in our parish Lady Mumford is to all intents and purposes the Church of England.

*Franklyn and Conrad come in.*

HASLAM [*to Franklyn*] By the way, sir, I think you ought to know. Would you mind if Savvy and I were to get married?

CONRAD. Hallo!

HASLAM. Yes: I know it sounds rather sudden. But theres no immediate hurry. Any time will do.

SAVVY. No it wont.

HASLAM. I dont mean our marriage, darling.

FRANKLYN. You mean only my consent, is that it?

HASLAM. Well, I suppose that is what it comes to. Ha! ha! Priceless!

FRANKLYN. Well, Savvy: you know your own business best.

CONRAD. There is no gainsaying the urge of Creative Evolution.

SAVVY [*desperately*] Oh, Nunky, do drop it for a moment. [*To Haslam*] Lets get married tomorrow. You can perform the ceremony yourself, cant you?

HASLAM. I think I shall ask the blooming bishop. It would be awful cheek; but I think he'd like it.

*Clara, Mrs Etteen, and Immenso come in.*

CLARA. Franklyn: go and play billiards. You will not digest your dinner if you sit there talking to Conrad.

FRANKLYN. Oh, goodness gracious, may I not have indigestion and intelligent conversation if I prefer it to running round a billiard table after my health?

[ 667 ]

CLARA. You will be very disagreeable if you get in-digestion. And Con wants to smoke. Off with you.

FRANKLYN. Oh, very well. [*He goes out sulkily*].

CONRAD. Anything for a quiet life. [*He goes out taking his pipe out of his pocket as he goes*].

CLARA. Savvy: take Rosie and Imm to the drawing room; and let us have some music. Imm hasnt heard Rosie play; and the sooner he gets it over, the better.

MRS ETTEEN [*moving towards the door*] Do you really want any music, Mr Champernoon?

IMMENSO [*going with her*] In moods of battle and victory I want the bagpipes, Mrs Etteen. My wife imitates them on the black keys of the piano. I do the drum, with a dinner gong. [*They go out*].

SAVVY. Come along, Bill.

*Haslam rises with alacrity.*

CLARA. No: Bill will stay and talk to me. You clear out.

*Savvy, surprised, looks at Haslam, whose coun-tenance has fallen; then goes out slowly.*

CLARA. Sit down.

*Haslam sits down.*

CLARA [*sitting down also*] Am I, too, privileged to call you Bill, Mr Haslam?

HASLAM. Certainly, if you like.

CLARA. You mustnt suppose because Mr Barnabas is blind, I am. What are your intentions, young man?

HASLAM [*his eyes twinkling*] I have just declared them to Mr Barnabas.

CLARA. What!!!

HASLAM [*enjoying his retort immensely*] Priceless!

CLARA. I see nothing priceless about it. I think it was great impudence of you to speak to Mr Barnabas before Savvy had said a word to me. What did Franklyn say?

HASLAM. You came in before he had time to say anything. But it seemed to go down all right.

CLARA. A nice father! Didnt he ask you a single question?

HASLAM. You didnt give him a chance.

CLARA. What means have you?

HASLAM. The stipend is £180; and the rectory lets for £300 a year furnished.

CLARA. Genteel poverty. And nothing to look forward to. They wont make you an archbishop.

HASLAM. I should think not. Ha! ha! Priceless!

CLARA. Very well. All I have to say is that if she is fool enough to marry you *I* cant stop her. So dont hope to get out of it that way. You have let yourself in for it; and now you must make the best of it.

HASLAM. It is rather awful. That is, of course, when it isnt delightful.

CLARA. What about your own people?

HASLAM. Oh, they expect me to make an ass of myself. I am the fool of the family. They look to my brother to marry money.

CLARA. Well, you seem to have a fairly sensible family: thats one comfort. I wish I could say as much for us. You know, dont you, that Con is as mad as a hatter, and that Franklyn is going soft in the same way? They think theyre going to live for three hundred years. I dont know what is to become of us. I have to keep up appearances; but—[*she almost breaks down*].

HASLAM [*much concerned*] Oh, dont take it that way, Mrs Barnabas. I had no idea you were worrying about it. I am really awfully sorry.

CLARA. Did you suppose I was a fool. Or did you think I believed all that stuff about creative evolution, or whatever they call it?

[ 669 ]

HASLAM. It's only a fad. I assure you men get the wildest fads without going a bit dotty. Jolly good thing for them, too. If they dont take to a fad they take to drink or to gambling on the stock exchange, or to the classics or something horribly tiresome.

CLARA [*a little consoled*] You really think that, Bill?

HASLAM. Quite sure of it. My brother's mad on golf. My mother's mad on gardening. Theyre not intellectual, you know. Mr Barnabas and the doctor have to go mad on something intellectual. This three hundred years stunt is a priceless refuge for them.

CLARA. Well, you comfort me. I need it badly, God knows. Thank you. For myself, I had far rather have a comforting son-in-law than one with lots of money. Savvy'd spend it all anyhow, if you had a million. The way she runs through boots! And theyre fortyfive shillings a pair now.

HASLAM. It's awfully good of you to take to me like this, Mrs Barnabas.

CLARA. There are not so many people in the world that one can take to. [*Looking at him critically*] After all, you may come to be an archbishop yet. Old Archbishop Chettle, who was my father's tutor at Durham, was just as ridiculous as you are.

HASLAM. People dont mind it so much when they come to know me.

CLARA. I am a little ridiculous myself, you know. I cannot suffer fools gladly. You dont seem to mind. Can you put up with me as a mother-in-law? I wont come too often.

HASLAM. You will suit me down to the ground. Fancy your turning out so pricelessly jolly as this!

CLARA [*pleased*] Very well. Now run off to the drawing room, and ask Rosie to play.

HASLAM. I'd a jolly sight rather hear Savvy play.

CLARA. Savvy doesnt want to play. Rosie is dying for an excuse to play Saint Nepomuk's Eve because it always fetches Franklyn from the billiard room to listen to her. Imm will never think of asking her to play: he will only talk her head off. Be kind to her, and ask her for something by Hugo Wolf.

HASLAM. Rather a lark it would be, wouldnt it, if Uncle Imm were to cut Mr Barnabas out with Mrs Etteen?

CLARA. Imm has no ear for music. She cant do it with the piano anyhow.

*A hollow chord of G flat and D flat is heard droning from the drawing room piano. Then The Campbells are Coming is played on the black keys.*

*A drum obbligato begins on the dinner gong, played at first with childish enjoyment, and proceeding, in a rapid crescendo, to ecstasy.*

HASLAM. She is doing it with the piano! Priceless!

CLARA [*indignantly*] Well!

SAVVY [*rushing in*] Mother: do come and stop Uncle Imm. If he starts dancing he will shake the house down. Oh, listen to them. [*She puts her fingers in her ears*].

CLARA [*rushing out*] Stop, stop! Imm. Rosie! Stop that horrible noise.

SAVVY [*shutting the door with a slam*] Did you ever hear anything like it? Uncle Imm is the greatest baby.

*The noise suddenly stops with the sound of the dinner gong being torn from Imm's grasp and flung down on the carpet, presumably by Clara. The piano takes the hint and stops too.*

SAVVY. What did mother want with you?

HASLAM. To ask me my intentions. Priceless!

SAVVY. Did she make a row?

HASLAM. Not a bit. She was awfully nice about it. She's a stunning good sort.

SAVVY. Bill!!

HASLAM. She is, really. I had no idea. We shall get on first rate.

SAVVY. Then I cry off. She has got round you.

HASLAM. Why? Arnt you glad?

SAVVY. Glad! When I am marrying you to get rid of her! Bill: the match is off. If she has got round you I might just as well stay at home. How does she get round people? Why am I the only person she doesnt think it worth her while to get round?

HASLAM. She didnt get round me: she went straight at me; and over I went. What could I do? I was prepared to hold my end up if she started fighting. But she fell on my neck. It wasnt my fault.

SAVVY. It's too disgusting. All men are the same: theyre no good when it comes to tackling a woman who can see nobody's point of view except her own.

HASLAM. She seems to like me in a sort of way.

SAVVY. She always wanted a son. All women do who like men: the women who want girls only want live dolls. I was a disappointment because I was a girl. And now she comes and grabs you from me, as she grabs everything.

HASLAM. I feel just the same about my father, you know. How mother ever stuck it out with him I cant imagine.

SAVVY. You neednt boast about your mother: look at my father! See how he has stuck it out.

HASLAM. Parents are a ghastly fraud, if you ask me. But theyre necessary, I suppose.

SAVVY. Bill: youre very aggravating. I want to quarrel; and you wont. You have no sand in you.

HASLAM. Whats the good of quarrelling? If I felt like

that I should jolly well punch your head and have done with it.

SAVVY [*throwing her arms violently round him and punctuating her epithets with savage kisses*] Pig. Fool. Idiot. Sillybilly.

HASLAM. Darling.

*The dinner gong is heard bumping against something outside. They spring apart. Immenso enters in the character of a Highland chieftain carrying the gong like a target, and a hockey stick like a claymore. He has heightened the illusion by draping his shoulder with a travelling rug. He marches about, humming The Campbells. Mrs Etteen follows, half annoyed, half amused, and sits down on the sofa.*

SAVVY [*still excited, to Immenso*] Sillybilly, sillybilly, sillybilly! Fat boy of Peckham! [*She snatches a ruler from the writing table. Immenso disposes himself immediately for combat. She makes a feint which he utterly fails to parry, and stabs him with the ruler. He falls ponderously and cautiously*]. Slain! slain! Mrs Etteen will receive your last breath. Come, Bill. [*She runs out*].

HASLAM. Priceless! [*He runs out after her*].

IMMENSO [*rising with difficulty*] "Unwounded from the dreadful close; but breathless all, Fitzjames arose."

MRS ETTEEN. Mr Champernoon: would you mind growing up for a moment, and condescending to treat me as an adult person?

IMMENSO. If you insist on our keeping up that dreary affectation I am bound to obey you. [*He throws down the hockey stick, the rug, and finally the gong*]. Farewell, ye real things. How good it is to hear your solid thump on the floor! The human boy sleeps with you there. The literary gasbag floats gently to your feet, madam. [*He sits down on the chair furthest away from her*].

MRS ETTEEN. But you have not floated to my feet. You have floated to the opposite end of the room.

IMMENSO. I need space if I am to treat you as a public meeting. I understand that you prefer that to Fitzjames.

MRS ETTEEN. There is a mystic region between the public meeting and the playground in which you have not been seen yet. It is the region in which men and women meet when they are alone together.

IMMENSO [*troubled and grave*] I had better say at once frankly, Mrs Etteen, that in that region I must put up a notice inscribed Nothing Doing. I am married; and I take marriage honorably and seriously. I am not putting this forward as a criticism of your attitude towards it. I only suggest that our attitudes are incompatible. Therefore will you allow me to continue to regard you as a public meeting?

MRS ETTEEN. By all means, if you can.

*A pause. Mrs Etteen bears the silence calmly. Immenso is embarrassed by it.*

IMMENSO [*at last*] The difficulty is that there is nothing before the meeting.

MRS ETTEEN. Just so. Come, Mr Champernoon! cant you get over this ridiculous shyness, and behave as Nature intended men and women to behave when they are alone together? Come and quarrel with me, or make love to me, or do something human. Search your soul for something to say to me that will not leave me cold and desolate.

IMMENSO. After searching my soul most carefully, absolutely the only remark that occurs to me is that we have been having wonderfully fine weather for the last fortnight. That is the commonplace but tragic truth.

MRS ETTEEN. That is the only thing you can find

words for. But there is something between us that you cannot find words for: even you, who are so great a master of words.

IMMENSO. What, for example?

MRS ETTEEN. Say, a sense of deadly peril.

IMMENSO [*slowly*] Mrs Etteen: there are certain things I cannot say to a lady. One of them is that I feel perfectly safe with her.

MRS ETTEEN. So much the better! Can you really talk to me exactly as you would talk to the baker?

IMMENSO. I cannot say that. The baker is an organic part of society. Without the baker I should perish or live on snails. I am not convinced that beautiful ladies—shall I call them love ladies?—are an organic part of society. Without them I should not perish. I should flourish.

MRS ETTEEN. Without love ladies there would be no love children. Have you noticed that love children, like love ladies, are very beautiful?

IMMENSO. The statistics of illegitimate children—

MRS ETTEEN [*quickly*] I did not say illegitimate children, Mr Champernoon: I said love children. There are more love children born in wedlock than out of it: at least I hope so. But there are very few born at all, either in or out of wedlock.

IMMENSO. I have known some very beautiful persons of the sort you mean. I may be prejudiced against them because I, alas! am not an entrancingly beautiful person; but some of them were infernal rascals.

MRS ETTEEN. Spendthrifts and libertines and so forth, eh?

IMMENSO. I am myself a bit of a spendthrift as far as my means allow. No: I should call them thieves, if people who order goods they cannot pay for are thieves. I should call them rascals, because people who borrow money heartlessly from poorer people than themselves on the security of false promises to pay are in my opinion rascals. And libertines, certainly, of both sexes.

MRS ETTEEN. And yet charming people, all the same. Centres of exquisite happiness. Living fountains of love.

IMMENSO. That is why I hate them. They bring these precious things into contempt. They are living blasphemies.

MRS ETTEEN. And so you have to put up with plain dowdy people, and have children as ugly as yourself. What sort of world is it where the ugly practical people, the people who can deal with money and material things, and be thoroughly mean about them, succeed, and the beautiful people who live in noble dreams and continually strive to realize them are ruined and despised? Do you suppose they like borrowing from poor people, who are the only ones simple enough to lend, or that they enjoy being dunned by tradesmen? Is it their fault that when they offer love, they are told that unless they steal it they must pay for it with all their worldly goods, with their liberty, with nearly the whole of their lives? Is that right? You are a clever man: you are a professional moralist. Is there nothing wrong in it? Give me an honest answer. Dont preach at me; but tell me as man to woman. Do you not feel sometimes that it is all wrong?

IMMENSO. As a professional moralist I can make out a case against it. I can make out a case for it just as easily. Cases do not impress me. They never impress people who have the knack of making them. It's no use giving tracts to a missionary.

MRS ETTEEN. Yes: I was wrong to argue about it.

The moment one argues one goes wrong at once. It is deeper than argument. You may say what you like; but can you feel that the beautiful people are all wrong and that the ugly people are all right? Would you think them beautiful and ugly if you really believed that?

IMMENSO. I have noticed that there are subjective and objective people; and—

MRS ETTEEN. Beautiful subjective people and ugly objective people?

IMMENSO [*uneasy under her greater conviction*] Beauty is a matter of taste, after all. One man's meat is another man's poison. Lots of people do not think my wife beautiful. They are nitwits; but they have a right to their opinion.

MRS ETTEEN [*with dignity*] Mr Champernoon: is it possible that you think I am discussing the question of sex with you?

IMMENSO [*taken aback*] Well—er— Well, good heavens! what else are we discussing?

MRS ETTEEN. *I* am discussing beauty, which is not a matter of taste at all, but a matter of fact as to which no difference of opinion is possible among cultivated people. Can you produce a single person of any culture who thinks that Venus of Milo or the Hermes of Praxiteles ugly? Can you produce a single person who thinks—

IMMENSO. Who thinks me beautiful? Not one.

MRS ETTEEN. I have seen worse, Mr Champernoon. [*He bows*]. You are very like Balzac, of whom Rodin made one of the greatest statues in the world. But dont you see that this sex attraction, though it is so useful for keeping the world peopled, has nothing to do with beauty: that it blinds us to ugliness instead of opening our eyes to beauty. It is what enables us to endure a world full of ugly sights and sounds and people. You can do without the Venus of Milo because the young lady at the refreshment bar can make you forget her. I dont want to talk about such attractions: they are only the bait in the trap of marriage: they vanish when they have served their turn. But have you never known really beautiful people, beautiful as girls, beautiful as matrons, beautiful as grandmothers, or men to match them? Do you not want a world of such beautiful people, instead of what the gentleman in Mr Granville-Barker's play calls "this farmyard world of sex"? Will you dare to tell me that the world was no worse when the lords of creation were monkeys than it is now that they are men, ugly as most of them are? Do you really want us all to become like ants and bees because ants and bees are industrious and goody goody?

IMMENSO. As I am myself a species of human bumble bee, I cannot give you an unprejudiced opinion.

MRS ETTEEN. No: you shall not ride off on a quip, Mr Champernoon. Stand to your guns. You thought I was going to entice you into a flirtation: you see now that I am trying to convert you to a religion of beauty.

IMMENSO. I am not sure that I do not think you all the more dangerous. You might pervert me intellectually; but on the other ground I am invincible. I cannot flirt. I am not what is called a lady's man, Mrs Etteen.

MRS ETTEEN. You cannot flirt! Mr Champernoon: you are the most incorrigible flirt in England, and the very worst sort of flirt too. You flirt with religions, with traditions, with politics, with everything that is most sacred and important. You flirt with the Church, with the Middle Ages, with the marriage question, with the Jewish question, even with the hideous cult of gluttony and drunkenness. Every one of your discussions of these questions is like a flirtation with a worthless woman: you pay her the most ingenious and delightful compliments, driving all your legitimate loves mad with distress and jealousy: but you are not a bit in earnest: behind all your sincere admiration of her priceless pearls and her pretty paint you loathe the creature's flesh and blood. You are all flirts, you intellectuals. If you flirted with housemaids and dairymaids, or with chorus girls, I could forgive you; but to flirt with ghastly old hags because they were the mistresses of kings and of all the oppressors of the earth is despicable and silly.

IMMENSO [*reddening*] I deny that innuendo. I was in a Liberal set, a Protestant set, an atheist set, a Puritan set. I had everything to lose by defending the Church and the Middle Ages, by denouncing Puritanism, by affirming the existence of God.

MRS ETTEEN. Then you had not even the excuse of wanting money or a knighthood. You flirted with these old, wicked, outworn things from pure devilment, because you were a born coquette.

IMMENSO. I do not admit that these institutions are wicked or outworn. I admit that they are old, which proves at least that they were not jerry built.

MRS ETTEEN. Cruelty is old. Slavery is old. Greed, ambition, plague pestilence and famine are old. They are not jerry built either. Are they any the better for that? I am not so clever as you, Mr Champernoon; but I can see that if we did not indulge you by stepping softly about the room because we want to admire your wonderful houses of cards, they would come down at the first resolute footfall. As often as not it is your own foot that comes down when some

abominable oppression stings you into earnestness;
and—

IMMENSO. And who can expect any house to stand
that earthshaking shock?

MRS ETTEEN. A jibe at your size has got you out of
many a controversial difficulty.

IMMENSO. I protest I have exploited it only in the
interests of good humor. I laugh at it with the
wrong side of my mouth. [*He sits down beside her*].
But I still defend the past. My roots are in the past:
so are yours.

MRS ETTEEN. My roots are in the past: my hopes are
in the future.

IMMENSO. The past is as much a part of eternity as
the future. Beware of ingratitude to the past. What is
gratitude? The cynic says, a sense of favors to come.
Many people would say that we cannot be grateful
to the past because we have nothing to expect from
it. But if we had no memory of favors from the past we
could have no faith in favors from the future. Why do
I uphold the Church: I, who know as much of the
crimes of the Churches as you do? Not for what the
Church did for men, but for what men did for the
Church. It brought us no gifts; but it drew forth
gifts from us. And that is just as it should be. I love
the Church because Michelangelo painted its churches. You complain of it because the churches did not
paint Michelangelo. Well, suppose they had painted
him! Suppose they had tarred and feathered him!
Would you not place the painting of Michelangelo,
with the burning of John Huss or Giordano Bruno
or Joan of Arc, among the crimes of the Churches?

MRS ETTEEN. That is a very pretty little juggle with
words, and very funny. But when you are talking of
Michelangelo you are talking of a man so great that he

was literally a demigod. When you talk of the Church, you are talking of a pack of common men calling themselves clergymen and priests, and trying to persuade us that they are demigods by wearing ugly black clothes. Michelangelo did not paint for them: he painted for me, and for people like you and me. We are the spectators for whom he painted: we are the Church which drew out his gifts. It was for us that Bach and Beethoven composed, that Phidias and Rodin made statues, that the poets sang and the philosophers became seers. It is you who are faithless and disloyal in giving the allegiance we owe to them to corrupt gangs of little lawyers and politicians and priests and adventurers organized as States and Churches and dressed up like actors to seem the thing they are not. They pretend to see events with glass eyes, and to hear the music of the spheres with ass's ears. [*She pauses. Immenso is staring before him like a man in a trance*]. Are you listening? [*He does not answer*]. I know. You are thinking how you can work this into an article.

IMMENSO [*waking up suddenly*] Damn it, I am. [*He salutes*]. Touché!

MRS ETTEEN. Plait-il?

IMMENSO. That is what a fencer says to his adversary when he acknowledges a hit. Yes: you got in that time. But why should I not make it into an article? It is my trade.

MRS ETTEEN. Couldnt you make it into an action of some sort. Couldnt you kill somebody, for instance, as all the people who are in earnest do?

IMMENSO. I am prepared to kill. You may think it boasting; but, like Hamlet, I do not hold my life at a pin's fee when my fate cries out. As I am not going to kill anybody—shall I say as we are not going

[ 681 ]

to kill anybody?—I suppose our fate does not cry out.

MRS ETTEEN. Oh yes: I am as great a coward, as futile a creature as you: dont think I dont know it. Shall I tell you why that is?

IMMENSO. You evidently will, whether I say yes or no.

MRS ETTEEN. It is because we have not really finished with the sensualities, the crudities, the vulgarities and superstitions that are holding us back. We have not had time to exhaust them, to survive them, to be forced to provide for a spiritual future on earth when they are all dead in us, just as we are forced to provide for bread in our present old age. We do not live long enough—

IMMENSO [*starting*] What! Are you on this Back-to-Methuselah tack too? Has all this been the craze of my brothers-in-law at second hand?

MRS ETTEEN. Oh, very manly man that you are, it does not occur to you that Franklyn Barnabas may have had this from me. Did he ever speak of it before he met me?

IMMENSO. Now that you mention it, no. But it began with Conrad; and you certainly did not work in his laboratory.

MRS ETTEEN. Conrad never saw the scope of his idea any more than Weismann, from whom he got it. He saw how it affected science: he knew that he had to die when he was just beginning to discover what science really is, and had just found out that the experience of people who die at seventy is only a string of the mistakes of immaturity. He had the skeleton of the great faith; but it was Franklyn who put the flesh on it. And it was I, the woman, who made that flesh for him out of my own. That is my relation to Franklyn. That is what Clara would call the intrigue between us.

IMMENSO [*gravely*] She should call it the tragedy of the man who does not trust his wife. He should tell Clara.

MRS ETTEEN. He tells her everything she can understand. If he tries to tell her more it is thrown back in his face like a blow. She is jealous of me; and with good reason.

IMMENSO. But why should he not explain to her the nature of his interest in you, or rather of your common interest in the great faith, as you call it? It is perfectly innocent.

MRS ETTEEN. Will you go home and tell your wife that you find me a very interesting person, and that though you began by keeping at the other end of the room, you have been sitting almost in my lap for the last five minutes?

IMMENSO [*springs up with an inarticulate exclamation. Then, with Johnsonian courtesy*] I beg your pardon, Mrs Etteen. [*He is about to sit down again further from her but corrects himself, and sits scrupulously as close to her as before*].

MRS ETTEEN. Have I won your interest fairly or have I not? Have I played a single low trick, or practised a single woman's wile?

IMMENSO. You are not a single woman, Mrs—

MRS ETTEEN. Tut! tut! tut! no puns, no jokes, no evasion. Was it fair play or foul play?

IMMENSO. You have landed a very large fish, Mrs Etteen. But you fished fairly. I wish to announce in all honor that I adore you [*he kisses her hand*]. I say it in all honor; and I mean it. And yet I know I shall not tell my wife. Will that be honorable?

MRS ETTEEN. You make too much fuss about it. Do

you suppose that there is not among our literary geniuses some writer whose best books she sometimes devours with just a tiny little more relish than your second best? But she does not tell you so. Is that dishonorable, or is it simply kindness—loving-kindness, as the Bible says.

IMMENSO. I hope so.

MRS ETTEEN. Every good wife should commit a few infidelities to keep her husband in countenance. The extent to which married people strain their relations by pretending that there is only one man or woman in the world for them is so tragic that we have to laugh at it to save ourselves from crying. But we shant be so foolish when we all live three hundred years.

How this conversation ended I cannot tell; for I never followed up the adventure of Immenso Champernoon with Mrs Etteen, and dont believe it came to anything.

# Postscript:
# After Twentyfive Years

One of the many summits in the mountain range of human selfconceit is the introduction by an author of his book as a World Classic. He cannot with any decency do it himself. And when he is invited to do so by a publisher whose prestige has been won in serious literature, his gratified compliance must be in the vein of apology and explanation rather than a fanfare of brazen exultation.

Therefore, though I am not addicted to what I have called "the modest cough of the minor poet" I will try to be as apologetic as my nature permits. I have never claimed a greater respect for playmaking than for the commoner crafts; and as every joiner is (or used to be) not only allowed but challenged to produce a masterpiece, I feel no shame in hawking my masterpiece without a cry of stinking fish.

Besides, I do not regard my part in the production of my books and plays as much greater than that of an amanuensis or an organ-blower. An author is an instrument in the grip of Creative Evolution, and may find himself starting a movement to which in his own little person he is intensely opposed. When I am writing a play I never invent a plot: I let the play write itself and shape itself, which it always does even when up to the last moment I do not foresee the way out. Sometimes I do not see what the play was driving at until quite a long time after I have finished it; and even then I may be wrong about it just as any critical third party may.

Take for examples the masterpieces of Dante, of Michael Angelo, and of John Bunyan. The three are beyond all question world classics notwithstanding the legendary fictions and childish superstitions which adapted them to the mental habits of their time, and still make them intelligible and interesting as stories, but which also aberrate them again and again into flat absurdity. Dante would have placed Mahomet in paradise had he realized that his Divine Comedy, with its ridiculous hell, its Sunday School purgatory, and its Feminist heaven, was driving at the same world Catholicism as the Koran. When Michael Angelo painted in the Sistine Chapel the series of Bible illustrations which culminated in the gigantic fable of the Last Judgement, he did not know that the series would be "continued in our next" by Nietzsche in his Thus Spake Zoroaster, the twain being driven more or less in spite of themselves to shew, Michael Angelo physically, Nietzsche mentally, not what mankind is but what it might become. Bunyan, when he was writing The Pilgrim's Progress, knew very well that he was being moved not by personal lust to become a Great Writer, but by "grace abounding to the meanest of sinners." Yet, if when his Holy War was sinking into the quicksand of sectarian nonsense in which it ends, he had been shewn a copy of Peer Gynt as an account of what his pilgrim would come to, or congratulated on having in The Life and Death of Mr Badman developed to a point not reached by Ibsen until three hundred years later, he would have been considerably scandalized.

I shall not go on to suggest that Goldsmith's Deserted Village should be used as a preface to Henry George's Progress and Poverty, and Keats's Isabella to Marx's Capital; but as a playwright I must not pass over my predecessor Shakespear. If he could be consulted as to the inclusion of one of his plays in the present series he would probably choose his Hamlet, because in writing it he definitely threw over his breadwinning trade of producing potboilers which he frankly called As You Like It, Much Ado About Nothing, and What You Will. After a few almost Ibsenish essays in As You Dont Like It, he took up an old play about the ghost of a murdered king who haunted his son crying for revenge, with comic relief provided by the son pretending to be that popular curiosity and laughing-stock, a village idiot. Shakespear, transfiguring this into a tragedy on the ancient Athenian level, could not have been quite unconscious of the evolutionary stride he was taking. But he did not see his way clearly enough to save the tons of ink and paper and years of "man's time" that have been wasted, and are still being wasted, on innumerable volumes of nonsense about the meaning of Hamlet, though it is now as clear as daylight. Hamlet as a prehistoric Dane is morally bound to kill his uncle, politically as rightful heir to the usurped throne, and filially as "the son of a dear father murdered" and a mother seduced by an incestuous adulterer. He has no doubt as to his duty in the matter. If he can convince himself that the ghost who has told him all this is really his father's spirit and not a lying devil tempting him to perdition, then, he says, "I know my course."

But when fully convinced he finds to his bewilderment that he cannot kill his uncle deliberately. In a sudden flash of rage he can and does stab at him through the arras, only to find that he has killed poor old Polonius by mistake. In a later transport, when the unlucky uncle poisons not only Hamlet's mother but his own accomplice and Hamlet himself, Hamlet actually does at last kill his enemy on the spur of the moment; but this is no solution of his problem: it cuts the Gordian knot instead of untying it, and makes the egg stand on end only by breaking it. In the soliloquy beginning "Oh what a rogue and peasant slave am I" Shakespear described this moral bewilderment as a fact (he must have learnt it from his own personal development); but he did not explain it, though the explanation was staring him in the face as it stares in mine. What happened to Hamlet was what had happened fifteen hundred years before to Jesus. Born into the vindictive morality of Moses he has evolved into the Christian perception of the futility and wickedness of revenge and punishment, founded on the simple fact that two blacks do not make a white. But he is not philosopher enough to comprehend this as well as apprehend it. When he finds he cannot kill in cold blood he can only ask "Am I a coward?" When he cannot nerve himself to recover his throne he can account for it only by saying "I lack ambition." Had Shakespear plumbed his play to the bottom he would hardly have allowed Hamlet to send Rosencrantz and Guildenstern to their death by a forged death warrant without a moment's scruple.

Two and a half centuries later the same thing occurs to the author of another world classic, Charles Montagu Doughty, who, compared to Shakespear, can be catalogued only as a bigoted simpleton when, undeveloped at the age of 32, he travelled in Arabia. To him the Arabs were dangerous and damned heathens, corrupted by a false religion invented by an imposter named Mahomet who had forged a spurious Bible called the Koran. To defend himself against them he armed himself with a loaded revolver and carried it wherever he went.

The protection seemed very necessary; for the Bedouins were so like himself (or he like them) that they regarded him as a damned infidel; and the fanatically pious among them considered it their religious duty to kill and despoil the Nazarene. Again and again his bags were rifled and the knife was at his throat. Yet with the revolver in his hand and his assailants at his mercy he did not discharge it. Like Hamlet he could not bring himself to judge and kill. Like Shakespear he could not see why: he could only record the simple fact. Yet his travel diary, published long after with the now famous title Arabia Deserta, is a world classic.

This logicless sequel puzzles the student of literature who is trying to find out what qualifies a book to rank as a classic. Doughty, when he began his two years roaming through the Arabian deserts, was what we call an educated English gentleman who had gone through a professional training in medicine. Yet he writes like a child of ten for the most part; and his diary, with scraps of memoranda stuck in anyhow in no order except the order of date, is in no sense a considered work of art. His interests are those of an amateur explorer only; and the comments on Bedouin life, character, and religion, which make his book so readable, change from day to day, from place to place, from meal to meal. On one page all the Bedouins he has known are "a merry crew of squalid wretches, iniquitous, fallacious, and fanatical." Two pages later the Beni Salim are "of gentle and honest manners; and I was never better entertained in nomad menzils." Many of his entertainers were more civilized, tolerant, and sceptical than he. His style is certainly unique; but it suggests the simplicity of a man who had never read a book in his life except the Bible, which he often quotes, less with any artistic appreciation than to shew that its descriptions tally with the facts of eastern life and thought as he found them.

There must have been something majestic or gigantic about the man that made him classic in himself. He was already a poet; for twice in his travel diary he explodes into half a page of prophetic rhapsody; and when he came home he spent the rest of his life in writing immense prophetic epics in blank verse of a Himalayan magnificence and natural eminence that would have made Milton gasp. Small wonder that when the knife was at his throat it got no farther; and when he arrived at the next oasis penniless and in rags, the rulers there clothed him and made those who had robbed him give him back their booty and repay him his stolen money to the last farthing. Englishmen who met him have described him to me as "a mountain of a man"; and extant portraits bear them out as far as portraits can.

It is clear then that in him as in Hamlet-Shakespear a step in evolution had occurred and taken all the vulgar fight out of him without taking any of the courage. And this brings me Back to Methuselah, and to the right of my "metabiological pentateuch" to be included in a list of world classics. Like Shakespear I had to write potboilers until I was rich enough to satisfy my evolutionary appetite (or, as they say, give way to my inspiration) by writing what came to me without the least regard to the possibility of lucrative publication or performance. Like Shakespear again, I was a born dramatist, which means a born artist-biologist struggling to take biology a step forward on its way to positive science from its present metaphysical stage in which the crude facts of life and death, growth and decay, evolution and reversion, consciousness and unconsciousness, self-preservation and selfsacrifice, defy the methods of investigation we employ in our research laboratories, and have to be made apprehensible by fictions, pictures, and symphonies in which they are instinctively arranged in a manner which gives a mysterious pleasure to some of the readers, spectators, and listeners, and provokes others to passionate denial and persecution. When I am not potboiling for myself or others I am being driven by my evolutionary appetite to write these fictions. Even when I have the box office in view I am not free to choose the most lucrative sort of fiction. Evolution keeps creeping in. I write such shameless potboilers as Pygmalion. Fanny's First Play, and You Never Can Tell, to oblige theatre managers or aspiring players; but at least I do not write detective stories to oblige publishers. I am clever enough at the tricks of my trade to be able to combine some worldly potboiling with my transcendental metabiology, but only up to an impassable boundary. If I could not do this, and had either to prosper as a stockbroker or starve as a metabiologist I should starve, as Mozart and Beethoven very nearly did when they composed symphonies instead of sentimental drawingroom ballads.

In writing Back to Methuselah I threw over all economic considerations, and faced the apparent impossibility of a performance during my lifetime. When a professional manager of whom I had never heard (though his name, by the way, was Barry Jackson, and he was already famous in the Midlands) approached me with a view to a performance, I asked him whether he had no regard for his wife and family. He replied that he was not married, and that he kept a theatre out of his private means as other similarly endowed plutocrats kept racehorses or steam yachts. In short, he was doing it to gratify his evolutionary appetite and could afford the cost. So I gave him my blessing and a performing licence; and he went ahead and produced the Methuselah cycle at his Birmingham Repertory Theatre, where he had made theatrical history by many notable experiments and revivals while London was barely marking time. When I asked him what he had lost by the Methuselah adventure he said with every appearance of satisfaction, "Only £2500." Later on, when he repeated it in London and I repeated my question, he answered exultantly "I have not lost: I have made twenty pounds." The twenty pounds did not give him a dock laborer's wages for his trouble; but it left him none the poorer, and my conscience all the lighter.

Clearly then, Back to Methuselah was not a commercial job: it came straight from the Life Force operating as an *élan vital* through myself and Barry Jackson. What, then, are world classics?

Well, they all try to solve, or at least to formulate, the riddles of creation. In them the Life Force is struggling towards its goal of godhead by incarnating itself in creatures with knowledge and power enough to control nature and circumstances. A classic author has to consider how far he dare go; for though he is writing for the enlightenment of mankind he may not be willing to venture as far as martyrdom for its sake. Descartes burnt one of his books to escape being burnt for having written it. Galileo had to deny what he believed to escape the same fate. The priests forced these alternatives on them not because they did not agree with them, but because they had to govern the people, and the people could be governed only by fictions and miracles, not by the latest steps in science. If the people will not obey their rulers unless they see the blood of St Januarius liquefy, then the priests must work that miracle for them or let them run wild. As long as civilization seems to stand or fall with the belief that God stopped the movement of the sun in its orbit to oblige Joshua as casually as the driver of a tramcar stops his vehicle to pick up a passenger, popes and emperors must take care that no physicist is allowed to tell the mob that it is the earth that moves round the sun and not the sun round the earth, even when they are entirely convinced that the physicist is right. When I was a municipal councillor I had to connive at bogus miracles, pretending that tubs of soap and water were as magical as the cauldron of Macbeth's witches, because my constituents believed in magic, not in soap and sunshine. It is useless to parrot the old saying that the blood of the martyrs is the seed of the Church, and expect scientific heretics to die to advertize their heresies rather than recant to save their lives. Descartes, when he burnt his book, knew that its truths would inevitably be rediscovered and become familiar, and that this would only be retarded by his being burnt for publishing them.

As for me I can write safely on the assumption that Galileo and Descartes knew much more about physics than Moses. But I am not therefore free to publish anything I like. Plays of mine have been banned for many years on grounds injuriously defamatory to myself; and at least one of my books is on the index in Eire, apparently because the heroine does not wear petticoats. The disciples of Pavlov would burn me if they had Torquemada's power. But State intolerance is founded, not now on crude fanaticism, but on the fear that if the people discover that the miracles they believe in are either fables or frauds, and that the scriptures they accept as Divine revelations are questionable in any sentence, they will empty the baby out with the bath water, and defy all religion and all morality. And in fact many of them have done so as far as such defiance is practicable, which is not very far, as disbelief in the Bible story of the ten commandments is no defence against being imprisoned for theft or hanged for murder.

Now it is hardly possible for men engaged daily in the starkly realistic practice of government, which is full of surprises for simpletons, to share the credulities of the crowd. They soon become arch heretics themselves; and as such they persecute heresy only as long as they believe that, as Ibsen put it, society is held together by chain stitched seams which will ravel out if a single stitch is cut. But they find out that this does not in fact happen. When experience taught them that Voltaire could laugh at Habbakuk and call on them to crush the Church as an infamy without immediately bringing down French civilization about their ears they inferred that their own scepticisms could be tolerated safely, and allowed the laws against them to fall into desuetude, without, however, daring to repeal them. It is fairly safe for me personally to fill my books and plays with heresies, and even be accepted as a world classic on the strength of them; but it is none the less within quite recent historical memory that the vogue of Voltaire and his fellow-heretic Rousseau was followed by the French Revolution, and that Rousseau's "Get rid of your miracles and the whole world will fall at the feet of Christ" has ended in whole States falling at the feet of Pavlov and Hitler.

The moral of this is that heretical teaching must be made irresistibly attractive by fine art if the heretics are not to starve or burn. I have to make my heresies pleasing as plays to extract the necessary shillings from those to whom they are also intensely irritating. Back to Methuselah, having begun its stage career by extracting £2500 from the pocket of Sir Barry Jackson, presently enabled him to extract a surplus of £20 from the pockets of his audiences.

Now the artistic attractions of the Methuselah cycle must operate in the theatre without explanation; but its hersies can be discussed on paper in prefaces or postscripts. First among them is the evanescence of God Almighty, and His replacement by a creative force striving by trial and error towards a goal of all-knowingness and almighty power over nature. But this aspiring fallibility is either indignantly rejected or personified and deified in an imaginary Supreme Being in the sky if not on earth.

Hence our gods, saviours, prophets, saints, heroes, and the like. It is through such conceits that we are governed and governable; yet only by debunking them can we evolve towards the goal. Most of us dont want to evolve. When God becomes too remote, too awful, and too cruel to be bearable, and we have to invent something more human, and call it Messiah or Christ, or Zoroaster or Buddha, we immediately destroy its humanity by insisting on its superhuman sinless perfection and unerring know-ledge and wisdom; so that it becomes as incredible as God was unbearable.

Our villagers, contemplating the mischief and horror of the Four Years war in 1917, said "Well, I suppose there must be a God; but what *is* He thinking of to let all this go on?" Now to admit that

God can err, or that He is powerless in any particular, is to deprive Him of the attributes that qualify Him as God; but it is a very healthy admission for the strongminded. It increases our sense of responsibility for social welfare, and is radiant with boundless hopes of human betterment. Our will to live depends on hope; for we die of despair, or, as I have called it in the Methuselah cycle, discouragement. What damns Darwinian Natural Selection as a creed is that it takes hope out of evolution, and substitutes a paralysing fatalism which is utterly discouraging. As Butler put it, it "banishes Mind from the universe." The generation that felt nothing but exultant relief when it was delivered from the tyranny of an Almighty Busybody by a soulless Determinism has nearly passed away, leaving a vacuum which Nature abhors.

Readers of my preface will remember that it was a remark by Weismann that set me on the track of Methuselah. He suggested that death is a result of Natural Selection, not "natural" in the ordinary sense, lifetimes varying in duration from the immortality of the eternally splitting amoeba to the brief span of the drosophila fly. Immortality is natural, death only an artifice to make it bearable as a burden and get rid of its garments of flesh as they wear out. The legend of Methuselah is neither incredible nor unscientific. Life has lengthened considerably since I was born; and there is no reason why it should not lengthen ten times as much after my death.

This possibility came to me when history and experience had convinced me that the social problems raised by millionfold national populations are far beyond the political capacity attainable in three score and ten years of life by slowgrowing mankind.

On all hands as I write the cry is that our statesmen are too old, and that Leagues of Youth must be formed everywhere to save civilization from them. But despairing ancient pioneers tell me that the young are worse than the old; and the truth seems to be that our statesmen are not old enough for their jobs. Life is too short for the experience and development needed to change romantic schoolboys and golfing sportsmen, or even prematurely forced Quakers, into wise senators. In the nineteenth century we reacted from an effete feudalism into a Cobden-Croce world in which the love of money is the root of all good, and freedom of contract and thought man's choicest treasure ("heartbreaking nonsense" Carlyle called it), and are now reacting into either a Marxist world in which the millennium will be guaranteed by a new Catholicism in which the proletarians of all lands are to unite, or an idolatry of imaginary Carlylean heroes and bogus Nietzschean supermen; but we have no sages old enough and wise enough to make a synthesis of these reactions, and to develop the magnetic awe-inspiring force which must replace the policeman's baton as the instrument of authority. Though I am very far from being as clever and well informed as people think, I am not below the average in political capacity; yet in my 89th year I am no more fit to rule millions of men than a boy of 12. Physically I am failing: my senses, my locomotive powers, my memory, are decaying at a rate which threatens to make a Struldbrug of me if I persist in living; yet my mind still feels capable of growth; for my curiosity is keener than ever. My soul goes marching on; and if the Life Force would give me a body as durable as my mind, and I knew better how to feed and lodge and dress and behave, I might begin a

[ 697 ]

political career as a junior civil servant and evolve into a capable Cabinet minister in another hundred years or so.

The Agnostics and Atheists and Determinist Diehards who have thrown over the creeds whipped into them in their childhood are surprised and alarmed to see Creative Evolution reviving much that they have discarded as superstitious. For example, the Creative Evolutionist believes firmly in Providence and in what used to be called the will of God. But he also insists strongly on the first of the 39 Articles of the Church of England, which, in a blinding flash of inspiration (it unfortunately did not last long enough to prevent its contradiction in the following articles) affirms that God has neither body, parts, nor passions, and is therefore not a Person but an incorporeal Purpose, unable to do anything directly, but mysteriously able to create corporeal organs and agents to accomplish that purpose, which, as far as we can see, is the attainment of infinite wisdom and infinite power. Instead of dwelling morbidly on the quite unedifying and not too interesting inference that in the beginning the earth was a wisp of blazing gas torn off from the sun, the votary of Creative Evolution goes back to the old and very pregnant lesson that in the beginning was the Thought; and the Thought was with God; and the Thought *was* God, the Thought being what the Greeks meant by "the Word". He believes in the thought made flesh as the first step in the main process of Creative Evolution. He believes in a new Jerusalem, and resolves, like Blake, that he will not cease from mental fight nor shall his sword sleep in his hand till he has built that paradise in England's green and pleasant land.

We are only just discovering that there is such a thing as wishful thinking; but the Creative Evolutionist knows that all thinking is wishful, and that we cannot think until our wishes or fears or cupidities or curiosities create what we call attention. I have known this since my childhood, when somebody shewed me that if I held up my two forefingers in a line from my eyes, I could see two of the nearest when I looked at the farthest, or vice versa, because I had on my two retinas two separate images of everything in sight except the thing I wanted to see. Yet I was conscious of them only when I co-ordinated them. Later on, when I threw over my childish belief in the infallibility of the Bible on discovering that much of it is obsolete or wicked, what struck me most was that the obsolescences and wickednesses had never been hidden from me: they had been staring me in the face all the time. I had simply not thought about them. There must have been an evolutionary growth in my mind which directed my attention to them. Attention is the first symptom of thought. John the Evangelist would have worded it so, had he been born a Victorian.

Civilization is at present an imposture: we are a crowd of savages on whom a code of makeshift regulations is forced by penalties for breaking them. They are never explained to us. When I was sent to school I was confronted by a new set of rules and made aware that if I broke them I should be punished. As no other reason for obeying them was given to me I concluded naturally that I could break them without the slightest loss of selfrespect, and indeed with some pride in my independence and cleverness, as long as I was not found out. My hero in fiction was the rebel, not the goodygoody citizen, whom I despised. This attitude became a habit which I have never been able to shake off quite completely. Yet it would have been easy without overstraining my childish powers of comprehension to make me understand that people cannot live together, and be fed, clothed, lodged, and protected from robbery and murder, unless they agree to do certain things at the same moments in the same order, and meanwhile abstain from doing certain other things however tempting: in short, that social behaviour is expected behaviour, and that to behave unexpectedly, to be original as we call it, though without this eccentricity there can be no improvement, is to assume a dangerous responsibility. A child must begin as a Conservative, and learn later that though it must tolerate change it must do so very critically. That is to say it must be an intelligent and voluntary Conservative and not merely a dunderhead with a stock of dictated habits. When I associated with other boys in secret gangs it was to do mischief for the fun of it, to wreck and steal and circumvent law and order, to emulate Dick Turpin and Jack Sheppard, and generally to defy the commandments and do whatever our teachers and the police told us we must not do. If we had had even the simplest lessons in citizenship we should, like the Boy Scouts and Girl Guides of a later time, have conspired to do good instead of evil. No doubt we should also have played at the cruelties of the criminal law; for children, who like exercising authority as their elders do, will, if not carefully policed, do diabolical things to one-another in imitation of the vindictive side of law and parental authority. To remedy this we must reform the law and re-educate the parents.

All this faces us with the dilemma that civilization means stabilization; and creative evolution means change. As the two must operate together we must carefully define their spheres, and co-ordinate them instead of quarrelling and persecuting as we do at present. We must not stay as we are, doing always what was done last time, or we shall stick in the mud. Yet neither must we undertake a new world as catastrophic Utopians, and wreck our civilization in our hurry to mend it. Professional science must cease to mean the nonsense of Weismann and the atrocities of Pavlov, in which life is a purposeless series of accidents and reflexes, and logic only a thoughtless association of ideas. Still less must it mean mere erudition in the scriptures of the saints, prophets, and metaphysicians from Augustin and Aquinas to Butler and Bergson and Shaw. It must renounce magic and yet accept miracle; for as biology is still in the metaphysical stage (all its new knowledge of chromosomes and hormones only sub-stitutes millions of miracles for the single mystery formerly called the soul or breath of life); and as physics, in spite of its miraculous electrons and its abolition of matter, is nearer to the positive stage, the metaphysicians and artist-philosophers must co-operate with the astronomers and physiologists in separate but friendly and at the edges overlapping departments of social service. Both are trying to see a little farther into the dark; and whether the electronic microscope or the philosopher's brain has pierced it farthest is not worth quarrelling about; for the darkness beyond still forces us to tolerate both microscopic revelation and metaphysical speculation with all its guesses and hypotheses and dramatizations of how far thought can reach. We must have a hypothesis as a frame of reference before we can reason; and Creative Evolution, though the best we can devize so far, is basically as hypothetical and provisional as any of the creeds.

The history of modern thought now teaches us that when we are forced to give up the creeds by their childishness and their conflicts with science we must either embrace Creative Evolution or fall into the bottomless pit of an utterly discouraging pessimism. This happened in dateless antiquity to Ecclesiastes the preacher, and in our own era to Shakespear and Swift. "George Eliot" (Marian Evans) who, incredible as it now seems, was during my boyhood ranked in literature as England's greatest mind, was broken by the fatalism that ensued when she discarded God. In her most famous novel Middlemarch, which I read in my teens and almost venerated, there is not a ray of hope: the characters have no more volition than billiard balls: they are moved only by circumstances and heredity. "As flies to wanton boys are we to the gods: they kill us for their sport" was Shakespear's anticipation of George Eliot. Had Swift seen men as creatures evolving towards godhead he would not have been discouraged into the absurdity of describing them as irredeemable Yahoos enslaved by a government of horses ruling them by sheer moral superiority. Even Ibsen, though his characters, like Shakespear's, reek with volition, perpetrated a tragedy called Ghosts, in which an omnipotent god is discarded for an inevitable syphilis. One of the masters of comedy among my playwright colleagues drowned himself because he thought he he was going his father's way like Oswald Alving. Even a mind so keen and powerful as that of Dr Inge has been troubled by the notion that Life cannot survive extremes of temperature, nor reach inconceivable heights long after the cooling of the sun makes a good riddance of Yahoo mankind. (The sun, by the way, is getting hotter by the latest guesses.) Discouragement does in fact mean death; and it is better to cling to the hoariest of the savage old creator-idols, however diabolically vindictive, than to abandon all hope in a world of "angry apes", and perish in despair like Shakespear's Timon. Goethe rescued us from this horror with his "Eternal Feminine that draws us forward and upward" which was the first modern manifesto of the mysterious force in creative evolution.

That is what made Faust a world classic. If it does not do the same for this attempt of mine, throw the book into the fire; for Back to Methuselah is a world classic or it is nothing.

*Ayot Saint Lawrence*
*1944*

# Birmingham
## as a Home of Dramatic Art

(Curtain speech after first performance of Birmingham Repertory Theatre production on 12 October, *Birmingham Gazette*, 13 October 1923)

I know my place as an author, and the place of the author is not on the stage. That belongs really to the artistes who give life to the creations of the author, and are the real life of the play. I have had the luxury of seeing my own play, which only existed until they took it and made it live.

I should like to ask one question, and that is whether, apart from a few personal friends of mine, there are any inhabitants of Birmingham in this house?

This has been the most extraordinary experience of my life. I have had five magnificent performances in four days, and, what is more extraordinary, this has been done in Birmingham.

I remember Birmingham when it was, dramatically and theatrically, the most impossible place in the world for work of this description.

That is why I ask—Are you all pilgrims or strangers here, or are there one or two genuine inhabitants of Birmingham?

It is astonishing to me that this, perhaps the crown and climax of my career as a dramatic author, has been seen in Birmingham.

I suppose Mr Barry Jackson must be a changeling, or is it that there is occurring in Birmingham some change such as that in this play?

The first two of the people who live 300 years, are people who never imagined it would be possible, and people whose friends never imagined it would happen to them.

Their surprise can be compared to my experience, for Birmingham, the last place in the world one would imagine to become the centre of dramatic art, has produced a play of an intensity I think unparalleled.

Without the co-operation of the audience such a feat would have been impossible.


# The Serial Play

(Interview drafted by Shaw, *The Observer*, London, 21 October 1923)


Mr. Bernard Shaw, interrogated as to whether his Birmingham experience suggests that the public can

be educated to serial plays, demanded, somewhat
testily, why people reserved all that solicitude for the
public.

"What difficulty is there for the public in a serial
play?" he asked. "A serial play gives it no more
trouble and costs it no more than the same number
of inconsecutive plays, and is far more interesting.
There is nothing new about serial plays. Shakespeare
gave us one serial of four plays: 'Henry VI.' in three
parts plus 'Richard III.,' and one in two parts:
'Henry IV.' Wagner's 'Ring' is a serial of four
dramas. The cinema is up to the neck in serials. What
man has ever seen the whole of 'Monte Cristo' or
'Felix the Cat'? The Chaplin films constitute a serial
biography of one hero. Look at the Sherlock Holmes
series and the serial orgies of crimes for small boys
which have done so much damage to the reputation
of the cinema! The public has no more objection to
dramatic serials than it had to the great serial novels of
Dumas and Trollope."

"Then you think we are in for a fashion of serial
plays in the theatre?"

"Certainly not. The Shakespeare serials are never
performed as serials. The 'Ring' is given as a serial
only under special circumstances."

"But you said that the public likes serials."

"Yes, but I did not say that the public performed
them. You forget the unfortunate people behind the
scenes. In the cinema they do not matter, because
the preparation of a film may go on for months practically without regard to time or expense, the performance being a mechanical reproduction, occurring
simultaneously in thousands of cities at a negligible
cost. That is why you have your serial 'Monte
Cristos' and the like on the screen.

"But the theatre is quite another pair of shoes. Take, for example, what has just happened in Birmingham with my 'Methuselah' serial. They had to rehearse and prepare scenery and costumes for five plays in what would be considered a short time for a single play in London. The manager had to risk five failures in a single week without the possibility of making more than is expected from one success. And yet some journalists are writing as if the theatre were about to be inundated with serial plays, and express pity for the poor public, for whose sake this prodigious effort and risk and sacrifice of lucrative alternatives was made. You might as well pity the author for having had five successful first performances crammed into four days instead of spread precariously over seven years—an experience unprecedented in the history of the theatre."

"But it happened, Mr Shaw. You cannot deny that. Why should it not happen again?"

"Because Barry Jacksons do not grow on the bushes; that is why. The manager was the pivot on which the whole thing turned. He designed the theatre, he built the theatre, he endowed the theatre out of his private fortune, he managed the business of the theatre so capably and enterprisingly that he kept the strain on his private fortune within bearable limits, and he directed it artistically with a judgment and devotion that has convinced his exceedingly hammer-headed fellow townsmen that he must be the most extravagant and unpractical of dreamers instead of the ablest and most public-spirited hard worker in Birmingham. The production of 'Methuselah' was a feat possible only to such a manager and such a company, and in such an atmosphere of enthusiastic artistic co-operation as he has created. And it was not even a *tour de force* for him: he took it in his stride, with no great straining of his routine, and with results that astonished me by their artistic perfection. Such work as 'Methuselah' goes to him inevitably because there is nowhere else for it to go. I can find elsewhere a manager with experience and traditions, another with business capacity, another with artistic enthusiasm, another with artistic judgment (they are not necessarily associated), another full of civic spirit, another capable of understanding the value of my work, and another—perhaps—with more than eighteenpence of his own in his pocket. But the combination of all these in one man is almost a miracle, and until miracles become common you need have no fear of an epidemic of serials, Shavian or other, in the theatre."

# Bernard Shaw Piqued

(Written statement, presented as interview,
*Daily Express*, London, 22 February 1924)

Mr George Bernard Shaw is thoroughly annoyed with those who regard "Back to Methuselah," his five-night play at the Court Theatre, as a joke.

"It is unthinkable," he said to a "Daily Express" representative yesterday, "that a man of my age would devote two whole years to a petty joke. I am only a leg-puller in so far as I pull crooked legs straight.

"The public are all mental cripples, and if they question the reasons that prompted me to write 'Back to Methuselah,' it only affords a striking illustration of my opinion expressed in that play that the English race never becomes fully adult."

Mr. Shaw does not see why the mere fact that the play takes five nights for its performance should be regarded as surprising. "Was not Wagner's 'Ring' composed for four nights?" he asked.

"If I felt like it," he said, "I would write a play that would take a month to perform. Why shouldn't I? The only objection is the purely technical one of the difficulty of rehearsing so many plays simultaneously, and paying for the large cast necessary."

Mr Shaw cannot understand why his plays are never taken seriously.

"When I wrote my first play thirty-two years ago," he said indignantly, "the critics and the whole town were in an uproar for a fortnight. Now people who see it cannot understand what all the fuss was about. It will be the same with 'Methuselah.'

"I wrote it because I meant it all. Why does Sargent paint pictures? Why did Shakespear write plays? Why do I write plays? I have the specific talent for being a dramatist and I choose to use the medium of the drama to say what I think.

"Many years ago perhaps there was some justification for calling some of my work ridiculous. But now, after I have written for over thirty years [Mr Shaw is sixty-eight], and my plays have been produced in all parts of the world, it is absurd to treat me as though I were a guttersnipe. Yet that is now the accepted way of treating me. Either that or saying that I am growing old and dull.

"Of course it is flattering to find columns written about the smallest details and changes in the food I eat and the clothes I wear, the fact that I am six feet tall, treating me, in fact, as though I am the one exception to the whole human race. It is, however, an infernal nuisance."

With a genial shake of his beard, Mr Shaw abruptly put out his hand.

"By the way," he said cordially, "of course your dramatic critic, A.B.B. [Arthur Beverley Baxter], is quite insane."

# Letters to the Editor of
## *The Times*

I

(25 February 1924)

Sir,—I am very reluctant to make any comment on the expressions of irritation which my play at the Court Theatre must inevitably provoke from the short-lived, but Mr Edward Marsh, whose sensibilities I have every personal reason for respecting, must not accuse me of "pouring scorn on a politician who actually allowed his own son to be killed in the war." In what sense did any man "allow" his son to be killed in the war? Would any man have allowed such a thing if he could have prevented it? Many men, who were more or less responsible for the war, had that responsibility brought home to them by the loss of a well-beloved son; but they will hardly, I think, regard that as a fact to be suppressed as shameful, or deny the son his right to his record and his share in the moral of the greatest tragedy of his time. Does Mr Marsh really believe that his delicacy is greater and more consoling than mine when he dismisses the son with the remark that "somebody must be killed in a war," and treats his fate as a mere personal episode in which a father "allows his own child to sacrifice himself," and is to be contrasted with "one who saves his family at the expense of others"? In the framework of my play such phrases would be heartless nonsense; the case is bigger and deeper than that.

As to "pouring scorn" on anyone, what I have done is to exhibit our Parliamentary politics in contrast with politics *sub specie aeternitatis*. If under this test they shrink to a ridiculous smallness and reveal a disastrous inadequacy, that is not a reason why the exposure should be spared; it is a most urgent reason for submitting them to it ruthlessly. And as the dramatic method requires that the politics should be expounded by politicians, and the test can be valid only if the politicians are recognizably true to historic fact, the politicians must to some extent share the fate of the politics. This inevitable effect may scandalize critics who, being innocent of political life, imagine that statesmen approach elections with their minds wholly preoccupied with abstract principles, oblivious of the existence of such persons as voters, and most undemocratically indifferent to their likes and dislikes. Such critics imagine that in representing two ex-Premiers, on the eve of a General Election, as keenly alive to such considerations, and only too bitterly aware of our electoral ignorance, folly, and gullibility, I am representing them as unprincipled scoundrels; but I can hardly be expected to defer to a judgment so ludicrously uninstructed. My play, as far as it goes outside the public history of public men, contains not a word against the private honour of any living person; and if I do not share the delicacy as to equally public and politically active women which restrained Silas Wegg from going into details concerning the Decline and Fall of the Roman Empire, I can only say that my blue pencil is at the service of any lady who can find a single reference to herself which is not within the privilege of the friendliest good humour.

I have been accused in your columns of "shouting scandal from the housetops." Is it scandal to say of one statesman that he is happily married? or of another, who has an almost embarrassingly clever and famous wife, and two daughters whose achievements in politics and literature threaten to eclipse his own, that he is in this fortunate condition? Surely my apology is due to these ladies for having given them minor and even mute parts in a drama in which they actually played much more important ones, and not to your critic, who grudges them any mention at all.

It is true that in stage fiction many marriages are scandalous, and most of them triangular. The critic's mind becomes at last like the dyer's hand: the wedding ring suggests nothing to him but the Divorce Court. But my plays are not theatrical plays in that sense; and I hope an honest woman may be mentioned in them without a stain on her character.

Finally, as Miss Eileen Beldon has been accused by your critic of mispronouncing the word "isolate" (perhaps he rhymes it, as many do, to "why so late"), may I ask him how he pronounces it himself? I once asked Thomas Hardy how he pronounced The Dynasts. He replied that he called it The Dinnasts, but that so many people knew no better than to call it The Die-nasts that he was getting shy about it, and preferred not to mention it at all. I appeal to your critic not to make Miss Beldon shy, and, after consulting the pronouncing dictionaries, to send her a suitable apology.

Yours truly,

G. BERNARD SHAW

## II

### (28 February 1924)

Sir,—Your critic's bluff is so magnificent that it would be unchivalrous to call it were not Miss Beldon's orthoepic honour engaged. He dares refer me to Murray, knowing well that Murray gives issolate as a received pronunciation, though he has the bad taste to prefer eye-solate. Webster gives issolate, Ogilvie gives isso-late, the invaluable Chambers, compared to whom and to the others Murray is the merest upstart, gives issolate and izzolate, and the monumental Anglo-German Muret-Saunders gives issolate also. Is a lady with these masses of authorities at her back to be told that she mispronounces, and, when she is vindicated, to be propitiated by an assurance that she is young and charming, and that I have taken advantage of her innocence? Your critic now owes two apologies instead of one.

For the information of your readers, let me say that ice-olate is a vulgar pronunciation, which has forced its way into acceptance by general use so effectually that nobody can pretend that it is incorrect or objectionable in private conversation. But for platform and stage use, and in poetry, the ambiguity and ugliness of the long "i" make it impossible for any speaker with an intelligent ear. On the stage, therefore, the received pronunciation is the old standard one of issolate; and your critic must reserve his I-so-late for the intimacies of the tea-table.

I have no further quarrel with your critic about the scandal. He has produced a specimen of which he has made the worst by audaciously omitting the clause that places its harmlessness beyond all question. But even as debowdlerized, I can safely say that if there is nothing more terrible behind his protest against "scandal shouted on the housetops," I forgive him for it, and leave it to the judgment of your readers, who have, I feel sure, received it with a unanimous cry of "Is that all?"

Your critic should not listen to my very mild chaff through a microphone, and put cotton-wool in his ears when Methuselah is shouting his loudest.

Yours truly,

G. BERNARD SHAW

# Shaw Has Become a Prophet

(Statement for Hayden Church on World's Classics edition of *Back to Methuselah*, *Evening Standard*, London, 8 February 1945)

*I wrote and asked Mr Shaw if it was true, as had been reported that he is writing a new, and, possibly, even lengthier, preface for Back to Methuselah. And if so, why for goodness sake? He replied:*

It is not a preface but a postscript after 25 years. The original preface, which I regard as one of my most important writings, still stands with a few changes of references that are no longer topical. The doctrine is unaltered; and the postscript enforces it much more confidently as the religion of the forthcoming century. The jester's disguise is now thrown off completely and the mantle of the prophet frankly assumed.

Methuselah takes three days for a complete performance. On Monday, Part One at a matinee and Part Two in the evening. On Tuesday, the same with Parts Three and Four. On Wednesday, Part Five in the evening.

In New York the Theatre Guild disregarded these instructions and played Adam and Eve and Barnabas at one performance, with the result that they had to send round buckets of coffee to keep the exhausted audience awake.

In Germany the Barnabas scenes—thanks to Asquith and Lloyd George—were such a success that the manager broke his contract and ran Barnabas as a single play, dropping the rest.

The first [British] performance, in 1923, was at the Birmingham Repertory Theatre by Barry Jackson. I did my utmost to dissuade him, knowing that his theatre, which could hardly bear the cost of the production of one play, could not possibly pay for the production of five, but he was determined to face any loss for the sake of the play.

He revived it later on [1924] at the Court Theatre in London, and, having the scenery and costumes in his wardrobe and scene dock, made this time a profit of £20.

Jitta's Atonement
by Siegfried Trebitsch
translated by
Bernard Shaw

WITH

*Translator's Note*

A free adaptation of Siegfried Trebitsch's *Frau Gittas Sühne*. Composition begun August or September 1920; completed 6 August 1921. Published in *Translations and Tomfooleries*, 1926. First presented at the Shubert-Garrick Theatre, Washington, D.C., 8 January 1923.

Mrs Billiter    *Phoebe Coyne*
Girl from the Florist's    (*Not named*)
Professor Bruno Haldenstedt    *John Craig*
Jitta Lenkheim    *Bertha Kalich*
Professor Alfred Lenkheim    *Francis Byrne*
Dr Ernest Fessler    *Walton Butterfield*
Agnes Haldenstedt    *Thais Lawton*
Edith Haldenstedt    *Beth Eliott*

Period—Vienna, 1920

ACT I    *The Drawing Room of a Flat in Mrs Billiter's Apartment House. Night*

ACT II    *Professor Lenkheim's Study. A Week Later. After Lunch*

ACT III    *Mrs Haldenstedt's Sitting-room. Morning*

# Translator's Note

Siegfried Trebitsch, a well-known Austrian novelist and playwright, was born in Vienna on the 21st December 1869. The list of his original works includes eight novels and volumes of stories, and six or seven plays, including Frau Gitta's Sühne, of which the present work is a translation. I have to stress the word original, because, with a devotion extraordinary in the case of a writer with a successful career open to him as an original writer, he has undertaken and carried out the heavy additional task of translating and introducing to the German-speaking public and to the German theatre the entire body of my own works, both literary and theatrical.

This enterprise is the more remarkable because it was begun at a time when my position in the English theatre was one not of good repute, but of infamy. I was rated in the theatrical world of London as an absurd pamphleteer, who had been allowed to display his ignorance of the rudiments of stage technique, and his hopeless incapacity for representing human nature dramatically or otherwise, in a few performances at coterie theatres quite outside recognized theatrical commerce. Trebitsch knew better. He also knew English. He was quite unknown to me when he appeared one day at my house and asked to see me with a view to his becoming my interpreter and apostle in Central Europe. I attempted to dodge his visit by asking my wife to see him and to explain politely that a proposal to translate could be entertained only when made by the responsible manager of a theatre with a view to immediate production. The evasion failed ignominiously. My wife came to me and said that the young gentleman, though he seemed a very nice young gentleman, had swept aside her excuse with explosive contempt, and would take no denial. If I was to get rid of him (which she already regarded as doubtful policy) I must go down and do it myself. I came down; and the result was that the young gentleman carried the citadel by storm as successfully as he had carried the outworks. I did what I could to dissuade him from what seemed a desperate undertaking; but his faith in my destiny was invincible. I surrendered at discretion; and the result was that I presently found myself a successful and respected playwright in the German language whilst the English critics were still explaining laboriously that my plays were not plays, and urging me, in the kindest spirit, to cease my vain efforts to enter a profession for which Nature had utterly unfitted me. In the last decade of the nineteenth century I was deriving a substantial income as a playwright from America and Central Europe. Not until the middle of the first decade of the twentieth could I have lived by my theatrical earnings in London. Today I have only to lift up my finger to attract a hundred translators. When Trebitsch volunteered for the job, the hundred would have fled from my invitation as one man.

It is not for me to say how far English drama is indebted to Herr Trebitsch for its present prestige abroad. It *is* for me to say that my personal debt to him is incalculable. When the horrible catastrophe of the war had torn Anglo-German relations to fragments, and only the fools who would not heed Mr Lloyd George's warning to "stop snarling" could doubt the vital European necessity for mending them, I could do no less than take advantage of the fact that Trebitsch has written plays of his own, to translate one of them from German into English for the man

who has translated so many plays from English into
German.

There were technical difficulties: how great I never
realized until I took the job in hand. At first I was
preoccupied with a quite minor matter. I can neither
claim knowledge of the German language nor plead
ignorance of it. I am like most literary persons: I
have spent several holidays in Germany (mostly in
Bayreuth), and have just managed to ask my way, and
get what I wanted in the shops and railway stations,
without the aid of an interpreter. The proverbial bits
of Goethe and Wagner and Nietzsche are familiar to
me; and when a German writes to me I can generally
make out what he wants provided he uses the Latin
and not the Gothic script. And that is all. When I
opened the pages of Frau Gitta's Sühne, I was driven
to the dictionary, only to discover that Trebitsch
apparently does not use words that are in the dictionary. It was not by any process known to men of
learning, but rather by some telepathic method of
absorption, that I managed at last to divine, infer,
guess, and co-invent the story of Gitta, or Jitta, as I
have had to spell her to avert having her name pronounced with a hard G. Trebitsch is amiable enough
to say that I have succeeded wonderfully; but even
a very bad translation may be a wonderful feat for a
translator who does not know the language.

However, when it comes to translating a play the
mere translation is only the tiniest fraction of the
business. I soon found that a literal translation would
fail completely to convey the play to an Anglo-
American audience. It was necessary to translate the
audience as well as the play: that is, to translate Vienna
into London and New York. And this involved translating one theatrical epoch into another. Vienna is

still romantic in the manner of Verdi's operas, and modern in the manner of De Maupassant and Baudelaire. And as the conqueror always acquires some of the qualities of the conquered, even now that he no longer eats him, there is a touch of the east in Vienna, not only brought by the winds along the Danube, but left by the Turks when Sobieski drove them back from the gates. Add to this that Vienna has never weaned itself from the sweet milk of eighteenth-century art, when even woe was a luxury, and the heroine could not die in gloom too deep to please the audience. When natural history (sometimes ambiguously called realism) is banished from the theatre, cruelty, horror and death become painless there, and even luxurious, because nobody believes in them. The most frightful torments may be heaped on the heroine until she dies of poison or a broken heart: the villain may, like the wicked Count in Il Trovatore, live only to *centuplicar la morte* of the hero in *mille atroci spasimi*, and the hero himself may not know a moment of happiness or security until misfortune dogs him to his death; yet no one will turn a hair: the more dreadful it all is the better it is liked, because romance can never come home to reality. To preserve this delicious anæsthesia there must be no bringing down to earth of the business by the disillusioning touch of comedy.

In England and America nowadays, such romance is privileged only in Italian Opera, and is not tolerated without the music. The Anglo-American audience wants a happy ending because it wants a credible ending, and therefore cannot bear an utterly unhappy one. It is true, as the late St John Hankin pointed out and illustrated by his Plays With Happy Endings, that the conventional happy ending is often as unhappy and disastrous as the marriages which foolish magistrates and police-court missionaries force on young people who have been no better than they ought to be. But the fact remains that in proportion as a play succeeds in producing an illusion of real life, it must dispense with the frantic agonies and despairs and poisonings and butcheries of the romantic theatre. Consequently, if you take a play written under the tyranny of a romantic audience and present it without modification to a comparatively matter-of-fact audience, it will miss its mark, and may even miss fire altogether.

To avert this result in the case of Frau Gitta's Sühne, I have taken advantage of the fortunate circumstance that in real life the consequences of conjugal infidelity are seldom either so serious as they are assumed to be in romantic tragedy or so trivial as in farcical comedy. I may as well confess at once that in the original play Jitta lives miserably ever after, and that her husband bears malice, and presents a character-study much subtler and more elusive than you will gather from my frankly comedic British version of him. Also Trebitsch, being a German poet, has a certain melancholic delicacy which escapes my comparatively barbarous and hilarious occidental touch. I could not help suggesting, by a few translator's treacheries here and there, that the ill-assorted pair settle down on reasonable human terms, and find life bearable after all.

Trebitsch goes so far as to say "You have made my last act almost a comedy"; but he is too amiable to reproach me, and tolerates my variations, which affect, not the story itself, but only the key in which it ends. Though the assumptions of the audience as to what will happen after the fall of the curtain will be more cheerful in England and America than they

were in Vienna, the action of the play remains unaltered. Nevertheless those who can should read the
original, to the idiosyncratic literary quality of which
I have been shamefully unable to do justice.

Frau Gitta's Sühne was first performed at the great
Burgtheater of Vienna on the 3rd February 1920.

# [ACT I]

---

*1920. The drawing room in a flat in Vienna. It is fashionably decorated and elegantly furnished, but not homelike, as there are no books nor personal belongings nor household odds and ends lying about. The two photogravure reproductions of pictures on the walls, symmetrically placed at equal distances from the door, are of the refinedly aphrodisiac character considered de rigueur in hotels. But the place is not quite like a hotel sitting room; because there is very little furniture: only two seats, a couch, and a small table with a glass flower-vase and a mirror on it.*

*It is an oblong room; and from the point of view of anyone looking towards the corner the long wall on the right has in the middle of it the door leading to the entrance hall; and the short wall on the left has an open door close to the corner through which a bed with rose-colored hangings is partly visible. In the same wall further forward from the same point of view is the fireplace.*

*The couch is in the corner, parallel to the longer wall, not quite close against it. A comfortable upholstered stool, really a chair without a back, is at the foot of the couch. This stool has a cushion on it which evidently belongs to the couch. The other seat, a chair with arms, is almost in the middle of the room, but nearer to the fireplace than to the door. The table stands near the corner of the fireplace.*

*It is almost dark.*

*Mrs Billiter, an elderly housekeeper, has something of*

*the same undomesticated air as the room. Her hair,
though not aggressively dyed, is still rather younger than
her face. She is well dressed, like a hotel manageress.
She opens the door, letting in some electric light from the
hall. She has a silver tray in her hands, with a siphon,
two tumblers, and a bottle on it. She switches on the
light at the door, and crosses the room to the table, where
she puts down the tray. She looks round the room to see
whether it is tidy. She goes to the stool; takes the cushion
from it; and puts it in its proper place on the couch.*

*Somebody rings at the outer door of the flat. Mrs
Billiter goes out to open it.*

---

A GIRL'S VOICE [*the accent is not that of a lady*]
Gentleman ordered these. Suppose it's all right, isnt
it ?

MRS BILLITER'S VOICE. Yes. Just bring them in,
and put them in the vase for me, will you ?

*Mrs Billiter returns, followed by a girl from the
florist's shop, carrying a handsome present of flowers.*

MRS BILLITER [*pointing to the vase*] There. I'll fetch
some water.

*She goes into the bedroom and switches on the light
there. The roseate hangings of the bed appear to great
advantage. The flower girl, on her way to the vase, stops
fascinated.*

*Mrs Billiter returns with a jug from the bedroom
washstand: a very pretty jug in rose color and gold.*

*The flower girl puts the roses into the vase; and Mrs
Billiter fills it with water.*

*Mrs Billiter takes the jug back into the bedroom; and
the girl steals after her to the door and peeps enviously in.*

*Mrs Billiter returns, putting out the bedroom light as
she does so, and finds the girl at the door.*

THE FLOWER GIRL. Just right for two, aint it?

MRS BILLITER [*incensed*] What do you mean, with your "Just right for two"?

THE FLOWER GIRL [*grinning*] Oh, it's nothing to me. But I know.

MRS BILLITER. You know too much, you do. Are they paid for?

THE FLOWER GIRL. Oh yes: thats quite all right. [*She grins again, shewing no sign of going*].

MRS BILLITER [*peremptorily*] Well? What are you waiting for? And what are you grinning at?

THE FLOWER GIRL. Aint the gentleman here? He promised to leave me something.

MRS BILLITER [*impatiently groping in her purse and extracting a tip*] Thats how they give themselves away, offering tips when they have no call to. [*She gives her some money*]. There! Now, out you go. I'm busy.

THE FLOWER GIRL [*sarcastic*] Sorry, I'm sure. Thanks awfully. [*She goes to the door, but stops on hearing the outer door opened by a latch-key from without*]. Oh, here is the gentleman.

*The gentleman enters. The girl ogles him. He recognizes her, and makes a gesture towards his pocket.*

MRS BILLITER [*very decisively*] Thats all right, sir: she's had what you promised. [*To the girl, sternly*] Good evening to you. [*She sails to the door so formidably that the girl, after an ineffectual grimace, has to go*].

*The moment the gentleman is left alone he shews signs of severe physical suffering. His ascent of the stairs has brought on an attack of angina pectoris. He makes his way to the stool, and collapses on it, struggling with the paroxysm. Mrs Billiter returns.*

MRS BILLITER [*running to him*] Oh dear, oh dear, has it come on again, sir?

THE GENTLEMAN [*a little better*] It's all right now,

Mrs Billiter. I took the stairs too fast. I rush at them without thinking. [*He rises, and tries to take off his overcoat. She helps him*]. Thank you, Mrs Billiter. I—I—I— [*gasping*] Just a moment. Whew! [*As the coat comes off he plunges to the armchair, and sinks into it*].

MRS BILLITER. How often have I begged you never to walk upstairs but always to take the lift? And now see the state you are in!

THE GENTLEMAN. Dont look at me: it will only distress you. Angina pectoris is a horrible thing; but it passes off soon. You can do nothing, thank you.

MRS BILLITER [*taking his hat and coat out into the vestibule*] Dear! dear! dear!

*Rather dazed by the attack, he sits up, straightening his collar and coat rather irresolutely, and looking very careworn indeed. He is well dressed, on the verge of fifty, going grey, very distinguished in appearance and kindly in manner.*

MRS BILLITER [*returning*] Why will you never take the lift, sir? It isnt as if anyone in this house knew you. And for that matter you meet people on the stairs as well as in the lift.

THE GENTLEMAN. I know; but I mustnt let the liftmen see me coming here too often. People talk, even when they have to live by holding their tongues.

MRS BILLITER [*reproachfully*] Oh, sir!

THE GENTLEMAN [*quickly saving the situation*] Except you, Mrs Billiter. You are an exception to all the rules.

MRS BILLITER. It's you who are the exception, sir. I wish all the other gentlemen that keep rooms here on the quiet to enjoy themselves were like you. There are people and people in this world; and I know a gentleman when I see him. And I feel sure your lady is a real lady, and always the same lady; though of course I take care never to see her.

THE GENTLEMAN. Thats very kind of you, Mrs Billiter. [*He rises to go to the table*].

MRS BILLITER [*stopping him*] Now do sit quiet a moment, sir. What was it you wanted?

THE GENTLEMAN. A mouthful of soda water.

MRS BILLITER. There: I'll get it for you. Sit down. [*He does so. She goes go the table and fills a glass from the siphon*]. If you would only let me put a drop of brandy in it?

THE GENTLEMAN [*shaking his head decisively*] It would probably kill me. I know. I am a doctor. [*He takes the glass from her*]. Thank you. [*He drinks*].

MRS BILLITER. You are not right yet. I can see it in your face.

THE GENTLEMAN [*hands her back the glass a little abruptly, and pulls himself together*] !!!!

MRS BILLITER. There! I shouldnt have said that. [*She replaces the glass on the table, snubbed*].

THE GENTLEMAN. Not at all. I know how anxious you are about me, and how kindly you mean it. But I am all right now; and I—I— [*he takes out his watch and looks at it*] I am expecting somebody.

MRS BILLITER [*taking the hint*] Yes, sir: I'm going. [*She crosses the room to the door, but turns for a moment appealingly before going out*]. But you will take the lift next time, sir, wont you? If anything were to happen to you—not that I think anything like that, of course; but—

THE GENTLEMAN. Of course not, Mrs Billiter. Still— [*he shrugs his shoulders*]!

MRS BILLITER. Yes, sir. And then what could I do but send for the police?

THE GENTLEMAN. Quite so, quite so. If I come again I will take the lift. I promise.

MRS BILLITER. Thank you, sir. Thank you kindly. [*She goes out, closing the door very softly behind her*].

*The gentleman, left alone, rises and goes to the table, where he takes up the mirror and looks at his wrinkles and his blanching hair. He shakes his head and puts the mirror down. Then he takes out a cigaret; puts it between his lips; takes out a match, and is about to strike it when the bell rings twice. His face lights up; he throws the match and the cigaret into the fire; and goes out eagerly to admit the visitor, leaving the door of the room open. Immediately afterwards a veiled lady hurries in like a hunted creature. He follows her; shuts the door; and comes to her in the middle of the room. They embrace.*

THE GENTLEMAN [*affectionately*] Why do you always look as if you were running away, and had just stumbled into my arms by chance?

THE LADY. I always feel as if my husband were lying in wait for me at the next turn.

THE GENTLEMAN. Well, suppose he were! You are not afraid of poor Alfred, are you? At home you are a perfect tyrant to him.

JITTA. I should have no courage if he caught me. Besides, if we are found out there will be an end of everything.

BRUNO. I almost wish we were found out.

JITTA. Why?

BRUNO. It would force us to stand by one another, and come out openly before all the world with our love.

JITTA [*embracing him impulsively*] Shall we?

BRUNO. There is my wife. Always my wife.

JITTA [*recoiling from him impatiently, and throwing her*

*cloak on the couch*] Oh yes: Agnes. Always Agnes, Agnes, Agnes.

BRUNO. She has done nothing to deserve our betrayal of her: she has sacrificed her life to me. I cant face what she would suffer.

JITTA. Has she sacrificed more for you than you for her? It is not the thought of Agnes that holds me back. But the scandal would ruin you. [*She takes off her hat, and puts it on the table*].

BRUNO [*with sudden energy*] I want to be ruined. Oh, the life of a University professor. His respectability kills his mind. His wife's respectability kills her soul. They both become mere shells of their former selves: going through life in grooves, on rails like tramcars, envying the tinkers and gipsies. If it were not for Agnes I should commit some disgraceful offence to free myself.

JITTA. I am afraid disgrace would not mend matters. I could not bear yours.

BRUNO. Nor I yours. We are in the net.

JITTA. Not here, Bruno. We have broken through the net into our dreamland. [*Now that her hat and veil are off Jitta is revealed as one of those attractively refined women whose wistfully sensitive unsmiling mouths and tragic eyes not only make imaginative men fancy unfathomable depths in their natures, and something undefinably sad and splendid in their destinies, but actually force this conception on the women themselves, however commonplace their characters and circumstances may be. Jitta is nothing more extraordinary than the wife of a college don, and has done nothing more heroic than fall in love with another and more poetic don (also married); but to her lover and herself her life is as dignified and beautiful as her face, and their relations as nobly tragic as her eyes. So, as we are all a little like that,*]

[ 731 ]

*let us share their dream for a moment whilst she continues, sitting down beside him*] You must brush off the bits of the broken net. [*Tracing on his brow*] There is a thread of it here, and here, and straight down here. [*She kisses his brow*]. No: they are not gone yet.

BRUNO. It is not the net. I can leave that behind when I come here into the dreamland. These last few months have been wonderful. But they have been terrible.

JITTA. Yes: wonderful and terrible. But they have been real, real. Life in the net is never real: it is all acting.

BRUNO. That is true. But there is something still more real than the dream.

JITTA. What is that?

BRUNO. The awakening.

JITTA. For me there will be no awakening.

BRUNO. There is always the tap at the door in the morning. The tap with bony knuckles. The caller.

JITTA. Death! Oh, why will you always harp on that? Death is nothing. Life with love is everything. Think, Bruno. We are here alone. There is nothing between us and happiness except the courage to grasp it. Can you never be happy?

BRUNO. Can any mortal be happy?

JITTA [*suddenly prosaic and impatient*] Yes: Alfred can. A glass of wine and a cigar can make Alfred happy. A vote of thanks can make Alfred happy. A cheque for £25 can make him happy. But I cannot make you happy.

BRUNO. Dearest love: you can, you do make me inexpressibly happy. So happy, that every time you go away from me, and I stand listening to your footsteps dying away in the distance—I always listen to them to catch the last sound of you—I am stabbed with a fear that I have held you in my arms for the last time. But when we have been parted for days, and I am here waiting for you and thinking the moments endless until you come, and at last I hear your ring, I suddenly become like a freshman just up from school. [*She laughs, smoothing his grey hair*]. Yes: I know; but grey as I am, I am still a hobbledehoy; just a student waiting for his girl at the corner of the street where her shop is.

JITTA [*moved*] And do you think it is any different with me? All day I long to be with you, to say a thousand things to you! And when at last— [*she finishes the sentence with a caress*]! When you are away from me, I plod through my housework, and just count the days until—until this [*she again presses him in her arms, and draws him down beside her on the couch*].

BRUNO. If only I were young! Then I could really begin a new life with you instead of merely thinking and dreaming about it.

JITTA. I like it better as it is. I dont want to see you every day and become a commonplace with you, Bruno.

BRUNO. But are you content with these heartbreaking stolen hours? I'd risk you becoming a commonplace: I want you to be a commonplace for me; but I daresay I should bore you.

JITTA [*sighing blissfully*] The happiness of these stolen hours is so delicious that it makes up to me for everything I have to endure between times. And who knows what would happen if I were to break up your home and shatter your career? Are you sure we should not be tired out, too broken by the effort, to enjoy our rest? One has to be young to do such things, Bruno: young enough to be able to forget.

BRUNO [*sadly*] You are right. Our love looks well only by candlelight. It wont stand daylight.

JITTA [*refusing to be discouraged*] Daylight is for your work, for your great book that is to be the crown of your career. But here in the candlelight you belong to me, and to me only.

BRUNO [*quickly*] Oh, not here alone. Do you think that my wife and my daughter put you quite out of my head when I am at home? They never do: you are everywhere. But what must it be for you? I often reproach myself—

JITTA [*softly*] You mustnt do that. I am not unhappy, Bruno. I was at first: I hardly dared go home and face Alfred's inquisitive eyes. But he saw nothing: his self-conceit is impenetrable. His cheerful grin killed my conscience. I hold up my head now everywhere: I am proud of belonging to you. When one is really happy, one is ruthless and shameless.

BRUNO. Jitta: do you know that you belonged to me before we ever saw one another?

JITTA. Yes. We were destined—

BRUNO. I dont mean that. I mean that we actually belonged to one another physically. I mean that my daughter—born before we knew one another—is your daughter.

JITTA. Edith! What do you mean, Bruno? You have the strangest fancies.

BRUNO. This is not a fancy, Jitta. It is a hard scientific fact: I worked out its theoretic possibility before Edith was born—before I ever set eyes on you. It strikes me dumb with wonder when I think how it has worked out between us. The daughter of my wife, my child and hers, not yours, resembles you, aye, loves you more than she loves her own mother, though she may not know it.

JITTA [*thoughtfully*] Strange. And I love your Edith as only a childless woman can love the child of the man she has interested and saved. I am not clever enough to share the rest of your science with you but this I believe and accept. But how can such a miracle come about?

BRUNO [*mystically*] Men do not yet realize that no prophetic aspiration of theirs can fall utterly without fruit if its roots lie deep enough in their innermost conviction.

JITTA. Bruno: that must be right. It is an inspiration. It takes hold of my heart with both hands. You really are great.

BRUNO. Not at all: it is not new: everybody knows it nowadays in the rough. But it has never been worked out scientifically far enough to explain this miracle of Edith and you. Well, I am working it out; and there is somebody else working at it with me.

JITTA [*jealous*] Somebody else!

BRUNO. You would never guess who.

JITTA. I do not want to guess. I do not care.

BRUNO. Think of the most hardened materialist you know: the very last man you could imagine lending himself to such a mystical speculation!

JITTA [*relieved*] Oh, a man! The most hopeless materialist I know is my husband; and I do not want to be reminded of him just now.

BRUNO. But it is your husband I mean. I have converted him.

JITTA. Oh, impossible. He would never believe a thing like that. Dont let Alfred deceive you, Bruno. He is only playing with your belief because he feels sure of discovering some grossly material explanation of it, and making you ridiculous. He does not believe it as you believe it.

[ 735 ]

BRUNO [*brightly*] I do not say he does: I do not say he can. Alfred is clever; but he is not me—or rather, not us two: two in one.

JITTA. Darling.

BRUNO. All the same, he is burning with ambition to have his name connected with a new departure in science. As he has failed to do it in physics he is willing to do it in psychology rather than not do it at all.

JITTA [*scornfully*] At your expense?

BRUNO. Not altogether, dearest. He really has given me some quite handy curve diagrams for my lectures. He knows everything: what he lacks is a sense of the significance of what he knows. I am really sorry for him, and should like to help him.

JITTA. You can help him without letting him rob you of your ideas.

BRUNO. It is not he who is robbing me of my ideas: it is I who am robbing him of his wife; and the less he is conscious of his loss the meaner thief am I. I feel that through and through. [*He kisses her hand passionately*]. I have taken a priceless treasure from him. I must make amends somehow: I must pay my debt. That sense of obligation is in my very bones.

JITTA [*looking hard at him*] Why have I never felt this sense of obligation to your wife? Have I no conscience? or have you too much?

BRUNO. It is not the same. You do not feel that you have taken anything from Agnes: you feel that she has taken something from you.

JITTA. I know that I have a divine right to you. And I know that she has not.

BRUNO. There are other rights beside divine rights. If I had never come into your life, you would perhaps

[ 736 ]

have come to some sort of understanding with Alfred; and he would have found some sort of happiness in possessing you.

JITTA. He has all the happiness he is capable of.

BRUNO. We have no right to say so. I have taken you from him.

JITTA. You have not taken me from him. I belonged to myself: and I gave you myself.

BRUNO. I have betrayed his trust.

JITTA. As I have betrayed your wife's trust.

BRUNO. That is quite different. Your relations with Agnes are mere society relations, conventional and superficial. But I am your husband's comrade: we were chums at school: we were at college together: we are professional colleagues. He knows me intimately; and if he were not such a confoundedly bad psychologist he would know that Nature meant you to be my wife. It is a stroke of luck for us that he knows nothing—if indeed it is only luck, and not his subconscious knowledge that he must not let himself know. Yes: he not only does not know: he will not know: he refuses to know. And that refusal, because it is unconscious, binds my sense of honor as if he spared us knowingly.

JITTA [*changing her tone, and trying to soothe and coax him*] Darling: you are tormenting yourself for nothing. Let me see whether I can cure you of all these scruples and fancies. They are only spooks. [*She draws him towards the bedroom*]. Come.

BRUNO. No, not yet. [*He gets away from her by standing up. She shrinks a little, wounded*]. I am telling you this once for all; so that I may never have to speak of it again. God knows it is not to involve you in my struggles with myself, nor to whitewash myself, that I am spending our priceless moments like this. I am as impatient as you are: I long for you beyond all expression. But there is something you must do for me. Something you can understand only when you know the rights of it.

JITTA [*repelled and anxious*] But what is it?

BRUNO [*pulling himself together*] I want to speak to you about my book. I have something very important to say to you about it.

JITTA [*a little disappointed*] Bruno: cant that wait a little? You know how I value your work; but we have so little time left this evening—

BRUNO [*resolutely*] It is just because I have so little time left that I dare not put this off any longer. You know the value of my book. Well, you must take charge of it.

JITTA. You need not trouble about that, Bruno: it will make your name famous without my help.

BRUNO [*looking hard at her, and forcing the emphasis of his words to the utmost*] Not my name. His name.

JITTA. God of Heaven! whose name?

BRUNO. Your husband's.

JITTA [*springing up*] Alfred's!

BRUNO. Listen to me. The book is finished: the typed copy will be found in my desk. And the title-page reads "Fetters of the Feminine Psyche, by Professor Alfred Lenkheim."

JITTA. Bruno! You are mad.

BRUNO. I burnt the original manuscript yesterday: there is not a word of it in my handwriting left to prove that I am the author. They will find a book by your husband among my things: that is all. [*She is about to protest*]. Promise me that you will leave this secret buried in my grave.

JITTA [*beside herself*] But why? Why? Why?

BRUNO [*seizing her hands, but now pleading like a*

*lover*] It is my deepest wish. It is my most urgent prayer to you, Jitta.

JITTA [*gasping*] You ask me to do that! to promise you this unheard-of thing! This man who has no soul; who has been guilty of everything to me that a man can be guilty of to a woman except the infidelity that I would welcome with delight to excuse my own (he is not man enough for that): the fruit of your life's work is to drop into his mouth! And I am to be your accomplice in such a crime! No. I cannot. Never.

BRUNO [*soothing her*] I know how hard it is for you, darling. That is why I have not been able to bring myself to tell you until today. But I know you will not fail me.

JITTA. Dont say that, Bruno, as if it settled everything. I cannot act like a madwoman. Give me a reason.

BRUNO. I will. Listen. A book by a dead man is an orphan. Orphans sometimes die when they are not adopted. Mendel's masterpiece lay dead for thirty-five years while the fame of the living Darwin spread over the world. If Alfred adopts my orphan it will not perish; for Alfred's wife will adopt it too.

JITTA. Oh, Bruno, Bruno, how can you? That is so clever, so damnably clever. Has it come to mere cleverness between us?

BRUNO. I asked for a promise. You asked for a reason.

JITTA. But I am thinking of your fame—

BRUNO [*snapping his fingers*] Psha! That for my fame! What does it matter from whose hands the new generation will take the torch to carry on the great race of science? The truth will be as true with Alfred's name tacked on to it as Bruno's.

JITTA [*impatiently*] Oh yes, yes: I know all that. It sounds like a sentence from your annual address to your students. It's not true, Bruno: I feel it. It is not human. There is something else at the back of your mind.

BRUNO. No—except this. When I finally and irrevocably sealed my resolution yesterday by burning the manuscript, there came to me a moment of extraordinary exaltation in which I saw this sacrifice as my atonement to Alfred. It is the price at which I buy his wife from him; and now at last I can take my happiness with both hands, free in my conscience, right in my heart, in all honor as well as in all affection to the very end. [*He clasps her to his breast*].

JITTA [*still wondering at him*] You throw the greatest achievement of your life to him like a bone to a dog; and then feel you have made us two one. [*Breaking away from him*] No, no, Bruno: you are asking too much. You know that I love you as my man, without a thought of your greatness and your work; but all the same your work, your greatness, are a part of you; and I love every bit of you, your body, your soul, your reputation, your work, everything that would not exist if you did not exist. All that is my treasure and my pride. When you take a handful of it and throw it into the mud, you make me so much the poorer. Have you thought of that?

BRUNO. When two people stand to one another as we stand, the children born from their intercourse are not always children of flesh and blood, but inspirations, intuitions, convictions that they cannot discard without unfaithfulness. This is such an inspiration. Will you be unfaithful to it?

JITTA. Bruno: you want to play at Providence. Alfred is far too conceited to let anyone play Providence to him. If he refuses, what then?

BRUNO. He will not refuse. I have thought all that

out. Why should he refuse to father a book which he already regards as half his own? He believes that I could never have written it without him. And you know how ambitious he is. I can depend on Alfred absolutely. Can I depend on you?

JITTA [*half beaten*] Who knows? I cannot depend on myself. This sacrifice is no child born of our intercourse, Bruno: you may be its father; but I am not its mother. I shall be its stepmother; and I shall hate it as no stepmother ever hated before. But the book is yours; and I have no rights over it: it must take the course you desire. I cannot go further than that. When you ask me to bind myself by a solemn vow, I— [*shuddering*] no, no: it is inhuman: a mockery, an impossibility.

BRUNO. I know I am putting your love to the cruellest test; but oh, Jitta, Jitta, do not fail me.

JITTA. So be it. [*He snatches her hands and kisses them*]. I promise you that if I survive the day that takes you from me, I will hide the truth as you demand, and take all the ghastly consequences just as you are mad enough to mean them. Are you satisfied now?

BRUNO [*clasping her convulsively to him and hardly able to speak*] I—I—thanks, thanks. My love.

JITTA [*extricating herself quickly from his embrace*] But if God wishes to be good to me he will never let me live to keep my promise.

BRUNO. I could not have pained you like this if I had the smallest doubt that I shall go first and go soon.

JITTA. Dont say that. Oh, do let us forget Death for one moment.

BRUNO. Death is nothing: if I could be sure that I should die tonight I should be unspeakably glad; for I should not have to strike the bitterest blow of all.

[ 741 ]

JITTA. Bruno! Another blow!

BRUNO. Yes, another. My strength is going from me; and I need it all to force myself not to play the coward.

JITTA. How?

BRUNO. By leaving you today without daring to tell you that I do not intend to meet you again.

JITTA [*struck to the heart*] Not meet me again! Leave me!

BRUNO [*with deliberate emphasis*] This must be the last time. [*Rising, with a sudden fanciful recklessness*] Come: let it be the best. Let it be so full of happiness that we can say "It is enough: farewell."

JITTA. You are going to give me up! You can bring yourself to do that!

BRUNO. Nonsense! I shall never give you up. But it would be a crime to let you meet me here again at such a risk.

JITTA. How is the risk greater now than it has always been?

BRUNO. It was only a risk of being caught here with a live man. That was nothing: only a secret that three can keep. What about the risk of being found with a dead one?

JITTA [*about to shriek*]!

BRUNO [*covering her mouth with his hand*] Hush—sh! [*She looks affrightedly at him: he looks gravely and significantly at her*]. It is all up with me, dearest. I could not stop working; and my heart—

JITTA [*with agonizing anxiety*] Is it worse?

BRUNO [*with a ghost of a laugh*] Worse! It has gone all to pieces. I had no right to let you come this evening. I have put off telling you too long; but when I climbed those terrible stairs just now, I knew. You would have to give your name to the police. Our relations would be shouted through the streets and posted on the newspaper bills if you were found here with a—with a [*he cannot say it, and indicates, by a gesture, the figure of a dead man lying on the floor*].

JITTA [*flinching at the image, but steadfast in her thought*] Have no fear, Bruno. Why did you not tell me sooner what was troubling you? I could have relieved your mind. I have known all along that you were ill; and my only fear was that that [*she repeats his gesture*] might happen when you were alone instead of in my arms. Does that sound as if I cared what would become of me without you?

BRUNO. But I care, dearest. That is why I am resolved on our parting before this crazy tired old clock [*he taps his left breast*] runs down and stops ticking for good and all.

JITTA. Never. There is only one thing that can part me from you; and that is not the stopping of the clock, but of your love for me. No other danger exists for me; and no forethought of ours can protect us against that if it comes. [*Abandoning herself to her passion*] All the more reason why we must make the most of our love while it is within our reach. I love you: I love you: we are alive, not dead: you are living with my life as well as your own: your blood surges to mix with mine: you cannot die while I hold you fast. All the rest is an uneasy dream that means nothing: this is love; and love is life made irresistible.

BRUNO [*carried away*] Life: yes: this is life, and this [*he kisses her eyes*], and this [*he kisses her lips*]. What a fool I was with my iron resolutions! one throb of your breast, one touch of your lips; and where are they? Nothing matters but Jitta, Jitta, Jitta [*he kisses her again and again*]. I am neither weak nor afraid now; and I promise you to live a hundred years.

[ 743 ]

JITTA. All the unhappinesses are forgotten: they never existed. [*She turns him round and draws him towards the bedroom*] Come.

BRUNO [*beside himself*] You trust me; and I must betray you. You thought me a young man; and I let you think so. But you shall not be deceived. You have made me young as I seemed to you. [*He seizes her round the hips, and lifts her up exultantly*].

JITTA [*terrified*] Oh God, no: take care, Bruno: take care.

BRUNO [*setting her down gaily*] Bah! Do I love you?

JITTA. Yes, yes. You love me. I love you. Come.

BRUNO [*pushing her towards the bedroom door*] Quick, quick.

JITTA [*running into the bedroom*] Yes, yes, yes.

BRUNO [*with a grim change of countenance*] Poor Jitta! That lift broke the mainspring. [*He staggers against the door frame; clutches at the wall to save himself; strikes the electric light out by chance; reels back into the middle of the room; and drops dead*].

JITTA [*running in: she has began to undress*] What is the matter? Where are you? [*She stumbles against the body*]. Oh God! [*She switches on the light*] Bruno. [*She rushes to him and kneels by him*]. Bruno: speak to me if you can: is it your heart again? What can I do for you? Shall I try to lift you?

*She tries to raise him by his shoulders; but they are too heavy. She puts her hand around his neck and pulls it up from the floor; but the back of his head remains hanging and his jaw drops. With a gasp of horror she replaces the head and closes the open mouth. Then she scrambles to her feet and runs to the other door, calling breathlessly and voicelessly Mrs Billiter, Mrs Billiter. She opens the door, and regaining her voice, cries Mrs— She checks herself, suddenly remembering the con-*

sequences to herself of being found with the body. She closes the door quickly and noiselessly. She tries to think, her strained senses shewing in her eyes. Her fingers clutch for a moment at her half-naked breast as she thinks of her disordered appearance. She dashes into the bedroom, and reappears almost immediately with her blouse on, arranging it with nervous hands. She puts on her hat and mantle anyhow. As she turns to rush to the door the hat falls off. With a little cry of misery she takes the hat-pins from the hat and pins it properly to her hair; then she looks at herself in the mirror and shakes her mantle straight. She turns, and is hurrying to the door when she finds the body in her way. A flush of remorse comes over her. She turns impulsively to the vase; takes out a handful of roses; and is stooping to lay them on his breast when she realizes that a man who drops dead cannot scatter flowers on himself. She shakes her head and puts the roses back; puts her hands distractedly to her head in an anguish of perplexity, feeling that she must not leave him without some ceremony of love. There is only one thing that comes into her mind that will not compromise her. She goes to him, and cannot touch him or kiss him; but she makes the sign of the cross over him; kisses her hand; crosses herself; and hurries out, closing the door very softly behind her.

# $\left[\text{ACT II}\right]$

*A week has elapsed. Bruno is buried, and his death from natural causes duly certified. Jitta has taken refuge in an illness, and is keeping her bed. Her husband, Professor Alfred Lenkheim, is sitting in his study after lunch with young Dr Fessler, who is engaged to Bruno's daughter Edith. Alfred lacks the distinction and heroic touch of Bruno; but prosaic as he certainly is, he is saved from being common, if not from being a little comic, by the stamp put upon him as a man of learning by his university training and his professorial Chair. His age is between forty and fifty. Fessler is just an ordinary nice-looking young doctor.*

*The room has two doors: one, in the middle of the wall behind the two men, opening on the corridor; the other, on their left, leading to an inner room. The window faces the inner door from the opposite side; and there is a window-seat before it. At right angles to this window-seat, further up the room, is a sofa. There are two tables: one a writing-table on the side near the window, at which the professor is sitting, and the other a round table on the side near the inner door. There is a chair at it with its back to the wall in which the entrance door is, and another, in which Dr Fessler is sitting, between it and the writing-table. The walls are crowded with book-shelves; and the writing-table is heaped with examination papers and manuscripts.*

LENKHEIM. Whats the matter? Going asleep at your age! You were not called up last night, were you?

FESSLER. No. But, by Jimminy, Lenkheim, I have gone through a lot this last week.

LENKHEIM. How?

FESSLER. Just consider. Imagine having to console Bruno's widow when I'm engaged to his daughter!

LENKHEIM. Why not?

FESSLER. Because theyre at daggers drawn. Every word that soothes old Agnes is an outrage to Edith.

LENKHEIM. Why? Whats wrong between them?

FESSLER. Oh, Mrs Haldenstedt is old-fashioned. She keeps up the convention that because Edith is a young unmarried woman she cant possibly understand about her father's death; and Edith has to pretend to be in the dark. But of course she knows as well as you or I; and it maddens her to have to hold her tongue and be treated like a child when all her feelings are boiling over about it. She was very fond of her father.

LENKHEIM. I knew the mother and daughter never got on very well together—jealousy, I suppose, as usual—but I thought this awful business would have brought them together.

FESSLER. Not a bit. It has set them more against one another than ever.

LENKHEIM. I suppose theyve no notion who the woman was?

FESSLER. None. She will never be found out unless she comes forward herself.

LENKHEIM. She wont do that. Why should she give herself away?

FESSLER. Women do, sometimes, God knows why! But meanwhile, poor Mrs Haldenstedt is most frightfully cut up. There she is, distracted by all sorts of surmises and suspicions, not knowing what to think, asking herself every minute whether he went on the loose and died in a vulgar street adventure, or whether there was somebody all along whom she never suspected, making her marriage a mockery. We are all as much in the dark as she is; for there never was a word against him: he seemed the correctest, most domesticated of men. That is, unless you know anything. You were so intimate with him, you know.

LENKHEIM. Was I really intimate with him? Certainly we were friends at college? and we kept it up afterwards. But he never told me much about himself.

FESSLER. He was not that sort of man. But he trusted nobody in the world as he trusted you: the widow is dead certain of that. By the way, she has asked me to prepare you for a visit she is going to pay you.

LENKHEIM. Why should you prepare me?

FESSLER. Well, she is going to ask you to act as his scientific and literary executor.

LENKHEIM [*pleasantly surprised and suddenly self-conscious*] Really! Of course I shall be delighted. I may tell you that in my own will I made him my literary executor. Who would have thought that he would peg out first?

FESSLER. But didnt you know that he was ill?

LENKHEIM. Oh, I knew about his heart and so forth. But many a patient with a heart disease lives to bury his doctor. As a matter of fact his case was not a very serious one. His heart would not have stood racing up two or three flights of stairs. But does any man of his age race upstairs? A very strong emotion or excitement might have killed him; but a settled married man with a wife and a grown-up daughter suffers more from too little excitement than from too

[ 748 ]

much. What emotions has a domesticated man of science to fear after forty?

FESSLER. Then why did he die?

LENKHEIM. Just so: why did he die? He wouldnt have died if he had been leading the quiet life we all gave him credit for. What sort of life did he really lead? That is the question.

FESSLER. Isnt it shocking that such a man should die under such—such—well, such shady circumstances?

LENKHEIM. Shady! I should call them disgraceful. Yes, my dear boy, we must face it: he came to a disgraceful end. An operatic tenor, or even a literary man, might be forgiven for dying in an adventure of that kind. But a man of science! Unfortunate, to say the least: most unfortunate.

FESSLER. At all events, since it was his luck to die in the dark, we are not called on to light the candle, are we?

LENKHEIM. We are not; but what about the police? And what about his wife?

FESSLER. They havnt the ghost of a clue.

LENKHEIM. It wont upset or delay your engagement, I hope. Not that I could blame you if you broke it off. Still—

FESSLER. *I* break it off! Good gracious, no!

LENKHEIM. I'm glad of that. Of course you must keep it up to Edith that there was nothing wrong.

FESSLER. But she wont have it that there was nothing wrong.

LENKHEIM. What!

FESSLER. You see, she adored her father. She sees him with a halo round his head; and nothing that he could do would be wrong for her. She has always felt that her mother could not live up to him; and she is persuading herself that this unknown woman was

[ 749 ]

some wonderful person who made him as happy as she thinks he deserved to be.

LENKHEIM. Thats funny. Very funny. Does she suspect anybody?

FESSLER. I dont know. I cant see through her; and the worst of it is, she can see through me. She will find out what I think.

LENKHEIM. Which is?

FESSLER. Well, just what you think. And when she finds out what that is, heaven help me!

LENKHEIM. She wont find out. All that a young girl sees in a death is the romance of it: the vulgar reality does not exist for her. What an eye-opener for us who know better! [*Sententiously*] And yet, whatever view we may take of the affair, we must admit that these moral problems are very difficult: in fact, insoluble. Is there any man who can say that he has never been in a position in which sudden death would have been extremely embarrassing?

FESSLER. I suppose not. [*Naïvely*] By the way, that reminds me that I forgot to ask how Mrs Lenkheim is.

LENKHEIM. Oh, Jitta is getting over it. She hopes to be able to get up for a couple of hours today. Just in a dressing-gown, you know, to sit about a bit.

FESSLER. Oh, good. Well, I must be off to the hospital. [*He rises*]. Tell her I asked after her.

LENKHEIM [*rising*] I will. How soon do you think I may expect the Haldenstedts?

FESSLER. Any time now, I should think. The old girl wont be easy until she has seen you.

*Lenkheim goes out for a moment through the inner door. Jitta comes in, languid, and dressed as Lenkheim has described.*

JITTA. Oh, so glad youve come, Doctor. [*She shakes hands with Fessler*]. Have you seen the Haldenstedts?

I was so sorry not to be able to call on them. I have been really too ill. I hope they know that.

FESSLER [*with affectionate deference*] They thoroughly understand that. You must take the greatest care of yourself.

JITTA. You are not running away, are you?

FESSLER. I must. I have to be at the hospital; and I am late already.

JITTA. Come again soon, Doctor.

FESSLER. I hope to find you quite well then, dear lady.

*He kisses her hand, and goes out. When he has gone, Lenkheim returns, full of excitement and curiosity.*

LENKHEIM. Jitta: old Agnes is coming to see us. Bruno has made me literary executor. That is what she is coming about.

JITTA. Has she recovered enough to bear discussing it with you?

LENKHEIM. She must. The world doesnt stand still when people die. I wonder what we shall find in his papers!

JITTA [*going white*] Has she found anything?

LENKHEIM. Yes: didnt I tell you? He has made me his scientific and literary executor.

JITTA. I mean about—about—

LENKHEIM. About his death? Absolutely nothing: Fessler has just told me so.

JITTA [*sitting down at the table, reassured*] Poor Fessler!

LENKHEIM [*resuming his seat at his writing-table*] Yes, poor chap: he is rather in a fright about Edith.

JITTA. Why?

LENKHEIM. He is afraid that her grief for her father will kill her feeling for him; so youd better take Edith in hand: you know how she clings to you. She is like her father in that: he clung to you.

[ 751 ]

JITTA. To me!

LENKHEIM. Yes: you know very well he did. If I had died you would have been up before this, I expect.

JITTA. Alfred: if you begin nagging I shall have to go back to bed.

LENKHEIM. Who's nagging? [*She rises. He jumps up apprehensively*] There now: for God's sake dont make a scene about nothing. All I meant was that if he ever told anything to anybody he would have told it to you. [*She sits down again*]. Jitta: have you really no suspicion?

JITTA. Of what?

LENKHEIM. Who the woman was.

JITTA. How could he tell anyone who she was? It would have been dishonorable to betray her.

LENKHEIM. Men do tell, all the same. They dont tell the newspapers; but they tell other women.

JITTA. I object to be classed with "other women."

LENKHEIM. Oh well, it's no use talking to you if you will be so touchy. I didnt suggest that he told you: you brought that in yourself. All that was in my mind was that as you were so much in and out of his house you must have met her one time or another if she was the wife of any of his friends. It usually is a friend's wife.

JITTA [*with affected listlessness*] Is it?

LENKHEIM. Well, it stands to reason, doesnt it? Unless it's a chance woman from the streets.

JITTA [*wincing*] I suppose so.

LENKHEIM. Did he never talk to you about love, or anything of that sort?

JITTA. The last time we were at the theatre he discussed the play with me. It was a play about love.

LENKHEIM. Well, what else would a play be about? Thats no clue. I wonder was she a patient of his?

JITTA. Does it matter? Need we gossip about it?

LENKHEIM [*impatiently*] Dont be so superior. I like gossip. Everybody likes gossip. You like it yourself as well as anybody. If she was a patient that would account for his being so reserved about her.

JITTA. Alfred: you are unbearable. I will go back to bed.

*She rises and makes for the door, but is checked by the entrance of Agnes Haldenstedt and her daughter, both in deep mourning. Agnes carries a small dispatch case. She is not really much older than Jitta; but she has retired so completely from the competition of women in attractiveness, and accepted so fully her lot as a good bourgeoise with a home to keep and a family to manage on a slender income that she is set down as much older and less distinguished socially. Her sense of duty has kept her upright; and her uprightness has given her a certain authority, as of a person of some consequence. She has been deeply wounded by the circumstances of her husband's death, and is stiff and suspicious in her manner.*

*Her daughter is young and ingenuous, with a strong character. A passion of grief for her father has set her on fire with pride and a sense of being ready for any sacrifice.*

*The conversation which ensues is solemn, artificial, and constrained. They condole with one another in low tones and unnaturally bookish sentences. Jitta has to draw the girl to her, and kiss her on the brow. Alfred leads Mrs Haldenstedt to the sofa. When she sits down, he sits on the window-seat near her. Jitta leads Edith to the chair she has just vacated, and goes to the sofa, where she seats herself on the widow's left.*

*All these movements are ridiculous; yet the mourning worn by the two visitors makes them seem, if not natural, at least becoming.*

LENKHEIM [*in hollow tones*] May I say again, dear Mrs Haldenstedt, how deeply I—

JITTA [*gushing*] At last, dearest Mrs Haldenstedt, I am able to tell you what I felt when I lay helpless, unable to pay the last respects to our dear lost friend. [*As she sits down, she seizes the hands of Mrs Haldenstedt, giving her no opportunity of refusing the attention*]. But in my sick room I was with you in spirit. Indeed I have never been closer to you and poor Edith than in that moment when I had to ask my husband to tell you what it cost me to stay away.

AGNES [*not at all disposed to allow Jitta so prominent a share in her grief, but conventionally resorting to her handkerchief*] Thank you. I'm sure it's very kind of you.

LENKHEIM [*clearing his throat and sniffing*] Under such a sudden blow, what can we say? We are all struck dumb. We all share your grief.

AGNES. When people are sick, and we can sacrifice ourselves completely to the duty of nursing them: when they can lean on us to the very last, then, when the parting comes, there is some consolation in the thought that we have done all in our power. But an end like this, so sudden, so dreadful—[*she breaks down*].

LENKHEIM [*making the best of it*] Still, I am not sure that a lingering death really spares the feelings of the survivors. Death often tortures its victims before it strikes the final blow. In your case, dear Mrs Haldenstedt, there was at least no torture.

AGNES [*staring at him*] No torture! What has the future for me but the torture of a widow's grief?

EDITH [*unsympathetic*] It has the honor of father's name. Is that nothing?

LENKHEIM [*effusively*] Which I will help you both to uphold, my dear Edith, believe me.

AGNES. He knew he could depend on you. I have a packet of papers marked "Professor Lenkheim's property: to be given into his own hands": That is why I have come today instead of waiting for Mrs Lenkheim to call.

LENKHEIM. Dear fellow: how conscientious of him! such papers as he had of mine were of no consequence. Shall we have a little quiet talk all to ourselves, in here? [*He rises and crosses the room, inviting her, by a gesture, to come with him through the door opposite the window*].

AGNES [*pausing between Jitta and Edith*] I wanted to come alone; but Edith insisted on coming with me.

LENKHEIM. She was quite right. She is now your only support.

EDITH [*proudly*] Thank you, Professor. I wish you could persuade my mother that I could do much more for her if she would tell me all her troubles. I am no longer a child. There is nothing now that cannot be spoken of quite frankly before me.

AGNES [*with a weary smile*] Of course not, dear. But there are things it is better not to know. I know them; and I only wish I could change places with you.

*Emphasizing this with an emphatic nod at Edith, she goes into the next room. Lenkheim follows her.*

JITTA [*throwing off her false manner, whilst retaining the patronizing suavity of an older woman to a younger one, holds out her hands to Edith with genuine sympathy*] Come, darling. [*Edith comes to her and takes her hands*]. Sit here, close to me. [*She makes room for her on the sofa beside her. Edith sits down on her left, and looks gratefully and longingly into her eyes*]. Do you remember when we were last here together? Your father brought you. He was radiant with joy and pride in you. We were all so happy.

EDITH [*thoughtfully*] How long was that ago?

JITTA. Barely three weeks.

EDITH. It seems an age. I was a child then. I can hardly remember how I felt. It is as if I had been asleep.

JITTA. Your father's death has awakened you: you are looking at life for the first time.

EDITH. I have been looking at death for the first time.

JITTA. My poor child! But dont lose courage. Life lies before you: it will make up to you for many sorrows. You will get over it, Edith.

EDITH. Why should I get over it? I dont want to get over it. Do you suppose I feel disgraced?

JITTA. Oh no, no: of course not. But such a grief as this always makes us feel that we have come to the end of everything: that nothing can ever be the same again. Yet next day we find ourselves at the beginning of everything instead.

EDITH [*impatient*] You need not speak to me like that. You know very well that what is the matter is not merely the loss of a father: a thing that happens to everybody sooner or later.

JITTA [*taken aback*] Edith, dear—

EDITH [*downright and indignant*] Why do you treat me as if I were a little girl, as my mother does? I did not expect it from you. Oh, I am so tired of all this humbug. I turned to you because I hoped you would understand me, and let me open my heart to you like a friend.

JITTA. My dear: I will be an elder sister to you—

EDITH [*fiercely*] I said a friend.

JITTA [*surrendering*] Oh, you are terrible. I will be everything you want, if I can. But why are you angry with me? I really meant what I said. Life has a great deal to offer you: dont forget that you are going to be married. I believe you can trust your man. He adored your father. He will regard you as a sacred legacy.

EDITH. Thats curious. He used that word himself the day we buried poor papa. But I dont intend to be taken as a legacy, sacred or not.

JITTA. Edith: he feels your loss as deeply as you do yourself. Some of us perhaps feel it more deeply, because we have more experience of men, and know how much better what he was than you are yet old enough to know.

EDITH [*rising and pacing restlessly across the room*] Oh, these commonplaces! How you keep throwing them at me! None of us know what my father was: he was thrown away among us. [*Turning on Jitta*] Why did he not die with us? Why had he no last word for us? I was nothing to him: none of us were anything to him.

JITTA. You know, dear, that you are unjust to him when you say so.

EDITH. Unjust! unjust! what has that to do with it? Why did he not come to us for help, for nursing, for care?

JITTA. He was too considerate to let you know how ill he was.

EDITH. He told everyone else. We were left in the dark.

JITTA. No, no. No one knew it except himself.

EDITH [*passionately*] My mother wont speak to me about it; but I know very well what she is thinking. They whisper all day at home. I see it in the eyes of the visitors; and it makes me furious. I never want to see anyone cry again as my mother cried that night when they brought him home. It wasnt only grief: there was a bitterness in her that had nothing to do with grief or love. I have often felt in my soul that papa never found in his home what he needed and longed for. There were moments when I somehow got beyond myself and became another person; perhaps the woman I am growing into; and he was so responsive to that flash of something different in me, so grateful for it, that I saw quite plainly how he was longing for something else, something more, than we were giving him. We were not good enough for him. [*She throws herself into the chair beside the round table, sobbing*].

JITTA [*rising and going to her*] Dearest: dont cry like that.

EDITH. It nearly killed me to see him sitting there, as he often did, staring right through me without seeing me, and sighing as he drew his hand across his eyes and through his hair.

JITTA. Dear child: you must not worry yourself because he sometimes looked straight at you and did not see you. Just think. He was a doctor: he knew his danger better than anyone. When a man finds himself condemned to death, his thoughts and feelings must be overwhelming. Well, if you were looking at the sea in a storm or at the heavens opening above it, would you see a tiny figure on the shore, even if it were your own child?

EDITH [*rising in a girlish rapture*] Thank you for that: it is beautiful, and quite true. [*She closes her eyes, silent for a moment, and a little breathless. Jitta smiles, and sits down in the writing-table chair*]. And now, wont you help me to find out the secret of his death?

JITTA. What secret?

EDITH. Who is the woman in whose arms my father died?

JITTA [*startled*] So that is what you think! Poor child!

EDITH [*angry*] I do not think it: I know it. You know it. Please let us have no more of the poor child business: it does not impose on me. How am I to find her?

JITTA [*remonstrating*] Edith, Edith, what could you say to her, even if you found her?

EDITH. Only that I love her.

JITTA. Love her! What for?

EDITH. For making my father happy. [*Restless again, pacing up and down*]. Oh, if you knew how infamously all those people who call on us misunderstand him. They insult my mother by condoling with her on her husband's unfaithfulness. They insult God by declaring that my father threw himself into the gutter, and was justly punished for it.

JITTA [*springing up*] What! They dare say such brutal things!

EDITH. Oh, not in those words: they are too polite to speak as horribly as they think; but I know. And my mother encourages them. She actually likes to feel that some unheard-of disgrace has fallen on her. She thinks it makes her interesting and revenges her. She positively wallows in it.

JITTA [*shocked*] Edith!

EDITH. Oh, it is the right word for it: why should I not use it? She never thinks of his sorrows: only of her own.

JITTA [*taking her arm persuasively*] My dear: you mustnt go on like this. Come: let me talk to you quietly. [*She draws her back to the sofa, and makes her sit down again*]. If you loved your mother as you loved your father, you would be kinder to her. You think of him as a man whose wife has failed him. Dont forget that she is a woman whose husband failed her.

EDITH. How did he fail her? If she had been worthy of him—

JITTA. Yes, yes, dear; but she was not worthy of him. Or stop: no: we have no right to say that.

EDITH. We have a right to say that she was not the right woman for him.

JITTA. Yes; but dont forget that that means that he was not the right man for her. He was her superior if you like; but that only made it worse for her. His superiority must often have wounded her self-respect; and as any weakness of his flattered it, she perhaps likes to think that he was not quite perfect, and even that he treated her badly.

EDITH. You think that an excuse for her! I call it abominable.

JITTA. Dont be impossible, dear. Abominable or not, it explains her readiness to believe the worst. You must not blame her because your faith in him is greater, and your consolation nobler. Remember: he did not betray you as he betrayed her. For he did betray her; and so did that woman. Tell yourself that, Edith, whenever you feel tempted to hate your mother. Promise me you will.

EDITH. I will never tell myself such a silly lie. I will take my father's memory and good name out of my mother's hands, and out of the hands of her tittle-tattling friends. I will make the world see him as he was, and as I loved him, not as she sees him, and as she hates him.

JITTA. The world will see him with its own eyes, dear, not with yours. All you can do is to save his memory from being blackened by that odious thing, a family quarrel. Come! promise me to stop worrying about your mother?

EDITH. I am not worrying about her: I am worrying about the woman my father loved. I cannot help it: she is always in my mind. Why was she not with him when they found him? Why did she run away like a criminal?

JITTA. Perhaps she is asking herself those questions every day in her shame and misery. Oh, Edith, we dont know what meannesses we are capable of until we are tried. The dread of a public scandal—of having to face a policeman prying into the most sacred and secret places in her soul—will drive a woman to anything. Remember: she had not only to save herself from the scandal, but his memory as well.

EDITH. No, no, no. She did not save him. She left him under the stigma of having died in the arms of some vile creature. I know in my soul that she was not that. The world would forgive him if it knew that she is what I know she must be if he loved her. Oh, why does she not defy all the silly world for his sake, and say "It was I."

JITTA. You ask too much from her. She may have been capable of great things when he was alive and at her side. What is the poor wretch now but a broken-hearted lonely coward?

EDITH. She is not broken-hearted: my father never broke any woman's heart. I loved him; and that makes even his death a glory to me. If she is lonely why does she not come to me? She shall come to me. We shall cure one another's loneliness, we two. Where is she to cry her heart out if not in my arms?

JITTA. No: she slunk away into the darkness. Let her be. She can bleed to death in her hiding-place.

EDITH. She shall not: she will be drawn to me: you will see. Remember that I have no longer any place at home. I cannot live with people who cannot feel about my father as I do; and there is only one such person in the world.

JITTA. That woman?

EDITH. Yes. I will give her every right over me that the woman who returned my father's love should have over his daughter: the right I deny to my mother. I swear it.

JITTA. How serious you are, Edith! But what will your mother say, and the man you are engaged to?

EDITH. My mother would never understand: I take nothing from her that she is capable of missing. As to the man who says he loves me, and asks me to share my whole life with him, if he cannot understand me and support me in this he will never have me for a wife. I can do without any man if I can find the woman to whom I am bound for ever and ever. You will help me to find her, will you not?

JITTA [*deeply moved, drawing Edith to her*] Oh, darling, darling, if only I could! If only I dared!

*Lenkheim throws the door open: he is returning with Agnes. Jitta and Edith move asunder and rise hastily. Agnes comes in, drying her eyes with her handkerchief. Lenkheim follows her solemnly with her dispatch case in his hand.*

EDITH [*stamping*] Oh, bother! Always at the wrong moment. Always spoiling everything. [*She turns impatiently to the window, and stands with her back to them, fuming*].

AGNES [*to Alfred*] Thank God I found strength for this. It is a great relief to me. But I am dead tired: I must go home. [*To Edith*] Come, child.

JITTA. Wont you sit down and rest for a moment?

AGNES. Thank you; but I shall be better at home. And I have so many accounts to settle.

LENKHEIM. Ah, yes, yes: of course you have. Well, if you must go, you must. And you may depend on me not to keep you waiting too long before I go to work on the scientific papers.

JITTA. I hope to be allowed to go out again in a day or two. May I come to see you if the doctor says I may?

AGNES. Do, of course. I shall expect you. [*To Lenkheim*] You will forgive me, wont you, all the trouble I am giving you? It has done me so much good to unburden myself to a real friend.

LENKHEIM. You have had a cruel experience, dear Mrs Haldenstedt; but we must all resign ourselves to our trials.

AGNES. Yes: I suppose that is a great consolation.

EDITH. My consolation is that nobody dares console me.

ALFRED [*pompously*] Proud words; and how true! how true! [*Unctuously, as he shakes her hand*] Goodbye, dear lady, good-bye.

AGNES. Goodbye. [*To Edith, laughing a little maliciously*] Since you are so strong, child, just give me your arm.

JITTA [*shaking hands*] Goodbye.

*Edith goes out with her mother leaning heavily on her. Jitta goes out with them.*

LENKHEIM [*relieved at being rid of the widow*] Ouf! [*He carries the dispatch case to his writing-table, and sits down to examine its contents. He is in no hurry. It contains nothing but the manuscript of a biggish book. He leans lazily back with his legs stretched, and turns over the cover without looking at it. He reads a bit, and makes a wry face. He disagrees intensely and contemptuously with every passage he reads, abandoning each with sniffs and pishes, only to be still more disgusted with the next.*

*Jitta returns; sees what he is doing; and halts between him and the round table, silently watching him.*

*Finally he gives the book up as hopeless; shuts up the pages; and stares at the mass of manuscript as if wondering what he is to do with such trash. Suddenly his expression changes. His eyes bulge in amazement.*

ALFRED [*after a stifled exclamation*] Jitta! Jitta! [*He turns, half rising, and sees her*]. Oh, youre there.

JITTA. What is the matter? [*knowing only too well, and very angry at his contemptuous air, but pretending to be listless and languid*].

LENKHEIM [*shewing her the manuscript*] Look at this!

JITTA. Well?

LENKHEIM. Look at the title.

JITTA [*reading*] "Fetters of the Feminine Psyche." Is that the book you worked on with him?

LENKHEIM. I! Certainly not: he wrote it all himself: I only gave him his facts. Read the next line.

JITTA [*reading*] "By Alfred Lenkheim." I suppose he meant you to finish it.

LENKHEIM [*turning over to the end*] But it is finished. Look. Was he mad? Did he suppose I would condescend to put my name to another man's work? I have some reputation of my own to fall back on, thank God. There is something behind this.

JITTA. I suppose he wished to leave you something valuable as a keepsake. You were his friend.

LENKHEIM [*scornfully*] A keepsake! Dont talk nonsense, Jitta: a man does not give away his biggest work as if it were his diamond pin, unless he is afraid to put his own name to it. But if he thinks he is going to put mine to his trash he is greatly mistaken.

JITTA [*boiling with rage, pointing to the manuscript*] He has sacrificed his immortality for your benefit.

LENKHEIM [*angrily*] Rot. Why should he? Nobody who can create sacrifices his creation. [*He throws the manuscript on the table.*] Not that he ever pretended to think much of the book.

[ 764 ]

JITTA [*indignantly*] He thought the world of it. It was his greatest pride.

LENKHEIM [*turning on her, a suspicion flashing on him*] How do you know?

JITTA [*checking herself, feeling that her temper has betrayed her*] He often spoke to me about this book, and about the hopes he had built on it.

LENKHEIM. To you! What do you know about psychiatry? Why should he sacrifice his reputation to add to mine? quite unnecessarily.

JITTA. The whim of an invalid, I suppose.

LENKHEIM [*out of patience*] Whim! He throws away his one chance of notoriety; and you call that a whim. Do you take me for a fool?

JITTA. Dont shout, Alfred, please.

ALFRED [*subsiding a little*] I'm not shouting: I'm asking you to talk sense. You say he spoke to you about this. What did he tell you?

JITTA. Of course I knew too little of the work you and he were doing together to be able to help or understand much. [*Decisively*] But in any case you must carry out his wishes.

LENKHEIM. What wishes?

JITTA. You must accept what he has left you.

LENKHEIM. Why must I?

JITTA. It was his last wish: we have no choice.

LENKHEIM. We! Me, you mean. What have you to do with it?

JITTA. Well, you if you like.

LENKHEIM. It's not me youre thinking of. Funny, the way women run after a dead man if only he dies romantically! Anyhow this thing is impossible. I wont do it.

JITTA. Why?

LENKHEIM. Because it would be nothing short of

swindling the scientific world to pass off his stuff on it as mine: thats why. And now, what the deuce am I to say to old Agnes? [*Grumbling*] Such an unreasonable thing to ask me to do! Such an ungrateful thing!

JITTA. Was it ungrateful to give you the whole credit when you were only his collaborator?

LENKHEIM. Collaborator! What are you talking about? He knew as well as I did that I was only waiting for the publication of his idiotic theory to tear it to pieces. You dont suppose I believe in it, do you?

JITTA. Then perhaps that was what he wanted to prevent.

LENKHEIM. Jitta: you are simply drivelling. Bruno was too jolly conceited to be afraid of me. Dont be childish.

JITTA [*irritably*] I am like yourself: I am only trying to guess why he did it.

LENKHEIM. Just so. Why did he do it? Where is the sense in it? I believe you know, Jitta.

JITTA. Really, Alfred—! I must go back to bed.

LENKHEIM. You havnt been up an hour.

JITTA. But I am dead tired.

LENKHEIM. You cant be as tired as all that. What do you want to run away for?

JITTA. Have you forgotten that I am ill? I can hardly stand. I must lie down.

ALFRED. Well, lie on the sofa.

JITTA. Dont be brutal, Alfred.

LENKHEIM. Bosh! You are hiding something from me: I havnt experimented with psycho-analysis for nothing. I notice that this crazy thing that bothers me doesnt bother you. You understand it: you couldnt take it so quietly if you didnt.

JITTA. I take it without shouting, if that is what you mean.

LENKHEIM. What did he say to you about the book and about his hopes? Why did you never say a word about them to me?

JITTA. I never thought about it.

LENKHEIM. If you had never thought about it you would have talked to me about it.

JITTA. I suppose I did not think it worth mentioning.

LENKHEIM. Psha! Would a man who told you all that not tell you plenty of other things? That love affair, now—?

JITTA [*shrinking*] Oh, Alfred!

LENKHEIM. Oh stuff! Who was the woman? You know all about her: I can see it in your eyes. [*He takes her by the shoulders and turns her face to face*]. Aha! You know who she was. You know all about it.

JITTA [*rising indignantly and letting herself go*] You are mad, and grossly rude.

LENKHEIM [*rising also*] I have had enough of being humbugged. Who was she?

JITTA [*closes her lips obstinately*]!

LENKHEIM. Was he so much to you that you will not give the other woman away, even to me, your husband? Were those his orders?

JITTA [*exhausted*] I have no orders. I go my own way [*she attempts to leave the room*].

LENKHEIM [*intercepting her*] You shant run away. If you dont tell me who she is, I will—I will—[*he makes a threatening gesture, not very convincingly*].

JITTA. Take care, Alfred. Your cunning is only a fool's cunning after all. The answer to your question is staring you in the face. Thank your stars you are too stupid to see it.

LENKHEIM. Am I? We shall see. Before you leave this room I will find out the part you have played in this dirty business.

[ 767 ]

JITTA [*starting as from the lash of a whip*] Dirty! Oh, never was anything purer, holier, nobler.

LENKHEIM [*screaming*] Ah! It was you! There was no other woman: it was you, you. He bought you from me, for that [*he bangs his fist on the manuscript*]. The damned thief! [*He collapses into his chair at the table, clasping his head in his hands*].

JITTA [*sitting down wearily on the sofa*] Leave the dead in peace. If you cannot hold your tongue, abuse me. I am alive, and can feel it.

LENKHEIM [*miserably*] You dont even deny it!

JITTA. No. Are you surprised? You lost me long ago.

LENKHEIM. My fault, of course. You worthless devil: what do you expect me to think of you?

JITTA. You can think what you like, Alfred. I dont grudge you that melancholy satisfaction.

LENKHEIM. Have you no conscience, no shame?

JITTA. Do you want me to make a scene for you, Alfred? I am sorry: I am too tired.

LENKHEIM. If I had him here—

JITTA. Threaten him to your heart's content. He is dead.

ALFRED. Yes; but I am very much alive. Dont forget that.

JITTA. Not so very much alive, Alfred.

ALFRED. Yah [*gnashes his teeth with rage*]!

JITTA. However, what I enjoyed I shall have to pay for. I know that.

LENKHEIM. You and he were lovers?

JITTA [*proudly*] Yes: you have found the right word at last. Lovers.

LENKHEIM [*whining pitiably*] And you could live in the house with me, and take my care and my nursing and my money, and even—[*He looks at her and chokes*]. How long has this affair been going on?

JITTA. Our love has lasted three years.

LENKHEIM. Love! Love in the sort of house he was found dead in!

JITTA. Love wherever we were. And wherever we were was paradise. Does that give you any idea of his greatness?

LENKHEIM. Of your meanness, more likely. Dont try to stuff me with big words: they only shew that you wont confess your caddishness even to yourself.

JITTA [*rising*] Oh, please! I cut a pretty contemptible figure—

LENKHEIM. [*triumphing*] You do. You do.

JITTA [*continuing*]—beside him.

LENKHEIM [*rising, goaded beyond endurance: threatening her*] You take care, do you hear?

JITTA [*wringing her hands*] My place was at his side. They should have had to tear me away from him by force. Yes; and I will tell you something more. The last beat of his heart would have broken mine if I had been any good. But I am no good; and here I am, as you see me. Oh, you are quite right. I have no right to be in any decent house [*she turns to the door*].

LENKHEIM. Stop: where are you going?

JITTA. I dont know. Into the streets, I suppose.

LENKHEIM. Oh, damn your heroics! You shant leave this room until you have told me everything.

JITTA [*bitterly*] Dont you know enough already?

LENKHEIM [*pointing to the manuscript*] What does that title-page mean?

JITTA. You know. You have said what it means.

LENKHEIM. I want to know what he said.

JITTA. That you are to be the father to his orphaned book. That the fame it will bring you will make amends to you—for me.

[ 769 ]

LENKHEIM. The blackguard! Not content with stealing you from me, he must dictate the rest of my life to me, as if I were a child.

JITTA. Yes: compared to him you are a child. He has provided for you.

LENKHEIM. Ha! And were you equally kind and thoughtful for his wife, eh?

JITTA [*earnestly*] Alfred: it was too strong for us.

LENKHEIM. What was too strong for you?

JITTA. Love. You dont understand love. Have you anything else to say to me?

LENKHEIM. No. [*He turns his back on her, and goes sulkily to the window*].

JITTA. Goodbye. [*She tries to go, but suddenly becomes weak, and reels against the head of the sofa*]. Alfred.

LENKHEIM. Whats the matter? [*He runs to her; and gets her safely seated*].

JITTA. Dont mind, Alfred. I shall be better soon: it is passing.

LENKHEIM [*turning brusquely from her like an angry child*] I am not sympathizing with you. It serves you right. [*He sits down at the round table, with his elbows on it, muttering and sulking*]. Treated me disgracefully. Disgracefully.

JITTA [*sighs wearily*]!!

LENKHEIM [*unaggressively*] Jitta?

*Her name and the change in his tone give her a shock. She turns and looks searchingly at him.*

LENKHEIM [*recovering his self-control by a rather broken effort*] This is no use. I have come to my senses. I—I will take it quietly and reasonably.

JITTA. I am glad you can: I wish I could.

LENKHEIM [*shaking his head*] But we cant leave it like this, can we?

JITTA. What can we do, Alfred?

LENKHEIM. You have done me harm enough. Do you want to ruin me as well?

JITTA. It is I who am ruined, as you call it, is it not? The sin is mine: I will pay the penalty by myself. Your life is only beginning: with that book you have a future. I have only a past. I will take it and myself out of your life. [*She rises*].

LENKHEIM [*out of patience, jumping up*] Look here: since you wont talk sense and be commonly civil to me, I'm going to assert myself. You cant settle an affair like this by looking like a martyr and walking out into the street. You must learn to consider other people a little. If you have no regard for me, at least remember that Agnes and Edith have a future, and have a right not to have it spoiled. For their sake I am prepared to endure your presence in my house.

JITTA [*with faint surprise and some irony*] You can bring yourself to that? You can still bear to look at me?

LENKHEIM. Make no mistake: all is over between you and me. For ever. I mean it.

JITTA. So do I.

LENKHEIM. Very well: be it so. But that does not mean that we need separate. People can live miles apart under the same roof. That is how you will have to live with me. If you have a spark of decent feeling left, you will not force a public scandal on me.

JITTA. Does it matter?

LENKHEIM. Does it matter! Are you utterly selfish? Dont you understand that if this miserable break-up of our marriage becomes known it will break up that poor woman's widowhood as well?

JITTA. Does she matter so much?

LENKHEIM [*playing his ace*] Well, what about Edith? Doesnt she matter? Do you suppose Fessler can afford to marry her if you drag her family through the mud?

JITTA [*staggered*] Oh! I was not thinking, Alfred. Give me until tomorrow to think it over. I can bear no more today. I can hardly stand.

LENKHEIM. You can stand as well as I can. [*She immediately sits down obstinately at the writing-table*]. Very well; but stand or sit, you dont leave this room until you give me your word to stay.

JITTA. With you?

LENKHEIM. Yes, with me. It is I who will have to pay the house-keeping bills. But dont be afraid: I am done with you, except before company. Not one word will I ever speak to you again when we are alone together.

JITTA. Oh, Alfred, you will tell me so ten times a day. Dont let us talk nonsense.

LENKHEIM. You will see. Not one word. Not a sound. I tell you I am done with you; and I wish I had never met you.

JITTA. It sounds too good to be true, Alfred.

LENKHEIM. Psha!

JITTA. But that part of it rests with yourself. [*Determinedly*] And now for my conditions.

LENKHEIM. Your conditions! Yours!!! You dare talk to me of conditions!

JITTA. You are in my hands, Alfred; and you know it. I can give the whole scandal away if you defy me. I will not be unkind; but if I am to keep up appearances, you must keep them up too. If I am to pretend to be a good woman, you must pretend to be a great man.

LENKHEIM. Pretend!

JITTA. Oh, be a great man by all means, Alfred, if you can. But you must pretend in any case.

LENKHEIM. How?

[ 772 ]

JITTA. You will pretend to be the author of that great book. That will be your share of the sham of our life together.

LENKHEIM. But I tell you I dont believe a word of the silly thing.

JITTA. Of course not. If you had the genius to believe it, you would have had the genius to write it.

LENKHEIM [*goaded*] I—

JITTA [*continuing calmly*] You cannot believe it, just as I cannot believe that you will never speak to me again;—

LENKHEIM. I never will.

JITTA [*still ignoring his protests*] —but you will come to believe every word of the silly thing, as you call it, when it makes Lenkheim as famous as Einstein.

LENKHEIM [*startled by the name*] Einstein! You are tempting me, you devil.

JITTA. You envied Einstein, Alfred. Well, all that you envied him for is within your reach. Stretch out your hand, and take it.

LENKHEIM. And you envied Einstein's wife, did you? I see. Why could not your stupid husband give you a triumphant tour through Europe? Why should you not shake hands with all the kings, and dine with all the presidents, and have gala nights at the Opera? To get all that you will be my accomplice in a fraud, eh? Since you cannot have a good time with him you will have one with me.

JITTA [*round-eyed for a moment at this new light on her conduct*] How clever of you, Alfred! You have found a reason you can really believe in. I should never have thought of it; but you are welcome to it if only you will father his book.

LENKHEIM [*desperately perplexed: yielding*] But, Jitta: I dont really believe that. It's not like you: you are not

[ 773 ]

clever enough, not ambitious enough. What is your real reason?

JITTA [*decisively*] He wished it: that is enough for me. He knew better than either of us what is best for us.

LENKHEIM. Did he indeed, confound him!

JITTA. He did indeed, Alfred; and I forbid you to confound him.

LENKHEIM. Well, if I do—and mind: I dont say I will—I—

JITTA. Yes?

LENKHEIM. I will think it over.

JITTA. Just so, Alfred. Goodnight. [*She goes out, tranquilly convinced that she will have her own way*].

LENKHEIM [*rushing to the door in a last effort to assert himself, and shouting after her*] If you think— [*He peters out; thrusts his hands desperately into his pockets like a cleaned-out gambler; trots back irresolutely to his writing-table; takes up the MS.; stares at it for a moment; and reads slowly*] "By Professor Alfred Lenkheim, Doctor of Philosophy in the University of Vienna." Well, I'm dashed!

# ⌈ACT III⌉

---

*Mrs Haldenstedt is in her sitting-room with Alfred and Fessler, all three very busy going through the papers of her late husband. She is feverishly reading letters, and tearing them up and throwing them into the waste-paper basket as they prove one after another to be of no interest. Her sighs and exclamations of disappointment and impatience are getting on the nerves of Alfred, who is trying to read a manuscript. He flinches at the sharp sounds made by her violent tearing of letters. Fessler, who is sorting some papers which he has already gone through, is sympathetic, and looks pityingly at the widow from time to time.*

*The room is lighted by a large bay window, with a window-seat under it. The table heaped with papers is in this bay; and Mrs Haldenstedt sits at the head of it with her back to the light, and Alfred and Fessler at the sides of it to her right and left respectively. The corner of the room behind them on their right is cut off by a double door leading to the study. Another door leading to the corridor of the flat is in the diagonally opposite corner, and is consequently before them on their left. On their right between the window and the study door, a console stands against the wall, with flowers on it, and above it a convex mirror. On the same side of the room, a couch.*

---

LENKHEIM [*unable to bear the noise any longer*] Do you mind my taking these manuscripts into the study and examining them there? They require a certain degree of quiet concentration.

AGNES. I am so sorry. Bruno always said that it was like trying to work in a shooting gallery when I cleared up his papers and tore up useless letters. But if you dont tear them what is there to prevent the servants and everyone else from reading them?

ALFRED. Just so. But why not leave the work to us? Why worry? Cant you trust us?

AGNES. Oh, Professor, how can you ask me that? Of course I can trust you.

LENKHEIM [*nodding*] Good. Then do trust us. [*He goes into the study, and shuts the door behind him*].

AGNES [*alone with Fessler, letting herself droop*] I have gone through this last batch of letters three times over in the hope of finding some clue. But it's no use: theres nothing.

FESSLER. You mustnt worry.

AGNES [*sitting up sharply*] Have you ever lost anyone you really cared for?

FESSLER. Well, my poor dear father—

AGNES. I'm not talking about poor dear fathers or poor dear anybodies. Bruno was none of your poor dears: he was three quarters of my life, even if half of it was being his slave and his household drudge. All the same, I cant spend my whole life doing nothing but grieving, can I?

FESSLER. Just so. Of course not.

AGNES. Life goes on, doesnt it? Housekeeping goes on: the future has to be thought for as well as the past. All my business and responsibilities and duties go on just as if nothing had happened.

FESSLER. I'm so glad you have recovered enough to be able to look at it in that way.

AGNES. Doctor Fessler: a widow is not an invalid; and

it doesnt help her to be treated as one when the first shock is over.

FESSLER. Quite so. Quite so.

AGNES. I am going to talk to you very seriously.

FESSLER. Of course. Of course.

AGNES. And you are going to talk to me seriously, I hope.

FESSLER [*surprised*] But certainly, my dear Mrs Haldenstedt.

AGNES. Yes; but that doesnt mean saying "Certainly" and "Of course" and "Quite so: quite so" to everything I say, as if you were soothing a baby.

FESSLER [*protesting*] But I assure you I—

AGNES [*gripping his hand on the table*] Tell me the honest truth. Did you consider Bruno a clever man?

FESSLER [*amazed*] Mrs Haldenstedt!!!

AGNES. Do you think he had anything to say more than any of the rest of the professors? [*Stopping him as he opens his mouth for a fresh protest*] Now if you dont, please dont begin to excuse yourself and spare my feelings. Ive had enough of having my feelings spared: I want the truth.

FESSLER [*whole-heartedly*] My dear Mrs Haldenstedt: he was a great man. His psychological doctrine was a revelation. It was the beginning of a new epoch in science.

AGNES. So I have always understood I know he thought so himself.

FESSLER [*indignant*] Oh no: he was the most modest of men. I am sure he never said so.

AGNES. Do you think a man's wife knows nothing about his thoughts except what he tells?

FESSLER. I am quite sure he did not know half his own greatness.

AGNES. Then will you tell me what has become of it

all? You and Professor Lenkheim have gone through his papers with me. Have we come across one word that could not have been written by an elementary schoolmaster?

FESSLER [*shaken a little*] Well, everything he wrote, even about trifles, has his peculiar touch.

AGNES. Everything he wrote is in his own handwriting, of course, if you mean that. But can you pick out from all that heap one single bit of paper which you could shew to a stranger and expect him to say "The man that wrote this must have been as great as Einstein"?

FESSLER. Well, not exactly Einstein, perhaps. But— [*he stops*].

AGNES. But what? Suppose he had left you a safe full of diamonds, and when you opened the safe it was empty!

FESSLER. Oh, you exaggerate!

AGNES [*rising, out of patience*] Doctor Fessler: if you can take neither me nor my husband's affairs seriously, I think you had better leave both alone.

FESSLER [*rising, greatly surprised*] Have I offended you?

AGNES [*disarmed by his naïve sincerity*] No, no. Never mind. Never mind. You are too young. You are not used to women. [*Sitting down again*] Sit down, wont you? I will talk to Professor Lenkheim about it. He will understand.

FESSLER [*standing stiffly, being now really offended*] By all means, Mrs Haldenstedt, though I really do not see what he can say more than I can.

AGNES. There! You are offended. But if you had been neglected as I have been for months past, while my husband spent hours and hours and hours in his study, writing, writing, writing, using up paper until it cost as much as the butter and eggs, you would want to know what had become of it all.

FESSLER [*sitting down again with a gesture of apology*] True. I should have thought of that.

AGNES. I never complained, because I thought it was a book that would make him famous and bring him in money. Well, is that heap of old letters and bills and prescriptions all that came of it? Dont tell me: there is a book somewhere; and I want to know where it is. Did he go mad and destroy it? If not, who took it from him? Did that woman?

FESSLER. Good gracious, Mrs Haldenstedt!

AGNES. Oh, this dreadful ending to all our happiness! It spoils everything that was nice in our lives. When the first and best of it was over and we settled down, troubles came I know; but I had my memories, and could sit and think of them. Now they are all poisoned for me.

FESSLER [*reflectively*] Dear Mrs Haldenstedt: may I speak quite frankly to you?

AGNES. Why, I am begging and praying you to. But I can get nothing out of you but sympathy, as if you were only a visitor instead of going to marry my daughter.

FESSLER. You see, though your husband will be remembered as a great psychologist, he had to practise as a doctor to make a living. Well, the wickedest and worst people have to call in doctors just as often as respectable people; and a doctor cant have them coming to his own house where his wife and daughter are. He has to keep a consulting room somewhere where they can come. The landlady said he rented the room to see his friends in occasionally. I daresay the women he saw there were common women; but how do you know that they were not his patients?

AGNES. Dont deceive yourself; and dont try to deceive

me. Whatever I may have said when I was upset, I knew very well all along that Bruno never went with common women from the streets. The landlady said it was always the same woman, and that she was a lady. When she ran away she took that book with her: you mark my words. [*She rises and goes moodily to the console*].

*They are interrupted by Lenkheim, who opens the door of the study and trots in flourishing a manuscript.*

LENKHEIM. See here!

AGNES. The book!

LENKHEIM. I have just found an unfinished lecture on varieties of sleep.

AGNES [*disappointed*] Only a lecture! [*Taking the manuscript*] Why, it's only six pages. And what can it mean? There is only one sort of sleep.

LENKHEIM. Not at all. He says that hardly any two people sleep in the same way. Every case is an individual one. You must read it, Fessler.

FESSLER [*eagerly*] How interesting! May I look? [*Taking it from Mrs Haldenstedt*] Thank you. I'll read it in the study. [*To Alfred*] Mrs Haldenstedt wants to speak to you. [*He hurries into the study*].

AGNES [*shaking her head*] You see, Professor, it doesnt account for anything.

LENKHEIM. What doesnt?

AGNES. The lecture about sleep. He could have written it in one evening. Thats not the book that he said might be my best insurance policy. It was part of his provision for me. He would never have given it to another woman. If she has it, she stole it. [*She sits down on the couch*].

LENKHEIM. You are still worrying about that woman. I shouldnt if I were you. [*He takes his former chair, drawing it from the table to the couch*].

AGNES. I shall worry about her until I find out who she is. And I will find her out some day.

LENKHEIM. If it is any comfort to you, you may take my word for it that with all his professional engagements it was utterly impossible for him to have given much of his time to any woman.

AGNES. What comfort is there in that? One hour is enough for a man. Then he can sit alone at his desk, thinking he is writing some great scientific work, when all the time he is thinking of her, living the hour over again, and looking forward to the next one, right in his wife's face.

LENKHEIM [*very uncomfortable*] Mrs Haldenstedt: do you suspect anybody?

AGNES. I cant see anything clearly. I thought I knew everybody that it could possibly be; but there's nobody. All I know is what he liked and what he wanted, and how easily he could get it by lifting up his little finger. Oh, I know exactly how he deceived us.

LENKHEIM [*rising, startled*] Us!

AGNES. Well, me and Edith, of course.

LENKHEIM [*sitting down, relieved*] Oh! Just so.

AGNES. She wasnt what you think she was, Professor: she was one of us. And I say that when a man has a wife and children and a home and a good position, he should think twice before asking any respectable woman to meet him in such a room in such a house. It was fit neither for him nor for her.

LENKHEIM [*drawing a little closer to her*] Dear lady: may I ask you a very indiscreet question? I shall not be in the least offended if you refuse to answer it.

AGNES. What is it?

LENKHEIM. Was your marriage a happy one?

AGNES. I always thought it was, at least until the last

[ 781 ]

few years. Then there was a sudden change. Up to that time he was full of interest in his home, in Edith's education, in our plans, our money, the chance of our being able to move into a better house, the furniture and pictures, in everything. Then he seemed to get beyond us somehow.

LENKHEIM. What were the symptoms?

AGNES. Well, he was sometimes very irritable, though he used to be a perfect lamb. I thought it was only his health; for of course neither of us was growing younger. I know better now. Oh, what a fool I was! But that is how things happen. They go on from year to year under your very nose, staring you in the face; and you never notice, never think, because your mind is off the track. And then suddenly your eyes are opened with a bang; and you could kill yourself for having been so blind. If I could only find out who she was! [*She rises restlessly*].

LENKHEIM. Mrs Haldenstedt: take my advice: give it up. What is the use of tormenting yourself? You will have no peace until you put that woman out of your head.

AGNES. I dont want peace. I want to find her out.

LENKHEIM [*rising*] But suppose you do find her. What then? Think of the scandal. Believe me, it's better not to know. You could not hurt her without hurting yourself and Edith worse.

AGNES. I dont want to make a scandal; and I dont want to hurt her: I want to find out from her what sort of life Bruno was really leading, and what has become of all that work he did.

LENKHEIM. But the lecture on varieties of sleep—

AGNES! Stuff! I know the variety of sleep he learnt from her. [*Looking at him queerly*] Why do you want to prevent me from finding her out?

[ 782 ]

LENKHEIM [*meeting her eye with imposing firmness*] Solely for your own sake, Mrs Haldenstedt. How could it possibly affect me? Banish this abandoned female from your mind; and trust to Time. Time is the great healer. Time will restore your happiness.

AGNES. Well, Time works wonders, they say. But it will never comfort me until I know for certain that the happiness he had with me was the right sort of happiness, and the happiness he had with the other woman the wrong sort. How do I know that she wasnt a cleverer woman than I am? I dont care that [*snapping her fingers*] how young she is, or how pretty she is: Time will bring her to my level in those ways soon enough. But I'm not clever at the things he was clever at. I dont understand science nor care about it. If I have to keep the house spick and span I cant always keep myself spick and span; and I know he was particular about such things. Thats where she might have cut me out. She might easily have persuaded him that she was the right woman for him, and that I was the wrong one.

LENKHEIM. No, no. You were an excellent wife to him, Mrs Haldenstedt; and he knew it.

AGNES. I dont say I wasnt. But she hadnt to keep the house for him. She had nothing to do but please him. And if she was clever into the bargain, what chance had I?

*Edith comes in from the corridor.*

EDITH. Good morning, Professor.

LENKHEIM [*relieved by the interruption*] Good morning. Will you excuse me, Mrs Haldenstedt: I have a few words to say to Fessler before Jitta comes.

AGNES. You have been so good. I will think over your advice: indeed I will.

LENKHEIM [*encouragingly*] Do. [*He waves his hand*

[ 783 ]

*to Edith, and goes into the study, leaving the mother and daughter alone together*].

AGNES [*looking after him bitterly as she goes back to her place at the table*] It's easy for him to talk.

EDITH [*wandering about restlessly between the table and the console*] Why do you listen to him? Why do you run to strangers when you want to talk about father? Why should our being mother and daughter keep us so far apart?

AGNES. What a thing to say, child.

EDITH [*going to her*] Of course if you dont want me, mother, I dont want to force myself on you.

AGNES [*dutifully, without real feeling*] Well, of course, darling, I want you.

EDITH [*irritated*] No, not of course, not in the way you think. Has it occurred to you that it is rather hard on me to be left entirely to myself when things are so serious with us?

AGNES. I dont know what you have to complain of. You used to trust me to know what was right for you, and now you have suddenly turned on me. Surely, child, nobody can be a better judge of what is best for you than your own mother. Here I am, worried to death almost; and you making it worse for me by setting yourself against me.

EDITH. I am not setting myself against you, mother. What I am setting myself against is being expected to go through life blindfold, or pretending to be blindfold. I am to be a good little child, and not know anything nor feel anything that little children ought not to know and feel, just when I, as a woman, most want the companionship of another woman to whom I can pour out my feelings and my sorrow on equal terms.

AGNES. I cant understand you, child; and I wont have you talking to me like that.

EDITH. I often wonder whether you have ever understood anybody. Perhaps you did not understand father.

AGNES. You dare—

EDITH [*continuing impetuously*] Oh, I know very well how tidy you kept his house for him, just as I keep my room. You did your duty: nobody can blame you. But was his house a home for him, as his heart made it a home for me?

AGNES. You are simply silly, child. Your grief and your crazy love for your father have turned your head. I wonder what you would say if you really knew.

EDITH [*scornfully*] If I really knew! Do you suppose any girl of my age nowadays does not know more than you were ever taught?

AGNES [*shrieking*] What?

EDITH. I know, as well as you do, where my father died, and how he died.

*Mrs Haldenstedt covers her eyes in horror. Fessler, opening the study door, appears on the threshold.*

AGNES. Oh, how dreadful! This will kill me. [*To Edith, rising*] Oh, now I know what you are. Just as bad as your father! Just as bad as your father!

FESSLER. What on earth is the matter?

AGNES. Dont ask me. Oh, this is beyond everything. Let me go [*she rushes from the room*].

FESSLER. What have you done?

EDITH [*coolly*] Told her I knew. I had to.

FESSLER [*closing the door, and coming softly to Edith*] My dear: you have dragged the poor woman down from her little heaven.

EDITH. My father's wife might have had a heaven on earth; but that poor woman, as you call her, did not know even how to begin.

FESSLER. Your grief is carrying you too far. Try not to be unjust to her.

[ 785 ]

EDITH. I am not unjust. It is my father who needs justice.

FESSLER. It is not much use, is it, giving justice to the dead and withholding it from the living?

EDITH. You need not lecture me: I am on my guard.

FESSLER. Against what?

EDITH. Against sharing my father's fate.

FESSLER [*terrified*] Dying!

EDITH. No. Living in utter loneliness.

FESSLER. Oh, that! How you frighten me! But you know, dear, you mustnt worry too much about your father. It's a sort of hypochondria; and it may make you really ill.

EDITH [*scornfully*] Yes, I know. What cant be cured must be endured; so let us get away from this unfortunate affair and fall back into the current of everyday life. That is what you want me to do. But I cannot do it. He was everything to me: I cannot describe what I feel: it is as if I were a branch broken off from him, a limb torn out of him, as if I were bleeding to death of the wound that killed him. As I see him now he is quite different from what he seemed to me when he was alive, and much greater. I think of him imprisoned in these walls, longing for his proper happiness, and then finding too late the woman who was his real destiny.

FESSLER. Ah yes: destiny! destiny! He had to fulfil his destiny, I suppose.

EDITH. He did not fulfil it. Life fulfils destiny, not death.

FESSLER [*prosaically*] Well, you know, death is a sort of destiny as well. If you are right, and he really was lonely here owing to your mother being incompatible and all that, then I quite agree it was a mercy he hit on somebody who could understand him and comfort him. Still, you must be careful not to idealize a person you dont know. You see, everybody is an ideal person to us until we meet them; and then, undoubtedly, some of the gilt comes off the ginger-bread. I am so desperately afraid that if you find her out, she will prove a horrible disappointment to you.

EDITH. Never fear. I know my father too well. [*Turning fiercely on him*] But that you can think so little of him as to believe what other people are whispering about him: yes, and about her: you! who have worked with him and had all his confidence! that digs a gulf between us.

FESSLER. Oh dont say that. You cant mean it, Edith. I love you. I have the truest respect for your father.

EDITH. Then how can you belittle him so?

FESSLER. My dear, I am a man; and I know more about men's ways than you do. A man is a very mixed sort of animal. Ask any experienced man, and he will tell you that there is a certain side to human nature that must just be ruled out in judging people's characters. Even the best men are subject to aber-rations, or at least commonnesses, in their relations with women, just as they will eat rotten cheese, and half-putrid partridges that are only fit for pigs.

EDITH. You are not making it any better by saying such disgusting things.

FESSLER. Yes: but you want the truth, dont you? You know very well that Goethe was a great man; but the fine ladies of Weimar were shocked by his marriage. Rousseau was a great man; but his Teresa married a groom after his death.

EDITH. My father was a gentleman. He was worlds above Rousseau in refinement, and even above Goethe.

FESSLER. Well, I could say something more; but I suppose I mustnt.

EDITH. What more can you say? Is it something more against my father?

FESSLER. Not exactly against him; but still—

EDITH. Well, still?

FESSLER. He married your mother.

EDITH [*staggered*] Oh! How mean of you to throw that in his face! Why do you not point out what is so clear to any unprejudiced mind, that a man who made a mistake like that once would be the last person in the world to make the same mistake again?

FESSLER [*with placid obstinacy*] Because I am sorry to say, my dear, that men's lives consist mostly of their making the same mistake over and over again. I see a lot of that as a doctor. Look at your mother: she knows that if she eats prawns and cucumbers she will have a wretched night; but she never can resist them. I knew a man who was married three times; and every one of his wives drank.

EDITH. The more you say, the more I see that we shall never understand one another, and that you will never feel about my father as I do. I could not have believed you could be so coarse. Nobody in this house understands me, neither my mother nor you nor anybody.

FESSLER. But if you want people to understand you, you must be reasonable. I often used to have to say that to your father. You take after him, you know.

EDITH. If I do I must take care not to make the mistake in marrying that he made. Doctor Fessler: I am sorry; but I cannot be your wife.

FESSLER. I dont mind that so much for the present if only you wont call me Doctor Fessler. It's ridiculous. You dont expect me to call you Miss Haldenstedt, do you?

EDITH. Yes I do.

FESSLER. Then I wont. You see, I dont know how long this mood of yours will last.

EDITH. Life is short: dont waste any more of yours on me. I shall not go back from what I have said.

FESSLER. Neither shall I. I can wait.

EDITH. I cannot prevent your waiting. Everybody seems to think they know my own mind better than I do myself. I can only tell you one thing. I have one object in life now, and one only.

FESSLER. And what is that, if I may ask?

EDITH. To find the woman who made my father happy, and to force you to confess that she is high heavens above your Goethe's Christiane, and your Rousseau's Teresa, and—you neednt remind me—above my own mother.

FESSLER. Well, I hope you may, darling. Does that please you?

*Jitta comes in from the corridor. Fessler pulls himself together into his best professional bedside manner. Edith rushes to Jitta and embraces her.*

EDITH. Oh, how good of you to come! How glad I am to see you!

JITTA. Is your mother at home?

EDITH. Yes: do you want her? I will send her [*she runs out*].

JITTA [*coming to Fessler in the middle of the room*] What is the matter with the child?

FESSLER. She is still fearfully upset. She is having a hard fight of it here.

JITTA [*looking at him with quick sympathy*] You are not looking very happy yourself, Doctor.

FESSLER. She has broken it off [*he narrowly misses a sob*].

JITTA. Oh, that mustnt be. Why, it was for your sake that I opened her eyes a little about her father.

FESSLER. I am afraid it had rather the opposite effect.

JITTA. I hope not. Tell me: does my husband know of this new turn?

FESSLER. Not yet. Perhaps you had better tell him. I dont know that I can go on working here every day if Edith sticks to it.

JITTA. Dont give in too soon, Doctor.

FESSLER. I am pretending not to—to her. But I am really afraid she may be in earnest.

JITTA. Is there nothing I can do?

FESSLER. It's very good of you, Mrs Lenkheim. But I must see this thing through myself, thank you. And now I must be off. [*He goes past her towards the door*].

JITTA [*shaking his hand*] Goodbye, Doctor. Dont despise my help.

FESSLER. Oh no, Mrs Lenkheim; but—

*Mrs Haldenstedt comes in.*

AGNES [*still distracted*] Oh, what is this that Edith tells me, Doctor?

FESSLER. We wont discuss it now, Mrs Haldenstedt. You had better talk it over with Mrs Lenkheim. Goodbye. Goodbye, Mrs Lenkheim. [*He bows to them and goes out*].

AGNES. Sit down, wont you? [*Jitta sits on the couch. Agnes sits down woefully beside her*]. He's gone; and Heaven knows whether he will ever come back. This is a marked house: everybody deserts it. Who knows how soon I shall be left alone here to haunt the place like my own shadow? I shall sit alone, going over and over that dreadful time in my imagination, with no relief but just thinking how I can catch that wretch that stole from me my right to be beside my husband when he died.

JITTA. She did not intend that. You may forgive her that, at least.

AGNES. Oh, you mustnt think it's mere spite and revenge. It's that I really loved Bruno to the last as I loved him from the first. He was all I had that I cared about. I am not like a man, to begin all over again with a new love: I shall never get away from it or get over it. Day by day all those years we lived together; sat at the same table; took it in turns to rock the cradle or take the child in our hands to pet it; and then he goes off to another woman without a word or a thought for me. [*Crying*] I didnt deserve it: I didnt indeed.

JITTA. There, dear, there! Dont torture yourself. After all, if he had died in your arms, you would still have had to grieve for him. It might even have broken your heart.

AGNES. Oh, if only it had! I could think of him then without bitterness and shame.

JITTA. Try to forgive him for the sake of the old days when you were young together. What does it matter what foolish things we old people do?

AGNES. I cant forgive him. Not while I am in the dark about her. Listen to me, Mrs Lenkheim. If I thought it was only her body that took him, I wouldnt care a straw. I have had thoughts myself about our young men at college sports: only fancies of course; and I wouldnt have indulged them for the world; but a man might. What I cant bear is the thought that she might have been somebody like you.

JITTA [*startled*] Like me!

AGNES. Yes; for he thought a great deal of you; and if you had been that sort of woman, I might have been jealous of you. You are clever in his way; and you could understand him when he was talking right above my head. You could talk about his work to him. I couldnt.

JITTA. Oh no, Mrs Haldenstedt: I knew better than that. Nothing annoys a man more than a woman who talks to him about his business and pretends to understand it. Do you know what Bruno always talked to me about? what it always came round to, no matter what subject he started with?

AGNES. What?

JITTA. You.

AGNES. Me!

JITTA. Yes, you, you, you, you. Do you know, I sometimes wanted to shake him for not taking a little more interest in me occasionally? His conscience was never easy about you. You had done everything for him; and he had taken it all and gone on with his scientific work: the work that did not pay, when he might have been making a fashionable practice for himself and leaving you comfortably off.

AGNES [*beginning to cry*] But I never grudged it to him. I wanted him to be great. I wasnt really as good a wife as I might have been. I worried him about things that he neednt have known anything about. It's in my nature: I cant help it.

JITTA. It was not in his nature to blame you for that. He understood. He was frightfully faithful to you. You possessed all his thoughts: you dominated his destiny: you haunted him. What right had you to take a great man like that all to yourself? I wanted a little bit of Bruno; but you stood always in the way. Marriage is a very wonderful thing. It held him as nothing else could hold him.

AGNES. But the other woman?

JITTA. Oh, the other woman! Need you make such a fuss about her? You dont even know whether she was not a patient who had to conceal the fact that she was consulting a doctor. There are such people, you know.

But suppose she was what you think! Would a woman who had any serious relations with him have coolly walked off and left him to die? A pet dog would not have done such a thing. They would have found it at his side.

AGNES [*excitedly*] You think then that though he forgot what was due to himself, he didnt forget what was due to me? that when he went into that disgraceful place with another woman he was only making a convenience of her? that it was a mere chance that she was there to close his eyes, like a chambermaid in a hotel?

JITTA. She did not close his eyes. She stole away from his side after coldbloodedly covering up her tracks. Could you have done that?

AGNES. I never thought of that. Of course: of course. Yes: that shewed what she was, didnt it?

JITTA. What does it matter what she was? She came out of the dark, and went back into the dark. Leave her there, as she left him.

AGNES [*shaking her head*] I cant imagine how women can bring themselves to behave so. What sort of women must they be? She must have known that he could never have cared for her.

JITTA. You dont know how she got him there. But I know that if he really opened his heart to her, he talked to her about you.

AGNES [*smiling*] Well, I am sure, Mrs Lenkheim, this talk has made the most wonderful difference to me. You dont know how much good you have done me. It only shews how little we can trust our own feelings and our own judgement when such troubles come to us. The weight you have taken off my mind! you cant imagine.

JITTA. Have I? Then I have done what I came to do. [*She rises*].

AGNES [*holding her*] Oh, dont go yet. You know, its very funny how one's mind works.

JITTA [*sitting down again*] How?

AGNES [*slowly and almost roguishly*] I'm so grateful to you, that I'm afraid of offending you if I tell you. But I am sure you will only laugh.

JITTA [*with a melancholy smile*] We both need a good laugh, dont we?

AGNES. Have you ever found that you have been all along thinking something that never came into your head for a single moment?

JITTA. That sounds a little difficult. I am afraid I dont quite follow.

AGNES. Of course you dont: it's too silly. But do you know that the moment you took that weight off my mind, and gave me back my peace and happiness—

JITTA [*murmurs*] I am so glad that I did.

AGNES [*nodding gratefully, and continuing*] Well, that very moment I knew that I had been believing all along—but I dont think I ought to say it; only it's so funny.

JITTA. What?

AGNES. Why, that YOU were the woman. [*She begins to chuckle*].

JITTA. No!!!

AGNES. Yes I did.

JITTA. But really?

AGNES. Really and truly.

JITTA [*beginning to laugh hysterically*] How funny!

AGNES [*her chuckles now culminating in hearty laughter*] Isnt it? Youre not angry, are you? Oh dear —[*laughing more than ever*].

JITTA. Oh no: of course not.

*Jitta has a paroxysm of agonizing laughter; and Agnes accompanies her without a suspicion that she is not enjoying the joke in good faith. Jitta at last recovers her self-control with a desperate effort.*

JITTA. Dont make me laugh any more: I am afraid I shall go into hysterics. I am still very far from well.

AGNES. It's such a shame to laugh at all at such a time. But for the life of me I couldnt help it.

JITTA [*looking hard at her*] You know, Mrs Haldenstedt, I was very very fond of him.

AGNES. I am sure you were, darling; and I shouldnt have minded a bit if it had been you: in fact I'm half disappointed that it wasnt, you have been such an angel to me. Isnt it funny, the things that come into our heads? But it's wicked of me to make you talk and laugh so much, and you so ill. Youre very pale, dear. Can I get you anything?

JITTA. If I might just lie down here for awhile. I—

AGNES [*rising to make room for Jitta to recline*] Yes, yes: of course you shall, dear. Make yourself comfortable.

JITTA. I dont want to go without seeing Edith.

AGNES [*taken aback*] Oh!

JITTA. What is it?

AGNES. I forgot all about Edith. Who is to tell her? She sees her father like a saint in a picture; and I could never put it to her in the wonderful way you put it to me. If only you would be so good as to tell her for me. Would you mind?

JITTA. Not in the least. Edith is like a child of my own to me: it would be the greatest happiness to me if I could set her mind at rest as you are good enough to think I have set yours.

AGNES. You have: indeed and indeed you have. I am sure what we owe you, with your dear husband coming here every day to set the papers in order, and you being more than an angel to me in spite of your illness, words can never say. Just lie quiet where you are; and I will send Edith to you. Oh, you have made me happy, dear! [*She goes out into the corridor*].

*Jitta, left alone, begins to laugh again hysterically, and is dissolving into convulsive sobs when she makes a great effort; springs up from the sofa; dashes the tears from her eyes with a proud gesture; goes to the glass; and has just made herself presentable when Edith appears. Her eyes are wide open and her expression one of joyful surprise and relief. She runs eagerly to Jitta.*

EDITH. What on earth have you done to mother? She is laughing. She is positively singing. Either you are a witch, or she has gone mad.

JITTA. Are you angry with her for daring to sing in this house of mourning? Or angry with me for making her sing?

EDITH. Oh no: it's rather a relief. But it's very odd. How did you do it?

JITTA. She made me laugh before I made her sing. You mustnt be shocked, dear. There is always a sort of reaction: Nature must have a relief from any feeling, no matter how deep and sincere it is. Have you ever seen a soldier's funeral?

EDITH. No. Why?

JITTA. They play the Dead March as they go to the grave; but they play the merriest tunes they know on their way back.

EDITH. How unfeeling!

JITTA. Yes; but how natural! Your mother would have gone mad if she had gone on as she was for another week. I am not sure that I should not have gone mad myself if she had not made me laugh. [*Taking Edith by the shoulders and looking straight at her*] And now what I want to know is how I am to

[ 796 ]

make you laugh. For you will go mad if you do not get back into everyday life again.

EDITH [*backing to the table, and half sitting against its edge*] Yes: I know. This house has been a sort of madhouse since my father died. We havnt spoken naturally, nor walked naturally, nor breathed naturally, nor thought naturally, because we were all so determined to feel naturally. Somehow, my mother's laughing and singing has made nonsense of it all suddenly.

JITTA. Then you are happy again? If so, I may as well go home.

EDITH. Happy! Oh no. But I am done with hypocrisy and conventionality; and that is such a relief that I seem happy by contrast. I suppose it is a sort of happiness to be able to give myself up at last wholly to my sorrow.

JITTA [*sitting down in Lenkheim's chair*] Which sorrow? The old sorrow that God made for you, or the new one that you have made for yourself?

EDITH [*straightening up*] I dont know what you mean.

JITTA. Doctor Fessler says you have jilted him.

EDITH. Did he call it jilting him?

JITTA. No. I call it that.

EDITH. But you cant think that. Do you know what he said?

JITTA. No. Anything very dreadful?

EDITH. He believes that my father died in the arms of a common woman of the streets.

JITTA. And he thinks your father must have been as worthless as the woman he died with. I see.

EDITH. Not at all. That is what is so dreadful. He thinks it makes no difference. He adores my father as much as he ever did; but he thinks you have to leave all that out when you are judging men. He thinks a woman doesnt matter. I cant forgive him for that. I couldnt marry a man unless he felt exactly as I do about my father.

JITTA. Is that reasonable, dear? How could poor Doctor Fessler feel as you feel? you! your father's daughter!

EDITH. Oh, of course I know that. I dont expect him to feel the same affection. But if he thought my father could go with low women—if he did not know for certain, as I know, that the woman my father loved must have been one of the best and noblest of women, I would rather die than let him touch me.

JITTA. My dear: how can he know for certain? You do not know for certain yourself.

EDITH. I know I cant prove it. But I am certain. And I will devote my life to proving it.

JITTA. How?

EDITH. I will find the woman: that is how. I have thought and thought about it. I know that she cannot be very far off. I know that her grief and desolation must be as great as mine: greater. I know she will love me because I am his daughter. And I know that she will be somebody worthy of him.

JITTA. Edith, Edith, how sentimental you are!

EDITH [*fiercely*] You call my feeling sentimentality! Are you going to disappoint me too?

JITTA [*sternly*] You must learn to expect disappointments. How do you know that if you found this woman she would not disappoint you? It is easy to imagine wonderful women worthy of your father's love. But the real person always kills the imagined person.

EDITH. He said that once.

JITTA. Well, is it not true? Can you think of any real woman among your acquaintances that you could bear to think of as that woman—even the best of them?

EDITH. You cant put me off that way. I tell you I know. There is some woman who was real to my father; and he loved her. I shall love her when she is real to me. Besides, I have a queer sense that I know her quite as well as a real person; that she is here within reach of my hands if only I could recollect. I—I sometimes wonder does everybody know? does my mother know?

JITTA [*quickly*] Your mother does not know. Your mother could never understand.

EDITH. Jitta: do you know?

JITTA. Yes.

EDITH. Jitta!!!

JITTA. Yes. I know that poor criminal. I know what has become of her. I know what she did. I know what she has suffered ever since.

EDITH. But how do you know? Oh, tell me. You must tell me now.

JITTA. When you are excited like that your voice is his voice. Oh, the agony of hearing it, and the happiness! You bring him to life again for me.

EDITH. Then it was—

JITTA. Only me, dear.

EDITH [*flinging herself into Jitta's arms*] Only you! Who better could it be? Of course it was you. I knew it all along, only I couldnt recollect. Oh, darling! Dont you want a daughter? Here I am. His daughter.

JITTA. Dearest, yes. You have been a daughter to me ever since I knew him. But we must be very careful, very discreet. You see, you are very young.

EDITH. Oh, dont begin that. I dont want that sort of mother.

JITTA. I know. But I mustnt take your devotion—it is devotion, isnt it?—

EDITH. Oh yes, yes.

[ 799 ]

JITTA. I mustnt take it under false pretences. Above all, you must not throw away your engagement because your lover does not feel about me as you do. He is right about me, you know: I am not a good woman. Have you quite forgotten that *I* have a husband, and that for your father's sake I was unfaithful to him?

EDITH [*naïvely*] Oh, but Alfred is such a chump!

JITTA [*a little shocked*] Edith!

EDITH. And papa was such a wonderful man! Nobody could blame you.

JITTA. I assure you a great many people would blame me so much that they would never speak to me again if they knew.

EDITH. More shame for them! Do such people matter?

JITTA. They do, dear. I am afraid they are the only people who do matter in this wretched world. So you musnt tell them. You mustnt tell anybody.

EDITH [*slowly*] I suppose not.

JITTA. Did you intend to tell everybody?

EDITH. No, of course not: I am not such a fool as that. But I did think that if I told Doctor Fessler he might see that he was wrong.

JITTA. And you might forgive him. Very well: I give you leave to tell him. But you understand that if you tell him you must marry him; for you mustnt tell anyone except your husband.

EDITH. You want me to marry him?

JITTA. I do.

EDITH. Then I'll telephone him. I suppose that will do. I am so happy now that it doesnt matter tuppence whom I marry. [*Lenkheim opens the study door and is coming in when Edith, not hearing him, goes on*] I'd marry anyone to please you. I'd even marry Alfred.

LENKHEIM. Thank you. [*The two women spring up in*

*dismay*]. Thats very kind of you, Edith, and very kind of Jitta to include me in the number of husbands she has apparently been offering you. But I have no intention of divorcing her at present.

EDITH [*not knowing what else to say*] It wasnt that. Mrs Lenkheim never offered you to me.

JITTA. Go off to the telephone, dear, and make it up with your man. I will make it up for you with Alfred.

LENKHEIM. Do, Edith. [*He crosses the room to the other door, and opens it for her with sardonic politeness*].

EDITH [*to Lenkheim, after kissing Jitta rather defiantly*] Mrs Lenkheim did not say a single unkind word about you. I did. [*She nods mockingly in his face and goes out*].

LENKHEIM. Have you told her?

JITTA [*her bored manner with her husband contrasting strongly with her warm interest in Edith*] She guessed. She knew. It is no use keeping secrets when they will not keep themselves. I have made her happy: that is all I care about. [*She goes listlessly to the window-seat, sits there looking out, with her shoulder turned to him*].

LENKHEIM. And have you told the old woman? Have you made her happy?

JITTA. I have made her happy. But I did not tell her. The strange thing is that she guesses it too; but she will never know it. She doesnt want to know it. Edith did. That makes all the difference. I have made them both happy. I wish someone could make me happy.

LENKHEIM. As I unfortunately am only your husband, I suppose there is no use my trying.

JITTA [*turning her face to him with open contempt*] You!

LENKHEIM. Funny, isnt it?

JITTA [*rising*] Dont be insufferable. You owe it to

[ 801 ]

your position as an injured husband never to speak to me when we are alone and there are no appearances to be kept up. You swore not to. And you have been talking to me ever since, except when there was somebody else present to talk to.

LENKHEIM. Make no mistake, Jitta: when I swore that, I meant it.

JITTA [*ironically*] So it appears.

LENKHEIM. When you swore to be faithful to me, you meant it, didnt you?

JITTA [*interrupting him curtly*] You need not remind me of that again. I have not denied it. I have not excused myself. But I do not intend to have it thrown in my teeth every time we meet. [*She turns away from him determinedly, and sits down in the chair between the table and the door*].

LENKHEIM. Very well, then, dont you start reminding me every time we meet that I swore to do a good many things that I find I cant do. Is that a bargain?

JITTA [*a little ashamed, feeling that she has allowed herself to descend to his level*] Yes. I beg your pardon. I should not have said it. But please remember that you can hurt me more than I can hurt you, because you have done nothing wrong. You are within your rights: you are above reproach: you have the superior position morally: no taunts of mine can degrade you as your reproaches can degrade me. [*Tragically*] I am a miserable creature. I betrayed you to please myself. I deserted him in his extremity to save myself. Please leave me to my disgrace. Nothing that you can say or think can add to the contempt I feel for myself.

LENKHEIM [*chuckling a little*] How you enjoy being miserable, Jitta!

JITTA. Enjoy!!

LENKHEIM. You just revel in it. You think yourself

such a jolly romantic figure. You think that everything that happens to you is extraordinarily interesting
because it happens to you. And you think that everything that happens to me is quite uninteresting because it hasnt happened to you. But what has
happened to you has happened to lots of women—
except, of course, the way it ended. And even that was
an accident that might have happened to anyone.

JITTA. No doubt. Unfortunately, I did not behave as
any decent woman would.

LENKHEIM. That is just where you are mistaken,
darling. When you were brought to the point and put
to the proof, you didnt behave romantically: you
behaved very sensibly. You kept your head, and did
just the right thing. You saved your reputation and
my reputation. You prevented a horrible scandal. You
have managed to make his wife and daughter happy.
And yet you think you are ashamed of yourself because you were not found stretched on his dead body,
with the limelight streaming on your white face, and
the band playing slow music.

JITTA. Oh, what a nature you have, Alfred! You are
prosaic to the core.

LENKHEIM [grinning] If you had only been clever
enough to take me in, your success would have been
complete. It wouldnt have been difficult. I always took
you in when I had an adventure.

JITTA [rising, very unpleasantly surprised, and not a
little furious] You! You have had adventures since we
were married? You have deceived me?

LENKHEIM. Now dont begin imagining that I am a
Don Juan. To be precise, I have kissed other women
twice. I was drunk both times. And I had a serious
affair with your dear friend Thelma Petersen. That
lasted until she and her husband went back to Norway.

JITTA. Oh, how disgraceful! And you call her my friend!

LENKHEIM. I call Bruno Haldenstedt my friend. So you see I am not your moral superior. I thought it might restore your happiness a little to know that.

JITTA. Alfred: I will never speak to you nor cross the threshold of your house again.

LENKHEIM [*more amused than ever*] Except when you call to tell me so. When you let out about Haldenstedt I felt just as you feel now. Tomorrow you will think better of it, as I have thought better of it.

JITTA [*more dignified than ever*] If you imagine that any relations that could exist between Mrs Petersen and yourself were in the least like my relations with Bruno, you only shew for the thousandth time how incapable you are of understanding either him or me.

LENKHEIM. I'm afraid you dont understand either Thelma or me as sympathetically as I could wish. Thelma was a very superior woman, let me tell you. If my taste did not lie in the direction of superior women I shouldnt have married you.

JITTA. I will not have it, Alfred. I will not be dragged down to your level.

LENKHEIM. Five minutes ago you were amusing yourself by pretending that you were beneath contempt.

JITTA. So I am, on my own plane, and on his. But not on yours.

LENKHEIM. I dont believe theres a woman alive who doesnt look on herself as a special creation, and consider her husband an inferior and common sort of animal.

JITTA. You forget that I did not think of Bruno in that way.

LENKHEIM. Yes; but then he wasnt your husband.

[ 804 ]

Thelma thought me a much finer fellow than Petersen.

JITTA [*exasperated*] If you mention that woman to me again, I will break my promise to you, and walk straight out of your house before all the world.

LENKHEIM. That will only make us quits, because, as it happens, I am going to break my promise to you.

JITTA. How?

LENKHEIM. About the book. I have read it.

JITTA. Well?

LENKHEIM. Well, I'll be hanged if I put my name to it. In the first place nobody would believe I had ever written it. In the second, it's the most utter tommy-rot that was ever put forward as a serious contribution to psychology. Why, it flatly contradicts everything I have been teaching for years past, and everything I was taught myself.

JITTA [*intensely angry*] Does that prove it to be tommy-rot, or does it prove that you are an idiot?

LENKHEIM. I may be an idiot; but my idiocy is the accepted idiocy taught in the University at which I am a professor; and his idiocy is not taught anywhere. Do you forget that I have to earn bread for the household, and that your own money hardly pays for your dresses? This book would ruin us both.

JITTA. It is a sacred trust; and I swore to him that it should be fulfilled.

LENKHEIM. *I* didnt. And the old woman has just told me that he said the book was to be her insurance policy. No doubt I am Bruno's inferior; but I draw the line at helping him to rob his widow for my own profit.

JITTA. Then you refuse to carry out his intentions?

LENKHEIM. I cant carry out his intentions.

JITTA. You mean you wont.

LENKHEIM. I mean what I say. When he left me this

book of his, he did so on the understanding that I was to know nothing of his relations with you. He hadnt quite such a low opinion of me as to suppose that I would take it as the price of my wife. Well, whose fault is it that I know all about it? Who let the secret out? You did.

JITTA [*collapsing into his chair*] Oh, how shamefully I have betrayed him at every step! How despicable I am!

LENKHEIM [*sympathetically*] Not a bit of it, dear. You have just said yourself that if secrets dont keep themselves, nobody can keep them. This secret wouldnt keep itself. Come! stop crying. If only you would be content to be a woman for a moment, and not a heroine! And oh Lord! if you only had the smallest sense of humor!

JITTA [*passionately*] You cant even try to console me without sneering at me. Do you know what Edith called you?

LENKHEIM. No. You can tell me if it will relieve your feelings.

JITTA. She said you were a chump; and so you are.

LENKHEIM. All husbands are chumps, dear, after the first month or so. Jolly good thing for their wives too, sometimes.

JITTA. What are you going to do with that book?

LENKHEIM. If I had any regard for his reputation I should burn it at our domestic hearth.

JITTA [*recovering her dignity; rising; and speaking with tranquil conviction*] You shall not do that, Alfred.

LENKHEIM. Perhaps not; but it would serve you right if I did.

JITTA. It would not serve Edith right. Besides, his work, his reputation, his greatness—for whatever you may say I know that that book is the greatest that ever

[ 806 ]

was written—belong not only to humanity, but to her. And I love her as if she were my own daughter. I have no other child.

LENKHEIM [*wincing a little*] My fault, I suppose. Oh, you can be nasty when you want to, Jitta.

JITTA. Oh, no, no. Will you never understand?

LENKHEIM. Probably not, being only a chump. Be a little amiable, Jitta: I havnt been so very hard on you, have I?

JITTA [*insisting*] You will not destroy the book? You will edit it? You will do everything for it that you could for a book of your own?

LENKHEIM. Well, if—

*Fessler and Edith come in arm-in-arm, followed by Mrs Haldenstedt.*

EDITH. Here he is. Kiss him.

FESSLER [*hastily*] Tchut! [*Taking Jitta's hand, and kissing it*] I owe you my life's happiness, Mrs Lenkheim.

AGNES. I am sure we all owe you the happiness of our lives. You are our good angel: indeed you are. Oh, you are a lucky man, Mr Lenkheim, to have such a wife.

JITTA [*striking in before he can reply*] I have one more piece of news for you, Mrs Haldenstedt. Alfred has found your husband's book. It is a masterpiece. He will edit it. He will do everything he could do for it if it were his own book.

FESSLER [*triumphant*] Splendid!

AGNES [*overjoyed*] Oh, think of that! Edith [*she kisses Edith*]! Doctor [*she kisses the Doctor*]! Professor [*she kisses Lenkheim*]! Didnt I say she was our good angel?

LENKHEIM. And now, may I take my good angel home?

AGNES [*to Jitta*] Oh, must you go, dear?

[ 807 ]

JITTA [*sweetly, to Agnes*] Yes, dear. [*Threateningly to Alfred*] Come home. [She goes to the door].

LENKHEIM [*cheerily, as he shakes hands with everybody*] Goodbye.

ALL [*shaking hands*] Goodbye. Goodbye. Goodbye.

JITTA [*sternly*] Alfred: come home.

LENKHEIM [*hastily obeying*] Yes, dear.

AGNES [*as the door closes sharply behind them*] She's too good for him.